The Making of a Township

Fairmount Township

Grant County
Indiana
1829 to 1917

Edgar M. Baldwin

HERITAGE BOOKS
2008

HERITAGE BOOKS
AN IMPRINT OF HERITAGE BOOKS, INC.

Books, CDs, and more—Worldwide

For our listing of thousands of titles see our website
at
www.HeritageBooks.com

A Facsimile Reprint
Published 2008 by
HERITAGE BOOKS, INC.
Publishing Division
100 Railroad Ave. #104
Westminster, Maryland 21157

Copyright © 1917 Edgar M. Baldwin

— Publisher's Notice —
In reprints such as this, it is often not possible to remove blemishes from the original. We feel the contents of this book warrant its reissue despite these blemishes and hope you will agree and read it with pleasure.

International Standard Book Numbers
Paperbound: 978-0-7884-1917-1
Clothbound: 978-0-7884-7293-0

EDITOR'S NOTE

It would be presumptuous upon the part of any one person to claim the authorship of this narrative. "The Making of a Township" is the joint production of many. Without the generous co-operation of friends the story would, indeed, have been lacking in essential elements of accuracy and interest. Credit will be given in the proper place for the work of each contributor.

Fairmount Township was literally hewn out of the wilderness. The forest, in its primitive purity, has given way to productive farms and splendid homes where modern conveniences abound. Measured in terms of days, months and years the record reaches back to but yesterday. Considered upon the basis of development and invention, it seems to cover centuries.

For more than thirty years the writer has thought that this account should be prepared. Ten years ago he commenced to assemble data for this purpose. Not until January 1, 1917, however, did he abandon the hope that others who had lived through the pioneer period, and were therefore better equipped by knowledge and experience to handle the subject, would take the matter up. Now that this information appears in permanent form, though the task be imperfectly performed, it is the hope of the editor that the book may in some measure preserve to posterity facts which otherwise might have been lost.

E. M. B.

Fairmount, Indiana, September 26, 1917.

TO THE MEMORY OF
MY NOBLE BROTHER DAN
WHOSE PATIENT
FRIENDSHIP AND STEADFAST LOYALTY
NEVER FAILED IN THE DAYS
OF MY ERRATIC YOUTH
THIS VOLUME IS AFFECTIONATELY
DEDICATED

McCORMICK'S TAVERN ON THE OLD STATE ROAD
From a drawing by Olive Rush made after a careful study of the building and its former environments and conversations with oldest settlers of that neighborhood.

EXPLANATION AND ACKNOWLEDGMENT.

In the preparation of this narrative two methods presented themselves for consideration.

First. The many communications received and published in The Fairmount News might have been revised and edited and set out in the editor's own language. It appeared that the work thus done would very likely take on a form entirely too prosaic and assume a style obviously too tedious, thereby losing much of its refreshing candor.

Second. The plan of treatment finally adopted, which seemed more appropriate to an effort of this character, speaks for itself. The reproductions of letters in substantially the identical language used by the contributor gives to the book, we trust, a more original significance, establishing an intimate or cordial relationship, so to speak, between narrator and the reader. This method seemed to meet with the approval of competent judges and it was therefore chosen.

Thanking you for your loyal support of this project, without which the volume could not have been added to your library, I am

Yours sincerely,

EDGAR M. BALDWIN.

LIST OF ILLUSTRATIONS

Page

McCormick's Tavern on the Old State Road
 (By Olive Rush) ....Frontispiece
Blazing the Way (Head piece by Olive Rush) 17
Victor A. Selby 19
Charles T. Parker 22
Hon. John T. Strange 32
Me-shin-go-me-sia 35
The Fankboner Graveyard 41
Original Site of McCormick Tavern 42
Old Coleman Homestead 45
Gabrille Havens 46
Daniel Winslow, Henry Winslow and Seth Winslow 49
Back Creek Meeting-house 51
Nathan Morris 53
Second and Third Generations 55
Mark Baldwin 56
John T. Morris 59
Asa T. Baldwin 64
William G. Lewis 67
Emeline Lewis 68
Solomon Thomas 69
John Smith 70
Mary Ann Smith 70
The Postoffice at A1 71
William S. Elliott 79
Lydia Morris Arnold 82
Aaron Newby 94
Major B. V. Norton 96
Members of the Wilson-Hill-Bogue-Baldwin Families 100
T. B. McDonald 113
William R. Woollen 121
David Stanfield 126
Elizabeth Stanfield 127
Site of Benbow Cabin 128
Cyrus W. Neal 129
Jonathan Baldwin 135

List of Illustrations.

	Page
Hon. James M. Hundley	136
First Frame Dwelling in Fairmount	137
The Old Baldwin Homestead	138
The Giant Hackberry	140
Mrs. Angelina (Harvey) Pearson	148
Herbert Pearson	150
The Pool of Siloam	153
Fac-simile of Scrip Issued by the Marion & Mississinewa Railroad Company	157
Rev. Herbert S. Nickerson	160
Daisy Barr	163
The Elijah Ward Cabin	165
William Hall	166
Berean Bible Class of the Friends Sabbath School	168
Mary Ann Taylor	179
John R. Little	180
Miss Stella Buller	190
Eli J. Cox	193
The Edmund Leach Homestead	196
William J. Leach	199
Claud Leach	200
Jonathan P. Winslow	203
Jane (Henley) Winslow	203
Palmer Winslow	204
Jonathan P. Winslow Homestead	205
Nixon Winslow	206
Levi Winslow	207
The W. H. H. Reeder Homestead	227
William Henry Harrison Reeder	228
Robert B. Reeder	230
Mr. and Mrs. O. M. Bevington and Family	231
Henry Simons	232
Jesse E. Wilson	238
Aunt Mary Wilson	240
Samuel C. Wilson	241
Lindsey and Jane (Davis) Wilson	244
Mrs. Eunice (Pierce) Wilson	245
Lin Wilson	247
Nathan D. W. Elliott	249
Clyde N. Wilson	250
Jesse Webster Wilson	250

List of Illustrations.

	Page
John Vetor	251
John B. Hollingsworth	254
Andrew Rhoads	258
Ephraim Bartholomew	267
James C. Thorn	269
Alson M. Bell	271
Modern Fairmount Home	272
W. Hort Ribble	273
Lieut. Col. Allen Parker	274
Joseph W. Relfe	276
Map of Fairmount Township	277
Thomas J. Lucas	278
David G. Lewis	281
Roland Smith	293
Last of Tanyard	294
H. W. Winslow	303
The Clodfelter Power House	306
The Old Swimmin' Hole	307
Joseph W. Baldwin	308
Nathan W. Edwards	311
Dr. Alpheus Henley	314
Dr. David S. Elliott	316
Hon. C. C. Lyons	319
Mrs. Gladys (Lyons) Knight	319
Dr. Carl D. Lucas	322
Dr. J. W. Patterson	323
Levi Scott	326
John Selby	327
John Flanagan	328
Robert A. Morris	329
Gilbert LaRue	332
Alvin B. Scott	334
Xen H. Edwards	336
Washington Street Looking East from Main Street	337
Main Street, Looking South from Washington Street	338
Nixon Rush	340
Graduating Class of Fairmount Academy (1888)	341
Garfield Cox	342
Joel B. Wright	344
Fairmount Academy Basketball Team (1915)	345
Fairmount High School Basketball Team (1915)	346

List of Illustrations.

	Page
Rev. W. D. Baker	347
Rev. W. J. Seekins	348
Ancil E. Ratliff	349
Alvin Seale	356
The Big Snow	358
Back Creek at Flood Tide	362
Back Creek on a Rampage	364
Hon. Edgar L. Goldthwait	382
David Jones and Family	417
In the Quaker Costumes of Their Grandmothers	435

THE MAKING OF A TOWNSHIP

CHAPTER I.

BLAZING THE WAY.

IT IS NOT definitely known when the first white man set foot upon the soil of Fairmount Township.

Until about 1823, according to best available authority, Indians were the sole inhabitants of Grant County.

It may be stated, however, for the meditation of thoughtful people, and as a matter simply of speculation, that James Marquette, noted Jesuit missionary, visited the northern part of Indiana about the year 1672; that within the same decade Joliet, intrepid French explorer, and LaSalle, with his band of adventurous spirits, passed through the region of the Kankakee swamps.

While it may be true that detachments from various expeditions, as sometimes happened with exploring parties, forayed into this section of the State, there appears to be no recognized authority bold enough to assert, as a fact, that any of these sturdy pathfinders penetrated the unbroken forest which in the first half of the nineteenth century covered this Township.

Flushed with victory over General Harmar in October, 1790, Indians had begun to terrorize the frontier settlements in Northwest Territory. Gen. Arthur St. Clair, a native of Thurso, Caithness-shire, Scotland, educated at the University of Edinburg, distinguished himself in the campaign which ended with the surrender of Cornwallis. General St. Clair was a delegate to the Continental Congress, serving part of the time as President of that body. He was the first Governor of the Northwest Territory.

As Commander-in-Chief of the U. S. Army St. Clair, in 1791, headed an expedition sent against Miami Indians on the Wabash. His troops, numbering 1,800 men, met with a disastrous defeat at the hands of more than 2,000 warriors led by Little Turtle. Though exonerated by Congress, General St. Clair resigned his command.

In 1792 St. Clair was superseded by General Wayne. On account of his many daring exploits he had come to be known by the people as Mad Anthony. He was a native of Waynesborough, Pennsylvania, and had served in the War of the Revolution. His dash and audacity as a commanding officer saved General Lafayette from annihilation in 1780 while the gallant Frenchman was operating in Virginia.

Major-General Scott, with about 1,600 mounted Kentucky Volunteers, joined the troops of General Wayne on July 26, 1794, at Ft. Defiance. Two days later the combined forces began their movement on Indian towns situated along the Maumee.

It may be remarked, in passing, that the reenforcements under General Scott might have been the soldiers who, tradition tells us, blazed the trail afterwards known as the Ft. Wayne road, passing in a northeasterly direction beyond and east of East Branch school house, in Fairmount Township.

This trail led across one corner of Willis McCoy's farm, passing through the southeast corner of Thomas Winslow's place, thence along the road by John H. Flanagan's land and through John Selby's tract, crossing the Mississinewa at Wilson's ford.

David Lewis, who came to this Township on November 18, 1834, always contended that General Wayne's troops left a quantity of supplies and equipment near this ford.

Thomas J. Parker, another early pioneer (father of Ex-County Treasurer Joseph H. Parker and Attorney Charles T. Parker), who lived at one time in the vicinity of Lake Galatia, frequently in his reminiscent moods talked to members of his family and to his neighbors of the accuracy of this statement with reference to what was known in the early days as "the Anthony Wayne trail."

Attorney Parker submits an interesting contribution to the literature on this subject, upon which there has been a wide divergence of opinion.

"In the years 1875 and 1876," Mr. Parker's statement reads, "my father, Thomas J. Parker, lived where the north side of what would be the east extension of Eighth Street intersects with the west bank of the prairie, east of the town of Fairmount. During the winter months he conducted a boot and shoe shop, making and mending boots for the people of that vicinity.

"Of evenings during the winter the neighbors would congregate there and pass the time in relating reminiscences and legends pertaining to that particular country, and especially with reference to the prairie part of it (which at that time was undrained, and during the greater part of the year was covered with water), this running for a considerable distance from a southwest angling on up to what is now known as Lake Galatia.

"On the brow of this prairie was a road following along the high bank, just above the prairie and meandering around with numerous crooks and turns, following the contours of the bank of the prairie.

"On many occasions I have heard my father and the old settlers along this road tell about that being the road which Anthony Wayne and his soldiers had cut out in their march from Maumee and Ft. Defiance to the relief of the settlers at the old fort, which is now the site of the city of Ft. Wayne, at that time besieged by the Indians. This was during the months of October and November, 1794.

"Among the old settlers living along the road at that time were Jacob McCoy, Major B. V. Norton, John Selby and Milton Winslow. This road, at that time—

VICTOR A. SELBY

Who possesses an old-fashioned flint-lock gun barrel said to have been left behind by one of General Wayne's soldiers as the troops passed through Fairmount Township.

in 1874 and 1875—was always called the Wayne, or Ft. Wayne road. In those days it was a common thing to pick up flint arrows and other stone implements, evidently having been used by the Indians of early times; also evidences of implements of warfare of various kinds were found. One which I had the opportunity of inspecting recently was an old flint-lock mustket barrel which had a hole blown in one side. It was found near this road, and is now in the possession of our fellow-towns-man, Victor A. Selby. The supposition is that it was one of the cast-off guns of Anthony Wayne's soldiers.

"A part of this road is still in use, following from the west bank of the Eighth Street road and angling round past the farm home of John H. Flanagan and John Selby, most of the other part of this road having been abandoned in straightening the lines along the different farms located on this thoroughfare."

"It is a reasonable conclusion," writes Dr. Alpheus Henley, "that the first settlers who came to Grant County from the South followed the road that was previously cut out, so far as it ran in the direction they wished to go.

"In talking with some of the first settlers, old Georgie Moore, Aquilla Moore's father, who settled where Abe Music lived, and Solomon Thomas, who settled a little farther north, I got the impression that Alexandria and Summitville were located on the old trail, and that Moore's, Thomas's and Henry Osborn's cabins were erected on the old road.

"When I first became acquainted with the Henry Osborn settlement, about seventy years ago, Henry had a field fenced in north of his cabin, along the east side of the road to his northwest corner. At that point where his north line intersected with the road, there stood a sign post, a board on it pointing to the northeast and southwest, which read:

    63 MILES TO FORT WAYNE
    63 MILES TO INDIANAPOLIS

"That post and sign were there some years later.

"At that time the land east of the then traveled road, and north to where Davis now lives, was all in woods. Isaac Stanfield then lived on the Ink place and Vernon Stanfield lived where Kaufman built his big barn.

"The Wayne trail led off from the sign post in a northeast direction, striking the prairie near eighty rods east of the Ink residence, and followed the meanderings in and out of the prairie, keeping on dry ground, to the Timothy Kelley residence. Here it left the prairie and made a more direct angle to the Wilson crossing of the Mississinewa River.

"Ft. Wayne* was the place of entry of all Grant County land, consequently there was considerable travel over the Wayne road by land

---

    *By an Act of Congress, approved by the President of the United States May 8, 1822, this office was established at Ft. Wayne. After the survey of the lands, President Monroe issued a proclamation for their sale, the minimum price being fixed at $1.25 per acre. The sale began on October 22, 1823.

buyers until the Government land was all taken up, that being the most direct route to the Land Office.

"In October, 1861, I drove a two-horse team from the then Kaufman place, due east through the middle of the farm, some eighty rods to the prairie, where I came on to the old trail, which I followed to the Billy Karwin place, and on by Jacob McCoy's, John Lee's, Otho Selby's and Timothy Kelley's, where the road left the prairie and ran north a little ways, then direct to the river. After crossing the river the road ran a pretty angle northeast to Warren and Huntington. After getting a little way from the river the land was quite level and covered with a dense forest. The farms were small and not always close together.

"My objective point was Huntington. My errand being accomplished, as I now recollect, it was almost 3 o'clock in the afternoon, and night overtook me near Warren. I drove to my starting place that night, or rather between 2 and 3 a. m., and I came to the conclusion that was about the most dismal drive I ever made.

"The old trail had not been changed much at that date, but ran on a direct angle."

"You no doubt have heard of old Dave Conner,* who established an Indian trading post on the river, some miles northwest of the present site of Marion," continues Dr. Henley. "Some time prior to the War of 1812 Conner was doing business there. The military authority over that district enjoined Conner from selling the Indians any more ammunition or guns. This order so incensed the Indians that they gathered up in force around the block house and demanded ammunition. Upon refusal to comply with their terms they threatened to tear down the house, kill Dave and help themselves to what they wanted. Conner was true to his country, and in the face of death refused to accommodate the Indians, who proceeded at once to carry out their threat by felling a small tree on the house that stood near the fort, up which a number of Indians climbed to the roof and commenced to make an opening in the top. When they had an opening sufficiently large to see what Conner was doing, Dave picked up a keg of powder and emptied it out on the counter, and with a piece of wood with fire on the end in one hand, told the Indians if they did not depart at once he would blow all of them beyond the happy hunting grounds. They took Dave at his word, knowing that he had always kept his word with them, and did not molest him again.

---

*This is undoubtedly the same man that Lieut.-Col. John B. Campbell refers to in his report on the Battle of the Mississinewa.

ATTORNEY CHARLES T. PARKER
Whose important contribution to "The Making of a Township" helps to define the route of the Anthony Wayne trail.

"Jep Sutton, one of Conner's clerks, was in the building with Conner at this particular time. He said when Dave picked up the stick with fire on it he fell down against the wall and closed his eyes, expecting every second to hear the crash that did not come.

"Sutton stayed with Dave until the latter died. I never saw old Dave, as he was called, but I did see Sutton, who was a rough backwoodsman, and I judge felt more at home with the Indians than with white men.

"Robert McClure and James Sweetser clerked for Conner at an early day, and learned the Indian language while selling them goods.".

Advancing from Ft. Defiance, General Wayne, on August 20, gained a decisive victory over the Indians and British, losing thirty-three killed and 100 wounded. Nine hundred Americans were actually engaged in this battle as against an estimated superior force of 2,000 of the enemy.

September 14, 1794, General Wayne, with his troops, proceeded in the direction of deserted Miami villages at the junction of the St. Joseph's and St. Mary's Rivers, reaching that point October 17th. Here the site of Ft. Wayne, named by Col. John F. Hamtramck, was selected. The fort was completed on November 22d.

General Wayne's complete pacification of the Indians was accomplished. The Treaty of Greenville was made on August 3, 1795. The principal chiefs present when the treaty was signed were Tarhe, Buckhongehelas, Black Hoof, Blue Jacket and Little Turtle.

General Wayne continued to serve until 1796 as United States Commissioner in the Northwest Territory. His career ended shortly after his successful campaign against the Indians. He returned to Ft. Presque Isle (now Erie), Pennsylvania, where he died, December 14, 1796.

Little Turtle was a natural leader of men. Skillful and courageous, he was a fearless and persistent enemy of frontiersmen. He won many victories over the whites. It was not until he encountered "the man who never sleeps," as he once described General Wayne in a council of war, that he met his match.

Little Turtle died at Ft. Wayne, July 14, 1812. A vast concourse of people attended his funeral. He was buried with the highest honors. The sword and medal presented to him by Gen. George Washington were placed in the coffin when his body was lowered into the grave.

CHAPTER II.

BATTLE OF THE MISSISSINEWA—BEARING UPON THE EARLY SETTLEMENT OF FAIRMOUNT TOWSHIP.

TECUMSEH, a Shawnee, perhaps the foremost man of his race, had in 1812 attained to a position of undisputed leadership. As warrior, statesman and orator, he was without a rival among his people. In all the country drained by the Mississippi his influence and power none questioned. His celebrated interview with Gen. William Henry Harrison, at Vincennes, which ended abruptly, convinced General Harrison that he had met a foe entirely worthy of his constant attention.

Tecumseh had for many years devoted his great powers of logic and persuasion to the proposition that all tribes must confederate, work together for mutual advantage and to maintain intact, at all hazards, every foot of their choice hunting grounds. His whole policy centered on this one end.

As a basic principle, Tecumseh held that the Great Spirit had given the tribes all these hunting grounds to keep in common, and that all treaties made with white men were null and void. With such diligence, resourcefulness and success did he propagate his doctrines that practically all Indians yielded to his leadership and rallied enthusiastically to his support.

The War of 1812 presented the opportunity and British machinations supplied the pretext which Tecumseh and his warriors seized upon in their resistance to further encroachment upon their territory. The Treaty of Greenville was disregarded. Indians once more left their peaceful pursuits, gathered up their guns and tomahawks and renewed their depredations and massacres.

It was during this period that the Battle of the Mississinewa was fought in Pleasant Township, on Grant County soil. The result of this battle was of supreme importance in its bearing upon the subsequent development of Fairmount Township.

The attention of thoughtful people is not attracted to that country for permanent settlement where life is not secure or where the peaceable possession of property is not assured. Men do not needlessly expose their own lives, much less the lives of their families, to pillage and rapine and murder.

It was not until fourteen years had elapsed after this battle had been fought that pioneers ceased to hesitate in forming their purpose and maturing their plans to gain homes in the new country. Gradually, satisfying themselves of ample protection in their property rights and of personal safety for themselves and their families, Fairmount Township became the objective point of those hardy people from the South and from the East.

In view of these facts, and without further explanation, it is not out of place to insert here a well-written account of the epoch-making Battle of the Mississinewa, prepared by Mr. Carl D. Hunt. This description, somewhat condensed, is taken from *The Indianapolis Star,* dated January 24, 1909. Details given in the article have been authenticated by competent critics who are familiar with ascertained facts relative to this engagement.

"It is the dead of winter," the story runs. "In the face of a blinding snow, and suffering intensely from the bitter cold, a company of soldiers is advancing into a wilderness broken in infrequent spots by a settler's cabin or a deserted camping ground. The men urge their stumbling horses forward, ever ready for the attack of the wary redskins, whom they have come to subject to the white man's rule.

"Imagine such a scene in Indiana but a short ninety-seven years ago, and once you have fixed in your mind the perils and hardships of that terrible march, the stage is set for the thrilling climax—the forgotten Battle of the Mississinewa.

"The valor of Harrison's heroes at Tippecanoe in their great victory over Tecumseh's hosts has been commemorated in song and story. But the heroism of the brave band of pioneer patriots who gave up their lives beside the Mississinewa that civilization might advance is an unknown story. Yet in all the annals of Indian warfare on Hoosier soil there was not a more picturesque struggle or one involving greater bravery and more privations upon the part of the soldiers than this Battle of the Mississinewa. It opened the way to Fort Wayne and Detroit on the north, and thus led to the final victory against the Indians of the Middle West.

"The battle-ground is in the corner of Grant County, not far from the Wabash County line and near the old town of Jalapa, on the Mississinewa River, along the banks of which is scenery not to be surpassed in Indiana. And it is not far, either, from the shaft which may some day remind future generations of the tragic story of Frances Slocum, the 'White Rose of the Miamis.'

"During the boyhood of men now living there were many marks

of the battle yet in evidence. Dr. T. R. Brady, of Wabash, lived near the scene of the battle, and as a boy used to go there in the summer time to gather plums from a grove of wild plum trees which marked the battle ground; and E. P. McClure, of Marion, as a boy, picked bullets from the trees on the battle ground, and remembers well the scene as it was then, before most or all of the original trees went down before the ax of the white man. His father and the Indians of that part of the State were good friends and in this manner Mr. McClure was informed in detail as to the manner of the fighting that marked the battle and of its great importance in opening up what was then the Territory of Indiana.

"The Indians of Indiana had been peaceable for many years—in fact, had been peaceable after their experiences with General Wayne in the neighborhood of what is now Ft. Wayne, and elsewhere. This peace had begun about six years before the Territory of Indiana was organized, in 1800. But when the War of 1812 beset the people of the United States, British representatives, as a part of the plan of that war, proceeded to stir up the Indians against the whites, and it was as the result of this that Gen. William Henry Harrison, the first Governor of Indiana, as a Territory, found much trouble with the Indians on his hands. General Harrison had been successful in his treaty making with the Indians and was satisfied with the progress the wilderness of Indiana was making until about 1806, when he found that Tecumseh, a Shawnee, and his brother, known in history as "The Prophet," were causing trouble. The Indians organized against the encroachments of the white man, and finally General Harrison was forced to order them to disband. They refused, and it was then that he led an expedition against them, which ended in the Battle of Tippecanoe, on November 7, 1811.

"The Indians were scattered, but the beginning of the War of 1812, about a year later, gave them new courage and a new opportunity for hostilities. As a result of their activities and the success of the British in the Northwest, an order was issued from Washington that General Harrison take charge of the forces in this part of the country, and this he did about a year after he had so signally distinguished himself at the Battle of Tippecanoe, making his headquarters at Piqua, Ohio.

"The importance of the engagement of the Indians in the Mississinewa region is shown in a letter then written by General Harrison to his superiors at Washington. Other expeditions had failed against the Indians in this territory and General Harrison was determined that a decisive blow should be struck. This letter, dated November 15, 1812, and addressed to the Secretary of War, was as follows:

"'I have received no information from General Hopkins, but there is no doubt of the complete failure of the mounted expedition under his command, and that measures must be immediately taken to prevent the evils which will otherwise flow from it. As soon as the information reached me I determined to direct an expedition against the Miami towns of the Mississinewa. The situation of this town as it regards my lines of operation, even if the hostility of the inhabitants was less equivocal, would render a measure of this kind highly proper, but from the circumstances of General Hopkins' failure, it has become indispensable. Relieved from the fears excited by the late invasion of their country, the Indians from the upper part of the Illinois River and to the south of Lake Michigan will direct all their efforts against Ft. Wayne and the convoys which are to follow the track of the left wing of the army. Mississinewa will be their rendezvous, where they will receive provisions and every assistance they may require for any hostile enterprise. From that place they can, by their runners, ascertain the period at which every convoy sets out from St. Mary's and with certainty intercept it previously to its arrival at 'Miami Rapids; but that place being broken up and the provisions destroyed there will be nothing to subsist any body of Indians nearer than the Pottawatomie towns upon the waters of the St. Joseph or Lake Michigan. The troops destined for the Mississinewa expedition are the dragoons, belonging to my army, with the addition of perhaps a single company of mounted volunteers. The dragoons will amount to about 600 men, but the greater part of them are to be entirely relied upon. The expedition will be commanded by Lieutenant-Colonel Campbell, of the Nineteenth Infantry. He has no military experience, but is brave, sensible and judicious, and will be ably seconded by the talents and experience of Major Ball. I am confident that you will not hear of any retrograde movement upon the part of this detachment until the object upon which they are sent is accomplished.'

"Leaving Greenville, Ohio, December 14, 1812, the men pushed forward through the wilderness into Indiana. It was cold when they left Greenville, but on December 16th it became much colder, and great were the hardships of the trip. On the morning of the 17th, after a long and hard march, they came upon a village of Indians on the Mississinewa River and surprised and routed them. They killed eight Indian warriors and took forty-eight prisoners, eight of whom were men and the rest women and children. Colonel Campbell left men to guard the prisoners, and, with horsemen, proceeded along the river, destroying Indian towns and dissipating the supplies the Indians had accumulated at this, their base of operations.

"On the following morning the camp was attacked by Indians, but Colonel Campbell, well aware of the likelihood of this, had prepared for it, and the redskins were routed. Then, having accomplished the purposes for which he was sent out, the Indians being driven from the base of operations from which they had done so much to harass General Harrison and thwart his plans, and being short of supplies, the Colonel and his men turned homeward. The march back was one of the most severe in the history of the country. Eight of the soldiers had been killed in the engagements and forty-eight had been wounded, and of the latter seventeen had to be carried, thus making the progress of the trip very slow. Seeing that he would not have provisions, the Colonel sent word ahead for relief, but it did not come until they were within forty miles of Greenville, and many of the brave men of the expedition, footsore and almost frozen, had not had food for three days when the relief party met them.

"That General Harrison was, indeed, well pleased with Colonel Campbell and his command, and was repaid for the confidence he had imposed in the young officer, is indicated in his report to James Monroe, Secretary of War, under date of January 3, 1813, in which he enclosed a detailed report by Colonel Campbell. In this General Harrison spoke in the highest terms of the bravery of the men who composed the expedition.

"General Harrison enclosed the report of the expedition which had been made to him by Colonel Campbell, under date of December 25, 1812. Colonel Campbell goes into detail regarding the privations suffered and the actual fighting. It is, perhaps, the best account of Indian fighting in the Hoosier wilds on record. Imagine what the Hoosiers a hundred years from now will think of such an article!

"In the course of his report Colonel Campbell wrote: 'On the march I occasionally formed in the order of battle to accustom the troops to it. They formed with the utmost celerity and in good order. The first two days I marched forty miles. The third day I pushed the troops as much as they could bear, marched the whole night, although excessively cold, stopping twice to refresh and warm. This day and night we marched forty miles. Early in the morning of the 17th I reached, undiscovered, an Indian town on the Mississinewa, inhabited by a mixture of Delawares and Miamis. The troops rushed into the town, killed eight warriors and took forty-two prisoners, eight of whom were warriors, the residue women and children. I ordered the town immediately to be burnt, a house or two excepted, in which I confined the prisoners; and I ordered the cattle and other stock to be shot. I then left the infantry to guard the prisoners, and with Simral's and Ball's dragoons advanced to some Miami villages a few miles lower down the Mississinewa, but found them evacuated by all but a sick squaw, whom we left in her house. I burnt on this excursion three considerable villages, took several horses and killed a great many cattle, and returned to the town I first burnt, where I had left the prisoners, and encamped. My camp was in the usual form, but covered more ground than common. The infantry and riflemen were on the line, Captain Elliott's company on the right, Butler's in the center and Alexander's on the left. Major Ball's squadron occupied the right and one-half of the rear line. Between Ball's right and Simral's left there was an interval which had not been filled up, owing to the unusual extent of the ground the camp embraced, it having been laid off in my absence to the lower towns. I now began to deliberate on our future movements, whether to go on further, encumbered with prisoners, the men much fatigued, and a great many severely frost-bitten; horses suffering from want of forage, which was very partially relieved by the scanty supplies of corn obtained in the towns. I determined to convene the field officers and captains of the detachment to consult, and then to take such a course as my own judgment might approve. At 4 in the morning of the 18th I ordered to be beaten the reveille, and the officers convened at my fire a short time afterward.

"'While we were in council and about an hour before day, my camp was most furiously attacked by a large party of Indians, preceded by and accompanied with a most hideous yell. This immediately broke up the council and every man ran to his post. The attack commenced upon that angle of the camp formed by the left of Captain Hopkins' troop and the right of Captain Garrard, but in a few seconds became general from the extremes of the right to the left of Ball's squadron. The enemy boldly advanced to within a few yards of the lines and seemed determined to rush in. The guards posted at the different redoubts returned to camp and dispersed among their several companies, this leaving me without a disposable force. Captain Smith, of the Kentucky Light Dragoons, who commanded at one of the redoubts, in a handsome military manner, kept his position until ordered in to fill up the interval in the rear line between the regiment and squadron. The redoubt at which Captain Pierce commanded was first attacked. The captain maintained his position until it was too late to get within the lines. He received two balls through his body and was tomahawked. He died bravely and much lamented. The enemy then took possession of Captain Pierce's redoubt and poured in a tremendous fire upon the angle, to the right and left of which were posted Hopkins' and Garrard's troops. But the fire was as warmly returned; not an inch of ground was yielded. Every man, officer and soldier stood firm and animated and encouraged each other.'

"The writer here continues at considerable length to detail the various maneuvers and formations for battle. Then he pays this tribute to his men:

"'Captain Butler, in a most gallant manner and highly worthy of the name he bears, formed his men immediately and in excellent order and marched them to the point to which he was ordered. The alacrity with which they formed and moved was never excelled by any troops on earth.

"'The battle had gone on in the night. At this time daylight had begun to dawn. I then ordered Captain Trotter, whose troop had been ordered by Colonel Simral to mount for the purpose, to make a charge. The Captain cried out to his men to follow him and they were tilted off at full gallop. Captain Trotter's first lieutenant, with eighteen of the men, were on guard. Lieutenant Trotter, Cornet Dishman and the residue of the troop, together with Lieutenant Hobson and four men of Elmore's Troop, Dr. Moore and a few other gentlemen, including Mr. Thomas Moore, my private secretary, advanced gallantly and charged a numerous body of the enemy. Major McDowell, with a small party, rushed into the midst of the enemy and exposed himself very much. I can not say too much for this gallant veteran. Captain Markle, with about fifteen of his Troop, and Lieutenant Warren's, also, made a daring charge upon the enemy. Captain Markle avenged the death of his relation, Lieutenant Waltz, upon an Indian, with his own sword. Captain Trotter and his Troop, and Captain Markle and his little band, performed a most dangerous duty in the bravest manner. Captain Trotter mentions to me as worthy of particular notice Robert Mitchell, a wagoner, who had volunteered for the expedition, and Christian Wilman, Trumpeter to Colonel Simral's Regiment, who blew two charges and hewed down an Indian with his sword. William Montgomery, Sergeant Major of the Regiment of Kentucky Light Dragoons, was in charge and distinguished himself as well as in the skirmish the day before. In this charge Captain Trotter was wounded slightly, Corporal Riddle shot through the body, David Stule wounded in the right thigh slightly and the brave Piatt received his mortal wound, being shot through the body and hand. Fearing that Captain Trotter might be too hard pressed, I ordered Captain Johnson of the Kentucky Light Dragoons to advance with his Troop to support him. I found Johnson ready and Colonel Simral reports to me that all his other Captains, to-wit: Elmore, Young and Smith, were anxious to join in the charge. But I called for only one troop. The Colonel had the whole in excellent order. Captain Johnson did not join Trotter until the enemy was out of reach. He, however, picked up a straggler or two that Trotter had passed over. The cavalry returned and informed me that the enemy had fled precipitately. I have on this occasion to lament the loss of several brave men and a great many wounded. Among the former are Captain Pierce, of the Ohio Volunteers, and Lieutenant Waltz, of Markle's Troop. From the enclosed list you will see names and numbers of the killed and wounded, eight being killed and forty-eight wounded, two of whom are since dead. The enemy paid dearly for their temerity. From the trails through the snow and those found dead we could not have killed less than thirty, which, with those killed the day before, amounts to thirty-eight. The enemy did not take a scalp. The Indian who killed Captain Pierce attempted to scalp him, but was killed. Major Ball informs me that he can say with confidence that there never were officers and soldiers who displayed more cool, firm and soldierly conduct than those of his squadron.'

"This concludes the principal account of the fighting written by the commanding officer. He then generously proceeds to give unstinted praise to his various officers, making personal mention of the deeds of each and also complimenting the valorous conduct of many privates.

"Colonel Campbell wrote of his return march:

"'I have now, my dear sir, detailed to you the particulars of an engagement bravely fought, and victory gloriously won, after contending most warmly for at least an hour. From the length of our line simultaneously attacked by them, I am persuaded there could not have been less than three hundred of the enemy. They fought most bravely. My strength on the morning of the action was about five hundred and ninety rank and file, a considerable portion of whom, amounting to at least forty or fifty, were almost rendered unfit for duty by the severity of the weather. Some were so badly frost-bitten as to be scarcely able to walk. There never was severer service performed by any troops, and yet there is not a murmur. Reports made to me yesterday morning inform me of three hundred who are so severely frost-bitten as to be entirely unfit for duty. On my march back I was compelled to move slowly on account of the wounded, seventeen of whom we had to carry on litters. I kept the troops always ready to meet an attack, which I daily and nightly expected, until I reached this place. I fortified my camp every night by a breastwork, which kept us very busily engaged. The scarcity of axes was now most sensibly felt. I have informed you how I advanced into the enemy's country. My return was much in the same manner. I determined to be always ready, to avoid surprises and falling into ambuscades. I assure you the responsibility attached to this command I most seriously felt. Being young in service, and inexperienced, I felt great diffidence in accepting this command. I, however, hope my conduct will meet your approbation. I will hasten to join you, but it will take the troops some time to recruit and heal. Some will lose their toes; others' feet are so swollen as not to be able to put on their shoes. The night march was most severe on them.'

HON. JOHN T. STRANGE

"The brilliant young Colonel, in the concluding paragraph of his report, gives us an estimate of the importance of the Battle of the Mississinewa.

"'I have learned, since my return, that General Hopkins had returned to Vincennes, after burning some Indian villages and driving them, supposed to be three hundred in number, up the Wabash. This still made my situation more perilous, and I shall not be surprised to learn that Tecumseh commanded in the action against me. Let him be who he may, he was a gallant fellow and maneuvered well. Conner thinks it was Little Thunder (nephew to the Little Turtle) from his loud voice, which he knew. He heard him ordering his men in the Miami language to rush on, that they would soon retreat. I think, sir, the Kentucky Cavalry will scarcely be in a situation to render you much more service. Their losses in horses are considerable and one hundred and thirty-eight frost-bitten severely. They are fine fellows with a few exceptions, and as brave as any men in the world. Captain Prince is here very sick, and was unable to get on with us; this was to me a great loss.

"'I am, sir, very respectfully, etc.,
"'JOHN B. CAMPBELL,
"'Lieut.-Col. Nineteenth U. S. Reg.'

"The valiant Campbell, for whom General Harrison predicted such a bright future, was promoted in the following year for his success in the Mississinewa expedition. In April, 1814, he was commissioned a Colonel in the Eleventh Infantry, but was fatally wounded in the battle of Chippewa, on July 5th, of that year, and died August 29th, following."

And these are the men and such are the deeds which prompted Senator John T. Strange, of Grant County, in January, 1909, to introduce a bill in the State Legislature for an appropriation to commemorate their achievements.

However much historians may differ as to the importance of the battle, there can be no question about the heroism displayed by Colonel Campbell's valiant band in an action which assured peace and safety for the pioneers on what was then the Western frontier.

BILL INTRODUCED BY SENATOR JOHN T. STRANGE BEFORE THE STATE LEGISLATURE IN JANUARY, 1909, TO PROVIDE MEMORIAL ON MISSISSINEWA BATTLEFIELD.*

Preamble.

Whereas, It has been almost one century ago since the Battle of the Mississinewa was fought, and

Whereas, Up to this time no action has ever been taken to purchase the ground upon which the battle occurred, or to erect a monument to commemorate the heroism of those engaged on behalf of the United States in said battle, or to commemorate the importance of the successful termination of said battle in the settlement of the great Northwest; and

Whereas, At this time it is deemed fitting and proper for the great State of Indiana to recognize in some suitable manner the vast importance of this event to the people of Indiana, and to the great Northwest; therefore,

1. Be it enacted by the General Assembly of the State of Indiana, That there is hereby appropriated out of any funds in the State Treasury not otherwise appropriated, the sum of $10,000 for the purchase of

---

*This measure failed to pass.

the Mississinewa Battle Ground and the erection thereon of a suitable monument in Grant County, Indiana, to commemorate the suffering, services and heroism of those engaged there in battle on the 17th and 18th days of December, 1812, and to perpetuate the importance of the event.

2. Three Trustees shall be appointed by the Governor, whose duty it shall be to carry out the provisions of this act, and said Trustees shall serve without compensation.

3. That said Trustees shall keep an accurate account of all disbursements and make a full report thereof and of the execution of their said trust to the Governor not later than January 1, 1910.

CHAPTER III.

ME-SHIN-GO-ME-SIA, CHIEF OF THE MIAMIS.

IN JUNE, 1861, Hon. Elijah P. Hackleman, a pioneer resident of Wabash County, upon request of John B. Dillon, author of Dillon's *History of Indiana*, visited the scene of the Battle of the Mississinewa. Mr. Hackleman made careful measurements of the ground and gathered considerable important information relative to this engagement. He obtained many facts from Me-shin-go-me-sia and William B. Richards, both of whom, it is stated, participated in the battle. Richards later moved to Liberty Township, where he lived until his death.

Me-shin-go-me-sia was born near the mouth of Josina Creek, in Wabash County, not very far from where the battle was fought. The year of his birth is given as about 1782.* He died December 16, 1879. There is a sharp difference of opinion prevalent regarding his participation in the Battle of the Mississinewa. This battle was fought on December 18, 1812. Me-shin-go-me-sia, if the year of his birth be correctly given, was then thirty years old. In order to properly qualify as chief of his tribe, an Indian must possess qualities which elevate a man somewhat in the esteem and confidence of his race. He must have stability, and skill, and bravery as a warrior. He must be able to inspire his followers and by personal example to stimulate courage. It is not very likely, therefore, that an Indian old enough to fight who skulked away at a time like that, when fearlessness, the most important attribute of all, was imperative, would ever be accepted or even tolerated as Chief of the proud Miamis. If, on the other hand, the year of his birth, as given, be incorrect, Me-shin-go-me-sia may have been a child when the battle was fought, and therefore might have been carried away with other children to a place of safety.

ME-SHIN-GO-ME-SIA

---

* *Kingmans' Atlas*, Page 16.

Me-shin-go-me-sia was the eldest of ten children. When his father, Me-to-cin-yah, passed away, Me-shin-go-me-sia became Chief of the Miamis. He managed the affairs of his people with wisdom; his prudence in business matters was recognized. He adopted the dress of the whites, but continued to use the Indian language; he spoke English fairly well. In all his habits he was strictly temperate. His conduct was manly and he was upright in his dealings. In his later years he joined the Baptist Church and lived a consistent Christian life. He was married about the year 1815.* No husband was ever more devoted or attentive to his wife. She was stricken with blindness before her death, and he was constantly by her side, ministering to her every need. At his death he owned 160 acres of good land. He enjoyed the respect of all who knew him.

"Me-shin-go-me-sia was a remarkable man," stated E. P. McClure, who knew him well. Mr. McClure's father, the late Samuel McClure, was intimately acquainted with the old chief. Samuel McClure settled on the Indian reserve in 1827, where he built one of the first cabins erected in Wabash County. He was implicitly trusted by the Indians. So highly was he esteemed that they gave him the name Che-cum-wah, meaning twin brother. "My father went to Washington City with Me-shin-go-me-sia several times on treaty matters. I recall, as a boy," remarked E. P. McClure, "that Indians made father's house their home when they came to Marion. The Miamis lived seven miles northwest of Marion, and this was their trading point. I used to get pies and cakes from mother's pantry for them to eat. They liked delicacies of this sort. I remember they used to wrap their blankets about them, eight or ten in a room, and lie down on the floor, their feet to the fireplace. That is the way they wanted to sleep, and father always let them have their wish about it. One day Sas-a-quas, sometimes called Sassafras, brought a gray pony to town and made me a present of it. I was a very proud boy. It was the first pony I ever owned. Sas-a-quas used to make bows and arrows for me. I have heard that the Miamis practiced polygamy. I have mingled with them a great deal, but I never knew of but two cases where the Miamis had plural wives. Shap-an-do-siah and Sas-a-quas each had two wives. I do not believe that Me-shin-go-me-sia took part in the Battle of Mississinewa. He was a peaceable man. I have heard my father in conversation with him many times on a wide variety of subjects, and not once do I recollect of hearing Me-shin-go-me-sia say anything about participating in that fight. My understanding has always been, and I am firmly of the opin-

---

Kingmans' Atlas.

ion, that he was not in that engagement. It is my impression that Me-shin-go-me-sia, with several squaws and their children, were over on Wildcat when the Battle of the Mississinewa was fought."

"I have been slower in making reply to your favor of the 13th inst. than I would have been excepting my inability to find data to bear me out in thinking that Me-shin-go-me-sia was a boy six years old, among other children, with women and men too old to accompany the warriors of the tribe who had gone north to do battle," writes Maj. George W. Steele, of Marion. "The latter returned in time, as we know, to give Colonel Campbell and his command all of the fighting he could stand.

"Of course Me-shin-go-me-sia was a young hero at any rate, and in due time a chief who proved to be the last of his tribe.

"As a boy, in 1849, was at their village at a round-up and separation of their ponies, which had become so numerous as to disturb our pioneer settlers, and were sold at public sale in surrounding towns, Marion, of course, among them."

The letter of Major Steele was prompted by an inquiry made in a communication by the writer addressed to him relative to the participation of Me-shin-go-me-sia in the Battle of the Mississinewa. Major Steele was a leading factor in the effort made looking to the purchase of the ground on which this battle was fought. It was planned to acquire this land with a view of converting it into a park, as was done in the case of the site of the Battle of Tippecanoe, located near Lafayette. The project failed for lack of proper interest on the part of men in position to make their co-operation effective.

A letter to Dr. Thomas R. Brady, of Wabash, who at one time represented Wabash County in the Indiana State Senate, elicited the following response:

Wabash, Indiana, January 31, 1917.

Edgar M. Baldwin, Fairmount, Indiana.

Dear Sir:—My father, Dr. Thomas R. Brady, received a letter from you recently asking for information concerning an Indian, Me-shin-go-me-sia, I think, and we are sorry that we have been so negligent in answering it.

Father has been very sick for some time and is unable to write a word, or I am sure you would have had a prompt reply.

He says: "I knew the Indian all my life. He was temperate and was a good citizen. He urged his people to work and be industrious. I have always understood he was not engaged in the Battle of the Mississinewa."

If he were able I am sure he could give you other and better information, and I am sorry I can give no more.

Hoping this may be of some little assistance, I wish to remain,

Yours sincerely,

JENNIE A. BRADY.

Dr. Brady, at the time the communication was written, was one of few men then living who knew Me-shin-go-me-sia intimately. It seems almost a hopeless task to connect the old chief with the engagement at Mississinewa. The safer plan, therefore, seems to be to submit such evidence as may be adduced and suggest that the reader use his own judgment in reaching a conclusion.

Referring to the matter, Hon. Edgar L. Goldthwait, for many years editor of *The Marion Chronicle,* says in a letter to the writer, under date of January 5, 1917:

"Relating to your inquiry of the old Indian's part in the battle: It is said that he spoke of it often to his friends. In one of the histories he pictured it. He was a boy; his duty was to look after the horses, to be ready when retreat was sounded."

Richard Dillon, of Fairmount, in a letter dated January 27, 1917, offers this interesting bit of information:

"Phineas Henley came to Indiana in 1837 and settled on forty acres now a part of the farm owned by Alice Thomas.

"The writer, a grandson of Phineas Henley, has often heard him speak of being acquainted with Me-shin-go-me-sia, and of hearing him tell about the Battle of the Mississinewa, stating that he was twelve years old at the time, and was hid in the woods behind a log, where he could hear the bullets whiz over him."

In a letter written on August 26, 1909, to Hon. John T. Strange, of Marion, Indiana, Mrs. John Flitcraft,* who lived at the time the communication was written at Macy, Indiana, says:

"Me-shin-go-me-sia told my father that he was fourteen years old at the time of the battle and held four ponies during the fight and then he lun and lun and lun and hid in sycamore log long time."

It is exceedingly difficult, owing to the well-known diffidence of the Indian, to obtain from him information which he sees fit to withhold from the white man. It is said that few Indians care to discuss

---

* Mrs. Flitcraft is the daughter of William L. Fields. William L. Fields lived in the neighborhood of the battlefield for over twenty-two years, and was well acquainted all through that section. His father built the old Conner mill and helped run it for years. His daughter speaks of Mr. Fields as possessing a fine memory.

in any way a battle in which he has been defeated. It may be stated, however, that Me-shin-go-me-sia was a man of considerable ability, firm, but not obstinate. His grave may be seen in the Indian burying ground near Jalapa.

CHAPTER IV.

THE FIRST SETTLERS.

IT WAS some time in the late fall or early winter that a family of eight arrived at a place about four miles from where Fairmount now stands and erected a booth by the side of a large fallen tree, under which and in the wagon that conveyed them there, they proceeded to make the best of the situation with the true pioneer spirit.

Their neighbors were few and far between in the then dense wilderness. The word soon became circulated for miles around amongst the scattered inhabitants that a family had moved in their midst and were living in the open forest. This aroused the neighborly chivalry. Runners were sent out all through that section to notify people that a family had moved in and were needing help.

No time must be lost in getting the exposed family under shelter. Accordingly a day was named. At the appointed time a dozen or more stout-hearted woodsmen met at the camp, elected their foreman and proceeded to business. Some felled the trees that stood plentifully near by. They were dragged in by a team as soon as felled. Four of the best ax men each took a corner of the building to notch and fit the corners together. This was considered a position of honor, requiring practice and a mechanical eye and steady nerve. Then two men must select a good oak tree, fell it, cut the blocks and rive the boards to cover the building.

When the noon hour had arrived they had the side walls to the cabin about done, for they did not meet there to play. Those first cabins were but one story, about eight logs high to the eve. The family was short of table supplies, and at dinner did not have cups to go around. Two and three must drink from one cup, use the same knife and fork and plate, and make a table of a chip.

Some of the men killed a deer on the way there and brought that along, which materially helped the dinner menu. By night they had the cabin up and covered, a place cut out for door and fireplace, which no doubt was soon occupied.

When I left Fairmount there was one man living in Marion who helped erect that cabin. That family proved to be good, honest, loyal citizens, but are all gone now. I have been on the place many times, but I think the original cabin was gone. This incident came before me today. I had not thought of it for a long time. So I sat down and

THE FANKBONER GRAVEYARD

Situated on a knoll about six miles northeast of Fairmount, near the old State road. In the foreground is Robert McCormick's monument. The inscription, which is not plain in the picture, reads as follows: "Robert McCormick. Died August 9, 1836, aged 57 years, 1 mo. 9 da." On Mrs. McCormick's tombstone appears the following words: "Ann, wife of John Fankboner, former wife of R. McCormick, died Jan. 23, 1880, aged 92 yrs. 4 mo. 7 da."

penciled it off in a hurry. It may interest you as a fraction of the history that was once one of the stage scenes in the making of Fairmount Township.

The walls of the cabin being up, the work of making the house comfortable was not near complete. An opening must be cut out for a door and fireplace and two small windows. Then the open spaces between the logs in the body of the house must be filled with chink and clay mortar to keep out the wind, snow and rain.

It will not be conducive to health to live on the ground in that damp country. There are no saw mills in the new country, and no roads one

ORIGINAL SITE OF THE McCORMICK TAVERN

The little pile of rock in the foreground indicates the location of the historic McCormick cabin, often in the first settlement of the new country the first stopping place of the pioneer who came to seek a home in the wilderness. This cabin was the center of hospitality in the early days.

could haul a load over. Consequently one must use such material as one has. Necessity is the mother of invention, it is said. They go into the woods, select three straight logs eight or ten inches in diameter, in length the width of the building on the inside, and with an ax make one side as true as possible, place one at each end on inside and one in the middle on which to rest the floor, which is to be made by selecting small, straight trees that will split easily, cutting sections half the length of floor, splitting them through the center and making the flat side as smooth as possible with the tools they may have, flattening the rounded ends so that they will lay evenly on the three sleepers, or joists, meeting in the middle, scalping the edges of the flooring so that they will come close together as may be.

The floor being down, a fireplace and chimney must be builded. There are no brick kilns or stone quarries awaiting them in the wilderness. What can the poor family do? Again they must appeal to the forest for material. They split out some boards three by ten inches wide, six feet long and three feet long, according to the size they wanted the fireplace, with which they would make a three-sided box by notching together at the corners, the loose ends to be nailed or fastened to each side of the opening for the fireplace and carried up to the mantle log, where they commence narrowing in for the chimney flue by splitting out pieces similar in size to plastering lath, but a little heavier, of the proper length to build a flue two by three feet, and plastering this lattice work on inside and out with clay mortar.

The fireplace must be lined with a stiff clay mortar about one foot thick, brought in to the edge of the wall and carried up to the lattice work of chimney flue to prevent the wood catching fire. Then, with split boards driven in the ground at front and sides of hearth place and filled with good clay well packed down, the family is ready to cook their first meal at home, if they have a skillet, boiler and coffee pot.

There was another way they had of getting out floor boards in those primitive days, when a man had some money and wished to build an extra fine log house. It was to employ two men with a whip saw to cut his boards. The saw was not quite so long as a cross-cut saw, with teeth set like a carpenter's rip saw. The log to be cut was placed on a platform of logs, some six feet from the ground, with one strong man below and one above, to work the saw up and down. This was slow work and took strong men to do the motor work. Charles Hinshaw, who settled on the Nate Wilson farm, did such work. I saw him operating his mill once.

Melbourne, Florida, December 26, 1916. A. HENLEY.

(Editor's Note.—It may be helpful, at this point, to consider carefully the pen picture so skilfully drawn of that struggling pioneer family in their efforts to gain a foothold and a home in the new country. How aptly it portrays the hardships of people who came here in the early days. How suitable as an introductory word to the fundamental purpose of this narrative. Expressed in words so simple and yet so comprehensive and so full of meaning, the little story stands out in front of you like a thing apart.)

In the fall of 1826, about the month of September,* Robert McCormick came from Fayette County, Indiana.

On August 15, 1829, he entered land and built his cabin soon after near the crossing of the Ft. Wayne, Muncie and Indianapolis State road, on the farm later owned by J. and M. E. Wilson, situated one-half mile south of Wilson's ford.

McCormick moved his family to their new home in October, 1829. His cabin became known far and near as McCormick's Tavern. As the State road in those days was the principal highway through this section of Indiana, the tavern enjoyed a good trade.

Near the site of this old tavern is Bethel Graveyard, the quiet spot where lie buried the early settlers of this neighborhood, including Daniel and Mary Coleman, the donors of the land, and Isaac Sudduth, who served in the War of the Revolution, and died at the Coleman home at the age of ninety-nine years. Mrs. Rachel Coleman Haynes, who lives at the Coleman homestead, takes great pleasure in bringing to mind the scenes about the old tavern house in the days when the girls wore poke bonnets and shawls and skirts of great fullness. Her father, Daniel Coleman, a son of Thomas Coleman, served for sixteen years as Justice of the Peace in pioneer days. Mrs. Haynes was married, August 26, 1868, to Francis Marion Haynes.†

---

*This information is supplied by Mrs. Gabrille Havens, whose parents, the Clarks, were neighbors and intimate friends of the McCormicks. The official records show that McCormick entered land on August 15, 1829. This was two years before Grant County was organized and three years after his arrival. The explanation is offered that there was no need for haste in that early day, since settlers were few and far between. Emigration had not commenced at this date to any considerable extent, and there was hence no likelihood of contention over property rights among pioneers who then peopled this sparsely settled wilderness. The discrepancy in the dates, therefore, is accounted for. McCormick simply deferred the long and difficult and often dangerous journey through the swamps and the forest to Ft. Wayne, where the land office was situated, to enter land.

---

†Francis Marion Haynes, farmer, who lives in the extreme northeast corner of Fairmount Township, was born in Franklin County, Indiana, August 22, 1842. His paternal grandfather came from England and on his mother's side of the house he is a descendant of Silas Andrews, of New York State. His parents were Solomon and Chloe (Andrews) Haynes. On December 6, 1864, he enlisted in the Second Indiana Battery and served with this command until July 3, 1865, participating in several hard-fought battles, among them the engagement at Nashville, Tenn. At the end of the Civil War he returned home, and in 1866 came to Grant County. In politics he has always affiliated with the Republican party, and for many years he has supported every movement to make Fairmount Township and Grant County dry. He is a member of the Methodist Protestant Church at Fowlerton.

The First Settlers.

OLD COLEMAN HOMESTEAD

Robert McCormick came from New York State to Indiana. He was born in Pennsylvania in 1779. He was the father of seven children, namely, Jacob, John, Katie, Eliza, Enos, Lewis and Jane. McCormick was of medium size, dressed plainly, was sober, industrious, thrifty, and exceedingly kind to his neighbors. He was helpful to others and popular with all. He kept tavern from 1826 until 1836, the year of his death. The funeral services, held at his tavern, were attended by a large number of people. The cause of his death was fever, the insidious disease which carried away, prematurely, so many pioneers. He was sick but a short time. McCormick was a member of the Baptist Church. In politics he was a Whig. At the time of his death he owned a section of land. This land was not all comprised in one body. It lay in several different localities within and adjacent to the boundary lines of what is now Fairmount Township. South Jonesboro is situated on part of an eighty-acre tract once owned by McCormick.

In 1829, according to official records, the first settlers came to Fairmount Township to make their permanent home.

On June 10, of that year, Josiah Dille purchased from the Government the south fraction of Section 10. James H. Clark, about 1834, bought this land of Dille. Josiah Dille was a brother to James Dille, who at one time lived in Fairmount. Josiah was a younger half-brother to Ichabod Dille, who was many years his senior. Josiah lived for about five years where he first bought land, then moved to what was known as the Dille neighborhood, two miles north of Jonesboro, on the river. In later years he moved West, with his family, where he died. As he was not given to writing letters, it is not definitely known which State he finally settled in, and there appears to be no information regarding his family now in possession of Grant County relatives.

Mrs. Gabrille Havens was born in Bradford county, Pennsylvania, near Luther's Mills, on February 25, 1820. She was the daughter of James H. and Susan B. Clark. There were nine children in the Clark family, namely, Polly, Gabrille, Rebecca, Visula, Weltha Ann, Emma Carline, Cynthia Mariah, Simon B., and James M. The father moved to Fairmount Township on February 3, 1838. Mrs. Havens was therefore eighteen years of age when she arrived. The Clark family came in two wagons, one drawn by horses and the other by an ox team. It required three days to complete the journey from Darke County, Ohio. Mrs. Havens has been of material assistance in connecting up past events with the present. At this writing (January 16, 1917), she is spending the winter with her granddaughter, Mrs. Frank McCombs, of Hartford City, Indiana. Although in her ninety-seventh year, her mind is as keen and active, apparently, as ever, and, barring unforeseen circumstances, she bids fair to live to see her one hundredth anniversary. Mrs. Havens has read the Bible through seventy times, besides the reading here and there at random in the Good Book. She completed the seventieth reading of the Scripture in the year 1915. The first President she remembers hearing her folks talk about when she was a girl at home was Andrew Jackson, when old Hickory was making his campaign in 1832, although, being always an omniverous reader, she was familiar with the name of the first President, and heard much of George Washington.

MRS. GABRILLE HAVENS

CHAPTER V.

LOCATING ON BACK CREEK.

Stories Grandfather Tells.

(By Mark Baldwin.)

OH, MARVELOUS tales can my grandfather tell
  Of wonderful times and the things that befell
When he was a boy, and roamed the wild wood,
Enjoying his life as a boy only could;
With vigor and health, and with pioneer blood
Flowing strong in his veins, he swam the swift flood,
Or hunted the sly, little, impudent beasts
That peopled the forests, and stole for their feasts
The corn from the crib, or took from the soil
The grain, making useless the pioneer's toil.

And I think to myself, then, how grand it must be
To live in a hut in the forest so free
From the vain, pompous ways of the life of today,
From the pace we are living at present. But say,
When grandfather tells of the woodticks and lice,
Of the fleas and the chiggers, the rats and the mice,
The fever and ague, I don't think I'd lose
My freedom from these to have been in his shoes.

We have observed that Robert McCormick and Josiah Dille came to Fairmount Township and settled over on the old State road. The center of pioneer activity is now changed. The scene shifts to a location a few miles to the west. The way is opened for settlement along Back Creek.

The earliest settlers of the Township are descendants of those idealists, and seekers after freedom, religious enthusiasts, and adventurers that left England in the seventeenth century for the new country of Pennsylvania and its neighboring states. Of the causes that led to their unrest after two or three generations, and exodus to Virginia and Maryland and almost immediately on to North Carolina, and the subsequent moving to the Middle West, there is an interesting account in "Southern Quakerism and Slavery," by Rufus M. Jones. No doubt all through the search for a place where absolute freedom of conscience could be exercised, a desire for larger and richer lands was another impelling motive, as it was perhaps the only one that had carried them South. This Southern experience turned out a bitter one in many ways, families of gentle blood being exposed to the rigors of mountain pioneering. It is small wonder if many of the more lax held slaves, and if, after conscience had bade them free them, they pushed out again for a new country, their fortunes crippled, but hearts resolute and purpose high. Yet, though they carried little away from the South in wagons through the dense wilderness, they ever kept in their hearts a tender regard for the Old State, which they had, for a brief period, helped to build. The counties of Guilford and Randolph were seats of advanced thinking in the early years of the nineteenth century; the first college in North Carolina was established there and there was a keen awakening even in those early days to the evils of slavery, war and intemperance.

Back Creek rises in Madison County, entering Fairmount Township in Section 6, and has a general northerly course, bearing a little to the east, entering Mill Township a little west of the half-mile corner on the north side of Section 17, emptying into the Mississinewa River at a point northeast of Jonesboro. The upper portion of the stream was, in 1829, very flat and rather marshy. It was cut wider and deeper about 1856. This was the first improvement of any extent done in the county. It is worthy of note that this work was carried on by private enterprise. The lasting benefits far exceeded expectations, both as to land drained and made tillable and as to the public welfare generally. This locality had been a series of beaver ponds. A channel was opened and a crude system of drainage introduced. This enabled farmers to raise grain and grass on soil where cattle had mired during the first settlement along the creek. The higher land and ground farther north were first choice for farming.

Joseph Winslow,* on December 28, 1829, entered the northwest quarter of Section 17, the farm now owned by Ancil Winslow.

---

*Joseph Winslow was by occupation a farmer and miller. He was born in Randolph County, North Carolina, in 1777. He came to Fairmount Township, with his family, in a four-horse wagon. He had been successful in the South. He brought with him to the new country $2,600 in cash, which was a considerable sum of money for that day. He entered land for himself and assisted his sons and daughters, supplying each with funds to enter a quarter-section at $1.25 per acre. He founded Friends meeting at Back Creek, in 1831, services being held at his home prior to this date. In 1841 the log meeting house gave way to the brick structure. For many years Joseph Winslow sat at the head of the meeting. He rarely ever spoke at the services, excepting at business sessions. He held to the Quaker idea of silent supplication to his Master, praying as his conscience directed. He was a liberal supporter of educational movements and figured prominently in all worthy enterprises which promised to advance the best interests of his neighborhood. One son, John, settled on Blue River, near Carthage, in Rush County. Daniel Winslow, a son, and Aaron Hill and Solomon Knight, sons-in-law, settled in Mill Township. Joseph Winslow died October 27, 1859, aged 81 years, 9 months and 22 days.

On the same date Matthew Winslow, son of Joseph, entered the west half of the northeast quarter of Section 17, the farm now partly owned by John A. Jones and partly by John Devine.

THREE OF THE FIRST SETTLERS ON BACK CREEK

Reading from left to right the men shown in the above picture are Daniel Winslow, Henry Winslow and Seth Winslow. They are sons of Joseph Winslow, who entered land along Back Creek on December 28, 1829. Joseph Winslow founded the Society of Friends in Fairmount Township. For a short time after the first settlement, according to Levi Winslow, son of Henry Winslow, Back Creek was known as Winslow Creek. Joseph Winslow, who was a plain, unassuming man, protested against the idea of calling this stream after his family for the reason that it appeared to him like exalting his own relatives over others equally entitled to consideration. Out of deference to his wishes, and upon his earnest solicitation, the name Winslow was dropped and it was called Back Creek, after a stream by that name in North Carolina, his old home. It has ever since been known as Back Creek. The sturdy men whose likenesses are shown above bore well their part in the primitive days of the Township.

Seth Winslow, another son of Joseph, on the same date entered the east half of the northwest quarter of Section 20. This farm was later owned by Mrs. Ruth Winslow Elliott, a daughter.

Henry Winslow, another son, settled on Section 17.

Exum Newby, on December 28, 1829, entered the southwest quarter of Section 17. This land is now owned by the heirs of Lewis Fankboner.

These men came from Randolph County, North Carolina. They formed the nucleus for a settlement which grew in numbers and prospered. They cherished high ideals. They possessed rugged characters and robust physiques. They were hopeful of the future. They were cheerful and they were helpful. They were made of the kind of material that did not hesitate to brave hardships and to surmount obstacles. They "toiled, and suffered and died that we might inherit the promise."

Among others who came in the early part of the thirties and entered land were:

Charles Baldwin, August 4, 1830.
Solomon Thomas, August 9, 1830.
Iredell Rush, March 16, 1831.
John Benbow, November 30, 1831.
Nathan Morris, April 9, 1832.
Thomas Morris, April 9, 1832.
Thomas Harvey, October 10, 1832.
Jesse Harvey, October 10, 1832.
Henry Osborn, August 27, 1833.
Thomas Baldwin, October 7, 1833.
Daniel Baldwin, December 16, 1833.
Benjamin Benbow, December 16, 1833.

A majority of these men entered land on Back Creek. Most of them came from North Carolina. All but two were of pious Quaker ancestry, and adhered strictly to the doctrines and discipline of the Quaker faith.

It may be remarked, by way of digression, that when the writer began his research for material for this narrative, he encountered a fact which seemed to him particularly significant. Nathan Morris, one of the pioneers whose name has been mentioned, was the father of twenty-two children. He was twice married. His first wife was the mother of fifteen children, and his second wife gave birth to seven. Carrying the inquiry a little farther, it was learned that the eldest daughter, then living, at the age of eighty-two, was the mother of nine, seven of whom survived to marriageable age. The seven sons and daughters, collectively, were parents of seven children, six sons and one daughter. At this rate of retrogression, numerically, if it be indefinitely maintained, Nathan Morris, father of the original family of twenty-two, should he return within two or three generations, would find his progeny practically extinct.

OLD BACK CREEK MEETING HOUSE
(From a picture taken by Oz B. Fankboner.)

Back Creek Monthly Meeting of Friends was opened and held, agreeably to the direction of New Garden Quarterly Meeting, on July 21, 1838. The membership had increased gradually from a small beginning, when meetings for worship were held from 1829 to 1831 at the cabin of Joseph Winslow. The building later erected for meeting purposes had proved to be inadequate for the accommodation of the membership.

On March 16, 1839, Friends nominated to make some arrangement in procuring lumber for a new meeting house reported to the monthly meeting that they had made "some engagements" for plank to the amount of about $100. Matthew Winslow, Thomas Hill, David Hiatt and Aaron Hill were appointed to have the matter in charge and report as occasion required.

On May 18, 1839, Aaron Hill, David Stanfield, Asia Peacock, Lewis Jones, Charles Baldwin, Jesse E. Wilson and Henry Winslow were appointed to make out a ratio of apportionment among the membership for the purpose of raising money to build the meeting house. This committee, on June 15, 1839, reported as follows:

Solomon Knight, Matthew Winslow, Exum Newby, Nathan Morris and Aaron Hill, 4½.

Jonathan Wilcuts, Joseph Winslow, Charles Baldwin, Daniel Baldwin, Timothy Kelley, Iredell Rush, David Stanfield, Thomas Harvey and Amaziah Beeson, 3.

Lewis Jones, Seth Winslow, Evan Hinshaw, Thomas Winslow, Thomas Baldwin, Henry Winslow and Asia Peacock, 2.

James Scott and Dugan Rush, 1¾.

Micajah Newby, Lindsey Baldwin, William Osborn, Charles Hinshaw, Thomas Hill, William Peacock, Daniel Frazier, Benjamin Benbow, Mahlon Neal and Job Jackson, 1½.

Peter Rich, William Stanfield, Jesse E. Wilson, David S. Stanfield, Henry Winslow, Jr., John Haisley, Ira Haisley, Jonathan Jones, Nathan Hammer, Elias Baldwin, Joseph W. Baldwin, Henry Harvey and Isaac Stanfield, 1.

John Rich, Allen Wright, Nathan D. Wilson, John Lee, Charles Stanfield and John Peacock, ½.

The ratio of apportionment having been agreed upon, the meeting proceeded at once to name Joseph Winslow, Exum Newby, Iredell Rush, Jonathan Wilcuts, David Hiatt, David Stanfield, Obadiah Jones, Charles Baldwin, Thomas Hill and Aaron Hill as a committee to devise a plan for the building of the meeting house "on the present lot of land."

On July 20, 1839, this committee reported as follows:

"We, the committee to propose a plan for a house, agree to propose the following: The house 40x80, to be built of brick, the wall 18 inches thick, 12 feet from floor to floor, to sink 18 inches below the surface of the ground and to be set on a stone foundation; three gallery seats to raise 9 inches each, the back part starting from the center and to raise 2 feet 3 inches; eleven 24-light windows in each apartment, glasses 8x10; three double doors in each apartment 4 feet in width, 7 feet in height, the house to be immediately east of the old one, with which the meeting unites and refers the subject to Back Creek Preparative Meeting."

The brick structure shown in the picture was constructed according to these specifications, and as nearly as it could be ascertained was ready for meeting purposes in June, 1841. In 1899 this house was torn down and the present church was erected at a location near the site of the old meeting house.

It is when we are confronted by these extraordinary facts that one is disposed to share with Col. Theodore Roosevelt his views regarding the far-reaching possibilities of race suicide and the apparent indifference of the present generation relative thereto.

After the year 1833 the country was settled up rapidly.

In 1835 Dugan Rush, Thomas Ratliff, William Payne, Clarkson Wilcuts, Timothy Kelley, Elijah Lucas, Lewis Moorman, James S. Wilson, Bingham Simons, Nathan Dicks, John Weston, Charles Hinshaw, Solomon Parsons, Franklin Davis, John Lee, Jr., John Lee, Sr., and Jonathan Wilcuts entered land.

In 1836 came Henry Harvey, Thomas Winslow, Thomas Edgerton, William Osborn, Eli Moorman, Charles Smith, Otho Selby, Wm. H. H. Reeder, Lewis Harrison, Harvey Davis, Jabez Moore, John Fankboner, William Leach, Jonathan Reeder, David Stanfield, Moses Benbow, Lancaster Bell, Carter Hasting, Joel Hollingsworth, William Harvey, David Bates and Lewis Jones.

In 1837 Phineas Henley, Peter Rich, David Lewis, Morris Payne, Joseph Weston, Sr., Amaziah Beeson, John Baldwin, Thomas Osborn, James W. Davis and Henry Simons entered land.

In 1838 Nathan Davis came to cast his fortunes with the people of the new country, and in 1839 Charles Beeson followed.

NATHAN MORRIS

Who was born in North Carolina in 1808. He moved with his parents to Wayne County, Indiana, in 1818, and from Wayne County to Fairmount Township in 1832, three years after marriage. In 1865 he moved to Marshall County, Iowa, and settled near Bangor. After five years' residence in Iowa he located in Jewell County, Kansas, and died at his home near Burr Oak, in 1880. He was a minister in the Society of Friends from his young manhood. He was liberal in his dealings with neighbors, and it is said that no needy person ever left his door empty handed. With all his natural generosity he prospered, and this fact again bears out the assertion often made that those who are the most thoughtful in their kindness to others are frequently the most blessed in their material fortunes.

Of these patient pioneers let the words of the poet speak—

> The world can easily spare the man
>   Who pauses a moment here or there
> To make a promise or form a plan,
>   Or to pluck some flower that may be fair;
> But the world has use for the man who gives
>   His best for the joys that he wins away—
> The world with a welcoming cheer receives
>   The determined man who has come to stay.
>
> There are few rewards for the pioneer
>   Whose thoughts are only of sudden gains,
> Who camps for a day on the far frontier,
>   Then journeys backward across the plains;
> But wood and valley and plain and slope
>   Yield their best to him who has blazed his way
> To the scene on which he has set his hope,
>   Who, having arrived, is there to stay.

Mr. T. B. McDonald, of Lovilia, Iowa, lived in Fairmount Township at a time when he witnessed many changes and improvements. It was during the period of the transition of this community from the rude agricultural implements of early pioneers and their primitive methods to a day when new devices were being gradually introduced for the better planting, cultivation and harvesting of crops.

The writer inserts at this place the comment of Mr. McDonald, which is prompted by his personal knowledge of affairs when he lived on his father's farm, located two miles southwest of Fairmount.

"The first thing the early settler did was to prepare a shelter for his family," writes Mr. McDonald. "He next cleared as much ground as was possible, on which to plant corn. This was the most important crop to be grown. With a crop of corn they had food for both man and beast. Wheat and oats were not thought of until considerable land had been cleared. Flax and buckwheat were the important products, however—one to make clothing and the other for food. With buckwheat cakes and maple syrup one could do fine.

"When wheat, oats and meadows were planted it took time and labor to harvest them. The wheat and oats were cut with a sickle or cradle. In fact, both were used, the sickle to get the grain around the stumps and places where the cradle could not be used.

"The grain was bound by hand and threshed either by flail or tramped out with horses or oxen. If a farmer had considerable grain, as soon as it was stacked he would prepare a threshing floor by leveling

THE SECOND AND THIRD GENERATIONS

Back row, standing, from left to right—Mrs. Jane Hobbs, daughter of Mrs. Jesse Dillon; Mrs. Roland Smith, daughter of Carter Hasting; Mrs. Elizabeth Bogue, daughter of Nathan Coggeshall; Mrs. Milicent Haisley, daughter of Iredell Rush; Mrs. Anna Hasting, daughter of John Smith; Mrs. Ruth Elliott, daughter of Seth Winslow. Middle row, sitting, left to right—Mrs. Julia Ann Dillon, widow of Albert Dillon; Mrs. Keziah Dillon, daughter of Phineas Henley; Mrs. Sarah Baldwin, daughter of Nathan Morris; Mrs. Huldah Bradford, daughter of Daniel Baldwin; Mrs. Mary Jane Winslow, daughter of Jesse Dillon; Mrs. Cynthia Winslow, daughter of Denny Jay. First row, sitting, left to right—Mrs. Leota Mozingo, granddaughter of John Smith; Mrs. Lucy Clark, granddaughter of Daniel Baldwin; Mrs. Kittie Smith, granddaughter of John Smith; Mrs. Myra Baldwin, granddaughter of Iredell Rush; Mrs. Lutie Newby, granddaughter of John Smith.

a piece of ground, making it as smooth and hard as possible. This floor would be in a circle. The grain would be placed on the floor and then two horses or oxen walked around this circle till the grain would all be out of the head. Then the straw was removed and another layer of grain placed on the floor as before. That would be repeated till all the grain had been taken from the straw.

"The next thing was to clear the chaff from the grain. This was done with a fanning mill, if one could be procured. The chaff, being the lightest, would blow away, thus leaving the grain practically clean.

"The next improvement was what was called the chaff piler, being

MARK BALDWIN

Scientist, was born in Ellis, Kansas, June 8, 1889. His paternal grandparents were Micah and Sarah (Morris) Baldwin and his maternal grandparents were Nixon and Louisa (Winslow) Rush. He is the son of Edgar M. and Myra (Rush) Baldwin. He was educated in the common schools of Fairmount, graduated from Fairmount Academy, in 1909, received from Earlham College, in 1912, the degree of Bachelor of Science, and later took a post-graduate course in the University of Chicago. He is the owner of 640 acres of land located in Georgia, near Albany, which comprises a part of the plantation belonging to the Albany Farming Company, consisting of 3,000 acres. This plantation was formerly owned by Ben Hill, the noted Confederate statesman of Civil War times. Mr. Baldwin is a member of the American Association for Advancement of Science and the American Forestry Association. In his early boyhood he wrote many clever verses which clearly indicated his poetic bent of mind. Two of these productions appear in this chapter.

a cylinder and a concave. This was run by horse power. Then came the separator, which pressed the grain and cleaned it.

"The next great improvement was the reaper. The first one that I remember was at Carter Hasting's. It was drawn by six horses. The grain was raked off the machine by hand. My recollection now is that the machine was owned by Jack Winslow, but I am not certain. One thing that I do remember is that people came a long distance to see the machine work."

BACK CREEK GRAVEYARD.
(By Mark Baldwin.)

Old, uncared for, 'most forgotten,
  Overgrown with weeds and grass,
Scarcely noticed, little thought of
  By the people as they pass,

Is an ancient Quaker graveyard,
  With its stones in quaint array,
Sculptured o'er with hopes eternal
  Of the resurrection day.

Yet beneath this sod are resting,
  Folded in their last, long sleep,
Men who toiled that we might prosper,
  Men who sowed that we might reap

Their glory not in martial deeds,
  Quiet, simple lives they led,
They built their faith on vital creeds,
  Not on ruins of the dead.

CHAPTER VI.

CLOTHING, FOOD AND SHELTER.

CORN, OATS, wheat and flax were staple products of the pioneer farm. Flax was raised for its qualities available in making articles of wearing apparel for both men and women.

There are three prime necessities of life, namely, clothing, food and shelter. These necessities are common to civilized mankind. In this connection it will be of interest to the reader to know how pioneers provided themselves with clothing. The following excellent description of the manner in which flax was converted into garments for women and into clothing for men will be found appropriate. This description is from the pen of John T. Morris,* than whom there was no one of that early period better fitted by education and personal observation to tell the story:

"During the first years of the settlement it was common for the people to produce nearly everything they consumed. Indeed, this was necessary, as most of the settlers were in limited circumstances—only able to command money enough to enter a small tract of land at $1.25 per acre. I suppose about eighty acres was an average entry for those who settled on the land at once. Some men who had the money to do so would take up larger bodies of land and hold it for speculation.

"So the situation demanded economy. The people manufactured most of their wearing cloths from the raw material. It was common for each family to cultivate a small plat of ground in flax, from which to manufacture their summer clothing and such other articles as towels, table linen, etc.

"The flax seed was sown early in May, and by some time in July it was ripe enough to pull. When flax was grown for fiber it was always pulled by hand—pulled out of the ground and spread in swathes on the ground where it grew, and left to cure, after which it was taken up, bound into bundles and put under shelter to remain until the fall rains commenced. It was then taken to some grass plot and unbound and again spread in swathes and left to take the rain and sunshine.

---

* John T. Morris, at the time this article was being prepared, lived at Carthage, Indiana. Mr. Morris was born near Fountain City, Indiana, November 22, 1821. With his parents, Aaron and Anna (Thomas) Morris, he moved to Grant County in March, 1830. He taught a number of terms of school and in numerous ways contributed liberally of his time, his talent and his energy to building for the present generation. Earl Morris, Clerk and Treasurer of Fairmount, is a grandson of John T. Morris. Mr. Morris died at his home in Carthage on May 3, 1914, in his 93rd year.

Clothing, Food and Shelter. 59

"This process was called 'rotting the flax.' This was necessary in order that the fiber might the more readily separate from the woody portion of the stalks, and at the same time the woody part of the stalks was rendered more brittle, hence more easily worked out from the fiber. When the action of the weather had sufficiently rotted the flax, it was again taken up, bound into bundles and put under shelter to await the farmer's pleasure to break and scutch it.

"The first machine in this process was called a 'flax brake.' This was made entirely from wood—not even a nail used in its construction. The flax was first put through the 'flax brake,' then to the scutching board. By the use of this and the scutching knife the schives were worked out from the fiber.

"After this the flax fiber was handed over to the women to complete the work of making it into cloth, or linen, which they did by the use of different machines, the first of which was the hatchel, an instrument used to comb out the coarse from the fine fiber. This machine was made by using a board seven inches wide and two feet long, in the center of which about thirty-six spikes were made fast in a space five by six inches. These spikes, or teeth, if you please, were about five inches long, made smooth and sharp at the point. This combing done, the fiber was ready for the 'little spinning wheel.'

JOHN T. MORRIS
Pioneer Fairmount Township school teacher and early friend of colored people. On April 10, 1843, Mr. Morris boarded a flatboat on the Mississinewa River, near Odd Fellows Cemetery, at Marion, and "staid with the boat," as he says, in his autobiography, "until I landed in New Orleans June 1st following."

"The reel was now brought into requisition, as it was always used in connection with the wheel. Reeled, spooled, warped and drawn through the sley, or put in the loom, the process of weaving was now in order. A nice fabric for men's pants and shirts was made by using cotton thread for the warp, filled in with flax thread. Trousers made from this, after it was nicely bleached, were fit for Sunday, and, indeed, your humble servant has worn such trousers when he went to see his 'best girl.' In those frontier times the women did the cutting and making, as well as spinning and weaving. It was some years after the first settlement was made before a fashionable tailor was in demand."

The Township originally was heavily timbered. There was an abundance of spice-wood, walnut, hickory, beech, cherry, sugar, ash, oak, sycamore, poplar, hackberry, etc.

The dense forest served as a refuge and feeding ground for all kinds of wild game, which was abundant in the early thirties. Bear, deer, porcupines, wild cats, raccoons, squirrels, 'possums, turkeys and quail were plentiful. The supply of meats was unlimited. The hunter and trapper had his choice "without money and without price."

Having referred to the manner of procuring necessary articles of clothing, the reader is again indebted to the late John T. Morris for the following well written description of methods employed by the pioneer in securing his food.

"In 1830," he says, "Martin Boots owned and was operating a corn mill, located a short distance above the mouth of Boots Creek.

"At the same time Jesse Adamson was running another such mill, on Griffin's Creek, about half a mile above the mouth of the creek.

"For a few years the settlers were dependent upon these corn mills to get their corn ground into meal. The water wheels were so made that they were liable to freeze up in the winter, and remain so for some time, and in that case the people would run short of bread stuff, and have to fall back on Irish potatoes and lye hominy as a substitute for bread. Corn bread was the rule and flour bread was the exception.

"Sometimes the neighbors would make up a team and go forty miles up the Mississinewa River, to what was known as Lewelling's Mill, and bring down a load of flour. Then, for a time, the settlers would have biscuits occasionally on Sunday morning.

"The diet throughout the community was plain and simple. Meat was had the easiest way of anything that entered into a living. Game was plentiful. There were but few groceries bought. Each family made their own sugar and molasses from the maple trees. A few people used coffee, but a substitute for store tea could be found within a few rods of every man's house—spice-wood.

"So far as hogs were concerned, when left on the range they were almost no expense, as they would live and do well all the year. During the fall and early winter they got fat on the mast. Acorns and hickory nuts were in such abundance that a large amount of this mast was still on the ground when winter came on. This would become covered with leaves, and maybe with snow, and be preserved, so that hogs could find it and feed on it all winter. There was, however, one trouble with the hogs. They would become as wild as deer on being left at large in the woods, where they would scarcely see any person.

"Those who had hogs on the range tried to keep them located by going out occasionally and finding their bed, which the hogs moved as occasion required. As the mast became scarce in their beat, they would move over into new territory.

"But the excitement was on when the men went out to butcher their meat. After deciding whose hogs should be killed first, a few neighbors would be on the way early, with dogs, guns and horses, prepared for the chase. They aimed to surprise the hogs in their bed. (A good snow was a prerequisite to this wild hog slaughter.) Arriving at the bed, the hogs were routed and the dogs turned loose. A hog was soon caught and held till the men came up and stuck it. This one was left to die while the dogs caught another. And so the chase went on until all were killed, or as many as were wanted.

"Of course the dead hogs were somewhat scattered, but at least one horse was provided with harness, single tree and loose chain, in order to drag the hogs together at some suitable place where they could get to them with a wood sled and haul them in where the dressing was to be done. In this manner of hog killing guns were not brought into requisition only as the hogs would rally and make a stand to fight, as was sometimes the case."

Mr. Morris has told how our ancestors hunted deer, and the reader is again indebted to him for this first-hand information:

"In those early times game was so plenty that it afforded both sport and profit to those who engaged in hunting. In the summer, hunters would go out on night expeditions on the river. They would equip a canoe for this purpose by placing a blind on the prow of the canoe. This was formed by using a few short boards. One was put down flat, crosswise. Immediately behind this was boarded up some twenty inches or more. The board planked down was for a candle to stand upon. The upright back was to break the light of the candle from shining upon the men. Their craft being ready, the next thing was to start up the river.

"This was called 'fire hunting.' It was their purpose to start early enough in the day to work their craft several miles up the river before nightfall. At that time the hunting was wont to commence. So they would stop and light their candle and turn about. The deer did not frequent the river much only at night.

"It was supposed that there were two things that caused the deer to go to the river. One was the need of water and the other was they fed upon a moss which was found growing in the water upon the rocks. This was called 'deer moss,' and was found only where the water was shallow. Those hunters asserted that they had seen the deer go down with their mouths into the water after the moss. Whatever may have been the inducement, the deer were largely found in the river at night.

"On starting down the river, one man would be seated in the stern of the canoe, paddle in hand. He made but little effort to give the craft headway, except to shape its course. The other man stood behind the blind, gun in hand, and far enough back so the candle would not shine upon him. By this arrangement the men were completely hid behind the blind. The hunters said that the deer would appear to be wholly oblivious to everything except the candle. They would stand and gaze at the candle until the canoe would approach within a few yards of them. It was also stated that a man could see a deer eighty rods or more from the light of a candle placed upon the blind.

"When the man that was on the lookout saw a deer, he would simply point towards it and the man who was working the canoe shaped its course accordingly, carefully avoiding noise, till the craft approached to within easy shooting distance before the old musket was turned loose.

"An old army musket was the style of gun used in this manner of hunting. They were wont to have the gun well charged with buckshot, as it was a random shot, not being able to see any sights. I remember to have seen one of these night expeditions on its return, in charge of Thomas Branson and Reuben Overman, with the canoe fairly loaded down with deer, lying on their backs with their legs up.

"It was claimed that the hotter the weather and the worse the flies the more the deer would be found in the river at night."

The coming of the pioneer for permanent settlement created the necessity for homes. The dwelling places took the form of log cabins. There could be no homes without shelter. As the cabins multiplied in number and the work of clearing the forest progressed, timber began to disappear.

Log rollings and house raisings were of frequent occurrence. Neighbors were, indeed, neighborly. Co-operation in the building of homes was the rule. The spirit of mutual helpfulness extended to quilting bees, corn huskings, spinning and weaving.

The main diversion for the boys was town ball and bull pen, while jumping the rope, hide and seek, and "William-a-trim-a-toe" were a few of the games in which both boys and girls participated.

Clothing, Food and Shelter.   63

Eye witnesses have touched upon the means of obtaining clothing and food. It is now appropriate to describe the methods of our ancestors in providing shelter and preparing food for their families. Again we rely upon authority which cannot be called into question.

The following is from the pen of Asa T. Baldwin,* residing, when these lines were written, at 2311 South Meridian Street, Marion, Indiana. Being one of the few men then living who learned how this was done by his own personal experience, this detailed account will be read with interest:

"The log cabin was made by cutting poles or logs 16 to 24 feet in length and notching the ends with an ax by men selected to carry up the four corners of the building, so that they would fit closely together and make a solid wall not easily thrown down. The open spaces between the logs were chinked with wood and daubed with mud or mortar to keep out the wind, rain and snow.

"The roof was covered with clapboards, or strakes, as the Yankees call them. These were split three or four feet long with a frow, and put on as evenly as possible, lapping them and breaking the joints so as not to leak. They were held on by weights called ridge-poles, secured in their places by large wooden pins, as nails were too scarce and high-priced in those days for the average settler to think of affording such an expensive plan as that of nailing the boards on. The stick-and-clay chimney was built a little higher than the comb of the roof and well lined with mud from top to bottom, to prevent getting on fire. The large, open fireplaces had jambs and hearths made of clay, sprinkled with water and thoroughly pounded with a maul to make them firm and solid when dry. The cooking arrangements were nothing like they are now. Tin reflectors were sometimes used for baking and roasting. Ovens made of a clay mortar were common. They were built on a platform of heavy plank placed on four posts about three feet high and quite large, so that several loaves and a dozen or more pies could be baked at once. Johnny cakes were baked on smooth boards at the sides of the jambs, and venison was dried in the flue of the chimney. There were no large, convenient cook stoves and ranges with numerous vessels to go along with them.

"Corn bread or wheat bread was frequently baked in a skillet by placing live coals of fire under the skillet and on the lid. Pork was

---

*Asa T. Baldwin was a native of Fairmount Township. He was born March 16, 1835, in a cabin which stood at the northeast corner of Mill and Jefferson Streets, in Fairmount. Mr. Baldwin taught several terms of school in his young manhood.

boiled with cabbage or beans in a kettle, hung, in the absence of an iron crane, on a wooden hook over the fire. Squashes and potatoes were often roasted by covering them with hot ashes in the fireplace. As a matter of economy, pewter plates were used by the early settlers, since

ASA T. BALDWIN
Who taught several terms of school in Fairmount Township from 1854 to 1864. His parents were Thomas and Lydia (Thomas) Baldwin. Thomas Baldwin entered land in Fairmount Township on October 7, 1833, less than two weeks after his marriage, at New Garden, in Wayne County, September 26, 1833. They traveled by wagon hitched to three horses. On the fourth day of their journey the wagon broke down. They had reached the Mississinewa River before the accident happened. Next morning their goods were loaded on an Indian pirogue, which had been hired for the purpose. The boat was pushed out into the middle of the stream to float with the current. The landing was made that same evening at a point near the old McCormick Tavern, and thence they proceeded to their destination in the forest. Thomas Baldwin taught four terms of school near where William A. Beasley now lives. Asa Baldwin died at his home in Marion on October 13, 1913. Lydia Baldwin died May 21, 1899, at the age of eighty-four years. Thomas Baldwin died May 25, 1899, aged eighty-six. This venerable couple were buried in one grave in the I. O. O. F. Cemetery at Marion, after a double funeral, held on May 27, 1899, having lived together more than sixty-five years.

they were not easily broken. Glass tumblers were out of the question, hence gourds were in frequent demand for drinking vessels.

"Many a cabin had not a single sawed plank in it. The floors were made with heavy puncheons, split out of logs and hewed as smoothly as possible with a broad-axe, and the loft was floored with boards similar to those on the roof. The joists were the straightest poles that could be found in the forest, and sometimes the bark was peeled off so as to make them have a clean, beautiful appearance.

"The doors were hung on wooden hinges, and, when closed, were fastened by a simple latch, which could be lifted by a string from the outside, so a neighbor could open the door on hearing the welcome 'Come in!' At night the door could be locked, if desired, by pulling the string through on the inside.

"Sometimes double cabins were constructed so as to have two rooms and a sort of open porch between them, but generally there was at first only one room, which served for many purposes. It was not an uncommon thing for a room of this kind to be occupied by a man and his wife, with eight or ten children, and sometimes nineteen, and they seemed to be perfectly happy."

Such were the camps that were built in the forest, and that served as shelter to the newcomers until such time as materials could be procured and leisure found to build better houses. No doubt the conviction, springing from a lively faith and hope that these cabins were only camps that soon would give place to better comfort, helped to give the dash of frolic and romance that most unmistakably spices up the tales of pioneer days.

CHAPTER VII.

DAVID AND NANCY LEWIS ARRIVE AT M'CORMICK'S TAVERN—SOLOMON THOMAS OPENS POSTOFFICE AT AI.

IT WAS at the hospitable McCormick Tavern that David Lewis* and family stopped over night when they arrived in Fairmount Township, on November 18, 1834. This family came from Franklin County, Indiana. Their household goods were loaded in a two-horse wagon, drawn by a couple of bobtailed horses owned by a man named Johnson. They were seven days on the road, the same distance now being covered by automobile in as many hours. The route was by way of Connersville and Muncie.

An accident befell the Lewis family as they were traveling along on their journey between Muncie and Granville that caused a delay of one day. An axletree broke, and it was necessary to make a new one before they could proceed. The delay occurred close by the cabin of a man named Wilson. Wilson owned an old black sow. A bear had viciously attacked the hog and lacerated it, but was driven off, and the wounds were now about healed.

The next morning after their arrival at the McCormick Tavern they moved into a cabin owned by Charles Baldwin, and later went to the McCormick farm to reside.

While living there the bread stuff gave out. Lewis went to a man by the name of Griffin, who owned a mill over on the river, to buy meal. Mr. Griffin asked Lewis if he had the money to buy with. Lewis told him he had. He was then informed that he would have to go down below Lafayette to get his meal, as they had plenty to sell there for money, Mr. Griffin being unable to sell him meal on account of so many settlers in the neighborhood depending on him who had no money and would suffer for want of food if he could not supply them.

In the spring of 1837, David Lewis, Henry Osborn, Thomas Osborn and John Weston hired a boat made of poplar logs, started from Wilson's ford down the Mississinewa River, then on into the Wabash River, four miles below Lafayette, and bought twenty-eight bushels of meal, loaded the meal in the boat, pulled up stream, arriving home after an absence of fourteen days, during which time they endured many hardships.

---

*David Lewis was born in Hawkins County, Tennessee, April 28, 1804 He came with his parents to Franklin County, Indiana, and there he was married to Miss Nancy George, a first cousin to Daniel Boone.

In his reminiscent moods Lewis had many thrilling stories to tell of his boyhood days. Being a cousin of Davy Crockett, one story, especially interesting to the children, was his visit with his father to the home of his uncle, John Crockett, during the absence of his cousin. Davy had run away from home to escape a whipping from his father and the schoolmaster.

WILLIAM G. LEWIS

Came to Fairmount Township with his parents, David and Nancy (George) Lewis. He was born in Franklin County, Indiana, May 13, 1825. He was nine years old when he came to this Township. William G. Lewis taught eighteen terms of school, served as Justice of the Peace and was for thirty-five years a minister in the Methodist Episcopal Church, later becoming connected with the Methodist Protestant Church, serving for fifteen years as local minister in this denomination. During his work in the ministry Mr. Lewis performed the marriage ceremony for more than a thousand couples. In early life he was a Whig, joining the Republican party when that organization was first formed. He was the original local advocate and agitator from a public platform of the abolition of the liquor traffic. As a young man of twenty-five, in the old Sugar Grove Methodist Episcopal Church, which stood on the land now owned by Daniel Johnson, Mr. Lewis made his first address attacking the liquor business. He was kind and hospitable, generous to a fault, aggressive in the right as he saw it, dealing justly by his fellow-man, living a modest life, full of usefulness and good deeds, leaving the world better for his having lived in it. He died January 13, 1907. Funeral services were conducted in the Congregational Church, Fairmount, the Masonic order being in charge. His remains were interred in Park Cemetery.

In the same year, and after the eventful journey, down the Wabash, Lewis went to Ft. Wayne and entered land located southeast of Fairmount. He became a pioneer resident of that community. He and his wife were charter members of the first Methodist Episcopal Church, of Fairmount Township, Lewis being chosen class leader.

His home was one of hospitality, where many ministers found a welcome. He was a man of medium size, and, like other pioneers of that day, a man of great endurance, plain of dress, and a Whig in politics.

His children were Wesley B., William G., Mary, James W., Morgan O., Evelyn, John S. D., Sarah, Rebecca J. and Elizabeth.

During the first years of his residence in Fairmount Township, David Lewis was ever ready to assist the new comers in selecting the best piece of land and securing the same of the Government for their future home. On several occasions he took them into his own home until a cabin could be built on their land. Being a thorough woodsman, he assisted the surveyors many times in establishing the lines which became some of the permanent roads of today in Fairmount Township. His death occurred November 13, 1855, at the age of eighty years.

MRS. EMELINE LEWIS

Wife of William G. Lewis, and a daughter of Henry Osborn, who entered land southeast of Fairmount, near the Lewis home, August 27, 1833. Mrs. Lewis was born January 12, 1835, in Fairmount Township. She was the first of a family of six children, others being Louisa, Jonathan, William P., Zimri C. and Rachel Ann. Although in poor health, enfeebled by the infirmities of old age, this noble woman in the latter months of her life, was mentally bright and alert, enjoyed company when strength permitted, and eagerly related interesting stories and incidents about first settlers and described the trials and joys of frontier life in the wilderness.

For a few years after he settled here, Solomon Thomas owned what was known as the Lake Galatia farm. In 1835 he sold this land and entered a tract about three miles southeast of Fairmount, the farm now owned by David L. Payne.

Here a postoffice, called AI, was established by Thomas, and he became postmaster. In that day the postage rate was twenty-five cents for a letter going out of the State and twelve and one-half cents for a letter addressed to a person within the limits of Indiana. The person receiving the letter paid the postage.

Previous to the opening of the postoffice at AI, mail was received and sent out from McCormick's Tavern. This was known as Greenberry Postoffice. Upon the death of McCormick and the beginning of a settlement at Jonesboro, in 1837, Greenberry Postoffice was discontinued, and moved to

Jonesboro. Joseph Jones, whose wife was a daughter of Robert McCormick; John Heavilin, Robert Wilson and a man named Furry were among the postmasters who handled mail at Greenberry.

Somewhat later, and before the town of Fairmount was laid out, Grant Postoffice was established in a frame house built by William Hall, in 1856, at the southwest corner of Adams and Main Streets. Here William Hall served as the first postmaster of the town.

The first public improvement recalled by the late William G. Lewis was a horse mill, erected about the year 1840 by Solomon Thomas. This mill was headquarters for farmers who wanted their corn ground. In that day it was a stroke of enterprise which was highly commended by the pioneer and liberally patronized.

A farmer would go on horseback to the mill with his corn, and by hitching his horse to the beam, together with Thomas's horse, the pioneer could get a grist ground out "in less than half a day." "It was a fine makeshift," comments Mr. Lewis in his reminiscences, now in possession of Trustee David G. Lewis, his nephew.

The first election held in the Township was that at the McCormick Tavern, soon after the organization of the County, in 1831. Charles Baldwin served as inspector. Ichabod Dille was the first Justice of the Peace. Elijah Lucas served next, and after him came Solomon Parsons.

SOLOMON THOMAS

Solomon Thomas was born in South Carolina in 1796. He entered land in Fairmount Township, August 9, 1830. The accompanying picture was copied from a tintype made of Thomas during the period of his residence in Iowa. This tintype was loaned by William R. Lewis, a great-grandson. The picture shows Thomas wearing a beard. Fairmount people remember him as a smooth-faced man.

Solomon and Anna (Morris) Thomas were parents of Mary Ann, Hannah, Edna, Sophronia, Isaac, Martha, Anna, Solomon, Jr., Nelson, John, Nathan and Rachel. "In physique," remarks a well known man

JOHN SMITH

Who for many years lived on the farm south of Fairmount at present owned by his grandson, Curtis W. Smith. John Smith was the son of Judge Caleb Smith, prominent in the early days of Grant County. John and Mary Ann (Thomas) Smith were the first young couple to secure a marriage license in Grant County. The wedding occurred in 1831 at the cabin home of the bride near Lake Galatia. John Smith died September 30, 1888, aged seventy-nine years, nine months and eight days.

know from the fact that he had a diversity of knowledge in general above the average pioneer. He had some knowledge of medicine and did some practice in Grant County, but when he saw there was much he did not know he gave up the practice. It could not be said of Solomon Thomas that he was not industrious and progressive, for he opened up a good farm in the wilderness and erected the first horse mill to grind corn in the Township. He loved to be in the woods with his gun, and was a good shot. He kept his large family supplied with wild meat while

who was intimately acquainted with him, "Solomon Thomas was rather corpulent. He would weigh near 200 pounds, was five feet, eight or nine inches tall, with a large, well proportioned head, nearly bald, with an abundance of good, natural ability. I do not know where he grew to manhood or his facilities for an education. That he had some education I

MARY ANN SMITH

Daughter of Solomon Thomas and the wife of John Smith. Mrs. Smith died February 16, 1890, at her home south of Fairmount, aged seventy-six years, seven months and seventeen days.

it was in the country. He was honest, kind, sympathetic, generous, ready to assist when called upon, and active in promoting the best interests in the organization of the new country. He was religiously inclined, being a member of the United Brethren Church from choice. He was a good conversationalist and enjoyed the visits of his neighbors. In dress, he was very plain, wearing home-made, brown jeans blouse and pants, with knit cap of same color while it was customary for the women to spin and weave and make the cloth for home consumption. He was a man without pride or ostentation. He was temperate in his habits, detesting profanity, but always used home-grown tobacco. He was classed among the good citizens of the country." He served as County Commissioner at one time from the First District. He died in Fairmount at the age of seventy-seven years and was buried at Back Creek Graveyard.

THE OLD POSTOFFICE AT AI

Above is a picture of the cabin owned and occupied by Solomon Thomas and family at the time mail was received and distributed by Thomas while serving as postmaster in the early part of the '40's. The cabin, no longer in existence, was located on the farm now owned by David L. Payne, who lives about three miles southeast of Fairmount. At this cabin Samuel C. Wilson, when a boy, got mail for his father, John Wilson, and other members of his father's family and for other neighbors. Wilson formerly received mail at Summit, but when the postoffice at AI was opened the Wilson family found it more convenient to go to the Thomas cabin for their letters. Not a great distance from AI, Thomas built a horse mill, and a little farther away, some years later, the United Brethren denomination built old Union Church and laid out a graveyard.

CHAPTER VIII.

BUILDING ROADS AND CONSTRUCTING DRAINAGE.

THE ROADS were the most serious handicap to the early settlers in getting their surplus grain to market," remarks T. B. McDonald. "Some time in the early '50's the Wabash & Erie Canal was constructed. This canal followed the course of the Wabash River for many miles. At this time the settlers along Back Creek had succeeded in clearing considerable land, and raised grain in excess of their needs. This they would haul in wagons to some point on the canal, usually Wabash town or Lagro, where a market could be found. This was the beginning of better times; but the wagon-road problem continued to be foremost, as only a short time in the year was it possible to haul any kind of a load.

"It was then that a few public-spirited men conceived the idea of building a plank road from Jonesboro to Wabash town by the way of Marion and Jalapa. This road was constructed by first leveling the roadway, then placing heavy oak planks two or three inches thick and fourteen feet long, which were laid across the road. This was a great improvement and worked fine when the road was new, but it was not long till it was found that this kind of road was not practical, as the boards could not be fastened in place. The effect of the sun would cause the boards to warp and get out of place. Hauling of heavy loads would occasionally break a plank or drag many planks out of place. The toll collected would not keep up the road repairs, say nothing of paying a dividend to the owners of the road. It was over this road that the farmers of Fairmount Township hauled their grain to market.

"No doubt the good old farmers along Back Creek saw where their neighbors failed, for they at once commenced to build a gravel road from Jonesboro to the Madison County line. This road is good to this day. It was practical, as time has shown. The plank road was replaced by the gravel road. So it was that the Back Creek farmer had a good road to market until the railroads came and brought the market to his very door.

"We have told how the farmers got their grain to market. Now we will tell how the hogs were disposed of. In those days the hog was a sturdy animal, capable of going a long distance, as we have previously stated. They were fattened on mast in the fall of the year and finished on corn. Hogs were marketed once a year, as a rule. I doubt there being a public scale in Grant County as late as 1854. Buyers went to the farmers and bought their hogs by the head. A time and a place were set for the same. After all the hogs had been delivered at the agreed point, then they were driven to the nearest shipping point. Sometimes there would be as many as five hundred hogs in a drove. It is my impression that Cincinnati was the market up to 1856, when Anderson became the market. It was no little task to drive so many hogs thirty miles. The weaker ones gave out and were hauled in the wagons that always followed the drove."

As the forest was cleared and acreage for crop purposes enlarged, the efforts of early settlers were quickened, and the making of farms progressed rapidly. As the yield of farm products increased from year to year, pioneers began to think about better facilities for reaching the markets with their surplus grain and live stock.

The first important step taken after corduroy roads had outlived their usefulness was the formation of an organization for the purpose of building a gravel road extending from Jonesboro to the Madison County line, to connect the settlement with markets at Wabash and Lagro. The Jonesboro & Fairmount Turnpike Company was the outgrowth of a strong sentiment, then practically unanimous, for improvements in this direction.

The old records of this company show that the shares were sold at twenty-five dollars each. The first officers of the new organization were Henry Winslow, President, and Thomas Baldwin, Secretary. Certificate No. 1 was issued on December 21, 1860, to Solomon T. Dailey, who bought two shares of stock.

Other shares were taken as follows:

	Shares		Shares
Ahira Baldwin	4	Seth Winslow	2
Santford Baldwin	2	Exum Morris	2
Thomas Baldwin	6	Nathan Morris	6
Thomas Winslow	2	Thomas W. Newby	4
John Winslow	2	Isaiah Pemberton	3
William R. Pierce	12	Daniel Winslow	6
Micajah B. Winslow	4	E. M. Tracy	1
Nathan Hill	2	Thomas Harvey	2
Benoni Hill	6	Henry Winslow	4
Aaron Hill	8	Jesse Dillon	10
Joseph W. Hill	4	Noah Harris	8

The Making of a Township.

	Shares		Shares
Thomas Knight	2	Josiah Bradway	3
Joseph Knight	4	James Lytle	4
John Russell	6	Nathan D. Wilson	4
Allen Winslow	2	Jonathan P. Winslow	4
Micajah Wilson	2	Elizabeth Rush	1
Harvey & Wilson	12	James R. Smith	1
David Smithson	4	Samuel H. Pierce	1
William Cox	1	Noah Brooks	1
Jesse E. Wilson	9	Jesse Reece	1
John T. Morris	1	Jonathan Baldwin	6
Levi Winslow	2	Carter Hasting	4
Margaret Puckett	10	Calvin Bookout	4
Wright & Brother	2	William R. Wright	2
Morris Payne	1	Samuel Dillon	11
G. H. Puckett	2	Henry Harvey	4
Eli Neal	1	Micah Baldwin	4
Lindsey Wilson	2	William Hall	1
Evan Benbow	4	Samuel Jay	1
Henry Wilson	1	Abraham Music	1
Samuel C. Wilson	1	David Jones	1
Barkley Hockett	4	William Macy	6
Henry Winslow, Jr.	½	Jacob Becht	2
Francis Lytle	4	Thomas Knight	2
David Stanfield	1	David Winslow	4
Eli and Adeline Haisley	32		

The office of Secretary was abolished and William R. Pierce was chosen to serve in the dual capacity of President and Secretary. He was succeeded by Jesse E. Wilson, who was elected President and Secretary and was serving as such on August 24, 1862. He continued in this position until August 5, 1881, a period of nearly nineteen years. Upon the death of Jesse E. Wilson the stockholders, on June 21, 1883, elected Joseph W. Hill, Jonathan P. Winslow and Daniel Winslow, Directors. On July 30, 1883, the Directors met and named Jonathan P. Winslow, President, Joseph W. Hill, Treasurer, and Jonathan P. Winslow, Secretary.

The position of an officer of the Jonesboro & Fairmount Turnpike Company was not regarded lightly. It was considered one of real responsibility and importance. This fact is evidenced by the action taken at a meeting of the Board of Directors held in July, 1883. The records show the following:

"State of Indiana, Grant County, ss.:

"We, Joseph W. Hill, Jonathan P. Winslow and Daniel Winslow, do truly affirm that we will support the Constitution of the United States and the Constitution of the State of Indiana, and that we will discharge the duties as Directors of the Jonesboro & Fairmount Turnpike Company according to law, to the best of our ability, for which we shall answer under the pains and penalties of perjury.

"Witness our hands and seals.
"JOSEPH W. HILL,
"JONATHAN P. WINSLOW,
"DANIEL WINSLOW.

"Subscribed and sworn to before me this 30th day of July, 1883.
"ALFRED BARNARD,
"Justice of the Peace."

On August 1, 1883, Jonathan P. Winslow purchased of Daniel Wilson, administrator of the estate of Jesse E. Wilson, thirty-eight shares of stock. At about the same date eleven shares of stock were assigned to Nixon Rush, Jr.

Jonathan P. Winslow continued to serve as President and Secretary of the Company until July 17, 1886, when he was succeeded by Christopher Hill.

On May 14, 1892, Jonathan P. Winslow was again elected President. Z. M. Gossett was chosen Secretary. On July 12, 1892, forty-one shares were assigned to Dr. A. Henley.

For the month ending August 1, 1892, the receipts for toll were as follows: Gate No. 1, $30.00; Gate No. 2, $52.66; Gate No. 3, $42.21. September, 1892, the receipts reached high-water mark. The report of receipts on October 1, for the preceding month, was as follows: Gate No. 1, $50.05; Gate No. 2, $98.62, and Gate No. 3, $39.72, making a total for the month of $188.39.

On April 27, 1893, one hundred and twenty shares were assigned to Sullivan T. Waite.

In 1899 the Interurban line connecting Marion and Anderson had been completed and was in operation. It was doubtless partly due to this new and more convenient means of travel and partly to the fact that other gravel roads had been constructed that the income from tolls became almost negligible.

The records show that on September 9, 1899, the receipts for two months, July and August combined, amounted to but $25.25. At this date Sullivan T. Waite was President and Adeline Wright, Secretary.

The Jonesboro & Fairmount turnpike was taken over by the county on January 9, 1901, at which time the officers of the company gave a quit-claim deed for the property to the County Commissioners. There are now no toll roads in Fairmount Township.

The construction of the Jonesboro & Fairmount turnpike marked the beginning of an era of rapid development along various lines of progress vitally important. It was, perhaps, the first gravel road built in Grant County. It enabled farmers more easily and more cheaply to get their products to market. It perceptibly increased the value of land. Perhaps no two things happened which worked more to the material advantage of pioneers than the drainage of farms and the building of gravel roads. The records show who blazed the way for better transportation facilities.

And thus we see that this pioneer road, as a profitable private business enterprise, under pressure of modern ingenuity and advancement, went the way of the pioneer corn cracker, the pioneer tanner and the pioneer boot and shoe maker. These institutions all served their purpose admirably in their day and generation. It is fitting that we of the present, in our moments of meditation, rejoice with hearts full of pride and gratitude that the persistent toil and uncomplaining sacrifice of men who have passed on before contributed so generously to a condition which has made life more pleasant and placed the possibilities of enduring happiness within the reach of all.

"Any one riding over Fairmount Township at the present day will note the very level surface of the land," writes Dr. A. Henley, under date of Melbourne, Florida, April 14, 1917. "It does not look nearly so level now as it did to the first settlers, before the forest trees and underbrush were cut away and the fallen timber removed that obstructed the natural drainage of the sloughs.

"I think one would be safe in saying that fifty per cent. of the landed surface was wet land, covered with water a portion of the year—too wet to cultivate until late in the spring—and was an uncertain proposition even then. For this reason the first comers selected land somewhat rolling, land that had the best natural outlet for the surface water, erected their cabins, cut out roads on the ridges and the driest ground and as direct from one neighbor to another as was practicable.

"They had the soil to bring abundant crops to please the appetite of man if they could get the surface water off. That was the leading question that agitated the minds of the people. A few farmers cut open ditches, which proved unsatisfactory, as the ditch would soon fill up by the stock passing over it. Then, again, the open ditch was a nuisance and obstruction when cut through a field, and also a waste of good land. Consequently, some of the more progressive farmers conceived the idea of making a blind ditch of split timber by cutting a narrow, deep channel, placing the oak timber in the bottom in different ways to suit the individual fancy, give a free channel for the water to flow beneath the timber, and filled the ditch to the top surface with the excavated dirt and clay. This scheme was a success and gave satisfaction so long as the timber remained sound and kept its place, which was not a great while.

"In the early seventies good timber began to be very valuable for export, so much so that other material was sought for to substitute wood as ditch timber. About this time a firm in Indianapolis, Chandler & Taylor, devised a machine that would press out of wet clay a tube from two to six inches in diameter, which was cut as it came from the machine into one foot lengths. The power used was a team of horses hitched at the end of a long sweep which was securely bolted to the top of the mill post, the team going round the mill, pressing out a length of the tube at every revolution of the machine, which was cut into proper lengths by the operator. Then the tile were placed on racks under a long shed to dry, and when sufficiently dry were removed to a round kiln, after the manner of pottery, to be burned to a dark red color.

"Thus the land owner was provided with an indestructible material for drainage purposes, if he could be convinced of the utility of the material.

"William S. Elliott was the first man to bring one of those machines into the Township and risk money in what was to most of the people a doubtful enterprise. Many people were incredulous. Mr. Elliott had to overcome all kinds of foolish objections to his new system of drainage. The very idea of paying out a lot of good money for material to bury in the ground for ditches had never been done, and it was a preposterous thing to do.

"Another objection was raised. The cost would be prohibitive. It would never pay interest, and the water could not get into the tiling any way. To overcome these and many other objections, Mr. Elliott, at first, let out many thousands of rods of tile on trial, with the understanding that if they failed to do the work he claimed for them they could have them free of cost.

"At first the farmers would lay the tile with the ends a little distance apart, fearful that the water would not get into them, and then cover the tile with straw to keep out the dirt while the ditch was being filled. No one believed the water could get through the sides of the tiling until

John Selby, with his ingenious turn of mind, determined to test that question by completely sealing one end of a tile and set it with the sealed end down in a tub of water not quite to the top of the tile. After twelve hours the water in the tile was on a level with the water in the tub.

"This, becoming generally known, the straw business was abandoned and the tile laid close end to end. It was soon observed that a tile ditch would run as full of water soon after a heavy rain as any timber ditch.

"The utility of the tile ditch was established, and Mr. Elliott's faith in putting out hundreds of dollars worth of tiling on trial was fully rewarded, as he did not lose a dollar in the end. Wide-awake farmers soon began to see that tiling their land, instead of being a financial burden, was a paying investment. They replaced their wooden ditches with tile, cleared and ditched more wet land, adding in excess of twenty-five per cent. to the acreage of tillable land in the Township. It was like putting a new and permanent foundation under an old building, making it safe and durable for all time.

"It will be remembered with a shudder by many that up to about this date chills, shaking ague, congestive fevers, dysentery, cholera morbus, cholera infantum, typhoid fever, and all malarial diseases were prevalent. Any one was liable to be prostrated from July to November. When the ponds and stagnant water were drained off and the surface water line lowered from two to three feet by means of the tile drainage, those malarious diseases first enumerated disappeared from the country and are not the factor to reckon with that they formerly were.

"To what or to whom shall we give credit for this great change and for this immunity from disease? Has not the tile drainage system been the real foundation upon which the prosperity of the Township rests? Who, then, is more deserving of gratitude as a benefactor of his race than he who introduced the tile system of drainage into the Township?

"Mr. Elliott did not use the horse-power mill, as described above, but devised a gearing out of an old portable machine which had been used for running a threshing machine in an early day. To this he attached steam power to the opposite end of the pinion shaft with the master wheel fastened in a saddle on the top of the mill post, and by driving the master wheel and also the mill with the little pinion he had adequate power, and just the proper speed for successful work.

"This was the first steam-power tile mill in Indiana. Mr. Taylor, of the firm at Indianapolis that made the mill, came over to see the manner of attaching steam power to his machine, after which his firm made no more horse-power mills. Tile mills and motor power went on improving until now a tile two feet in diameter can be made as easily as the six-inch tile in the first place."

William S. Elliott is a native of Grant County. He was born January 28, 1844, at the Elliott cabin, which then stood on the present site of the Mess Hall of the National Military Home. His grandparents, Isaac and Rachel (Overman) Elliott, with two children, came originally from Virginia, settled in Wayne County, Indiana, and in 1822 traveled in wagons to a point near the Mississinewa River, where they entered land since taken over by the Government and now included within the grounds forming the Soldiers' Home property.

William S. Elliott as a boy attended the public schools, as well as the schools conducted by the Society of Friends in that day. His ancestors for many generations were Quakers. He engaged in agricultural pursuits in his boyhood, until August, 1862, when he volunteered his services to his country. He enlisted in Company C, Eighty-ninth Indiana Regiment of Infantry, at eighteen years of age.

WILLIAM S. ELLIOTT

This company was in the latter part of the war in command of Capt. J. F. Jones, lately deceased. The term of service for which Mr. Elliott had volunteered was three years. The regiment was captured by the Confederates while guarding a railroad bridge at Mumfordsville, Kentucky, before he had been out six weeks. In a short time he was paroled and sent home, under instructions not to take up arms against the Confederacy until properly exchanged.

In six weeks this exchange was arranged by the authorities and Elliott again joined his command at Indianapolis. After some time of hard drilling the command was ordered to Memphis, Tennessee. Here he did post duty while the Union Army was sent on to Vicksburg. In the weeks following he did much important service, being promoted for his fidelity and efficiency.

With twelve men he was detailed to escort a dozen captured Confederate officers to Johnson's Island, in Lake Erie, near Sandusky, Ohio. The prisoners were taken in a separate car set aside for the purpose. At Centralia, Illinois, and Bellefontaine, Ohio, the prisoners attracted numbers of Southern sympathizers, several offering pistols to the prisoners. As one of the guards on duty at Centralia Elliott, with gun and bayonet, pressed the crowd back from the car.

At another time, after the surrender of Vicksburg, July 10, 1863, he was detailed with others to guard iron safes containing $2,000,000 sent by the Government on the "City of Madison" from Memphis to Vicksburg to pay off Union troops.

In October, 1864, Elliott was with his command in Missouri, then under General Pleasanton, in pursuit of the Confederate General Price. Captain Jones had responded to a detail to guard a water tank twelve miles west of Sedalia. General Pleasanton reminded Captain Jones that it would be a dangerous undertaking, telling him that he and his entire command might be killed or captured.

"You may have all the men you require for this work," remarked General Pleasanton, "but they must be picked men. You now realize the dangerous character of the duty you are about to perform. Are you ready?"

Captain Jones hesitated.

"Why do you hesitate?" asked the General.

"I am not hesitating because of the hazardous character of the mission," replied Jones, "I was simply wondering, General, if you would allow me to take my own company with me."

The General agreed to the suggestion. So Captain Jones, with Company C, made up principally of Fairmount Township and Grant County men, went to the water tank and held this important source of water supply until relieved.

After more than three years' service, mostly with the Sixteenth Army Corps, Mr. Elliott was mustered out on July 26, 1865, at Mobile, Alabama. Returning home he was married in September, 1865, to Miss Ruth Wilson, daughter of Jesse E. Wilson. She died in 1867. Later he married Miss Alice Radley, daughter of Samuel and Mary (Bull) Radley, by whom he is the father of eleven children, all living. Mr. Elliott has been uniformly successful in his various pursuits, and has retired with a competency ample to insure the comfort of himself and wife. He has been and is now useful in the church and enterprising in his work for educational and civic progress. He has for several years devoted considerable time and attention to the welfare of White's Institute, located in Wabash County, of which institution he is at present trustee. In all his activities he has been a conspicuous factor. As soldier, as farmer, as church man, as promoter of educational and civic welfare, Mr. Elliott is not only a many-sided man, with a broad experience and a thorough understanding of public affairs, but he is a type of the useful citizen of whom there are entirely too few in the average American community.

CHAPTER IX.

GLIMPSES OF PIONEER LIFE.

(By Mrs. Lydia Morris Arnold.)

BEING the wife of a contractor and builder, changing from one State to another, one job to another, it will be hard for me to concentrate my mind in order to give anything accurate of happenings of early days. In writing of my early childhood and what I remember, will say that I was born in 1844, on the farm called the Sammy Dillon place, in a two-story hewn log house with a fireplace in the west end. There was a road on the east. Daniel Baldwin joined on the south. Then north of us the houses on the main road were on the east side of the road.

MRS. LYDIA MORRIS ARNOLD

First was Jesse Dillon, then Charles Baldwin. He had a log cabin in the south corner of his orchard, where Samuel Jones lived awhile. His wife was Jane Jones, a gifted minister of the Friends Church. Then Charles Baldwin lived next, and Matthew Winslow and Aaron Hill.

West of the road were farms on Back Creek, with the houses up on the hill west of the creek. First, going south and across the creek from Aaron Hill's farm were Solomon Knight and Joseph Winslow, then south was the road turning east across the bridge, then the old meeting house and school house, and the Newby farm south. We cross the creek to go up to Rachel Newby's, then we cross the road running west to Oak Ridge. Going on south we crossed the road, then passed the Seth Winslow farm, then Iredell Rush's, then Jesse Wilson's, and next Nathan Wilson's farm, west of the town.

Most of the houses first built in Fairmount were one-story, about thirty feet square, then shedded off back for a kitchen. They had a fireplace in the large room and one or two bed rooms. Some put a bed in the kitchen.

Two stores were built, one on the east side of Main Street, and one on the west. Joseph W. Baldwin had his goods on the east, Isaac Stanfield on the west. These two buildings were a little larger, with gable facing street and a small attic. They had the store in the big room.

A saw-mill was built south of the road running west to Little Ridge. James Cammack, who owned the mill, lived in the house west of Stanfield's store.

The first meeting house was built on the vacant ground north of Cammack's. It was a small frame, and was also used for school purposes. Father and David Stanfield helped to lay out the ground for the house.

Father bought the first clock and cook stove in the Township. The clock was a wooden clock. It had these letters on the door, "Time is Money." The stove was what they called a step stove.

I went to school at Back Creek before Fairmount was prepared with school facilities. The school house was west of the meeting house. It was a square frame about thirty feet, with a door in the north and one in the south, two windows in east, two in west, one on each side of the door in south, a blackboard on north and east and west as far as the windows. There were two posts in the middle of the room, on each side of the big box stove, heated by wood, and they were big sticks at that. The teachers were paid by the scholar, so the larger the attendance the bigger his wages.

The first teacher I went to was William Neal. He had no bell, and when he called us in he beat on the side of the house and shouted:

"Books! Books! Books!"

And away we scampered for our seats. There we spent about fifteen minutes with our books, in the manner they called "studying out loud." What would one of our modern students think to be ushered into such a babel as that?

I can shut my eyes and fancy I hear them spelling:

"Baker, shady, lady."

"Ab, eb, ib, ob, ub."

"The old oaken bucket, the iron bound bucket, the moss covered bucket that hung in the well."

"Twinkle, twinkle, little star."

"Twice one are two."

"Indiana is bounded on the north by Lake Michigan, State of Michigan, on the east by Ohio, south by Kentucky and west by Illinois."

"Silence! Silence!" by the teacher.

"First class in spelling."

And so forth, on until noon.

We ate our lunch in silence, and then we were given an hour of play. Our games were "black man," "town ball," "three-cornered cat," "base," "drop the handkerchief," "little lame dog," "pussy wants a corner," and on stormy days we had "cross questions and crooked answers," "smiles," "thumbs up," and many other simple games.

They used the Elementary Spellers and McGuffey's Readers, Tolbert's Arithmetic, Olney's Geography, Thompson's Higher Arithmetic, Brown's Grammar and Walker's Dictionary. A teacher, in order to pass examination, must be able to make a good writing pen out of a goose quill and "do sums up to the rule of three."

The girls wore flannel dresses and big aprons in winter, heavy cotton in summer. The boys wore a cloth called jeans in winter and tow or flax in summer. In the middle of the week we went to meeting. Often, now, when I hear the "whinney" of a horse, it brings to my remembrance those times as I sat in meeting (as it was sometimes very quiet in doors), the restless neighing of the horses anxious to return to their mates. The women rode often with a child on behind and one in her lap, the men most always walking.

About the first one to arrive would be Solomon Knight, walking, his wife, Betsy, riding. He would lead the horse up to where they had a wide slab leaning up to a tree, with a deep notch cut to hold it secure, and two pegs driven in the ground down south of the tree. Those who came across the creek got off here, and those on the north on a big stump, with places cut on one side for steps. On the south was a big log with notches for steps. They were generally on time, and when one we all called Uncle Josie Winslow came, we knew it was time for our teacher to say:

"Prepare for meeting."

That meant for us to put away our books and march, the girls first, two and two, the boys next. The teacher led the way, and at the door he let us all pass, the girls on the west of the aisle and the boys east. The teacher sat back of us, as the seats were arranged a little on the incline. He would be able to see over us. We had to be decorous, sure, for there were the old people in the gallery looking down on us and the teacher behind us.

The gallery had three seats on each side of the aisle. Josie Winslow was first and then Nathan Morris, David Stanfield, Solomon Knight and John Carey. Next row, Jesse Harvey, William Osborn, Aaron Hill, old Thomas Harvey, Lindsey Baldwin and Thomas Winslow. Now, I will leave the next bench for comers and goers.

On the west, first, was Eunice Baldwin, as Charles was now dead. After Eunice Baldwin there were Sallie Knight and Anna Harvey. When a woman minister came with her companion they moved over and gave place for them. (When men came on the other side two men moved down for them to the next seat.) On the second seat on the west was Rachel Newby, Miriam Morris, Lydia Carey and Anna Winslow. I will not locate others (too tedious).

The preaching was generally spoken without a text, but occasionally a text was given. When prayer was offered we all stood up and turned our backs towards the gallery.

Nathan Morris was not much for changing his dress and address. He wore his hair cut the style he wore when a young man. It was cut square across the forehead, then slanting down to his ears, down a little, then it was a little longer in back. His collar was attached to his shirt. In winter he wore a black tie, in summer a white one. His vest was buttoned up within about four inches of his chin, coat in the shad style, pants made with a flap buttoned up about two inches of the pockets on each side, and his suspenders were knit of yarn. They were called galluses. His hat was a beaver. Aunt Polly Henley made his "meeting clothes," as she was a fine needle woman. She was a sister of Betsy Rush and Martha Winslow, and mother of Dr. Alpheus Henley, grandmother of Angelina (Harvey) Pearson. Father never did receive money for his services as a minister. He said if he was faithful the necessary things would be forthcoming. His crops would grow and the stock increase and flourish. He had a good, roomy house, large barn and cribs, a cattle pen for drovers to put their cattle in, and a hog-tight pen for the hog drovers to put their hogs in. We had one large room with a fireplace and a large, brick hearth to let people stay in on stormy nights.

Travel was by wagon. There were no railroads. The boats came up the Wabash River, north, over forty miles away, and south the Ohio River made Cincinnati a great trading point. So the cattle, sheep and hogs were driven to those points.

Father's place was one of the stopping points on the route. The wagons were the old stiff-tongued affairs, with wooden axles, the wheels fastened on with linchpins, and the bed looked more like a boat on wheels than anything I can think of. The harness was the chain style, with high hames, and the teamsters often had a set of what they called hame bells, so when they were coming we were well aware of it. If the tar-bucket was forgotten, what a squeaking noise we could hear, nearly a mile away, on a clear day in winter! They nearly always hung the tar-bucket on the hind axle. A hole was made in the lid for the tar-paddle. A leather whang was used to fasten the lid to the bucket to secure it. If there was more than one span of horses the driver rode one of the horses at the tongue. Oxen were used for logging and other heavy work. One Indian often came to town driving a team of oxen with a set of chain harness on, he sitting in the wagon guiding them with lines.

In the winter they made wooden sleds from the timber of a crooked tree, split and hewn for runners, with cross-pieces mortised in, plank laid on and straw and comforters. We packed in sardine fashion, as happy as larks in June.

There were the spelling schools, quilting bees, log rollings and quiltings combined, wool pickings, apple cuttings, and sometimes writing schools. To tell how these social gatherings were conducted would be too lengthy. Will mention the wool picking event.

They took their turns in the neighborhood and invited all to "come and help with the wool." Now, this was a gala time, and a good, old-fashioned dinner was spread. The teacher was invited to come after school for supper. The wool, having been washed and dried, it was brought in and spread out in the center of a large room. Then each put on her big apron. And such a hubbub all around the room, exchanging the last news, and each busy with the wool. There were burrs, Spanish needles and trash to be extracted. Then it was tied in sheets or old blankets to be taken to the woolen mill at Jonesboro, in my time, but earlier it was made into rolls at home with hand-cards about fourteen inches in width, with wire teeth, and handles like curry-combs. They combed the wool until it was in smooth layers, then with forward and backward movements formed it into rolls ready for spinning.

One day I found grandmother's cards and asked mother to teach me how to make rolls. You ought to have seen some of my awkward movements before I got anything like a roll. The rolls made at the carding machine are over two feet long. They were in bunches of from fifty to a hundred. Then they were put in layers on the sheets the wool was brought to mill in, then rolled up very tight and pinned with thorns. My brother earned his "first big money," as he thought, by gathering thorns to sell to the proprietor of the mill at so much a dozen. Most everyone raised sheep, and the women spun and wove cloth for their clothing and blankets, knit their own hosiery, and the men's, too.

The farmers raised flax. It was pulled up by the roots, cured and put through the flax-brake. The coarse fiber was called tow, which was used for ropes, kite strings, twine, and to spin into carpet warp. The fine fiber was done up in twists and laid away, to be spun into thread for sewing and weaving into bedding, towels, tablecloths, shirts, dresses, pants and other useful things. Grandmother made a substantial button out of flax thread. It looked a little like a crocheted button of this time.

For weaving, there was the spool-holder, warping-bars, loom, quill-wheel, winding-blades, shuttle-quills, spools and yard-string. To try to describe all the attachments pertaining to a loom would be a task.

The spinning of wool was done on a big wheel, on a bench of three legs, two at back end, one longer in front. They spun the thread and wound it on a broach on a spindle. When full it was wound on a reel. One hundred and twenty rounds made a cut. The skein consisted of four cuts. Each cut was tied or cross-threaded. The girls often tried to see who could make the most in a day. Sister Sarah could get her twenty-four cuts.

In spinning flax they used a little wheel with a distaff, on which the flax was held while spinning. The thread was so stout it could not be broken. They used to cut it. I will not describe a flax-wheel, as you can examine some old book or painting and see the way they look at the little wheel.

One woman east of the Mississinewa River raised the silk worms and made silk thread. It was very good, stout thread. People raised most of what they used, both eatables and wearing apparel. All the sewing was hand work, and they borrowed patterns one of another, so there was no kick on high cost of living.

Hog killing time was a neighborhood affair, as they helped one another. There was an old colored man, Robert Brazelton, who was adapted to such occasions. He could knock a hog in the head and stick it with ease. The hogs were scalded, scraped, and then hung upon a long pole. A chip was put in the hog's mouth. Father was an adept in drawing them. The entrails were carried to a long table for women to extract the fat. They thoroughly washed out the inside. There were generally about eight to twenty hogs slaughtered at a killing, as the meat was cured and the farmers sold some to help run the expenses in summer. By the time the last hog was hung the first was ready for cutting up and salting away in the smoke-house to cure ready for smoking. They hung the joints on wooden hooks made of forked limbs of hickory. They used corn cobs or hickory wood to smoke with.

The women cut up the fat leaf lard and entrail fat. It was cooked down to make lard.

In making sausages there were no grinders, so it was all chopped by hand on a big chopping block. They made head cheese, pickled pigs feet, and hung the ribs before the fire and roasted them. Oh, they were fine!

Corn-planting time was a busy month. First, they plowed the ground, then run a single-shovel plow the longest way of the field, then they mustered all the help available to get the corn in one run, the single plow the other way of the field forming check rows. Following him was a dropper, putting four grains in each hill, followed by one with a hoe, covering it. Sometimes we made a bee of it. Then a lot of us girls would drop and the boys with hoes covered. Then we got a good dinner and supper, sure. The cultivating was mostly by the hoe. Some run the single plow a few times through it.

When the corn was ripe they snapped it, hauled it into the barn, or crib, to be husked at leisure. Sometimes they had a husking bee. It was an interesting sight, with those tin lanterns hanging here and there and the busy men and boys at their work. Women prepared them a treat of doughnuts, apples, pie and some coffee.

When they wanted to take the grist to mill a few sacks of corn were brought to the house after supper. All hands set to and did the shelling by hand. It was taken to the water mill, ground between two stones, and was sifted at home in a round-wire sieve. The corn bread and pones were fine.

Sugar and molasses were made of the sap of the sugar maple. They cut a downward-stroked notch in the south side of the tree, bored a hole so as to run into the notch, inserted a spile to let the sap run into a trough made of a log split and hewn out for a receptacle for the sap. They built a place to boil it by putting clay and rocks around the big iron kettles, put wood in the north end, as it was mostly south wind in spring. Father would build a shed, put in some straw and a few comforters, so we could take turns watching the kettles. The first sap was used to make sugar. The last end of sap time it was made into molasses.

One night sister Millie, Charlotte Peacock and I helped father "sugar off." We slept until he was ready for putting it into crocks to cool and stir. The more we stirred it the whiter it got. Sometimes it was as light as coffee A sugar we get nowadays. This was our "company" sugar. Some was darker for common use. Then we molded some into cakes and stacked it away.

Father waked us up to feast on wax. We put it on plates to cool. Soon we had our fun, pulling and eating. Then father told us to lie down until he was ready for us. So Millie said, "Shadrach, Meshach and Aebednego," or, "Get up, eat wax, and to bed we go."

Most of the farmers raised ducks and geese. The duck feathers were used to make pillows and the goose feathers to make feather beds. There was a good market for feathers when not wanted for home use.

They raised broom-corn, made their own brooms, and for scrubbing, sweeping the yard and barn floor they made a split broom by taking a pole of hickory wood and shaving it down within three or four inches of one end and then turn the splits over that stub, tie it and trim off even. It made a stout, serviceable broom.

They did their plowing for wheat as soon after haying as possible, then harrowed it. Those who had no harrow used a brush as drag. They sowed the wheat broadcast by hand, then brushed it in. To harvest the wheat, those who had no cradle used a sickle in cutting it. Then it was tied into bundles and put up in shocks ready for the barn.

When ready to thresh, they swept the floor (and here was where the splint broom came into good play). They used a flail. Some tramped it out with horses. Father had a fanning-mill. Some used the fire bellows. Some took it out on a windy day, spread it on a wagon cover or sheets and passed it from one vessel to another to get the chaff out. It was taken to the old water mill to be made into flour. The miller took his toll.

The farthest back that I can remember is when old Sorrel and Charley ran away while one of my brothers was eating a lunch before he started to Jonesboro with his wheat. He had been hauling rails for father to lay fence. The people laid the first row in the "right time of the moon." He took two planks, put them on the running gears of the wagon and piled his sacks of wheat thereon. The other brother and Millie were on the wagon when the horses started. They ran against a plum tree in the front yard, turned over wheat and all, with sister underneath. She was hurt. I was two years and a half old, but it was indelibly stamped on my memory.

The lanterns they used were made of tin, with oblong holes punched outward to emit the light. They used candles placed in a tin socket. Those who didn't have a lantern took the scaly bark of the hickory tree, tied it with a tow string and lighted it at the fire. There were no matches. People covered up live coals of fire with ashes to start fires. If the coals went dead on them, over to the nearest neighbor they would go to "borrow fire." Smokers carried a tin box lined with ashes to keep coals for a pipe lighter.

Fairmount was a temperance town. I never saw a drunk man until I was eighteen years old, and that was at a colored camp-meeting. A young man from Marion was lying on his face dead drunk. It had a disgusting look to me.

People made their own soap. They saved the ashes and put them in an ash hopper, poured water on and it ran through into a trough similar to a sugar trough, boiled the lye down to where it would eat a feather, then put in old meat trimmings, old grease and such, and boil it until it roped from the paddle In washing, they used wide, flat paddles, soaped the clothes in strong suds made of this soap, and then laid them on a block, or slab, to be "paddled out." When I was past seven years of age they got to using a pounding barrel, as barrels were made by Jackson Reel and other men around there. This barrel was about a third full of water. The clothes were soaped and put in. Then a wooden pestle was used to extract the dirt. Then they were boiled, rinsed, starched and hung out to dry on a line made of tow. The starch was made by scraping potatoes, then washed. The part that settled made a good starch when cooked.

Blacksmiths in those days could make irons. These were heated in front of the fire in the fireplace. Most of these fireplaces had what they called a crane-iron attached, with different lengths of hooks to hang kettles on to boil dinners, cook pumpkins and other things. Grandmother Benbow had a reflector. It was a bright tin frame with slanting shelves toward the fire and used to roast sweet potatoes, squashes and meats, and to bake the Johnnie cakes and other things.

They made chairs, baskets, wooden spoons, bowls, churns and wooden tubs. On each side was left an extension of the staves to make openings for handhold. William Wellington made us a good wood washboard with a kind of plane he brought with him from England. He made our bedsteads and did other carpenter work. He was a well-read man and he brought his Advent books with him, and many other books. My brother-in-law, Micah Baldwin, did have some of his books when I was young. "Religious Emblems and Allegories" and "Daniel and the Prophets" were among them.

Now, I will write some of my recollections of father Nathan Morris. He was born in Guilford County, North Carolina, Tenth month 8, 1806. He was the son of Thomas and Sarah Morris. He moved, with his widowed mother, to Wayne County, Indiana, when a young man. Some time after his mother's death he married the eldest daughter of John and Charity Benbow. After their eldest child, Sarah, was born they moved to Grant County. He entered eighty acres just north of Daniel Baldwin. After building a one-room log cabin, in the middle of the claim, he cleared out a garden and corn patch and set out an orchard. This was the old one (on the forty acres Allen Dillon bought of father afterwards). He lived in that cabin some years, until he built a large two-story house, which had a splendid brick fireplace and wide hearth. In this house I was born.

Father planted a fine orchard west of this house—apples, pears, peaches, cherries. West of the house, inside of the picket fence, he planted some plum trees for shade for his string of bee hives.

The garden was on the south. There were roses on each side of the gate and currant bushes in the back of the garden.

Now, father had a hobby for planting orchards, and every time I write of a change in farms just think there he was looking after fruit supplies, for no one had better fruit than he had. He lived in the two-story house and continued adding a room or two until it was quite a roomy place. (It was burned down after we left there.)

My father sold the north forty to Sammy Dillon and the south forty to Allen Dillon, and moved to a farm near Marion, in the spring of 1852.

In 1857 father traded this farm for the old Charles Baldwin farm, near Back Creek meeting house. Charles and Eunice Baldwin lived in the west end of this house. There were three orchards, as father bought three other farms. Grandmother had half of the west one, near the road. So I went to school at the old stamping ground.

The turnpike was made while we lived there. Father had a share of stock in the road when he left. He sold his share to Jonathan P. Winslow in time of the war.

In the spring of 1869 we went to Iowa by way of the old covered wagon.

In September we went back to Indiana. I went to normal at Back Creek and boarded at William Pierce's, then stayed in Fairmount with sister Sarah that winter. Father lived in the little town at Oak Ridge, as his farm was occupied until March. Father attended Oak Ridge meeting. His farm joined the meeting-house yard on the north. The next spring I took the school for the summer and stayed at home. The next winter I stayed with Sarah, as Micah had moved into the Jonathan Baldwin hotel.

In the spring, father took a notion he would go back to Iowa. He had interests there. We went by train this time.

Father died in 1880. He walked over three miles to meeting, preached as usual, returned home, and in a few days he passed away, and was laid to rest in the Oak Creek Graveyard, near Burr Oak, Jewell County, Kansas. He had preached fifty-one years. He was liberal in every good cause. I have seen a cart load of eatables, clothing and things go out of the house and cellar at one time, and in his rounds among the poor, if he saw children too thinly clad would go to the store and buy cloth for us to make up, telling us the size and sex, so we could fit them. My mother died in the fall of 1850, and father later married Abigail Peacock, widow of John Peacock.

Father Morris had three brothers and five sisters. Elizabeth married a man by the name of Moorman. I forget his name, for he died about twenty years before I was born. Aaron married one of the Thomas girls. Hannah and Anna were twins. Hannah married John Lee and Anna married Solomon Thomas. Caleb married Polly Conner, Mary married Benjamin Benbow, father married Miriam Benbow, Thomas married Nellie Osborn, and Celia married Henry Carter.

Aunt Hannah Lee and Aunt Anna Thomas looked as near alike as two peas. There was such a strong, sisterly tie between them that they never were widely separated. The only way I could tell them apart was by the horses they rode. When one of them was sick the other would say, "Now, get the horse ready, for I know sister is sick." It never did fail.

Solomon Thomas and John Lee moved to Iowa when I was small, so I don't know much about them except that Uncle John lived to be over one hundred years old. Uncle Solomon married the second time. Father and I visited him and his last wife in southern Iowa, in 1862, and after that he moved back to Fairmount. When I was back on a visit I went to see him. Solomon was living at the tollgate. He was getting quite old, but was able to look after the collection of toll.

Now, I will tell of a few persons around Fairmount. There was one Bob Level, who was quite eccentric. When he came to town he always got off a pun or two. One day he came into Henry Harvey's store and said:

"Henry, I want a set of knitting-needles. Be sure not to put in the seam-stitch needle, for no difference how big a hurry I am in, the old woman says, 'wait till I get to the seam-stitch needle, then I will help you'."

Another time Bob said the flies were so bad out to his house they moved out on the porch. "I drove all the flies into the house but one. I killed it, then we ate dinner with pleasure."

When father went to Iowa the first time, Bob came to town one day. He said:

"Now that Uncle Nathan has gone we won't know when to sow wheat or plant our other crops or nothing. We are all broke up." Well, father was always considered quite a weather prophet, and hardly ever missed it. He was a close observer and people had faith in his predictions.

There was Joseph Knight. He was a regular bookworm. Often he would go in from his morning work to prepare for meeting, get his book, and forget the matter until the rest were ready to start and he was reminded of it . So, after meeting had begun here he would come in. One time, when he was clerk of the meeting, he did not come until late. He had the clerk's book under his arm and his hat in his hand. But he got there before the business had begun. One night we were at Martha Winslow's for supper. After supper the young folks proposed we all go to Fairmount to geography school, as we had them often in those days. This school was taught by Alpheus Weaver. Well, Joseph had forgotten his overcoat, cold as it was. So he picked up a buffalo robe off the lounge (one Jack Winslow brought home from the Territory now Kansas). This he wrapped around him and said he was ready. We marched two and two down the turnpike on through town, the end of the robe going clip-clip on the frozen sidewalk, on into the meeting house (for then we used the meeting house as an educational center). He never took it off until seated. He was a learned man, taught at several places, went to Iowa and married a widow with two boys, then came to Kansas and settled in Jewell County. He was living there when I went to visit my brother, Exum, and mother, in 1891.

Ottawa, Kansas.

THOMAS W. NEWBY.

(By Aaron Newby.)

Thomas W. Newby was born May 7, 1824, in Randolph County, North Carolina. When about three years of age his father, Eleazar Newby, died, leaving his mother, Mary (Winslow) Newby, a widow with two small children, Thomas, about three years old, and Eleanor, about one year old. When a boy, Thomas Newby made his home with his uncle Micajah Newby, who was the father of the late Nancy Thomas, wife of the late Amos Thomas. When a small boy, he moved to Indiana, first living in Henry County, then later moved to Grant County, where his uncle, Micajah, settled on the farm known as the Amos Thomas farm. When a young man, he hired to Uncle Nathan Morris, who was a Friends minister of the Gospel.

AARON NEWBY

Sarah Hill was born in Randolph County, North Carolina, on December 7, 1824. When a little girl about three years of age, her father, Aaron Hill, loaded his belongings and family into a wagon and started for Indiana, and settled on what is now known as the Henry Harvey farm. The writer of this article remembers hearing his mother often tell about riding over the Blue Ridge Mountains in the feed-box on the back end of the wagon. Quite different from the ways of conveyance of today with automobiles and aeroplanes.

I think it was while Thomas Newby was working for Nathan Morris that his courtship began with Sarah Hill, which resulted in their marriage, the ceremony being performed in Back Creek meeting, the contracting parties walking from the home of the bride to the meeting house, and then back home again after meeting and the ceremony had been performed according to Friends discipline.

About the year 1847, Thomas Newby bought the eighty acres that

Aaron Newby formerly owned for ten dollars an acre, went in debt for the whole amount, and the writer has often heard him remark that if all his belongings had been sold at that time for one hundred dollars it would not have left a shirt on his back. The farm had no land cleared on it, there being seven acres deadened on the northwest corner of the eighty, the balance in green woods and swamps. He built a hewed-log house, of one large room, but built it tall enough so that it contained one large attic about three and one-half feet from loft (we called it those days, to the eaves), making it about six and one-half feet to the comb of the house. He also built a log barn and stable, with barn on one end, and stable on the other, into which three horses could be crowded, with shed between barn and stable, the barn being ten or twelve rods from the house. They could not see the barn from the house, the timber and bushes being so thick, deer often passing by in sight of the house.

At the time he bought the farm, his father-in-law, Aaron Hill, told him he was foolish, that they could not make a living on the place; but he had too much energy and perseverance to be discouraged, and set to work clearing the land and ditching, and by his every-day habits of industry, and living very economically, he soon had the farm paid for; and going right forward, performing such work each day as he could, and using close economy and good management, with his good companion giving all the aid she could in performing her part of the work, keeping house, cooking, washing, ironing, spinning, weaving and making the clothes for the family, they added, acre by acre, until they had bought over eight hundred acres of land, which is the choice of Grant County land today, there having been as high as ninety bushels of corn raised to the acre and fifty bushels of wheat without the use of commercial fertilizers.

In the year 1903, December 7th, Thomas Newby, at the age of seventy-nine years and seven months, passed away. After his death, it was agreed among the heirs to keep the estate in one body while mother lived. She remained in good health, most of the time, until March 7, 1911, when she passed from works to rewards, at the age of eighty-six years and three months. After the death of both, when the heirs met to settle the estate, it was found to be valued at over sixty thousand dollars, besides giving each of the six children eighty acres of land, which was worth about one hundred and forty dollars per acre. With the improvements the children had made on their land the entire estate rose from less than one hundred dollars in 1846 to about one hundred and thirty thousand dollars in 1911—all by steady habits of industry and economy and keeping money at usury at only a reasonable rate of interest.

Thomas Newby was a man who liked to accommodate his neighbors, and was always willing to aid those in need. He had a great reputation for selling persons who were in need of feed and did not have the money, to let them have the feed on time and pay when they got the money. He was not a man to go security on notes or give security. He was a man who paid the cash for what he bought, outside of land, and in settling his estate we found only one account against him, of fifty cents.

MAJOR B. V. NORTON

When first starting up housekeeping they had neither cookstove nor clock for quite a while; had a large fireplace in the west end of the house that would take in a backlog three and one-half feet long. Up over the fireplace was a long bar of iron reaching from one jamb to the other, with hooks hanging down on which mother would hang kettles to boil meat, cabbage, potatoes, turnips, etc., and to bake bread she had an oven. She would pull out fire coals on the hearth, put her oven on, and would then put her corn dodgers, biscuits or corn pones, whichever she was baking, then would put the lid on the oven and cover with good, live fire coals and let set until they were baked. I can almost see mother lifting that lid to see how the bread was baking. To make mush, they would hang a kettle of water over the fire until the water would begin to boil, then mother would have her tray of meal served ready, then take the kettle of boiling water from over the fire, shovel some good, live coals out on the hearth, setting the kettle on; then she would begin adding the meal; father, with a wood paddle about three feet long, would keep constantly stirring the water as mother added the meal, until they got the mush as thick as they wanted it, then they would let it boil until it was done. The only cupboard mother had for years was made by boring holes in the logs of the house and driving long pins in them, then laying clapboards on the pins for shelves, on which to put her dishes and victuals. The first clock they owned they traded a milch cow for. Father did not have any wagon to start out with, using a hand-made sled for some time.

I well remember the two large beds setting in the east end of the room, one on the north side and the other on the south side, with the trundle-bed run under the one on the north side. I imagine I can hear that trundle-bed squalling now as it is pulled out from under the large bed. But when the children grew large enough father hired a carpenter to build a stairway by using two rough boards, nailing cleats on the inside of them, then nailing steps on the cleats. The loft floor, as we called it those days, was made out of rough boards, with great cracks between the boards, and the roof was of four-foot clapboards riven out. The roof must have been put on the wrong time of the moon, as the boards curled up.

Now just imagine one sleeping up there on a stormy night in the winter and wake up in the night with snow sifting down in his face, and next morning when he went to arise, roll the cover back and hear the snow squeak like rolling a snowball; then think of wading through snow down to the big fireplace, where he would receive a warm greeting.

Fairmount, Indiana.

CHAPTER X.

PERSONAL CHARACTERISTICS OF FIRST SETTLERS.

(By Dr. A. Henley.)

EVER since the descendants of Noah passed out from the plains of Shinar to people the whole earth and the islands of the seas, there has not been a land discovered by a record-making people that did not find a race of beings which had preceded them and taken possession and made themselves homes. This disposition to seek a new country seems to have been a God-given impulse that has come on down through the ages, and manifested itself in the Anglo-Saxon race of the eighteenth century.

We have records of but few of the early emigrants to Fairmount Township who became discouraged by reason of privations and hardships they had to endure in the new country and returned to their native land. This proved that they were in possession of that energy, perseverance and stick-to-itivenesss which triumphs over all difficulties.

Just why the people of North Carolina and Virginia should have selected Grant County for a future home without a forerunner to spy out the land I cannot say. Certainly the move demonstrated good judgment as to fertility of soil and favorable surroundings for the making of desirable homes and the development of a sturdy, loyal progeny.

In my location of the first settlers of Fairmount Township I will take up the district lying between the Range line on the west and the State road, or old pike, on the east, from the county line north. Later I may take up that part of the Township lying east of the old pike.

John Wilson and wife, Mary, with a family of twelve children, eight sons and four daughters, came over the mountains from Randolph County, North Carolina, in May, 1837, and bought a half-section of land that was bounded on the south by the present County and Township line (it will be remembered that the Grant County line once extended a half-mile south of where it now is), erected a cabin and proceeded to the making of a farm. The family consisted of Jesse E., Nathan D., Cyrus, Henry, Nancy, Micajah, Elizabeth, Eliza, John Milton, Lindsey, Samuel and Abigail.

John Wilson was an energetic, enthusiastic farmer, and with the low cost of labor of those days and the assistance of his boys, he in a few years had a self-sustaining farm, with grain and stock to sell to those that came in later. John had the reputation of raising good horses, good corn and large melons.

He had the advantage of some in receiving a good education, and was a fine scribe. Very few excelled him with a pen. He was a good writer and composer, and wrote the life history of Joseph in poetry, which was worthy of preservation. At the beginning of each chapter there was a verse different in style from the balance, but appropriate to that chapter.

John met with quite a misfortune on election day, as I now recall it. The election was held in the woods near my father's house. John had ridden a spirited animal to the election which he hitched to a limb or bush not far away. The animal managed to get loose and started for home. The way was but a trail for near a mile through the thick woods. The animal evidently was running, and in making a short, quick turn, struck one hind leg against a sapling and broke the bone below the knee. The only remedy was to shoot the horse and relieve its suffering. I passed by that skeleton many times.

John Wilson gave each of his children a good start in life, and lived to see the country develop into good farms, and when too feeble to longer attend to his farm work, sold out and moved to town, where he died, in June, 1864, at the ripe old age of eighty years.

Hanley Broyles and wife, Betsy, came from North Carolina near the time John Wilson did, and took land in the southwest corner of the intersection of the County line and the Range line, where they made a farm and lived many years, esteemed by all who knew them, and died leaving no posterity.

The first man to take up land north of John Wilson was Dempsey Bailey, who did not remain there long, but sold to Jonathan Wilcuts, who, in a year or two, sold to Martin Bates.

There seemed to be considerable trading in land at that early date. The first settlers who came into the new country before mills were erected to grind corn had their resources severely taxed at times to provide for large, dependent families. Green corn, beans, potatoes and squash would substitute for bread for a short season, but soon the roasting ears were too hard. Then they must resort to other means to prepare the corn for the palate. One device was to cut a section of a tree twenty inches in diameter and three feet long, set it on end in some convenient place and with an axe or chisel and fire work out a depression in one end to hold a quart or more of corn. Then with a pestle made of hard wood beat the corn in this improvised mortar until one could run it through a sieve or blow the bran off and make a cake or pot of hasty pudding, commonly called mush. He who has not read Will Carleton's poetical production on "Hasty Pudding" has missed a treat.

While Wilcuts was on this place he decided to have a wheat cake.

HEADS OF WILSON-HILL-BOGUE-BALDWIN FAMILIES
(1910)

Hon. Samuel C. Wilson, son of John Wilson; Joseph W. Hill, son of Aaron Hill; Jesse Bogue, son of Barnaba Bogue, and Asa T. Baldwin, son of Thomas Baldwin.

He had grubbed out a few acres in the green woods in the spring and put it in corn, and gave it some kind of cultivation, but the squirrels got a good part of the grain. When wheat sowing time came round, the wild weeds and wild pea vines were taller and much thicker than the corn. Wilcuts made an effort to get between the corn rows with horse and plow, but after making quite an effort he gave it up as a bad job. He determined not to be beaten out of his wheat bread without one more trial. Shouldering his sack of wheat, he got on his horse and rode between the corn rows, sowing the grain over the tops of the weeds as he went, trusting that the weeds would soon fall down and protect the wheat, which they did, rewarding him with a fair yield the next harvest.

I have written of this incident to show future generations that may chance to read this what difficulties the early settler had to contend with. Wilcuts sold to Martin Bates, who, I think, put up the first frame house I recollect of seeing on Back Creek.

Bates had a half-section of land and took stock for all of it in a scheme to build a railroad from Cincinnati to Chicago. The bubble burst and nearly all that took stock in the road lost every dollar or acre of land they put in. Bates moved to Iowa, and from there to Kansas. I was near where he lived in Kansas, in 1858. It was said Martin was doing quite well there.

John Phillips lost eighty acres west of Little Ridge in that same railroad.

Bernard McDonald next bought the Bates land of the railroad creditors. Since then it has been divided up somewhat and may now be owned by Henry Davis's heirs.

James Lytle settled on the Cal Dean place. He sold to John Smith some time in the '60's and moved to Iowa, where he died some years ago.

The next place north was taken by Frank Lytle, Jr. He, too, emigrated to Iowa. The place has since been owned by a number of persons, namely, Nixon Winslow, David Stanfield, Lindsey Wilson, and others.

The next eighty acres was taken by Benjamin Benbow and traded to Thomas Baldwin. Then, Calvin Bookout owned it; then, a Mrs. Dickey, I think.

The next man north of the Bates place was David Smithson, who took up three hundred and twenty acres, in length one mile north and south. Wilson, Bates and Smithson owned a block of land two miles in length, reaching from the County line north to Perry Seale's south line, or directly west of Washington Street, Fairmount.

David and Betsy Smithson had a family of twelve children, six sons and six daughters, namely, Mahala, Judiah, John, Jehu, Sarah, Jonathan, Isaac, Anna, Margaret, Seth, Nancy and Adeline. Four of his sons were in the Civil War. They were Judiah, Isaac, Seth and Jehu. David was a good citizen and died on his farm. He set each of his children off with forty acres of land.

In 1833, Thomas Baldwin and Lydia, his wife, came from Wayne County, Indiana, and took up the land that reached to the center of Fairmount, later known as the David Stanfield homestead. Baldwin sold to Stanfield, who came, in 1836, from Tennessee, with a family of seven children, who later married and settled near Fairmount.

The land now owned by W. A. Beasley was first taken by Thomas Morris, April 9, 1832, and later sold to Benjamin Benbow. Thomas Baldwin, in the early day, taught three terms of school on that place.

Benbow sold the place to Daniel Thomas, who lived there from 1841 until his death.

Thomas Baldwin afterwards bought the farm later known as the Jesse Dillon place, north of town. From there he moved to the Deer Creek settlement.

Jesse E. and Nathan D. Wilson, sons of John and Mary Wilson, married sisters, Hannah and Mary, daughters of Aaron Hill, in 1838, and settled on the land given them by their father, south of the Rush farm and west of Back Creek. They both reared large families and were energetic, progressive farmers, useful members of church and community, and were much used in the church, giving freely of their time and substance to promote the cause of righteousness, temperance and peace, and were in the front ranks when anything was to be done for the betterment of the community. They led exemplary lives, and left the world better for having lived in it. They died on their farms, after enjoying the fruits of their labor for many years. Their widows died in Fairmount with relatives. Their children are scattered many miles apart. Some went on the long journey where life is full of joy and bright hopes. A majority of both families now rest with the silent dead.

Daniel Baldwin and wife, Christian, with a family of ten children, came to Fairmount Township, in 1833, and settled on the quarter-section of land embracing what is now the north half of Fairmount. He erected a cabin near where J. H. Wilson's residence now stands. Here they lived, and here they died some years later, leaving five of the family yet unmarried. They subsequently married and lived in Fairmount.

Nathan Morris and wife, Miriam, with a family of children, came in 1832 and took the quarter-section lying immediately north of Daniel Baldwin, where he made a good farm. Nathan was energetic, progressive, and made a good and useful citizen. He was the father of twenty-two children. He emigrated west, in 1865, and died in Jewell County, Kansas, in 1881, having been a minister in the Society of Friends from early manhood. His old farm has been divided up and is now owned by different parties.

In 1835, Dugan Rush and wife, Elizabeth, took up the land now owned by John Kelsay. He was a hard worker, would pile his brush during the day and burn it at night. Mostly by his own labor, he made a nice farm and had passed over the most trying period of pioneer life. The alluring reports from the great West of the ease with which one could make a farm on the prairie so enthused him that he sold out to Thomas Powell and moved to Iowa, where he purchased land and proceeded to make a new home. They had not been gone more than a year, I think, when word came that Dugan was dead and the family was anxious to return to Indiana. A brother of Dugan's went after them and moved the family back. Having to dispose of their holdings out there at a reduced price, they had but little left when they arrived at their old home.

In 1835 came Thomas Winslow, wife and four children, Milton, Lydia, Milicent and Nixon.

In 1836, Phineas Henley and Mary, his wife, and four children came and took land lying between Dugan Rush and the Range line west and the Oak Ridge road on the north.

Thomas Winslow lived there until some time in 1850, when he sold to Robert Carey, and purchased the farm east of the pike formerly owned by Jesse Bogue.

Phineas Henley remained on his land until no longer able to work it, and moved to town.

Thomas Winslow's original farm is now owned by Mattie Wright and Phineas Henley's by Mrs. Alice Thomas.

Thomas Winslow died on the Bogue farm and Phineas Henley passed away at the home of his son, Dr. A. Henley, in Fairmount.

Seth Winslow and Mary, his wife, in 1829, entered land directly north of Iredell Rush's northeast forty and Nathan Morris's northwest forty. They had four children born to them, namely, Sarah, Elizabeth, Jesse and Ruth. Jesse died when about twelve years old, I think. Sarah lived to be a young woman and died. Elizabeth married and died, leaving four children. Ruth lived to care for her parents and soothe their pathway through the decline of life. Ruth has since joined her loved ones to give an account of her stewardship, and thus that family has become extinct.

In 1835 came Jacob Hale and Dorinda, his wife, from North Carolina, with a family of eight children, namely, Nancy, Elizabeth, Dorcas, Samuel, Asenath, William, Jane and George, and located on the eighty acres north of Josept W. Baldwin, the land now owned by John Flanagan and W. P. Seale. Jacob's wife was a sister of Iredell and Nixon Rush. Hale sold to a man by the name of Townsend, he to Robert Corder, and Corder to W. P. Seale. Hale emigrated to Iowa, and from Iowa to Kansas, in 1858, where a remnant of the family is now living, near Leroy, Coffey County.

In 1837, Peter Rich and wife, Sarah, and six children, mostly of age, namely, Aaron, George, Rebecca, Mary, Martha and Isaac located directly east of Hale. Peter was a wagon maker by trade. He did all his work by hand and with few tools. His work was strong and lasting. He was a useful man in the new country. They were a stout family and industrious workers. The mother and daughters spun, wove, colored and made all the material they wore. The father, mother and Isaac died a mile west of Fairmount. George, Rebecca and Martha died in Kansas. Aaron and Mary died in Iowa.

The land joining the Rich farm on the east was taken by Iredell Rush, in 1831. He and his wife, Elizabeth, were also from the old North State. They had a family of eight children born to them in the new country, namely, John, Calvin, Nixon, Jr., Thomas, Jane, Milicent, Anna and Mary. Iredell was an energetic farmer and was forging ahead rapidly when he was taken violently sick and died, in the prime of life, leaving a widow with a large family. She nobly cared for them and lived to see all of them married but two, Thomas and Jane, who died unmarried. After many years of widowhood, the mother married Thomas Jay, a minister of the Society of Friends, where she had held an honorable position as elder for many years. They were a mutual help to each other, and passed down the shady side of life happily together, and now await the trumpet's call.

In 1836 came William Osborn and wife, Keziah, and took up the land that Mary Rich now lives on, directly north of Dugan Rush. William's wife was a sister of Thomas Harvey, Sr., and Jesse Harvey, Sr. They brought up a family of six children, namely, Mary, Abigail, Ruth, Lindon, Mahlon and Lydia. They were a very nice family of people, dressed and lived very plain, as most people did in the new country. Mary married Lindsey Baldwin, Abigail married George Shugart, Ruth married Samuel Roberts, Lydia married Milton McHatton, Lindon married Mary Reeder and Mahlon married Arcadia Phillips. I think not one of the family is now living.

Characteristics of First Settlers.

Thomas Harvey, Sr., and Anna, his wife, came the same year, with a family of five, four sons and one daughter, namely, Jesse, John, Henry, Thomas and Mary, and took the land directly north of William Osborn and a forty west of the road that Jesse settled on, where Cyrus and Ephraim were born. Thomas Harvey, Sr., was a very industrious, quiet, inoffensive man. He had a large orchard and fruit nursery at an early day, and sold his fruit and young trees over the newer parts of the country. Thomas and his boys were great friends to the colored race, and assisted many on to freedom. The old homestead has passed out from the Harvey name, I think. All of the original family have passed away. A few of the second and third generations yet survive the ravages of time, but are widely scattered.

Directly east of William Osborn's old home lies Exum Newby's one hundred and sixty-acre farm, given him by his father-in-law, Joseph Winslow, in 1829. Here two children were born, Eleazer and Rebecca, when the young mother died, leaving a little babe that was taken by Grandmother Newby, and as years rolled by became the wife of Zimri Richardson. Caroline Newby was the first one of the new colony to be taken away. Her little boy was taken by an uncle and reared until he was of age, when he met with an accident that ended his life. Later on, Exum married Rachel Knight and reared a family of seven children. Exum Newby was a carpenter by trade, and was a No. 1 workman. He and Thomas Hill, a brother of Aaron Hill, another good workmen, did the carpenter work on the old Friends brick meeting house at Back Creek. Anyone who has seen that work would say that it was a marvel of accuracy. The matching of the flooring, and especially the ceiling, has not been excelled by the late machine work. Many a time I have sat and looked for a bad joint in that ceiling, but found none, and yet it was all worked out and gauged by hand.

The old road that ran diagonally through the Newby farm has long been closed up, and the old frame house, one of the first that was put up on Back Creek, that was wont to resound with the cheerful voices of all the young people of that section, even for miles away, may now be the home of the bat or barn swallow.

The old Back Creek meeting house should never have been torn down, but kept as a lasting monument to the memory of the loyalty and energy of the founder of that church. What a great place that could have been made for recreation and public meetings!

North of the Newby farm, and joining the same, lay the Joseph and Peninah Winslow home, with their son, Henry. Joseph has been quite well written up and I will not detract from what has gone before.

His farm is now occupied by Ancil Winslow, a grandson of Thomas Winslow, one of the first settlers of the country.

Matthew Winslow (son of Joseph) and his wife, Anna, came with his father and took the land directly east of his father, where he made a farm and prospered. Later, he decided he must have more land for the boys. He sold out and moved to Iowa, where land was cheap. The change did not prove to be a good one. The two elder boys sickened and died, leaving him but one son. The bereavement cast a shadow over the remainder of their days. The old farm is now occupied by John A. Jones and John Devine.

Charles Baldwin (a brother of Daniel Baldwin) and Eunice, his wife, came in 1830 and took land joining the Newby farm on the east. Charles was married twice. By his first wife he had five sons and three daughters, namely, Thomas, Ahira, Lindsey, John and Quincy, Mary, Jane and Rachel. All of them came to the new colony, marrying and making homes near by. Thomas married Harvey Davis's daughter, Ahira married Jane Newby (a sister of Exum Newby), Lindsey married Mary Osborn (a daughter of William and Keziah Osborn), Mary married Lancaster Bell, Jane married David Stanfield, Jr., and Rachel married Jesse Dillon and was the mother of the preacher, Josiah Dillon. The younger son, Charley, as we always called him, married Malinda Knight, a daughter of Benjamin Knight, near Marion. Thus we see the two elder Baldwins and Nathan Morris did a Roosevelt's part in populating the new country. Charles Baldwin was rather dignified, but courteous and kind-hearted, kept close to the old style of Friends' plain dress and address, never wearing suspenders, and, I think, but few buttons. He and his wife rode to meeting in a two-wheeled covered gig, the only vehicle of the kind in the country at that date. His last wife was a fleshy woman, a sister of the Pembertons. Some twenty or thirty rods north of the LaRue brick house stood the old Baldwin residence, partly log and partly frame, a few rods east of the public road, and an open lane ran by it down east beyond where the Big Four railroad now crosses the farm. Just over there once stood a cabin that was occupied by Evan Hinshaw and family, then John Baldwin, and later Joseph Baldwin for a brief time. Across the lane from the residence the woodhouse and carriage shed stood, where Carlotta Peacock ended her life.

The field east, south and west of this house contained some eight or ten acres, and was sown to wheat, which was ripe and ready for harvest. At that date wheat had mostly been cut with a sickle or cradle scythe. This field of grain had been put in the shock ready for threshing out. At that period threshing machines were in their development stage and rather crude affairs.

A man by the name of Jesse Morris, from near Marion, had a machine that was fashioned somewhat on the principle of the later-made ones, not so long in body, but set on four wheels, the two hind wheels being the drivers for the motor power, the whole thing drawn by four or six horses. It was to pass over the field by the shocks, where the pitchers would toss the sheaves to the band-cutter and feeder, who stood on the machine. They had just made a start when it was discovered that the machine was defective. The band that ran the straw-carrier would slip off the pulley every few rods, necessitating the feeder to climb over the top of the machine to adjust the band. In doing that he went over once too many times and let one foot slip into the cylinder, when one or more teeth hit his foot, tearing it to pieces. It was necessary to take the foot off above the ankle. That was done before the day of anæsthetics. Dr. William Lomax, a young man then, did the operation.

Whew! Just think of lying down and having a leg taken off without an anæsthetic. I think that machine was not moved out of its tracks for some time. I saw it standing in the field later.

Thomas Hill and Daniel Frazier were among the early arrivals, and located east of Aaron Hill and Matthew Winslow. Frazier's land joined Samuel C. Wilson's farm on the north and Hill's land lay north of Frazier's. It later was occupied by Lindsey Baldwin and family. Baldwin died there and his family are scattered.

Thomas Hill was a brother of Aaron Hill and was a first-class carpenter and joiner. As has been said, he was one of the builders of the old brick church at Back Creek. What became of Thomas Hill and family I do not know.

Daniel Frazier had a wife and family of three sons and two daughters that I can recollect, who attended church at the old brick house in an early day. One son and one daughter were grown, two were in their teens and one boy eight or ten years old. This little fellow, in some way I do not now recollect, got lost in the forest. If anything will arouse sympathy and energy in a people it is for a child to get lost in the wilderness. As soon as the word was circulated that the Frazier child was lost, the whole settlement was out looking for him. The clearings around the settlers' cabins were small, then, with a heavy forest all round and wild animals prowling about looking for something to devour. Night came on, with no tidings of the lost boy. The nights were dark. Anxiously, they waited for the light of another day, when they could renew the hunt. A little way north of the cemetery grounds and halfway between the creek and public road stood a large, hollow sycamore tree, with an opening near the ground. When dark came on the lad chanced to come across that tree, and, looking in, saw it was very dark in the hollow, and decided it was so dark that no animal could see him in there. So he went in, laid down, and slept until day, when he was soon sighted by some one on the search for him. At no time was he far from a cabin, but made no noise, and hence was not sooner found. The family emigrated to Iowa and passed out of our knowledge.

Lewis Moorman, who married Sarah Thomas, of Wayne County, Indiana, a sister of the wife of Thomas Baldwin, Sr., came to join the new colony in 1835, and took land a mile east of Charles Baldwin. The land between was very wet. Lewis was a stout-built, heavy man, with a coarse voice, and somewhat eccentric, but made a good, loyal citizen. He had two sons and two daughters. I do not know who now owns the original home place. I think his sons are dead. The daughters moved to the West years ago. The Moormans lived the farthest east of any family of Friends, but were regular in attendance at meetings.

The same year, 1835, came Jabez H. Moore, and took land joining Moorman on the south. Moore was an educated man, and put on a little more style than many others. He always went dressed well when away from home, wearing a tall, silk hat and cravat. He had two sons and two daughters, namely, Isaac, John, Lacy Ann and Martha. Jabez and his wife have been dead some years. One son and one daughter were living in Kokomo a few years ago. Jabez made a good citizen and was active in the organization of the Township and County, rarely ever missing an election.

Directly south of Charles Baldwin, on the east side of the public road, Lancaster Bell, who married Mary Baldwin, a daughter of Charles Baldwin, took up eighty acres, in 1836. Bell sold, or traded, to Thomas Baldwin. Later, Jesse Dillon bought the place and established a gun-making shop there, where he and his boys changed all the flintlock guns for miles around into caplocks. The place is now owned, I think, by some of the Winslow family. Lancaster Bell and wife moved to Iowa many years ago, where they died. Jesse Dillon and wife died there.

The eighty acres just east of the Bell place was taken by Jesse, Sr., and Lydia Harvey, in 1832. He was a brother of Thomas Harvey and Solomon Parsons' wife. Jesse died early in the '40's. His wife lived there alone for many years and passed from there to the Great Beyond. They were two very quiet, kind-hearted bodies, liked by all who knew them. They left no children.

In 1835, Solomon Parsons and wife, Rachel, took the land joining Harvey on the south. Rachel was a sister of Thomas and Jesse Harvey, Sr., and Keziah Osborn. Solomon was a valuable man in the new country, as he was an excellent workman with leather and made a nice boot or shoe. He was a fast workman. They reared a family of five children, namely, Keziah, Elizabeth, William, Anna and Henry. Keziah married Henry Wilson. He died. Later she married Reece Haisley, and they moved to Jewell County, Kansas. Elizabeth married Gonner Knight, an Englishman, and lived for some years on what is now the north end of John Peacock's farm. They are both dead, leaving two sons and two daughters. Dr. John C. Knight, of Jonesboro, is one of the family. William married and moved to Iowa many years ago. Anna married Dr. White, a young physician who practiced in Fairmount a short time in an early day. He emigrated West and we lost track of him. Henry fought for the Union in the Civil War, was badly wounded, but recovered sufficiently to live until a short time ago. He settled in Iowa after the war, reared a family, and was an honored citizen. Parsons sold to John Beck. The writer went to school with all the children many a day.

The land directly east of Parsons, to the prairie, was taken up by Eastern speculators, held for some years, and for this reason was not improved for some time.

In 1835 we find John Lee and wife a mile and a half east of Parsons' south line. The cabin stood a little east of the old Wayne trail, west of the slough. Amaziah Beeson located a little way across the slough, to the southeast of Lee. John Lee's wife was a sister of Nathan Morris and a twin sister of Solomon Thomas' wife. The Lees and Beesons were members of the Friends church and attended Back Creek meeting. Lee and Thomas emigrated to Iowa, in 1850. Lee died out there.

Beeson remained on his prairie farm and brought up a family there. Beeson and the Lees were related in some way. Amaziah was a chemist, to some extent, and had a small distillery, where he manufactured sassafras and peppermint oil, which he sold at a profit. He built the first brick residence in Fairmount Township, I think, which certainly indicated energy and perseverance. I think he and his wife died on the farm. Charles Beeson was their son.

In 1835 Timothy Kelley settled on the Lake Galatia land. He and his wife, Avis, had five children, namely, Jane, Mary Ann, Alfred, Samuel and Anna. They were from Pennsylvania, I think, members of the Friends Church, and a degree more aristocratic than most of the early settlers. A portion of their land was covered by a cranberry marsh before the country was drained. This was a source of considerable revenue to them. They were good, honest, Christian people, and have all passed away.

Between the John Lee place and the Kelley farm Otho Selby settled, in 1836, on the north side of the prairie, where he reared a family of three children. Otho was an industrious man, uncompromising in principle, and an educator and promoter of the best interests of the country. His children are all living, and retain the old farm, which but few descendants of the original pioneer stock can truthfully say.

A half mile southeast, across a branch of the prairie, Henry Winslow, Sr., and Jesse, his son, settled in 1836. They were Friends, and their location was a long way back in the woods, with bad roads, yet they were regular attenders of Back Creek meeting. They were compelled to go on horseback. Aunt Penny made a fine appearance in the saddle. Old Henry, as we always called this one, because there were four of that name—Joseph's Henry, or Big Henry, Ryer's Henry and John's Henry. Old Henry, the father of Thomas, Jesse, John, Henry, Polly Wilson, Elizabeth Powell-Dillon and Susie Crowell, died on the prairie farm. Jesse sold out over there and bought the Elijah Harrold place, where Foster Davis now lives, east of Fairmount. Jesse and his wife, Peninah, were excellent people. I would that we had more like them today. Their influence will roll on until it reaches the golden shore.

The farm now owned by Nate Wilson was taken in 1835 by Charles Hinshaw and wife. Charles was a strong, hard worker and had the only whipsaw in the country. He cut out floor-plank for people. It was a slow, expensive process, and was not resorted to very much. While Hinshaw lived at that place, a son, a young man about seventeen, I think, was drowned in the river north of Jonesboro, a little southeast of Jesse Jay's place, where the road makes a turn to the northwest. He had been, or was on his way, to the Deer Creek mill, had reached that point, and decided to have a bath, not knowing that it was a deep hole of water. He hitched his horse, left his clothes on the river bank and plunged in where the water was deep, but could not swim. Some time later a man was passing, and, seeing the horse tied and clothes lying near by, surmised what was wrong, got help and fished the body out. Not long after this, Charles sold out and moved to Iowa. In 1858 I met Charles in Kansas. He was wearing the same hat he wore the first time I ever met him, at Back Creek meeting. He was a Friend. It was a round-crowned, broad-brimmed beaver hat and would last one hundred years.

The Clint Winslow place was taken by a man named Ratliff. The house was on the north side, near where the old original road ran.

Ratliff, I think, sold to Hopkins Richardson, and Hopkins gave it to his son, Jonathan.

In 1833, Hopkins Richardson and wife, Elizabeth, with two sons, Jonathan and Zimri, located directly west of Ratliff. Richardson was of medium size, dark skin, black hair, and full of energy. He was a great hunter and would find a deer where other people failed. Hopkins gave the most of his land to his two sons. His wife died at the old place and he sold what land he had left, married again, bought a place on top of the Deer Creek bluff, west side, and died there. He was quite a trader for that early day. He would buy a lot of good horses—he was a good judge of horse flesh—take them to Kentucky or Georgia, sell them to the wealthy planters at a good profit, return and invest in more land. Thus he became owner of a fine body of land. His sons are dead. Elmer Buller, I think, holds the old homestead.

Directly west of the Richardson homestead, William Winslow (black Bill, or Uriah's Bill, as he was always called to designate him from the other Bills) took land. He was a brother of Jesse, Thomas and John Winslow. He had quite a family of girls. He sold his land to Richardson and moved to Iowa. The old road ran east and west, near the middle of his place, and near his cabin, some thirty rods west of the public road that passed by Richardson's house, and intersected the road that crossed the creek on the line of Third Street, or what is now Bogue's corner.

This brings us back to the center of Fairmount again.

CHAPTER XI.

HAVING TO DO WITH A WIDE VARIETY OF SUBJECTS.

(By T. B. McDonald.)

MY FATHER, Bernard McDonald, moved to Grant County the fall of 1854. He bought what was known as the Martin Bates (now the John Davis) farm, three hundred and twenty acres, mostly heavy timber. Bates never received a dollar for this farm.

About the year 1849, a railroad was projected to run from Cincinnati to Chicago. The land, as surveyed, ran east of Fairmount, through Galatia and Jonesboro. A part of the right-of-way was cut out. Immense piles of crossties and bridge timber were piled up along the right-of-way, were not paid for, and rotted where the material was piled.

A great many farmers subscribed for stock in this railroad and gave their farms in payment for the stock. Not a single subscriber ever received a penny for his farm or stock. The farms were sold to innocent purchasers and there was no recourse for the people who lost their farms. Martin Bates was one of those who lost a good farm. There were many more.

Bates had planted an orchard of about twelve acres in apples, peaches and pears. This orchard was a great source of profit for my father. There were but few orchards west of us for many miles, and for several years we sold apples at Kokomo, Windfall and Elwood. Those were our nearest railroad towns, west of us, at that time.

The west half of Fairmount Township was settled by Friends, mostly from North Carolina. The east half of the Township was settled by good, sturdy people who were not Quakers.

We had not been in the country long until I became acquainted with Morris (Mallegan) Payne's boys, and they were friends of the Lewis and Leach boys. In that way I met those of my own age.

I remember Esom Leach, a short, fat man, who once told me he had no use for an Irishman, as a rule. I soon learned that he was in fun.

William G. Lewis was a kind man—generous to a fault. The Osborns, Paynes, Thorns, Harrisons and Fears were all names which I recollect as being early settlers.

Thus it was, in the first settlement of the Township, they were all sturdy men, able to cope with the hardships that were necessary to succeed. What was once a wilderness is now the finest farming community in the world. The entire Township cannot be excelled in this glorious country.

T. B. McDONALD

Has had an interesting career. He was born near Liberty, Union County, Indiana, December 6, 1846. His father, Bernard McDonald, was born in County Carlow, Ireland, August 25, 1812. At the age of eight Bernard McDonald went to sea as a cabin boy on a ship with his uncle. He followed the sea for twenty-five years, when he came to America. T. B. McDonald's mother, Elizabeth McDonald, was the daughter of Samuel Heavenridge, of Rock Bridge County, Virginia. He settled at Cincinnati, Ohio, where Mr. McDonald's mother was born in 1824. Samuel Heavenridge was a Quaker of the old school. He was an elder in the church at Fairmount when he died. Bernard McDonald moved to Henry County, Indiana, when the son was one year old, and to Grant County in 1854, where the latter spent his boyhood days on a farm. When he left the farm Bent went to Jonesboro and worked in a woollen mill owned by Pemberton & Baldwin.
From there he went to work for Noah Harris, and assisted in building the first grain elevator at Harrisburg (now Gas City). It was while this elevator was being built that John Evans killed John Brinegar. T. B. was a witness to the killing. This unexpectedly changed his plans for life. He had intended to go to Kansas with John Rush, but was held as a witness to the tragedy, and could not go as he had planned. He then went to work on the Panhandle railroad as a brakeman on a gravel train, then on a local freight train for about ten months, when he went to Nebraska City with Dr. J. N. Converse, who was building the Midland Pacific railroad. He remained there, employed as a conductor, until the road was finished to Lincoln, Nebraska. He was the first conductor to run a train into Lincoln. This was on April 24, 1871. He went to Iowa October 9, 1871, the day of the great Chicago fire. He was employed by the Burlington Railroad as a conductor for ten years. Since that time he has been engaged in farming, merchandising and banking, and is now President of the Lovilia Exchange Bank. He owns 965 acres of valuable coal lands, contented with his lot, never held a public office, has often been a member of the third house (lobby), has always taken an interest in politics, votes the Republican ticket, believes in prohibition and woman suffrage. He is proud of the fact that he is a native of Indiana and lived in Fairmount Township, "where," as he puts it, "more good people live and have lived than on any other six miles square on earth."

Among the early settlers there was not a single sluggard to be found —every man a Christian according to his belief. There were Solomon Thomas, the Winslows, Wilsons, Newbys, Harveys, Baldwins, Solomon Parsons, the Jays, Peacocks, Joseph Rich, Spencer Reeder, Lindsey Buller, the Scotts, John Ferree, the Wrights, Harvey Davis, William Cox, David Smithson, Eli and William Neal, Carter Hasting, David Stanfield, William Hall, William Pierce, Joseph Hill, Nixon Rush, Phineas Henley, Iredell Rush, Mahlon Harvey, John and William P. Seale, Samuel Radley and John Bull. Were there ever so many good, solid, well-meaning men in one neighborhood? We think not. It does me good to think of those sturdy men and their wives. God bless them! They, too, were the equals of their husbands.

Clothing the family was a problem in those days. It was difficult to raise sheep in the heavy timber, and for that reason wool was scarce. The wool was carded by hand and spun into yarn, reeled into skeins, and from the skeins it went to the large roller in the loom. Then the ends of the thread were placed through a reel, when it was ready for the shuttle. Sometimes the chain would be all cotton and the filling all wool.

This cloth was called linsey, and when both filling and chain were wool it was called flannel, or jeans, as the case might be.

Remember, the work was all done by hand, and a great deal of it by night with but little light, sometimes a tallow dip, sometimes a greasy rag placed in a pan and set on fire.

The first houses were built of logs, some hewed and some round. A big fireplace at one end of the building served for both heat and light, and a place to cook what they had to eat.

The manner of cooking was certainly crude. Those who could, had cranes in their fireplaces. There was a bar of iron fastened at one side of the fireplace, fixed so it would swing out or in as needed. This bar extended almost across the fireplace. Hooks were placed on this bar, on which the kettles would be hung while the food cooked. Then there were covered skillets, in which the baking was done, such as corn bread or wheat bread, as the case might be.

Those skillets were set on the hearth and live coals put on top and around the bottom, and kept there until the food was done. I don't believe the stove was ever made that would cook food to taste as good as those good old-fashioned pots and kettles.

Wheat bread was not within the reach of all the early settlers. Wheat bread was rather a luxury in 1850.

Stoves were few and far between. Everything that the pioneer had in the shape of clothing was made at home. Bed ticks and sheetings were made of linen, so were towels and grain bags.

The flax was sown with a view of getting as long a fiber as possible. When the flax had gotten ripe enough it was pulled up by the roots, the seed knocked off, then a nice, clean piece of meadow was selected, the flax spread out and left until the fiber had rotted sufficiently, then the rotted flax was tied up in bundles and placed in a dry place until spring.

When the flax was prepared for the loom first, it was broken, that is the wood part of the stem was separated from the fiber. An ugly piece of machinery called a flax brake was used to do the work. The machine consisted, first, of five pieces of wood about six feet long and six inches wide. The top edge of those bars was shaven to a sharp edge, then they were matriced into a heavy block of wood. Into those blocks were placed wooden legs about two feet long. Then there was another set of only three bars. These fitted between the first named bars. The top set was hinged at one end. The operator would raise the top set of bars and place the rotted flax on the bottom set of bars. When the top set of bars came down it would break the flax straw so that the woody parts would separate from the fiber. The next thing to be done was to scutch the fiber.

This was done as follows: A board about eight inches wide was shaven to a sharp edge at the top, then fastened to a block. A piece of board two feet long and four inches wide was shaven so that both edges were sharp. This was called a scutching knife. A bunch of the fiber would be taken in the hand, laid across the top of the board, and used against and down the side of the board would soon prepare the fiber for the hackle.

This instrument of torture was made by driving a lot of sharp spikes in a solid board. These spikes were driven as close as possible. The tops of the spikes were as sharp as possible.

This machine was about six inches square. The fiber was drawn through those teeth until all the coarse fiber had been separated from the finer fiber.

Then came the spinning of the thread. This was done on what was called the little wheel, which was run by foot power. The thread passed through what was called flyers. The fiber was placed on what was called a distaff. The operator would take a small piece of the fiber in her hand and start it through the flyers, which twisted the thread. The operator regulated the size of the thread by the deft feel of her fingers. Some were more expert than others. When sufficient thread was produced then the weaving was done.

We have no doubt that some pieces of linen made as above described can now be found in Fairmount. You who have it just take a look at it, and think what toil it required to produce it. Yet it was done cheerfully. It does not seem possible that such wonderful changes could take place in a space of sixty years.

The next step necessary to keep the family of the pioneer in good health was to provide shoes. If he be fortunate enough to have cattle, then one or more would be killed for meat. The hide would be taken to the tanner and made into leather. It took one year to complete the tanning. If the farmer had money enough he would pay the tanner the cost and take all the leather. If not, the tanner would take one half for his labor. Aaron Williams, where Summitville now stands, had the first tanyard that we recollect. There was one, we think, at Fairmount, but we have forgotten who owned it. However, we do remember Micah Baldwin and Rariden Smith as tanners, because we have driven the old horse in the bark mill many an hour. We also remember being thrown bodily into one of the vats filled with filthy ooze. A school house stood just east of the tanyard and we were going to school there at the time.

After the leather was procured, the itinerant shoemaker came and stayed until the entire family was shod for the winter. However, there were a great many men who made all the shoes for the family. One pair of shoes for each person was about the limit for each year.

The early settler had plenty to eat, such as it was. Game was plentiful. Not many years after the first settlers came wild hogs were numerous, and in the fall of the year those hogs were fat. They lived on mast, as it was called—nuts, such as beechnuts, acorns, hickory nuts, hazel nuts, walnuts. The ground would be literally covered with nuts—and hogs could live all winter on them.

The man who did not have hogs of his own would take his trusty flintlock rifle and soon have sufficient meat to last all winter. There was no excuse for killing more than he needed, as there was no market for cured meat and salt was scarce. Bear in mind, there were only a few persons who had to get their meat as we have described.

Wild turkey were plentiful, as were deer, squirrels, pheasants, opossums and raccoons. The pioneer had no difficulty in bringing home game when needed.

Powder and lead were scarce and were never wasted. There were none of the modern guns in use—no percussion caps. Such a thing as a shotgun was never seen, unless it was an old musket that had been used in the War of 1812, or earlier. The guns were fired by a spark made by a flint striking a piece of steel, which was a part of what was called the pan. A small portion of powder would be placed in the pan.

When the trigger was pulled the hammer, which had a flint fastened in it, would make a spark which would ignite the powder in the pan, and cause the gun to go off. Sometimes the gun would fail to fire. Then it was called a flash in the pan, and it was then that the hunter said uncomplimentary things, especially if he missed getting the nice turkey he had expected to take home with him.

The hunter's outfit consisted of his gun, powder-horn, bullet pouch, bullet moulds, string of patchen, knife, powder measure and a bunch of flax tow.

The first store that we now recollect of being in was kept in Fairmount by Henry Harvey. The building, we think, stood where the Citizens State Bank now stands, and his residence about where the News office is now located. This store was a small affair in comparison with the stores now in Fairmount. The principal stock was green coffee, brown sugar, rice, dried herring, salt crackers, a few cut nails, grain pepper, cloves, powder and lead, a few pieces of blue denim, some cotton thread, and possibly two or three pieces of wool cloth suitable for men's pants, three kinds of tobacco (home grown), a twist called dog-leg, and a plug black as night. If you asked Henry for tobacco, he would say:

"Will thee have flat plug or dog-leg?"

There were no canned goods, no cereals such as oatmeal, corn flakes, etc. No bottled goods, no olives; in fact, nothing except what I have mentioned above.

Henry Harvey was a good man in every sense of the word. He did just as the merchants of today do. He granted credit to those who never paid him for his goods or appreciated his kindness for extending credit

I remember only John, Avis and Kelley Harvey. Possibly there were others.

Joseph W. Baldwin kept store in Fairmount, and, I believe, Seaberry Lines. John Scarry kept a grocery.

George Doyle came later on, kept a grocery, and was accused of selling wet goods. We always thought he was guilty for the reason that at that period my father was in the habit of taking a nip of the "Oh, be joyful!" He thought a great deal of Mr. Doyle and usually after calling at Doyle's grocery showed the effects of John Barleycorn. Therefore, we thought that wet goods were sold at Doyle's. We think that no liquor was sold in Fairmount after Doyle left until after 1868.

Fairmount was as dry as the Sahara Desert for years, except possibly when a drug store sold 4-X bitters and London gin. That did not last long.

We forgot to mention the fact that the first settlers had no oil lamps —only tallow candles, some of which were made in moulds and some were what were termed dips.

The candle-mould consisted of three, six or nine round tin tubes shaped like a candle. Those were joined together at the bottom and top. The bottom of the tube had a small hole through which the wicking was drawn. The wick was prepared as follows: It was cut twice the length the candle was to be made, then doubled and placed in the tube and the ends drawn through the hole in the bottom of the tube. After a round stick had been placed through the folded wick at the top of the moulds, the wick was then drawn tight and tied at the bottom. The melted tallow was then poured into the mould and allowed to cool, when the candles were pulled out of the mould and stored away ready for use.

The dip was made by preparing the wick and placing them on a round rod. Then a kettle of melted tallow was prepared and the wick was dipped in the melted tallow and taken out and hung on a support until the tallow that had adhered to the wick had hardened. This process was continued until the candle had become the desired size. This style of candle could be made only in cold weather. We have assisted our mother in making this style of candle.

A lamp flue or lantern globe was not thought of. A lantern made of tin, punched full of holes of various sizes, was to be found occasionally. A candle was placed on the inside of this lantern. You can imagine about how much light it would give. Later a lantern was made which had glass sides. This was an improvement over the old tin lantern. There may have been a lantern that burned sperm oil, but we never saw one. When we wanted a light to go to the neighbors, or coon hunting, a hickory bark torch was used, and it made a good light.

Fairmount Township was covered with heavy timber, the finest that ever grew. If we were to state the size of some of those immense poplar and oak trees that were to be found along Back Creek the reader might say:

"That fellow is out of his head."

It was a serious problem with the early settlers to know how to dispose of the timber. In order to clear the land for cultivation the most common method was to deaden the trees. After they had become dead and dry it was easier to burn them. This was done and it involved a great amount of labor. A farmer would either burn or cut a large number of logs in lengths that could be handled. Then he would invite his neighbors to a log rolling. They would come early and stay late. You would see them with their favorite handspike in hand ready to roll logs and out lift their neighbor.

It was at the log rollings that many contests were had as to the strength of those hardy pioneers. There was much care exercised to see that no advantage was taken in the contests. If a man won honors it must be done fairly. Great numbers of logs would be piled by the men, to be burned at the pleasure of the owner. The women of the neighborhood would come in and assist the good wife in preparing a sumptuous dinner for the men. And so it went all over the country.

The people of those days were genuine neighbors in the strictest sense of the word. When a few acres were cleared they were fenced with rails. This was done to keep the stock out, as all kinds of stock ran at large. Bells were put on cows, horses and sheep, so that the owner could find them more readily when he wanted them. Each owner knew the sound of his bell as well as that of his neighbor.

When we moved to Fairmount Township, David Smithson owned six hundred and twenty acres of land that joined my father's farm. We do not think that more than sixty acres of this immense farm was clear and in cultivation. This was about a fair sample of the entire Township at that time. Tanbark finally became a commercial factor in the community. In the spring of each year hundreds of the finest oak trees would be felled and the bark taken from them and hauled to the tanyard. The trees were either made into rails or left to rot.

The best log house ever built on Back Creek was built by Seth Winslow about two miles north of Fairmount. It was built of hewed logs, was two stories high, and there were only seven logs on a side, as we recollect it. Each log was thirty inches wide when hewn. We think the building was twenty by thirty. What immense trees it must have taken to get such logs! Who but Seth Winslow would have undertaken such a task? Anyone who ever saw this house could not help praising its builder.

Uncle Seth could pinch the hardest of any man I ever saw and derived the most pleasure out of seeing his victim get out of his reach. We have good reason to recollect him. The last time the writer saw him he was sitting outside of his house on Main Street, in Fairmount. I had just arrived from Nebraska, and was talking to some friends near where he sat. He reached out and pinched me until I winced with pain. He laughed heartily at my discomfort. No one could get angry at him. If he is not with the angels then there are none.

The first school I attended in Grant County was taught by Milt McHatton. He was a small man. My recollection is that the school house was a little old log cabin that stood on the southwest corner of my father's farm. Then a new, hewed-log school house was built on Henry Wilson's farm and called Wesleyan Back Creek school house. It was the pride of the community. The seats were linden logs hewed flat and pins driven in for legs. Then there were long pins driven in the walls and a wide board placed on them. This was where we practiced writing. Once or twice a week the teacher set the copy and the scholars tried to imitate it. Steel pens were a scarce article. The pens were usually made by the teacher out of a goose or a turkey quill. The ink was of home manufacture.

At the first school the studying was audible—reading and talking aloud—a regular bedlam. This method soon gave way to more sane ideas. In those days there was very little money for educational purposes. The majority were subscription schools. A teacher would go through the neighborhood and get as much patronage subscribed as possible, with the understanding that the teacher should board around among the patrons. The result was the patron who had the best accommodations had the teacher to board most of the time. The net amount usually received by the teacher was fifteen to twenty dollars per month. The term usually lasted four months. It did not require a great deal of preparation to be a teacher. If you could write a fairly good hand, knew a little arithmetic and read fairly well, you could teach school. Grammar, algebra, history and geometry were not necessary in the first schools.

John Rush was our second teacher. He taught in the new school house. He was a frail man and very sedate. He came to school the first day with a big beech limb, or whip, laid it on his desk, then read the rules of the school. In those days the teacher made his rules without any reference to patrons of the school. He was the lord of the manor. The whip, or gad as it was called, was used unmercifully by many teachers. I have witnessed some brutal whippings in the old log school house.

WILLIAM R. WOOLLEN

Was born in Dorchester County, at Johnson's Cross Roads, now Oak Grove, on the eastern shore of Maryland, September 5, 1818, and died at his home on Mill Street, in Fairmount, August 31, 1911. He was a son of Jacob and Nancy (Cockran) Woollen. In early life he had acquired a practical education obtained by his own personal experience and observation. In 1836, at the age of eighteen, his parents having died, he went to Baltimore. From Baltimore he walked to Wheeling, Virginia, and at this point he took a boat, making Ohio River towns, arriving at Cincinnati with only seventy-one cents in his pocket. Here he found employment in a brick yard. After a short stay at Cincinnati he went by boat, working his passage to Quincy, Illinois, where his cousin, Isaac Woollen, resided. He remained here two years, doing such work as came to hand in this new Mississippi River town, when he decided to return to his old Maryland home. He traveled horseback. While on this journey he joined some cattle men and assisted them in driving their stock as far as Connersville, Indiana, where he parted company with the drovers and went on to Wayne County, Indiana, to visit Robert and Jane (Woollen) Whitely, his sister, who had but recently emigrated from Maryland and settled at Milton. He abandoned the idea of returning to Maryland and joined Robert Whitely in agricultural pursuits. It was at Milton that he met and courted Julia Ann Oldfield, a daughter of William Oldfield, also a native of Maryland, who with his daughter and two sons, James and Luther, had found a home in the new West. James subsequently bought a farm near Summitville, Indiana, where he lived until his death, Luther continuing to reside at Milton. On May 24, 1842, at Milton, William Woollen and Julia Ann Oldfield were married. Five years later, in the fall of 1847, they moved to Madison County, and with savings accumulated by hard labor and the strictest economy, purchased a farm near Summitville. He commenced at once to improve his land, passing through all the hardships and successfully meeting the discouragements which were the common lot of all pioneers in that early day. In 1852 he bought and operated the first chaff piler brought to that section, later purchasing a separator from a Richmond concern, one of the first separators manufactured, and for that time an innovation which attracted the attention and excited the wonder of his neighbors for miles around in that sparsely populated settlement. In 1864 he sold his Madison County farm and bought of John Rush two hundred acres of land in Grant County, situated southwest of Fairmount, where John Woollen now lives. Here he remained until his wife's health failed, when he retired from active work and moved to Fairmount. In politics he was first identified with the Whigs, casting his ballot in 1840 for Gen. William Henry Harrison, who was elected the ninth President. In 1856, upon the formation of the Republican party, he supported Gen. John C. Fremont. Late in life he became a member of the Society of Friends, and as often as health would permit he was found in his place at all services. William and Julia Ann (Oldfield) Woollen were the parents of five children, namely: James H., born May 24, 1843, who died in January, 1894, at his home in Clay County, Nebraska; Jacob, born November 30, 1845; Edward, born September 22, 1847; William L., born August 6, 1851, who died June 22, 1873, at his father's home, and Mrs. Elda A. Trader, born September 1, 1857, wife of Harvey Trader. They reside in Fairmount. Jacob lives in Fairmount, and Edward owns and manages a farm about three miles southwest of Fairmount. August 13, 1886, the wife and mother, after a prolonged illness, passed away. On the 14th day of December, 1887, William Woollen was married to Miss Lizzie McConnell, of Marion, who was a true companion and faithfully attended her husband's care and comfort in his declining years. William Woollen was a man of sterling qualities and noble characteristics. His strict integrity and absolute honesty none questioned. His life was replete with kindly deeds and manifestations of consideration for the welfare of others. To his progeny he left the memory and example of a career in every respect worthy of emulation.

We think George Pierce taught several terms. Foster Davis was well liked as a teacher. He was one of the first teachers at Wesleyan Back Creek to get away from the old idea that "he that spareth the rod spoileth the child." I do not think that he ever kept a whip in the schoolroom. All the others prior to him did.

No woman had ever taught school at Wesleyan Back Creek until a little English miss of about seventeen applied for the school. Mary Taylor was her name. The old heads said it was not possible for a woman to teach the school, but Eli Neal, Harvey Davis and my father were willing to try, and employed Miss Taylor. She was a success from the very first, and taught one of the best terms ever held in the old school house.

About this time, 1854 to 1866, the people became more enlightened, and waked up to find that women were just as competent to teach school as men. Angelina Harvey and Mary Winslow, both, were teachers who never had a superior and few equals.

When we attended our last school in Fairmount Township the term was taught in the new two-story frame building. It stood just opposite Jonathan P. Winslow's brick house, at that time the finest in Fairmount.

No wonder Fairmount has such good schools. The foundation was of the right kind of material. The early teachers were none of them more advanced than the eighth grade of the present time. They made good use of what knowledge they did have and laid the foundation for the present-day methods.

In the earliest days the school house did not have stoves, but a big fireplace that would take a four-foot backlog. The teacher (man) and the big boys cut the wood in the timber around the school house and carried it so it could be used when needed. A backlog twelve to eighteen inches in diameter would be put in the fireplace, then smaller wood would be placed in front, fire started, and all in the room would be comfortable. A backlog would last a day.

Schoolbooks were scarce. They would not average more than one book to the scholar. Not all children of school age attended school. As soon as they were able to work they were compelled to assist in clearing the land, that a crop might be raised.

The roads of Fairmount Township were almost impassable, especially in the spring and fall. As is well known, the surface of the land is very level, and at an early date was not drained. Therefore, it was not possible to have good highways. I will describe the thoroughfare running east and west from the old pike at Carter Hasting's, and this description will answer for all the roads in the Township.

All the worst places were called corduroy. This kind of road was made by cutting rails, poles and logs about twelve feet long. These were placed across the road and a little dirt thrown on them—just enough to hold them in position. This kind of road could be found for miles. Often, when the waters were high in the spring, these logs would float out of place. Then the road would be impassable until the logs were replaced or the water receded.

Commencing at the home of James Nixon, running west for miles, this pole road could be found. To say that it was rough would be putting it mildly. Just imagine going over those logs or poles in a wagon (no spring seat) for miles at a time, with seldom a smooth piece of road to break the jolt, and water on both sides full of frogs and snakes. Such were the country roads of Grant County prior to 1860.

The first gravel road built was started about the year 1857. As we now recollect, it was a toll road commencing at the Madison County line and running north to Jonesboro, where it was to connect with a plank road that was to run from Jonesboro to Marion, and on to Wabash. This road was built by private parties. We fail to recollect all of the original owners, but Nathan D. Wilson, Jesse E. Wilson, William Pierce, Samuel Radley, Joseph W. Hill, Henry Harvey and my grandfather, Samuel Heavenridge, were among those who built the first gravel road in Fairmount Township and Grant County.

This road is a monument to the men who built it. They were eighteen carat fine in brains and integrity. They anticipated the wants of the country long in advance of the time. Tollgates were established at points where travel coming from cross roads would be intercepted and toll collected. For a long time a tollgate was maintained just south of where Dr. Glenn Henley's office now stands, that being the south side of Fairmount. Solomon (Toddy) Thomas kept this gate for years. There was a gate not far south of Joseph W. Hill's, near Jonesboro. William Winslow kept this gate. Later on, a gate was established near Allen Dillon's and one at the cross roads south of Carter Hasting's. (I use the names that were familiar to me.)

There were always people who would try to avoid paying toll. They would run past and do a dollar's worth of dodging to avoid paying a few cents. I have known men who lived south of Fairmount, and near the pike, who, rather than pay a toll of say, ten cents, would go west out of town, then south to the County line, then east, miles out of their way. They pretended that their rights were infringed upon. I am told that there are no toll roads in Indiana now.

The farmers soon discovered that drainage was very important. Back Creek and Deer Creek were splendid outlets for almost the entire west part of Fairmount Township. It soon became evident that those creeks must be cleaned out to make drainage perfect. There was no such thing as tile to use in draining the farm. The ditches were dug about two feet deep and twenty inches wide. An oak rail about six inches wide was put on one side of the ditch and stakes driven to hold it in place. Then puncheons of oak were made and one end placed on the rail, the other end resting on the ground. This made a good drain. My father was among the first who drained his farm. We always had corn when anyone in the vicinity did.

The first settlers depended on maple sugar almost entirely until 1856-'57, when sorghum was first introduced in the United States. My father received a package of sorghum cane seed from the Patent Office at Washington, D. C., the spring of 1857. He decided to give it a trial. Sorghum was an entire stranger in the United States, being a native of China. No one knew how to get best results. There were no mills in existence to crush the stalk and get the juice. Neither did they have evaporators or other means to reduce the juice to syrup.

Grandfather Heavenridge and my father conceived the idea of making a mill of wood. They took a wheelwright by the name of Jack Reel in with them. They went to the timber, selected a perfect maple tree about two feet in diameter. They turned two rollers eighteen inches through, one with a long shaft, the other shorter. They placed wooden cogs near the top of the rollers, then a heavy oak frame was made and the roller placed in it. The frame was made so that by means of a wedge the rolls could be made either loose or tight, just as needed. After the rolls were in place it was necessary to have something to turn them. A crooked tree was procured and made into what was called a sweep.

In the meantime, the cane had grown splendidly and was ready for the mill. The next problem was, "Could the juice be boiled in iron kettles?" We had two iron kettles and one large coffee kettle, and decided to try both.

The cane was cut and business commenced. The result was the molasses was as black as it was possible to be, but tasted all right. People came from far and near to taste the new syrup. The mill was a success. We think it possible that one other person tried the same experiment the same year in Grant County.

This was the year that a paper dollar would be good when you started to town, but would be worthless before you got to spend it. The merchant kept a book in which the values of paper money then in circulation were listed. Nothing but gold and silver had a real value, and there was but little of either in circulation.

There were no markets for the products of the farm, for the reason that farmers would not take money of uncertain value. A great many merchants issued their own script. This was used in the vicinity where it was issued. If the merchant was good the scrip was redeemed. Many merchants failed, many banks went out of business, but the sturdy farmers of Grant County went along as usual.

CHAPTER XII.

DAVID STANFIELD AND THE NAMING OF FAIRMOUNT.

DAVID STANFIELD, son of Samuel and Lydia Stanfield, was born about nine miles above Greenville, in Greene County, Tennessee, on the Second day of the week, Fifth month 13th, 1793. From a little private diary, made by himself of an excellent grade of paper, each page 3x4 inches, the writer is permitted by Dr. Glenn Henley, a great-grandson of David Stanfield, to copy the information given herewith. As nearly as is practicable the items are taken verbatim from this diary as David Stanfield himself entered them:

DAVID STANFIELD

"David Stanfield's Family Record of his own and his wife and family's births, marriages, removals and deaths. 1824."

Omitting information in regard to David and Elizabeth already given, this diary reads as follows:

"David Stanfield and Elizabeth Beals, aforesaid, were married by Esq. Miller, at her father's house, in Washington, Tennessee, aforesaid, on the 13th of 5th mo., 1813.

"Births of David and Elizabeth Stanfield's children, the 2 eldest, William Williams and David S. Stanfield, both born at his father's house, nine miles above Greenville, Green County, Tennessee State. The other children as far as the now youngest, namely, Lydia Jane, were all born on Big Sinking Creek, Green County, five or six miles above Greenville, Tennessee, as follows:

"William Williams Stanfield was born 1st day of week and 13th of 2d mo., in the year of Christ, 1814.

"2d child, David S. Stanfield, was born on 1st of week and 7th of 5th mo., 1815.

"3d child, Charles Stanfield, was born 5th of week and 18th of 12th mo., in the year of Christ, 1816.

"4th child, Isaac Stanfield, was born on 5th of week and 27th of 8th mo., 1818.

"5th child, Samuel Vernon Stanfield, was born on the 4th of the week and 29th of 3d month, in the year of Christ, 1820.

"6th child, Hannah Jones Stanfield, was born on 6th of week and 28th of 12th month, 1821.

"7th child, and last, until the successor, Lydia Jane Stanfield, was born on 4th of week and 12th of 11th mo., 1823.

"8th child, Elijah Stanfield, was born on 24th of 10th mo., and 3rd day of week, in the year of Christ, 1826.

"Clayton Reeve Stanfield was born 1st day of the week and 3d of 6th month, 1832."

No entries are made under the headings of the different pages left for "Marriages," or "Wedlock yet Perpetuated." Under the heading "Removals" we find this entry:

ELIZABETH (BEALS) STANFIELD

Daughter of Isaac and Hannah Beals, and wife of David Stanfield, was born three miles above Leesburgh, on the Abington Road, Limestone Creek, Washington County, Tennessee, on the first day of the week and first of sixth month, 1794. She died fifth month, twenty-first, 1881, aged eighty-six years, eleven months and twenty days. Her remains lie in Back Creek Graveyard, where repose in their last resting place all that is mortal of many of her pioneer friends and acquaintances.

"David Stanfield moved from Tennessee to Indiana in the year 1833, and from Madison County to Grant County in 1837."

David Stanfield was of English stock. He bought a piece of land not quite a mile east of Fairmount, which is now a part of the Foster Davis farm, where he lived for a short time prior to buying the land south of town, where he made his permanent home. In stature, he was erect, five feet, ten inches tall, square-built, of a commanding appearance, weighed about 175 pounds, big forehead, dark hair and grey eyes, pleasing address, and when speaking in public used good English. His habit was to go smoothly shaven, hair cut short, was neat and clean in his dress and appearance, wearing the Friends regulation cut of clothes and using the plain language at all times. As a recorded minister of the Society of Friends, he traveled some in ministerial service, always paying his traveling expenses, which all preachers did not do. He held advanced views in reference to the resurrection of the dead to what was generally accepted by his church in his day and time, hence some objected to giving him liberty to travel, as was Friends usage. His faith is now quite generally accepted by all orthodox churches. He was a man of energy and perseverance. He did not wait for opportunities to come to him, but got out and turned something up. He was strictly fair and honest in his dealings with men, but wanted what was his by right. He loved to trade in real estate, owned a number of farms at different periods of his active life, and gave each of his sons a good start in life. At one time he kept a large fruit nursery, from which many of the orchards of this section were stocked. He was kind and considerate

This picture shows the old house which once stood at the southwest corner of Main and Eighth Streets. It was on this lot that John Benbow commenced the erection of the first log cabin on the present site of the town of Fairmount. Before the cabin was completed Daniel Baldwin came from Wayne County, Indiana, with his family, and in 1833 purchased the property and finished the cabin, which he occupied for several months.

as a neighbor, courteous in his manner, given to hospitality, lived out the Scriptural injunction to live in peace with all men as much as laid in his power. David Stanfield was a man of splendid spirit and of singular purity of character. The foregoing is an estimate of his career by a prominent citizen who knew him intimately for many years.

David Stanfield's monument, a plain stone slab, erected at his grave in Back Creek graveyard, bears the following inscription:

"David Stanfield, proprietor south half of Fairmount, Minister of Friends Church, died 10th mo. 24th, 1868, aged 75 yrs., 5 mo. 11 da."

(By Cyrus W. Neal.)

As David Stanfield was one of the persons who did not come to Fairmount, but Fairmount came to him, I will give a little information as regards this fine man and much-loved citizen. He came from Green County, Tennessee, was an authorized minister in the Friends Church before he came to Fairmount, and so continued until his death. He was the first preacher I remember of hearing preach. In the fall of 1856 he preached at my mother's funeral at old Back Creek (I was five years old at the time). Margaret Pucket also preached at the same funeral.

David Stanfield appeared to be quite an old man at that time. He lived about two blocks south and two blocks west of where Dr. Glenn Henley's office is now located. His family consisted of himself and wife and nine children, seven boys and two girls. The boys were William, Vernon, Elijah, Clayton, Isaac, Charles and Samuel. The girls were Lydia Jane (wife of Joseph W. Baldwin), and Hannah (wife of William Hall).

CYRUS W. NEAL

David Stanfield was a great man for fruit and had a large nursery and orchard that came to Dr. Henley's residence. He was exceedingly fond of good horses, and they did not come too lively for him. He was a good man with young horses, and always had the very best. He was what we would call an up-to-date farmer. He was not a rich man, but for that day was considered "pretty well fixed," and was ready and willing, as were all the early settlers in the Township, to divide the last bushel or the last ham with a neighbor without money and without price.

My wife, who was a daughter of Joseph W. Baldwin, and a granddaughter of David Stanfield, has in her possession a diary kept by her grandfather in 1831, before he came to Fairmount. The book was made by cutting heavy, plain white paper seven inches square, which was sewed together with white flax thread, and the writing was very fine, indeed. It would be interesting to some of our young people to see this splendid penmanship made by him eighty-six years ago. Not many persons of today could duplicate it. He says:

"In the year 1831 had a concern to attend Indiana Yearly Meeting and the meetings constituting it, and obtained a certificate for that purpose. On the fourteenth of the Ninth month, in the same year, pursued the project, accompanied by my worthy friend, Aaron Hammer." He says they held no meeting while passing through Kentucky, and arrived at that great city in the State of Ohio, Cincinnati, Ninth month, twenty-fifth. (Eleven days on road, and I suppose traveled horseback, a distance of about three hundred miles.)

A meeting was appointed for him in Cincinnati at the First Presbyterian Church. Many English Friends were present. He felt very much embarrassed at the prospect of facing a congregation made up of persons so intellectual and distinguished, in such a large city, and wished himself among country people. He says that Friends told him that Cincinnati, according to the last census, contained twenty-eight thousand people. He had his meeting, and many older Friends came to him after the service and encouraged him, saying he did well.

On the seventh day, first of the Tenth month, they attended Yearly Meeting at New Garden (doubtless Indiana Yearly Meeting was held at New Garden and not at Richmond, at that date, as he says nothing about Richmond in his book).

On the way from Green County, Tennessee, to Cincinnati, they stopped over night at taverns, I suppose similar in construction and hospitality to the one kept by Robert McCormick in Fairmount Township. The bills itemized are: Bobbs, 25 cents; Lowe's, 50 cents; Johnson's, 50 cents; Calvert's, 50 cents; Sails, 62½ cents; Rose, 62½ cents.

As these bills were for two men and two horses, it would seem that the high cost of living did not figure much in those days. After preaching in Indiana and Ohio, at many places, they returned home.

David Stanfield was a persistent Bible student. Any person going to his home to see him on matters of business would find him reading his Bible.

Marion, Indiana, March 13, 1917.

Fairmount had in 1850 attained to a position of some importance as a business point. It was in this year that citizens began to cast about for a suitable name for the embryonic town. David Stanfield suggested that the place be called Kingston. Joseph W. Baldwin, who owned the corner store, had heard much of Fairmount Park, Philadelphia, and favored Fairmount. Stanfield and Baldwin, after due consideration of the matter, being unable to agree, decided to leave the controversy to the decision of William Neal. Neal agreed with Baldwin, and this is how the town came to be called Fairmount. This, at least, is the conclusion arrived at by the writer, after conferring with a pioneer who knew Stanfield, Baldwin and Neal intimately, and was closely allied with the three men and held frequent conversations with them at the time the matter was under consideration. However, there appear to be other ideas in reference to it, and expressions bearing upon the subject are here submitted:

Joseph W. Baldwin, when talking about the early days of Fairmount, always claimed that he gave the infant town its present name. There were three of them that had the matter in controversy. They were William Neal, surveyor, William Hall and Joseph W. Baldwin. They all had names to offer. I have forgotten what they were. Joseph presented the name of Fairmount and won the others over to his choice and thus it was recorded Fairmount.

A. HENLEY.

Melbourne, Florida, March 27, 1917.

Editor News: I see that somebody says Joseph W. Baldwin gave Fairmount its name. I have always thought that my father, William Neal, named Fairmount. I am sure he was County Surveyor about that time. MRS. ALVIN WILSON.

Los Angeles, California, February 26, 1917.

(Editor's Note:—The best information at hand shows that before a name was selected for the town Joseph W. Baldwin had a little store on the Seth Winslow corner (the northeast corner of Main and Washington Streets), located where the Borrey Block now stands. David

Stanfield, father-in-law of Baldwin, was planning to have a part of his farm surveyed and an addition laid out and platted for the sale of lots. It was suggested by one of the two men that the time had come to select a name for the town. Both agreed that this should be done. Stanfield preferred that the town be called Kingston. Baldwin, who had been reading about Fairmount Water Works, at Philadelphia, favored Fairmount. After discussing the matter at some length they agreed to let William Neal decide the controversy when he came to make the survey. When Neal arrived Stanfield and Baldwin put the question up to Neal, and he took the view that, all things considered, Fairmount would be the best choice of names. Bill Wright had previously given the struggling village the name of Pucker, and the place was so designated until the name Fairmount was finally agreed upon.)

Editor News: Some years ago, while Joseph Baldwin, William Hall and James R. Smith were yet living, I remember one afternoon these three worthy pioneers were sitting at the front of our store (Oakley & Elliott's), discussing with others the question as to who gave Fairmount its name. My recollection is that William Hall made the following statement (the other two concurring), that William Neal, who just at the time the people were seeking a name for the prospective town, returned home from Philadelphia, where he had visited Fairmount Park, and being greatly delighted with its beauty and grandeur, he proposed the town be called Fairmount, which was generally accepted by the community.
                                                                J. N. ELLIOTT.
St. Petersburg, Florida, March 9, 1917.

(Editor's Note:—It will be observed that there exists a difference of opinion as to who named Fairmount. However, there is honor enough to go around, and it is very likely that several had a hand in it.)

The south part of Fairmount was platted and subdivided into lots by David Stanfield, December 28, 1850. At first only four blocks lying south of Washington Street were surveyed by William Neal, who had been engaged for this work.

The original town plat was located in Section 29, Township 23 north and Range 8 east, consisting of fifteen lots. The following additions have since been made: David Stanfield's; Jonathan Baldwin's

First, Second, Third, Fourth and Fifth; Nixon Winslow's; J. P. Winslow's First, Second and Third; Henley's First, Second and Third; Baldwin and Nottingham's; Phillips's; Winslow, Ellers and Bogue and Winslow and Osborn's.

The first home built inside the present corporation limits was a log cabin started in November, 1831, by John Benbow, and completed later by Daniel Baldwin, at the southwest corner of Eighth and Main Streets. It was a typical pioneer cabin built of round logs, with a stick and clay chimney, puncheon floor, chinked and daubed to protect the family from wind and cold.

In December, 1833, Daniel Baldwin and family arrived from Wayne County, Indiana. Baldwin had visited Grant County the year before, and while here he purchased the Benbow cabin.

The second cabin built was erected by Thomas Baldwin, on the lot at the northeast corner of Madison and Mill Streets.

CHAPTER XIII.

EIGHTEEN FIFTY-TWO TO EIGHTEEN SIXTY-THREE.

(By James M. Hundley.)

IN COMPLIANCE with my promise I will attempt to describe things as I remember them in 1852 and up to 1863, when my acquaintance with Fairmount and Fairmount Township terminates.

In order that the reader may know why I assume to speak of early conditions in your town and Township I will say that I make no claim to having been a pioneer in your community. As a matter of fact the hunters and early pathfinders who contended with the haughty savages that inhabited your almost impenetrable wilderness had gone many years before I came. But the home builders and early settlers, the sturdy characters who cleared away the forest, built the roads, constructed the drains, erected the log school houses, the primitive church and their plain and simple habitations were here when I came. It is of these that I shall attempt to write.

I was born in Clinton County, Ohio, July 6, 1847, and came with my father, William Hundley, to your Township in the late fall of 1851. I have no distinct recollections of the journey from Ohio, which was made in a two-horse wagon to a point a short distance south of the Back Creek meeting house, where the road running east and west crosses the road leading to Marion.

It was here, in the early spring of 1852, that memory first dawns upon me. I found myself living with my father in a log cabin which was owned and also occupied by a man named Sam Jones and his family (not the Sam Jones of Gospel fame, but the husband of Jane Jones, who was a preacher of some note in the Friends Church). Sam Jones had a small frame blacksmith shop located at the crossroads, and, as my father was a blacksmith, they joined their fortunes and we remained there until the year 1853, when we removed to Fairmount and father, with Isaac Roberts, built the first smith shop in your town on what is now North Main Street.

I want to say before proceeding further that I am writing wholly from memory, which for one so young as I was at the period about which I write, would seem an unreliable source of information at this time. It has been said, and I think truly, that early impressions are the most lasting. I am sure that in my mind the surroundings and the men and events of that day are more clearly impressed upon my mind than events happening but a few brief years ago.

I am conscious of the fact that I am writing for a generation of men and women who can have but a faint conception of the conditions which surrounded your beautiful and prosperous town and your splendid and progressive Township when I came. I have already stated that I was not a pioneer or first settler, but only one who remembers those sturdy and splendid men and women who laid sure and fast the foundation and assured the making of your splendid town and Township.

They it was who overcame obstacles which would seem to characters less stern and hardy, insurmountable. Their industry, privations and hardships changed an unhealthy and unfriendly environment and made your fertile fields to blossom as the rose. If we trace the progress of civilization in the past we shall find that environment has largely determined the advance of man in the attainment of the highest and best of which he has been found capable.

JONATHAN BALDWIN

Son of Daniel and Christian (Wilcuts) Baldwin, was born in Wayne County, Indiana, September 30, 1823. He came to Fairmount Township with his parents in December, 1833, his father having entered the land now comprising the larger portion of the north part of Fairmount. This land extended from Washington Street north to Eighth Street, and from the Big Four railroad west to Back Creek. The cabin home originally stood near the hackberry tree on the Bogue lot. After the death of his parents Jonathan Baldwin purchased the home place and added much to its appearance. He was a man of medium size, not of robust build, but with more energy than physical endurance. He was public spirited, and always in the front rank in promoting public improvements. No man did more in the building of the town, the public schools and the church of his choice than Jonathan Baldwin. He was extremely hospitable and kind-hearted, generous in charitable calls. He was religiously inclined, a consistent member of the Wesleyan Methodist Church, to which he was a liberal contributor. He kept several yoke of cattle and for some years did a great amount of heavy teaming. He greatly exposed himself to inclement weather, thus contracting lung fever, from which he never recovered, but lived a number of years afterwards. He was no shirker. If there was a hard piece of work to do he went at it, confident of success. He did Cammack's heavy hauling in building the first steam saw-mill in that country. He was one of the original promoters of the Jonesboro and Fairmount turnpike. He was married twice. His first wife was Sarah Ann Dillon, daughter of Jesse Dillon. By this union four children were born, namely, Isaac, Elizabeth, David and Mary. Isaac died at fourteen years of age. The others are still living. His wife died in 1861. Later he married Mrs. Emeline (Tharp) Hockett. Jonathan Baldwin died April 8, 1877. His funeral was a large one. The minister, Rev. Elijah Coats, who preached his funeral, said of him: "As to his real worth to his church and the community in which he lived, he stood head and shoulders above his fellow men; that he lived a contented, joyful, happy life, spent in doing good."—Dr. A. Henley.

I think I am safe in saying that your Township had made more progress when I came than had Fairmount. There were scattered all over your Township small farms and clearings. Fruit-bearing orchards gave evidence that their owners had been there several years when I came. The town and Township were, however, covered largely with a dense growth of magnificent forest trees. The houses were chiefly of logs, some of them hewed logs, but by far the most of them were round log cabins, with puncheon floors and stick and clay chimneys. I do not mean by round-log cabins that they were circular in form, but that they were constructed of round logs. A puncheon floor was one made of split logs. The man who was fortunate enough to have a comfortable frame house was considered an aristocrat in those days.

HON. JAMES M. HUNDLEY

Who has contributed leading articles to this story, is one of the able writers and speakers of the State. He is a son of William and Jane (Martin) Hundley. James M. Hundley enlisted in August, 1863, at Indianapolis, in Company C, Eleventh Ohio Volunteer Infantry. He served with this regiment till April, 1864, when he was discharged and sent home. In August, 1864, he again enlisted, this time as a member of Company E. One Hundred and Fortieth Indiana Infantry, serving with this command until July 11, 1865. Mr. Hundley is a lawyer. He has served as a member of the Indiana Legislature, from Madison County. He was for eight years postmaster at Summitville.

The most formidable task which confronted men of the early day was the clearing away of the forest and the draining of the land, which was very much of it covered with stagnant water for a large portion of the year. And this produced an abundance of fever and ague, which, during the fall of the year, would prostrate entire families. I think it was Col. Robert G. Ingersoll who said that "the world was not a very good place in which to raise people, because it was three-fourths water and much better adapted to raising fish." I am sure that this was true of Fairmount Township when I first saw it. Back Creek, which runs through Fairmount, was an almost impenetrable swamp, and in a good many places it was more than one-half mile in width, and for the greater part of the year it was very difficult to locate the channel. In the year 1854 the ditching of this creek was commenced, and a drain twenty-five feet wide and of sufficient depth to carry the water and furnish an outlet for lateral drains was constructed. This work was done by some fifty

FIRST FRAME DWELLING IN FAIRMOUNT

Owned and occupied by James Cammack and family. Built by Joseph Peacock, then a carpenter and contractor here, now a citizen of Kokomo.

James Cammack, who owned the mill, lived in the house west of Stanfield's store. The picture above shows this house, which until torn down in 1916 stood almost opposite The News office on West Washington Street. This house was at one time the home of George W. Butler and family, when Butler was associated with his son-in-law, J. N. Wheeler, in the ownership and operation of the old flouring mill, located in the building which still stands at the southeast corner of Washington and Mill Streets, and now occupied as a coal office. The old dwelling was used in later years as an office by the late Squire John F. Jones. It was also a sort of headquarters for veterans of the Civil War, who were in the habit of congregating here during leisure hours for the purpose of exchanging reminiscences and telling stories of their service during the Rebellion. Squire Jones himself was a brave soldier, having served as Captain of Company C, Eighty-ninth Indiana Volunteer Infantry, a command in which many Fairmount Township men were enlisted. Captain Jones was popular with all comrades, enjoyed their respect and confidence, and for many years after the close of the War worked faithfully to secure and did secure pensions for hundreds of veterans and their widows.

Irish laborers, brought from Cincinnati, and was superintended by Jesse E. Wilson, Seth Winslow and Jonathan Baldwin. It was the first public improvement undertaken aside from cutting out and making some corduroy roads.

"Well," some of our young people will ask, "what was a corduroy road?" Simply a road constructed with logs thrown crosswise and covered with brush and dirt in order to prevent vehicles from sinking in the mire. Anyone who has traveled over one of these roads in a wagon will not soon forget his experience.

THE OLD BALDWIN HOMESTEAD

On North Main Street, now owned and occupied by Mrs. Elizabeth Bogue, widow of Robert Bogue, a grandson of Daniel Baldwin. This house, which consisted originally of twelve rooms, six below and six above, is finished in native walnut taken from the forest. It was built by Jonathan Baldwin, son of Daniel Baldwin, in 1858, and was for many years the center of characteristic pioneer hospitality dispensed with a lavish hand by Jonathan Baldwin and wife. This house has at different times been used for hotel purposes. Across the road east of this house, in a beautiful grove, political and other meetings were held during summer and fall months.

The first saw-mill in Fairmount was built by James Cammack, and was there when I came in 1853. A little later he put in burrs and ground corn. Solomon (Toddy) Thomas had a horse mill for grinding corn, but this was southeast of Fairmount.

Isaac Stanfield, who was a pioneer merchant, built the first flouring mill a little way south of the present mill site, in the year 1854. This was a two-story structure and equipped with the most modern machinery known in that day. This mill blew up by a boiler explosion and was never rebuilt.

The building of a woolen mill was commenced in the year 1860 and completed in 1861. I am now unable to say who was the builder and operator of this mill, but think Jonathan P. Winslow was one of the chief promoters. In any event, this mill supplied a long-felt want, carding, spinning and weaving wool, making jeans and linsey, the fabrics out of which the clothing of this time was chiefly made. Prior to the building of this mill the carding, spinning and the weaving had been done by hand, and the woolen clothing for winter and the linen clothing for summer had been spun and woven by the good women who then lived in your Township.

I cannot here describe the old-fashioned spinning wheel, your grandmother's loom or the cards used in preparing the wool for spinning. You may find these in some collection of curios. The flax-brake and the hackle have long since disappeared and can only be found in some collection of relics.

I cannot describe the process by which the home-made garments were colored. Certain it is, however, that many variegated and beautiful colors were obtained, and the miss of that period, costumed in her homespun dress, was quite as comely and fair to look upon as her latter-day sister, arrayed in her frock of silk which in many instances seems to have failed to attain its growth at both ends.

I wish I could paint a pen picture of an autumn day in your Township in 1853. In all the humble homes would be heard the hum of the spinning wheel, the sound of the loom, and in the clearings would be heard the sound of the woodman's ax and the crash of falling timber. At night the sky would be illumined by the burning of brush and logs piled high by your sturdy home builder in his effort to clear away your virgin forest and bring it under a state of cultivation. Then we were seeking to obliterate the forest and to destroy millions of dollars worth of valuable timber. Today we are talking about conservation and spending millions in promoting forestry. But I am digressing. I have been attempting to describe the public improvements and the private enterprises which at an early day contributed to the making of your Township.

In 1854 or 1855, Daniel Ridgeway came with a tanyard and located in your community. He continued to operate this place for a few years, when he sold it to Micah Baldwin, who continued to make leather so long as the writer remained in or near Fairmount. Nathan Little established a tanyard in your town some time after Daniel Ridgeway came, and these two places furnished the leather to make the boots and shoes for your town and the surrounding community. This was an important and indispensable industry.

In 1859 or 1860 a stage line was established from Marion to Anderson, and trips were made from each place three times a week, carrying mail, merchandise and passengers. I cannot now remember who estab-

THE GIANT HACKBERRY

Which stands on the Bogue lot, near the present residence of John Harvey Wilson, on North Main Street. This tree is one of the largest in the Township. A few of its spreading branches extend out seventy-five feet, making an interesting and picturesque object contributed to the present generation from the primitive forests of Fairmount Township.

lished this line, but know that Walker Winslow operated it during the Civil War and for some years afterwards. It went out of business when the Cincinnati, Wabash and Michigan Railroad came, in 1874.

In 1862 or 1863 was built the first gravel road in your Township, running from Jonesboro to the Madison County line. This was a toll road, and was promoted and owned by men of your Township until bought by the County and made a free gravel road. I think Jonathan P. Winslow was one of the chief promoters and owners of this road.

I have thus far confined myself to matters that in my opinion were of a more or less public character and in their operation served to promote the growth and making of your Township in a material way. I have said nothing about schools, churches, trades or business enterprises, all of which are vitally essential to the growth and progress of a town or Township.

When I came to your town the frame Quaker meeting house furnished the only school room in town. In 1855 was built on East First Street a frame building in which was opened the first free school in town. William Neal was the teacher. There were in the Township, at that time, some five or six public schools located in various parts of the territory. I cannot now locate all of them, but remember that one was located near the William G. Lewis homestead, another east of town, not far from the William Karwin farm, one at Sugar Grove, on the Madison County line, another southwest of town, near the Liberty Township line.

The Quaker meeting house was the only place of public worship in town when I came. Nixon Rush and Milton Winslow were the ministers connected with this church whom I remember most distinctly. William Hall was, I think, a United Brethren minister and George Bowers was a Methodist minister. The last two were what were known in that day as circuit riders and covered a wide extent of territory.

All of the above ministers were worthy exponents of the Master's cause, and were preaching in the interest of a fallen humanity and for the upbuilding of the cause of Christ.

The merchants in town during the period about which I write were Joseph W. Baldwin, Isaac Stanfield, William and Vincent Wright, Seaberry Lines, George Doyle, Ezra Foster, Jonathan P. Winslow and Micajah Wilson. I think, perhaps, Henry Harvey may have had a store there during this period.

The physicians were John White, Philip Patterson, Alpheus Henley and David S. Elliott.

The blacksmiths were Isaac Roberts, William Hundley, Joseph Bennett, William A. Walker, Elisha Cook and Solomon Macey.

The carpenters were William Hall, Nathan Vinson, Joshua Foster, Miller Martin, Alfred Waldron and Dennis Montgomery.

The shoemakers were Solomon Parsons, James Martin, William G. Lewis, Logan Fear and Micajah Wilson. Richard Mott was a traveling shoemaker, and went from house to house in the fall and winter, making the shoes for the entire family while he remained.

The first cabinet maker was William Hollingsworth. He made the furniture which adorned the primitive homes, as well as the caskets in which the pioneer fathers and mothers were consigned to their final resting place.

Lawyers we had none, and needed none. Men were then capable of settling their own affairs.

Bankers were not necessary, for everybody was poor. The good housewife was the tailor and dressmaker.

Robert Kelsay, Smith Kelsay, Granville Mott and Bert Mott were the early stone cutters and builders of monuments.

The early hotel keepers were Seaberry Lines, Solomon Parsons, Nathan Vinson and John Scarry.

I have now traced briefly many of the men and events which my boyhood recollections connect with the early making of your Township. I have not stopped to comment upon the individual characteristics of these men, nor to point out, except in a general way, the part they played in obtaining the high and advanced position your town and Township now occupy in all that is best in our present day civilization.

These men were ruggedly and scrupulously honest in their dealings with their fellow men, loved their homes and their families, as well as their neighbors. They recognized the fatherhood of God and the brotherhood of man. They were charitable and generous to a fault. They knew and recognized no law except the law of right, and during all the period about which I write no crime of any kind dims the fair record of your Township.

To these rugged pioneers courts and jails were unnecessary and for them held no terrors. These hardy pioneers have long since gone to their final reward, and most of the men who were contemporaneous with me have also crossed the Great Divide.

As I close this review of a long-gone past there come unbidden to my mind some stanzas of Gray's immortal Elegy Written in a Country Churchyard:

> Beneath those rugged elms, that yewtree's shade,
>   Where heaves the turf in many a mold'ring heap,
> Each in his narrow cell forever laid,
>   The rude forefathers of the hamlet sleep.
>
> The breezy call of incense-breathing morn,
>   The swallow twitt'ring from the straw-built shed,
> The cock's shrill clarion, or the echoing horn,
>   No more shall rouse them from their lowly bed.

For them no more the blazing hearth shall burn,
  Or busy housewife ply her evening care;
No children run to lisp their sire's return,
  Or climb his knees the envied kiss to share.

Oft did the harvest to their sickle yield,
  Their furrow oft the stubborn glebe has broke;
How jocund did they drive their team afield!
  How bow'd the woods beneath their sturdy stroke!

Let not ambition mock their useful toil,
  Their homely joys, and destiny obscure;
Nor grandeur hear with a disdainful smile
  The short and simple annals of the poor.

The boast of heraldry, the pomp of pow'r,
  And all that beauty, all that wealth e'er gave,
Await alike th' inevitable hour.
  The paths of glory lead but to the grave.

These men who linger only in memory, whose lives and deeds you seek to perpetuate in "The Making of a Township," which is, after all, but the making of a State and Nation in miniature, have left to their descendants who largely populate your town and Township a glorious heritage. No act of theirs can bring aught but pride, no deed of theirs can mantle the cheeks of their children and grandchildren with shame. They are gone, but not dead. They live in the glory of the blessings they have transmitted to posterity.

Summitville, Ind., January 30, 1917.

CHAPTER XIV.

THE UNDERGROUND RAILROAD.

(By J. M. Hundley)

I CAME into your community when the great questions which afterward shook the very foundation of our Nation were beginning to be discussed and agitated. I mean the extension of human slavery and the doctrine of State's rights.

Reference has been made in your story to the Underground Railroad, but I doubt very much if young people have any adequate conception of what is meant by the Underground Railroad.

Slavery, in some form, existed in all Nations from the earliest dawn of human history, but it is not my purpose in this communication to discuss the different forms of this monstrous and inhuman custom, except in so far as it has affected our political history in the past.

Our English ancestors established negro slavery in this country in 1620, at Jamestown, Virginia, and at one time it extended throughout the New England states.

It was soon found to be unprofitable in New England, and finally found its abiding place in the cotton-growing states, where we find it at the period about which I am writing.

As early as 1807 the great British statesman, Fox, worked aggressively against human slavery in England and her colonial possessions. He was preceded by Wilberforce, Buxton, and Elizabeth Heyrick, a Quaker lady, who wrote a pamphlet entitled "Immediate, Not Gradual Emancipation."

The arguments of this good Quaker lady finally prevailed, and on August 1, 1834, England emancipated her 800,000 slaves and paid their owners $100,000,000 for them. At the same time England emancipated her slaves in her East Indian possessions, making a grand total of 12,000,000 slaves who obtained their freedom.

I have recited the brief history of England's emancipation of slaves in order that I may the more easily get the reader to understand what I am going to say in relation to the Underground Railroad and its operations in Fairmount Township, as well as with the political history of our common country.

It will be understood that the United States failed to be impressed by the humane arguments which induced the mother country to give freedom to her slaves. On the other hand, the Southern States, finding slavery very profitable in the growing of cotton and other Southern staples, sought to have this institution extended to newly-formed states, and even succeeded in having this degrading practice recognized in our Federal Constitution.

Canada, lying along our Northern border, was the mecca of bondmen fleeing from slavery in Kentucky and border slave states. As early as 1800 Congress had declared the importation of slaves to be piracy, and had abolished slavery in the District of Columbia. But at the same time the slave power was growing more arrogant and was extending slavery to new states and demanding additional laws to assist in the recapture and return of escaping slaves.

The Fugitive Slave Law, which made every free man in Indiana or any other free State a slave catcher, and provided that anyone who should feed or shelter one of these poor black men fleeing to Canada in order to obtain his liberty should be subject to fine and imprisonment.

This obnoxious law was soon followed by the infamous Dred Scott decision, which declared that the negro belonged to an inferior race and had no rights which our Constitution was bound to respect. These two actions on the part of the slave power which was then dominant in our Government fanned to a white heat the flame of hatred against the curse of slavery which already prevailed in the free states.

As love laughs at locksmiths, so liberty depises and defies oppression. The immediate effect of the laws to which I have referred was to foster the organization of societies in the free states to render aid and comfort to escaping slaves.

The most potent and effective agent in assisting slaves to obtain their freedom by reaching Canada was the Underground Railroad, which consisted of organized societies extending across Indiana and Michigan, with stations at convenient intervals where escaping slaves could be secreted by day and transported by night from one station to another on their way to Canada and Liberty.

This railroad had no track but the rude trail through the wilderness, and no train or trolley car, but the means of transportation was a farm wagon, on horseback, or on foot, as the case might be. The fleeing slave, with the north star as his beacon to liberty, and three or four of these hardy Hoosier pioneers as guides and protectors, made his slow and painful way to freedom.

One of these Underground Railroad stations was in Fairmount, and the Winslows, Wilsons, Baldwins, Rushes, Davises, Henleys, Stanfields, Richardsons, and many others were active agents on this railroad.

Pendleton, south of Fairmount, and Marion, north, were stations, and when an escaping slave was brought from Pendleton in the night time he was concealed in Fairmount or vicinity until the next night, when he was conveyed to Moses Bradford or Samuel McClure, at Marion, who in turn would convey his charge to Ashland, now Lafontaine. In this way fugitive slaves were housed, fed and conveyed to their destination in Canada.

The writer well remembers the last escaping slaves he saw. It was in August, 1856, and for some reason two runaway slaves had found it necessary to change their hiding place in the day time, which was an unusual and dangerous thing to do. They came to my father's smith shop about two o'clock in the afternoon, but in a few moments disappeared and were concealed in Dr. Philip Patterson's hay mow—none too soon. Shortly after their disappearance James Buchanan, who was, I think, the sheriff of your county at the time, appeared upon the scene, accompanied by four or five other men, two of whom were the masters of the fleeing negroes. Inquiry was made as to whether any one had seen the escaping slaves, but, of course, no one had seen them, and in a short time their pursuers disappeared. That night my father, William Hundley, Jonathan Baldwin and Seaberry Lines conveyed them to Bradford's, at Marion.

Many instances of this kind occurred, and men, women and children were conveyed in the above-described manner to Canada and freedom.

I think a large number of your pioneer citizens were connected with the Underground Railroad, and I am sure a very large majority of them were in sympathy with its operation. While many of them came from North Carolina, Kentucky and Tennessee, they were not of the slaveholding class and detested the institution of slavery and loved liberty for all mankind.

I have traced briefly the history of slavery as it affected your community. While I have shown that there was an overwhelming sentiment in your town and Township in favor of human freedom and opposition to the institution of slavery, it is only fair to say that this institution had in your midst a few defenders.

The writer has traced in a hasty manner the action being taken everywhere throughout the North to nullify the odious laws which had been enacted in order to perpetuate human slavery. Nowhere was the feeling against slavery stronger than among the Quakers of your Township, but it was seen that this institution could not be eliminated by compromise or by the assistance of the Underground Railroad. The time was rapidly drawing near when this institution was to be shot to death on the field of battle, and in the accomplishment of this result Fairmount and Fairmount Township were to offer on the bloody field of carnage many of their best and noblest sons, who gave their lives in order that human freedom might prevail everywhere in our fair country, and that the doctrine enunciated in the Declaration of Independence "that all men are created free and equal, endowed with certain inalienable rights, among which are life, liberty, and the pursuit of happiness" might be true for the first time in our history.

I shall not attempt in this article to trace the formation of political parties or to describe the National campaigns which immediately preceded the Civil War. I want to here advert very briefly to what was known in 1856 as the Know Nothing party, which made its appearance in Fairmount Township in that year. It was also known as the American party, because of its opposition to foreign influence. This party was characterized by its secrecy and the reticence of its members.

I remember that when this party organization came to your Township there were no secret societies of any kind in Fairmount. As the members of this party held their meetings in secret, and as there were no public halls or lodge rooms the meetings were held at night in barns and shops. The women of the town upon one occasion became greatly excited and pursued their liege lords to Bill Wright's barn and demanded admittance. This was refused, whereupon the women proceeded to break into the star chamber session and of course broke up the meeting and took their spouses home, where they were taught that they must at least know one thing, and that was that they could not keep late hours in barns without the consent of their wives.

I have been writing much about slavery and the black man, but have failed to say that the first colored man I ever saw was in Fairmount in 1852. His name was Nelson Brazleton, and he was a wagonmaker and worked in my father's shop and lived at our home for some time. He was a sober and industrious man, and was universally respected. I do not know whether he was the first man of African descent to make his home in your Township or not, but he was the first man of that kind that I had ever seen. In 1858 and 1859 Brazleton had a small shop on Jesse Winslow's farm, east of town, and did wagon repair work and some blacksmith work. I think he died here in 1860 or 1861.

I am sure that I have only touched upon the great subject of the Underground Railroad and have failed to mention scores of your early pioneers who were identified with this cause and did valiant service in advancing human liberty.

Summitville, Ind., February 27, 1917.

(By Mrs. Angelina Pearson)

The Friends everywhere worked by speech and by writings against the institution of slavery. The Underground Railroad became a means of escape for human chattels. Levi Coffin, a Friend, who lived in Cincinnati, was the reputed president. There were hundreds of branch lines running through various sections of the free states, reaching northward to Canada, the only territory the runaway slave could flee to and be safe from the pursuit of his master.

MRS. ANGELINA (HARVEY) PEARSON

One of the capable teachers to whom frequent reference has been made, is a native of Fairmount Township, where she was born, February 17, 1845. Her paternal grandparents were Thomas and Anna (Sadler) Harvey, and her maternal grandparents were Phineas and Mary (Bogue) Henley, all of North Carolina, who came in the early day to this community. John S. Harvey, the father, was born in Randolph County, North Carolina, February 24, 1821, and died August 18, 1850; Lydia (Henley) Harvey, the mother, was born July 21, 1827, and died July 29, 1845. Mrs. Pearson was their only child. On her father's side she is of English, Irish and Welsh extraction, while her maternal ancestors were a mixture of English, French and Indian blood. She was educated in the common schools of Fairmount Township and attended Earlham College in 1863. With the exception of three years' residence at Converse, Indiana, she has always lived in Fairmount Township. Mrs. Pearson was engaged in teaching from 1862 until 1870, her school work being confined mostly to her own native Township, with the exception of brief engagements at Blue River Academy, in Washington County, Indiana, in Howard County, near Greentown, and one summer session in Greentown. Her most notable success, perhaps, was at the Lake School, in Fairmount Township, during the Civil War, when management of the highest order was required in the maintenance of discipline. On December 30, 1869, she was joined in marriage to Lemuel Pearson, born at West Milton, Ohio, December 17, 1843. His death occurred September 15, 1914. His parents were Isaac and Mary (Pemberton) Pearson. Lemuel and Angelina Pearson were parents of six children, namely: Herbert, born June 25, 1871; Harvey, born August 18, 1873; Mary, born February 22, 1878; Ethel, born December 30, 1880; Ernest, born April 26, 1883, and Susan, born April 24, 1886.

The Dred Scott decision covered the entire United States. This decision made it unlawful for anyone to harbor, feed or protect a runaway slave.

The Underground Railroad had one of its best officered organizations in Fairmount Township. All the way from Cincinnati there were stations where the slave was befriended. As far back as 1833 there was a station at the farm just opposite the Friends meeting house at Back Creek. It was occupied by Charles Baldwin and family, he having several stalwart sons who were ready, day or night, to give their lives, if need be, for the cause of abolition. I will relate one incident.

Often there were runaways brought in for Baldwin to aid. On one occasion there were nine men brought, and for one week Baldwin kept them concealed in a thicket, in a little log cabin which had been built for the purpose, one-quarter mile east of his home. These men were closely pursued by their masters. They belonged to three different owners in Kentucky. Baldwin had brought them to the house with the intention of conveying them on north. Upon looking out towards the road, which is now the tarvia road, he saw three men and two officers stop at the end of the lane. One of the slaves ventured out far enough to look at them and recognized them as their masters. He informed his comrades and they formed a circle in the center of the living room, taking hold of hands, looked upward, and in concert they swore:

"By the God of Eternal Justice we will die in our tracks right here before we will go back into slavery!"

And they stood there firm.

After parleying for a half hour the men at the end of the lane turned their horses and went back to Anderson without a single sight of their slaves, after pursuing them to within speaking distance.

The Back Creek neighborhood was wholly one of anti-slavery sentiment, and was always glad to aid in any way it could.

Charles Baldwin often said:

"I could not do what I am doing if it were not for my kind neighbors. I often have to inform them when I have a consignment. Sometimes I am eaten out, but when we open the kitchen door in the morning there will be great baskets of cooked food, clothing and medicines as our needs may be."

The kitchen door had not been locked at night.

It was no uncommon thing for the slave owner to follow the track of the Underground Railroad, but it was rare for him to recover his human property. Many were the cunning artifices used to delude him.

On one occasion there were three men to be conveyed to Moses Bradford, three miles north of Marion. The owners were in the neighborhood. It was undertaken by John S. Harvey, my father, and Quincy

Baldwin, two young men then about twenty years of age. The work must be done that day. They dared not travel the public road, but walk, and go a round-about way through swamps and a jungle of underbrush. As there had just been a deep "thaw out" and a heavy rain, it was impossible to travel in any other way. They selected a position where there was a thicket on each side, what is now a stone road, in front of where Isaiah Thomas now lives, and every man kept hid while John Harvey crossed the road and reported that nobody was in sight. Then one man would cross at a time, being careful to step in the same track. Quincy Baldwin was the last to cross. By sunset they were at Bradford's, torn by brush, clothing in tatters, cold, hungry and wet with mud and water above their knees. Oh, what a price for liberty! But that was better than the lash of the whip, or being branded by hot irons, like cattle, as many slaves were.

HERBERT PEARSON

Is another Fairmount boy who is occupying a responsible position. Mr. Pearson has for several years been located at Balboa Heights, Canal Zone, where he is employed as Auditor of the Commissary and Railroad Departments of the Panama Canal. Here his services are so eminently satisfactory to the Government that he finds no difficulty in holding his position. Mr. Pearson is a son of Mrs. Angelina Pearson and the late Lemuel Pearson.

As well as the writer remembers, until January 1, 1861, the date of his death, at the age of sixty-two years, Aaron Hill lived on the farm now known as the Harvey farm, and his home was another station. For some time after Aaron Hill's death the business was successfully carried on by his son, Daniel. One Sabbath afternoon Daniel Hill called upon the writer of this article and excused himself for not staying but a few minutes, saying:

"I took seven runaway slaves to Bradford's last night. There was the father, mother and five children. I had them four days. I put hay in my deep wagon bed, then had them get in and lie down. Then I put hay over them and ordered them not to speak. The only road was through both Jonesboro and Marion, and it was a bright, moonlight night. In driving through these towns I drove slowly. I passed through Marion just at midnight. I had my horses walk through town slowly, but when I got beyond town at a safe distance I whipped them into a gallup and delivered them safely."

This was the last "consignment" that ever passed over the Underground Railroad through Fairmount Township. Some one calculated that as many as fifteen hundred runaways passed over the road while it existed. Daniel Hill was a frail, delicate-looking man, but it is due him to say he was heroism personified. He, like many others, hoping that the war then raging would end slavery, enlisted in Company C, Eighty-ninth Indiana Volunteer Infantry, and laid down his life at Alexandria, Louisiana, on that fruitless raid up Red River.

CHAPTER XV.

THE SPIRITUALIST MOVEMENT AND ACTIVITIES AROUND LAKE GALATIA.

IN 1851 Spiritualism swept over this part of the country. William Chamness started the movement for a town at Lake Galatia.* As early as 1833 Solomon Thomas had built a tannery in the neighborhood, and Micajah Cross, son-in-law of William Chamness, and Moses Hollingsworth had erected cabins there. Chamness insisted that all his followers should have everything in common. All believers were required to subscribe to the idea that there should be a mutual interest in all human necessities.

In this way a proper community spirit would be developed, and all would labor for the common good of the faithful.

Otho Selby, well known surveyor of his day, was employed to locate streets and blocks. Circles were formed and services were conducted by writing mediums. It was the design of Chamness to make this a seat of learning and headquarters for the propagation of Spiritualism.

William Wellington and Joseph Hollingsworth erected a saw-mill and grist-mill. William Chamness and son started a store and built a residence. A little later James Lancaster erected a small frame building and put in a stock of merchandise.

A printing office was soon located, and a periodical called *The Galatia Messenger* was published.‡ *The Messenger* was a four-page paper, each page being about eleven by seventeen inches in size. Eli Selby was the managing editor of the periodical, which contained news of spiritualistic movements, accounts of local happenings, items in reference to the seances held, and frequently referred to the excellent healing properties of the waters in the Pool of Siloam, otherwise known as Lake Galatia.

Joseph Hollingsworth and Peter Havens were two of the strong characters connected with the movement. Mrs. Eleanor Hollingsworth, wife of Enos Hollingsworth, was one of the strong mediums. Charles Stanfield was another active supporter.

---

*Micajah Weesner at one time ran a tanyard near Lake Galatia. An epidemic of cholera broke out in the neighborhood. Weesner and Alex Dolman, who had been stricken, were moved to a point north of Jonesboro, and died of the disease.

---

‡Louise Payne Thorn once related that on many occasions, as a girl, she visited the printing office and watched the printers and publishers at work on their paper.

Robert Nose relates that in 1855 a man named Gerard created considerable excitement in the neighborhood by announcing that on a certain day he would make his ascension into heaven. Gerard had for a number of days been preparing for his flight by remaining in bed and abstaining from all food. E. B. Chamness, son of William Chamness, who was teaching in the vicinity, adjourned school in order that his scholars might see the flight of Gerard. At the appointed hour the children and other neighbors formed a circle around the bed. Gerard,

THE POOL OF SILOAM

It was asserted in articles published by the *Galatia Messenger* and claimed by followers of William Chamness, that the waters of Lake Galatia possessed healing properties. Thus the lake became known among faithful Spiritualists of the early day as the Pool of Siloam.

his arms akimbo, slowly arose, shook himself violently for a few minutes, and by various other means attempted to arise. He did not succeed in making the ascension as promised, and his failure created much unfavorable comment in the settlement.

All went well for a time with the little colony. A minister of one of the orthodox churches, believed to have been Rev. George W. Bowers, one day gained the consent of leaders of the Spiritualists to preach a sermon to members of the faith. The minister chose for his text:

"Oh, foolish Galatians, who hath bewitched you?"

The sermon is described as one of great power. Bowers was an orator of unusual ability and considerable persuasiveness. His unanswerable logic appealed with such irresistible force to his hearers that the sermon started an agitation which eventually proved to be the beginning of the end of the enterprise. The movement began to disintegrate in 1857, and in time gradually disappeared.

The proposed metropolis soon faded away, and few of the present generation are aware of the movements of its ambitious but misguided promoters. Today not a vestige remains of this exploded enterprise, which in its energetic infancy promised far-reaching results.

One of the most aggressive opponents of Spiritualism as practiced in that day was Morgan O. Lewis, who openly ridiculed their doctrine and their practices.

Rev. Bowers was a Methodist Episcopal minister. He was combative when it became necessary to enforce respect for religious services. Upon one occasion, it is related, an intoxicated hoodlum made bold to walk up to the platform and take his seat in the pulpit with the minister. Bowers remonstrated with the drunken man, who promptly replied that he had as much right in the pulpit as Bowers had, whereat Bowers took hold of the ruffian by the nape of the neck and forcibly escorted him to the door, putting the boot to the disturber as he went out. After this circumstance became known throughout the settlement Bowers was never known to have been again interrupted in his meetings.

Eli Selby, soon after the enterprise began to wane, went to Missouri and settled in the Ozark Mountains. When the Civil War broke out Selby is said to have sympathized with the South. He and his son, George, joined a party of bushwhackers and were both killed in the Ozarks in operations against the Union forces. It is not known what became of other members of the family.

E. B. Chamness, son of William Chamness, lived for many years at Alexandria, Indiana. He died in 1910. The widow, Mrs. Clara K. Chamness, at one time owned a cottage at Chesterfield, headquarters of the Indiana Association of Spiritualists, where their annual meetings are held.

Lake Galatia afforded fine fishing for the pioneer. There used to be an abundance of black bass and plenty of fine perch here. A hard freeze in 1862 killed them off, and fish has not since been so plentiful in the lake. Attention was turned to the Mississinewa River, later on, where there were plenty of pike, red horse, suckers, bass and perch.

The scattering settlers thought the gig, or hook, was too slow for catching fish, so they devised a brush drag long enough to span the river, and with grape vine and hickory bark improvised into a rope they pulled the drag down to a deep hole where they landed with all the fish they could take care of.

"In December, 1847, in the village of Hydeville, New York," writes Mrs. Angelina Pearson, "a family by the name of Fox heard strange rappings about their house, which increased in loudness and frequency, and which were more of an annoyance at night than during the day time, and were noticeable in different parts of the house. It was annoying to Mr. and Mrs. Fox, who became worn out with sleepless nights. Not until in 1848 did they discover that so many raps meant 'yes' or 'no.'

"Such mysterious doings could not be kept secret. The news spread in the village and elsewhere, and finally extended over the United States and to Europe. Great excitement prevailed wherever it made its appearance, and people would go long distances to see and hear its mysterious manifestations.

"Finally, an alphabetical code was established, the letters corresponding to the number of raps. Thus the mediums believed a communication was established between the living and the dead. The first communication thus given, it is claimed, was:

" 'We are all your dear friends and relatives.'

"The public press took hold of the subject and printed much literature. Now, Spiritualism had gained a strong hold, and had multitudes for its advocates. The Banner of Light, a magazine published in advocacy of Spiritualism, was issued in an Eastern city.

"The definition of Spiritualism, as given in some of the literature on the subject, is as follows:

" 'Spiritualism is based on the cardinal fact of spiritual communion and influx. It is the effort to discover all truth relating to man's spiritual nature, capacities, relations, duties, welfare and destiny, and its application to a regenerate life.'

"But to all honest-thinking minds who watched its final outcome it was a decided farce.

"It reached Grant County some time previous to 1860, and found many believers. It had many strong advocates in Fairmount Township in that day, especially in the neighborhood of Lake Galatia, and persisted in keeping up its operations until some time in 1865 or 1866.

"The writer began teaching school in that neighborhood, in January, 1864, and boarded at a house which had formerly been occupied by a family that had encouraged it. Often large crowds would gather at this home to witness its noisy manifestations. The family who then owned the house was not friendly to it, yet it was there to annoy them. Every evening about 9 o'clock there would be a noise begin near the floor, between the ceiling and weather boarding, like the climbing up of an animal as large as a cat, or small dog. On reaching the upper floor it proceeded to run, making a noise with its feet, and also another noise as if it was dragging a heavy garment with large buttons attached, which scraped and bumped on the floor. Then it jumped off down into the ceiled partition on the north side of the room. Then all was quiet till next evening at just the same time. At the exact hour it would be there and perform the same mysterious operation.

"The woman of the house informed the writer that this was kept up just one year without missing a single night, but it gradually died out. At that time, in Fairmount Township, there were hundreds of people, as well as the writer, who saw and knew to a certainty something of the mystic nature of Spiritualism, but who did not believe it had its source in anything good, and only a few aged persons are living today who were witnesses. Latter-day Spiritualism has but little resemblance to that of 1847."

For a number of years a lane was visible through the forest where the right-of-way had been blazed and graded ready for the Marion & Mississinewa Valley Railroad, which was projected to connect Galatia with the outside world. Many people subscribed to a fund which it was proposed to loan to the promoters of the railroad at ten per cent. interest. Thousands of cross ties were bought and hauled to the scene of operations. There are still slight evidences of the grading done on the James Carroll farm, near the lake, but few traces of the right-of-way remain. The Chesapeake and Ohio Railway later took over and now traverses for several miles practically the same route as that indicated by the original survey.

The article in relation to the railroad which was surveyed and partly constructed through the eastern part of Fairmount Township brings to my mind that I have seen the bridge which Mr. Tingley mentions and many piles of cross ties along the right-of-way, which, if I remember rightly, ran near the farm then owned by Otho Selby, near Lake Galatia, writes J. M. Hundley.

I also remember that many men in the southern part of Grant County were induced to put their farms into this scheme. I think much litigation arose over these farms, and I believe that a few farmers recovered their lands, but of this I am not quite sure.

Mr. Tingley is right in saying that this railroad was the first attempted in Fairmount Township, and, for that matter, in Grant County;

Fac-simile of scrip issued by the Marion & Mississinewa Valley Railroad Company. For a number of years a lane was visible through the forests where the right-of-way had been blazed and graded ready for the Marion & Mississinewa Valley Railroad, which was projected to connect Galatia with the outside world. Many people subscribed to a fund which it was proposed to loan to the promoters of the railroad at ten per cent. interest. Thousands of cross ties were bought and hauled to the scene of operations. There are still slight evidences of the grading done on the James Carroll farm, near the lake, but few traces of the right-of-way remain. The Chesapeake & Ohio Railway later took over and now traverses, for several miles practically the same route as that indicated by the original survey.

and had it succeeded would no doubt have changed the whole aspect of your Township. Galatia would no doubt have been the leading town instead of Fairmount.

I remember that this railroad bubble burst a short time after the scheme to build a canal from Wabash to the Ohio River through Grant and Madison counties had collapsed. These failures, with the failure of the State Bank of Indiana, which came about the same time, almost completely prostrated the little business there was at that time. (I am a little hazy about whether it was the State Bank of Indiana or the Bank of the State of Indiana, which failed, as there were two of them, and one was good and the other worthless.)

I know my father had a lot of this money taken in at the smith-shop, and it was worthless. It was given to the children to play with. This was the day of wildcat banking, so called, and I remember that every merchant in Fairmount had what was called a "detector," or a book in which was given the amount of discount or the value of the several kinds of paper money.

Dad Lines would say, when my father would go into his store with a paper bill:

"We will take down the investigator and see how much this darned thing is under repair."

And it was almost invariably under repair from a few cents on the dollar to half of its face value.

This was one of the difficulties with which your pioneers had to struggle—the want of a stable currency. Imagine, if you can, our bankers and business men of today attempting to do the present vast volume of trade with a currency of this character. It would simply be an impossibility.

CHAPTER XVI.

TEMPERANCE AGITATION AND EPISODES FOLLOWING—ORGANIZATION OF CHURCHES.

THE FIRST temperance meeting of which there is any knowledge was held at the old Sugar Grove Church, in the Lewis settlement, about five miles southeast of Fairmount, in 1848. It was at this meeting that William G. Lewis made his first effort to speak in public. The sentiment expressed in his address created a furore in the neighborhood, and almost broke up the peace and harmony that had for many years prevailed among the early settlers. A few of the neighbors claimed that Lewis was advocating a plan that would take away the liberty that their fathers had fought for and bled for and died for.

The movement grew rapidly, however, and ended in the formation of a division of the Sons of Temperance. The agitation spread and the enthusiasm created at that first meeting bore fruit.

As time went on all denominations united on this question and stood out aggressively against the liquor traffic. Ever since there has been in this Township a general feeling of hostility toward the sale and use of intoxicating beverages. This sentiment manifested itself in a striking manner on more than one occasion in the years that followed.

In the late summer of 1874 Andy Morris, who lived at Summitville, encouraged by representations of an acquaintance that Fairmount might be a profitable location for a saloon, thought by a ruse to test the matter of putting in a stock of liquors.

It was highly important to ascertain the feeling of ultra temperance folks with regard to his proposed enterprise. Induced by Fred Cartwright, a well known character of that day, to make a reconnoiter, Morris put some articles of furniture resembling saloon fixtures into a wagon and brought them to Fairmount.

No sooner did Morris reach the southern outskirts of the town with his conveyance than he was surrounded by a crowd of determined, but angry men, led by Dennis Montgomery and Alex Pickard, who notified him that he had better take his traps and move out at once.

Morris was reluctant to do so. He hesitated too long. He was placed astride a rail, Alex Pickard holding one end and W. A. Planck the other, and was carried for a considerable distance along Main Street. He was told, after a pause in the proceedings, that he might have his choice, get out of town immediately or be tarred and feathered.

REV. HERBERT S. NICKERSON
Former Pastor Methodist Episcopal Church

Morris promptly acceded to the arbitrary terms laid down, and promised to leave at once if released. He was taken off the rail and with his wagon and other belongings he started south. Morris never returned to Fairmount after that.

June 1, 1875, Dave Capper, of Harrisburg, planned to open a saloon in a one-story frame structure built by Capper for that purpose east of the Big Four Railroad. There was a door in the west end of the building, and another opening out on the north side. When the structure was being erected Capper claimed that it was intended for a blacksmith shop.

Jonathan P. Winslow suspected the motives of Capper, and kept vigilant oversight of the structure as the work was being completed and the building made ready for occupancy.

A circus was billed for the town. It was on the night before that Capper brought his liquors by wagon from Harrisburg.

Failing in his efforts to persuade Capper to desist from his purpose, Winslow went to the home of Frank Norton.

Norton immediately left his bed and plans were formulated. It was agreed that the ringing of the Wesleyan Methodist Church bell would be the signal for the ringing of every other bell in Fairmount. When this bell pealed forth in the early dawn of that summer day church bells and dinner bells in the town and country joined in, and a great commotion among the people was the result.

Nixon Rush was among the first to respond. The people were thoroughly aroused, and a number of men assembled to ascertain the cause of the excitement. As each man appeared upon the scene the matter was fully explained. In a short while the crowd had gathered at the old frame school house on East Washington Street.

Norton was promptly elected leader of the crowd. He formed the men in line, and at their head marched northeast, crossed the Big Four tracks, and were soon at the building, where they halted.

Capper, who was a Civil War soldier and a courageous man, appeared at the west door with a cocked revolver in each hand. He swore that he would shoot the first man who came near or who molested him in any way.

Norton was acquainted with Capper. He knew that Capper meant what he said, and that he would shoot. However, Norton, who himself was a soldier in the Civil War, and just as courageous and equally determined, quietly notified Capper that citizens meant business, that they did not propose to allow a saloon to be run in the town, and that he would advise Capper, on behalf of the people, to pack up his goods and get out immediately.

Capper stepped back, again notified the crowd that he would shoot the first man who interfered with him, and closed the door.

After a short consultation with Jesse Bogue, J. P. Winslow and Nixon Rush, Norton shouldered a fence rail, took a running shoot, and knocked the door about half way through the building. Jesse Bogue was at the time right at the side of Norton and remained with him through the mix-up.

When Capper discovered that further resistance was useless, and that the citizens would not be bluffed or bulldozed, he capitulated.

The citizens loaded up his stock of liquors on a two-horse wagon owned by Jonathan P. Winslow, and, driven by his son, John, who held the lines, forced Capper to sit on one of the whisky barrels, and in charge of a committee, at the tolling of a bell, was hastily started back to Harrisburg, amidst the jeers and hoots of an indignant but hilarious crowd.

In 1886 Ira M. Smith, of Marion, was making plans to open a saloon on the west side of North Main Street, between Washington and First, in a two-story frame building which stood where the Marion Light and Heating Building is now located. Smith had secured his license. One night, in the summer of that year, the building was destroyed by dynamite, and Smith abandoned his project. He returned to Marion.

Luther Morris secured a license in 1892 and opened a saloon in a one-story frame residence at the northeast corner of First and Main, which had been occupied by Mrs. Eleanor Thomas, widow of Daniel Thomas. Prior to this year, for about fourteen months, Morris had been engaged in taking orders for liquors and beer, delivering his goods by wagon from Marion. In the latter part of 1892 Morris had erected a one-story frame building on East Eighth Street, and was preparing to move his stock of liquors to this location. Before the structure was quite ready for occupancy it was destroyed by dynamite one night and a few days later the pile of debris was burned. In 1900 Morris erected the two-story brick building now occupied by the Marion Light and Heating Company, on North Main Street. He continued to operate his saloon in this building until 1906, when the citizens of the Township, by petition, remonstrated the business out of existence, Morris being the first and the last man to own a licensed saloon in Fairmount.

A Friends meeting was held as early as 1831 at the cabin of Joseph Winslow, on Back Creek, two miles north of Fairmount. In the same year a double hewed-log cabin was built, where services were continued, on the Exum Newby farm, and this meeting was known as Back Creek. Nathan Morris was the first preacher. Among early members were the Winslows, the Morrises, the Newbys and the Baldwins. In 1833, by direction of New Garden Quarterly Meeting, of Wayne County, a meeting for worship was regularly established. A monthly meeting was set up here in 1838 by direction of the same Quarterly Meeting.

The construction of the old Back Creek meeting house was started in 1840, and completed in 1842.* Charles Osborn sat at the head of the meeting and preached the first sermon. The land on which it stood was donated by Exum Newby, and the ground for the graveyard was donated by Henry Winslow. David Stanfield and Nathan Morris were prominent preachers among the Friends at that time. The early settlers along Back Creek and the supporters of Quakerism as well, were the Winslows, the Baldwins, the Hills, the Newbys and the Harveys.

DAISY BARR

In the early day, Northern Quarterly Meeting of Friends, held at Back Creek, in June, was one of the important events of the year, not only among Quakers, but with people of every shade and variety of religious thought and denominational attachment. For a number of years people from miles around, on foot, on horseback, and by means of wagons and every kind of vehicle then known, would attend these meetings. On Sunday the capacious brick meeting house would always be filled to overflowing. Those who were unable to gain admittance attended services outside. It was not an uncommon thing to see preachers up in wagons out in the shade of the beautiful grove exhorting sinners to forsake their evil ways. Platforms were provided for the use of

---

*In that day it was necessary to mold and burn brick by hand. It was a tedious process, and accounts for the delay in completing the structure.

ministers. These platforms were surrounded by roughly improvised seats. From such rude elevations the Gospel was ardently expounded and the power of the Holy Ghost vigorously proclaimed. Vast throngs would assemble on these annual occasions, drawn thither by motives as varied as the individual mood differed. Some had pious promptings, others came to mix and mingle, while young beaux brought their best girls to "see the sights," and a few attended as a matter of idle curiosity. Thrifty men, anticipating the needs of the multitude, would erect tents and sheds from which were retailed sandwiches, ice cream, lemonade and other eatable knickknacks. These "stands" naturally were liberally patronized. From year to year others similarly inclined were attracted, and the gatherings began to take on the appearance of ordinary Sunday outings, thereby to a great extent defeating the main purpose for which Friends established the quarterly assemblies, and assuming the air and aspect of "worldliness." The crowds, as they grew in numbers with each recurring June, finally became noisy and unmanageable. The sessions were transferred to Fairmount and the name changed to Fairmount Quarterly Meeting.

The first Methodist Church in Fairmount Township was organized at the home of Joseph Weston, about 1835. The charter members were Elijah B. Ward, Elizabeth Ward, Joseph Weston, Lydia Weston, David Lewis, Nancy Lewis, William Payne, Celia Payne, George Crist, Martha Crist and Ann Austin. The latter taught the first term of school ever held in this part of the Township. Elijah Ward was the first class leader at old Sugar Grove.*

The class later moved the place of meeting from Joseph Weston's, Joseph Weston being the first class leader. The class was organized by Wade Posey. Rev. G. W. Bowers was the second preacher. These people were the earliest supporters of Methodism in this part of the country. The Methodists held services at the cabin of Henry Osborn, southeast of Fairmount, as early as 1837.

In 1849, Methodists held services at Henry Osborn's hewed-log cabin, which still stands, and is situated on land now owned by Zim Payne, three miles southeast of Fairmount. Caleb Morris, of Marion, an exhorter of that day, would sometimes be present and assist in conducting the meetings. Those who attended meetings at Osborn's were Jesse Brooks and wife, Thomas Morris and wife, David Jones and wife, Henry Osborn and wife, Charles Stanfield and wife, Emeline and

---

*This church was then located on land now owned by Henry Roberts. It was later moved to the David Lewis farm, on the County Line Road, now owned by Daniel Johnson.

Louisa Osborn, and Caroline, Martha and Aaron Taylor. In that day it was no uncommon thing to keep house and hold religious services in a room eighteen by twenty feet.

THE ELIJAH WARD CABIN

Located about four miles southeast of Fairmount. Elijah Ward, who was the grandfather of Mrs. David G. Lewis, about the year 1835, helped to organize the first Methodist Church established in Fairmount Township. He was the class leader at old Sugar Grove.

A United Brethren Church, known as Union Chapel, was built in 1839 on the Solomon Thomas farm, three miles southeast of Fairmount. Rev. John Pugsley was the first preacher at this church.

Standing in Union Graveyard, as if to keep mute vigilance over the remains of pioneer dead, is a wild cherry, a hickory, a sycamore, a walnut, an elm, and a buckeye tree. The graveyard is situated just south of where Union Church stood.

The United Brethren, in 1844, organized a class at Carter Hasting's home, one mile south of Fairmount. The charter members were Solomon Thomas and wife, John Thomas and wife, Isaac Anderson and wife, Carter Hasting and wife, William Hall and wife, John Buller and wife, and John Smith and wife. William Hall was the first class leader. Services were held later on at the home of William Hall, in Fairmount. He was called to the ministry, and for a number of years preached at different points in this section of Indiana.

WILLIAM HALL

First Postmaster of Fairmount, was in his younger manhood a carpenter and tanner. For a number of years he lived at the southwest corner of Third and Main Streets, occupying the dwelling house now used by his daughter, Mrs. John Burgess Hollingsworth, and family. William Hall was a native of Greene County, Pennsylvania, where he was born, February 28, 1814. He died at his home in Fairmount on October 4, 1900. His father's name was Josiah Hall, born in Greene County, Pennsylvania, where he died, in 1825; the mother, born in the same county and same State, died in 1828. William Hall was a Republican in politics. He served as a member of the Indiana State Legislature in 1861-62. For fifty years he was a minister of the United Brethren Church, and had much to do with the organization of this church at various points in this section of Indiana. He was known widely as a circuit rider, doing a vast amount of missionary work among the pioneers. His wife was Hannah Jones Stanfield, born in Tennessee, December 28, 1821. She died August 3, 1873. Her parents were David and Elizabeth Stanfield. William and Hannah Hall were the parents of seven children, namely, George W., Malissa, Mary, Jane, Levi, Sarah Ann and David. Mary Hall Hollingsworth lives in Fairmount; Levi is a well known business man of Marion, and David resides in Wichita, Kansas. The others are deceased. William Hall was a man of considerably more than ordinary ability. He lived a long and useful life, and as minister and legislator earned by good works and disinterested service the respect and gratitude of his neighbors. William Hall was a potential factor in many of the most important movements which resulted in the moral, educational and business welfare of the community.

The Wesleyan Methodist Church was organized about 1848 at the home of Harvey Davis, who at that time lived about two miles and a half southwest of Fairmount. The charter members were Lindsay Buller and wife, Elijah Harrold and wife, and Henry Wilson and wife. The class was organized by Rev. Alfred Tharp. Meetings were continued at the home of Harvey Davis until 1850, when William Cox, David Smithson, James Farrington and Harvey Davis built a school house on the Davis farm, where services were held for ten years or more. Robert W. Trader* and wife and Bernard McDonald and wife became members soon after the services were started at the school house.

The first Baptist Church was organized at the home of William Leach, which was a commodious two-story log structure, located about five miles southeast of Fairmount. This was the beginning of the church that is now known as Harmony Church, which holds services in a brick building standing on the pike northwest of Matthews. The first members, when the church was originally formed at the Leach home, were William Leach and wife, Benjamin Furnish and wife, William McCormick and wife and James Gillespie and wife. Benjamin Furnish was an associate judge of the circuit court, 1845 to 1852.

Fairmount Friends meeting for worship was set up in 1851. Preparative meeting was established in 1852, and a monthly meeting in 1869, with a membership of 547. The first brick church was built in 1860. It had a seating capacity of 800. Fairmount Monthly Meeting was composed of Little Ridge, East Branch, Upland and Fairmount Preparative meetings.

The little frame church that the Friends first put up in Fairmount, where they held their first school, stood, according to Dr. A. Henley, about where the late Henry Davis lived, now the home of Mr. and Mrs. Lewis Mittank, on the south side of First Street.

(Editor's Note.—Dr. Henley's recollection of Fairmount Township

---

*Robert W. Trader, prominent in the early days in the Wesleyan Back Creek neighborhood, was born in Clinton County, Ohio, June 30, 1828. His grandfather was Arthur Trader, of Virginia. His father was William Trader, born in Virginia in 1801, and died in October, 1867. Robert Trader was the son of William and Elender (Wiley) Trader, the father born in Virginia in 1801 and died in October, 1867, and the mother born in Clinton County, Ohio, in 1801 and died in 1855. Robert Trader came to Grant County in 1842, and with the exception of sixteen years spent in Alexandria, Indiana, he has lived in Fairmount Township all his adult life, engaging continuously in farming with the exception of one year he sold merchandise in Fairmount. He cast his first vote for the Free Soil candidates, and when the Republican party was organized in 1856 he supported Gen. John C. Fremont, remaining loyal to this organization until 1884, when he affiliated with the Prohibition party. He was converted in 1848 and became one of the organizers of the Wesleyan Methodist Church in Fairmount Township, being a charter member. The denomination held its first meeting, led by Rev. Tharp, in Harvey Davis's home, southwest of Fairmount. The organizers were Harvey Davis and wife, James Lytle and wife, Lindsay Buller and wife, John Buller and wife and Robert Trader and wife. Jane (Davis) Trader, the wife, was born in Madison County, Indiana, in 1829, and died May 9, 1862. They were married in February, 1849. Four children were born of this marriage, namely: Harvey, Mariah, Mary and Eunice. The second wife was Phebe Ann Wright, daughter of Jesse Wright, and of this union three children were born, namely, Etta, Oscar and Luther. There were no children by the third marriage to Nettie Sater, of Alexandria, Indiana.

BEREAN SABBATH SCHOOL CLASS FRIENDS CHURCH (1913)

This picture of the Berean Class of the Friends Church, Fairmount, was taken in October, 1913. One hundred and thirty-two members and one visitor were present on that day, and all filed out in front of the church at the close of the lesson and were back in their places at the close of the school, after the picture had been taken. Following are the names of those present:

Back row, left to right—John W. Smith, Edgar M. Baldwin, Caleb A. Starr, Hude Dyson, John W. Naylor (deceased), William Bell, Albert W. Kelsay, Roland Mahoney, John Kelsay, James Bell, Charles E. Carey, Horace Reeve, Alvin J. Wilson, O. R. Scott, John Hasty, Rev. Wilson Bond, Levi Winslow, Prof. William M. Coahran, David G. Lewis, Alonzo Thomas, Rev. Elwood Davis.

Second row from back, left to right—Riley Jay (deceased), Mrs. Riley Jay, Mrs. John W. Naylor, Mrs. J. E. Duncan, Mrs. C. E. Carey, Mrs. W. M. Coahran, Mrs. W. B. Pickard, Mrs. Will Taylor, Simon Barber, M. A. Hiatt, G. E. Mabbitt, Fred Macy, Joseph A. Roberts, William R. Lewis, Oliver P. Buller, William H. Lindsay, Arthur Throckmorton, Mrs. A. Throckmorton, Mrs. Thomas Winslow, Thomas Winslow, Thomas Butler, Charles Kelsay, Samuel Fritch, John E. Duncan, Charles D. Adams.

Third row from back, left to right—Mrs. A. W. Kelsay, Mrs. E. J. Seale, Mrs. H. F. Presnall, Mrs. Lydia Washburn, Mrs. Lizzie Woollen, Mrs. Isaac Moon, James Lynch, Joseph Holloway, Ralph Little, J. C. Long, Jabez Winslow, Webster J. Winslow, Edwin Harvey, James Clark, William Hickman, E. J. Seale, Alvin B. Scott, Dr. N. F. Davis.

Fourth row from back, left to right—Mrs. Alice Thomas, Mrs. J. A. Roberts, Mrs. Luther Davis, Luther Davis, Mrs. Marcus Gaddis, Mrs. Ralph Little, Mrs. N. A. Armfield, Mrs. Elizabeth Hane, Adam Hane, Joshua Hollingsworth, O. J. Stevick, Rev. Eli J. Scott (deceased), Mrs. J. R. Little, John R. Little, Addison Scott (deceased), C. D. Overman, Walter Luse (deceased), Henry Barber, Joseph Ratliff (deceased).

Fifth row from back, left to right—Mrs. O. P. Buller, Mrs. G. E. Mabbitt, Mrs. Wilson Bond, Mrs. Louisa Haisley, Mrs. James Clark, Miss Rena Fritch, Mrs. A. B. Scott, Mrs. Fred Macy (deceased), Mrs. William Lewis, Mrs. W. L. Henley, William L. Henley, Aaron Newby, Harvey F. Presnall, Paxton Wilson, W. B. Pickard, Isaac Lemon, Jr., Isaac Lemon, Sr., Seth Cox.

Sixth row from back, left to right—Mrs. Nimrod Brooks, Mrs. M. A. Hiatt, Mrs. May Carter, Mrs. Jennie Jones, Mrs. Jabez Winslow, Mrs. Leroy McHatton, Mrs. Joseph Ratliff, Mrs. A. J. Wilson, Mrs. E. J. Scott (deceased), Mrs. James Bell, Mrs. John Foster (deceased), Mrs. Tom Miller, Mrs. William Lam, Mrs. Paxton Wilson, Mrs. C. D. Overman, Mrs. Gas Wood.

Seventh row from back, left to right—Mrs. Addison Scott, Mrs. Martha Gossett, Mrs. O. J. Stevick, Mrs. N. F. Davis, Mrs. Charles Altice, Mrs. C. D. Adams, Mrs. Roland Mahoney, Mrs. John Kelsay, Mrs. Susie Cassell, Mrs. Ethel Shuey, Mrs. Joshua Hollingsworth, Mrs. J. W. Smith, Mrs. D. G. Lewis, Mrs. Isaac Lemon.

Sitting in front—Barnaba P. Bogue, Ellwood O. Ellis.

runs back seventy years or more. This fact makes his contributions of more than average importance. The writer may add, at this point, in connection with the location of the frame meeting house, there is excellent authority for the statement that this structure stood close to the spot where the late Henry Davis had his office, on the lot now owned by his daughter, Mrs. Lewis Mittank.)

Following is a paper read at the Friends Church, Fairmount, in the autumn, 1916, by Elizabeth Peacock:

I have been asked to give a little history of the local Friends Meeting at Fairmount, but as it will have to be given almost entirely from memory I fear that it will fail to be of much interest.

Whenever my thoughts turn back to the early days of Friends in Grant County, and especially in and near Fairmount, and remember how earnestly they toiled to clear the forests, ditch the swampy ground, build school houses and churches, and improve the almost impassable roads, I am always reminded of one text in the Bible, which is this: "Other men labored and ye are entered into their labors," John iv: 28.

I often wonder if the young people, and even the middle-aged, ever stop to consider what it really meant to do so very much under such trying circumstances.

And then I think, well, is it possible for them to realize what the early Friends and citizens endured to make the pleasant surroundings that we are enjoying today?

Let us all, young and older, try to be thankful for these things.

Fairmount local meeting of the Friends church was established in the year 1851, and was composed of a few families, about fifty persons, adults and children, who were members of the Back Creek Monthly Meeting of Friends and had been attenders of the Back Creek local meeting.

The first church was a small frame building, and to my recollection, nearly square. It stood a little east of where Lewis Mittank's residence now stands. It was used for a place of worship and also for a school house. On meeting days school kept on until near 11 o'clock, the hour of meeting, when books and slates were put away until after the service was over, the scholars remaining for the service.

Isaac Cook and Peninah Hill Binford, I remember, were among the early teachers.

After some few years, a larger house, of brick, was built, as the frame house was found to be entirely too small to comfortably accommodate the growing congregation and Sabbath school. It was quite an undertaking, as there was but very little money to be found among the members. But Friends helped willingly with their teams and in every way they could.

The brick and lime were hauled from Jonesboro, and that was quite a task, as there were no gravel, tarvia or crushed-stone roads at that time.

My father, Samuel Radley, and Phineas Henley laid nearly all, if not all, the brick, and my father did the plastering. The house was torn down to make room for the house occupied today. We did not have electric lights, but these first two churches were lighted with candles and lamps.

We did not often have night meetings in the first church, only when ministers came from a distance. But some wonderfully good sermons were preached in the dimly lighted church, for the ministers who came were filled with the Spirit and preached with power.

David Stanfield, to my recollection, was the only minister of the Gospel who became a member of this meeting when it was first set up, and I think the first person I ever heard preach a sermon. He lived on a large farm where the south part of Fairmount now stands.

David Stanfield's land reached to Washington Street on the north, and west to the William A. Beasley land, east to Main Street. His house stood not far from where Dr. Glenn Henley's residence now stands.

The meeting grew in numbers and interest. So much so that a monthly meeting for the transacting of the business of the church, composed of Fairmount, East Branch and Little Ridge local meetings, was established, in the Eleventh month, 1869. Nathan D. Wilson and myself were the first clerks.

No doubt, through the faithful efforts and preaching of some of the ministers and workers who went there nearly every Sabbath, there is now a monthly meeting at Upland. Its members were for some time members of Fairmount Monthly Meeting, and are still members of Fairmount Quarterly Meeting.

Later, largely through the influence and faithful labors of Nixon and Louisa Rush, ministers of the Gospel, a meeting was begun, and is still kept up, at Vermillion, in Madison County, Indiana. The members of that local meeting now belong to Fairmount Monthly Meeting.

In the early days of Fairmount meeting, ministers and Christian workers used to go on Sabbath afternoons and hold Gospel meetings in the school houses in the country, where much good was done.

You ask me if those early Friends made a mistake in asking for a meeting for worship at Fairmount? I answer, "No, indeed, they did not, but did just right."

No doubt a great deal of good has been done, and many souls saved. But perhaps much more might have been done if every one of the members had done their duty faithfully.

A Sabbath school was started some time after. It was established largely through the earnest efforts of Milton Winslow. To my recollection, he was the first superintendent.

The Making of a Township.

Jesse Reece, also a minister, as I remember, was the first superintendent to begin the practice of keeping up the school all the year. The bad roads and the distance some lived from church made it impossible, as some thought, for it to be done. But he succeeded, and it is still being done.

For several years the Friends Church was the only church in Fairmount.

I remember well when Isaac Meek, a minister of the Wesleyan Church, and a very good man, held a revival meeting in the brick church, and in the winter of 1864 a woman belonging to the United Brethren Church held another meeting. She went from here to Jonesboro, and died there. John Lewellen, a Methodist minister from Jonesboro, also held a meeting in the brick church.

The following named persons were married by Friends ceremony in the first two Friends meeting houses in Fairmount, as I recall them:

Isaac Cook and Susannah Moorman.
Calvin Rush and Elizabeth Winslow.
Amos Thomas and Nancy Newby.
Thomas Bogue and Emily Wilson.
(The last two was a double wedding.)
John Seale and Amy Davidson.
Jesse Rich and Mary Ann Radley.
Elwood Haisley and Milicent Rush.
Samuel Dillon and Elizabeth Powell.
James Foust and Rachel Little.
Jonathan Binford and Anna Wilson.
Thomas Jay and Elizabeth Rush.
Ephraim O. Harvey and Eliza Jane Dillon.
George Shugart and Harriet Hollingsworth.
William P. Seale and Elizabeth W. Henley.
Charles V. Moore and Mary Baldwin.
Elijah Elliott and Deborah Wilson.
William S. Elliott and Alice C. Radley.
Joseph H. Peacock and Elizabeth Radley.

The following persons have been recorded ministers of the Gospel by Fairmount Monthly Meeting: Milicent R. Haisley, Susannah Cook, William H. Charles, Enos Harvey, John W. Harvey, Thomas Elsa Jones, Perry B. Leach, Eli J. Scott, Oscar H. Trader, Hiram Harvey, Charles Everett Davis, Bernice Oakley Riddle, Ola Smithson Oatley, Evelyn Overman, Grace B. Hobbs and Garfield Cox.

(Editor's Note.—Mrs. Peacock was for many years clerk of the Northern Quarterly Meeting, afterwards known as Fairmount Quarterly Meeting of Friends, and until about 1913 was officially connected with the Friends church practically all her adult life.)

East Branch Preparative Meeting of Friends was established in 1869, and was held in a school house until 1871.

The ministers accredited to the Friends in Fairmount Township in 1877 were John Carey, Ruth T. Carey, Back Creek; William H. Charles, Thomas Jay and Nixon Rush, Jr., Fairmount; and Milton Winslow, East Branch.

The Methodist Episcopal Church, of Fairmount, was originally organized in 1861. The first services were held in the old frame school house,* which, at that time, stood on the east side of Walnut Street, between First and Second.

The charter members were William H. Broderick, class leader; Agnes Broderick, Joseph Broderick, Martha Broderick, David Baldwin, Elizabeth Baldwin, Martha A. Wilcuts, Hannah Wilcuts, M. M. Mason and Anna Mason.

In 1864 the membership had increased by the addition of the following names: John R. Kirkwood, Phebe Kirkwood, George N. Eckfeld, Sarah M. Eckfeld, Mary H. Moreland, Mahala Ward, Martha A. Smith, Thomas J. Parker, Rebecca Parker, John Shields, Martha Shields, John S. Bradford, Louisia Williams, Rachel Fankboner, Sarah Moreland, Jane Knight, Delilah Hollingsworth, Wesley B. Hollingsworth and Isabel Hollingsworth.

A frame building was constructed for worship at the southeast corner of Second and Main Streets, in 1871, and used for services several years.

In 1886, a one-story brick church was built at the southeast corner of Madison and Walnut. In this church services were held until 1910, when the present magnificent structure was dedicated. The building committee having charge of its erection consisted of James F. Life, Charles T. Parker, J. W. Dale, Dr. J. W. Patterson, Palmer Winslow, Curtis W. Smith, J. W. Parrill, Dr. W. N. Warner, Asa Driggs, O. M. Bevington, Capt. Hugh Weston, with Rev. Benjamin Kendall, then pastor. This building cost ten thousand dollars and is modern in design and construction.

---

*This structure was later bought by William Hollingsworth and moved to the south side of East Washington Street, between Main and Walnut, and occupied by him for many years as a cabinet shop. The building was later purchased by N. W. Edwards and in July, 1908, was torn down.

In 1865, the Fairmount Wesleyan Methodist Church was organized by Isaac Meek, who continued as pastor for eleven years. Among the first members were Jonathan Baldwin and wife, Nathan Vinson and wife, Joseph Rush and wife, Mrs. Margaret Henley and Joseph Bennett and wife. Jonathan Baldwin donated the ground on which the church was built.

The Baptist Church was organized April 25, 1888. The charter members were Cornelius Price, Hannah Price, William Price, F. C. Creek, Catherine Creek, William Mulford, Joseph Leach, Louisa Leach, James M. Fowler, Lucretia Fowler, Ida Fowler and Albert Fowler and wife. James E. Price was selected clerk and R. J. Gorbit, moderator. The present brick church, on the corner of First and Sycamore streets, was built in 1891. Emory Swindell, Joseph Leach and James M. Fowler comprised the building committee. The church was dedicated in November, 1891, by Rev. A. J. Hill.

St. Cecilia's Catholic Church was organized in 1878. The services were held at private homes for several years, Father Kelley, Father Struder, Father Grogan and others being in charge at different times. In 1900, the present building on North Vine Street was dedicated, and Father Joachim Baker became the first priest. The prime movers in the erection of the new church were John Shaughnessy, L. L. Coyle and Jerome Coyle. The charter members were J. P. Shaughnessy and family, Patrick McCone and family, Martin Flanagan and family, William Monahan and family, James Monahan and family, L. L. Coyle and family, Jerome Coyle and family, Mrs. Isaac Delph and children, Andrew Ulrich and family, Mrs. James Fenton, John Pfarr and family, Joseph Kearns and family, J. H. Flanagan and family.

The Congregational Church was organized in 1888 by Rev. William Wiedenhoeft, who was the first pastor. The charter members were H. H. Wiley and wife, Wesley B. Hollingsworth and wife, Mrs. Phoebe LaRue, Mrs. S. F. Ink and Mrs. Elizabeth Nelson. The church which now stands on the east side of Walnut Street, between Washington and First, was dedicated December 15, 1889. Levi Scott, Dr. A. Henley and William Lindsay were members of the building committee. Members of all denominations contributed liberally of their means to the fund for the building.

The Christian Church was organized in 1907. The members were Noah Henigar and wife, A. R. Long and wife, Mrs. C. N. Brown, Ab Jones and wife, John Strubel and wife, Mrs. J. C. Albertson, William Cox and wife, Rockafeller LaRue and wife. Rev. W. A. McKown was the first pastor. The church building at the corner of Second and

Walnut Streets was erected in 1912. The building committee consisted of the pastor, Rev. J. Ray Fife, A. R. Long, Ab Jones, Jason B. Smith, N. C. Henigar, Ed Stout and John Strubel. The church was erected at a cost of five thousand, five hundred dollars.

The African Methodist Episcopal Church was organized in 1901 by Rev. Chambers. The charter members were Reuben Jones and wife, Mrs. Luzena Frazier, Minnie Wallace, Rosa Wallace, Lucien McMillan and Lydia E. McMillan, Homer Dicken, Willis Dicken and Virte Lee Jones. Bishop Grant dedicated the church on East Seventh Street in 1903. Rev. Jerry Nickels was the first pastor.

CHAPTER XVII.

EARLY SCHOOLS AND SCHOOL TEACHERS.

SUSANNAH BALDWIN, daughter of Charles Baldwin, who setled in the Township in 1830, taught school at the Back Creek Friends meeting house in 1831. Others who taught here were Mahlon Neal, Thomas Winslow, Henry Harvey, Jesse Harvey and John Harvey.

The first school house was built on the Benjamin Benbow farm, later known as the Daniel Thomas farm, now owned by William A. Beasley. It was a log structure, erected in 1836. The next school building was erected on the Jacob McCoy farm in 1839.

In 1844 a frame school house was built on the Edmund Leach farm by popular donation. A store and a saw-mill were also started at about the same time, and the community took the name of Leachburg. Joe Broyles taught here. Among the scholars at different times were Elizabeth and Louisa Reeder, William M. Duling, John Duling, George W. Reeder, Henry Carpenter, Charles M. Leach, Clark Leach, Frank Brewer, James Terrell, John W. Furnish, Milt Brewer, Mary Brewer, William, John H. and Adrial Simons and Morton and Oliver McCormick, the two last named being grandsons of Robert McCormick.

The earliest teachers in the Township upon the building of log school houses were David Stanfield, Thomas Baldwin, Joseph W. Baldwin, Solomon Thomas, Thomas Gordon, Rachel Lee and John T. Morris.

In his young manhood Thomas D. Duling, Sr., was Township Trustee. He was broad in his views and tolerant of the religious and political opinions of others. When he leased land for the erection of a school house, it was definitely stipulated in the agreement that the building should be open free to all denominations for service when not in use for school purposes. This school house stood three-quarters of a mile due north of Fowlerton.

Edmund and Eliza (Hubert) Duling came to the Township in the same year, 1845, with the former's brother, Thomas D., Sr. Edmund Duling's family consisted of five children, namely: Maria, Asa, Mary Jane, Solomon and Emily. Mary Jane died at an early age. Edmund Duling bought eighty acres of land of Nathan Dicks, who in the early

Early Schools and Teachers.   177

day owned a half-section, this tract lying about one mile northwest of Fowlerton. Edmund Duling was a successful farmer and a minister in the Methodist Protestant denomination. In his younger days he, like his brother Thomas, was a teacher. One of his schools was taught at the old Myers school house, then situated at a point about one-half mile northwest of Fowlerton. The old Duling school house, frequently called Liberty, a frame building twenty-four feet square, erected in 1856, was located on the farm now owned by J. O. Duling, three-quarters of a mile northwest of Fowlerton. The first teacher at this school was William H. H. Reeder, followed in consecutive order by George Bowers, Milt McHatton, Columbus F. Lay, John Heal, David H. Bowers, Mary Taylor, Lydia E. Brelsford, John M. Littler and John Daily. There was an enrollment of sixty at the first school taught there in 1856. Among the scholars were Thomas, Ellis, Lemon, Mary Jane and William Jones, children of Jacob Jones; Mary Ann and Simon Small, children of Josiah and Sarah Small; Laura, Hiram and Elijah Simons, children of George W. and Mary Simons; Wesley, Henry and George Roberts, children of Matilda Roberts; Newton and Stephen Brewer, children of Stephen and Jane Brewer; Sarah and William Searl, children of Elijah and Rachel Searl; Nancy, Charles, John and Robert Nose, children of George Nose; Washington and Minerva Reynolds, children of Thomas and Rebecca Reynolds; Charles Wright, son of Charles and Nancy Wright; George W., Hiram A., Burtney R. and Robert L., sons of Joseph and Catherine Jones; John C., Thomas, Minerva, John M., Lewis and James Littler, children and step-children of James and Sarah Nottingham; Joshua, Andrew and Deborah Bishop; Eliza and Cenia Reeder, daughters of Franklin and Fannie Reeder; William and Adrial Simons, sons of Henry and Elizabeth Simons; Joseph W. Parrill, step-son of Henry Simons; Jasper, Charles M. and George Leach, sons of Edmund and Emily Leach; Jane, Joseph and Eunice Barclay, children of Henry Barclay; Maria, Asa and Solomon Duling, children of Edmund and Eliza Duling; William M., Mary, John W., Barbara Ann, Elizabeth, Thomas D., Jr., and Joel O. Duling, children of Thomas D., Sr., and Nancy Duling. The winter term of school continued for sixty days, from December to February. W. H. H. Reeder, the teacher, walked two miles through woods and swamps, built his own fires, boarded himself, received one dollar a day for his services, and on the last day of school gave each boy and girl a present. William H. H. Reeder was one of the strong, efficient teachers of the early day. He was a foremost man in promoting the best interests of the Township. He took great pride in his work when he set out to do a thing. He always contended that it was his duty to perform any task set before him with all the care and intelligence of which he was capable. Several of the boys whose names are mentioned served in the Union Army during the Civil War, and some of them never returned from the front.

In 1865 there were 495 children in Fairmount Township of school age. The amount of tuition fund drawn during the year was $908.98.

In 1875 the number of children of school age was 445. Amount of tuition fund drawn during this year was $1,353.68. The tuition fund increased in ten years $444.70.

In 1876 there were 447 children enrolled in the Fairmount Township schools, 264 male and 183 female. The average daily attendance was 283. In this year there were eight school districts and nine teachers, six male and three female. The salary of the teachers was $2.18 per day for male teachers, and $2.02 for female teachers. The number of days taught during the year was seventy-five. There were two brick and six frame school houses, having an estimated value of $5,000, and $100 worth of apparatus.

In 1866 Jonathan P. Winslow, who was at that time Township Trustee, built the two-story frame school building* which stood on the square, donated by Jonathan Baldwin for the purpose, on East Washington Street previous to the time that the present brick structure was erected to replace it.

Winslow met with considerable opposition. Citizens at that time thought the Trustee was too ambitious, that his plans were too elaborate, and that the building he planned was too big and entirely too expensive. But with characteristic energy and persistence Winslow went forward with the work. He lived to see his judgment vindicated by later developments, as it was not many years before his critics discovered that he rightly interpreted and foresaw the needs of the time. His neighbors in later years gave him full and proper credit for his foresight. William Pusey and Mary Winslow Bogue were engaged as the first teachers in the frame building. In 1891 the present commodious brick building was constructed.

MARY ANN TAYLOR.

Some incidents are here related in the life of Mary Ann Taylor, who was one of the teachers of Fairmount Township in the years of

---

*Squire Caleb Moon afterwards bought the old frame building, which had been turned into a dormitory, and moved it to his farm, west of Fairmount, in November, 1898, where it was worked over into a barn.

the past. She was of English birth, born in Stebbing, England, in August, in 1843, coming to the United States when a little child, being the youngest of a family of five children, who with their father, William Taylor, set sail for the new world some time in the spring of 1849. The mother, for whom Mary Ann was named, had been laid away three years previous, in one of the beautiful cemeteries of England. William Taylor chose a sail boat for this journey of almost three months, as much safer, as he believed, than a steamboat, of which there were few at this time. The little Mary Ann, then five years old, remembers her disappointment at leaving on shore her small dog, named Keeper, whom she had hoped to take with her.

MARY ANN TAYLOR

She remembers during a funeral on shipboard her father holding her up to see the shrouded figure lowered into the water, and of her fright at a great storm at night. There was great distress during the voyage from sea sickness, and her elder sister said to her when she refused to eat:

"Oh! but you must or you may die, and we might have to bury you at sea."

The child remembered the family coming to Lagro, Indiana, by canal, although the connecting link between the Atlantic and the canal is lost; and also that Aaron, who was next to her in age, after crossing the ocean without serious mishap, fell overboard into the canal and was rescued with more or less difficulty. At Lagro friends met them with a wagon and brought them to Grant County. This was some time in June. William Taylor, with his motherless children, settled in Fairmount Township and lived on the little farm that he purchased until his death, in 1854. It was in these years that the people of Fairmount Township endeared themselves by many acts of kindness to this lonely family. The children left were never without home and friends.

The first school attended was a subscription school at Back Creek, which was taught by William Neal. The school advantages being bet-

The Making of a Township.

JOHN R. LITTLE

Taught thirteen terms of school in Fairmount Township. In 1905, when Mr. Little wrote for teacher's license, his examination papers showed an average grade of 100 per cent. He served one term of six years as Trustee of Fairmount Township. John R. Little is a son of Thomas and Susannah (Foust) Little. Thomas Little served during the Civil War, first in the Eighty-fourth Indiana Infantry, and later in the Seventh Indiana Cavalry. John R. Little's people were Quakers for many generations back.

ter in Jonesboro, after a time Mary Ann found her way into the Jonesboro schools and took advantage of every thing offered at that time in the way of education. Such teachers as Sarah Jay, Terah and Asa Baldwin, Cornelius Ratliff, with his wife, Susan Jay Ratliff, and Cornelius Shugart, have left a pleasant memory. Just before the Civil War she attended the Indiana College, at Marion, for a time. After leaving college Miss Taylor, who had intended to become a teacher, went back to Fairmount Township to begin her work. Her favorite pastime as a child had been make-believe school teaching, when she would gather the children of the neighborhood around her during vacation time, keeping them happy and out of mischief for hours. She speaks of her first school in the summer of 1859, at Wesleyan Back Creek, as a real school, taught by a little girl, as she was not much more than that. She may have inherited somewhat the teaching instinct, as two of her maiden aunts were life-long teachers in England, having taught until past four-score years.

After teaching at Wesleyan Back Creek she taught in Fairmount a summer and fall school. These were subscription schools. In the winter of 1863-1864 she taught the Duling district school, east of Fairmount. In March, 1864, she was married to Joseph A. Morrow, of Jonesboro. In 1866 they moved to Marion, Mr. Morrow having been elected Clerk of the Circuit Court of Grant County. They identified themselves with the Methodist Episcopal Church, of Marion, having been members of that church in Jones-

Early Schools and Teachers. 181

boro since early in life. Here Mrs. Morrow took up active church work, in the Sunday school as teacher and assisant superintendent in the Woman's Foreign Missionary work and wherever duty called her. At the present time she lives in Marion and is still interested in all work for the benefit of humanity, although of necessity not so active as in former years.

NAMES OF TEACHERS OF FAIRMOUNT TOWNSHIP

Tacie Pemberton Adell
Charles Atkinson
Ann Austin
Lydia Morris Arnold
Joy Anderson
Agnes Anderson
Mary Winslow Bogue
Alonzo A. Burrier
Narcissa Luther Bundy
Elias Bundy
Andrew Buller
David Baldwin
Mattie Carter Bogue
Burton Bradfield
Joseph Broyles
Frank C. Brown
Millie Bogue
William Bowers
Frank Bundy
Lancaster D. Baldwin
William Baldwin
Robert Beauchamp
Stella Buller
Zola Neal Brunt
Asa T. Baldwin
Charles Baldwin
Susannah Baldwin
Mary Baldwin
Quincy Baldwin
John H. Baldwin
Arcadia Baldwin
Huldah Baldwin Bradford
Peninah Hill Binford
Terah Baldwin
Thomas D. Barr
Thomas Baldwin
Joseph W. Baldwin
George W. Bowers
David H. Bowers
Lydia E. Brelsford
Ella Brightenfelt
Anna Bogue
Zola Beasley
Dora Bogue
Emma C. Beals
Vashti Binford
Aaron Cosand
Milicent Cosand
Sarah Cammack
Cassie Lamm Carter
Will Calhoun
Pearlie Champ
Mrs. Amy Carroll
Hugh Clark
John Carter
Keturah Baldwin Crawford
Eli J. Cox
William J. Caskey
John H. Caskey
James E. Caskey
Sallie Clark
William Cammack
Mosilean McFarland Crilley
John W. Cox
Eliza Coffin
Mahlon Cook

Truxton Coggeshall
Clark Calderwood
Charles H. Copeland
Will Coahran
Lelia Davis Coahran
Charles L. Coffin
Professor Carr
Gertrude Coyle
Elmira Dillon Charles
Mattie Carter
Edna Calvert
H. L. Carter
Mrs. Mattie Charles
Ava Cope
S. C. Cowgill
Bernice Conner
Katie Coahran Dillon
Alice Coahran Dillon
Georgia Dickens
Hazel Duling
Estella Davis
Millie Cosand
Ellwood O. Ellis
Dora Ellis
Xen H. Edwards
Ora E. Eiler
Vina French
John Furnish
Joseph Furnish
Ada Hill Felton
James Flanagan
Forrest Foraker
Prof. Daniel Freeman
Evan H. Ferree
Rachel Moreland Fankboner
John Flanagan
John D. Ferree
Hortense Glass
Murton Glass
Treva Seale Gaddis

Hamilton Dean
Joel Davis
Thomas Duling, Sr.
Edmund Duling
Alex Deeren
Nathan Davis
Foster Davis
J. M. Dickey
Dorinda Rush Davis
Lucy Davis
Wyllis Davis
R. B. Duff
Everett Davis
John Dailey
Homer L. Dickey
Nelle Denney
Professor Dean
Mr. Douglass
Hannah Beeson Davis
John Evans
Martin Evans
Elwood Garner
Flora Reeder Glass
Addie Dare Goodall
Mahala Gordon
Edward Gardner
Thomas Gordon
W. C. Goble
Eugene Goble
Neil Good
Grace Bevington Guinnup
Rebecca Garrison Hayden
Elizabeth Hollis
Clinton Hockett
Jarett Horine
Joseph A. Holloway
Thomas Harris
Eliza Jane Dillon Harvey
Charles M. Hobbs
Albert Haisley

Robert W. Himelick*	Anna Harvey
Louisa Baldwin Henley	Lida Millikan Haisley
W. J. Houck	Oscar Hockett
Icy Horton	Grace Hobbs
Rose Horton	Waldo E. Haisley
Oliver Hockett	Mr. Hadley
John Harley	Kate Holliday
Sallie Price Harvey	Gusta Whitney Johnson
H. A. Hutchins	Cerena Wright Jay
Benajah Harris	Berry Johnson
Elwood Harvey	Cassie Jennings
John W. Himelick	Henry Jeffrey
Cyrus W. Harvey	Ben Jones
Jesse Harvey	Thomas Elsa Jones
Henry Harvey	Orpha Jones
Thomas Harvey	Ora Jones
Miriam Henley	David Jay
Mamie Ellis	Elizabeth Johnson Rush
Lydia Hussey	John Jones
Ephraim O. Harvey	Walter L. Jay
Avis Harvey	Edith Johnson
John W. Harvey	Beulah Knight Kaufman
Susannah Harvey	Samuel Knight, Sr.
Gertrude Hinshaw	Thomas Knight (Long Tom)
Thomas Hutchins	Estella Davis Kirk
John Heal	Robert Kearns
Richard Haworth	Louvenia Winslow Kelsay
Nettie Baldwin Hollingsworth	Sallie Hollingsworth Kelsay
Tillman Hutchins	Mrs. Thomas Knight

*Robert W. Himelick is a native of Madison County, Indiana, where he was born December 16, 1869. He was educated in the common schools, at Fairmount Academy, State Normal School, Indiana University, DePauw University and New York University. He received the degree of Master of Arts at Indiana University. He is a member of the Congregational Church. Mr. Himelick is principal of the Cleveland (Ohio) Normal School. He graduated from the State Normal School in 1898; Bachelor Arts, Indiana University, 1909; Master of Arts, Indiana University, 1910; superintendent of Fairmount schools; Jonesboro, Indiana; Monessen, Pennsylvania; supervising principal, Indianapolis schools; summer school instructor, Indiana University; superintendent training school, State Normal, River Falls, Wisconsin, and principal, Cleveland Normal School since 1914. Mr. Himelick was married, in 1895, to Miss Meda O. Tyler, at Fairmount. They are the parents of two interesting children, namely: Francis and Jesse Himelick. Mr. Himelick has attained to his high position in educational achievement by thorough preparation and conscientious effort, ever mindful of the importance of keeping his profession at the highest standard of efficiency and practical usefulness.

Joseph Knight
Thomas Knight
Cly Knight
Julia Kelsey
Mary Ladwig
John R. Little
William J. Leach
William G. Lewis
Frank Livesy
Myrtle Leach
Norman Leasure
Preston Lucas
Thurman Lewis
John Lewis
Marie Lyons
Matilda Lassiter
Charles Lloyd
Thomas Ladd
J. D. Latham
Morgan O. Lewis
Daniel W. Lawrence
Dorothy Luther
Leonard Little
A. R. Long
Rachel Lee
Columbus F. Lay
John M. Littler
Homer D. Long
Lee O. Lines
Lucinda Mendenhall
Maggie Moore
Thomas Morris
Emma Phillips Martinez
Frank Monahan
William Modlin
Mary Ann Taylor Morrow
Deborah Moore
Mina Hollis McCone
Ed Monahan
Morton McCormick
Milton Millspaugh

Mollie Sherwood Murphy
Earl Morris
Jay McEvoy
James Merritt
Miles Moore
C. V. Moore
Columbus Moore
Marion Moore
Ada McCormick
Nora Mart
Milton McHatton
Exum Morris
Rachel Moon
Sallie Merritt
Thomas Morris
Millie Morris
John T. Morris
Mrs. Miles Moore
Elizabeth Moreland
Benson Millard
Mary Latham McTurnan
Gertrude Mills
R. Nelson
Samuel M. Nolder
William Neal
Winslow Neal
Thomas J. Nixon
Annie Newby
Alice Nixon
Mahlon Neal
Miss Nagle
Dea Nolder
Berry Oliver
William P. Osborn
L. M. Overman
Mahlon Osborn
Ruth Osborn
Lydia Osborn
George A. Osborn
Margaret Lindley Overman
Calvin W. Pearson

Edith Philippy
J. W. Parker
Frank M. Presnall
George M. Pierce
Thomas Pusey
Seth T. Parsons
Lucia Parrill
Margaret Wright Phillips
Rena Price
Jane Pruitt
Fidella Pierce
Levi Pierce
Enos Presnall
Charles T. Parker
W. L. Pearson
Joseph W. Parrill
Mary Pearson
William Pusey
Ella Pearson Patterson
Angelina Harvey Pearson
Malissa Pierce Morris
Phoebe Pemberton
Tod E. Paulus
Samuel Radley
William Stover
Otho Selby*
John H. Simons
Ella Exelby Steele
Frank Sherwin

Nancy Reece
Jesse Reece
Seright Roberts
Grace Ratliff
Russell Ratliff
Frank H. Rigdon
William H. H. Reeder
Joseph A. Roberts
Ovid Reeder
Ancil M. Raper
John Rush
Ryland Ratliff
Ancil E. Ratliff
Milo E. Ratliff
Anna Rush
Calvin C. Rush
Frederick Rauch
Ora Searls
Ada Scott
Mary Spangler
Joseph Shugart
Nellie Simons
Henry Stover
Sallie Stretch
W. S. Seaford
John Smithson
Adrial Simons
Osha Starr
David Stanfield

---

*Otho Selby, one of the prominent and successful teachers of pioneer days, was a native of Westmoreland County, Pennsylvania, born in 1805. His paternal grandfather was Samuel Selby, a native of Maryland, who emigrated to Pennsylvania. It was in this State that Samuel Selby, Jr., father of Otho Selby, was born; his mother, whose maiden name was Agnes Bernhard, was also a native of Pennsylvania. Her death occurred in Grant County, in 1855. Otho Selby died at his home in Fairmount Township in 1880. He was educated in the common schools of Pennsylvania, came to Franklin County, Indiana, in 1832, and later to Fairmount Township, where he made his home, and where he at one time owned 200 acres of good land. Before he came to Fairmount Township he taught school in Franklin County thirteen years in one school house, a part of this time passing the summer seasons in Grant County on land which he had entered. In politics he was a Democrat, and was a member of the Presbyterian Church. His wife's maiden name was Jane C. Allen, born in Ohio, in 1821, who died in Fairmount Township in 1878. Her father's name was Joseph B. Allen.

J. R. Sherrick
Prof. W. E. Schoonover
Frances Sheppard
Geneva Sanders
Catherine Stanfield
Frank Smith
Anna Simons
L. O. Slagle
Katie Coahran Slone
Irma Smith
Martha Townsend
Martin Tracy
Alice Test
Elon W. Tucker
Maggie Tracy
David Thomas
George Thorn
Aaron Taylor
Jesse J. Thomas
L. L. Tyler
Solomon Thomas
Martha Townsend
Bert Thomas
Delia Truman
Jennie Phillips Whitney
Cassie E. Wiltsie
J. H. Wilson
Murt Woollen
Robert L. Wilson

W. W. Ware
Roland Whitney
J. M. Wilson
Cyrus Wilson
Enos Wilcuts
Helen Weston Wells
Eunice Pierce Wilson
Joel White
P. H. Wright
Asenath Winslow
Joseph Wilson
Millie Wilcuts
Herman Wimmer
Thomas Winslow
Lillie Watson
Margaret Neal Wilson
David Weesner
Flaud Wooten
Belle Van Arsdall
Jennie Van Arsdall
Myrtle Ellis Winslow
Mary Wright
Addie Wright
Dora E. Wilson
E. Leona Wright
Carrie Wantland
Alfred Waldron
William Young
Lizzie Zink

Charles Baldwin taught in the log house at Back Creek about 1836; Beulah Knight Kauffman in new frame. There were no desks, only benches; no backs, and a long plank for those who wrote. William Neal next.

Then I went to Fairmount, as the meeting house was now built, and Millie Wilcuts taught there. I will not soon forget it was in this school I made my first public effort in speaking. They were speaking poems, so I asked Jennie Rush if she knew "Twinkle, Little Star." She said, "Yes." So we went out on the floor. She commenced with "Tinkle, tinkle, 'ittle 'tar," so fast I burst out laughing after saying "Twinkle" once, and ran to my seat. (Now, that was different from today, being in the Matron's Medal Contest for the W. C. T. U. work.)

We now moved to Marion; were gone five years. Back again to Back Creek, close to the school house. David Thomas was teaching when we returned. Miriam Henley, next Quincy Baldwin, a Winslow (forget his given name), from another county; Melissa Pierce, Joel Davis, Anna Newby, Mahlon Osborn, then the war came on. I taught one winter at East Branch. We then went to Iowa.

MRS. LYDIA ARNOLD.

Ottawa, Kansas, February 6, 1917.

(Editor's Note.—Mrs. Arnold is a daughter of Nathan Morris. Mrs. Arnold moved away from Fairmount more than fifty years ago. Since her marriage to Isaac Arnold she has lived in Missouri, Kansas and Oklahoma. In another part of her letter Mrs. Arnold states that besides herself, Thomas Morris, Exum Morris and Millie Morris were other members of her father's family who taught school in Fairmount Township. Mrs. Arnold has for years been active in work as teacher among the Indians, in Sunday school associations, in Women's Christian Temperance Union matters, in suffrage organizations and other lines of endeavor having to do with the betterment of civic and social conditions.)

I have been reading your letters and notes which I have enjoyed very much. I can remember a few teachers who have not been mentioned, especially my first.

In 1860 a small frame school house stood in Nixon Winslow's grove just across the road from his late residence east of town. This school was taught by Huldah Baldwin Bradford. Other teachers I remember going to were Anna Rush, Asenath Winslow, Joseph Wilson. They taught in the Quaker school, across from the Quaker Church, Here the Quaker children went in preference to the other school. Fourth-day meeting was observed and teacher took her flock to church. Sometimes this seemed a day, and how many times we sought for excuses, mostly always in vain.

CAROLINE SMITH PICKARD.

Marion, Indiana, February 21, 1917.

(Editor's Note.—Mrs. Pickard is a daughter of Rariden and Rachel (Baldwin) Smith, and a granddaughter of John and Mary Ann Smith, early settlers. Mrs. Pickard's grandparents were the first couple to obtain a marriage license in Grant County. Rariden Smith was at one time interested in a tanyard located here.)

My father, Exum Elliott, bought the farm north of the Solomon Knight farm in the fall of 1864. My mother was Solomon Knight's eldest daughter, therefore I am a great-granddaughter of Joseph Winslow.

Though living in Mill Township we went to Back Creek to meeting, and the greater part of the time from 1864 to 1874 I went there to school. Several have spoken of the "gads" and the "whippings," but I never witnessed a child whipped at school. Neither did I hear of one being whipped at any school I ever attended, though this may have happened.

Several have spoken of all the school attending mid-week meeting at 11 o'clock, a custom which was faithfully kept up at Back Creek until the fall of 1888. The teacher, although a Friend, decided not to take the children to meeting, and as the patrons did not ask him to let their children go, the custom of so many years was dropped.

Now, I never remember of attending school but that it was a part of the program of the day to begin school with a Bible reading. A few of my teachers offered prayer occasionally after the reading, and sometimes a pupil would pray. One teacher especially I remember that read from the Bible and prayed every morning, often explaining to us children the lesson read. One morning she read the twelfth chapter of Ecclesiastes and gave from it such a vivid picture of an old man without God that I have never forgotten it.

RUTH T. CAREY.

Jonesboro, Indiana, April 10, 1917.

Once there stood a little school house in the corner of a large woods near where Perry Seale's house is now located. In that school house Elmira Dillon taught a summer term. If memory does not fail, she was the daughter of Sammy Dillon, and she afterwards became the wife of William Charles. Mr. Charles had a gift in public speaking, and was recorded a minister of the Friends Church in his young manhood days. Mrs. Charles died soon after her marriage. Are these memories correct? To that school among the trees went Misses Mary and Hannah Wilson, the writer and her sister, Emma, and it probably was the first school for each of us. We had great fun making clothes and hats during recess hours out of pawpaw leaves and even roofing our play houses with the same big leaves.

MYRA BALDWIN.

Fairmount, Indiana, March 6, 1917.

Do you have the name of Joseph Knight, son of Solomon Knight, as one of the early Fairmount teachers?

In examining my scrap book I find the following that I believe was published in *The News* the middle of 1908:

"Joe Knight is still living and is seventy-nine years old. His eyesight did not fail until last winter. He has never used glasses to aid his sight. He can still read without them. He enjoys telling of early days in Grant County, and remembers many who are now living at Fairmount and Jonesboro.

"This evening he told some of us about the first license he got to teach school. It was in 1853. William Neal was the Examiner. He asked only this question: 'Why do you invert the divisor in divisions of fractions?' Mr. Knight said he did not know, but he told the Examiner something, he had forgotten what, and got a two years' license.

"He taught school at Back Creek on this license. He afterwards taught in Fairmount and Oak Ridge.

"Mr. Knight is considered the best read man in the vicinity of North Branch, Kansas, he having an excellent memory."

Mr. Knight died a few years ago, over eighty years old. He was a good citizen.

I well remember old Milt McHatton, and frequently heard him spoken of as a man of some attainments.

My mother went to school to William Neal. She thought he was an excellent teacher. Has any one told you of Pike's Arithmetic and Talbert's Arithmetic and Pineo's Grammar? Have they told of singing geography?   D. W. LAWRENCE.

Deepwater, Texas, April 14, 1917.

(Editor's Note.—Prof. Lawrence is a former Liberty Township man, and a brother of Mrs. Jacob Briles. For many years he has been engaged in educational work, a profession in which he has met with notable success.)

Old Liberty school house was built in 1856, on the northeast corner of the land now owned by Joel O. Duling. During the time the house was situated there I went to the following teachers: William H. H. Reeder, George Bowers, Milton McHatton, Columbus Lay, David Bowers, John Heal, Mary Taylor, Eliza Brelsford, John Daily, Frank Smith, John Litler, and Maria (Duling) Hollingsworth taught a subscription school.   SOLOMON DULING.

Jonesboro, Indiana, March 24, 1917.

(Editor's Note.—Solomon Duling is a son of the late Edmund and Eliza Ann (Hubert) Duling, who came to Fairmount Township in 1845 from Coshocton County, Ohio, and settled on the farm situated about four miles east of Fairmount, now owned partly by Solomon Duling and partly by Joshua Hollingsworth. Edmund Duling served as a County Commissioner during the Civil War, when the county was paying bounties in order to induce men to enter the Union Army. He was an ardent supporter of the Republican party, and he and his family were affiliated with the Methodist Protestant Church. The Dulings have been known from the very early days of the Township to be active in promoting educational and church matters in their neighborhood, and foremost in supporting the best and most substantial things in civic affairs.)

I see the folks are contributing quite freely to the list of early teachers for "The Making of a Township." They have missed my teachers entirely. I always have a warm spot in my heart for them.

They were Seright Roberts and Martin Tracy, winter teachers, and Rebecca Garrison Hayden and Mrs. Elizabeth Hollis, summer teachers.

They all taught at old Leachburg prior to 1874. Miss Garrison taught there about the summer of 1869.

I will never forget my first day at school. The teacher stopped to talk to my mother, and as I was not always good, mother said:

"Harry, you go with Miss Garrison to school."

And I balked. So mother came out and made a little history right then and there.

And Rebecca took me gently by the hand and led me to school. And I always loved my teachers ever after.

HARRY SUMAN.

MISS STELLA BULLER
Fairmount Township teacher. Miss Buller is a great-granddaughter of David Stanfield, founder of the south half of Fairmount, and one of the Township's progressive pioneers.

Hunter, North Dakota, February 5, 1917.

Early Schools and Teachers. 191

(Editor's Note.—This is a contribution which relates an experience familiar, doubtless, to many others on their initial introduction to the school room. Mr. Suman, who is a son of Abner Suman, lived when a boy and young man in the Leachburg neighborhood. Mrs. Suman is a daughter of the late William G. Lewis and Mrs. Emeline (Osborn) Lewis.)

I have your recent favor, together with two copies of your paper. Glad to hear from you.

Yes, as they used to say, I "kept school" in Fairmount Township. I am not so certain whether I taught anybody or not, but I did keep order.

It was in the years of 1874-75. I was master over the Back Creek school, with Miss Fidella Pierce as my sole assistant. It was in the old brick school house, with two rooms, one upstairs and one down, which you no doubt remember when you were a small boy.

Since that time I have seen a lot of this old world, and now have the honor of holding down a seat in the Minnesota State Senate, which is now in session, and it is likely to be "some session" at that.

I live two hundred miles northwest of this place, at Frazee, in Becker County, and a very fine country that is.

Hoping this may answer your question, I am,

J. H. BALDWIN.

Senate Chamber, St. Paul, Minnesota, February 6, 1917.

(Editor's Note.—Mr. Baldwin is a grandson of Charles Baldwin, and a son of Lindsey Baldwin, both of whom at one time lived in the Back Creek neighborhood.)

In the summer of 1852 I went to a school taught by Rachel Jane Fankboner, then Rachel Moreland, who now lives in Fairmount. The school house stood on the Abraham Myers farm, a little more than one-fourth mile northwest of the present school house in Fowlerton. There had been schools taught there before by Thomas Duling, Edmund Duling, Bertley Bradfield and Joseph Broyles. You have their names. In the winter of 1852-1853, while George Thorn was teaching there, the house burned down, and was never rebuilt.

In 1854 there was a frame school house built just one mile south of the Fowlerton school house that was known as Leachburg. One of the teachers who taught there, in 1857 I think it was, whose name I have not seen in the list, was Benson Millard. He was a brother-in-law to George W. Bowers, the pioneer Methodist preacher who was known by all Methodist people in early times for many miles, especially as far north as Marion and east to Hartford City and Eaton. Millard was a well-educated man, from the East I think, but his ways and manner of teaching were so far different from what the pioneers were used to that his school was not as much of a success as it should have been.

In the summer of 1854, Anna Simmons taught a subscription school in a log dwelling house, which was vacant at the time and stood near one-fourth mile west of the present brick Leachburg school house.

I well remember of being at the last day of her school. I remember of going with my parents to a basket meeting held at a log school house that stood on the Jonesboro and Muncie road in Fairmount Township, about one-fourth mile west of the Gabriel Johnson farm, where the Hartford City pike now intersects the old road. I don't know who any of the teachers were that taught there.

Gabriel Johnson and John Heavilin, east of him, were early settlers on the old road. Johnson kept a tavern and Heavilin had a blacksmith shop and did lots of work for travelers on the State Road in early times, such as mending wagons and shoeing horses. He also made almost everything in the way of hardware. I have in my possession at this time a pair of barn-door hinges that Byram Heavilin, son of John Heavilin, made in 1851 for Joel Littler, then living on the farm that I now own. They are the hook-and-strap hinge.

ADRIAL SIMONS.

Fairmount, Indiana, May 16, 1917.

Mrs. Mary R. Haisley,

Dear Friend: Some one very kindly sent me two copies of *The Fairmount News*. In each copy there was a reference, one by yourself and another by your brother, to a little girl who years ago taught school in your neighborhood.

You will think this statement true when I tell you that at that time I was less than sixteen years of age (friends told me then I was older than my years), and until I was twenty years old I taught at intervals in Fairmount Township. The school to which your brother refers, when I "boarded around," was my first school.

"The Hoosier Schoolmaster" is no joke. There are advantages in boarding around, which I enjoyed. I learned my scholars better, and the people generally, and they, in turn, became better acquainted with me. There is a friendship in this, too, not found in the school room.

Do your remember one evening that I went home with you? On our way there came up a thunder storm. We were in the woods. Other children were with us and we all were drenched. That was my sixteenth birthday, and I suppose the reason I remember it, and maybe

ELI JONES COX

Born near Fairmount, in 1853, is a son of William and Elizabeth (Wilson) Cox, the parents natives of North Carolina. The Coxes trace their ancestry back to England and Scotland, having originally come to the new country with Friends who settled in Pennsylvania. Eli J. Cox was educated in the common schools of Grant County and attended Normal School at Marion, Indiana. As a young man he taught school a short time and then traveled West, where he remained for one year. He later went to Florida, where he engaged in the business of growing, buying and shipping citrus fruits, becoming an active member of the Florida State Horticultural Society. He has found time in his busy career to devote considerable attention to the study of astronomy, and is deeply interested in this science. He has kept abreast of the discoveries made from time to time, and with the theories of leading astronomers, never tiring of the study of the wonders of the heavens. He is a member of the Astronomical Society of Los Angeles, California. In politics Mr. Cox is a loyal Republican, and affiliates with the Friends Church. Mr. Cox, who owns a home in Fairmount, with Mrs. Cox, spends his winters at his orange grove near Maitland, Florida. Mr. Cox, as a small boy, was a pupil of Mrs. Mary (Taylor) Morrow when the latter taught school at Wesleyan Back Creek in the days when the teacher "boarded 'round."

that is why Eli remembered my age. If I remember correctly, he was of the younger scholars. His memory is better than mine.

I do not recall standing him on the stove with a little girl, or of making him wear a dunce-cap. "Poor little man," I would say now. I'm glad if he has forgiven me. I suppose the punishment was not unjust. I know I did not like to use the whip, but usually kept a supply on hand, for order was requisite to my teaching.

After teaching this first school, the following winter I went to school to a former teacher of mine, Cornelius Shugart. Then I taught the summer school again at Wesleyan Back Creek, with an increased attendance and some larger pupils.

I have been told since that at the first (and I am not surprised) older and wiser heads thought I would not be sufficient for the place, as there had been some trouble in the government of the school. I do not recall now of having any serious trouble.

I do not mention this to take any credit or glory to myself. Before I began to teach others I had learned in whom to trust for needed help. I believe now that I did the best I knew at the time, and lived to feel the "touch of His hand on mine."

The last year I taught in Fairmount. In the fall it was arranged for me to continue the school and draw my salary from the district funds.

I well remember a pony ride down to Marion to meet the county superintendent and pass an examination for a teacher's certificate. After this, I felt better equipped for teaching, and in the winter of 1863 I taught my last school in the Duling settlement, east of Fairmount.

Marion, Indiana.   Mrs. Mary A. Morrow.

CHAPTER XVIII.

WILLIAM LEACH AND HIS DESCENDANTS.

(By David G. Lewis.)

WITHIN a year after Grant, as an organized county, had been placed on the map of Indiana, the Leach family name was spoken in the wilderness long since supplanted by the cultivated fields, in the immediate vicinity of Fowlerton.

In their early ancestry history the Leach family is of English and Scotch descent. Coming to America in the Seventeenth century, like pioneers of other households, the ancestral members were busy with the every-day economic problems, and they did not leave much record of their effort—simply the fact that their posterity is here and enjoying the fruit of their labors. We have little knowledge of the family back of Esom Leach, father of William Leach, and great-grandfather of William J. Leach. Esom Leach came from Virginia to Ohio, and into Indiana early in the Nineteenth century.

It is a family tradition that in 1803 or 1804 Esom Leach located in Franklin County, and that six children were born in his family. William Leach, who came in 1832 to Fairmount Township, was the founder of the local branch of the Leach family. We trace him back to the Franklin County family, and to the household of Esom Leach. He was one of the four sons and two daughters. His brothers were Reuben, Archibald and James. His sisters were Martha and Rebekah. Those who remember Uncle Billy now know whom he left behind him when he came to Fairmount Township.

Privation and dire necessity, which were the common fate of all, must have been the portion of Esom Leach's family in the Territorial days of Indiana history. The Leach family was in Indiana a dozen years before it became a State, and in Grant County within a year after its organization. The name Leach appears early in the annals of both the State of Indiana and Grant County.

The name Esom—the name of the family's earliest Indiana ancestor—has been handed down in several Grant County families, and it is a name peculiar to the Leach family. Where is there an "Esom" outside the Leach family relationship in Grant County?

There was a time when Leachburg seemed to describe the locality —the neighborhood now occupied by Esom Leach's descendants in Grant County. William Leach entered seven eighty-acre tracts of Fair-

THE OLD EDMUND LEACH HOMESTEAD

Located about one-half mile south of Fowlerton. This property is now owned by Mrs. Naomi Deeren. William Leach, father of Edmund Leach, was born in Virginia May 5, 1793, and when a young man moved to Ohio. He was married in Ohio to Sarah Harrison. Their marriage occurred on December 23, 1813. About 1820 they moved west to Franklin County, Indiana. During the thirties he left his wife and some of the children on the Franklin County farm and with his son, Edmund, and a daughter, Rachel, came to Grant County and entered a half-section of land where the town of Fowlerton now stands, his wife and the other children joining him later. William Leach and his wife remained in this Township until his death, February 23, 1851. His wife survived him until about 1865. Religiously, they were of the old school Baptist faith. Edmund Leach was born June 22, 1821, in Franklin County, Indiana. He came to Fairmount Township with his father in 1832. Edmund Leach married Miss Emily Brewer, daughter of Stephen Brewer, one of the early settlers of Fairmount Township. To this union were born twelve children, namely: Jasper, now living in Gordon, Nebraska; Charles M., now living in Delaware County, Indiana; Stephen and Esom, living in Sullivan County, Indiana; Rachel Ann, deceased; Edmund, Jr., living in Gordon, Nebraska; Lucinda, of Culver, Indiana; George, of Sullivan, Indiana; four dying in infancy. Edmund Leach, Sr., moved to Sullivan County, Indiana, in 1864, and died there in 1901. Charles M. Leach, son of Edmund Leach, Sr., was born in Fairmount Township in 1846, and moved with his parents to Sullivan County in 1864. Charles M. returned to Fairmount Township in 1872, and married Miss Malissa J. Caskey. Mr. and Mrs. Leach are the parents of Edmund, Claud and Iva, the latter the wife of Leo Underwood, all of whom live at Gaston, Indiana; William O., best known as Wick Leach, of Fairmount Township; Addie, of Wheeling, Indiana, and Bertha, wife of Oscar Roberts, also of Wheeling.

(Editor's Note.—Claud Leach, who kindly supplied the writer with the above facts, is at present the Trustee of Washington Township, Delaware County, an official position which evidences the esteem in which he is held by his neighbors and the citizens of the community where he resides.)

mount Township's most fertile and productive land, all of which lie in the immediate vicinity of Fowlerton, and most of which are yet in the possession of his posterity. The peaceful village of Fowlerton nestles securely on one of those tracts. There was a Leach school, a Leach store, and a Leach saw-mill. In short, the name Leach was coupled with about all the industries of the community, and the name Leach is still a synonym for thrift and industry, the Leach family occupying an honorable place in the history of the community.

William Leach married Sarah Harrison, who was born in October, 1793. Mrs. Leach belonged to a pioneer family with an honorable history, her brother, Lewis Harrison, father of Luther Harrison, having been a soldier in the War of 1812. The span of fifty-eight years seems short, now that so many older men and women have succeeded him in the history of the Leach family. William Leach lived when the settlers of Fairmount Township were enduring hardships. Longevity seems to have been the rule in all families, now that the comforts of civilization are secured, and the men of three-score years do not seem old. Three score and ten is the allotted life of man, and many reach the four-score milestone in Grant County history.

William Leach, who was a soldier in the War of 1812, came when Fairmount Township was a dense forest, and he certainly had his part in its transformation. Along with the Lewis, Ward, Todd, Simons, Duling, Powers, Crist, Reeder, Ice, Corn, Furnish, Mason, Harrison and Payne families, the Leach family had its opportunity, and William Leach was the man of the hour in planting the family tree in the virgin soil of the Township. Three sons, namely, Esom, John and Edmund, and four daughters, Rachel, Mary, Jane and Martha, constituted his family circle, and his children and children's children unto the third and fourth generations assemble in annual reunion in the comfortable little grove generously bequeathed to Fowlerton, the town of his founding, by William J. Leach, who is in the second generation of his family in Indiana, but in the first generation as far as the history of Fairmount Township and the immediate family tree is concerned. Those who point to him as a relative are numbered among the good people of the community. With the coming of railroads came changes in the family and community history, and Leachburg became Fowlerton.

In the days of William Leach the McCormick Tavern was a landmark. The pioneers along the Mississinewa—the McCormick, Wilson and Coleman families—knew all about self-denial and privations. The pioneers in all these early-day families knew what it meant to procure venison from the woods, and to shoot wild turkeys if unexpected company arrived for dinner, when the family repast was cooked before the fire. Some of those old hearth-cooking vessels are still treasured in many households.

David Lewis was not the only man who secured corn meal for family use from the settlers along the Wabash when the resources of the Mississinewa farmers were exhausted. Our forefathers all told of the long trip to Wabash and the canal when they had something to offer on the market. They hauled grain to Wabash until the railroads came and changed the whole situation. Fairmount Township was then in touch with the outside world.

William Leach went the way of all the world many years before the whistle of the locomotive or the telephone bell had been heard in the land to which he brought the family name. He and his contemporary neighbors should be honored, inasmuch as they made this community a possibility. The history of the sons and daughters of William and Sarah (Harrison) Leach is, in a measure, the present-day history of Fairmount Township.

Rachel Leach, born December 13, 1814, married Elijah Searles, and their children are William, Ruth and Sarah.

Esom Leach, born December 8, 1816, married Lucinda Corn, and thirteen children were born to them, namely, William J., Nancy E., Sarah A., Joseph J., Edmund C., Martha P., John G., Mary E., George W., Wilson T., Benjamin F., Reuben J., and Simon B. Leach, who have all been factors in this community.

John Leach was born January 23, 1819, married Martha Fear. One son, Harvey, was born to them. Martha died and John married Mary Lewis. There were born to them David, who died in infancy; Nancy, Esom O., Sarah J., Mary E., Edmund S., and Martha Ann.

Edmund Leach, born June 22, 1821, married Emily Brewer, and their children are Jasper, Rachel Ann, Charles M., James S., George W., Esom, Lucinda, and Edmund, Jr.

Jane Leach, born October 26, 1823, married Stephen Brewer, and their children are William N., Stephen, John, Emily, and Mary.

Mary (always called Polly) Leach, born October 24, 1825, married James McCreery, and one son, Samuel, was born. After the death of McCreery, Mary was joined in wedlock to Jehu Stanley, and two sons, William and Joseph, were born of this union.

Martha Ann Leach, born July 9, 1833, married Thomas Edward Smith, and their children are William Henry, James Edward, Louisa Jane, John Lewis, Esom Leach, Mary Emeline and Rachel Olive.

The Leach family history is an open book and new pages are constantly being added to it. William Leach was a God-fearing man, and, with his wife, was instrumental in organizing the first Primitive Bap-

WILLIAM J. LEACH

Son of Esom and Lucinda (Corn) Leach, is a native of Fairmount Township, where he was born on February 2, 1840. Esom Leach, the father, was a native of Franklin County, Indiana. Esom came with his father, William Leach, to Fairmount Township, in the early day. William Leach stopped the first night in the new country at the McCormick Tavern. From this friendly cabin he went forth with a compass and blazed his way through the forest to the location where he afterwards made his home. On August 24, 1838, Esom was married to Miss Lucinda Corn, who was born in Kentucky, December 15, 1823. She was a daughter of Joseph and Nancy (Said) Corn, pioneers of Fairmount Township. Joseph Corn lived to be eighty-three years of age. His wife died at fifty-four. Bred to farming and stock raising, William J. Leach has never been permanently engaged in any other occupation. In 1865 he married Miss Sarah E. Havens, the daughter of Jonathan and Gabrille (Clark) Havens. Mrs. Leach, like her husband, was a native of this county, where she was born April 23, 1843. Four children were born to this union, namely: Lucinda A., Anna J., Charles E. and Martha C. The wife and mother died April 17, 1888. March 16, 1890, Mr. Leach was again married to Miss Jennie Wood, of Bluffton, who is a native of Ripley County.

tist Church in Grant County. He established a pace for the family, and the men and women of today owe him an obligation. Harmony Primitive Baptist Church had its inception within the Leach family, having been organized in the home of William Leach, a large, two-story hewn-log house located about one-half mile south of Fowlerton, on the farm now owned by Simon B. Leach. Today, descendants of this pioneer family are members at Harmony, while others are identified with the church in Fowlerton.

William Leach was an Andrew Jackson Democrat, and the family has always clung to his political faith. In an early day he gained the confidence and esteem of his pioneer friends, and was chosen by them the first justice of the peace in Fairmount Township. He was an aggressive, enterprising citizen, an obliging neighbor and a good friend, although firm in his convictions and determined in his stand for the right as he understood it. The name Leach will always live in the annals of this community. The founder of this family was a strong advocate and a liberal supporter of all projects for the extension of educational advantages in the early day. He was an especially good friend of David Lewis, grandfather of the writer, and proved himself a man of tender sympathies under many trying circumstances. William Leach was born May 5, 1793, and died February 23, 1851, in his fifty-eighth year.

At the age of twenty-two William J. Leach was employed by Henry Harvey, then Township Trustee, to teach the winter term of school at Sugar Grove. As an evidence of the economical habits formed in early life, Mr. Leach now has in his possession, in the shape of a $2.50 gold piece, a part of the first money he ever earned, which was paid to him by Henry Harvey.

In 1855, led by William H. H. Reeder, who had energetically advocated the improvement, the first effort was made to drain the big sloughs of the Leach neighborhood by the construction of ditches leading to Barren Creek, and in this work Mr. Leach, as a boy, had a part. In the winter of 1863 he split about five thousand rails. It was by means of the hardest kind of labor that he gained his first start in life.

CLAUD LEACH
A former Fairmount Township man, member of the well known pioneer family of that name, now a prosperous farmer of Delaware County and Trustee of Washington Township.

All his life William J. Leach has been a prominent factor in the development of his neighborhood, and it is largely due to his untiring efforts and his ceaseless enterprise that the town of Fowlerton was built. Throughout his long and busy career he has, in season and out of season, with his influence, his energy and his purse, supported every well-directed movement which promised to redound to the advantage of the people of his community and of his Township, even doing so at times when it resulted in personal and financial sacrifice.

Mr. and Mrs. Leach reside at Fowlerton, where they live in comfort amidst the friends and descendants of many who were his associates in his young manhood, enjoying the surroundings of his earlier activities and the scenes of his boyhood, blessed with a full measure of contentment and happiness, which he richly deserves in the evening of a life well lived.

CHAPTER XIX.

AN INFLUENTIAL PEOPLE.

JONATHAN P. WINSLOW, active promoter for many years of all movements tending to benefit Fairmount and surrounding community, was a farmer and merchant. He was born in Randolph County, North Carolina, June 11, 1818, and died at his home in Fairmount, August 18, 1899. His paternal grandparents were William and Quinea Winslow, and his maternal grandparents were Jonathan and Mary Phelps. Jonathan P. Winslow was a son of Hardy G. Winslow, who was born in North Carolina August 15, 1791, and died December 30, 1871; the mother, Christina (Phelps) Winslow, was born in North Carolina, August 8, 1793, and died June 21, 1861. Hardy G. and Christina (Phelps) Winslow were the parents of twelve children, namely: Mary, Martha, William, Jonathan P., Thomas, Quinea, Jesse, James, Alison, Hilkiah, Griffin and Eliza, all deceased except the youngest, Eliza Walker, who still resides in North Carolina. Jonathan P. Winslow was educated at New Garden Boarding School, now Guilford College, North Carolina. He first came to Fairmount Township in 1840, when he was twenty-one years of age, driving the horses and carriage for Dougan Clark, an uncle of Jane (Henley) Winslow. Dougan Clark, accompanied by his wife, Asenath, both recognized ministers in the Friends Church, visited most of the Friends meetings in the United States, traveling either on horseback or by carriage. Dougan and Asenath Clark were the parents of Dr. Dougan Clark, of Richmond, and Nathan Clark, of Westfield, ministers in the Friends Church, both now deceased. On his

JONATHAN P. WINSLOW

visit to Indiana Jonathan P. Winslow remained in Fairmount Township a few months and worked for Daniel Winslow and Matthew Winslow, who owned farms on Back Creek. He worked at splitting rails and as a farm hand. He helped to make the shingles that covered the old brick meeting house at Back Creek. He was reared in a Methodist home in North Carolina, but as a matter of religious conviction joined the Friends at Back Creek, September 19, 1840, during his brief stay here. The same year he returned to his native State and attended New Garden Boarding School. He afterward taught the Oak Grove school, in the neighborhood where he was reared. This was the first term of school Sarah (Stewart) Luther, of Fairmount, ever attended. In politics he voted the Whig ticket until the formation of the Republican party. In 1884 he left the Republican party and supported Governor John P. St. John, Prohibition candidate for President. He was loyal and enthusiastic in his support of this party until his death.

In 1843, at the age of twenty-five years, the subject of this sketch was united in marriage to Jane Henley, at Back Creek, North Carolina. She, too, was reared a Methodist, but united with the Friends when a young woman. Jane Henley was born in Randolph County, North Carolina, May 12, 1823, and died May 17, 1908. Her parents were Esquire John Henley, born January 3, 1793, and died February 18, 1854, and Margaret (Clark) Henley, born February 7, 1794, and died during the Civil War. They were the parents of nine children, namely: Martha, William, Henry, Jane, Mary, Thomas, Rebecca, Alexander and John, all deceased except John. Jonathan P. and Jane (Henley) Winslow were the parents of eight children, namely: Mary M., Margaret L., Thomas J., Martha J., William Clark, John Henley, Joseph A. and Oreanna E.

JANE (HENLEY) WINSLOW

M͞ married Jesse Bogue; Margaret married Enoch Beals; Thomas ͞rmount in 1864 for the Civil War, and never returned; Martha married Henry M. Shugart; William married Adeline Patterson; John died at the age of forty years, unmarried; Joseph married Margaret Gurnea, and Ora married Webster J. Winslow.

By hard work and economy, which continued to characterize their lives, they succeeded in gaining a competency. The first $1,000 they saved, however, had to go to pay security for a friend. With undaunted courage they kept right on, owned different farms and held stock in the Union Factory cotton mills. Just before the Civil War broke out he disposed of his business interests at High Point, being at that time a partner with Sewall Farlow in the mercantile line, and owning a half interest in the brick hotel at that place. This hotel was subsequently converted into a female seminary.

Having always cherished a desire to return to the North, he, with his wife and seven children, started in the spring of 1860 to their future home. They came via Baltimore, Chesapeake Bay, Cincinnati, Richmond and Anderson, thence by stage coach, driven by H. Walker Winslow to Fairmount. Arriving at Fairmount, then a very small village, they met a warm reception at the home of Seth Winslow, corner of Main and Washington Streets, where the Borrey block now stands. Until a house could be procured they found most hospitable entertainment at the homes of the Winslows, Wilsons, Rushes and Thomases. They soon located in a house on North Main Street, the only vacant one to be found, now owned by Isaiah Jay, who purchased it of Dr. J. W. Patterson.

PALMER WINSLOW

Son of W. C. Winslow and grandson of Jonathan P. and Jane (Henley) Winslow, is a native of Fairmount Township. He is president and manager of the Winslow Glass Company, located at Columbus, Ohio. Mr. Winslow is one of the best known manufacturers in the country, and has amassed a fortune.

Mr. Winslow soon opened a general store on South Main Street, afterwards locating at the corner of Main and Washington Streets, later building the two-story brick building now owned by John Flanagan. He purchased forty acres of land of David and Elizabeth Stanfield. This land extended from what is now Walnut Street east to the Big Four railroad and south of Washington Street to the fair grounds, all of which is included in the town of Fairmount. In 1861 they burned the brick and that summer built the house in which he and his wife continued to reside until their deaths. The youngest daughter, Oreanna E. Winslow, with her husband, Webster J. Winslow, continue to reside in the old homestead, which was left as a part of her inheritance. Out of a family of eight children, four sons and four daughters, only three survive,

JONATHAN P. WINSLOW HOMESTEAD
(East Washington Street)
Now owned and occupied by Mr. and Mrs. Webster Winslow. Mrs. Ora E. Winslow is a daughter of Jonathan P. Winslow, who came into possession of the property as an inheritance.

namely: Mary M. Bogue, of Fairmount; Joseph A., of Ontario, Oregon, and Ora E. Winslow.

The grandparents of Mrs. Jane (Henley) Winslow on her father's side were John Henley and Keziah Nixon, who were also the paternal grandparents of Dr. Alpheus Henley. Her grandparents on her mother's side were William Clark and Eleanor (Nellie) Dougan. William Clark was a captain in the Revolutionary War. He lived to a ripe old age, but ever regretted the fact of having taken human life, although the cause for which he fought seemed a just one. The spectacles worn by William Clark are in the possession of the Winslow family and are prized by them as an heirloom of Revolutionary times.

Nixon Winslow, farmer and banker, humanitarian in principle and in practice, benevolent in his tendencies and by inclination a community builder, was born in Randolph County, North Carolina, June 28, 1831, and died at his home in Fairmount, May 23, 1910. His paternal grandparents were Henry and Elizabeth Winslow and his maternal grandparents were John and Lydia Bogue. He was a son of Thomas Winslow, born July 14, 1795, and Martha (Bogue) Winslow, born August 30, 1805. Thomas and Martha Winslow were parents of six children, namely, Nixon, John, Nancy, Peninah, Charles and David, all deceased. Nixon Winslow came with his parents to Fairmount Township in 1836, when he was five years old. He was educated in the common schools of the log-cabin period, when reading, writing and arithmetic were about the extent of the mental training received. At twenty-one years of age he began to carve out a fortune of his own. His first investment was the purchase of eighty acres of land, bought with money earned at hard labor. He kept adding to this possession until at one time he had acquired over five hundred acres. He was President of the Citizens Exchange Bank from 1893 to 1909, being a heavy stockholder in this institution. In politics he was affiliated with the Republican party, in later life identifying himself with the Prohibitionists. He was, all his life, a member of the Friends Church, being for many years an elder. During the Civil War he was drafted, but faithful to the principles of the Society of Friends and true to the doctrines of his forefathers, he paid $300 rather than enter the army. His wife's maiden name was Cynthia Ann Jay, born in Miami County, Ohio, May 5, 1832. Her parents were Denny and Mary Jay, he born April 24, 1809, and she on January 18, 1809. Their children were Susan Ratliff, Cynthia A. Winslow, Keturah Rush, Elisha J. Jay, Elvira Small, Jesse Jay, Thomas Ellwood Jay, David A. Jay, Mary J. Nixon, Denny Jay and Lambert B. Jay. October 25, 1854, Nixon Winslow and Cynthia Ann Jay were married at Jonesboro. To this

NIXON WINSLOW

union seven children were born.: Luvenia, February 24, 1856, married John Kelsay; Webster J., January 15, 1858, married Mary Jean, and after her death was wedded to Ora E. Winslow; Mary Ella, October 31, 1859, unmarried and at home with her mother; T. Denny, October 28, 1861, married Anna Ellis; Ancil, December 29, 1864, married Ida Elliott; Clinton, June 1, 1869, married Myrtle Ellis, and Marcus A., September 24, 1871, who passed away July 12, 1874. The sons and daughters of this esteemed couple all reside in Fairmount and the surrounding community.

John Kelsay and wife are parents of seven children, three now living, namely, Guy Kelsay, of Anderson, and Oren and Mary, at home. Webster and first wife had three children, one living, Mrs. Will Jones. Denny and wife had four, three living; Ancil and wife, two, and Clinton and wife, one.

Nixon and Cynthia Winslow lived together fifty-six years, were life-long Friends, and all their children are members of this denomination. There are ten living grandchildren and sixteen great-grandchildren. If recorded in detail the good deeds of this worthy man and wife would fill many columns. It is enough to say that they built wisely and well in their own day and generation. The example of their noble lives will be an inspiration to those who follow in the years to come.

LEVI WINSLOW

Levi Winslow, son of Henry Winslow and grandson of Joseph Winslow, was born in Fairmount Township on July 20, 1836. Levi Winslow remembers the old log meeting house which was the place of worship for Friends until 1841, when the red-brick structure was ready for use. Joseph Winslow sat at the head of the meeting for many years. He was a Quaker of the strictest sort, very plain in manner and dress. Levi Winslow lives near Jonesboro, on the farm formerly owned by the late Jack Winslow, who was a son of Thomas Winslow, another pioneer. In early life Levi Winslow was a carpenter and has helped to build many of the homes still standing in this Township. He is a member of the Society of Friends, and attends services as often as health will permit.

CHAPTER XX.

CAPT. DAVID L. PAYNE.

CAPT. DAVID L. PAYNE was the son of William and Celia (Lewis) Payne, who lived four miles east of Fairmount.

Payne received a rudimentary education in the schools of his boyhood days. Perhaps no other man born and reared in Fairmount Township attained to such distinction in frontier work and in the building up of the great West as did Captain Payne. He was as dashing and picturesque in real life as he was in his personal appearance. Long after he had departed for the West he continued to make visits periodically to his old home. He was born in 1836.

Gabrille Havens, who remembers Payne quite well as a small boy, relates that he was precocious, witty, and possessed an abundance of initiative.

THE WILLIAM PAYNE HOMESTEAD

Located about two miles southwest of Fowlerton. In the foreground of the above picture is shown Trustee David G. Lewis, a nephew of the pioneer. It was on this farm that Capt. David L. Payne was born and reared to manhood. William Payne was born in Georgia. He was a farmer throughout his life. He had a common school education. He was a close observer and a strict disciplinarian. The original homestead comprised one hundred and twenty acres, entered in 1835. In politics William Payne was a Democrat. He was a member of the Methodist Church, and attended services at Sugar Grove. His wife was Celia Lewis, sister of David Lewis. Mrs. Payne was a native of Franklin County, Indiana. William and Celia Payne were the parents of ten children, namely: Jack, Morgan L., James G.,* Wesley, David L., John, Allen W., Margaret, William and Jennie. William Payne died at his home September 10, 1875. Celia, his wife, passed away May 16, 1870. Their remains lie in the Fankboner Graveyard, where rest all that is mortal of many of their relatives and friends of pioneer days.

It is related that in the early day a plant had been discovered over on the river that was good for rheumatism, which in that time was a common complaint. Payne had a little touch of rheumatism, and when it was suggested one day that he try the new remedy he replied that it would not do for him, though it might be good for others, as he had understood that the medicine was a Payne killer, and he wanted to live a long while yet.

Mrs. George W. Bowers was among Payne's early teachers. Captain Payne and John W. Furnish, who until recently resided at Jonesboro, were intimate boyhood friends. Furnish is a grandson of Benjamin F. Furnish, well known as a pioneer associate judge of the Circuit Court.

Furnish relates that his first acquaintance with Payne was formed when they attended a school taught by William H. H. Reeder in John Brewer's kitchen, about the winter of 1851-1852. There were about twenty other children in attendance at this school.

In 1859, having secured what was for that day a fair education, Payne, accompanied by his brother, Jack, went West and located in

---

*Henry Elsberry Payne was born in Fairmount Township on October 10, 1862. His paternal grandparents were William and Celia (Lewis) Payne. His maternal grandparents were Henry and Mary (Parsons) Osborn. James G. and Louisa J. (Osborn) Payne, the father and mother, were both natives of Fairmount Township, the former born in 1832, and died November 28, 1877, and the latter, born April 22, 1833, died October 16, 1915. James G. and Louisa J. Payne were the parents of nine children, namely: Amanda, Henry E., W. Zimri, David L., Emma O., Joseph C., Minnie M., Mark and James G., Jr. H. E. Payne was educated in the common schools of Fairmount Township. From boyhood he has always worked on a farm, and with such industry and ability has he applied himself that today he is the owner of seventy-two acres of good land, situated three miles southeast of Fairmount. He is a stockholder of the Citizens Telephone Company. In politics he is a Prohibitionist, and his church affiliations are with the Methodist Protestant denomination. He has been honored by his party friends with the nomination for Township Trustee, polling the full strength of his party, with many accessions from other political organizations. He also has been frequently called upon to act as administrator and executor of estates, thus attesting to his sound business judgment and absolute integrity. February 29, 1884, he was married to Miss Effie C. Smith, born in Fairmount Township June 7, 1863, and a daughter of Roland and Nancy (Hasting) Smith. Mr. and Mrs. Payne are the parents of six children, namely: Myrtle, deceased; Stella, Wessie, Lucille, Nellie and Madeline. Myrtle, who married Will Leach, died October 27, 1910.

Brown County, Kansas. He took part in the Border-Ruffian War in 1859-1860, in Kansas and Missouri.

In 1861, upon the outbreak of the Civil War, he enlisted in the Seventh Kansas Cavalry. During his service in this command Payne distinguished himself by his courageous conduct and was promptly promoted to the rank of captain. He was with General Fremont in the latter's operations through the West, and was serving under Colonel Sullivan at the time Sullivan was in pursuit of Price in Missouri. Colonel Sullivan was killed at Springfield in a hot engagement.

After the Civil War Payne went with the command of Gen. George Custer and fought the fierce Comanche Indians with that brave officer through Kansas and Colorado.

In 1865, having returned to his Kansas home, Payne was elected from Brown County to the Kansas State Legislature.

In 1870, having taken up his residence in Sedgwick County, he was elected Senator from this county in the State Legislature.

In 1881 Captain Payne conceived the idea of starting an agitation for the opening of Oklahoma Territory to settlement. It was at this time that Furnish was called by Payne to the position of private secretary. Payne caused to be printed and circulated many thousand bills and circulars announcing his purpose to open Oklahoma to settlement. Payne stated in his circulars that he would locate parties on the land, and proceeded to form a stock company for the purpose of securing the necessary funds with which to push his enterprise. Headquarters were established at Wichita. The shares were sold at five dollars each. About three

CAPT. DAVID L. PAYNE

thousand different investors became interested in the movement, and in 1883, headed by Payne, these stockholders moved into the Territory. Captain Payne, Couch, Smith and two other leaders of the colonists, were promptly arrested by the Government police and taken to Ft. Smith. Payne offered no resistance to the orders of the Territorial police, and quietly instructed his people to calmly submit to lawful authority.

The arrest of Payne, Couch and Smith had the desired effect. Payne's purpose was to start an agitation which would create a sentiment favorable to his project. Events which followed later showed his calculations to have been correct. He was at no time hostile to the Government. He always recognized the right of properly constituted authority to eject his people from the Territory, but it was his firm conviction that Oklahoma should be opened to the public for settlement, and he was impressed with the idea that already this important step had too long been deferred by the Government. A few days after Payne and his comrades were taken to Ft. Smith they were released.

Returning to Wichita, Payne again renewed his agitation, and was again organizing his following for another entry into the Territory. Before the expedition began its march, Payne had prepared a plat for the location of Oklahoma City. Entering the Territory again in 1883, Captain Payne was promptly arrested. The Government police took into custody ten or twenty of the leaders, and they, with Payne, were confined in the prison at Ft. Smith.

Being again released, Payne organized the third expedition for the trip into the Territory. Again he was seized and sent to Ft. Smith, this time for thirty days, when he was released under bond.

Returning again to Wichita, he began once more to organize a company for another invasion. His headquarters were changed to Wellington, Kansas. Before his plans were fully completed for the fourth effort to reach Oklahoma he died suddenly in 1884 at his hotel in Wellington.

During this prolonged fight, which covered a period equal to the duration of the Civil War, Captain Payne became a National figure. He had the sympathy and support of many followers in various parts of the United States.

His printing press, on which he printed the first newspaper ever published in Oklahoma, was seized by the authorities and thrown into the Chickaskia River. It is related that he was once chained behind a slowly moving ox-cart and compelled to walk the entire distance across eastern Oklahoma to Ft. Smith.

In a short time final action was taken by the Government for the opening of the Territory. Had Payne lived to see the Territory thrown open to settlement, he would undoubtedly have been elected Governor or one of the first United States Senators from Oklahoma.

Captain Payne was a natural orator of great magnetism and considerable power. His language, though not of the finest quality, was nevertheless logical and convincing. His power over men was rarely equaled. He was liberal to a fault. No worthy person ever appealed to him in vain for financial assistance. He was a friend of the poor. In the West, when he was in the midst of his tempestuous career, he was known among the people as "Ox-Heart" Payne. He was always considerate and courteous to all with whom he came in contact. In his personal relations he was always a gentleman, never quarrelsome or rude, and it is said that he was never known to take part in an argument of any kind.

Mr. Furnish, Payne's secretary, who gave the writer these facts, served three years in the Thirty-fourth Indiana Infantry during the Civil War under Col. Ab Steele. Furnish lost his left arm while in the service, at Algiers, Louisiana.

The writer is indebted to William Z. Payne, nephew of Captain Payne, for the following very interesting narrative written by E. C. Cole, an intimate friend and follower of Captain Payne. The story was printed first in book form, in 1885, and is replete with illustrations showing the camp life and the many daring exploits in which Captain Payne had a leading part. Mr. Cole says:

"With the recent death of the Hon. David L. Payne, the great interest already agitating the people, and in fact the whole world on both sides of the Atlantic—the Oklahoma country and the Indian Territory—is increased tenfold. That the great mass of the people are crazed over this most beautiful country is no wonder to the average man of today.

"Among the statesmen, soldiers, and pioneers, David L. Payne's name stands foremost in the history of this country—Oklahoma. His sterling qualities, his faithful friendship, unwavering in devotion and constant as a polar star, have endeared him to those who knew him best. Who ever spent an hour in his friendly company without feeling his life's burdens as a feather? Conscious that you were with one whom you were proud to call your friend—a convivial companion, and a true gentleman in every sense that the word implies. Rudeness and vulgarity were never a portion of your entertainment in his company. His camp was your home; his noble heart your solace. He had the generosity of a prince. His purse was ever open in behalf of those around him who were more in need than himself. When more was needed his industry would procure it. He had friends—indeed, who was not his friend? Of his enemies, they were few, and of them we need not speak. He was brave and true. He had a heart, when touched, full of love and the pity of a woman. He had faults that were his own; they were few and easily forgotten. He had more brains than books, more sense than education, more courage and strength than polish. Hatred can not reach him more. He sleeps in the sanctuary of the tomb, beneath the quiet of the stars. He did not live to see the sunshine of his dearest hope matured, but left the field for his successor to see his great ambition attained—that noble country —Oklahoma—opened up for settlement by the white man, and the millions of acres of land made into bright and happy homes, occupied, free and unmolested, by the poor and struggling homesteaders.

"David L. was born in Grant County, Indiana, on the thirtieth day of December, 1836, where he received the usual country school education in the winter, working upon his father's farm in the summer time. He was bright and forcible in character from his youth, and became more than an average scholar. Being a lover of hunting and adventurous sports, he, in the spring of 1858, with his brother, started West with the intention of engaging in the Mormon War, which was creating great excitement at that time throughout the whole country, and especially in the West. Reaching Doniphan County, Kansas, he found the excitement somewhat abated. Inducements being offered, Payne pre-empted a body of land and erected a saw-mill thereon. This investment, while flattering at the start, proved an unfortunate enterprise, and young Payne found himself entirely destitute of means. He was placed, so to speak, upon his own metal. With an active brain that would acknowledge no defeat, he soon found an occoupation of a most congenial character.

"At the time of Payne's settlement, Doniphan County, now a fertile and thickly populated section, was the grazing ground for vast herds of buffalo, deer, antelope, wolves and other wild animals native to the plains. He became a hunter. There he hunted with much success, as well as profit. He gradually extended his field to the southwest until he had penetrated the Magillion Mountains of New Mexico and explored the course of the Cimarron River through the Indian Territory, and so became familiar and acquainted with the topographical situation of the great Southwest. He naturally drifted from hunting to that of scouting. He was soon engaged by private parties on expeditions, and after a time, by the Government. He became the comrade of all the distinguished trappers, guides and hardy characters of that wild country. His intimacy with Kit Carson, Wild Bill, California Joe, Buffalo Bill, General Custer, and many others of national reputation, approached companionship.

"When the Civil War came Payne was one of the first to volunteer his services, joining the Fourth Regiment of Kansas Volunteers, which was subsequently consolidated with the Third Infantry; shortly afterwards the two were formed into the Tenth Regiment. He served three years as private, refusing during the time six different tenders of commission. At the expiration of his three years' term he returned to Doniphan County, Kansas, and, in the fall of 1864, was elected to the Legislature of Kansas, serving in the sessions of 1864 and 1865, during which time, while never courting the part of an orator, his influence was pronounced. At the close of the Legislature he again volunteered as a private, taking the place of a poor neighbor who was drafted. He felt that he was better able to stand the hardships, and leave his friend and neighbor at home with his large and dependent family. Payne, upon re-entering the service, assisted in recruiting a company for General Hancock's corps of volunteers, and succeeded in enlisting one hundred and nine men, all hardy frontiersmen, who were devotedly attached to him. Again Payne refused to accept a commission, preferring to remain a private and with his friends.

"Payne's services in the volunteer army extended over a period of eight years, first as a private in Company F, Tenth Regiment, Kansas Infantry, from August, 1861, until August, 1864. His second enlistment was in Company G, Eighth Regiment of Western Volunteers, and as a private from March, 1865, until March, 1866. His third service was as captain of Company D of the Eighteenth Kansas Cavalry, where he served from October, 1867, until November of the same year; and his last service was in the Regular Army, as captain of Company H, of the Nineteenth Kansas Cavalry, in which he served from October, 1868, until October, 1869. In the meantime he performed other services of great value to the State. He was at one time Postmaster at Fort Leavenworth; also appointed Sergeant-at-Arms, for two terms, of the Kansas State Senate; and in 1875 and 1876 he was doorkeeper to the House of Representatives in Congress, at Washington, D. C. Besides engaging in political campaigns that gave him social and acknowledged influence as a leader, he was an ardent supporter of Gen. Tom Ewing, who, after serving a term as Chief Justice of Kansas, sought the great honor of United States Senator. It is credited to Capt. D. L. Payne that General Ewing received his nomination through his influence and support; and such were his efforts in behalf of General Ewing that they remained ever afterwards warm and steadfast friends.

"During the Rebellion, Captain Payne was attached to the Army of the Frontier, under General Blunt, and was engaged in nearly all of the memorable conflicts that took place in Missouri and Arkansas, distinguished for the desperate fighting and mortality of men. He was a participant in the battle of Prairie Grove, Arkansas, which occurred on the seventh day of December, 1862; and in this engagement he performed an act of gallantry which entitled him to a place in history. In the hottest of the fight his first lieutenant, Cyrus Leland, was shot through the arm, and then through the right shoulder. The enemy, having recovered from the charge, and reinforced, poured a deadly fire into the ranks of Captain Payne's company. The commanding officer ordered his men to fall back. Captain Payne, seeing his brave comrade lying upon the ground, while the maddened enemy was charging and ready to trample him under, stepped out of the ranks and lifted up the almost lifeless lieutenant and bore him upon his shoulders for fully one-half mile to his own tent, where surgical attendance saved the life of his friend. Lieutenant Leland was afterwards appointed Adjutant-General upon General Ewing's staff, and is now a wealthy citizen of Troy, Kansas, a living evidence of Payne's heroism and devotion. During the session of 1864 and 1865 Payne opposed the Special Bounty Act, purely upon patriotic grounds. However, the act was passed; but he refused to accept it for his own use, but donated it to the county which he represented, thus sustaining his honesty and consistency.

"After the close of the War, Payne again resumed the occupation of plainsman, hunting, scouting and guarding caravan trains. From nature he was congenial; from his commanding figure and ways, he was held in respect by the most daring desperado and the wild Indians of the plains, and earned for himself the name of the Cimarron Scout. The Indian Territory, the courses of the Cimarron River and the Great Salt Basin were as familiar to him as his childhood playground. But few men knew as well the Indian character as he, and his numerous conflicts with the Cheyennes, Arapahoes, Kiowas and Navajoes were numerous and beyond description.

"In the year 1870 Captain Payne removed to Sedgwick County, Kansas, near Wichita, and the following year he was again elected to the Legislature, from Sedgwick County; and during that session through his influence Sedgwick County was divided and a new county formed from the northern portion and called Harvey County. In the redistricting, one of the longest townships was called Payne Township, and for many years it was his home, where he owned a large ranch, about ten miles east of Wichita.

"In 1879, Captain Payne became interested in a movement for the occupation and settlement of a district in the Indian Territory known as Oklahoma, which, in the Indian language, signifies Beautiful Land. This Beautiful Land is located in the center of Indian Territory, and comprises an area of fourteen million acres of the finest land on the American continent. Captain Payne claimed the right to settle on this land under the treaty made by the Government with the Indians, in 1866, by which this district ceded to the United States and became a part of the public domain, and was actually surveyed and set apart as such. Through his personal endeavors a large colony was organized for the purpose of entering and settling upon these lands. The colony moved, early in December, 1880, and first assembled upon the borders of the Territory, near Arkansas City, on the banks of Bitter Creek; and after organizing upon a military basis moved along the State line to Hunnewell, where they went into camp. The colony was closely followed by the United States Cavalry under command of Colonel Copinger, who had previously informed the intending colonists that any attempt to enter the Indian Territory would be forcibly resisted, the President of the United States having issued a proclamation to that effect. At Hunnewell the troops occupied one side of the creek and the colonists the other. The latter remained in camp for three days, receiving a great many recruits from western Kansas. On Sunday, the 12th, the camp was crowded during the day with the inhabitants of the surrounding country, who came, some from sympathy and some from curiosity. In the afternoon there was a dress parade by the colonists, and fully six hundred men were in line. The wagons numbered three hundred and twenty-five, with a goodly number of women and children. During the afternoon of this memorable Sabbath day the colonists held Divine service, conducted by the colony chaplain. The United States troops were invited to attend, which they did, officers and soldiers. The services were opened by that old familiar air, 'America,' and the text was from Exodus: 'The Lord commandeth unto Moses "to go forth and possess the promised land."' Appropriate hymns were sung, and the services were closed with the rendition of 'The Star-Spangled Banner.' The feelings and emotions were visibly manifested on all sides, and officers and soldiers affected alike. The Stars and Stripes were fanning the breezes of a beautiful day from both camps. The wagons were covered by banners with such mottoes as:

"'Strike for Your Homes!'

"'No Turn Back!'

"'On to Oklahoma!'

"And sundry other devices. In the evening, council was held as to what course to pursue. It was decided to wait a few days for some modification of the President's orders. Receiving no answer from the petition that had been forwarded to the President, and getting somewhat uneasy, some proposed to enter the land in spite of the military. A meeting was held on the thirteenth day of December, at which Dr. Robert Wilson, of Texas, was appointed a committee of one to go to Washington, D. C., and see if something could be done at once to relieve the critical situation of the colonists. On the fourteenth day of December the colony moved on to Caldwell, some thirty-five miles, where they were joined by five more wagons and twenty men. The mayor and a long processsion of citizens escorted them through the town, ladies waving handkerchiefs and men and children cheering. The troops moved along with the colonists without interfering with their progress. The day following, a mass meeting was held by the citizens of Caldwell, resolutions were adopted indorsing the movement to settle these lands, and asking the President to order the troops to accompany the colonists to Oklahoma as an escort. Being unable to induce Congress or the President to move in their behalf, the colonists became restive, and shortly afterwards—Captain Payne having been arrested by the United States authorities, charged with trespassing upon Indian lands, and thus deprived of their leader—the colonists temporarily disbanded. Captain Payne was taken to Ft. Smith, before the United States District Court, Judge Barker presiding, and on the seventh of March, 1881, was tried before the Court. Captain Payne was ably represented by Judge Barker, of St. Louis, Missouri, who argued at length the Treaty of 1866. The question raised by Captain Payne's arrest involved directly the nature and validity of that treaty, and hence means were offered for testing a point upon which the Secretary of the Interior and the ablest lawyers of the country were at variance, the latter holding that Oklahoma was a part of the public domain and subject to settlement the same as other public lands. Captain Payne at this trial was nominally bound over under bonds of $1,000 not to re-enter the Territory, and returned home.

"Since the above arrest Captain Payne has made four well-organized expeditions into the Territory, each time safely landing upon the Oklahoma lands, and there laid out towns, located farms, plowed and planted, built houses, and has as often been turned out by the United States military, seen his property destroyed before his eyes, and forced to the Kansas line, and there turned loose, he each time demanding a trial before the courts. His last expedition was in the spring and summer of 1884. He had with him two hundred and fifty wagons and about five hundred men, all being again dispersed by the United States troops and escorted to the Kansas line. Captain Payne and his officers were arrested and dragged through the Territory to the Texas line, thence back to the interior of the Territory, marched on foot, and often suffering for the want of food and water, the object seeming to be to wear them out; and then taken to Ft. Smith, and there refused a trial; then taken from there to the United States Court at Topeka, Kansas, where public sentiment finally demanded a trial, which he was accorded at the fall term of 1884, and which resulted in a decision that he was guilty of no crime; that the lands upon which he sought to settle were public lands. Elated with this decision, he returned to Wichita, Kansas, and, though shaken in health from exposure and exhaustion, he at once proceeded to gather about him his faithful followers. He soon found himself with the largest and strongest expedition that he had ever yet organized; and in a few days he would have marched at its head to the promised land, when, suddenly, on the morning of November 28, 1884, while at breakfast at the Hotel de Barnard, in Wellington, Kansas, he fell dead in the arms of a faithful servant. He died without pain or struggle. His body is buried in a metallic casket at Wellington, Kansas, and was followed to its present resting place by the largest concourse of people that ever gathered together for a like purpose in southern Kansas. They numbered many thousands. The time will come when his body will find a permanent resting place beneath a monument erected to him in the great square of the capital of the State of Oklahoma.

"Personally, Captain Payne was one of the most popular men on the Western frontier. He was a natural-born scout, and inured to the hardships of the Western frontier. His mother was a cousin of the celebrated David Crockett, for whom he was named. Captain Payne was never married."

CHAPER XXI.

DULINGS, REEDERS AND SIMONSES.

THOMAS D. DULING, SR., was born in Hampshire County, Virginia, November 22, 1811. With his parents, Edmund and Mary (Dean) Duling, he moved in the fall of 1815 to Coshocton County, Ohio. On February 4, 1836, he was married to Nancy Meskimen, daughter of William and Anna (Shryock) Meskimen, her father a merchant of Baltimore, Maryland, where she was born. John Meskimen, great-grandfather of Thomas D. Duling, Jr., was a soldier under Gen. George Washington, serving through the entire period of the Revolutionary War with a regiment of Maryland colonial troops. Thomas D. Duling, Sr., came to Fairmount Township in the spring of 1845. He bought of Nathan Dicks eighty acres of land located about one-half mile north and west of Fowlerton. Here he built a hewed-log cabin eighteen by twenty feet, with one door, two windows and a fireplace. Having made preparations for a home, he returned to Ohio, and on October 3, 1845, with his wife and family, namely, William M., Mary, John and Barbara Ann, came in a two-horse wagon to settle in the wilderness. This wagon Duling traded to George Nose for clearing twelve acres of ground. Here Elizabeth, Thomas D., Jr., Joel O. and George E. W. Duling were born. Elizabeth passed away at fifteen years of age, and George died September 2, 1894. The father and his family shared the hardships common to pioneers of that day. The first season he cleared six acres of land out of the green woods and planted a crop of corn. Each season he added more acreage to his cleared ground. Being industrious and thrifty he began to accumulate. He bought, in 1849, another eighty of Aaron Vestal, and about 1860 he

THOMAS D. DULING, SR.

purchased of the William Chamness estate eighty acres more. In politics Mr. Duling was a Republican and a pronounced Abolitionist. The Dulings are members of the Methodist Protestant Church, and have given liberally of their means and have devoted their activities to the firm establishment of this denomination in their neighborhood.

Thomas D. Duling, Sr., to whom extended references have been made in former articles, came to this Township in 1845. He taught two terms of school in the early day, the attendance one winter being so large that he was obliged to employ an assistant, who was Oliver Meskimen, of Linton, Ohio. In 1846 Mr. Duling was named one of the Township Trustees for a period of three years. On October 31, 1846, he gave bond for the faithful performance of his duties, with Henry Simons as his surety. Mr. Duling continued to serve in this position until 1860. The old log school house having burned in 1855, steps were taken at once to build a new one in his district. He offered one-half acre of land free as a site. This site was situated on the northeast corner of the west half of the northwest quarter of Section 25. He provided that this school house, which was known as the Liberty school house, should be open for all religious meetings, no denomination barred, when not occupied for school purposes. This building was completed in 1855. It was in this building that Mary Ann Taylor taught when a very young woman. Mr. Duling's home was the scene of much hospitality. It was here that teachers usually made their home, and itinerant ministers of all denominations found a characteristic pioneer welcome. Thomas Duling was a man of considerable education for his day, and in a few instances young men would not undertake to teach school in his neighborhood unless first assured of Mr. Duling's assistance and advice. It was he, with the help of his sons, William M. and John W. Duling, who

EDMUND DULING

Was a pioneer who settled in Fairmount Township in 1845. Mr. Duling served as Commissioner from the Third District during the Civil War, and in many ways did his part to make this community what it is today.

got out the huge timbers, sills, posts and beams that were used in the construction of the old Duling home which was burned last winter. In finishing the interior of this house the best walnut lumber obtainable in that day was used.

William M. Duling, son of Thomas D. and Nancy (Meskimen) Duling, is a native of Coshocton County, Ohio, where he was born on May 22, 1837. He came with his parents to Fairmount Township in 1845. He was educated in the common schools of Coshocton County, Ohio, and Grant County, Indiana, being a pupil at different times of William H. H. Reeder, George W. Bowers and Columbus Lay. Mr. Duling has all his life been engaged in agricultural pursuits and has been quite successful. In politics he first affiliated with the Republican party, later identifying himself with the Prohibtionists. He has been for many years a prominent member of the Methodist Protestant Church. During the Civil War he served from 1864 to 1865 as a private with Company I of the Seventy-ninth Indiana Volunteers. On September 3, 1862, he was married to Miss Matilda J. Wilson, born in Jefferson Township, June 30, 1844. She was the daughter of John M. and Mary Ann (Lucas) Wilson, early settlers in Grant County. Mr. and Mrs. Duling are the parents of seven children, namely: Mary, John M., Flora L., Frank, Eva, Oliver and Effie, all living. They have sixteen grandchildren and five great-grandchildren. Much of the information appearing in this story regarding the Lake Galatia neighborhood was supplied by, or has been verified by Mr. Duling, who is still hale and hearty, though eighty years old.

WILLIAM M. DULING

Thomas D. Duling, Jr., son of Thomas D. Duling, Sr., was born in Fairmount Township October 22, 1849. His paternal grandparents were Edmund and Mary (Dean) Duling, and his maternal grandparents were William and Anna (Shryock) Meskimen. Thomas D., Jr., was educated in the common schools of Fairmount Township, one of his teachers being William H. H. Reeder, frequently mentioned as a highly efficient teacher of the pioneer period. Mr. Duling has lived his entire life in his native Township. He owns a splendid farm of eighty acres, and has served as director, part of the time as treasurer of the Barren Creek Gas Company, which he helped to organize and became one of the first stockholders. In politics he identified himself with the Republican party when he attained his majority, later joining the Prohibitionists. He is an active and influential member of the Methodist Protestant Church at Fowlerton.

THOMAS D. DULING, JR.

On February 13, 1875, he was married to Miss Laney Ellen Dean, born in Owen County, Indiana, July 29, 1850. Mrs. Duling died December 25, 1900. Mr. and Mrs. Duling were the parents of three children, namely: Melissa H., now the wife of Milton A. Rich; Sina Emily, wife of Lowry Glass, and Barbara L., who died February 27, 1891, aged about five years. Mr. Duling remembers many of the pioneers who have been mentioned in this story, and has lived his entire life in Fairmount Township.

REEDER FAMILY.

(By Bishop Milton Wright)

Jonathan Franklin Reeder and William Henry Harrison Reeder were among the pioneers of Grant County. They entered the land of which they afterward made homes for life in the year 1837. They settled in the southeastern part of Fairmount Township, and did their part in clearing up the forests. Both of them were of Rush County,

Indiana, to which their parents had removed when they were young from Montgomery County, Ohio, where William was born, November 15, 1813, Franklin having been born in Hamilton County, Ohio, June 18, 1806. The removal of their parents to Rush County was in the fall of 1822, where the father, George Reeder, died May 13, 1845, and the mother, September 12, 1858, both quite aged.

This George Reeder's ancestors, for the four generations preceding him, had the name of Joseph. The first Joseph Reeder was the grandson of William Reader (Wilhelm Leser), of the Kingdom of Hanover, in Germany, who removed to England, probably before the year 1600, and his grandson Joseph came to Newton (Township), Long Island, New York, about 1650. He had with him John Reeder and perhaps other brothers. From this John is descended, in the sixth generation, Governor Andrew H. Reeder (1854), of Kansas, the true Free State man. The descent was thus: 1. John; 2. John; 3. Isaac; 4. John; 5. Absalom; 6. Andrew H.

The four successive ancestors by the name of Joseph followed agricultural pursuits on farms of their own, and all of them, except the first Joseph, were members of the Presbyterian Church, and citizens of industry and much respectability. The last two were deacons in the church and noted for good sense, honesty and piety, as was George, who was an elder in the church nearly all his life. All the Joseph ancestors had each two or more sons, who married, and from them are descended many of the Reeders of the different states. The second Joseph ancestor, probably late in life, removed to Morris County, New Jersey. His son, Jacob, is celebrated in the early history of Newton for his education, fine character and usefulness. (Reeder was formerly spelled Reader.)

Joseph Reeder the third married in Hopewell, New Jersey, about 1740, as his second wife, Susana Gano, daughter of Daniel Gano, and great-granddaughter of Francis Gano, a wealthy Huguenot, of Rochelle, France, who, after the revocation of the Edict of Nantes, barely escaped martyrdom by fleeing with his children and their families, about 1686, first to Guernsey Island, and thence to America, and he died at New Rochelle, New York, aged one hundred and three years. Joseph and Susana had a large family, of whom six sons lived to have large families, and all of them settled in the Miami Valley, Ohio. In 1763 he had settled in Loudoun County, Virginia, and his son, Joseph, the fourth, having married Anna Huff, in New Jersey, removed to the same county in 1766, and a number of years later removed to Hampshire County, now in West Virginia, and lived on the Great Cacapon

River, whence with all his family he removed to Hamilton County, Ohio, in 1789. His son, George, married in Cincinnati, June 2, 1796, Margaret Van Cleve, daughter of John Van Cleve, who was killed by Indians there June 1, 1791. John was descended, in the fourth generation, from John Van Cleve, a Hollander, who came to Long Island, New York, in 1650; and, in the fifth generation, from John Vanderbilt, also a Hollander, who settled at Gravesend the same year, and New Utrecht, Long Island, in 1659. This John Vanderbilt was the father of Aris Vanderbilt and grandfather of Jacob Vanderbilt, the ancestor of Commodore Cornelius Vanderbilt. The foregoing is an abridged sketch of the ancestral history of Franklin and William Reeder, pioneers in Fairmount Township.

The Reeders had one brother and four sisters who lived to have families, the brother, George, the last surviving of his father's family, dying in Hutchinson, Kansas, August, 1900. One of the sister's husbands was Dan Wright, father of Rev. Harvey Wright, Bishop Milton Wright and Rev. William Wright, whose son, Ellis, resides on a farm owned by him east of Fairmount. Another was Prof. Ryland T. Brown, of Northwestern Christian University, now Butler University, father of Capt. George Reeder Brown, who commanded the Ninth Indiana Battery through the Civil War. Another is John Braden, a retired merchant, of Greensburg, whose sons are merchants of Watseka, Illinois.

J. Franklin Reeder married in Rush County, Indiana, July 19, 1827, Nancy Furnish, and they had Mary Jane, Margaret, Phebe Catharine, Eliza and Asenath, all of whom married and have since died, except Eliza, and all had children. His wife, having died some years previously. Mr. Reeder, about 1853, married Fanny Broyles, by whom he had one son, George, and a daughter, the latter dying within a few years. The son married, removed to Michigan, and died some years afterward, leaving a widow and several children. Mr. Reeder's descendants are scattered, but those living in Fairmount Township are the children of Asenath, William Millspaugh, a former merchant at Fowlerton, and Mrs. Horace Reeve.

William H. H. Reeder, the pioneer, was of a fine mould mentally, morally and physically. Physically, of fine symmetry, handsome features, and of a magnetic temperament; mentally, of an active, acute and strong cast; morally, having a deep sense of the right and an abhorrence of anything unjust or wrong; with a ready tongue, accurate utterance and good voice, his conversational powers were fine; and if they had been so used he would have made an able and eloquent public speaker. But his ideas of the necessities of education forbade his entering public life, and probably his taste did not incline him to it. He was, however, a successful school teacher a small part of his long life. He died in honor among the best people, and having a very humble opinion of his own worthiness of everlasting life.

William H. H. Reeder married, in Decatur County, Indiana, August 18, 1847, Miss Elizabeth Dealy, and they were the parents of the following children, all born in Fairmount Township: Margaret Elizabeth, who married John W. Broyles, of Delaware County; Eliza Catharine, who married Joseph A. Broyles, of Delaware County; George, who died at thirteen years of age; Madora, who died at four; William Henry Harrison, who married Mattie Parks, of Jefferson Township, and who has served as Justice of the Peace; Flora M., who married Oliver A. Glass; Robert B., who married Hattie Glass. The older daughters have children and grandchildren. The two youngest children have each several children. William, who has no heirs, Flora, who resides on a farm of their own near Lincolnville, Wabash County, Indiana, and Robert all live on parts of the old homestead in Fairmount Township.

(Editor's Note.—Milton Wright, a pioneer of Fairmount Township, was born in Rush County, Indiana, in 1828, and died at his home, Oakwood, Dayton, Ohio, April 3, 1917. His paternal grandfather was Dan Wright, Sr., who was a soldier in the War of the Revolution, and participated in the Battle of Saratoga. His paternal antecedents traced their ancestry back to Samuel Wright, of England, whose descendants probably settled originally in Connecticut. His maternal grandparents were George and Peggy Reeder, of Ohio, the former born September 24, 1767, and died May 13, 1845. Dan Wright, Jr., father of Milton, was born September 3, 1790, at Centerville, Ohio, and died October 6, 1861. The mother, Catherine (Reeder) Wright, was born March 17, 1800, and died September 24, 1866. Dan Wright, Jr., and wife were the parents of five children, namely: Samuel Smith Wright, Harvey Wright, Milton Wright, Sarah Wright and William Wright, the latter the father of Ellis Wright, who resides southeast of Fowlerton. Milton Wright passed the early part of his life on the farm, attending country schools and for a time was a student at Hartsville College. When about twenty-one years of age he was a licensed exhorter in the United Brethren Church; in 1852 he was granted a license to preach; in 1856 he was ordained by Bishop David Edwards. In 1857 he was sent as a missionary to the Pacific Coast, and taught and preached in the region of Salem, Oregon, for two years. Returning East in 1859 he taught school a short time, and then served under the White River Conference until 1869 as pastor and presiding elder. He was the first authorized professor of theology in the church and taught at Hartsville College. He was elected to the general conference in 1861 and served forty-four years as a member of this body. In 1869 he was chosen editor of the

THE OLD W. H. H. REEDER HOMESTEAD

Located about one mile and a half southwest of Fowlerton. This hewn-log cabin was built by William Henry Harrison Reeder out of native timber in 1844, three years before his marriage. In the early day it was pointed out as the finest home in that part of the Township. Up to the time of its construction there were but very few two-story cabins in the new country of like dimensions and elegance. This cabin is still standing on the farm, which is yet in the hands of members of the original family, being now owned by a son, William H. H. Reeder. For many years the son occupied this comfortable cabin, until it was recently replaced by his present modern residence. The elder Reeder served in the Indiana State Militia before coming to Fairmount Township. It was in this cabin that the well known pioneer frequently presided as the arbiter in matters which came before him while serving as Justice of the Peace. In the early day William Henry Harrison Reeder was known far and near as a peacemaker. Upon many occasions he adjusted differences between neighbors which promised endless litigation and bitter enmities if carried into the courts. Well poised, with a mind keenly analytical, of discriminating judgment, and possessing a broad view of justice and equity, his upright character and profound knowledge of men and affairs enabled him to command the respect and confidence of all who knew him. In several disputes where there were prospects of contention and strife he proved to be the man of the hour. His tact and resourcefulness served him in good stead in rendering quietly and unobtrusively a good deal of important service to his pioneer friends. It was at this cabin home that many contentions were satisfactorily settled and friendships which might have been abruptly ended were made permanent and beneficial.

Religious Telescope, official publication of the church, in which capacity he served for eight years. In 1877 he was elected Bishop of the

Church, serving as such the remainder of his life. He was an ordained minister of the Gospel for sixty-one years, a record seldom equalled in the work for religious and moral uplift. In politics Bishop Wright was a Republican. November 24, 1859, he was married to Susan Catherine Koerner, of Union County, Indiana, who died in 1889. By this union five children were born, namely, Reuchlin, Lorin, Wilbur, Orville and Kathrin. Reuchlin was born in a two-story log cabin located northeast of Fowlerton; Lorin was born near Dublin, Indiana, and Wilbur, Orville and Kathrin were born at Dayton, Ohio. Wilbur and Orville Wright achieved world-wife fame by their invention of the aeroplane. This machine is now being utilized, with telling effect, in the greatest war of all history. It was an invention designed by these modest young men to bless and benefit mankind. It has by the exigencies of the hour been diverted from its original purpose to a potential agency of terrorism and destruction in the fiercest of all human conflicts.)

William H. H. Reeder was one of the most capable and conscientious teachers during the early period of the Township's history. The writer has the register of a school taught by this pioneer instructor in Union (now Fairmount) Township, commenced December 17, 1862. This record was kept by Mr. Reeder with scrupulous care. His penmanship is plain, easily understood, and would be a model for the present day. The record is kept on a blank arranged in his own way, and is concise. The names of his pupils are given. In most cases the age is accurately indicated. The names appearing are those of the best known families of that day, as follows:

W. H. H. REEDER

Name.	Age.
Elizabeth A. Adams	17
Sarah D. Adams	15
Avis Adams	10
Timothy Adams	12
Hannah L. Adams	7

John Wood	12	Mary Wood	14
Arnalda C. Wood	7	Elizabeth J. Payne	12
Catherine E. Mann	14	Martha A. Furnish	4
Mary J. Mann	6	Nancy A. Payne	13
George Mann	11	Martha E. Payne	11
William A. Mann	8	James Terrell	16
James W. Furnish	12	William Shields	8
Joseph M. Furnish	11	John Harris	20
Thomas J. Furnish	7	Sarah A. Payne	6
William F. Ward	11	Sylvester Payne	
David O. Ice	7	Andrew Mann	16
John S. D. Lewis	20	Charles Ice	17
Elizabeth Lewis	17	Margaret Payne	16
Susan Mason	15	Catharine A. Payne	6
Sidney J. Mason	13	Margaret E. Reeder	
Matilda Burk	13	Eliza C. Reeder	
Louisa Shields	17	John Payne	23
George Shields	13	John Rhoads	4
Alphis Shields	10	James B. Mann	
Allen W. Payne	17	Nancy Terrell	
William Payne	14	Sarah Terrell	
Sarah E. Wood	13	Luther Harrison	

McGuffey's Readers, Webster's Elementary Spelling Books, and Ray's and Talbots' Arithmetics were used as text books in that day.

ROBERT B. REEDER

Robert B. Reeder, one of the enterprising farmers of Fairmount Township, resides one mile and a half southwest of Fowlerton. He is a son of William Henry Harrison and Elizabeth (Dealy) Reeder, the father born at Centerville, Ohio, November 15, 1813, and the mother in Buckeye County, Kentucky, December 29, 1824. William Henry Harrison Reeder died at his home in Fairmount Township on June 24, 1885, and Mrs. Reeder passed away on May 6, 1892. George Reeder, the paternal grandfather, was born September 24, 1767, and married Margaret Van Cleve, at Cincinnati, Ohio, June 2, 1796. She

MR. AND MRS. O. M. BEVINGTON AND FAMILY

died September 12, 1858. George Reeder served as a captain in the American Army during the War of 1812. He died May 13, 1845.

Robert B. Reeder is a native of Fairmount Township, where he was born June 13, 1864. He was educated in the Township, attending school in winter and working on his father's farm in the spring and summer months. He owns a farm of one hundred acres, part of which is the original Reeder homestead, and has been quite successful in its management. In politics, Mr. Reeder is a Progressive Republican and has served several terms as a member of the Grant County Republican Central Committee. In 1912 he was the choice of the Progressive party for the nomination of Representative in the Legislature. As a member of Fowlerton Lodge No. 848, Independent Order of Odd Fellows, he passed all the chairs and was a delegate at one time to the grand lodge. On February 5, 1892, he was married to Miss Hattie Glass, a native of Rush County. Their children are Crystal, George S., B. Dora and Edgar C., all graduates of high school or common school.

SIMONS FAMILY.

(By John H. Simons.)

My father, Henry Simons, was born in Bradford County, Pennsylvania, May 15, 1815. He moved, with his father, about the year 1819, to Darke County, Ohio, where he grew to manhood. In the summer of 1837, probably July, he started West, on foot, to find some place to locate, where he could make himself a home for the future. He walked to Grant County, where, after spending some time looking for a location, he found eighty acres in Section 36, Fairmount Township, which had not been taken of the Government. Most of the land at that time which was thought to be of much account had been entered or bought by people hunting for homes. It was so wet and swampy that it was supposed to be nearly worthless for agricultural purposes.

After getting the description of the eighty acres, he started on foot to the Land Office at Ft. Wayne. He went north through the wilderness, traversing Grant and Huntington Counties, striking the canal at Lagro or Huntington, after which he walked along the towpath used for the mules and horses pulling the canal boats. These boats conveyed the products of the settlers to market, and bringing back such things as they could use. It took about three days to make the trip from southern Grant County to Ft. Wayne. Father said he never

HENRY SIMONS

Pioneer farmer, was a native of Bradford County, Pennsylvania. His father, Adrial Simons, was born April 9, 1792, and died February 26, 1876; his mother, Patsy (Merit) Simons, was born September 30, 1795, and died March 21, 1863. Henry Simons was persevering, industrious and thrifty, and at the time of his death, March 31, 1902, owned one hundred and sixty-five acres of good land. In politics he was a Republican. He was a member of the New Light Church, and did much in the early days of the Township toward the organization and establishment of this denomination. The influence of Henry Simons in his neighborhood was always exerted for the best interests, both material and moral, of the community.

suffered from thirst more than he did while walking on the towpath on his way to Ft. Wayne. There was plenty of water in the canal, but it was not fit to drink, and the settlements, where he could get a drink, were a great ways apart. After reaching Ft. Wayne, he found the Land Office and closed up the deal for the eighty acres. He left as payment for the land $100 in gold, which he had carried all the way on his trip from Ohio. After his purchase was made, he started on the return trip to Grant County, covering practically the same ground. Reaching the farm, he put out a deadening, after which he returned to Ohio to earn money and prepare to move to his newly acquired possessions.

By the summer of 1840 he was prepared to go West, he having previously married Phebe Thomas, who set out with him for Fairmount Township. Their mode of travel was by horses and wagon. They brought all of their possessions with them. They arrived at the home of their uncle, Bingham Simons, who lived a mile north, in the edge of Jefferson Township.

Leaving their goods at the home of their uncle, with the help of the early settlers he set out to cut logs and build a house in which to move his belongings. After three or four days they had logs cut and the house built and a door cut through the wall. Then they were ready to move into their own home. They were obliged to prop up clapboards to close the doorway at night while they slept, the wolves howling on the outside of their cabin.

To Henry and Phebe (Thomas) Simons were born six children, five sons and one daughter, namely, Jonathan, Martha Ann, Ransom Ellis, William and Adrial. One infant child was buried in the Fankboner Graveyard in 1841. Three others died of scarlet fever within one month of each other. William and Adrial Simons are still living. William resides in Fairmount and Adrial lives on his farm near the old home.

Phebe Simons was born in 1820 and died February 3, 1852.

In February, 1854, Henry Simons was united in marriage to Elizabeth Ann (Walker) Parrill. To this union were born seven children, five sons and two daughters, four of whom are living, namely, John H. Simons, Levi P. Simons, Mata M. Buller, and D. Wilson Simons, Morris, Arthur, Walker and a daughter having passed away in infancy.

Mata Buller and her husband, Oliver Buller, own the eighty acres bought of the Government by my father. There never has been but the one transfer made—the conveyance to Oliver and Mata Buller.

Elizabeth (Parrill) Simons died on March 29, 1899.

Henry Simons died March 31, 1902. He was the grandfather of twenty-three children, seventeen still living. Donna Jean Simons, first great-grandchild, daughter of Harry L. and Jessie Simons, was born on his one hundredth anniversary.

My great-grandfather, Adrial Simons, was a soldier in the Revolutionary War.

Below are the names of some of the pioneers of Fairmount Township fifty years or more ago, as the writer recollects them: Joseph Corn, Edmund Leach, I. N. Miller, Esom Leach, William H. H. Reeder, John R. Minton, Thomas Estell, John Leach, David Lewis, Elijah Ward, John Brewer, Stephen Brewer, Benjamin Ice, Edmund Duling, Thomas Duling, George Simons, George Nose, John Heavilin, Sr., Abraham Reeve, Elwood Smith, William Maynard, Milton Wright, William Payne and Absalom Furnish.

The only one living at the time this article is written, to my knowledge, is Bishop Milton Wright, who resides at Datyon, Ohio. (Bishop Wright has passed away since Mr. Simons prepared this matter.)

One of the first churches, if not the first, organized in the east end of the Township was organized at my father's house in 1842. Among some of the old records I have in my possession I find the following:

"September the 26, in the year of our Lord one thousand eight hundred and forty-two. We this day at Henry Simons', unite ourselves together as a branch of the Christian Church to take the Holy Scriptures as our only rule of faith and practice, as we have hereunto set our names. E. S. PARKS.

Samuel Todd.	Elizabeth Todd.	Sarah Ann Ervin.
Henry Simons.	Abraham Rader.	Christopher Mittank.
Anna M. Simons.	Martha Jane Rader.	Elizabeth Mittank.
William Ervin."		

This organization was called Barren Creek Christian Church. They built a log church on my father's farm soon after this organization. The pews were made by taking logs and splitting them and then they were hewn off smooth on the flat side, then a hole bored on the rounding side and wooden legs put in. They were then turned over and set in position ready for occupancy. This organization was kept up for a number of years, until better churches were built in the country nearby. Then the organization was abandoned, but the old log church stood near a half century.

CHAPTER XXII.

THE WILSONS.

RACHEL WILSON was born February 6, 1719, and departed this life January 5, 1785, aged sixty-nine years and eleven months. John Wilson was born January 10, 1725, and departed this life October 23, 1776, aged fifty-one years and nine months. John and Rachel Wilson were married January 16, 1758.

Joseph Wilson, son of John and Rachel, was born November 9, 1760. Sarah Charles, daughter of Samuel and Abigail Charles, was born April 20, 1761. Joseph Wilson and Sarah Charles were married June 11, 1780.

Rachel Wilson, daughter of Joseph and Sarah, was born September 20, 1781, and departed this life July 13, 1784, aged two years, nine months and twenty-three days.

John Wilson, son of Joseph and Sarah, was born July 13, 1784.

Samuel Wilson, son of Joseph and Sarah, was born January 28, 1787.

Joseph Wilson, son of Joseph and Sarah, was born September 8, 1788, and departed this life October 17, 1788, aged one month and nine days.

Henry Wilson, son of Joseph and Sarah, was born April 8, 1791.

Mary Wilson, daughter of Joseph and Sarah, was born August 31, 1793.

Abigail Wilson, daughter of Joseph and Sarah, was born March 22, 1796.

Nathan Wilson, son of Joseph and Sarah, was born November 29, 1800, and departed this life January 3, 1801, aged about five weeks.

Sarah Wilson departed this life October 10, 1803, aged forty-two years, five months and twenty days.

Joseph Wilson departed this life October 20, 1803, aged forty-two years, eleven months and ten days.

Mary Winslow, daughter of Henry and Elizabeth Winslow, was born July 20, 1797.

John Wilson, son of Joseph and Sarah Wilson, was born July 13, 1784.

John Wilson and Mary Winslow were married.

Jesse Ewell Wilson, son of John and Mary, was born on Sunday, July 14, 1816, at about half after 3 o'clock in the afternoon.

Nathan Darwin Wilson, son of John and Mary, was born on Sunday, December 21, 1817, at about half after 2 o'clock in the afternoon.

Cyrus Wilson, son of John and Mary, was born November 21, 1819.

Henry Wilson, son of John and Mary, was born December 27, 1821.

Nancy Wilson, daughter of John and Mary, was born December 15, 1823, about 10 o'clock in the evening.

Micajah Wilson, son of John and Mary, was born February 17, 1825, about 9 o'clock at night.

Elizabeth Wilson, daughter of John and Mary, was born February 22, 1827, about eighteen minutes past 2 o'clock in the morning.

Eliza Ann Wilson, daughter of John and Mary, was born May 2, 1829, about half after 2 o'clock in the morning.

John Milton Wilson, son of John and Mary, was born Friday, January 8, 1831, about half past 11 o'clock in the evening.

Lindsey Wilson, son of John and Mary, was born on Wednesday, December 19, 1832, about 8 o'clock at night.

Samuel Charles Wilson, son of John and Mary, was born on Tuesday, October 14, 1834, about five minutes after 4 o'clock in the evening.

Abigail Wilson, daughter of John and Mary, was born Tuesday, December 13, 1836, about 2 o'clock in the morning.

(By Webster Parry)

In eastern North Carolina, what is now Perquimans and Pasquotank Counties, the Wilsons were a prominent family of Quakers before the year 1700. Among the Friends families there in very early times were those of Michael, Jesse, Edward, Robert, James, Isaac and Benjamin Wilson, and probably others that I know nothing of. I suspect the Fairmount Township Wilsons were there as early as 1695 to 1700. I cannot certainly trace your family further back than to thy great-grandparents, John and Rachel Wilson. In fact, I know nothing further about them than that Rachel, the wife, was born February 6, 1719, and died January 7, 1785, and that they had at least one child, Joseph, thy grandfather, who married my great-grandfather's sister, Sarah Charles, on June 11, 1780. He, Joseph Wilson, was born November 9, 1760, and died October 20, 1803. His wife, Sarah Charles, was born April 2, 1761, and died either the same day as her husband or ten days previously. The records did not agree as to that. They were married at Symons Creek Meeting and lived in Perquimans County, North Carolina, near Nixonton, where most all of their children were born. Later they moved to Randolph County, North Carolina, where they died and were buried.

The Wilsons.

Samuel Wilson and Ruth Thornburgh were married at Uwarrie Meeting, Randolph County, North Carolina, in 1809. They had a family of thirteen children, eleven of whom married and generally had large families. They lived in Hamilton County, Indiana, and Ruth died there on March 15, 1860. Samuel then moved to Leavenworth County, Kansas, where he died. His descendants are widely scattered throughout Indiana, Missouri, Kansas, Nebraska, California and others of the far Western States. I think it likely that his sons, Henry, Eleazer, Samuel and Nathan, may still be living, as I have not heard of the death of either of them. Henry, born in 1815, was not long ago living at Santa Ana, California, almost totally blind.

Henry Wilson settled in Washington County, Indiana, and died there. By his first wife, who died in 1855, there were six children, of whom, I believe, but two daughters married. One of them, Priscilla, wife of Samuel Trueblood, may be still living. If so, she is eighty-one years old this month. Henry Wilson's second wife was a minister in the Society of Friends, and died in 1894. Henry Wilson's father and mother having died when Henry was a boy of twelve years, he was taken and reared by Benajah Hiatt, at New Garden, Guilford County, North Carolina. His first marriage occurred October 9, 1816, at Springfield Meeting, and on the twenty-eighth of the same month he and his bride started on the long and tedious trip to Indiana. He was a saddler by trade, and the shop which he built soon after arriving in Washington County, this State, was still standing a few years ago.

Mary Wilson and Owen Lindley were married in Washington County, Indiana, on the last day of September, 1819, and settled in Orange County, Indiana, where their seven children were born and where three of them were still living a few years ago. Owen Lindley came with his parents from Orange County, North Carolina, in 1811, when eighteen years of age, and died in 1871.

Abigail Wilson and Thomas Symons were married in 1818, in North Carolina. They moved to Indiana and Thomas died in 1839 near Dublin, in Wayne County. Abigail died near Carmel, Hamilton County, Indiana. They had seven children, of whom some are living, one or two of them in Hamilton County, Indiana.

The Wilsons are, I think, all of Irish descent, and I imagine that almost or quite all of the members of the family who were Friends (Quakers) and went to the Carolinas in early times were closely related to each other, but I have had no occasion to study the matter and it would be a task that would take both time and money to learn, if, indeed, it could be done at all. There were Wilsons who came with or about the time of William Penn and landed at Philadelphia. Some of these settled there, and in the country near there, and others moved south to Virginia and the Carolinas.

Richmond, Indiana, May 29, 1905.

(Editor's Note.—This matter was prepared by Webster Parry, of Richmond, Indiana, who for many years has been engaged in tracing the genealogy of different prominent families of Indiana for interested relatives. Mr. Parry is regarded as one of the best authorities in the State in matters of family antecedents, and has earned a wide reputation for his careful research along this line. It will be well to note that this letter was written in 1905. It was addressed to Samuel C. Wilson.)

Jesse E. Wilson, an early settler in Fairmount Township, was born in North Carolina, July 14, 1816, and came with his parents to Grant County in 1838. He made this trip in the saddle, driving a four-horse team.

JESSE E. WILSON

On June 21, 1838, he was married to Hannah Hill, daughter of Aaron Hill. They settled on the farm that remained his the rest of his life. It was a one hundred-acre farm eighty rods wide, extending from what is now Mill Street west along Eighth Street and Fairmount and Western gravel road for two hundred rods. Their home buildings were located on the hill, where Joe Shane now lives.

Jesse Wilson was long identified with the history of Grant County and Fairmount Township. He was for many of the later years of his life head of the Society of Friends in Fairmount. His seat was seldom vacant. Only sickness prevented him from being in his place at church at the stated times for meeting. Horses were taken from the plow in the middle of the week, as well as from the binder in harvest. All work ceased on his farm on meeting day from 10:30 a. m. to 2 o'clock p. m., and all went to meeting.

Jesse E. Wilson's name stood at the head of the list of active temperance and Sabbath school workers. He was for twenty years an elder in the church, and for several years belonged to the representative body of Indiana Yearly Meeting. His ability and honesty in settling decedents' estates were qualities well known in the County and Township, and his services were sought by both court and people.

While being progressive, as shown in the lines just written, he was especially so in other ways. The best, up-to-date farm tools and machinery were always at hand on his farm. The public improvements in the way of ditching and road building found a ready helper in Jesse E. Wilson. He was for years an official in the Fairmount and Jonesboro Gravel Road Company, and at the same time he was President of the Fairmount and Western Gravel Road Company. These activities antedate all laws for free gravel roads.

There was a great struggle to obtain the Big Four Railroad through the County and Township. A tax of fifty-six thousand dollars for a subsidy had been voted by the people. There arose quite a talk of enjoining its collection. This coming to the ears of the railroad officials, they refused to proceed with the building of the road unless this subsidy was fully guaranteed by reliable real estate owners. One hundred and fifty farmers signed the bond. Jesse E. Wilson was the first. He was liberal with his means in assisting the poor. Lending money and endorsing for neighbors who found themselves in close places for funds were very characteristic of him. His credit at the only bank in the County was limited only by his own judgment.

WILLIAM S. ELLIOTT.

Fairmount, Indiana.

(Editor's Note.——Jesse E. Wilson died at his home, near Fairmount, April 5, 1883, aged sixty-seven years, nine months and twenty-one days.)

Nathan D. Wilson was born in Randolph County, North Carolina, December 21, 1817, and with his parents came to Fairmount Township in May, 1837. Shortly after he settled on the farm now owned by the heirs of John Seale, situated west of the corporation limits of Fairmount, he was married to Mary Hill, daughter of Aaron Hill.

This land was heavily timbered. In clearing this farm there was enough good poplar and walnut burned and made into rails to pay for the land today. After living in a log cabin several years he decided to

AUNT MARY WILSON

build a frame house. He bought twenty-five large poplar trees of Nixon Winslow for twenty-five dollars. Either one of these trees would bring one hundred dollars now.

Nathan D. Wilson was a man of considerable ability, and was used in both church and business affairs. He was an elder in the Friends Church for thirty-five or forty years and served for many years as clerk of Back Creek Monthly Meeting. He settled many estates, one of which was David Stanfield's, giving bond in the sum of twenty-five thousand dollars for the correct handling of the business. He assessed Fairmount Township several times and served on juries in county courts quite frequently. He went through many privations that people now would not know how to endure. Jonesboro had the nearest water-power mill. He would put a boy on a horse with two bushels of wheat. Sometimes they would fall off. In the dry season pioneers had to go to the nearest steam flouring mill, which, then, was at Chesterfield, Indiana. When he had wheat to sell he hauled it to Wabash. Thirty bushels made a good load for two horses in those days. It took two days to make the trip, and he got a yard of calico for a bushel of wheat. He was one of the company that went to Cincinnati with teams for the equipment to be installed at James Cammack's saw-mill that was built in Fairmount in the early day. The company was gone nearly four weeks, in the winter time, when the roads were very bad. Nathan and Mary Wilson were parents of thirteen children, namely: Joseph, born February 11, 1840; Emily, born June 21, 1841; Sarah, born June 12, 1843; Deborah, born June 26, 1845; Anna, born July 26, 1847; Peninah, born April 12, 1850; Henry, born April 12, 1852; Rufus, born September 10, 1854; Margaret, born June 26, 1857; Alvin J., born November 20, 1859; Jane, born August 30, 1862; Thomas, born October 7, 1865; Hannah, born June 24, 1868. All are deceased except Joseph, who lives at Newberg, Oregon; Thomas, who resides at Formosa, Kansas; Henry, who lives in Fairmount, and Alvin J., former Township Trustee, who owns a good farm northwest of Fairmount, where he lives.

Nathan D. Wilson died at his home, near Fairmount, February 14, 1881, aged sixty-three years. His wife, Mary, who was born February 11, 1822, died on November 19, 1909, aged eighty-seven years, surviving her husband more than a quarter of a century.

The influence of this worthy man and wife will extend into the future generations, and their piety and rectitude are a memory and a heritage of which their progeny may be justly proud.

Samuel C. Wilson, farmer and pioneer, was born in Randolph County, North Carolina, October 14, 1834. His paternal grandparents were Joseph and Sarah (Charles) Wilson, also natives of North Carolina, and his parents were John and Mary (Winslow) Wilson, who came to Fairmount Township in 1837 from Randolph County, North Carolina. John Wilson was born July 13, 1784, and died in Fairmount in 1864, lacking one day of being eighty years old. Mary, his wife, was born July 20, 1797, and died in 1871. They were parents of twelve children, namely: Jesse E., Nathan D., Cyrus, Henry, Nancy, Micajah, Elizabeth, Eliza Ann, John Milton, Lindsey, Samuel C., and Abigail, all deceased except Samuel C.

It is a tradition in the Wilson family that their early ancestors came to this country with William Penn, landing at Philadelphia. From this point members of the family drifted to different sections of the Colonial States, some to New Jersey, others remaining in Pennsylvania, while many settled

SAMUEL C. WILSON

in Virginia and North Carolina. The Fairmount Township family of Wilsons are descendants of the North Carolina branch.

Samuel C. Wilson attended the common schools of this Township, his first teacher being David Stanfield, about the winter of 1840-1841. Stanfield had charge of a school in a log cabin southwest of where Fairmount now stands. John Wilson had settled on a three hundred and sixty-acre farm about two miles southwest, now partly owned by Joel B. Ware and partly by John Dare, Ed Woolen and Lon Payne. The first recollection Samuel Wilson has of the new country as a child was when a clock peddler came through the forest selling Seth Thomas clocks, driving from cabin to cabin with an ox team. His father bought a twenty-four-dollar clock. Another incident he recalls was the noisy approach of several Indians, with painted faces and wearing their moccasins and blankets. They came dashing up to his father's cabin one day, whooping and yelling like mad. The Indians announced that they were hungry and demanded something to eat. After a short parley the father provided each one with a case knife and turned them into his turnip patch. After satisfying their hunger they mounted their horses and single file galloped away in good humor.

"I was five years old at the time," remarked Mr. Wilson, in speaking of this visit of the red skins, "and to my childish mind the hideous noises made by this band of Indians were terrifying. I could not see much chance for a Tar Heel or a Hoosier in this country if that sort of thing happened very often. We got our mail at Summitville, where John Kelsay, uncle of John and A. W. Kelsay, was then serving as postmaster. My father was for many years a subscriber of the *Louisville Journal*, edited in that day by George D. Prentice, one of the great American journalists and a contemporary of Horace Greeley. The *Journal* printed many descriptions of fugitive slaves, mostly copper-colored.

"When we were getting our mail at Summitville, Solomon Thomas established a postoffice called AI in his cabin about two miles southeast of Fairmount. We then changed our postoffice, as it was nearer to the Thomas cabin. It was while we were getting our mail here that James Cammack came into the neighborhood in quest of a location for a saw-mill. The building of this saw-mill in Fairmount was really the first start of the town.

"In 1847, Grant Postoffice was established at Fairmount and John Scarry was then in charge of it. Scarry went to Indianapolis from here.

"I recall, as a boy twelve years old, in 1846, I went to Wabash with father. We traveled in a four-horse wagon. We took a load of bacon. It required four days to make the trip. Once we stuck in the mud in front of Elizabeth Bogue's house on North Main Street.

"Father sold a great deal of stuff in Cincinnati. He sold wheat there for forty-five cents per bushel and brought back salt. It took twelve days to make this trip with a four-horse wagon.

"My brother, Cyrus, who had a good education for that day, taught school in a log cabin southeast of Fairmount, then at the Benbow cabin. I recall the Underground Railroad station at Aaron Hill's quite well. One station was also located at Solomon Knight's."

Mr. Wilson bought one hundred and three acres of land, now owned by his son, Lin Wilson, as productive a farm as there is in this Township, which he drained and cleared. With the exception of fourteen months spent in Carthage, he has lived in the Township practically his entire life. He was one of the original stockholders in the Jonesboro and Fairmount Turnpike Company. He served four years as Trustee of Fairmount Academy. Believing that women should have representation on the board, he finally withdrew in order that a place might be provided for Mrs. Anna K. Rook.

Mr. Wilson is a Republican in politics. His first vote was cast for John C. Fremont. He has served as Township Assessor, and was a member of the Indiana State Legislature during the session of 1890-1891, serving on six important committees, among them being the committee on railroads, the committee on swamp lands, and the committee on natural gas. He has been a lifelong member of the Society of Friends.

Mr. Wilson's first wife was Rachel Overman, born near Marion, who died in 1865, aged twenty-two years. On January 10, 1867, at Carthage, Indiana, he married Elizabeth Jessup, a native of Rush County, who died in June, 1913, aged seventy years. Her parents were Thomas and Rebecca Jessup, to whom were born four children, namely, Elizabeth, Ann, Sarah, and Micajah, the latter being the only one now living. Samuel and Elizabeth (Jessup) Wilson were parents of three children, namely: Lin, born March 19, 1870; Jessup, born November 21, 1872, and Thomas, born December 19, 1874. Thomas died in 1880.

Lindsey Wilson, who lived during the last fourteen years of his life in Fairmount, was by training and occupation a farmer. He was born in Randolph County, North Carolina, December 19, 1832, and died at his home in Fairmount on May 20, 1906. His ancestry for nearly two hundred years has been traced.

Lindsey Wilson attended the common schools of the Township, and, considering the advantages of his early life, was well educated. He was industrious and thrifty and owned a splendid farm of one hundred acres south of Fairmount, retiring from active pursuits only when advancing years and failing health required him to do so. In politics he was a Republican. He was a birthright member of the Society of Friends. After his marriage he joined the Wesleyan Methodist Church, his wife being a member of this denomination, and for many years they were among the leading members of the Back Creek congregation, southwest of Fairmount. He entered the Union army as a member of Company D, Thirty-third Indiana Infantry, but was taken sick, and

LINDSEY AND JANE (DAVIS) WILSON

afterwards assigned to hospital work, he being physically unable for army service. On December 13, 1854, he was married to Miss Jane Davis, born in Wayne County, Indiana, February 6, 1836. She died July 26, 1908. Her parents were Harvey and Maria Davis, and their children were Thomas, Philip, Henry, Foster, Jane, Harvey and Mary, all now deceased.

Lindsey and Jane (Davis) Wilson were parents of nine children, namely: John H. Wilson, of Fairmount, born October 5, 1855; Mary M. Harvey, born February 8, 1858, wife of Rev. Enos Harvey, of Noblesville, Indiana; Lucy Rush, born February 28, 1861, wife of Miles Rush, of Fairmount; Rachel, deceased, born December 13, 1863; William E. Wilson, of Huntington, Indiana, born August 22, 1866;

Elizabeth, deceased, born March 22, 1869, married John Dobson; Charles S., deceased, born March 30, 1872; Martha J., born April 24, 1874, married Carson Payne, deceased; and Merton L., deceased, born April 2, 1878. There are sixteen grandchildren and nine great-grandchildren.

John Wilson and family left North Carolina in April, 1837, to find a home in the State of Indiana. Their journey was not attended by the difficulties which so frequently beset the path of other pioneers. It is evident that the circumstances of the Wilsons, from a material point of view, were more prosperous than those of a great many who settled in Fairmount Township and Grant County at that early date. They located on Section 6, of Fairmount Township, where the father bought 360 acres of land.

Lindsey Wilson was a good citizen, seeking to promote that which is best in government and best for his country and his community. He was a good neighbor, kind and accommodating to all. He was a man of sturdy characteristics, exceedingly conscientious and scrupulously honest. He gave good quality and full measure in what he sold and paid promptly for what he bought. Every contract, whether verbal or written, he endeavored to fill to the letter. He was always willing and anxious, when convinced of error, to make confession and proper restitution. He welcomed the stranger and visited the sick and needy. He was a kind father, an indulgent husband and a splendid type of American.

Mrs. Eunice (Pierce) Wilson came to Fairmount Township with her parents, William and Prudence (Pemberton) Pierce, on November 10, 1851. When the family arrived, from their home in Ohio, the weather was cold and they found acres of water and ice as they passed along the winding roads of the forest.

MRS. EUNICE (PIERCE) WILSON

"There's land that will never be worth anything," remarked one member of the party, as they traveled on their way to the site of the new home near Back Creek. And the prospects were not the most flattering.

Mrs. Wilson was born near West Milton, in Miami County, Ohio, July 8, 1848. She began teaching school at fifteen years of age, and taught several terms at Back Creek, Oak Ridge, and near Greentown, Indiana. On September 30, 1871, she was married to Robert L. Wilson.

About 1886, a local organization of the Woman's Christian Temperance Union was formed at Back Creek, Mrs. Wilson becoming one of the charter members and served as President for several years. In 1889 she was chosen President of the Grant County Woman's Christian Temperance Union. She filled this position with such skill and ability for eighteen or twenty years that her reputation as organizer and speaker spread to other sections of the State. Under her splendid guidance the Grant County organization attained to a prominent position in reform work in Indiana. She was honored by her associates in this movement, and in 1900 was elected President of the Indiana Woman's Christian Temperance Union. For three years—1900, 1901, 1902—she was President of the Indiana Woman's Christian Temperance Union, declining re-election because of pressing household duties requiring attention. In this position she again demonstrated her capacity as a leader, and under her intelligent guidance the membership grew and the power of the women of the State became more potent and their sphere of work and usefulness was broadened and deepened. Mrs. Wilson recently stated that the Woman's Christian Temperance Union has given the best opportunity for the development of woman's talents of any reform organization ever created. Discussing this matter, she said:

"What is wanted in the Legislature, in the Congress and on the school boards is the home influence, and that is represented by the women. This is why woman needs representation on the various boards which have to do with the welfare of women and children."

Mrs. Wilson has done a vast amount of good work for humanity, and her official connection with the Woman's Christian Temperance Union of the County, State and Nation has been of benefit in a large way to this splendid organization, which has played so important a part in making this a Prohibition State.

LIN WILSON

Lin Wilson, son of Samuel C. and Elizabeth (Jessup) Wilson, is one of Fairmount Township's prominent farmers. Born March 19, 1870, he has lived all his life on the home place. He was educated in the common schools of the Township and attended Fairmount Academy. He has always affiliated with the Republican party, is a member of Masonic Lodge No. 635, of Fairmount, and of the Friends Church. On December, 1894, he was married to Miss Effie G. Davis, a native of Fairmount Township, born August 8, 1869, and a daughter of Foster and Dorinda (Rush) Davis. To this union two children were born, namely, Dora E., now a member of the faculty of Fairmount Academy, and Hubert D., a graduate of Fairmount Academy. Lin Wilson is interested in all phases of up-to-date farming, and has for several years done his part in promoting the agricultural welfare of the Township. He has served as President of the Fairmount Township Farmers' Institute, secretary of the Grant County Farmers' Institute, treasurer Grant County Farmers' Mutual Insurance Company for several years and also a director of this organization. His farm shows the energetic and painstaking care given to it, and the results of his labor from year to year bespeak the diligent student of agricultural matters combined with the capacity of applying in a practical way the best and most modern methods of farming.

Nathan D. W. Elliott, son of Elijah and Deborah (Wilson) Elliott, was born at Marion, Indiana, August 28, 1866. His paternal grandparents were Isaac and Rachel (Overman) Elliott and his maternal grandparents were Nathan D. and Mary (Hill) Wilson. The subject of this sketch was educated in the Fairmount Public Schools and at the Holmes Business College, Portland, Oregon. He learned the printer's trade, working in the office of *The Fairmount News,* being employed later at Warren and Marion. In 1887 he went West, working on *The Newberg (Oregon) Graphic,* and later on *The Daily Statesman* and in the State printing office at Salem, the capital of the State. In 1903 he engaged in the printing business at Salem, and has been quite succesful. In politics he is a Republican, serving as Secretary of the Republican County Central Committee 1914-1918; member of Salem City Council 1908-1912, and again elected for the term of two years, 1916-1918. In 1910 he was chairman of the committee that installed a seven hundred and fifty thousand-dollar sewer system; in 1917 he is chairman of the committee that is building over one hundred thousand dollars' worth of new pavement. He is a member of Pacific Lodge No. 50, Ancient Free and Accepted Masons; Multnomah Chapter No. 1, Royal Arch Masons; Hodson Council No. 1, Illustrious Royal and Select Masters, and the Benevolent and Protective Order of Elks, No. 336. He is a member of the Society of Friends at Salem. He was a charter member of the Marion Light Infantry, in 1886, and was first sergeant in 1891 and captain in 1892. Mr. Elliott was married in Newberg, Oregon, April 19, 1898, to Miss Clara E. Hodson, born at Carthage, Indiana, a daughter of Gideon and Delphina (Coffin) Hodson, both natives of Indiana, and of the same family of Coffins that played an important part in the Underground Railroad in early days. For generations back the Hodsons and Coffins were Quakers. Mr. and Mrs. Elliott are parents of one daughter, Maxine, born February 20, 1899, at Salem. They have

NATHAN D. W. ELLIOTT

an adopted daughter, Marjorie Elliott, born September 8, 1907, and a granddaughter of Dr. Henry Charles, pioneer Fairmount physician.

Clyde N. Wilson,, son of Alvin J. and Margaret (Neal) Wilson, and a grandson of Nathan D. Wilson, is a native of Fairmount Township. Mr. Wilson now holds an excellent position as head of the Business Department of the Sheboygan (Wisconsin) High School.

Jesse Webster Wilson, son of C. M. and Olive (Charles) Wilson, was born at Fairmount, Indiana, October 23, 1884. He attended the common schools, finishing his education at St. Louis and Paragould, Arkansas. While at Paragould he graduated in a business college and then accepted a position on *The Paragould Soliphone,* a daily newspaper published there. He remained with this paper until he was seventeen

CLYDE N. WILSON   JESSE WEBSTER WILSON

years of age, at which time he accepted a position as assistant bookkeeper with the Stewart-Alexander Lumber Company at Gifford, Arkansas, and was soon promoted to assistant manager and was later transferred to Memphis, Tennessee. Mr. Wilson proved his efficiency and was soon again promoted, this time to the main office of the firm at St. Louis. For a time he was manager of their plant at Mangham, Louisiana. Since May, 1913, he has occupied the important position of manager of the Mississippi Lumber Company; he is now located at Meridian, Mississippi, at which place he resides with his family.

CHAPTER XXIII.

FAIRMOUNT TOWNSHIP SOLDIERS.

WAR OF THE REVOLUTION.

Isaac Sudduth, buried in East Bethel Graveyard.

WAR OF 1812.

*Lewis Harrison.
*William Leach.
*James Martin.
*Capt. George Reeder.

MEXICAN WAR.

*John Hubert, corporal, Company B, Third Ohio Infantry.
*John Plaster, private, Company I, First Indiana Infantry.
*John Vetor, private, Third Michigan Infantry.

While the Society of Friends do not encourage war and strife, as a denomination, but stand, instead, as a church, for peace and arbitration among nations, this community, where peace principles then largely predominated, contributed as many volunteers to the Union Army during the Civil War as any other locality of similar population.

Following are the names of Union soldiers who lived in Fairmount Township at the time of their enlistment or who have resided in this community since the close of the Civil War:

Elijah Alexander, private, Company I, One Hundred and Thirtieth Indiana Infantry.

JOHN VETOR

*Deceased

George N. Allred, corporal, Company K, One Hundred and Thirtieth Indiana Infantry.

*Moses Allred, private, Company F, Thirty-fourth Indiana Infantry.

*Lindley Arnett, private, Company K, Forty-seventh Indiana Infantry.

*L. D. Baldwin, sergeant, Company C, Eighty-ninth Indiana Infantry.

Henry Barber, private, Company D, One Hundred and Thirty-sixth Indiana Infantry.

Ephraim Bartholomew, first sergeant, Company A, Nineteenth Indiana Infantry; first lieutenant, Company I, Twentieth Indiana Infantry.

*George Bates, private, Company D, Second Indiana Cavalry.

*Enoch Beals, private, First Indiana Cavalry.

Newton Beals, private, Company K, First Indiana Cavalry.

*James W. Beidler, private, Company A, One Hundred and Fifty-sixth Indiana Infantry.

*Joseph Bennett, private, Twenty-fourth Indiana Battery.

*Randolph Boggess, private, Company C, One Hundred and Fifty-third Ohio Infantry.

*Jonathan Bogue, unassigned.

*James Brewer, private, Company K, One Hundred and Thirtieth Indiana Infantry.

*Willis Brewer, private, Company C, Eighty-ninth Indiana Infantry.

*Jesse Bright, private, Company H, One Hundred and Forty-second Indiana Infantry.

Thomas Brookshire, corporal, Company E, Ninth Indiana Cavalry.

James Brown, private, Company I, Second Ohio Cavalry.

*Charles F. Buck, private, Company C, Thirty-third Massachusetts Infantry.

Frank Buck, private, Company C, Thirty-third Massachusetts Infantry.

*Harmon Buller, private, Company C, One Hundred and Eighteenth Indiana Infantry.

*John Buller, private, Company K, Forty-seventh Indiana Infantry.

*Gabriel Bumpus, private, Company I, Thirty-third Indiana Infantry.

*John Busing, private, One Hundred and Fifty-third Indiana Infantry.

---

*Deceased

*Isaac Carter, private, Company G, Thirty-third Indiana Infantry.

Robert Carter, private, Company C, Fifty-first Indiana Infantry.

Nathan D. Cox, private, Company A, Thirty-third Indiana Infantry.

*Cyrus Crawford, first lieutenant, Company I, Sixteenth Indiana Infantry.

*H. M. Crilley, corporal, Company C, Fourteenth New Jersey Infantry.

*Milton Crowell, private, Company H, Twelfth Indiana Infantry; Company K, One Hundred and Thirtieth Indiana Infantry.

*William P. Crowell, Company H, Twelfth Indiana Infantry.

James W. Curtis, private, Companies M and A, Sixth Indiana Cavalry.

Robert Dare, corporal, Company G, Sixty-ninth Indiana Infantry.

*Foster Davis, private, Company H, Twelfth Indiana Infantry; second lieutenant, Company G, One Hundred and Fifty-third Indiana Infantry.

*G. W. Dealy, private, Company F, Thirty-second Indiana Infantry.

*Harrison Dean, private, Twenty-second Indiana Infantry.

*Alex Deerin, private, Company C, One Hundred and Seventy-second Ohio Infantry.

*Amos Deshon, private, Company D, Seventy-ninth Indiana Infantry.

R. H. Dickerson, private, Company F, Thirty-second Indiana Infantry.

W. A. Dolman, private, Company C, Eighty-ninth Indiana Infantry.

*John L. Douglass, private, Company F, Fortieth Indiana Infantry.

Levi Dove, private, Company A, Nineteenth Indiana Infantry.

William S. Elliott, corporal, Company C, Eighty-ninth Indiana Infantry.

*M. S. Friend, private, Company K, Seventy-ninth Ohio Infantry.

*John Gambriel, Company D, Thirty-fourth Indiana Infantry.

*Henry Gardner, private, Company K, One Hundred and Thirtieth Indiana Infantry.

Henry Garrison, private, Company A, Eighth Indiana Infantry.

Leander Geeding, private, Company G, One Hundred and Thirty-sixth Indiana Infantry.

*John Gibson, private, Company K, One Hundred and Thirtieth Indiana Infantry.

*Charles Gift, private, Company I, One Hundred and Fifty-ninth Ohio Infantry.

---

*Deceased

Jesse Haisley, private, Company F, One Hundred and Thirty-ninth Indiana Infantry.

JOHN B. HOLLINGSWORTH

Retired monument dealer, was born in Hudson County, Ohio, August 5, 1836. His grandparents were natives of Pittsburgh, as were his parents, William Hollingsworth, born June 25, 1811, and Lucinda, born May 8, 1814. William and Lucinda Hollingsworth were the parents of six children, namely: Wesley B., John B., Gilmore, Mariah, Isabel and William. In 1856 John B. Hollingsworth came to Fairmount Township with his parents, locating in Fairmount, then a village of about a dozen houses. The father opened the first cabinet shop in the Township, making household furniture of all kinds by hand, and supplying pioneers with coffins for their dead. John B. went to school at White Hall and also at Summitville. He started to learn the carpenter trade with his uncle, William Wellington, then living at Summitville, remaining with his relative about one year, then returning to Fairmount and working at odd jobs until the spring of 1861. On April 23, 1861, he enlisted in Company K, Eighth Indiana Volunteer Infantry, for the three months' service, remaining with this regiment until the command was mustered out on August 6, 1861. He, with Smith Kelsay and Isaac Smithson, were the first three Fairmount Township men who at the outbreak of war responded to President Lincoln's call for troops. October 1, 1861, Hollingsworth enlisted in Company F, Twelfth Indiana Volunteer Infantry, serving seven months in this regiment. With this command he was discharged May 18, 1862. On August 10, 1862, he volunteered for the third time, enlisting in Company H, Eighth Indiana Volunteer Infantry, for three years, or until the close of the war. The Eighth was mustered out June 14, 1865. He was with his regiment at the battle of Rich Mountain, West Virginia, July 12, 1861. During his second enlistment his regiment was on guard duty, being stationed near Sharpsburg, Maryland, guarding the Potomac River. During his third enlistment he saw hard service with the Eighth Indiana Infantry, participating with his command in the battles of Blackwater, Missouri, Port Gibson, Champion Hills, Jackson, Big Black, Vicksburg, second battle of Jackson, Hall Town, Oppequon, New Market, Cedar Creek and Fisher's Hill. At Cedar Creek, on October 19, 1864, just before Gen. Phil Sheridan arrived to rally his demoralized army, Hollingsworth met Harry Norton, who was then sick. Hollingsworth helped his comrade along as far as Norton was able to go. The Confederates had at this point flanked the Union forces and it was a case of every man for himself. Norton insisted that Hollingsworth go on and take care of himself, explaining, after much effort, that he was too sick and too weak to go farther. Hollingsworth reluctantly left his comrade. The Confederates were upon them. Hollingsworth wheeled around, fired at his pursuers as he retreated, and took to his heels, making his escape to the Union lines as bullets were "throwing up dirt all about him." Norton fell into the hands of the Confederates, and was taken to Libby Prison, where he died. In June, 1865, Hollingsworth returned home and for many years successfully carried on a monument business in Fairmount. On February 17, 1876, he was married to Mrs. Hary Hall Hathaway, daughter of William and Hannah (Stanfield) Hall, who was born February 11, 1844, in Fairmount Township. To this union four children were born, namely: Martin L., Morton, Joseph B. and Sarah L., all deceased except Morton.

Robert Hart, private, Company G, One Hundred and First Indiana Infantry.

*Cyrus W. Harvey, sergeant, Company C, Eighty-ninth Indiana Infantry.

F. M. Haynes, private, Second Indiana Light Artillery.

*John Helton, private, Company C, Eighty-ninth Indiana Infantry.

Alpheus Henley, private, unassigned, Eighty-ninth Indiana Infantry.

*Daniel Hill, private, Company C, Eighty-ninth Indiana Infantry.

*Thomas Hobbs, private, unassigned, Thirty-second Indiana Infantry.

*Joseph Hockett, private, Company F, One Hundred and Thirtieth Indiana Infantry.

Joseph Hoggatt, private, Company C, Seventy-ninth Ohio Infantry.

J. B. Hollingsworth, private, Company H, Eighth Indiana Infantry.

Cyrus Hollingsworth, private, Company I, One Hundred and First Indiana Infantry; private, unassigned, Thirty-second Indiana Infantry.

*Wesley Hollingsworth, musician, Company K, One Hundred and Thirtieth Indiana Infantry.

*Gilmore Hollingsworth, musician, Company H, Twelfth Indiana Infantry.

*Abner Holloway, private, Company E, Eighty-third Indiana Infantry.

Polk Hosier, private, Thirty-sixth Indiana Infantry.

*John Hubert, corporal, Company C, Fifty-fourth Indiana Infantry.

J. M. Hundley, private, Company E, One Hundred and Fortieth Indiana Infantry.

Nathan W. Hunt, private, Company C, Twelfth Indiana Infantry.

*Henry Jeffrey, corporal, Company H, One Hundred and Eighteenth Indiana Infantry.

*Gabe Johnson, private, Company A, Eighth Indiana Infantry.

*John F. Jones, private, Company H, Twelfth Indiana Infantry; captain, Company C, Eighty-ninth Indiana Infantry.

Hiram Jones, private, Company C, Eigthy-ninth Indiana Infantry.

---

*Deceased

John Jones, private, Company C, Eighty-ninth Indiana Infantry.

*Thomas Jones, private, Company G, One Hundred and Twenty-ninth Ohio Infantry.

*Thomas Jones, private, Forty-second Indiana Infantry.

*Smith Kelsay, private, Company K, One Hundred and Thirtieth Indiana Infantry; Company H, Eighth Indiana Infantry.

A. W. Kelsay, private, Company H, Twelfth Indiana Infantry; corporal Company K, One Hundred and Fifty-third Indiana Infantry.

*Henry D. Kepler, private, Company E, Fifty-seventh Indiana Infantry.

*Lawson Kimes, private, Company A, Fourteenth Indiana Infantry.

William G. Lamm, private, Twenty-fourth Indiana Battery.

Andy Leverton, private, Company C, Tenth Indiana Infantry.

*John S. D. Lewis, private, Company H, Twelfth Indiana Infantry.

*Eli B. Lightfoot, private, Company G, Twenty-sixth Indiana Infantry.

*Albert Lytle, private, Company C, Eighty-ninth Indiana Infantry.

*Enoch Lytle, private, Company H, Twelfth Indiana Infantry.

*Henry Lytle, private, Company H, Eighth Indiana Infantry.

Newton Lytle, private, Company H, Eighth Indiana Infantry.

*Stanton Lytle, Company C, Eighty-ninth Indiana Infantry.

*John Lillibridge, private, Company F, One Hundred and Thirteenth Ohio Infantry.

Alex Little, private, Company H, Twelfth Indiana Infantry; private Company B, Seventh Indiana Cavalry.

*Azel Little, private, Company H, Twelfth Indiana Infantry; Twenty-fourth Indiana Battery.

*Thomas Little, private, Company H, Eighty-fourth Indiana Infantry; private, Company B, Seventh Indiana Cavalry.

*Byram Love, private, Company D, Thirty-fourth Indiana Infantry.

*Joseph Mahoney, private, Company F, One Hundred and Forty-seventh Indiana Infantry.

*Andrew Mann, private, Company E, One Hundred and First Indiana Infantry.

Frederick Mason, private, Company G, One Hundred and Fortieth Indiana Infantry.

*Jacob McCoy, Company D, Thirty-third Indiana Infantry.

*Jesse Milner, Company F, One Hundred and Thirty-ninth Indiana Infantry.

---

*Deceased

Michael Mittank, private, unassigned, Thirty-second Indiana Infantry.

*George Modlin, private, Company C, Eigthy-ninth Indiana Infantry.

Caleb Moon, corporal, Company K, One Hundred and Thirtieth Indiana Infantry.

Lewis Moon, private, Company C, Seventy-ninth Ohio Infantry; captain, Company G, One Hundred and Eighteenth Kentucky Infantry.

*Albert P. Mott, corporal, Company H, Twelfth Indiana Infantry.

*William Newby, private, Company C, Eigthy-ninth Indiana Infantry.

Daniel Nicholson, private, Company G, Sixty-ninth Indiana Infantry.

A. F. Norton, private, Company C, One Hundred and Eighteenth Indiana Infantry; private, Company D, Thirty-third Indiana Infantry.

*George Norton, private, Company H, Eighth Indiana Infantry.

*Harry Norton, private, Company H, Eighth Indiana Infantry.

*James Norton, private, Company D, Thirty-third Indiana Infantry.

*Henry Odell, private, Company K, Thirty-fifth Ohio Infantry.

J. H. Parker, private, Company G, One Hundred and Fifty-third Indiana Infantry; private, Company K, Sixteenth United States Infantry.

*Harper Parsons, private, Company I, One Hundred and Forty-seventh Indiana Infantry.

B. S. Payne, private, Company K, One Hundred and Thirtieth Indiana Infantry.

*Ephraim Payne, private, Company H, Twelfth Indiana Infantry; sergeant, Company K, One Hundred and Thirtieth Indiana Infantry.

*James Payne, private, Company C, One Hundred and Fortieth Indiana Infantry.

*Thomas Payne, private, Company G, One Hundred and Fortieth Indiana Infantry.

*Wesley Payne, private, Company H, Twelfth Indiana Infantry.

*Lemuel Pearson, private, Company K, One Hundred and Eighteenth Indiana Infantry.

James Phillips, private, Company A, One Hundred and Twentieth Indiana Infantry.

*Alex Pickard, private, Company K, Sixteenth Indiana Infantry.

*William Powell, private, Thirty-ninth Indiana Infantry.

---

*Deceased

*A. W. Ray, private, Company D, Seventy-ninth Indiana Infantry.

*Joe Reeves, private, Company C, Eighty-ninth Indiana Infantry.

*Andrew Rhoads, private, Company G, Fifty-seventh Indiana Infantry.

ANDREW RHOADS

Who was a shoemaker, was a native of Pennsylvania, where he secured a common school education. He was a splendid mechanic. It is said of him that he could take a man's measure for a pair of boots one morning and have them ready to wear the next. In politics he was a Republican. He was a member of the Methodist Episcopal Church, and took an active part in religious work; he was very conscientious and always endeavored to do what was right. At the beginning of the Civil War he closed his shop and volunteered his services, going at once to the front. He was killed December 31, 1862, at the Battle of Stone River, being the first man from Fairmount Township to lay down his life in defense of his country. His remains were buried in the Stone River National Cemetery. Andrew Rhoads married Sarah Mann, born in Indiana, and a daughter of Andrew and Martha Mann. To this marriage was born John L. Rhoads and Jennie (Rhoads) Thorn. John L. Rhoads was born November 19, 1858. He was married November 14, 1887, and his children are Glen, Bessie, Alta, Blanche and Lillian. Their present home is at Fairmount. Jennie was born December 6, 1860; married August 17, 1889, and her children are Hassel, Walter and Lloyd, all of whom reside near Gaston, Indiana. Sarah (Mann) Rhoads had two brothers in the Civil War, namely, John and Andrew. They contracted the measles while in the service and died. Andrew Jackson Mann, father of Sarah, John and Andrew, also served in the Union Army during the War.

*Lewis Ricks, private, Company K, One Hundred and Thirtieth Indiana Infantry.

*Elias Roney, private, Company A, Fifty-seventh Indiana Infantry.

Calvin Scott, private, Company C, Twelfth Indiana Infantry.

Jesse Scott, private, Company F, One Hundred and Thirty-ninth Indiana Infantry; private, Company G, One Hundred and Fifty-third Indiana Infantry.

*John Scott, private, Company C, Twelfth Indiana Infantry.

Levi Scott, private, Company C, One Hundred and Eighteenth Indiana Infantry.

---

*Deceased

John Selby, private, Company F, One Hundred and Thirty-ninth Indiana Infantry.

William Simons, private, Company C, Eighty-ninth Indiana Infantry.

Ichabod Smith, sergeant, Company C, Eighty-ninth Indiana Infantry.

Jason B. Smith, private, Company B, One Hundred and Twenty-third Indiana Infantry.

Leander Smith, private, unassigned, Eighty-third Indiana Infantry.

Moses Smith, private, Company G, Sixth Indiana Infantry.

Roland Smith, sergeant, Company H, Twelfth Indiana Infantry.

*J. B. Smithson, private, Company B, One Hundred and Thirtieth Indiana Infantry.

*Seth Smithson, private, Company E, One Hundred and Fortieth Indiana Infantry.

Caleb A. Starr, private, Company K, One Hundred and Thirtieth Indiana Infantry.

B. F. Stevens, private, Company I, Sixtieth Indiana Infantry.

John H. Stewart, private, Company C, Twelfth Indiana Infantry.

*Samuel Stewart, private, Company G, One Hundred and Fifty-third Indiana Infantry.

*Elijah Stover, private, Company D, Thirty-fourth Indiana Infantry.

R. Sutton, lieutenant, Company B, Seventy-second New York Infantry.

Isaiah Thomas, private, Company F, Thirty-fourth Indiana Infantry.

*George Thorn, lieutenant, Company K, One Hundred and Fifty-third Indiana Infantry.

James Thorn, private, Company B, Thirty-sixth Indiana Volunteer Infantry; private, Company I, Nineteenth Veteran Reserve Corps.

George Turner, private, Company I, Thirty-third Indiana Infantry.

James Turner, private, Company C, Eighty-ninth Indiana Infantry.

Lewis Turner, private, Company F, Thirty-fourth Indiana Infantry.

*E. Vancanon, private, Company B, Thirty-third Indiana Infantry.

*Philip Waggy, Company H, Twelfth Indiana Infantry.

*Alfred Waldron, private, Company K, One Hundred and Thirtieth Indiana Infantry.

*John B. Wells, second lieutenant, Company C, Eighty-ninth Indiana Infantry.

*Tom Wilson, private, Company C, Eighty-ninth Indiana Infantry.

---

*Deceased

*Cyrus Winslow, private, Company D, Thirty-third Indiana Infantry.

*Henry Winslow, private, unassigned, Thirty-second Indiana Infantry.

*Walker Winslow, private, unassigned, Seventy-ninth Indiana Infantry.

Joseph Wright, private, Company I, Sixty-third Indiana Infantry.

Julian Wright, Company K, One Hundred and Thirtieth Indiana Infantry.

ADDITIONAL NAMES.

The following is a list of names of old soldiers that we have never seen named in your reports, who were from Fairmount Township:

William Fogleman, of the Twelfth Indiana Infantry.

John Evans, of the Eighth Indiana Infantry, who was poisoned at Otterville, Missouri, with a number of other Indiana soldiers. Evans was the boy whom my father reared and who came to Fairmount with us.

Thomas Heavenridge, of Company A, Thirty-sixth Indiana Infantry, who was an uncle of mine.

Samuel Puckett, of the First Indiana Cavalry, who was an own cousin, and a brother of Cyrus Puckett, who was drowned, and William Wright was a grandson of William Said. His mother will be remembered as Susan Wright, who married Frank Lytle, Sr.

T. B. McDonald.

Lovilia, Iowa, March 21, 1917.

I am sending you some additional names of soldiers and think I may have duplicated a few of your names on printed list. I am sure I have omitted many names.

The names of Andrew Mann and Andrew J. Mann are two different persons—father and son.

The names of John Buller and John Buller, Sr., are different persons—uncle and nephew.

Lewis Payne is father of Bailey S. Payne.

George Brewer, Willis Brewer and James Brewer are brothers and sons of William Brewer, and all lost their lives in the service.

Joseph Little, Azel Little and Zachariah Little (you have it Zimri) are brothers, and sons of Nathan and Nancy Little.

---

*Deceased

Joseph Bennett and Josephus Bennett are father and son.

Milton Crowell and William P. Crowell are brothers and sons of John Crowell.

John B. Hollingsworth, Wesley Hollingsworth and Gilmore Hollingsworth are brothers and sons of William Hollingsworth.

The Norton boys are brothers, and sons of Major Norton.

The Montgomery boys were brothers, as were also the Lytles, Paynes and Thorns, with the exception of Bailey S. Payne and Lewis and Wesley Payne.

The Smith boys, William, Roland and Leander, are brothers and the sons of John Smith.

I could furnish you much more information, but find it hard and slow work.

I omitted to say that John B. Wells, James A. Wells and Newton Wells are brothers, as are also the Stewart boys, John and Samuel, and the Beals boys.

I hope what I have written may be of some assistance to you.

J. M. HUNDLEY.

Summitville, Indiana, May 6, 1917.

Here are the names sent in by Mr. Hundley:

William McCombs, corporal, Company F, Thirty-fourth Indiana Infantry.

Iredell B. Rush, second lieutenant, Company F, Thirty-fourth Indiana Infantry.

Charles Felton, private, Company F, Thirty-fourth Indiana Infantry.

*David Y. Hoover, corporal, Company F, Thirty-fourth Indiana Infantry.

John F. Furnish, private, Company F, Thirty-fourth Indiana Infantry.

*John Garrison, Company F, Thirty-fourth Indiana Infantry. Died February 13, 1862.

Milford Jones, private, Company F, Thirty-fourth Indiana Infantry.

Lewis Jones, private, Company F, Thirty-fourth Indiana Infantry.

Josephus Bennett, private, Company K, Thirty-fourth Indiana Infantry.

John R. Harrold, private, Company D, Thirty-fourth Indiana Infantry.

---

*Deceased

Jacob D. Cry, private, Company D, Thirty-fourth Indiana Infantry. Wounded. Leg amputated.

Nelson Thomas, corporal, Company K, One Hundred and Thirtieth Indiana Infantry.

Lemon Jones, private, Company K, One Hundred and Thirtieth Indiana Infantry.

Andrew J. Smith, private, Company K, One Hundred and Thirtieth Indiana Infantry.

Stephen Morman, private, Company K, One Hundred and Thirtieth Indiana Infantry.

Caleb McCoy, private, Company K, One Hundred and Thirtieth Indiana Infantry.

*William Dillon, captain, Company K, One Hundred and Thirtieth Indiana Infantry.

*William Smith, sergeant, Company K, One Hundred and Thirtieth Indiana Infantry.

*Andrew J. Mann, private, Company E, One Hundred and First Indiana Infantry.

John Mann, private, Company E, One Hundred and First Indiana Infantry.

*John C. Montgomery, private, Company E, One Hundred and First Indiana Infantry. Died November 27, 1862.

*Solomon Montgomery, private, Company E, One Hundred and First Indiana Infantry. Died February 22, 1863.

*John R. Henley, private, Company I, One Hundred and First Indiana Infantry.

John A. Horner, private, Company I, One Hundred and First Indiana Infantry.

William H. H. Conger, private, Company I, One Hundred and First Indiana Infantry.

*James S. Bradbury, private, Company I, One Hundred and First Indiana Infantry. Killed at Chickamauga, September 19, 1863.

Mansfield Felton, private, Company I, One Hundred and First Indiana Infantry.

*James A. Wells, private, Company I, Eighty-fourth Indiana Infantry.

Newton J. Wells, private, Company C, Eighty-ninth Indiana Infantry.

---

*Deceased.

*George Brewer, private, Company C, Eighty-ninth Indiana Infantry. Died December 15, 1862.

William A. Bradbury, private, Company C, Eighty-ninth Indiana Infantry.

*John B. Wells, second lieutenant, Company C, Eighty-ninth Indiana Infantry.

*Lewis Payne, wagoner, Company C, Eighty-ninth Indiana Infantry.

*Hugh Weston, captain, Company A, One Hundred and Twenty-third Indiana Infantry.

*Marion Wood, private, Company K, Eighth Indiana Infantry; lieutenant, One Hundred and Forty-seventh Indiana Infantry.

Jacob M. Plow, private, Company B, One Hundred and Thirtieth Indiana Infantry.

*John Lytle, private, Company H, Eighth Indiana Infantry. Killed at Cedar Creek, Virginia, October 19, 1864.

*Robert W. Hasting, private, Company H, Eighth Indiana Infantry.

*William J. McNabney, private, Company A, Eighteenth Ohio Infantry.

Abner Leach, private, Company H, Eighth Indiana Infantry; also Company B, Eighth Indiana Infantry.

William Sapp, private, Thirty-second Indiana Infantry.

Frank Furnish, Thirty-second Indiana Infantry.

*John Buller, Sr. Died in service.

*Isaac Smithson, private, Company B, Eighth Indiana Infantry. First three months' call.

James Terrell, private, Company G, One Hundred and Fortieth Indiana Infantry.

*Hubbard Stanley, Thirty-second Indiana Infantry. Substitute. Killed by accident.

*Jonathan Winslow, private, Company C, Eighty-ninth Indiana Infantry.

*Lindsey Wilson, private, unassigned, Thirty-third Indiana Infantry.

Emanuel Duncan, private, Fifth Indiana Cavalry.

Thomas Milholland, private, Company B, Fifty-second Indiana Infantry.

*James Monahan, private, Company K, Thirty-third New Jersey Infantry.

---

*Deceased.

*John Manning, private, Company G, Thirty-fourth Indiana Infantry.

*David L. Payne, private, Company F, Tenth Kansas Infantry; Company G, Eighth Regiment Western Volunteer Infantry; captain, Company D, Eighteenth Kansas Cavalry.

*Simeon Rader, private, Company B, Eighty-fourth Indiana Infantry.

*Daniel Richards, unassigned, Thirty-second Indiana Infantry.

John Roberts, private, Company I, One Hundred and Seventeenth Indiana Infantry.

*Theodore Stansbury, first sergeant, Company K, Second Ohio Infantry; first sergeant, Company D, Sixty-sixth Ohio Infantry.

*George W. Vaughn, private, Company C, Seventh Michigan Infantry.

William M. Duling, private, Thirty-second Indiana Infantry.

*John W. Duling, private, Company D, Thirty-third Indiana Infantry.

The writer is indebted to Jesse Haisley for the additional names given below of men who served in the Union Army during the Civil War:

William Penn Beals, second lieutenant, Company F, One Hundred and Thirty-ninth Indiana Infantry.

*Joseph Rush, sergeant, Company F, One Hundred and Thirty-ninth Indiana Infantry.

*Lindley Hockett, sergeant, Company F, One Hundred and Thirty-ninth Indiana Infantry.

*Thomas Cox, private, Company F, One Hundred and Thirty-ninth Indiana Infantry.

*Hezekiah Miller, private, Company F, One Hundred and Thirty-ninth Indiana Infantry.

*Ephraim Poole, private, Company F, One Hundred and Thirty-ninth Indiana Infantry.

Henry (Tobe) Winslow, private, Company F, One Hundred and Thirty-ninth Indiana Infantry.

*Thomas Mann, private, Company F, One Hundred and Thirty-ninth Indiana Infantry.

*Henry Nichols, private, Company F, One Hundred and Thirty-ninth Indiana Infantry.

---

*Deceased.

John J. Carey, private, Company C, One Hundred and Eighteenth Indiana Infantry.

Hiram Reel, private, Company F, One Hundred and Thirty-ninth Indiana Infantry.

Charles A. Carey, private, Company C, One Hundred and Eighteenth Indiana Infantry.

FOUR SOLDIERS.

Please correct the statement about the Smithson boys who were in the army. There were four in the army during the Civil War, namely, Judiah, Jehu, Isaac and Seth. Jonathan was drafted and got exempt on account of a crooked finger. Jehu and Seth died in the army.

LYDIA SMITHSON.

Fairmount, Indiana, March 22, 1917.

(Editor's Note.—Mrs. Smithson is the widow of Jude Smithson, and although eighty-six years old, is enjoying good health for a person of her age. Her father was the late Mahlon Neal. She was born in Miami County, Ohio, and came to Grant County with her parents in 1839, when she was about eight years old. In her father's family there were six children, namely: William, Margaret, James, Eli, Lydia and Caleb. Judiah and Lydia Smithson commenced housekeeping in Fairmount in 1851, shortly after their marriage.)

Joseph Whybrew, unassigned, was drafted in September, 1864. He reported at Indianapolis, took sick and died in Camp Carrington Hospital in October or November, 1864. I went to General Carrington's residence at late bed time and procured an order to take the body home for burial, with a detail for two comrades, Henry Winslow and Thomas Hobbs, to accompany the remains and see that he had a soldier's burial, which instructions were carried out, and he was laid to rest in Back Creek Graveyard.

John Winslow, a brother of Nixon, was drafted, reported at Indianapolis, obtained a furolugh to return home, and hired Silas Cook to substitute. When they both reported at headquarters at Indianapolis Cook was examined and accepted and Winslow was released. So we have Silas Cook, Elisha Elliott, Henry (Tobe) Winslow and David L. Payne.

Have you Frank Jones's brother? I believe his name was Clark.

A. HENLEY.

Melbourne, Florida, May 29, 1917.

ANDREW RHOADS.

(By John L. Rhoads)

In speaking of the early shoemakers of Fairmount will say that my father, Andrew Rhoads, had a shoeshop at the time the Civil War broke out, which he closed up and went to the front.

The building he was in was a low, wooden structure, located where the John Flanagan store now stands. He had the shop in the front and we lived in the rear rooms. Our living room door faced Washington Street.

Just across from us, where the Hahne drug store is now located, lived Uncle Seth and Aunt Mary Winslow, as I always called them. Their south door faced our north door, and Uncle Seth often coaxed me over there with a nice red apple or something tempting, and I will always remember them as jolly good friends of my childhood days.

I have been told that father would take the measure of a man's foot one morning and by the next morning the man would be wearing his boots. My father taught the round notes in early days, also played the violin by note. Sometimes they would bring a violin to the shop and have him play, but, after he was converted and joined the Methodist Church and became a class leader, they did not sanction such things, so he quit playing.

I was a small boy, but remember quite well when the stage brought the letter to mother saying my father had been killed at the Battle of Stone River, on December 31, 1862. Uncle George Mann was staying with us at the time. My sister, now Mrs. Will Thorn, of Gaston, and myself, were the only children in our family.

After father's death mother sold the shop. He belonged at his death to Company G, Fifty-seventh Indiana Volunteers. We have in our home an enlarged picture of him, taken in his uniform.

Fairmount, Indiana, April 17, 1917.

Ephraim Bartholomew, retired farmer, is a native of Devonshire, England, where he was born on July 29, 1842. With his mother he came to Fayette County, Indiana, in 1854. In 1860, with his parents, he located in Liberty Township, on the farm now owned by William Lindsey, about seven miles southwest of Fairmount. He went to school in Devonshire before leaving his native land, and also attended the common schools as a boy in Fayette County. In politics he is a Progressive Republican. Mr. Bartholomew is Commander of Beeson Post, No. 386, Grand Army of the Republic, having become a member of this Post in 1903, by transfer from Andrews, Indiana. He is a member of the Baptist Church. On July 28, 1861, he enlisted in Company A, Nineteenth Indiana Volunteer Infantry, then organizing at Camp Morton, Indianapolis, Col. Sol. Meredith commanding. No regiment, perhaps, saw more hard fighting during the Civil War than the Nineteenth, which was mustered into the service July 29, 1861. On August 9 the command arrived at Washington, D. C. In an engagement with Confederates at Lewinsville, Virginia, September 11, 1861, three men were killed and wounded. The winter was passed at Fort Craig, brigade headquarters being established at Arlington House, formerly the home of Gen. Robert E. Lee, now known as the National Cemetery. On March 10, 1862, moved with the First Army Corps, under General McDowell, to Fredericksburg, Virginia, and on August 5 made a raid to Spottsylvania Court House, reaching Cedar Mountain August 10. August 28, 1862, the Iron Brigade, of which the Nineteenth Indiana formed a part, and General Gibbons' brigade, six regiments in all, withstood General Jackson's corps of twenty-six regiments from 5 p. m. until 9 p. m., the regiment losing one hundred and eighty-seven killed and wounded and thirty-three missing, Maj. Isaac M. May being among the killed. On August 30, at Groveton (second Bull Run), they were engaged with slight loss. September 14 the Iron Brigade was engaged to carry the

EPHRAIM BARTHOLOMEW

pike at South Mountain, center of the position under General Hooker, losing forty killed and wounded and seven missing. On September 17, at Antietam, the regiment went into battle with two hundred officers and men and came out with but thirty-seven officers and men. Colonel Meredith was promoted to brigadier-general and Lieut.-Col. Samuel J. Williams promoted to colonel. Participated in the Battle of Fredericksburg, December 12 and 13. April 28, 1863, was in the fight at Fitz Hugh Crossing. The Nineteenth was one of the first regiments to launch pontoons and carry the rifle pits, losing four killed and wounded. May 21 went to West Moreland Court House to relieve some cavalry on a raid. June 12, 1863, crossed the Potomac River at Edwards' Ferry. The Iron Brigade was on picket duty June 30 in front of the Army of the Potomac. July 1 this brigade was the first infantry to engage the Confederates at Gettysburg, capturing Archer's Brigade and General Archer during the forenoon. On this day Bartholomew was promoted to the rank of first sergeant. About 3 p. m. Gen. A. P. Hill's corps in full force attacked the First and Eleventh corps. The Eleventh corps had arrived at about 12:30 p. m. The Nineteenth Indiana went into the engagement with two hundred and eighty-eight men, losing two hundred and ten killed, wounded and missing. July 2 and 3 the regiment was entrenched on Culp's Hill, near Cemetery Ridge. Its loss was but two wounded. Moved to Culpepper, Virginia, then to Mine Run, in November. While in winter quarters at Culpepper the regiment re-enlisted and was granted a furlough to Indiana. Moving with General Grant's army May 4, 1864, was engaged in the battles of the Wilderness, Laurel Hill, North Anna, Spottsylvania, and Cold Harbor. May 5 Colonel Williams was killed and Lieut.-Col. John M. Lindley was given command of the regiment. Losses from May 4 to July 30: Killed, thirty-six; severely wounded, ninety-four; slightly wounded, sixteen; missing, sixteen; total, two hundred and twenty. In the seige of Petersburg, Virginia, the regiment was constantly under fire. August 19-21 was in the capture of the Weldon railroad below Petersburg. September 23 the Seventh Indiana was consolidated with the Nineteenth Indiana. October 18 they were consolidated with the Twentieth Indiana and Bartholomew was promoted to first lieutenant of Company I, and served as such until the Twentieth Infantry was mustered out of the service July 12, 1865. Bartholomew was wounded twice, the first time in front of Petersburg, on June 16, 1864, and again on April 6, 1865, while leading his company at Amelia Court House, Virginia a few days before General Lee surrendered at Appomattox, Bartholomew was severely wounded and left on the field to die. He regained consciousness, was picked up and moved by his men to the hospital. And this is the story of a man and of a regiment which did their part in the great Civil War to restore the Union. On February 4, 1864, Mr. Bartholomew was married to Miss Sarah E. Gibson, daughter of George Gibson, she a native of Hamilton County, Indiana, born June 26, 1845. They were the parents of six children, namely: Frances Ann, George, William, Mary, Linnea, Albert and Annie Gussie, all deceased except William and Albert. Mrs. Bartholomew died in March, 1903. In 1913 Mr. Bartholomew was married to Miss Emma F. Davis, of Tipton, and they now reside on North Buckeye Street, Fairmount.

James C. Thorn is the son of Stephen and Jane (Lewis) Thorn, who settled in Van Buren Township, Madison County, about 1840. The Thorns came from Boone County, Indiana. Stephen and Jane Thorn were parents of five children, namely, Joseph, George, Charles, Jacob and James, all deceased except the latter. On August 1, 1861, at Fairmount, he enlisted in the Thirty-fourth Indiana Infantry, but on August 16, of the same year, was transferred to the Thirty-sixth Indiana Infantry, commanded by Col. William Grose, of New Castle, and Lieut.-Col. O. H. P. Carey, of Marion. Thorn served with this regiment until April 12, 1864. He was transferred from the Thirty-sixth on April 13, 1864, to the Nineteenth Veteran Reserve Corps, at Washington, D. C., and on November 16, 1865, was mustered out at Buffalo, New York, having completed a service of more than four years in the Union army.

JAMES C. THORN

He was one of the youngest men who volunteered during the Civil War, being but sixteen years old at the time of enlistment. Before tendering his services he had taken the precaution to prepare for any objections on account of his youth. He had marked the figures 18 on the soles of his shoes. When the recruiting officer inquired his age he replied that he was "over 18," and no further questions were asked. The Thirty-sixth Infantry took part in several important engagements, among them Chickamauga, Stone River, Pittsburg Landing and Mumfordsville.

"At Washington, on July 12, 1864," stated Mr. Thorn to the writer, "the Confederates under Gen. Jubal A. Early and General Breckinridge, had they known it, could easily have taken the capital. Outside the city about three miles the breastworks were held by a small force of hundred-days' men, unseasoned and without military experience. The Confederates came up Saturday afternoon, but on account of heavy marching stopped to rest over Sunday. By Monday, when the attack was started, Early and Breckinridge found themselves confronted by a considerable force of Union troops, who had in the meantime manned the works with artillery and seasoned infantrymen, Gen. Lew Wallace and his Sixth Army Corps coming up in time to save the day. The Confederate attack, which occurred at a point about three miles north of Washington, was repulsed."

During the four years Thorn was in the service he was injured four different times. He was wounded at Chickamauga, where he lost a finger on his left hand. The Thirty-sixth was under fire one hundred and twenty-eight days in succession on the Atlanta campaign.

On October 7, 1868, Mr. Thorn was married to Miss Elizabeth J. Dame, in Clinton County, Indiana. In 1882 he located in Fairmount, and in 1884 they moved to his farm, situated two miles and a half southwest of Fowlerton. Assisted by John George and Jacob Dame he circulated a petition for the building of the Thorn pike, extending from the Interurban line to John W. Himelick's corner, a distance of four miles. When Mr. Thorn first moved to his farm, land in that neighborhood was valued at fifty to sixty dollars per acre. He constructed timber ditches and put in about seventy rods of tile to get an outlet to Barren Creek and the Harrison ditch. In a few years his land was worth one hundred and fifty dollars per acre. The farm developed into a splendid oil territory, four good producing wells being put down. Thorn and Capt. David L. Payne were relatives and schoolmates. He speaks of Captain Payne as a boy of considerable native ability, always fond of jokes and pranks. These characteristics were not entirely lacking when Payne became a man. Mr. Thorn relates that upon one of his visits to his old neighbors, while on his way from Washington,

D. C., to his Western home, Captain Payne brought with him a quantity of what he described to be very choice yam sprouts. Two of his old friends were eager to try out this new variety for a change, and proceeded to plant the sprouts. The result was a pestiferous growth of wild morning glories, which are still found in spots in the vicinity of Payne's old home. Captain Payne had simply resorted to this plan of getting even with some of his old school-day friends who had on many occasions in the past played tricks on him in his boyhood. Mr. and Mrs. Thorn are now comfortably situated at their home in Fowlerton, where they are passing their last years in peace and plenty.

Alson M. Bell, who lived in Fairmount Township for many years, was born June 7, 1842. He was a Confederate soldier during the Civil War, serving in Company H, Thirty-eighth North Carolina Infantry, in the Army of Northern Virginia, under Gen. Robert E. Lee.

ALSON M. BELL

WAR WITH SPAIN.

*J. Frank Deshon.
John H. Crow.
Burl W. Cox.
*Leroy R. Smith.
Murton Woolen.
*Hollis R. Hayworth.
Louis O. Chasey.
Allen D. Parker.
*David Tappan.
Charles T. Payne.
Edgar M. Baldwin.

All members of Company A, One Hundred and Sixtieth Indiana Volunteer Infantry.

Hal V. Dale, Sixth United States Cavalry; Ed Stover, J. D. Latham, Dr. C. B. Vigus.

Cyrus Pemberton, Company F, Twenty-ninth United States Volunteer Infantry.

---

*Deceased.

272   The Making of a Township.

W. Hort Ribble, sergeant, Company H, Thirty-fourth United States Volunteer Infantry.

MODERN FAIRMOUNT HOME
Residence of Xen H. Edwards on North Walnut Street

WAR WITH GERMANY.

Clyde Scott
Louis Freital
Burr Stephens
J. Dyson Stuckey
Ora Alberts
Quincy Cox
Alfred Gore
Marion A. McCorkhill
Lewis Cline
Charles Creek
Troy Eaton
George Ellison
Cecil M. Payne
Ray Lynch
Henry Stradtman
Mark Leach
William Owens

Edwin Tomlinson
Lewis Brunker
Floyd Payne
Watt Fallis
Roy Collins
Roscoe George
Alva Huston
Frank A. Beasley
Paul N. Fred
Ira Anderson
Lieut.-Col. Allen Parker
Russell Dale
Russell Ricks
Raymond Barr
Xen Creek
Francis Hardesty
Roy Frankford

C. V. Hearn
Will Gregg
Wayne Sizelove
Floyd Woodruff
Bert Ward
Carter Helms
Earl Ricks
Garl Munsell
Cleo Thomas
Clyde Monahan
Ray Myers
William Archer
William C. Powell
Harold Griffin
Austin Fear
Archie Curtis
Adam Bates
Raymond Dicks
Paul Whitely
Emil Mostart
John Oakley
Fred A. Smiley
Charles Hill

Frank Allred
Ora Cline
Kenneth Huston
Harry Foster
Ray Odell
Robert Winslow
Ora A. Eiler
Richard Bright
Fred Langsdon
Daniel R. Payne
Leo Bundy
Russell Wright
George Foster
William Benner
John A. Painter
Leslie Winslow
Dale Nicholson
Jesse Welch
Forest Frantz
Harry Fitzpatrick
Bloomer McCoy
Basil Underwood
Charles Heater

W. HORT RIBBLE

W. Hort Ribble is a native of Delaware County, Indiana, graduating from the Muncie High School. In April, 1899, at Pueblo, Colorado, he enlisted in Company H, Thirty-fourth United States Volunteer Infantry. In July following he was promoted to corporal, and in 1900, while serving in the Philippines, he was again promoted to sergeant. Sergeant Ribble took part in seventeen skirmishes and participated in the engagement at San Quintin, in the Island of Luzon, where he saw service for nearly two years.

Lieut.-Col. Allen Parker is a native of Fairmount, where he was born April 9, 1877. He was educated in the Fairmount public schools,

LIEUT. COL. ALLEN PARKER

attended school at Marion during one year while his father, Joseph H. Parker, was serving as County Treasurer, and for over three years a student at Fairmount Academy. In April, 1898, he enlisted as a private in Company A, One Hundred and Sixtieth Indiana Volunteer Infantry, Col. George W. Gunder, commanding. When this regiment returned from Cuba, at the close of the Spanish-American War, Colonel Parker was ordered to Fortress Monroe, where he passed a rigid examination and was commissioned, on his twenty-first birthday, as second lieutenant in the United States Army. He has been promoted several times since that date. In 1917 he was assigned to duty with the new army and brevetted lieutenant-colonel, the only Fairmount Township man to attain to this military honor.

CHAPTER XXIV.

FAIRMOUNT TOWNSHIP AND FAIRMOUNT CORPORATION.

IN SEPTEMBER, 1851, Fairmount Township was organized by authority of an order issued by the Board of Commissioners of Grant County. This Board consisted of Robert H. Lenfesty, William C. Miles and Spencer Reeder, the latter being the Commissioner from the Third District.

The territory set aside for this purpose had been included within the boundary lines of Liberty Township since May, 1839. The Township lines were then indicated as follows:

"Commencing at the northeast corner of Section 16, in Township 23 north, Range 8 east; running thence south on section line to the southeast corner of Section 4, in Township 22, in Range 8; thence west to the southwest corner of Section 6, in Liberty Township and Range; thence north to the northwest corner of Section 18, in Township 23, Range 8; thence east on the section line to the place of beginning."

In describing the topography of Fairmount Township, William Neal, who for many years followed his occupation, that of a Surveyor, and was reputed to be familiar with practically every section of land in the Township, in 1886 wrote as follows:

"This Township presents some variety on the surface, but is generally level except in the neighborhood of the streams, where it is somewhat rolling, the greater portion consisting in a state of nature of black, level lands, where the ash, elm and maple grow in great abundance, yet a great deal of the soil produced the walnut, poplar, beech, sugar and lin, all growing together in the fullest perfection, and arriving at great size. Along Back Creek grew the poplar (tulip) in large proportion. Along Barren Creek grew the oak in full size and perfection. In the eastern and southeastern portions grew in great plenty all timber mixed in together, so that the lumberman could get whatever he might want without going off the section where he might be located. The surface along Barren Creek and along the prairies is peculiar, and more or less uneven as compared with the other parts, and is almost exclusively covered with oak, mostly white oak mixed in with black and red and even some jack oak. Barren Creek enters the Township in Section 4, Township 22, Range 8, and has a general northeasterly course and leaves the Township a little south of the northeast corner of Section 24, Township 23, Range 8; then comes the prairie on the west of the creek and extending to the lake, a distance of four and a half miles, and the valley of one is sometimes not more than forty to sixty rods

JOSEPH WARREN RELFE

Who lives on Route 3, southeast of Fairmount, is one of the Township's splendid farmers. He was born August 25, 1854, near Linwood, in Madison County. His paternal grandfather was Malachi W. Relfe, born in Perquimans County, North Carolina, who died March 5, 1870, aged fifty-nine years, five months and seventeen days. The maternal grandfather was George Smith, who died in 1858. Albertson Relfe, the father, was born in Perquimans County, North Carolina, October 1, 1833, and died at his home in Marion County, Oregon, October 1, 1899. The mother, Virginia (Smith) Relfe, was born in Madison County, Indiana, May 22, 1834, and died at the family home southeast of Fairmount, February 2, 1879. To Albertson and Virginia Relfe were born three sons, namely: Joseph Warren and Wilson Worth, who now live in Fairmount Township, and Grant, who lives in Jefferson, Oregon. It is a tradition in the Relfe family that through the maternal side of the house they are descendants of Captain John Smith, the founder of Jamestown. Warren Relfe attended school near Linwood, in Madison County; near Amboy, in Miami County; and after his parents moved to Grant County, in October, 1869, he went to the Fairmount Township schools. When he left school he engaged in farming, in which occupation he has been successful. He was one of the original stockholders of the Barren Creek Gas Company. In the spring of 1896 he was elected Township Assessor, serving in this position until 1900. Again, in 1904, the people turned to Mr. Relfe, and he was for the second time honored by their confidence, the term of Assessor being by act of the State Legislature extended from four to six years, making the total length of time ten years for the two terms for which he was elected. In politics Mr. Relfe is a Progressive Republican. He is a member of Pleasant Grove Methodist Protestant Church. February 22, 1877, Mr. Relfe was married to Miss Mary Ann Buller, born in Liberty Township, January 5, 1857, a daughter of John and Jane (Thomas) Buller. She died January 12, 1912. Four children were born of this marriage, namely: George M., January 22, 1878; Nellie, June 16, 1880; Frank E., February 16, 1882, and Mary E., March 10, 1887. George died April 1, 1881; Nellie died October 25, 1914; Frank E. and family reside on the Hubert farm, in the northeast corner of the Township. March 20, 1915, Mr. Relfe married for his second wife, Miss Ida Ink, daughter of a well known pioneer family of the Township.

from the other. The space between lies high and is covered with oak, as are also the eastern and western banks of creek and prairie."

In June, 1855, the Board of County Commissioners made a general reorganization of the Township. Union and Fairmount Townships were consolidated, the territory comprising the new division taking the name of Union Township. Again, before the close of the year 1855, another change was ordered, and the old lines restored. Being again consolidated in 1858, the new arrangement re-established the original boundaries and the territory thus created was called Fairmount Township.

At the September session of the Board of Commissioners, in 1863, a part of Township 25, situated west of the Mississinewa River, was

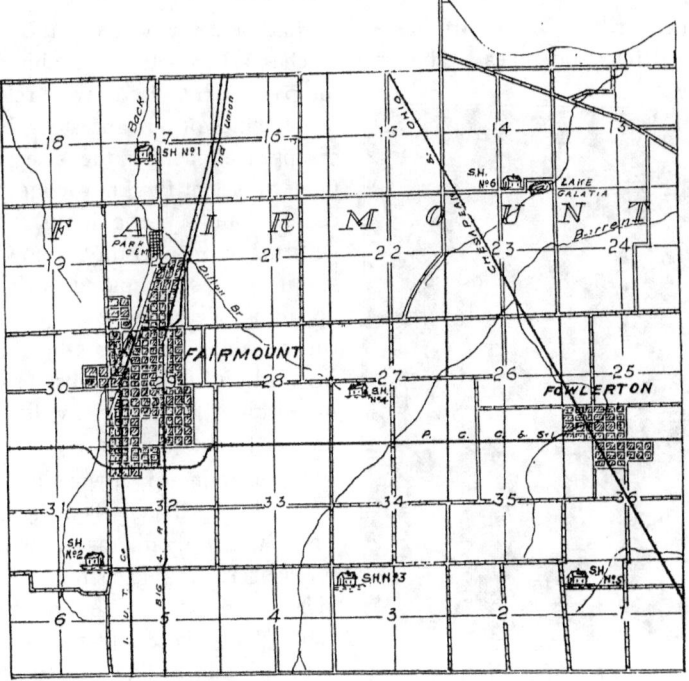

MAP OF FAIRMOUNT TOWNSHIP
(1917)
Courtesy of Marion Title & Loan Company.

added to Center Township, and at a later period that part of Sections 11 and 12, in Township 23, Range 8, which lies south of the Mississinewa, was annexed to Fairmount Township. There has been no change in the boundary lines of the Township since 1863.

It may be remarked, in passing, that inasmuch as Fairmount Township, while yet in her infancy, partook freely of the soil of Liberty and Union, seed fell upon good ground. The natives of this community point with a pardonable pride and satisfaction to the unusually heavy enlistments from Fairmount Township in the Union Army during the Civil War and the War with Germany.

Considering territorial area there is comparatively little or no unproductive land in the Township. Practically every foot of cleared ground is under cultivation. The earnest labors of the pioneer, reenforced at a later period by the industry and enterprise of his sons and daughters, have transformed the bogs and the beaver dams of the early day into the fertile farms of the present.

The corduroy roads of more than half a century ago have been replaced by good pikes. The open ditches are practically a thing of the past. Chills and fever, relentless enemies of our ancestors, have disappeared before the sweep of modern scientific knowledge and correct sanitary conditions. The percentage of mortality is now insignificant as compared with the appalling death rate of former times, when large families were invaded and homes almost broken up within a few weeks by diseases known to the pioneer.

THOMAS J. LUCAS

At a meeting of Township Trustees held April 11, 1853, the bond of William Hall, as Township Treasurer, was accepted as sufficient and filed. The Trustees at that date were Jesse Brooks, Nixon Rush, Sr., and Joseph Hollingsworth. Ezra Foster was the Township Clerk. At this session of the Trustees seventy-five cents was allowed as compensation for one full day's service. This is the first meeting of Township Trustees, the law then providing for the election of three, instead of one, as shown by the official records of the Township now in possession of the present incumbent, Trustee David G. Lewis.

In April, 1854, there were six road districts in the Township. The list of road hands eligible for service was classified as follows:

District No. 1, James M. Ellis, Supervisor—Joseph W. Hill, Jesse Harvey, John Carey, Thomas Harvey, Jr., Henry Winslow, Linden Osborn, Joseph Carey, Robert Carey, Robert Corder, Samuel Radley,

Allen Wright, George Rich, Samuel Dillon, Seth Winslow and James M. Ellis.

District No. 2, William Pierce, Supervisor—William Pierce, Clarkson Pierce, Thomas Newby, James Harrison, Andrew Lytle, John Phillips, Joel Phillips, Jesse Pemberton, Mordecai Davidson, Moses Larkin, James Davidson, Milton Winslow, Jesse Dillon and John Knox.

District No. 3, Hopkins Richardson, Supervisor—William Winslow, Isaac Wright, Henry Level, Aaron Kaufman, Charles Stanfield, George Lewis, John Benbow, Isam Portice, Walker Winslow, Daniel T. Lindsey, Henry Winslow, Jonathan D. Richardson, Zimri Richardson, Simon Kaufman, Isaac Roberts and James Quinn.

District No. 4, Phillip Patterson, Supervisor—Andrew Buller, Carter Hasting, James Nixon, Judiah Smithson, Daniel Thomas, John Seale, Nathan D. Wilson, Jesse E. Wilson, Jonathan Baldwin, Nathan Little, Isaac Hawkins, David Baldwin, Phillip Patterson, Mahlon Cook, John Henley, Joseph W. Baldwin, Isaac Stanfield, James Cammack, William Hundley, William Wright, Nixon Rush, Sr., Nathan Vinson, Seaberry Lines, William Hall, Solomon Parsons, Joshua Foster, Andrew Leverton, Calvin Dillon and Iredell Rush.

District No. 5, Lindsey Wilson, Supervisor—Hanley Broyles, Henry Wilson, Eli Neal, Micajah Wilson, Henry J. Reel, Andrew J. Mann, Albert Dillon, James Lytle, Calvin Bookout, Clayton L. Stanfield and Alfred Waldron.

District No. 6, William Fear, Supervisor—William Fear, John Smith, John W. Ridge, Aaron Cosand, James Williams, Isaac Thomas, William Parsons, Isaac Johnson, Clark A. Johnson, Jr., Henry Osborn, Jonathan Osborn, Charles A. Johnson and Nelson Thomas.

April 7, 1856, Phineas Henley was elected Justice of the Peace, William Hall, Treasurer, A. R. Williams, Clerk, and Samuel Dillon, Daniel Thomas and Micajah Wilson were chosen to serve on the Board of Township Trustees.

In 1858 Thomas D. Duling, Samuel Dillon and Seth Winslow were elected to the Board of Township Trustees, John S. Carey, Township Clerk and William Hall, Township Treasurer. This was the last year that a Board of Township Trustees was elected.

In 1859 the law was amended so as to provide for the election annually of one Township Trustee, for a term of one year.

On April 4, 1859, Henry Harvey was elected, being the first man to serve under the new law.

The following Township Trustees have served since the election of Harvey:

1860-1865—Jonathan P. Winslow.
1865—M. C. Wilson.
1866—Jonathan P. Winslow.
1867—Samuel Dillon.
1868—Jonathan P. Winslow.
1869—J. F. Jones.
1870—Morgan O. Lewis.
1871-1872—J. Nixon Elliott.
1873-1874—Joseph H. Wilson.
1875-1877—Eli Neal.
1880—Lemuel Pearson.
1884—Joseph Ratliff.
1888—Lemuel Pearson.
1890—John Kelsay.
1894—Joseph Ratliff.*
1900—Joel O. Duling.
1904—Alvin J. Wilson.
1908—John R. Little.
1914—David G. Lewis.

The census of 1860 shows that Fairmount Township had a population of one thousand, three hundred and six, two colored. In 1870 the census shows a population of one thousand, five hundred and seventy-three, one thousand, five hundred and forty-three native, thirty foreign; one thousand, five hundred and twenty white and fifty-three colored.

The taxable property of the Township in 1876 amounted to five hundred and sixty-three thousand, three hundred and twenty-five dollars.

*Joseph Ratliff, for many years Trustee of Fairmount Township, serving in this important office at different times, was a native of Henry County, Indiana, born March 27, 1838. His parents were Gabriel and Catherine (Pearson) Ratliff, natives of North Carolina, who came to Indiana and settled with their parents while small children, near Richmond. Joseph Ratliff came to Fairmount Township in 1870, and bought the farm one mile northeast of Fairmount, which he owned until his death. He was educated in Miami County, Indiana, where he was married, in 1859, to Miss Mary A. Lamb, a native of Madison County, Indiana. They were the parents of eight children, but two of whom, Ancil E., a prosperous Liberty Township farmer, and Dr. Milo E. Ratliff, a prominent citizen and dentist of Cassopolis, Mich., are the only survivors. Joseph Ratliff and family were consistent members of the Society of Friends, and were always active and influential in the church. He was during his entire lifetime engaged in farming. His broad experience and strict integrity in all the affairs of life soon won the confidence of the people of the Township and this confidence was fully justified by a number of years of faithful and efficient service rendered.

In 1876 four hundred and forty votes were cast in the Township for the different candidates for President, of which number Rutherford B. Hayes received two hundred and ninety-six; Samuel J. Tilden, one hundred and twenty-one, and Peter Cooper, twenty-three.

DAVID G. LEWIS

Township Trustee, was born two miles and one-half southeast of Fairmount, on what was known as the John Leach farm, August 16, 1862. His paternal grandparents were David and Nancy (George) Lewis; his maternal grandparents were Morgan and Susan Lewis. Morgan O. Lewis, the father, and a former Township Trustee, was born in Fairmount Township, January 21, 1836, and died January 18, 1884. The mother, Maria Lewis, was born at Narvou, Illinois, May 4, 1844, and died in November, 1901. David G. Lewis was educated in the common schools of Fairmount Township. In 1868 he attended his first school at Sugar Grove, which was taught by his father. All his life he has followed farming. For twenty-five years he has studied tree culture. His nursery on South Mill Street is an evidence of his perseverance and industry. For several years he was a stockholder and director in the Fairmount Fair Association. Mr. Lewis is a self-made man. By his own unaided efforts he has met with success from humble beginnings. As Trustee of Fairmount Township he was the first to secure State aid for vocational training, which enables boys over fourteen and under twenty-five to secure competent instruction in various vocations. In politics he is a Democrat, and has served his party as precinct committeeman, Secretary of the Township Committee, and as a member of the Finance Committee. He has been active in all organized movements looking to the elimination of the saloon from County and Township. The esteem in which he is held is evidenced by his election as President, repeatedly, of the Grant County Township Trustees' Association. He was reared in the Methodist Protestant Church. In June, 1899, he was married at Jonesboro, to Miss Mintie Ward, only child of Austin P. and Lucinda A. Ward, and a granddaughter of Elijah Ward, who helped to organize the first Methodist Church in Fairmount Township. Mr. and Mrs. Lewis are the parents of one son, Iliff Ward Lewis, born January 30, 1903. All his life, with the exception of eleven months spent in Hand County, South Dakota, has been passed in Fairmount Township.

In September, 1870, a petition, properly drawn, and signed by a sufficient number of voters of Fairmount, was presented to the County Commissioners, requesting that an election be authorized for the purpose of determining whether or not the town should be incorporated.

The election was held on September 26 of that year. The total vote cast was sixty-five. Of this number, forty-four were in favor of incorporation and twenty-three voted against it.

The first election of officers, on December 10, 1870, resulted as follows: Trustee First Ward, Enoch Beals; Trustee Second Ward, Elwood Haisley; Trustee Third Ward, Milton Gossett; Trustee Fourth Ward, Dr. P. H. Wright; Trustee Fifth Ward, C. T. Schooley. A. M. Raper was elected Clerk; Micajah Wilson, Town Assessor, and Foster Davis, Marshal.

The Board of Trustees met January 23, 1871, and adopted By-Laws. At a meeting held on April 4, 1871, William Hall, Alex Pickard and Joseph N. Rush were elected School Trustees.

BY-LAWS ADOPTED.

Fairmount, Indiana, Monday Evening, January 23, 1871.

The Board met by call of the President and the following members were present, viz.:

First District—Enoch Beals.
Second District—Elwood Haisley, President.
Third District—Milton Gossett.
Fifth District—C. T. Schooley.
P. H. Wright, of the Fourth District, was absent.

The Clerk then presented the bonds of Clerk, Treasurer, Marshal and Assessor, which were accepted by the Board.

On motion the Board adopted the following By-Laws, viz.:

Article One.—It shall be the duty of the President to call the members to order and conduct all business before the Board to a speedy and proper result.

Article Two.—He shall state all questions to the Board before putting it to vote, shall ask, "Are you ready for the question?" Should no member of the Board offer to speak, he shall rise to put it and after he has arisen no member shall be allowed to speak on it without the consent of all the members present.

Article Three.—A motion must be seconded and afterward repeated from the chair or read aloud before it is debatable.

Article Four.—The President shall have a casting vote in case of a tie, but in ordinary cases shall not vote. He shall announce all votes and decisions and his decision shall not be debatable, unless he invites discussion.

Article Five.—He may speak to points of order in preference to other members, rising from his seat for that purpose, and he shall decide points of order subject to an appeal by any member of the Board.

Article Six.—When an appeal is taken from the decision of the President, he shall put the question thus: "Shall the decision of the chair be sustained?"

Article Seven.—It shall be the duty of the presiding officer to call any member to order who violates any established rule of order.

Article Eight.—It shall be the duty of the Secretary, or Clerk, to call the roll of the members at each meeting, note absentees, and read the minutes of the previous meeting, and keep a true and accurate record of the proceedings of the Board of Trustees.

Article Nine.—When a member is called to order he shall take his seat until the point is settled.

Article Ten.—When two or more members rise to speak at the same time, the presiding officer shall decide who is entitled to the floor.

Article Eleven.—No member shall speak more than twice, nor longer than five minutes each time, without consent of the Board.

Article Twelve.—While the member is speaking no one shall interrupt him, except for the purpose of an explanation.

Article Thirteen.—Any conversation by whispering or otherwise, which is calculated to disturb a member while speaking or hinder the transaction of business, shall be deemed a violation of order and if persisted in shall incur censure.

Article Fourteen.—When a question is before the Board the only motion in order shall be, first, to adjourn; second, the previous question; third, to lay on the table; fourth, to postpone indefinitely.

Article Fifteen.—A motion to adjourn shall always be in order, except, first, while a member is in possession of the floor; second, while the yeas and nays are being called; third, while the members are voting, and fourth, when any business of importance is before the house.

Article Sixteen.—The Board shall be called to order by the President within fifteen minutes of the time the Board agreed to meet at its last session, or if he is not present, the Board will be allowed to call one of its members to the chair, for the transaction of business.

Article Seventeen.—It shall be the duty of the Treasurer to receive all money assessed by the Board, and pay it out on an order from the Board attested by the President and Clerk.

Article Eighteen.—It shall be the duty of the Marshal to execute and put in force all the ordinances and laws passed by the Board of Trustees, and perform all the duties prescribed by law for the action of the corporation.

Article Nineteen.—It shall be the duty of the Assessor to make a true and correct assessment of all the property, both real and personal, within the corporation limits, and make a return to the Board of the same, according to law.

Article Twenty.—The Marshal shall be allowed one dollar per each arrest he may make and sustain, and for serving subpoena, or other writs, such fees as are allowed constables by law, and for collecting taxes he is allowed five per cent. on the amount collected.

Article Twenty-one.—The Assessor shall be allowed one dollar and a half a day for each day he may be occupied in making the assessment of the corporation.

Article Twenty-two.—The Clerk shall be allowed one dollar and fifty cents for each regular meeting and for each called meeting and for other services he shall receive a reasonable compensation to be allowed by the Board.

Article Twenty-three.—The Treasurer shall be allowed a reasonable compensation by the Board for his services.

Article Twenty-four.—It shall be the duty of each member to vote on every question before the house, either for or against.

On motion the Board adopted Ordinance No. 1, which is recorded in Ordinance Book, Page 1; also Ordinance No. 2, recorded in said Book, Page 2; also Ordinance No. 3, recorded in said Book, Pages 2 and 3; also Ordinance No. 4, recorded in said Book, Pages 3 and 4.

On motion Ordinance No. 3 should not take effect until thirty days after its publication.

On motion the Clerk was requested to ascertain whether two blank books for the use of the Board could be obtained for an order from the Board for their cost, and if so to order such books.

On motion the Board adjourned to meet on Thursday evening, January 26, 1871, at 6:30 o'clock p. m.

E. HAISLEY, President.
A. M. RAPER, Clerk.

The 1870 census shows that Fairmount had a total population of three hundred and thirty-four native and three foreign; three hundred and thirty-one white and six colored.

In 1875 there were two hundred and fifty-three children of school age in the corporation. The amount of tuition fund drawn during the year was seven hundred and eighty-nine dollars and thirty cents.

In 1876 Fairmount corporation had enumerated two hundred and thirty children of school age, one hundred and twenty male and one hundred and ten female. The average daily attendance was one hundred and thirty-five. There were three teachers, one male and two females. The teachers' wages per day average, male four dollars and female two dollars and a half. Days taught during the year, one hundred. One frame school house was sufficient to accommodate the pupils. The estimated value of the school building and school apparatus was two thousand and fifty dollars.

NAMES OF OFFICIALS OF FAIRMOUNT CORPORATION
From 1871 to 1917
BOARD OF TRUSTEES

Year	First District	Second District	Third District	Fourth District	Fifth District	Clerk and Treasurer
Jan. 1871 to May 1872	Enoch Beals* Willis Spenny† Wm. Wilkinson	Elwood Haisley* A. R. Williams	Milton Gossett	P. H. Wright* Foster Davis	C. T. Schooley	A. M. Raper
May 1872 to May 1873	W. J. Neal† Wm. Fogelman Alex Little	Isaac Smithson	W. B. Hollingsworth	Jacob Woollen	Wm. Wilkinson	J. N. Elliott
May 1873 to May 1874	John Lillibridge	Isaac Smithson* W. D. Montgomery	W. B. Hollingsworth	Jacob Woollen* Joseph Wilson Thomas Beck	Wm. Wilkinson	J. N. Elliott
May 1874 to May 1875	John Lillibridge	Micajah Wilson	Dr. Alpheus Henley	J. H. Shepard	Wm. Wilkinson*	J. N. Elliott
May 1875 to May 1876	Jonathan Baldwin	James Tuttle	Dr. Alpheus Henley	Wm. Woollen	H. W. Winslow	Samuel Knight
May 1876 to May 1877	J. B. Hollingsworth	A. Frank Norton	Dr. Alpheus Henley	Wm. Woollen	Wm. Hasting† Joseph Wilson	Samuel Knight
May 1877 to May 1878	D. M. Nottingham	A. Frank Norton	Dr. Alpheus Henley	Wm. Woollen.	Levi Scott* Wm. Hasting	Robert Bogue
May 1878 to May 1879	D. M. Nottingham† Nathan Vinson	Isaac Smithson	J. N. Wheeler	Wm. Woollen* Eli J. Scott† Levi Scott	Henry Love	Robert Bogue
May 1879 to May 1880	Nathan Vinson	A. D. Bryan	J. N. Wheeler	Levi Scott* Irvin Galloway	Wm. Hasting	Robert Bogue
May 1880 to May 1881	Nathan Vinson	Albertson Relfe* Gabriel Johnson	W. D. Montgomery	Wm. Hasting	Wm. R. Woollen	Benj. F. Frazier
May 1881 to May 1882	Foster Davis	Gabriel Johnson	Thomas J. Nixon* John F. Jones	Wm. Hasting	Dr. Chas. V. Moore	Benj. F. Frazier (a) Nathan W. Edwards
May 1882 to May 1883	Henry M. Crilley	Gabriel Johnson	W. D. Montgomery	David A. Baldwin	Jasper N. Wheeler	Nathan W. Edwards
May 1883 to May 1884	Henry M. Crilley	Enoch Beals* Alex Little	W. D. Montgomery	Geo. W. Butler	Wm. Woollen	Nathan W. Edwards
May 1884 to May 1885	Jacob Adell	John S. Baker	M. A. Hiatt†	Geo. W. Butler	Wm. Woollen	Nathan W. Edwards
May 1885 to May 1886	Jacob Adell	H. H. Wiley	Thos. P. Latham Thos. J. Nixon	Ryland Ratliff	Cornelius R. Small	Nathan W. Edwards

Fairmount Township—Corporation.

May 1886 to May 1887	Asa Carter	H. H. Wiley	Thos. J. Nixon	Ryland Ratliff	Cornelius R. Smal	Nathan W. Edwards
May 1887 to May 1888	Asa Carter	H. H. Wiley† Daniel Baldwin† Chas. T. Parker	Thos. J. Nixon	Wm. F. Fink	Cornelius R. Smal	Ephraim Smith
May 1888 to May 1889	Matthew M. Symons	Micajah Wilson	Wm Hosting	Wm. F. Fink	Cornelius R. Smal Wm. R. Pearson† Joel B. Wright	Ephraim Smith
May 1889 to May 1890	Matthew M. Symons	J. Hamilton Dean	Wm. Hasting	Wm. F. Fink	Theo. W. Bryan	Ephraim Smith
May 1890 to May 1891	Josiah G. Worley	J. Hamilton Dean	Joseph W. Patterson	Wm. F. Fink	Lew A. Cassell Theo. W. Bryan	Ephraim Smith
May 1891 to May 1892	Josiah G. Worley	John H. Wilson† Jehu Hardwick	Joseph W. Patterson	Wm. F. Fink	Theo. W. Bryan	Ephraim Smith
May 1892 to May 1893	Matthias S. Friend	Jehu Hardwick	Joseph W. Patterson	Wm. F. Fink	Wm. R. Pearson	Ephraim Smith
May 1893 to May 1894	Matthias S. Friend	Jason B. Smith	Joseph W. Patterson	Gabriel Johnson	Wm. R. Pearson	Ephraim Smith
May 1894 to May 1895	Matthias S. Friend	Jason B. Smith	Joseph W. Patterson	Gabriel Johnson	Wm. R. Pearson	Ephraim Smith
May 1895 to May 1896	Matthias S. Friend	Samuel Fritch	Joseph W. Patterson	M. A. Hiatt	Wm. R. Pearson	Ephraim Smith
May 1896 to May 1897	Harry Davis	Samuel Fritch	Isaac Elliott	M. A. Hiatt	N. A. Wilson* Wm. R. Pearson	J. H. Winslow (b)
May 1897 to May 1898	Harry Davis	Samuel Fritch	Isaac Elliott	M. A. Hiatt	Wm. R. Pearson	Ephraim Smith
May 1898 to May 1899	Henry M. Crilley	Samuel Fritch	Isaac Elliott	M. A. Hiatt	Lee R. Whitney	Geo. A. Fletcher
May 1899 to May 1900	Henry M. Crilley	Nathan W. Hunt	Isaac Elliott	Robert J. Beals	Lee R. Whitney	Geo. A. Fletcher
May 1900 to May 1901	James Phillips	Nathan W. Hunt	John H. Simons	Robert J. Beals	A. M. Presnall (a) Robert Dare	Jacob Briles
May 1901 to May 1902	James Phillips	Nathan W. Hunt	John H. Simons	Robert J. Beals	Albert Paulus	Jacob Briles
May 1902 to May 1903	James Phillips	Nathan W. Hunt	John H. Simons	Robert J. Beals	Albert Paulus	Jacob Briles
May 1903 to May 1904	James Phillips	Alonzo Thomas	John H. Simons	John Borrey* Fred H. Macy	Albert Paulus	Jacob Briles
May 1904 to Dec. 1905	J. W. Kester	Alonzo Thomas	Frank Andrick Harmon T. Newby* E. J. Seale	Fred H. Macy	Albert Paulus	Jacob Briles
Jan. 1906 to Dec. 1909	M. S. Friend	Alonzo Thomas		F. M. Wood (a) Oliver R. Scott	Wm. L. Henley	Jacob Briles
Jan. 1910 to Dec. 1911	Lemuel Pearson	Oz B. Wilson	Clark D. Overman	Thos. J. Lucas	J. C. Albertson	Walter L. Jay
Jan. 1912 to Dec. 1913	Lemuel Pearson	Oz B. Wilson	Clark D. Overman	Curtis W. Smith	J. C. Albertson	Earl Morris
Jan. 1914 to Dec. 1915	Lemuel Pearson (a) John W. Smith	Wm. Z. Payne	James T. Hill	Curtis W. Smith	Homer L. Leer	Earl Morris
Jan. 1916 to Dec. 1917	John W. Smith	Wm. Z. Payne	James T. Hill	John M. Harvey	Homer L. Leer	Earl Morris

* Resigned.   † Moved from district.   (a) Deceased.   (b) Sick.   Deputy Clerk, Ephraim Smith.

SCHOOL TRUSTEES
From 1871 to 1917

Apr. 1871 to Apr. 1873	William Hall	Alexander Pickard	Joseph N. Rush
Apr. 1873 to Apr. 1874	William Hall*	Jesse Reece	Dr. Henry Charles
	Jos. K. Bennett (a)	Isaac Smithson	
April 4, 1874		Isaac Smithson (b)	
April 3, 1875			Dr. Henry Charles*
June 6, 1876 (c)	J. N. Elliott		James Tuttle
August 15, 1876	J. N. Elliott	Andrew Buller	Enoch Beals
April 24, 1877	J. N. Elliott	Andrew Buller	Enoch Beals
June 10, 1878	J. N. Elliott	Andrew Buller	P. H. Wright
June 3, 1879	J. N. Elliott	Andrew Buller	P. H. Wright
June 1, 1880	J. N. Elliott	Andrew Buller	P. H. Wright
June 6, 1881	J. N. Elliott	Andrew Buller (d)	Alpheus Henley
		Thomas J. Nixon	
June 3, 1882	Foster Davis	Thomas J. Nixon	Alpheus Henley
June 11, 1883	Foster Davis	Enoch Beals	Alpheus Henley
June 7, 1884	Foster Davis	Enoch Beals	Alpheus Henley
June 1, 1885	Mrs. Alice Nixon	Enoch Beals	Alpheus Henley
June 7, 1886	Mrs. Alice Nixon	Enoch Beals	Alpheus Henley
June 6, 1887	Mrs. Alice Nixon	Enoch Beals*	Elwood Davis
		Clarkson D. Overman	
June 4, 1888	A. R. Long	Clarkson D. Overman	Elwood Davis
June 3, 1889	A. R. Long	Clarkson D. Overman	Elwood Davis
June 9, 1890	A. R. Long	Clarkson D. Overman	N. W. Edwards
June 1, 1891	Oliver R. Scott	Clarkson D. Overman	N. W. Edwards
June 9, 1892	Oliver R. Scott	John H. Wilson	N. W. Edwards
June 7, 1893	Oliver R. Scott	John H. Wilson	N. W. Edwards
June 6, 1894	Oliver R. Scott	John H. Wilson	N. W. Edwards
June 1, 1895	Oliver R. Scott	Gurney Lindley*	N. W. Edwards
		Fred H. Macy	
June 10, 1896	Oliver R. Scott	Fred H. Macy	Nathan W. Edwards
June 8, 1897	Gabriel Johnson	Fred H. Macy	Nathan W. Edwards
June 15, 1898	Gabriel Johnson	Fred H. Macy	Nathan W. Edwards
June 3, 1899	Gabriel Johnson	Fred H. Macy	Nathan W. Edwards
July 5, 1900	Dr. J. W. Patterson	Fred H. Macy	Nathan W. Edwards
June 6, 1901	Dr. J. W. Patterson	John Flanagan	Nathan W. Edwards
June 5, 1902	Dr. J. W. Patterson	John Flanagan	Nathan W. Edwards
June 1, 1903	Dr. J. W. Patterson	John Flanagan	Nathan W. Edwards
June 6, 1904	Dr. J. W. Patterson	John Flanagan	Nathan W. Edwards
June 5, 1905	Dr. J. W. Patterson	John Flanagan	Nathan W. Edwards
June 18, 1906	Dr. J. W. Patterson	John Flanagan	Nathan W. Edwards
June 3, 1907	Dr. J. W. Patterson	Oscar M. Bevington	Nathan W. Edwards
June 1, 1908	Dr. J. W. Patterson	Oscar M. Bevington	Nathan W. Edwards
June 7, 1909	Dr. J. W. Patterson	Oscar M. Bevington	Nathan W. Edwards*
			Xen H. Edwards
June 7, 1910	Dr. J. W. Patterson	Oscar M. Bevington*	Xen H. Edwards
		Oliver R. Scott	
June 6, 1911	Dr. J. W. Patterson	Oliver R. Scott	Asa Driggs
June 4, 1912	Walter L. Jay	Oliver R. Scott	Asa Driggs*
			Oliver Buller
June 3, 1913	Walter L. Jay	Oliver R. Scott	Oliver Buller
June 2, 1914	Walter L. Jay*	Oliver R. Scott	Enos M. Lafler
	Mrs. Helen Wells		
June 1, 1915	V. A. Selby	Oliver R. Scott	Enos M. Lafler
June 6, 1916	V. A. Selby	Oliver R. Scott	Enos M. Lafler
June 5, 1917	V. A. Selby	Oliver R. Scott	Dr. Charles N. Brown

* Resigned.   (a) Removed from corporation.   (b) Moved to Marion, Ind.   (c) On August 15, 1876, Board of Trustees declared all school board offices vacant.   (d) Deceased.

ASSESSORS AND MARSHALS

Year	Marshal	Assessor
Jan. 1871 to May 1872	Foster Davis* Joel O. White* D. H. Crawford	Micajah Wilson* Foster Davis* D. H. Crawford
May 1872 to May 1873	D. H. Crawford* James R. Smith* Frank Norton	D. H. Crawford* James R. Smith* Frank Norton
May 1873 to May 1874	Henry Winslow John Ried Elwood Haisley	Henry Winslow John Ried Elwood Haisley
May 1874 to May 1875	Elwood Haisley* J. F. Jones	Elwood Haisley* J. F. Jones
May 1875 to May 1876	J. F. Jones* David B. Mason	
May 1876 to May 1877	Charley Hasty (a) George Modlin* Jonathan McDonnell	
May 1877 to May 1878	John Kelsay*	
May 1878 to May 1879	Adam M. Miller	
May 1879 to May 1880	Adam M. Miller	
May 1880 to May 1881	Elwood Gardner* Adam M. Miller	
May 1881 to May 1882	Adam M. Miller	
May 1882 to May 1883	Adam M. Miller	
May 1883 to May 1884	Adam M. Miller	
May 1884 to May 1885	Adam M. Miller	
May 1885 to May 1886	J. W. Kester (b)	
May 1886 to May 1887	J. W. Kester Alexander Little	
May 1887 to May 1888	Adam M. Miller (c) Sylvester Smithson* J. W. Kester	
May 1888 to May 1889	John W. Symons	
May 1889 to May 1890	John W. Symons* William M Kennedy	
May 1890 to May 1891	William M. Kennedy	
May 1891 to May 1892	William M. Kennedy	
May 1892 to May 1893	Seth Cox	
May 1893 to May 1894	David O. Ice	
May 1894 to May 1895	Elmer E. Hiatt	
May 1895 to May 1896	Elmer E. Hiatt	
May 1896 to May 1897	Riley Jay	
May 1897 to May 1898	Esom O. Leach	
May 1898 to May 1899	Esom O. Leach	
May 1899 to May 1900	Esom O. Leach* W. E. McCoy	
May 1900 to May 1901	Thell Crabb	
May 1901 to May 1902	Esom O. Leach	
May 1902 to May 1903	Esom O. Leach	
May 1903 to May 1904	James J. Payne (c) C. V. Hadley	
May 1904 to Dec. 1905	C. V. Hadley	
Jan. 1905 to Dec. 1909	James A. Jones	
Jan. 1910 to Dec. 1911	George Bannister* James L. Collins	
Jan. 1912 to Dec. 1913	William H. Eastes	
Jan. 1914 to Dec. 1915	James A. Jones	
Jan. 1916 to Dec. 1917	A. M. Seright	

* Resigned   (a) Removed from town.   (b) Moved away.   (c) Deceased.

HEALTH OFFICERS
From 1873 to 1917

July 2, 1873, to January 2, 1882—Dr. Alpheus Henley.
May, 1883, to May, 1884—Dr. P. H. Wright.
May, 1884, to May, 1887—Dr. C. V. Moore.
May, 1887, to May, 1889—Dr. William B. Thomas.
May, 1889, to May, 1891—Dr. Allen Moon.
May, 1891, to May, 1893—Dr. J. O. Lowman,* Dr. J. W. Patterson,† Dr. A. F. Marlow.
May, 1893, to May, 1894—Dr. A. F. Marlow.
May, 1894, to May, 1895—Dr. Alpheus Henley.
May, 1895, to May, 1901—Dr. Joseph W. Patterson.†
May, 1901, to May, 1903—Dr. J. P. Seale.
May, 1903, to May, 1905—Dr. S. G. Hastings.†
January, 1906, to December, 1909—Dr. William M. Warner.†
January, 1910, to December, 1911—Dr. J. P. Seale.†
January, 1912, to December, 1917—Dr. C. N. Brown.

* Moved to Anderson, Ind.
† Resigned.

CHAPTER XXV.

THE TANYARD—HOME GUARDS AND QUAKER ARSENAL—CAMMACK'S SAW-MILL—THE EXPLOSION.

IN 1846 William Hall built and operated a tannery south of town on the ground where the late J. W. Parrill lived for many years. In 1853 Daniel Ridgeway started a tannery at the northeast corner of Second and Main Streets. In 1856 Micah Baldwin purchased an interest of Ridgeway. They operated the tannery until 1860, when James R. Smith took over the interest of Ridgeway. Baldwin & Smith conducted the business until 1876. In this year William Thomas bought Smith's interest and the enterprise was thereafter managed by Baldwin & Thomas. After disposing of his interest to his partner, Ridgeway started a tannery southeast of Fairmount, where John H. Caskey now lives.

Nathan Little, who had been employed by Ridgeway, in 1861 opened a tannery on East Washington Street. A striking object displayed over the south door of this tannery attracted considerable attention from passers-by. A lynx had been killed by Billy Brewer on land now owned by Charles Allred, situated one mile and a half northeast of Fairmount. The lynx was skinned, prepared, stuffed and mounted, and used as an advertising device for the business carried on within.

It required about a year to tan, properly, a cowhide. The skin was first placed in a lime-vat. After it had remained in this vat a few days it was taken out and the hair removed with a scraping-knife, then to a vat of clean water, where the lime was thoroughly soaked out, and then through a succession of vats containing hen manure, weak oak ooze, strong oak ooze, this process being continued until the skin was thoroughly tanned and turned over to the finishing-room, where an application of "dubbin" was put on, one side blacked and dressed and made ready for the market. The hair was saved and sold to put in mortar for plastering.

Oak bark, called tanbark, was plentiful in those days. Farmers would peel this bark off of trees and cord it up to dry. When thoroughly dried, it was hauled in, and found a ready cash market. The price ranged between two and four dollars per cord. At the tanyard it was corded up under sheds so as to be kept perfectly dry. When needed, it was taken to the grinder, located upon the upper floor, known as the bark-mill. In the center of this room was a large iron hopper, something near three feet in diameter at the top and eighteen or twenty inches at the bottom, and about three feet deep. Inside was a succession of iron teeth, and there was fitted in the hopper another iron small in proportional size and iron teeth fitted on it. This hopper was used to grind the tanbark into a fine powder. It was operated by a large beam, to which was attached one horse going about in a circle. This mill was usually operated by a boy, sometimes the proprietor's son. His work was to get the bark up into the mill and with a wooden mallet break the bark over the edge of the hopper in small pieces two or three inches in length. After being ground the powder fell below into another room, and from there taken out in a wheelbarrow to the yard and placed in the vats.

The tannery was in that day an important institution. It was headquarters in War times for men who were interested in the issues of the day. Abolitionists, especially, would meet here to discuss the slavery question and the progress of the War. It was the stopping-place for refugees, both white and colored, and during the entire War was the center of interest for people from miles around. It was in 1867 that Thomas Harvey, one of the prominent anti-slavery men of his day, suddenly died in the beam-house of the Baldwin-Smith tannery.

According to older residents, it was the housing-place for quantities of arms and ammunition of the Fairmount Company of Home Guards, organized to maintain law and order in the community and to assist in repelling any stray bands of guerrillas that might happen to ride in this direction.

There were one hundred members of this organization. Roland Smith, who had served in the Union army, was the captain; Joseph Macey, first lieutenant, and Dennis Montgomery, second lieutenant.

Regular drills were practiced every Saturday afternoon in the north part of town, which was then known as Christianville. Here on several occasions the company was divided into two forces and sham battles were fought. Often during the week the company would be assembled for military drills, conducted in the evenings after supper on the yard of the school building which then stood on North Walnut Street, near the present home of George Montgomery.

The corner building of the tanyard shown in the picture came to be known as the Quaker Arsenal.

Roland Smith, retired farmer, son of John and Mary Ann (Thomas) Smith, was born four miles northeast of Fairmount, on a farm then owned by his father, on April 20, 1839. On his mother's side he is a grandson of Solomon Thomas. His paternal grandfather was Judge Caleb Smith, both grandparents natives of North Carolina. Roland Smith was educated in the common schools of Fairmount Township, his first teacher being John T. Morris, who, in 1845, was in charge of the school at Back Creek. For many years Mr. Smith owned ninety-six acres of land located south of Fairmount, now known as the Cal Dean farm, which he managed successfully. He has always voted in Fairmount Township, his first ballot being cast for Abraham Lincoln. In politics he is a Progressive Republican. For twelve years he served as road supervisor.

ROLAND SMITH

He is a charter member of Beeson Post, Grand Army of the Republic. For many years he has been a member of the United Brethren Church. In May, 1861, he enlisted in Company H, Twelfth Indiana Infantry, serving with this regiment twelve months. For meritorious conduct he was promoted to sergeant. Returning home in 1862 he organized a company of infantry and was elected captain. When he called upon Governor Oliver P. Morton to tender his services and arrange for his commission, the Governor suggested that he remain at home for duty in Grant County. Accordingly, Smith formed a company of Home Guards, known as the Fairmount Militia Company, composed of one hundred volunteers, and on July 16, 1863, was given a commission for four years as captain of this company. The Home Guards did duty in Fairmount Township during the period of the Civil War, the organization disbanding in 1865, with the close of the Rebellion. The members of the company, so far as Captain Smith is able to recall them from memory, follow:

Captain, Roland Smith
First Lieutenant, Joseph Macey
Second Lieutenant, Dennis Montgomery

William Hasting
Nelson Thomas
Alfred Waldron
Berry Farrington

Eli J. Scott
Jesse Scott
Jesse Haisley
William Smith
Andrew Buller

Elias Rich
Samuel Kirk
T. B. McDonald
Morgan O. Lewis
Moses Adams

LAST OF THE OLD TANYARD

Above is an excellent picture of the finishing room of the tanyard which stood at the northeast corner of Main and Second Streets, on the lot now owned by Victor A. Selby. The house was occupied for many years by Ben Thomas and his sister, Mina. The picture shows Ben Thomas standing in the foreground. Here the pioneers of the early day brought their cowhides and here they hauled oak bark and sold to the tanner at two dollars per cord. In the Garfield campaign, 1880, it was used as a voting place.

Evander Farrington
Levi Scott
Stephen Scott
Elwood Scott
J. M. Hundley
Charley Howell
Jonathan Smithson
Calvin Dillon
Wesley B. Hollingsworth
Philip Davis

Zimri Richardson
Leander Baldwin
Gilmore Hollingsworth
Solomon Duling
Jesse Milner
Harvey Davis, Jr.
David Y. Hoover
Azel Little
William Dillon

Many of the men named volunteered their services and were at the front in the Union army. In the fall of 1863 a dozen shots were exchanged between unknown parties and members of the Home Guard on the Jesse Winslow farm, now owned by Foster Davis, about a mile east of Fairmount. In 1862, Captain Smith was married to Miss Nancy Hasting, daughter of Carter and Elizabeth (Roe) Hasting, pioneers of Fairmount Township, where Mrs. Smith was born, in May, 1844. Eight children were born to this marriage, namely, Effie, Mary Elizabeth, Dailey Henley, Cora, Bertha, Thomas Edwin and Clista. Effie married H. E. Payne; Mary Elizabeth married W. H. Underwood; D. H. married Elizabeth Gimmer; Cora married Lon Payne; Bertha married C. B. Fry and Thomas Edwin married Grace Brattain.

(By J. M. Hundley.)

I was a member of the Fairmount Militia Company referred to as the Home Guards for a short time in 1863, and while I belonged we took our equipment home with us. This equipment consisted, as I now remember it, of a Belgian musket, bayonet, cartridge-box and sixty rounds of fixed ammunition. Very few of this company had uniforms. They were boys from fifteen to sixteen and men from forty to fifty-five, most of them clad in homespun, with straw hats made from straw plaited by mother, and now and then would be seen a coon-skin cap. Some one, whose name I do not now remember, would come to drill practice wearing a stovepipe plug hat. Several of the members had been in the service and had been discharged for disability or because of expiration of term of service, and had a fairly good idea of military tactics. The Belgian muskets with which they were armed were quite as dangerous to the man behind the gun as to the man in front. The boys at the front used to say that there was death at one end and six months' sickness at the other end of these weapons.

I am reminded that some time in June, 1863, I was ordered to report with my blunderbuss for immediate duty. We were drawn up in line and told that Fairmount was to be invaded and burned on that night. Details were made and a cordon of men established around the town. I was placed on duty southeast of town, in the shadow of a dense woods, situated on the farm which formerly belonged to James Tuttle, and told to shoot anything that approached me from the east or south. Captain Smith failed to relieve me during the night and I remained there from 6 o'clock in the evening until 7 o'clock the next morning. I never could quite understand the action of the captain in this matter, as I should have been relieved in two hours; but perhaps the captain thought I might shoot him if he came my way in the darkness of the night. I think it perfectly certain that had any luckless bovine or elm-peeler hog strayed in front of me there would have been an explosion and a hasty retreat, and I am not quite sure what other casualties might have ensued. I think it perfectly safe to say that the men who were suspected with intentions of making war upon your town were soundly sleeping in their homes, with no intention of doing harm to anyone while I stood there alone in the darkness.

I want to say in conclusion that some of these Home Guards had seen service and many of them went to the front and remained until the close of the War. The writer had seen service before and left this organization after some three or four months and again entered the service in the field. I am sure that I left my Guard equipment at the home of my father when I entered the volunteer service and never at any time had it in the Quaker Arsenal.

Summitville, Indiana, April 2, 1917.

James Cammack, who came in the winter of 1848, built a saw-mill the following year on the ground at the southeast corner of Washington and Mill Streets. Cammack had been induced by Iredell and Elizabeth Rush to come to Fairmount. They had been neighbors in Wayne County, Indiana. In 1857 the saw-mill was owned by Albert and Allen Dillon. Jonathan P. Winslow later purchased the mill of the Dillons, and a grist-mill was started in connection. The two occupied a frame building, the grist-mill using the lower floor and the saw-mill the upper one. In 1870, J. N. Wheeler & Company purchased the property of Winslow, and it was for many years successfully operated by J. N. Wheeler and George W. Butler, his father-in-law, under the firm name of J. N. Wheeler & Company.

In August, 1861, occurred the first big sensation that the people of the sparsely settled community had known. The boiler in a grist-mill exploded, scattering fragments of iron and brick and timber in every direction. The mill, which was located on the west side of Mill Street, just north of where Jesse Bogue's house now stands, had been built a few years before by Clayton and Isaac Stanfield and Thomas Lytle. Ward McNeir, of Anderson, known in that day as a trader, owned the mill. A man named Frank Brindle was the miller. John Brandon was the engineer and Hugh Finley was in charge of the mill.

It appeared that Brandon had neglected to keep the proper amount of water in the boiler, and the result of his carelessness was disastrous. The heavy balance-pea was sent by the force of the explosion to the creek bottom on Nathan Wilson's farm, a distance of a quarter of a mile. A piece of the boiler was blown a distance west of the creek on Daniel Thomas's farm. John Smith was passing by at the time in a wagon with his son, William Smith. The father was struck in the head by a piece of brick and the sight of one eye was temporarily destroyed. Dr. Elliott was summoned to take care of Smith, the physician extracting particles of bone and brick from Smith's face. George Doyle, at the time, was conducting a grocery store in a frame building located at the northeast corner of Mill and Adams Streets. A fragment of the debris passed through this building, leaving a hole in its path 18x24 inches square. The mill was so completely demolished that it was never rebuilt.

"Fairmount was scared for once," writes M. A. Hiatt, under date of January 29, 1917.

"In the year 1861 the writer was standing on the front porch at the J. P. Winslow residence. Although I was only eight years old, I can remember the time well. It was a fairly warm, still day, in the afternoon. Everything was quiet. Some were taking their naps. The corner whittler had left his box and retired to the shade, when all at once a very loud noise was heard. It sounded as though there was a great earthquake, or a great volcano had broken loose on the banks of quiet Back Creek. I do not know how high I jumped, but I landed on my feet. I looked down Main Cross (now Washington) Street toward town, and I could see people running and coming from all directions. You should have seen this boy scooting into the house where my mother and Mrs. J. P. Winslow were. Mrs. Winslow said it must have been a keg of powder that had exploded at the store. My mother said she would guess it was the steam mill that had blown up. And she was right.

"If ever a mill blew up that one did. It stood a little south of where Van Arsdall's coal office now stands, on West Washington Street. The boiler blew up while the engineer was up town. If he had been attending to his business it might not have happened. The lower story was blown all to pieces, letting the roof down on it, making it look like a one-story building. It is a wonder no one was killed. The miller and one boy were in the mill. I do not know their names, as I did not live here then. I was visiting here for a few weeks. They were rescued from the mass of broken timbers, and, strange to relate, they were not dangerously hurt.

"Uncle John Smith, living south of town, had just driven up in front of the mill. A brickbat struck him in the face and broke his jaw. He was hurt the worst of any. The pea off the safety-valve was thrown a long distance, alighting in a field on the Jesse Wilson farm. One end of the boiler fell into a pig pen, killing two hogs."

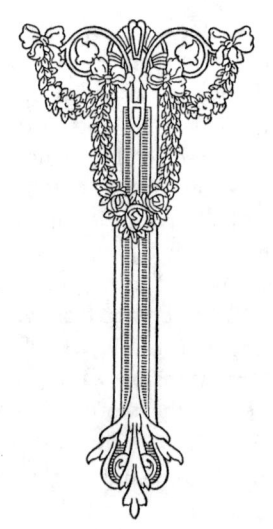

CHAPTER XXVI.

TRANSPORTATION PROBLEM AND PIONEER MERCHANTS.

"TRANSPORTATION was a problem hard to solve in the first settlement of Fairmount Township," writes T. B. McDonald.

"They were compelled to go to Cincinnati for their supplies, such as coffee, salt, powder and lead. This was hauled in wagons drawn by four and six horses over all kinds of roads. They would start from the settlement with what barter they might have to sell, such as fur, ginseng, beeswax, tallow, dry hides, etc. This they would exchange for such goods as were really necessary—shoe pegs and boot and shoe lasts.

"If the men of Fairmount today could see the harness that the teamsters of the early days used they would wonder where all the leather came from. It took an able-bodied man to put the harness on a horse. The back band was from six to eight inches wide. The hames were of wood, three to four inches wide, with high tops, on which bells were often placed. This was done by having an iron arch on which three bells were fastened. There were staples driven in the hames to receive the arches. The collars were immense—leather, usually stuffed with corn husks. The bridles were very heavy with big blinds. The tugs were iron chains housed or covered with leather. The breeching was heavy to match the balance of the harness. A large leather housing went on the top of the collar, and this was for the protection of the horse's neck and shoulders.

"All harness and wagons were made at home. By this I mean they were made by local talent. A saddle was placed on the near, or pole horse, from which the driver directed the lead horses by a jerk line (a single line). An immense leather whip called a black snake was always to be found on the driver's saddle horn. This was used more as a reminder than to punish the horse.

"The wagons had wooden axles and wooden spindles. Pine tar was used as a lubricator. A bucket of tar was always found suspended from the coupling pole at the rear end of the wagon. A feed box was fastened on the rear of the wagon and a tool box on the front. The wagon was always covered to protect the contents. The men who drove these freight wagons usually calculated to reach a given point to stay over night, but if they failed to reach the desired point they would camp out, as they always carried feed and provisions for an emergency.

"In those days almost every house was open to the traveler. If but a one-room house, all were welcome as long as there was room to lie down.

"We have tried to describe the method of transportation in the early days of Fairmount Township. The farmers, however, as a rule, did not have many wagons or horses. The ox team was used because they cost less and were better adapted to clearing the immense forests. There were no harness to buy, nothing but a yoke and a log chain. A team of oxen could be driven where a team of horses could not go with safety. An ox team was perfectly reliable except when thirsty. An ox would go to water at any cost. Often, in cases of necessity, a cow would be broken and used as an ox, as well as supplying milk for the family.

"When we moved to Fairmount Township carriages were scarce. In fact, I do not now remember one. No doubt there were a few, but I failed to recollect it. Most people went horseback or on foot. Saddles were not plentiful. You would often see a sheep skin fastened on with a surcingle. A young man who was fortunate enough to have a saddle horse thought nothing of going to call on his sweetheart, and, if there was church, spelling school or any other social function that she wanted to attend they would go. The young lady would be mounted behind the young man and they would strike out, care free."

I have read with much interest the contribution of T. B. McDonald describing early transportation facilities. I think the Wabash and Erie Canal was built in the thirties, writes J. M. Hundley. I know the canal had been in operation many years before the Indianapolis & Bellefontaine (or Bee Line) Railroad came to Anderson, and this was in 1852.

The Pan Handle (or Pennsylvania) Railroad came to Anderson in 1856. Many men now living will remember that there was no railroad in Grant County during the Civil War, and that soldiers going to the front were transferred in wagons to Anderson, where they took cars for the State capital. What would our military authorities of today think of that kind of mobilization?

I think that for many years after the railroads came to Anderson the farmers of Fairmount Township hauled their wheat to Wabash, probably because the cheap transportation afforded by the canal enabled the buyers to pay a better price for this commodity. Sure I am that this was the chief market, and quite well I remember of having made the trip with my father and some of his neighbors. It required three days to make the round trip, and they generally went four or five teams together, so they could splice and pull up the hills, especially

Deer Creek hill, just this side of Marion. The first day they would drive to the Indian village and camp. The next day they would drive to Wabash or Lagro, dispose of their grain, do their trading, and return to the place where they camped the night before. On the third day they would drive home.

I wish to speak of one of the primitive methods of transportation—"The Mill Boy of the Slashes," and his gray mare. I have no reference here to the historic character distinguished by the above sobriquet whose life and character your schoolboys and girls will no doubt recall. I have reference to the Hoosier boy, who, mounted on the gray mare with a bag of shelled corn under him, rode through the slashes of Fairmount Township to mill.

It was in January, 1861, and the weather was intensely cold. The slashes were covered with a coating of smooth ice. I then lived on the John Eaton farm, near what is now Hackleman. It was necessary to go to mill at Little Ridge, some two or three miles away. The road was an angling track through the woods, following the high ground in ordinary times to keep out of the water, and at this time to keep off the ice. I was mounted on the gray mare with a bag of corn, and in due time reached the mill, which was, I think, operated by Joel B. Wright, an honored and long time resident of your city.

When I reached the mill a number of Hoosier lads had preceded me, and I was compelled to await my turn, which came after the sun had gone down and darkness was approaching. The jolly miller put my grist (I mean the corn meal) on the mare, and me on top of it, and I started for home. I got along quite well until darkness came and I reached the ice in the woods. The mare missed the way, got on the ice and slipped and fell with me and the bag of meal. Fortunately, I was not injured, but my plight can better be imagined than realized. There I was, in the dense woods, in the bitter cold, surrounded by darkness, and unable, for want of strength, to put my meal back on the mare.

I was crying, bitterly, when there came to my aid a good Samaritan, Eli Smook, a pioneer preacher, who was passing through the woods and heard my cries and came to my rescue. He put my meal on the mare, mounted me on top of it, and led the mare to high ground and safety. I reached the cabin in the clearing about nine p. m., and after a good supper of mush and milk was ready to forget the hardships of my adventure.

Mike Beck and Benny Adams hauled freight from Anderson in the early day, this being their occupation in 1860 to 1865. Beck brought the remains of the first Union soldier home from the War on the cold New Year in 1864. The body was taken to the residence of John Smith.

As some indication of the severe weather it is stated that this was the first time in his career that Walker Winslow left the harness on his horses all night for fear they would be so stiff from freezing as to make it impossible to harness the horses next day.

In 1866 David Baldwin commenced hauling freight from Anderson, which was then the nearest shipping point. He used a two-horse wagon. In 1868 the Pan Handle was built to Harrisburg. This being then the nearest railroad station, Baldwin continued to transport freight by wagon from that point, until 1872. During this year he met with an accident which left him a cripple for life. In 1873, J. W. Patterson, nephew of Baldwin, quit school and at the age of thirteen succeeded his uncle in the work. Patterson continued to haul merchandise from Harrisburg until 1875, when the Cincinnati, Wabash & Michigan Railroad was built to Fairmount, this line then taking over the freight business. In 1875 Patterson purchased a dray outfit and continued to carry on this business in Fairmount until 1878, when he sold the dray line to Eli J. Scott and Uriah Ballard.

Before the Civil War O. H. P. Carey owned and operated a stage coach for passengers and freight between Marion and Anderson. His drivers were Coon Slagle and Caleb May. These men were occasionally relieved by Thomas Hobbs and Henley Winslow. They changed horses at Johnny Moore's, just north of Summitville, at a point called Wrinkle. Upon the outbreak of the war Carey volunteered his services, becoming in a short time the colonel of a regiment. He sold his stage coach to Rode Hammill.

About the same year a stage line was established and in operation on the State road from Marion to Muncie. This line changed horses at Wheeling.

About 1860 Walker Winslow bought the stage of Hammill and continued the business. It was not a great while before he owned two Concord stages. One he named "Artemus Ward," after the famous humorist, and the other he called the "Lincoln." In those days it required four horses to pull the load, and occasionally, in bad weather, it required six.

In 1861 Winslow secured a contract from the Government to carry the mail. The compensation agreed upon for this service was three hundred dollars a year, and his route was from Marion to Anderson.

While the work of carrying the mail was important, Winslow soon discovered that the profitable part of his business was the transportation of passengers and express between these points. The coach left Marion every Monday morning, and he made three trips to Anderson every week. The stage would comfortably accommodate twelve passengers, but he has hauled as high as twenty-four when travel was heavy.

Winslow handled large sums of money by express and never lost a dollar. Upon one occasion he had charge of thirty-five thousand dollars in gold and silver, which was billed to Jason Willson's bank, at Marion.

At that time but nine miles of the thirty-four lying between Anderson and Marion were piked, and it frequently required eight hours to cover the distance between the two towns, with six horses pulling every pound they could. In the summer months the distance could be covered in much less time. The old corduroy roads became at times almost impassable. In such an emergency as this he would be compelled to leave his coach behind and use a lighter vehicle to proceed with the mail, riding horseback.

In an interview given to the newspapers shortly before his death, in 1911, Mr. Winslow relates this interesting story:

H. W. WINSLOW

Son of John and Elizabeth (Henley) Winslow, was born in Randolph County, North Carolina, January 16, 1827. With his parents he came to Fairmount Township and resided here until his death, except for a brief time passed in Minnesota and Iowa. The minutes of Back Creek Monthly Meeting of Friends show that on September 19, 1840, a certificate was received for John Winslow and sons, Jesse H., Hugh W., Henry, William and Hezekiah, from Back Creek Monthly Meeting, North Carolina. On February 22, 1848, H. W. Winslow was married to Miss Martha Newsom, a native of Randolph County, North Carolina, born July 24, 1826. Mr. Winslow died at his home in Fairmount on September 6, 1911, and Mrs. Winslow passed away February 4, 1912.

"In addition to being carrier of the mail I invariably carried all important news northward from Anderson, and my route was lined with people daily asking for the latest news from the War. I brought the first news of President Lincoln's assassination into Marion, and I can tell you it was a sorry task for me. People along the route became so excited that frequently men mounted horses and galloped ahead of me for miles, spreading the news to their neighbors.

"In coming through Alexandria that day a big soldier was occupying the seat by my side, and upon reaching the main part of town I called out to the waiting crowd that I had sad news for them, imparting the information of the President's death. The words were scarcely uttered before a man in the crowd shouted:

"'It should have been done long ago!'

"The Union soldier, angered, looked at the man a minute, then crawled down from his seat, and, grabbing him by the throat, fairly hissed into his ear that he and several other passengers in the stage had just come from the South, where they had been very busy shooting such reptiles as he was, and that if he did not get down on his knees and apologize and give a loud cheer for the American flag he would kill him in his tracks. The man fairly groveled in the dirt at the soldier's feet and gave a lusty hurrah, as instructed. This action undoubtedy saved his life."

Winslow continued his stage line until the Cincinnati, Wabash & Michigan Railroad was built, in 1875.

I have read all the articles in the "Making of a Township" with great interest, as I remember so many of the things mentioned in the write-up. It brings back memories of long ago, of friends that have gone beyond, till it occasionally makes one homesick for ye olden times.

If my father, H. W. Winslow, was living, he could give you many thrilling accounts of his life during the War, as he drove the stage coach from Marion to Anderson. He carried the United States mail, also passengers, for that was the main transportation in those days. It was he who brought the War news. He carried *The Indianapolis Journal* and sold them readily at ten cents a piece. He always carried a brass horn on the stage, which he blew when about a mile from town. Then the men would gather, ready to get the papers for the War news. He would get into Fairmount at 1 or 1:30 p. m., when the roads were good. Then he would change his team, which consisted of four horses, and get the other driver started on to Marion. He would stay there till the next morning, gather up the passengers (for they would leave word the night before) and the mail. Then, when they would get to Fairmount, change horses again. Father would then drive to Anderson.

Father was the first person to burn a coal oil lamp in Fairmount. When they came to Anderson he bought one, and when he got home with it people came in to see it burn. They were afraid of it, for fear it would explode. Then he was the first person to burn natural gas after it was drilled in at Fairmount.

In reading the article about David Stanfield I well remember being at church one day when he was the only one who preached, and his sermon was this:

"The young may die and the old must die."

That was all that was said at meeting that day.

JENNIE W. JONES.

Niles, Ohio, March 27, 1917.

(Editor's Note.—Mrs. Jones is the daughter of Walker Winslow and the widow of Capt. John F. Jones. Mrs. Jones lived through the trying times of the Civil War, when most Fairmount people had relatives or friends at the front. It was a period of great anxiety. As the fortunes of war would shift from time to time, and the destiny of the Nation seemed to be hanging in the balance, interest was intense. Walker Winslow was a prominent figure in those days. He was the principal means of communication and the only medium of news which connected the great outside world with the isolated settlement in the wilderness.

In 1896, when promoters first began to talk about building an Interurban line to connect Marion and Anderson, the scheme was put down as a foolish project, fantastic, chimerical and visionary, the dream of a poetic mind.

A meeting was called of men interested in the matter at the Claypool Hotel, in Indianapolis. There were present at this conference Noah Clodfelter, William R. Pearson, Dr. Sullivan, Dan Mustard, Burr Sweetser, John H. Winslow, V. C. Quick and Harvey Painter. Three New York financiers met with this party. Arrangements were made with a New York Trust Company to underwrite $500,000 worth of bonds to begin the work of construction. The conditions arising from the panic of that year rendered it impossible for the Trust Company to sell the bonds.

At a subsequent conference William R. Pearson was directed to go to Chicago to interview the President of the Trust Company of Iowa.

This man's father was a Wall Street capitalist. An attorney and one other representative of the Iowa people were sent to inspect the route of the proposed line. After going over the ground carefully these men returned to Chicago and reported the prospects first class. The President of the Iowa Company went to New York to see his father regarding the matter and the father turned down the proposition on account of the financial stringency then generally prevailing.

L. N. Downs was then interested by the promoters of the enterprise, and he went to Kalamazoo, Mich., where a $92,000 loan was arranged

THE CLODFELTER POWER HOUSE

All that remains of the equipment bought by Noah Clodfelter, original promoter of the Interurban line between Marion and Summitville. This old building stands on the Jonesboro and Fairmount turnpike, opposite Park Cemetery.

for. Immediately upon the consummation of this deal, William R. Pearson went to Cleveland, Ohio, where seventeen carloads of rails were purchased to begin construction work. While at Cleveland Mr. Pearson received a telegram to return at once. Upon his arrival home announcement was made that a proposition had been submitted by Mr. McWhiney, Eli and Charles W. Halderman and Phil Matter for the purchase of the property, the proposition having been accepted. These men financed the enterprise, and in 1898 the line was opened for passenger traffic between Anderson and Marion.

In 1851, Joseph W. Baldwin built a small frame house at the northeast corner of Main and Washington Streets, where the Borrey block now stands. Here a store was opened, and Baldwin became the first merchant in the town.

Other merchants of the early day were Joseph Hollingsworth, Isaac Stanfield, Aaron Kaufman, Paul Williams, William and Vincent Wright, Solomon Parsons, George Doyle, Skid Horne, Seaberry Lines, Henry Harvey, J. P. Winslow, Micajah Wilson, Harmon Pemberton and Robert Bogue, Milt Crowell, Eph Wilson, John Busing, Joshua Hollingsworth, William P. Osborn, A. D. Bryan, Charlton Thomas, Nathan Johnson, John Lillibridge, Thomas Baldwin, B. S. Payne, Mrs. Maria Hollingsworth, Charles W. Hasty, Frank Norton, A. P. Harvey,

THE OLD SWIMMIN' HOLE
(Down by the saw-mill)
Looking north from the West Eighth Street bridge.

D. M. Nottingham, Wilson, Dove & Co., Winslow & Co., H. H. Wiley, Fields & Co., woolen-mill; Winslow & Beals, warehouse; Charles R. Fleming, hotel, and Parker & Relfe, hardware.

A business directory prepared and printed in 1877 shows the following:

William Azbel, proprietor hotel; Enoch Beals, grain dealer; Henry Charles, physician; Asa Carter, carriage and wagon maker; Foster Davis, justice of the peace; W. J. Dove, miller; William S. Elliott, farmer and tile maker; Alpheus Henley, physician; John B. Hollingsworth, monument dealer; Cyrus Haisley, farmer; Jabez H. Moore, retired farmer and mechanic; Eli Neal, farmer and Township trustee; Maj. B. V. Norton, farmer; Thomas J. Parker, dealer in boots and shoes; Samuel Radley, farmer; Aaron Taylor, farmer and teacher; James Underwood, farmer; J. P. Winslow, merchant and county commissioner; Jesse E. Wilson, farmer; John Wilson, engineer; H. H. Wiley, proprietor planing mill; C. A. Wood & Son, proprietors stave factory; Lewis Moorman, retired farmer, and Joel B. Wright, farmer.

Joseph W. Baldwin, son of Daniel and Christian (Wilcuts) Baldwin, was born in Wayne County, Indiana, January 13, 1818. He came to Fairmount Township in the fall of 1833, with his parents. His father entered land on December 16, 1833. When he became of age his father gave him eighty acres of land, then in the woods, now owned by the heirs of Perry Seale. Joseph immediately put out a deadening and built a cabin. On April 15, 1840, he married Lydia Jane Stanfield, a daughter of his neighbor, David Stanfield. They moved on the land and proceeded to make a farm, where he lived for some years, and where three of his children were born. When they moved into their cabin there was an unbroken wilderness for many miles directly west of them, and from that direction they could hear the wolves howl almost any night.

In ten years there was a great change made in that neighborhood. Emigrants came in, taking up land and clearing the forest. The people soon began to think of public improvements; but no prophet, or son of a prophet, had yet given the projected village a name. Joseph W. Baldwin was getting a little tired of the slow progress of farming and conceived the idea of

JOSEPH W. BALDWIN

being the first man to start business in the prospective town. He was short of funds.

About this time James Cammack arrived upon the scene, looking for a location to erect a steam saw-mill. Previous to this date there was no mill nearer than Jonesboro, about five miles distant, where the good people could get lumber for buildings.

The heavy forest of fine saw timber and the growing settlement of a good class of citizens made a very favorable impression upon Mr. Cammack. At a called meeting of the citizens of Fairmount and surrounding community to ascertain the feeling and the support that would be given such an enterprise, the Township was well represented. Cammack made them a proposition that if they would sell him a piece of ground on which to locate a mill and dwelling, and guarantee a certain number of logs to be on the ground when the mill was ready for operation, he (Cammack) would build and operate the mill.

Cammack's proposition was so much more favorable than was expected that the citizens were jubilant over it and a contract was soon entered into by David Stanfield offering to sell a mill site on his north line and Jonathan Baldwin offering to sell him a piece of ground on his south line for a residence building.

At this date the county road east and west had not been opened out and the travel was on the line between Jesse and Nathan Wilson's farms. They realized that work must be done at once or they could not even establish a cross-roads postoffice or blacksmith shop. Consequently, the people and road supervisor got busy and established that road and laid a corduroy and bridge over the creek, which at times reached from Rush Street to near Mill Street, a regular bog, set with willow maple, ash and buttonwood shrub. Long before Cammack had his mill ready to cut lumber his contract with the people for saw-logs was filled and duplicated.

John Bull had come over from England a short time before, bringing a bag of gold with which to buy land. Accordingly, Joseph struck Bull for a trade. Baldwin sold out to Bull and got his money all in cash. He at once proceeded to put up a small frame house (hauling his lumber from Jonesboro) on the corner where the Borrey block now stands. In this house he fitted up a room in the southwest corner for dry goods and groceries. He procured the assistance of Thomas Jay, a merchant of some experience from Jonesboro, to help him in the selection of his first stock of goods, and was soon established as the first citizen and first merchant of the village. Here he made some money, but when competition got too sharp and the patronage divided up, he sold out and bought a farm near Marion, where he ended his days. He died June 26, 1893. DR. A. HENLEY.

Following are the names of business and professional people in different firms at present located in Fairmount:

Bee Hive Cash Store
Xen H. Edwards
Ribble Bros.
R. C. Shoffner
M. W. Hunt
W. H. Parrill
Fallis Bros.
Hiatt & Ware
John Flanagan
Charles C. Hackney
J. W. Dale
Claud Jones
S. A. Hockett
Henry W. Hahne
Charles Keifer
L. E. Nolder
J. R. Busing & Co.
Mrs. Bessie Cooper
John Osborn
W. Frank Buller
Hollingsworth & Co.
Charles H. Stephens
Fritz & Son
Marion Light and Heating Co.
   L. A. Wagoner, Manager
Hill Brothers
John L. Conrad
L. H. Kimes
P. H. O'Mara
Oz Fankboner
J. C. Albertson
C. L. Salyers
L. E. Montgomery
Montgomery & Buchanan
Will R. Lewis
Elmer Pennington
Elmer Jay & Son
Mercer, Brannum & Bevington Co.
Ab Jones
Charles F. Naber
John Winslow
A. D. Bryan
E. H. Parker
N. A. Wilson
Fairmount State Bank
Citizens State Bank
A. M. Seright
Kelly & Son
Clinton Sellars
W. P. Van Arsdall
Dr. J. G. Yerkey
Dr. Sidney T. Rigsbee
Dr. C. N. Brown
Harley Winsett
David G. Lewis
Walter Jones
Charles L. Buller
Arley Addison
C. C. Brown
Dr. Harry Aldrich
Seth Cox
A. R. Long
Charles Brown
Myron Parker
E. O. Ellis
Dr. L. D. Holliday
Dr. D. A. Holliday
Rev. P. W. Raidabaugh
S. H. Buchtel
McNeil & Jay

Mrs. Ella Patterson
Wilbern & Briles
Charles T. Parker
Joseph A. Roberts
C. D. Overman
O. R. Scott
R. C. Smith
J. W. Smith
A. L. Dreyer
John Winslow

Central Indiana Gas Company,
   Charles Wingate, Manager
Dr. D. M. Woolen
Dr. J. P. Seale
Isaiah Jay
John T. Howell
Walter S. Ellis
Dr. Glenn Henley
Elmer Flint
Bowman Pickard

Nathan W. Edwards, for more than thirty years a leading citizen and successful business man of Fairmount, was a native of Madison County. He was born near Alexandria, October 27, 1847, and died at his home in Fairmount, May 24, 1910. Peter Edwards, his paternal grandfather, was one of the early pioneers of Madison County and the first citizen to build a brick residence in his neighborhood. During those primitive days in the wilderness the builder and owner of a brick house usually marked its possessor as a man of substantial taste and discrimination and he was regarded by his neighbors as a person unusually thrifty and prosperous.

Henry and Thurza (Ellis) Edwards were natives of North Carolina. They were parents of eight children, namely, Wesley and Benson, both of whom died of injuries received in the Union army during the Civil War; Granville, Orville, Nathaniel, Mary, Isabelle F. and Nathan W.

The latter years of his life were spent by Henry Edwards at the home of his son, in Fairmount, where he passed away August 21, 1900, at the ripe old age of eighty-six years. Though stricken with total blindness during the latter part of his life, he remained cheerful and optimistic to the last day, an example of patience and fortitude. Mrs. Thurza Edwards died at the home of her daughter, Mrs. William Tilden, in Miami County, in 1887, at the age of sixty-seven years.

NATHAN W. EDWARDS

Nathan W. Edwards was educated in the common schools of Madison and Starke Counties, and also attended Richmond Business College. He taught a number of terms in Starke and Madison Counties. He gave up the teaching profession for a business career and entered a drug store at Alexandria. He later owned and managed drug stores at Rigdon and Elwood. In 1877 he bought the Pioneer Drug Store of Dr. P. H. Wright and made Fairmount his home. In politics he never wavered in his support of the Republican party. In recognition of his capacity and fitness for the position, voters of Fairmount, in 1881, elected Mr. Edwards Town Clerk and Treasurer. He served in this office as the practically unanimous choice of citizens from July, 1881, to May, 1887, almost six years. On June 9, 1890, in appreciation of good work performed as Clerk and Treasurer, he was unanimously elected for a term of three years as member of the School Board, an office he filled with exceptional diligence and ability for many years, until June 21, 1909, when he was forced by failing health to resign the position. He was succeeded on the Board by his son, Xen H. Edwards, who filled out his father's unexpired term.

N. W. Edwards served as receiver for Rau Bros., and for a brief time was connected with the reorganization of the Farmers' and Merchants' State Bank. The exactions and confinement of this work were not suited to his tastes or desires and he relinquished his connection with the institution. He was at one time a member of the Knights of Pythias and the Independent Order of Odd Fellows orders. He was affiliated with the Methodist Episcopal Church, having served as one of the trustees and a member of the official board.

On May 21, 1879, Mr. Edwards was married to Miss Lenora Galloway, born at Ogden, Henry County, Indiana, March 6, 1860. Her parents were Irvin and Jeannetta (Daniels) Galloway. They were parents of five children, namely, Frank (deceased), Elmer, Lenora, Alice and Ella, the latter deceased. Nathan W. and Lenora (Galloway) Edwards were parents of three children, namely, Xen H., who married Miss Ethel Harvey, January 15, 1905; Gladys, who married Burl W. Cox, June 27, 1907, now residing at Alexandria, and Forrest, who resides with her mother in Fairmount.

Nathan W. Edwards was always interested in the welfare of the community, and was especially efficient in his efforts on behalf of improved educational facilities. He was among the first to see the need of higher learning, where boys and girls who passed out of the grades might have a chance without leaving home for increased knowledge and additional equipment for the life before them.

CHAPTER XXVII.

FAIRMOUNT PHYSICIANS—FIRST POSTMASTER—NEWSPAPERS—ORGANIZATION OF CORNET BANDS.

DR. ALPHEUS HENLEY, last survivor of that period when physicians of Fairmount Township rode horseback to see their patients and carried their medical supplies in saddle-bags, was born in Randolph County, North Carolina, July 21, 1836. His parents, Phineas and Mary (Bogue) Henley, came to Fairmount Township the following year. They were natives of North Carolina, where they were born in 1802. Dr. Henley's paternal grandparents were John and Keziah (Nixon) Henley, natives of Randolph County, North Carolina; the maternal grandparents were John and Lydia Bogue, natives of Perquimans County, North Carolina.

The Henley family is of English origin, and as far back as their history can be traced they were prominent members of the Society of Friends. The progenitor of the family in America was Patrick Henley, who came to this country in the Seventeenth century and located first in Philadelphia, subsequently removing to North Carolina, where several generations of the family were born.

Phineas Henley entered land, in 1837, one mile and a half northwest of Fairmount, this land now comprising a part of the Alice Thomas farm. Here a cabin was built and a clearing made in the wilderness. Here his family of five children was reared, and here Dr. Henley grew to manhood, attending school in winter in the primitive log school house of that day, with its slab benches and broad fireplace.

In 1857 Dr. Henley, in company with Nixon Rush, went to Coffey County, Kansas, where they entered a claim and lived two years, securing title to same. Dr. Henley did his part during those border ruffian days in the West to pave the way for the admission of Kansas as a free State. He was the first man to join Capt. David L. Payne's enterprise to settle Oklahoma.

In 1859 Dr. Henley returned to Fairmount, entering Bloomingdale Academy, Indiana, with the intention of preparing himself for a professional career. In 1862 he commenced the study of medicine with Dr. David S. Elliott. In 1863 he was a student at Michigan University, Ann Arbor. In 1865 he graduated at Sterling University, Columbus, Ohio. In the fall of 1864 he entered the Union army as an assistant surgeon and was stationed at Indianapolis.

DR. ALPHEUS HENLEY

At the close of the War Dr. Henley returned home and commenced the practice of medicine in Fairmount. For forty years, with the exception of one year spent in Oklahoma (1870) as Government surgeon for the Cheyenne and Apache Indians, being stationed at the time at Darlington Post, he followed his profession in Fairmount Township. As a physician he rose rapidly in popularity and grew in the confidence and respect of the people, reaching a position in the esteem of his neighbors and acquaintances which he uniformly maintained throughout the entire period of his extended active professional life.

During the many years of his busy life Dr. Henley was always prompt to respond with his energy and his means to all well directed efforts intended to advance the industrial, business, educational and religious movements worthy of support. All his life he has been a member of the Society of Friends.

Dr. Henley has served as President of the Town Board, President of the School Board and President of the Board of Trustees of Fairmount Academy, an institution he helped materially to establish. He is a member of the Grant County Medical Society, of which organization he has served as President, a member of the Indiana Medical Society and of the American Medical Association.

Dr. Henley has led a long and honorable career. His kindness of heart, his thoughtful regard for the welfare of others, his helpfulness by counsel and in substantial assistance given, his interest in many struggling young people and his exemplary personal and domestic life have been an inspiration to hundreds of people in this community. Can more be said of any man who has attained to his years? The writer does not deem it always wise to reserve kind words for the obituary, and so in this instance we pay our tribute to the living. While in order to escape the rigors of our Northern climate, he has for the past few years maintained a home in the Southland, Dr. Henley is nevertheless affectionately regarded by our people here at his old home as Fairmount's grand old man.

Among the physicians from the earliest days of the town to the present may be mentioned Philip Patterson, 1850-1860; John White, 1852-1855; David S. Elliott, 1858-1866; Dr. Beckford, 1854; John T. Horne, 1860-1865; Dr. Boyden, Dr. McDonald, Thomas Davis, 1865-1866; Silas W. Camp, 1867-1870; Alpheus Henley, 1865-1904; Cyrus V. Gorrell, 1875-1880; P. H. Wright, 1868-1888; Dr. Wetherell, 1875-1878; Thomas S. Beck, Henry Charles, 1868-1875; W. H. Hubbard, 1884-1886; Charles V. Moore, 1874-1884; M. F. Baldwin, J. W. Patterson, W. A. Frazier, S. M. Nolder, Olive Wilson, Allen Moon, Stephen A. Marlow, Glenn Henley, J. P. Seale, Nathan Davis, Charles B. Vigus, William B. Thomas, C. N. Brown, W. M. Warner, D. A. Holliday, L. D. Holliday, J. H. Stephens, Harry Aldrich.

Not only has Fairmount Township been the home and the field of work for many physicians who have passed on to their final reward as well as members of the profession now located here, but the community has supplied to other cities and towns members of this noble calling who received their elementary education in this Township. Among those to be mentioned are a few who have been notably successful. Dr. Etta Charles, of Alexandria, Indiana, lived in Fairmount many years and attended the common schools here. She is a daughter of Dr. Henry Charles, Friends minister as well as a physician. Her paternal grandparents were Samuel and Sarah Charles, and her maternal grandparents were Elijah and Ann (Puckett) Jackson. Her parents were Henry and Olive Ann (Jackson) Charles, the father born in Wayne County, Indiana, August 10, 1822, died July 17, 1884; the mother was born in Randolph County, Indiana, in 1828, and died on April 12, 1869. Dr. Etta Charles matriculated at the Woman's Medical College, St. Louis, and in 1895 she received

DR. DAVID S. ELLIOTT

Native of Deep River, Guilford County, North Carolina, an early Fairmount physician who practiced medicine here during the years 1858 to 1867. He was a brother to J. Nixon Elliott. It was in the office of Dr. Elliott that Dr. Alpheus Henley commenced the study of medicine. In the spring of 1864 Dr. Elliott went with other Fairmount men to Wabash to enter the Union Army as a surgeon. While quartered at Wabash he met with an accident which resulted in permanent injuries, from the effects of which he died. He continued to reside in Fairmount, doing an office business, as his health permitted, until the spring of 1868, when he removed to Richmond, Indiana, with his wife and only daughter, Miss Hettie Elliott, and lived in Wayne County until 1869, when he passed away, at the home of his parents, Elias and Martha (Sanders) Elliott, at the early age of thirty-six. At the time of his death Dr. Elliott was President of the Grant County Medical Society.

her diploma. On June 10, of that year, she located at Summitville, and remained at this point until November 13, 1913, at which date she located in Alexandria, where she has prospered in her chosen profession. Dr. Charles is a member of the Madison County Medical Society, Indiana State Medical Association, Eighth District Medical Society and the American Medical Association. She has served the Madison County Society as President and also in the capacity of Secretary for four years. She has read many papers before her State, District and County societies, besides contributing valuable articles to important medical publications. Dr. Charles is examining physician for the Woman's Auxiliary of the Modern Woodmen of America, known as the Royal Neighbors of America. She is one of a very few physicians who has discovered a case of typhus fever in an inland town. In the midst of her busy life she finds time for club work and is an active member of the Ladies' Art Circle and of the Riley Club, of Alexandria, and an honorary member of the Priscilla Club at Summitville.

Dr. Calvin C. Rush, son of Nixon and Louisa (Winslow) Rush, resides in Philadelphia. Born on February 16, 1876, he attended the public schools of Fairmount, and graduated from Fairmount Academy in 1894; received from Earlham College the degree of Bachelor of Science in 1900; graduated from Haverford College in 1901 and from the Medical Department of the University of Pennsylvania in 1907. At present Dr. Rush is taking a post-graduate course in the Polyclinic Hospital and Wills' Eye Hospital, Philadelphia. Dr. Rush was located at Portage, Pennsylvania, from 1909 to 1916, where he met with considerable success, retiring from the general practice and taking up his residence in Philadelphia, in November, 1916. He is a stockholder in the First National Bank of Portage. He was a resident physician in the University of Pennsylvania Hospital from 1907 to 1909. Dr. Rush is a member of the Pennsylvania Medical Association and the American Medical Association. He is a member of the Society of Friends. Dr. Rush was married to Miss Annette Johnson, at her home in Fairmount, on June 20, 1910. She is the daughter of Barclay and Sylvia Anna (Lindley) Johnson. Dr. and Mrs. Rush are parents of three children, namely, Sylvia Louise, born April 5, 1911; Norman J., born August 26, 1913, and Eleanor, born March 16, 1916.

Robert Benjamin Jones, physician and surgeon, is located at Laporte, Indiana. Dr. Jones was born in Fairmount Township July 21, 1884. His paternal grandparents were Robert Jones and wife, and his maternal grandparents were Amos and Nancy Thomas. David and Sallie (Thomas) Jones, parents of Dr. Jones, were both born in Fairmount

Township. Dr. Jones was educated in the schools of his native township, and graduated from Fairmount Academy, later receiving his degree of Doctor of Medicine from Indiana University School of Medicine. On July 23, 1909, he located at Laporte, Indiana, where he has met with excellent success in his profession. He is a stockholder in the First National Bank at Laporte, Moore & Richter Lumber Company, Laporte, and the American Standard Motion Picture Company, Chicago. In politics Dr. Jones is a Democrat, and he holds a birthright membership in the Quaker Church. He is a member of Phi Delta Theta and Phi Rho Signa college fraternities, and also of the Independent Order of Odd Fellows and the Benevolent and Protective Order of Elks at Laporte, Indiana. He is a member of the Laporte County Medical Society, the Indiana State Medical Society and the American Medical Association. On March 26, 1910, Dr. Jones was married to Miss Mabel Child, daughter of Charles and Mary Child, at their home in Fairmount. Dr. and Mrs. Jones are parents of two children, Helen Marie Jones, born May 26, 1912, and Robert Benjamin Jones, Jr., born September 12, 1916.

Thomas J. Carter, M. D., son of Robert L. and Mary (Rush) Carter, is a successful practicing physician at Wichita, Kansas. Dr. Carter was born in Fairmount Township in 1876. He attended the Fairmount public schools, graduated from Fairmount Academy in 1897, received his degree from the Medical Department of Indiana University in 1902, and located in League City, Texas, in 1904. In June, 1917, he removed from League City to Wichita. He served as President of League City School District and as a member of the Board of Education of Galveston County, Texas. Dr. Carter is a birthright member of the Friends Church. In 1900, at Fairmount, he was married to Miss Sula Edgerton, daughter of Jesse and Sarah (Shugart) Edgerton, prominent residents of Grant County. Dr. and Mrs. Carter are parents of three children, namely, Stuart R. Carter, born June 4, 1904; Esther H. Carter, born June 9, 1907; Willard E. Carter, born November 15, 1911.

Others who have entered the profession and are attaining a large measure of success are Dr. Wilbur Lucas, of Pueblo, Colorado, and Dr. Eli Jones, located at Hammond, Indiana. Dr. Lucas is a son of former County Commissioner Thomas J. and Mrs. Amanda (Dunn) Lucas. Dr. Jones is a son of David and Sallie (Thomas) Jones, both well known families of Fairmount Township.

The first postoffice was located in a frame house built by William Hall, situated at the southwest corner of Adams and Main Streets. This was the third frame house built in Fairmount. The second frame dwelling was built by David Stanfield, on the northwest corner of Adams and Main Streets.

HON. C. C. LYONS
Former State Senator and Postmaster

MRS. GLADYS LYONS KNIGHT
Former Postmistress

William Hall was the first postmaster. In 1844 he had been elected class leader and then ordained a minister in the United Brethren Church. His duties as a circuit rider took him away from his home a large part of the time, and as he thought the work of the office was too arduous for his family during his enforced and many times prolonged absence, he gave up the office and turned it over to Joseph W. Baldwin, who kept it in his storeroom.

Others who served as postmaster since the days of William Hall and Joseph W. Baldwin may be mentioned Alex Henley, Al H. Johnson, Ephraim Smith, T. P. Latham, W. H. Campbell, J. D. Latham, C. D. Overman, C. C. Lyons, Miss Gladys Lyons, W. P. Van Arsdall.

The Galatia Messenger was issued in 1852 by William Chamness and associates for the primary purpose of advocating the movement to establish a city near Lake Galatia. *The Messenger* was established as part of a plan to propagate in a large way the doctrine of Spiritualism. It was the first publication issued in Fairmount Township.

In December, 1877, Joel Reece, who had been publishing *The Jonesboro News*, finding that field unprofitable for a newspaper, moved his outfit in a wagon to Fairmount and issued the first edition of *The Fairmount News*. The question of starting a newspaper occupied the attention of business men for several weeks, and was discussed by citizens, who held frequent meetings for the purpose of considering the matter. Among the active promoters of the enterprise were Robert Bogue, N. W. Edwards, E. N. Oakley, J. P. Winslow, and others. The paper was issued from a room in the rear of the second story of the Pioneer Drug Store. An old-fashioned Washington hand press, the nucleus of an equipment for the average country weekly in that day, was used to print the first edition. Reece conducted the paper for about one year, when he sold his plant to Charles Stout and moved to Stafford County, Kansas, where he has since died.

For a short time William S. Seaford, who was a teacher in the Fairmount public schools, was associated with Stout in the publication of the paper.

In May, 1885, *The News* was taken over by Edgar M. Baldwin, who continued as the publisher until April, 1888, when the property was purchased by Jack Stivers.* Stivers was in charge of the paper until July, 1903, when it was again taken over by Edgar M. Baldwin, who, assisted by his wife, Myra Rush Baldwin, has since been actively engaged in its management.

The Fairmount Times was started in 1888 by Edward A. Morgan. The paper was later discontinued. About 1900, Morgan entered the

---

*J. Stivers, editor of *The Fairmount News* from April, 1888, to July 28, 1903, was born at Pt. Isabel, Ohio, June 14, 1854. His father's name was J. M. Stivers, both parents being natives of Ohio, where the elder Stivers was a school teacher and surveyor. In 1866, as a boy twelve years of age, J. Stivers came to Indiana and lived with his brother, Charles W. Stivers, at Liberty. Later, with his brothers, C. W. and Scott Stivers, he was for several years engaged in the newspaper business at Liberty and Brookville. In 1886 he went to Grass Lake, Mich., and after two years of successful publication of a weekly newspaper at that point he came to Fairmount and purchased *The News*. Mr. Stivers' father was one of the early Prohibitionists of Ohio, when adherents of this cause were few and far between. During his editorial control of *The News* Mr. Stivers stood out boldly against the liquor traffic in the face of the fact that there were at the time ten saloons in Fairmount, and he takes pardonable pride in his aggressive and effective work against the liquor business. In politics Mr. Stivers is a Republican. He is a member of the Independent Order of Odd Fellows, and has passed all the chairs of a subordinate lodge. He now resides in San Francisco, California, with his wife. His daughter, Georgia Dell, is married to J. L. Schleimer, a native of San Diego, California.

Fairmount field with *The Daily Journal,* which flourished for several years, suspending publication in 1906. Several other newspapers have been started in Fairmount in the intervening years, with indifferent success.

The Child's Golden Voice, a juvenile religious periodical issued monthly by Rev. G. P. Riley, was published here in 1885.

James Chapman published *The Index* at Fowlerton from 1902 to 1906. Mr. Chapman discontinued *The Index* in order to assume charge of *The Gas City Journal.* *The Index* was succeeded by *The Independent,* and then by *The Review,* both publications at different times edited by Cal Sinninger. Sinninger was an aggressive writer, sometimes vitriolic in his utterances, and was noted for his independent views on religion, politics and business.

The first Cornet Band in Fairmount was organized in October, 1870, by Blanche Hockett. The first instructor was D. K. Elliott, who then lived at Anderson. The members of this band were Blanche Hockett, Walker Crowell, Dennis Montgomery, Cyrus W. Neal, Joel Puckett, Zep Gossett, Isaac N. Gossett, Gilmore Hollingsworth, Lawrence McDonald, Will Carson, Henry Jeffrey, J. B. Hollingsworth and Wesley Hollingsworth. In that day the first-class bands that had wide reputations for the kind of music played were located at Indianapolis (The When), Peru, Noblesville and New Castle.

The next band was organized September 14, 1884, by William St. Clair. The members of this organization were J. W. Patterson, leader; John S. Baker, John Montgomery, Dennis Montgomery, Orlando F. Baldwin, Gilbert LaRue, George Gibson, William Hollingsworth, Charles Hollingsworth, Pet Gift, William Galloway and Lewis Mittank. When Gen. John A. Logan spoke at Indianapolis, during the campaign of 1884, this band was assigned to the position of honor in the line of march, and escorted the speaker to the platform.

In December, 1904, Quinton LaRue organized the present Fairmount Band. Birney Allred, Walter Briles and LaRue met in the old light plant, on East Washington Street, for their first practice. Since this first meeting of the original members rehearsals have been held once, and many times twice, each week. The result of their persistent work is the splendid band which now is a credit to Fairmount. Prof. C. R. Tuttle was for several years the efficient instructor. The organization progressed rapidly under his direction. Prof. George L. Payson, of Alexandria, succeeded Professor Tuttle. Other members of the band at different times were Charles L. Kiefer, Leslie Davis, Burr Holmes,

Ed Guinnup, Albert Riggs, Homer Williams, John W. Montgomery, Oscar Dickey, Orville Wells, Earl Morris, Ellis Wright, Louis Bender, Otto Morris, Omar Brewer, Luther Davis, Russell Stephens, Ancil Wright, Ward LaRue, Russell Dale, Roy Wells and Kenneth Morris.

In the profession of dentistry several former Fairmount Township young men have gone out into other cities and towns and proved their worth. Perhaps the most notable success is that of Dr. Carl D. Lucas, of Indianapolis. Dr. Lucas is a native of Jefferson Township, where he was born October 24, 1879. His paternal grandparents were Thomas M. and Mary Lucas, and his maternal grandparents were Thomas and Mary Dunn. His parents are Thomas J. and Amanda (Dunn) Lucas, the father having served six years as a member of the Board of Grant County Commissioners. Dr. Lucas attended the Fairmount public schools, and, in 1899, graduated from Fairmount Academy. In 1902 he received from the Indiana Dental College the degree of Doctor of Dental Surgery. For fourteen years he did general practice in the capital city, but since 1914 his practice is limited to oral surgery.

DR. CARL D. LUCAS

Dr. Lucas is a member of the Indiana State Dental Association, Indianapolis Dental Society, Chicago Dental Society, Kentucky State Dental Association, Louisiana State Dental Association; Corydon Palmer Dental Society, Youngstown, Ohio; Associate Fellow of American Medical Association; member American Institute of Dental Teachers; member of National Dental Association, having held two offices in this organization; Chairman and Supervisor of Operative Surgical Clinics in 1917 at National meeting in New York City; member Scientific Foundation and Research Commission of the National Dental Association. In politics Dr. Lucas is neutral, exercising his own personal judgment as to candidates and measures appealing to him for his support. He is a member of Fairmount lodge, Free and Accepted Masons, also of the Delta Sigma Delta fraternity. His skill and knowledge of his profession are recognized throughout the United States, and especially in Indiana, where he is best known. Dr. Lucas is lecturer at the Indiana Dental College on oral surgery, anatomy, histology and embryology and clinician at the Indiana Dental College in oral surgery. Dr. Lucas was married on June 29, 1910, at Arcadia, Indiana, to Miss Effa Jane Carter. They are parents of one son, Carl D. Lucas, Jr., born September 5, 1911.

Other former Fairmount men who are practicing dentistry in different localities are Dr. Milo E. Ratliff, Cassopolis, Michigan; Dr. Charles E. White and Dr. Trosseau Heck, at Indianapolis; Dr. Mark Struble and Dr. Laurence Shaughnessy, at Chicago, and Dr. Will E. Ferree, at Pittsburgh, Pennsylvania.

Dr. Joseph W. Patterson, deceased, son of Dr. Philip and Mary (Baldwin) Patterson, was born in Fairmount, October 28, 1859. His paternal grandfather, William Patterson, was a native of Ohio and a veteran of the War of 1812 who, in 1830, came to Madison County, Indiana, and settled near Anderson, where he died. The father was born in Ohio, in 1825, was reared at Anderson, received his education in the old Franklin College, south of Indianapolis, and graduated from the Ohio Medical College, at Cincinnati, in 1846. He later took a course in the Jefferson Medical College of Philadelphia. About 1847 he located in Fairmount, then a sparsely settled community, where he practiced his profession for about eleven years. Soon after the death of his wife, in 1860, he moved to Frankton, in Madison County, where he continued to live until his death, in November, 1870. Mary Patterson was born in Wayne County, Indiana, December 21, 1825. She was a daughter of Daniel Baldwin,

DR. J. W. PATTERSON

one of the early pioneers of the Township. Dr. J. W. Patterson's mother having died when he was but five months old, he was taken into the home of David and Elizabeth (Coleman) Baldwin, by whom he was reared as one of their own. He attended the Fairmount public schools, during the summer months worked for his uncle, David, and early began to earn and save money as a plasterer and bricklayer with which to attend medical college. His ambition to be a doctor was gratified, and in 1889 he graduated from the Indiana Medical College with honors, being awarded the Taylor anatomical prize. He located in Fairmount the year of his graduation and commenced the practice of his profession, meeting with success. He served as health officer of Fairmount. He was a member of the Grant County Medical Society, Delaware District Medical Society, State Medical Society, and for two years President of the Harvey Medical Association of Indiana Medical College. In politics Dr. Patterson was a Republican. At twenty-one years of age he was elected justice of the peace; he served several terms as member of the corporation Board of Trustees, suggesting the names adopted for the streets; as President of the Board he advocated the installation of the water works; was a member of the School Board for twelve years, giving loyal and efficient service to the educational interests of the community; on July 7, 1906, he was appointed a member of the Grant County Board of Examining Surgeons, a position he held at the time of his death. As a manifestation of the esteem in which he was held by survivors of the Civil War he was unanimously elected an honorary member of Beeson Post, Grand Army of the Republic. In 1883 he was married to Miss Moslen Pickard, daughter of Alexander and Mary Pickard. They were parents of two children, namely, Fred P., of Columbus, Ohio, and Mrs. Charles E. Hutchins, of Marion, Indiana. The wife and mother passed away on April 28, 1896. On June 26, 1898, he was joined in marriage to Miss Ella Pearson, daughter of Henry and Minerva Pearson, this union proving to be a most congenial and happy one. Dr. Patterson died on December 26, 1913, aged fifty-four years. His funeral, conducted at the Methodist Episcopal Church by Rev. H. S. Nickerson, was one of the largest ever held in Fairmount.

CHAPTER XXVIII.

ORGANIZATION OF BANKS—DEVELOPMENT OF NATURAL GAS—BUILDING THE WATER WORKS—LOCATING INDUSTRIES.

IN 1883 Dr. A. Henley and Levi Scott, perceiving the need of local banking facilities, proceeded to organize the Fairmount Bank as a private institution. They purchased ground on South Main Street and erected a two-story brick building.

On June 24, 1886, the capital stock was increased to twenty-five thousand dollars and the bank was reorganized and incorporated under the laws of the State, and became known as the Farmers and Merchants State Bank, with Dr. A. Henley, President, and Levi Scott, Cashier. The directors met in 1887 and decided to increase the capital stock to fifty thousand dollars.

The institution continued to operate successfully as the Farmers and Merchants State Bank until June, 1893, when the panic of that year brought disaster to many enterprises throughout the country, carrying this bank down in the general crash.

On July 15, 1893, the Citizens Exchange Bank was organized with Nixon Winslow, President; John Selby, Vice-President, and W. C. Winslow, Cashier. Other stockholders were A. A. Ulrey, John Seale, Sr., and William J. Leach.

On June 10, 1911, this bank was reorganized and incorporated as a State Bank, with John Selby, President; Charles F. Naber, Vice-President, and Victor A. Selby, Cashier.

The Fairmount Banking Company was organized as a private institution on December 18, 1902, with Aaron Morris, President; John Flanagan, Vice-President; R. A. Morris, Cashier, and C. R. Small, Assistant Cashier.

In 1905 the bank was organized under the laws of the State and the name changed to the Fairmount State Bank. John Flanagan was elected President; Aaron Morris, Vice-President, and R. A. Morris, Cashier. The present officers are W. F. Morris, President; R. A. Morris, Cashier, and Tony Payne, Assistant Cashier.

On March 4, 1887, the Fairmount Mining Company was organized for the purpose of making explorations for natural gas. Other communities in Grant and adjoining counties had formed similar companies for this purpose, and the results were such as to encourage local men to believe that the Fairmount field offered as good prospects for developing this fuel as others that had been successfully opened up.

LEVI SCOTT

Former prominent Fairmount citizen and business man, is a native of Wayne County, Indiana, where he was born January 21, 1846. His parents, Stephen and Mahala (Arnett) Scott, were among the pioneers of Liberty Township. Levi Scott passed the early years of his life working upon his father's farm, attending the common schools in winter. August 1, 1863, at seventeen, he enlisted in Company C, One Hundred and Eighteenth Indiana Volunteer Infantry. At the conclusion of his service in the army he returned home, engaged in farming, and later in retail merchandising in Huntington County, in which he was successful. Disposing of his stock of goods he purchased a farm near Pleasant Plain, and once more followed agricultural pursuits. In 1865 he was united in marriage with Miss Emily Davis, daughter of George Davis, of Liberty Township. They were the parents of twelve children, namely: Melissa M., Alvin B., Irvin, Arthur D., Lillie, Lemuel, Eliza A., Alonzo, Charlotte, Clelia, Elois and Harrison. Melissa, Arthur and Lemuel are deceased. The wife died in 1891. For his second companion he married Emily R. Hill, of Carthage, Indiana. Mr. Scott, in 1877, engaged in general merchandising in Fairmount, entering actively into the support with his means, his time and his influence of various enterprises promoted for the good of the community. In November, 1882, with surplus funds not otherwise invested, he established the Fairmount Bank, giving local people their first banking facilities. This institution did a general banking business, dealing in exchange, receiving money on deposit, discounting notes, etc. He built Scott's Opera House in 1884, with a commodious stage, scenery and all necessary equipment to accommodate the best theatrical troupes touring the smaller towns and cities of that day. The Fairmount Bank was later reorganized under the laws of Indiana and became known as the Farmers and Merchants State Bank. The business grew as Fairmount increased in population and industry. In 1893, as the result of a liberal policy adopted by the bank toward the encouragement of local manufacturing enterprises, a policy which in time proved to be unwisely generous, owing to the panic of that year, the financial drain became too great for its resources and the institution was forced to close its doors. This action became necessary on account of the inability of the management to quickly realize on paper then in its possession. In 1896 Mr. and Mrs. Scott disposed of their interests here and moved to Missouri, then to Texas, and later to California, where they are comfortably situated.

J. P. Winslow, T. J. Nixon, C. R. Small, Levi Scott, Dr. W. H. Hubbard, M. Mark, John Flanagan, Kimbrough Bros. and Dr. A.

Henley were the original stockholders. The Board of Directors consisted of Dr. A. Henley, President; T. J. Nixon, Secretary; C. R. Small, Treasurer; J. P. Winslow, W. C. Winslow and Levi Scott. On March

JOHN SELBY

Is the son of Otho Selby, born in Pennsylvania, September 24, 1805. Otho Selby entered one hundred and sixty acres of land near Lake Galatia on May 30, 1837, subsequently, on August 20, 1838, adding by entry forty acres adjoining. Before he came to Grant County he had sold a tract of land in Franklin County, which he had entered there on August 14, 1834, this tract comprising eighty acres, southeast of Indianapolis. He owned the Fairmount Township farm until his death, February 16, 1881. Otho and Jane (Allen) Selby were parents of three children, John, Mrs. Sarah Smith and Mrs. Emma Compton. John Selby was born June 10, 1846. He attended the common schools and remained on his father's farm until fifteen years of age, when he learned the tinner's trade, following this vocation in Jonesboro and Fairmount. In 1864 he enlisted in Company F, One Hundred and Thirty-ninth Indiana Volunteer Infantry. Upon his return from the war Mr. Selby again engaged in the stove and tinware business, remaining in this line until he went back to the farm. In 1894, associated with others, Mr. Selby organized the Citizens Exchange Bank, with the late Nixon Winslow as President and himself as Cashier. June 10, 1911, this bank was reorganized under State laws, the name changed to the Citizens State Bank, and Mr. Selby was selected to serve as President, a position he has filled acceptably ever since. The officers of this strong institution are: John Selby, President; Victor A. Selby, Cashier. Directors are John Selby, A. A. Ulrey and Charles F. Naber. Mr. Selby owns one hundred and seventy acres of the farm originally entered by his father. In politics he is a Democrat, and a member of the Congregational Church. He was married in 1874 to Miss Hattie M. Allen, born in Ohio in 1853. To this union two sons were born, namely: Victor A., who is married and resides in Fairmount, and William A. Selby, deceased. Mr. and Mrs. Victor A. Selby are the parents of two children, namely, Victor A., Jr., and Virginia.

9 the Secretary was directed to contract for the work of putting down a well.

Pursuant to instructions, Mr. Nixon contracted with W. A. Walley, of the firm of O'Neill & Walley, of Muncie. Mr. Walley placed Steve A. Irwin in personal charge of the work. The big derrick was speedily erected, equipment secured and operations commenced.

On Tuesday, April 26, the drill penetrated Trenton rock at a depth of 965 feet. The well yielded an abundance of gas. Professor Orton,

Ohio State Geologist, after much difficulty, succeeded in making a test of the pressure. He found that its flow was eleven million five hundred thousand cubic feet every twenty-four hours, or, in the language of

JOHN FLANAGAN

Is a native of Preble County, Ohio, where he was born August 10, 1853. His father, James Flanagan, was born in County Mayo, Ireland, about 1820, came to the United States in 1848 and settled in Grant County in 1865. He died in 1880, at his home northeast of Fairmount. John Flanagan was educated in the common schools of Preble County, Ohio, and in Grant County, attending a Normal School later, teaching in winter and farming in summer. April 1, 1879, he entered the mercantile business with E. N. Oakley, a partnership which continued for three years. In April, 1882, he joined the firm of Henley & Nixon, grain dealers, and took over a grain elevator at Summitville, operating this enterprise under the name of John Flanagan & Company, for one year. The same firm, Flanagan, Henley & Nixon, bought the stock of merchandise at Washington and Main streets and conducted this store from 1883 to 1888, when the firm name was changed to Flanagan & Henley, Mr. Nixon having retired. The two-story brick building was bought in 1889, and the business has continued at this corner ever since. In 1893 Mr. Flanagan bought Dr. Henley's interests and he has since conducted the business as sole proprietor. In addition to his mercantile interests Mr. Flanagan owns considerable land. For six years he was President of the School Board. He was one of the organizers and for seven years President of the Fairmount State Bank; a director and Secretary of the Fairmount Mining Company, which put down several productive wells in the oil and gas districts of this section; President of the Commercial Club during the period of its greatest activity; President of the Fairmount Building & Loan Association for several years, and for many meetings of that organization he was an official of the Fairmount Fair Association. In politics Mr. Flanagan is a Republican, and while not a member of any church he has always contributed liberally of his means to the support of all. He was married to Miss Sarah E. Winslow, daughter of Levi and Emily (Henley) Winslow, on March 8, 1860. Mr. and Mrs. Flanagan have no children.

Professor Orton at the time, "nearly sufficient gas to supply the three largest cities in Ohio."

The well was located on the south side of East Washington Street, near the old brick elevator formerly owned by Winslow & Beals.

In the fall of 1888 a special train bearing James G. Blaine and a party of friends stopped nearby. The pressure was turned on and the distinguished Maine statesman expressed astonishment and admiration as the well roared thunderously and the gigantic flames leaped skyward.

The pressure was so great that it was with considerable difficulty

ROBERT A. MORRIS Cashier of the Fairmount State Bank, was born at Milton, in Wayne County, Indiana, May 16, 1877. His paternal grandparents were George and Rhoda Morris, natives of North Carolina, and his maternal grandparents were Lewis W. and Priscilla M. Thomas, Pennsylvania people. The parents of Robert A. Morris were Aaron and Martha M. Morris, the father, born at Milton, November 23, 1834, having died February 15, 1907. The mother (who was a direct descendant of Thomas Lloyd and Samuel Preston, both councilors of William Penn, Lloyd serving as first Governor of Pennsylvania), was born February 3, 1839, and now resides at Pendleton. Mr. and Mrs. Aaron Morris were the parents of four children, namely: Louella Burdsall, of New York; W. F. Morris, of Pendleton, Indiana; Robert A. Morris, of Fairmount, and Elizabeth Lantz, of Pendleton. Robert A. Morris was educated in the public schools at Milton, his home, and at Earlham College. Early in life, at nineteen years of age, he entered the banking business, being associated with his father in the Pendleton Banking Company. In 1902, with his father, he came to Fairmount and assisted in organizing the Fairmount Banking Company, this institution being later incorporated as the Fairmount State Bank, under which name it is now doing business. Mr. Morris is a stockholder and director of the Pendleton Banking Company, of which concern he is President; director of the Citizens Telephone Company, and a director of the Fairmount Commercial Club. In politics Mr. Morris is a stanch Republican, and a member of the Hicksite Friends. He has served his party as Treasurer of the Grant County Republican Central Committee, and was a member of the Grant County Council. He is an active member of Fairmount Lodge, Free and Accepted Masons, No. 635, having served the local lodge in all the chairs, being now a Trustee. On October 21, 1908, Mr. Morris was married in Fairmount to Miss Artie Suman, a native of Fairmount Township, and daughter of Harry and Rachel (Lewis) Suman, now residing at Hunter, North Dakota. Mr. and Mrs. Morris are the parents of one son, William Suman Morris, born January 2, 1913.

the flow of gas was harnessed and gotten ready for use. Excursion trains came loaded with passengers from every direction to see the well. In a few weeks, because of its enormous capacity, which was said to be greater than that of any other well in Indiana, it was given the name of Jumbo, so called after Barnum's elephant.

The gas was finally put under control and piped, and the expense of light and fuel for many years did not exceed twelve dollars per year for each family for domestic purposes. Walker Winslow was the first man in Fairmount who introduced natural gas for cooking purposes, and it was not many months before its use was general among Fairmount people.

Attracted by the cheapness, cleanliness and convenience of the new fuel, several glass factories located in Fairmount. By the year 1890 the town began to increase in population and grow in industrial importance. In 1894 the census showed approximately five thousand inhabitants.

Foreign corporations, seeing the opportunity presented, began to lease land in the neighborhood. Lines were laid and gas was transported into Chicago by means of great pumping stations erected for the purpose. These stations pulled strongly upon the entire field, diminishing the supply, and finally exhausing the entire territory.

Far-seeing men wisely discouraged people from leasing land to outside syndicates, but the advice went unheeded and the pressure began to weaken and then gradually to disappear.

The discovery which promised at the outset to dot the gas belt with connecting cities eventually came to naught. There are now but few scattered families in this part of the State using natural gas.

Fairmount had reached the point in population and industry by 1894 where the need of a system of water works seemed imperative.

The Board of Trustees of the corporation at this time consisted of Dr. J. W. Patterson, President; M. S. Friend, Jason B. Smith, William R. Pearson and Gabe Johnson.

Immediately upon his election as Trustee, Dr. Patterson began an agitation for water works. At first he encountered considerable opposition among citizens. However, after considering the matter with care, the Board decided to investigate the question. Dr. Patterson and William R. Pearson were named as a committee to make a thorough investigation and report back to the Board. The committee visited a number of towns, inspecting many plants and examining closely details relating to operation and construction. A public meeting was called. This meeting was held in Parker's Opera House. It was addressed by Dr. Patterson, who made an exhaustive explanation of the plans by which the system could be installed.

A petition was circulated calling for an election and the required number of signatures secured. The result of the election which followed showed a practically unanimous sentiment favorable to the proposition, there being but thirty votes registered in opposition to it. Work was started immediately after the bonds were sold, and the plant was soon in operation.

H. H. Wiley came from Jonesboro in 1876, and located a saw and planing-mill near the railroad, which he operated until he retired from active business.

In 1882 Cyrus Winslow and Lemuel Pearson bought the saw-mill which had previous to that time been owned and operated by Winslow, Pearson & Beidler. The mill was located north of Fairmount.

William S. Wardwell came to Fairmount in 1876 and took charge of the Woolen Mills,* which for many years had been operated previous to his arrival. Mr. Wardwell manufactured blankets and stocking yarn. He later moved the machinery to Converse, Indiana.

In 1878 C. A. Wood and son, Mark, built a stave factory east of the Big Four railroad. The business flourished. In the year 1879-1880 the factory dressed two million oil-barrel staves, made from timber obtained in this locality.

In 1881 J. P. Winslow and son, W. C. Winslow, bought the building vacated by the Woods and installed a flax-mill. The venture proved to be a profitable enterprise until people quit growing flax. The mill was then abandoned and the machinery shipped to Odebolt, Iowa.

The Cincinnati, Wabash & Michigan Railroad was constructed as far south as Fairmount in 1875. This station remained the southern terminal point until 1876, when the line was extended to Anderson. Jonathan P. Winslow and Jesse E. Wilson were active in promoting this railroad. The latter served as one of the directors for a time. A. G. Wells secured the contract for the construction of the road from Wabash to Fairmount. The line had previously been extended from Goshen to Wabash. In 1893 the Big Four Company took over the property, and since that year the road has been known as the Michigan Division of the Big Four. The property has since been acquired by the New York Central system, and is now operated by the New York Central people, having been extended to Louisville, Kentucky, on the south, from Benton Harbor, Michigan, on the north.

---

*The Woolen Mills occupied a two-story frame structure which stood at the southwest corner of First and Sycamore Streets. Prior to 1878 this industry had been owned and managed at different times by Vincent and William Wright, Jesse Reece and Elwood Haisley.

The Chicago, Indiana & Eastern Railroad was built from Matthews to Fairmount in the year 1892. In 1901 the line was extended from Matthews to Muncie. In 1898 it was extended from Fairmount to Swayzee; in 1899, from Swayzee to Converse, where connection was established with the Pennsylvania line to Chicago. In 1907 the road was taken over by the Pennsylvania Company, and is now operated by this company as a short line from Muncie to Chicago. The Chicago, Indiana & Eastern was projected by Harry Drew, manager of the Matthews Land Company, and the surveyor of the line was Frement Wilson, who was afterward elected Surveyor of Grant County. For a considerable period the line had headquarters in Fairmount, and the extension work west to Swayzee was largely carried on from the offices here.

In 1876 the amount of taxable property located within Fairmount corporation was seventy-nine thousand five hundred and fifty dollars.

In 1885-1886 Brady & Allred Bros. owned and operated a chair factory east of the railroad, north of the Big Four depot.

In 1885 the Fairmount Machine Works was established by J. H. Harrington and M. A. Hiatt. Later Mr. Hiatt retired from the firm and was succeeded in the ownership by Elwood Davis and Wiliam Fink.

In January, 1881, Gilbert LaRue, associated with two brothers, came to Fairmount from Anderson and started a saw and planing-mill, which

GILBERT LARUE

Was one of the successful manufacturers and business men of Fairmount. He was part owner of a sawmill at the beginning of his career, later engaging in the manufacture of excelsior. He installed in Fairmount the first electric light plant, which furnished light for commercial and domestic use. Governor J. Frank Hanly, impressed by Mr. LaRue's reputation as a builder and practical mechanic, appointed him Superintendent of Construction of the Southeastern Hospital for the Insane, located at Madison. The building of this institution by the State involved an outlay of more than a $1,000,000. The buildings stand as an enduring monument to the skill and executive ability of Mr. LaRue, who was in personal charge of their construction. Mr. LaRue died in December, 1910.

was later converted into an excelsior factory. The enterprise prospered under the management of Mr. LaRue, who in the meantime had purchased his brothers' interests.

In January, 1885, Kimbrough Brothers established a saw-mill, which operated for many years, supplying dressed lumber in large quantities to the Graham & Morton Transportation Company at St. Joseph, Michigan, owning and managing a line of vessels on Lake Michigan plying at that time between St. Joseph and Chicago.

The Fairmount Manufacturing Company was incorporated February 2, 1886, with a capital stock of three thousand dollars. This company was organized for the purpose of manufacturing the Lancaster corn planter and ditching machine. The officers of the company were J. P. Winslow, President; C. R. Small, Secretary, and Levi Scott, Treasurer. There were twenty stockholders.

In 1887 T. J. Nixon owned and operated the flouring mill located where Ulrey & Company's mill now stands. Mordecai Nixon was in personal charge of the mill.

In the same year T. J. Nixon and Dr. A. Henley composed the firm of Henley & Nixon, grain dealers, who carried on an extensive business among the farmers. This firm had, in 1881, purchased of Robert Bogue the grain elevators. New machinery was bought and installed and the equipment improved.

Jonathan P. Winslow and Enoch Beals, under the firm name of Winslow & Beals, in 1887, occupied the two-story brick elevator at East Washington Street and the Big Four Railroad. The building was erected in 1875. In addition to the grain business the firm handled salt, lime, hair, flour, etc.

In 1887 various means were adopted to induce manufacturing industries to locate in Fairmount.

Levi Scott and W. C. Winslow were appointed a committee to solicit donations of money to be expended in properly advertising the town and presenting its claims to the attention of parties desiring locations for factories and other suitable enterprises.

Dr. W. H. Hubbard and John Flanagan were selected by the Fairmount Improvement Committee to solicit donations in the way of real estate to be offered for the location of shops, factories or other industries that would be of benefit to the town.

The owner of the Nixon Winslow land offered ten acres to an institution that would employ one hundred and fifty persons.

ALVIN B. SCOTT

Manufacturer, is a native of Fairmount Township, where he was born March 27, 1868. His grandparents were Stephen and Mahala (Arnett) Scott and George and Charlotte (Baldwin) Davis, and his parents were Levi and Emily (Davis) Scott. Alvin B. Scott was educated in the common schools of Fairmount Township.

The owners of the Wilson farm offered eight acres for a factory that would employ one hundred men.

Levi Scott offered five acres for one hundred hands.

Allen Dillon offered four acres for desirable factory or shop.

J. P. Winslow offered ten acres to shop or factory working one hundred hands.

Others stood ready to co-operate when necessary.

In 1888 William H. Lindsey built a planing-mill and saw-mill. Afterwards, Lindsey and Julian Swaim owned a lumber yard under the firm name of Lindsey & Swaim.

In 1888 W. C. Winslow, John Rau, Frank Taylor and Charles Tigner established a bottle factory.

In 1889 Charles Tigner, Allen Dillon and Frank Taylor built a fruit-jar factory, which became known as the Dillon Glass Factory.

In 1890 F. B. Ziegler, Harry Gable and Al Reed built the Big Four Window Glass Factory.

In 1890 Dr. A. Henley and Charles Tigner started what was known as the "Dinkey" Bottle Factory.

In 1893 John Borrey and others started the Bell Window Factory.

In 1894 Headley & Co. started a window house.

In November, 1906, E. C. McKever, a representative of the T. A. Snider Preserve Company, arrived in Fairmount looking for a factory location. After he had satisfied himself as to the adaptability of the soil for tomatoes, coupled with the best class of farmers, who gave their earnest support, the Snider Company, at a special public meeting, made known their proposition.

The offer proved to be a satisfactory one, and it was speedily and successfully handled through the co-operation actively of a number of the leading business men, among them being Dr. J. W. Patterson, John H. Wilson, John Flanagan, E. M. Baldwin, Hill Brothers, R. A. Morris, James F. Life, Charles T. Parker, John Selby, Goldstein Bros., Xen H. Edwards, David G. Lewis, J. W. Parrill, and all the business and commercial interests of the community. The following named farmers contributed their part, which was considerable, toward the success of the enterprise: John W. Cox, W. V. Cox, Joe Shane, E. J. Seale, Nixon Rush, John H. Caskey, Hiram Harvey, Wick O. Leach, Elsberry Payne, Thomas Winslow, Joe A. Winslow, Harvey Trader, Charley McCoy, Will M. Jones and John L. Weaver.

While the tomato crop was new to the farmers of Fairmount Township, they began to make tomato growing a business, and started to grow them right. Today there is no more successful tomato-growing section than Fairmount Township.

The Snider Company, although erecting a magnificent factory in the start, has added to and enlarged it from year to year until it is one of the largest and best equipped plants of its kind in the country.

XEN H. EDWARDS

Among the younger element of successful Fairmount business men has chosen to remain at his old home and here make a career where he is best known, among his life-long friends and acquaintances. Born in Fairmount, February 8, 1880, he attended the Fairmount schools and graduated from Fairmount Academy in 1897. In 1902 he received his degree of Bachelor of Science at DePauw University. Immediately upon his graduation from DePauw he returned home and engaged in the drug business with his father, the late Nathan W. Edwards. Xen Edwards has been quite successful in the drug trade, and is now owner of the Pioneer Drug Store, at Upland, Indiana, and an equal partner in the Bailey-Edwards Drug Store at Alexandria, Indiana. During his student days at DePauw he was President of the State Oratorical Association and a member of the Glee and Mandolin Club, also an active member of the Phi Delta Theta fraternity. In politics, Mr. Edwards is a Republican, and has given much time to his party. He has served on the School Board. He is a member of Fairmount Lodge, No. 635, Free and Accepted Masons, and of Alexandria Chapter of Elks, No. 478. He is a member and Trustee of the Fairmount M. E. Church. He was Secretary of the Fairmount Fair Association at the time of its widest popularity, and his efficiency and energy were recognized when he was elected President of the Fairmount Commercial Club. Mr. Edwards has served as President of the Indiana State Rexall Club, and was Vice-President of the National Association of Rexall Clubs. On January 25, 1905, he was married to Miss Ethel Harvey, daughter of Rev. Enos and Mary (Wilson) Harvey. To this union two sons, namely, Frederick and John Ethan, were born. Mr. Edwards owns a comfortable home on South Walnut Street, which is locally known for the hospitality extended.

It is largely due to the conscientious efforts of the Snider Company to comply with the plans originally laid down by them when locating in Fairmount, together with the co-operation of the farmers of Fairmount Township and the citizens of Fairmount, that the concern is enabled to fulfill all promises. This company now pays out annually in the community ninety thousand to one hundred thousand dollars for raw material alone, besides wages and other expenses.

In 1910 the Bell Bottle Company was established by Alvin B. Scott and others.

The Commercial Club was organized in 1904. John Flanagan was elected President; J. F. Life, Secretary, and R. A. Morris, Treasurer. The directors chosen were, in addition to the officers, Al Goldstein and John Rau. The organization did good work for a time. The location

WASHINGTON STREET
Fairmount, looking east from Main Street.

of the Bell Bottle Company and the Snider Preserve Factory is largely due to the harmonious and united efforts of the club.

In 1884 the Fairmount Union Joint Stock Agricultural Association was organized. In the summer of that year the fairground was laid out on what was known as the Stanfield land, adjoining the corporation limits on the southeast.

The ground selected included a beautiful grove, which afforded plenty of shade and water, an open space on the south edge of the land making a splendid location for the race track.

The first fair was held in September, 1884, the following officers being in charge of the meeting: Enoch Beals, President; W. C. Winslow, Secretary; Levi Scott, Treasurer; M. S. Friend, Superintendent, and Philip Davis, Marshal.

The stockholders reorganized in 1904, the name was changed to the Fairmount Fair Association, and Dr. J. W. Patterson elected President; John Flanagan, Treasurer; Xen H. Edwards, Secretary, and Gilbert LaRue, Superintendent. These men infused new life and vigor into the association, which enabled the fair to go forward with added prestige and improved prospects.

The Fairmount Telephone Company was promoted by S. B. Hill and operated by him successfully for several years.

The Citizens Telephone Company was organized in October, 1901, with John Kelsay, President. The directors elected for the first year

MAIN STREET

Fairmount, looking south from Washington Street.

were Aaron Newby, Ancil E. Ratliff, C. R. Small, Dr. D. A. Holliday, W. A. Beasley, I. S. Benbow and John Kelsay.

This company purchased the plant and equipment of the Fairmount Telephone Company, which at the time was under the management of Harry Miller.

Fairmount has about twenty-five miles of cement sidewalks and approximately five miles of brick streets. The business blocks are modern in arrangement and substantial in structure.

CHAPTER XXIX.

FAIRMOUNT ACADEMY—HIGH SCHOOL—WESLEYAN THEOLOGICAL SEMINARY.

MOVED by the urgent need of a secondary school in this locality, and inspired by the example set before them by the splendid work done at Spiceland Academy, where they had been students, Dr. P. H. Wright and wife and Samuel C. Cowgill and wife, in the year 1883, began to consider the possibilities of establishing such an institution in Fairmount.* The result of their meditations was communicated to others.

In December, 1883, at a business session of Northern Quarterly Meeting of Friends held at Back Creek, Jesse Hiatt arose at his place and suggested to the meeting that it take under consideration the proposition of establishing an academy. The suggestion was favorably received by those present.

A committee was appointed to consider the matter and make report of judgment to a future meeting. This committee consisted of Dr. Alpheus Henley, Joel B. Wright, Jonathan P. Winslow, Milton Winslow, Asa Bond, Elwood Haisley, Abel Knight, Henry B. Rush, Levi Hiatt, James M. Ellis, Enos Harvey, Nixon Winslow, Lewis Hockett, Samuel C. Cowgill, James L. Williamson, Willis Cammack, Mattie P. Wright, Louisa Rush, Eunice P. Wilson, Adeline Wright, Millie Little, Thirza Howell, Mary Bond, Sallie Harvey and Keziah Haisley.

On March 15, 1884, the committee reported to the Quarterly Meeting that they favored the proposition.

On June 21, 1884, the committee reported that the location selected for the Academy consisted of three acres of ground twenty-two rods south of the public school grounds, which would cost six hundred dollars. The amount of money pledged by subscription reached the sum of four thousand dollars. Elwood Haisley, James M. Ellis, Thomas J. Nixon, Ivy Luther and Mahlon Harvey were named as a committee to look after the incorporation papers.

Jesse Haisley and Samuel C. Wilson, to serve one year; Dr. P. H. Wright and Enos Harvey, to serve two years, and Abel Knight and William C. Winslow, to serve three years, were elected Trustees.

---

*The writer acknowledges his indebtedness to Ellwood O. Ellis for much of the information about Fairmount Academy here recorded.

NIXON RUSH

Educational Institutions. 341

On September 20, 1884, the building was in process of erection.
On September 21, 1885, Fairmount Academy opened for instruction,

Among the makers of Fairmount Township the name of Nixon Rush must take a prominent place, symbolizing all that is of the best in civil, educational and religious affairs of the community. His broad understanding of practical matters was reinforced by a keen sense of justice and fairness in all human relationships. The faith of his fathers

GRADUATING CLASS OF FAIRMOUNT ACADEMY
(1888)

Reading from left to right—Dr. Milo E. Ratliff, Cassopolis, Michigan; Asa Wimpy, Marion, Indiana; Will W. Ware, Fairmount, Indiana.

and the teachings of his pious Quaker parents molded his mind and heart and found expression in his dealings with people. His parents, Iredell and Elizabeth Rush, were among those pioneers who had fled from a slave State to a new country where slaves were not considered a necessity in well-ordered homes. They were descended from English and from French Huguenot families, who had, in their day, sought religious freedom in the new world of Pennsylvania and Virginia, whose going to North Carolina in the Eighteenth century, in the general migration that took vast companies to that State in search of larger lands, only brought them into a thorny wilderness, and before a problem bitter and difficult, a problem destined to tear the Nation with Civil War.

Benjamin Rush, great-grandfather of Nixon Rush, was a son of

Crafford and Mary Rush, of Virginia, who had migrated thither from Pennsylvania. He was born April 19, 1752, and at the age of twenty went to Randolph County, North Carolina. He was married, in 1772, to Dorcas Vickery. Azel, one of his six sons, born in 1780, was married, in 1806, to Elizabeth Beckerdite. He owned a large number of slaves, whom he liberated in 1833. They were valued at one hundred thousand dollars. He subsequently sold his plantation and came to Indiana, in the '50's, when he entered land near Little Ridge. His son, Iredell, who entered the Rush Hill farm, was born in Randolph County, North Carolina, in 1807, was married, in 1828, to Elizabeth Bogue, daughter of John and Lydia (White) Bogue. These heads of one of the oldest families in the Township receive further mention elsewhere in this book.

Nixon Rush was born at Rush Hill, March 30, 1836, and died there January 30, 1915. He was married on October 21, 1861, to Louisa Winslow, daughter of Daniel and Rebecca (Hiatt) Winslow, and granddaughter of Joseph Winslow, the story of whose coming to the Township is told in Chapter V. For many years Nixon and Louisa Rush were ministers in the Society of Friends and traveled not only over this and neighboring townships, tirelessly carrying a gospel of love and cheer, but also over many States of the Union, wherever a struggling and discouraged people sought help; and not by Spiritual means alone, but also in a substantial way, they were ever ready, continually giving aid of which the world never knew. The land on which Fairmount Academy stands was originally a part of the Rush Hill place, and they gave to that institution sums amounting into the thousands.

GARFIELD COX
A graduate of Fairmount Academy who has won many oratorical honors.

All churches built, all reforms and improvements and public enterprises started and kept up found them ready and liberal supporters. They traveled extensively and both left journals of absorbing interest. Their flower-bordered home at Rush Hill attested to their love for the beautiful. Their children, Axelina, Myra, Emma J., Walter W., Olive,* Calvin C., and Charles E.,* with the exception of Axelina, lived to maturity. Rush Hill is now occupied by Walter W. Rush, who was married, in 1895, to Elizabeth Johnson.

---

*Fairmount Township has contributed its share of talent to the various fields of useful occupation. In many cities and States our young men and young women are taking active and often leading parts in different lines of endeavor. Perhaps no other community of equal population and like environment has sent forth into the world a larger proportion of successful workers. In industry, in science and in the professions our people are busy and effective. While notable examples are not so numerous in art circles as in other callings that might be mentioned, those who have followed her efforts closely have reason to be gratified with the triumphs scored by Olive Rush. The early pioneers who came up from the old South and out from the old East carried with them into the new country more love for the beautiful than they knew, or cared to recognize. They satisfied their souls by contemplation of nature which in those days of big trees and unspoiled wilderness they found full of moody grandeur, and by an intensely spiritual religious life. They were too busy building homes in this same wilderness to long for more than these outlets, and the leanings of their children toward artistic pursuits were quickly and firmly discouraged. The following extracts from the journal of Nixon Rush vividly show the early attitude toward art in the Township, and the longing for artistic expression, which was not uncommon among its children:

"There was a school house built on the north side of our farm, on Uncle Seth Winslow's land, made of logs and with a long desk across the room which gave us boys a good chance to study geography and to play. I loved to make pictures. I had a natural taste for art. The children would have me make pictures of all kinds, such as pigs, cats, dogs, birds, monkeys, babies, boys or men. One day a committee came to the school and talked to the teachers about it and said I would have to leave school or quit drawing, so I had to stop, and lost my interest in drawing.

"One evening, in the year 1857, on shipboard on the Mississippi, I had a long talk with a doctor and a merchant from New Orleans. We were talking about the difference between the North and South. They thought the South had the advantage over the North. Just then I picked up a sheet of paper, began to make the picture of a lion in the act of leaping on his prey. They looked, and the doctor said:

"'You are an artist. Where did you go to an art school?'

"'I did not know anything about art schools; did not know that an art school existed in the United States. I knew they had such things in France and England. I said:

"'When I went to school the Trustees compelled me to stop drawing or be expelled.'

"The doctor said:

"'That is your life work!'"

Not only from her father, but also from her mother does Miss Rush inherit her love of the artistic, and she treasures drawings of great charm made by her mother. Well knowing what it meant to care to paint and to be denied the opportunity, her parents sent her to the best schools in the East. Finding her talent sufficiently rewarded financially to pursue her studies, she went abroad and studied in the Ateliers of Paris and painted in the quaint villages and countrysides of France and England. Among her principal works are the altar decorations in the church of St. Andrews, at Wilmington, Delaware, two stained glass window designs, one of which was bought for the country house of a New York millionaire. She has painted a number of portraits and sketches of her parents, group portraits of children, besides many easel pictures poetic in feeling that have been seen at exhibitions in the Paris Salon, New York, Washington, Philadelphia, Indianapolis, and other cities. Her cover designs and illustrations in leading American magazines, as well as her illustrated verses for children are well known not only in the Township, but in every State.

*Charles Everett Rush, son of Nixon and Louisa (Winslow) Rush, is another Fairmount Township young man who has displayed exceptional energy and ability in his chosen profession, that of Librarian. Born in the Township on March 23, 1885, he attended the Fairmount public schools, graduating in 1899. In 1902 he graduated from Fairmount Academy, and in 1905 from Earlham College, receiving the degree of Bachelor of Art; student at the Wisconsin Summer Library School in 1904; in 1908 received the degree of Bachelor of Laws from the New York State Library School, at Albany. In 1908 he was appointed Librarian of the Jackson, Michigan, Library, remaining here for two years; in 1910 he was placed in charge of the Public Library at St. Joseph, Missouri, serving in this position until 1916, when he was unanimously chosen as Librarian at Des Moines, Iowa, remaining in Des Moines until 1917, when he was called to the capital of his native State and placed at the head of the new Indianapolis Public Library. Mr. Rush's success in his field of work has been rapid, and he is now in charge of the most important collection of books in Indiana. He is ex-President of the Missouri Library Association, and chairman of the Library section of the International Association of Rotary Clubs. In politics he is independent. He is a birthright member of the Society of Friends. He is a member of the American Library Association, member of the Council of the American Library Association, and a member of the American Economic League. Mr. Rush receives a handsome salary and has acquired considerable prominence in his line of work for marked efficiency and progressive achievement. He was married, September 7, 1910, at Albany, New York, to Miss R. Lionne Adsit, of Voorheesville, New York, and they have three interesting children, Alison Adsit, Frances Marie, and Myra Lionne.

JOEL B. WRIGHT

Joel B. Wright, for twenty-six years a member and for many years Treasurer of the Board of Trustees of Fairmount Academy, was a native of Greene County, East Tennessee, where he was born July 7, 1832. His parents were Jesse and Charity (Reece) Wright, who moved to Liberty Township in 1855. Joel B. Wright was for many years prior to his death a resident of Fairmount Township. All his active life he devoted himself to farming, in which he was successful. In politics he was a Prohibitionist and in religious affairs a consistent member of the Society of Friends. His death occurred on September 27, 1910, at the age of seventy-eight years, two months and twenty days.

with J. W. Parker, A. B., as Principal, and Ellwood O. Ellis as teacher in the Grammar Department, each receiving an annual salary of six hundred dollars. The school opened with forty pupils, but before the first term of fourteen weeks had ended the enrollment had increased to sixty-five. Before the close of the first year the attendance had reached one hundred and thirteen.

The present building stands on land at the northwest corner of Rush and Eighth Streets, donated by Nixon and Louisa Rush. In 1895

ACADEMY BASKET BALL TEAM
(1915)

Left to right, top row—Lester Wright, guard; Herman Jones, center; Prof. Albert B. Hall, coach; Ozro Cunningham, forward.
Left to right, lower row—Clarence Christopher, sub-guard; Alva Smith, guard; Ralph Mittank, forward; Ralph Trice, sub-guard.

the new structure was occupied. In 1911 an addition was built, a commodious gymnasium provided, equipment installed, all of which greatly facilitated the work of teachers and increased the spirit and efficiency of the school.

While Fairmount Academy is supported by Friends, the institution is non-sectarian. Presbyterians, Christians, Congregationalists, Episcopalians and Baptists have had their turn as members of the faculty.

In 1898 the High School received its commission. The present High School Building was completed in 1902. R. W. Himelick was the first

HIGH SCHOOL BASKET BALL TEAM
(1915)

Left to right—Prof. Neil Good, coach; Orla Harris, forward; George Ramsey, forward; Harry Davis, center; Burr Stephens, center; Harold Craig, forward; Ralph Parker, guard and captain; Raymond Coss, guard; Prof. D. H. Carter, manager.

Superintendent of Schools, he in turn being succeeded by C. H. Copeland, who held the position for fifteen years. The first graduates from the High School were Grace Crilley, Eliza Frazier, Verna Hardwick, Grace Hobbs, Albert Knight, Moses Morrison, Emma Parrill, Irwin Winslow and John P. Starr.

The matter of starting a High School was first discussed by Dr. J. W. Patterson, E. D. Lewis and J. W. Parrill. Finally, the Town Trustees advised the School Board to proceed, and the result is the structure on South Vine Street.

The Fairmount Bible School had its origin in a Theological Institute of the Indiana Conference of the Wesleyan Methodist Connection of America. The first session of this institute was held at Sheridan, in 1884, under the leadership of Rev. Eber Teter, at which meeting there were twelve elders and licentiates present. A ten-day institute was held annually on the various circuits of the Indiana Conference until June, 1906, when, by an order of the previous annual conference, a thirty-day institute was provided for and held on the Wesleyan camp-ground, near Fairmount.

This Institute body, at the close of the session, framed a memorial, which was presented to the next annual conference of the same year, asking for the establishment of the Fairmount Bible School, which was granted.

The purpose of this Institute is the training of an efficient ministry in the spreading of Bible holiness.

REV. W. D. BAKER
Former Pastor of Fairmount Wesleyan Church, and one of its most popular ministers.

Among its promoters we find the names of Eber Teter, Aaron Worth, George Reber, William J. Seekins, Thomas P. Baker, Jacob Hester and James O. Baker.

REV. W. J. SEEKINS

Formerly a resident of Fairmount, has been an influential man in the Wesleyan denomination for many years. His home is now at Stockton, Illinois, where he is serving three churches, in addition to doing evangelistic work. Rev. Seekins was at one time in charge of the Wesleyan Publishing House, located at Syracuse, New York.

This school had a small beginning. The first enrollment numbered twelve, with one teacher. Since that time the institution has been able to enroll from thirty to sixty and to maintain a faculty consisting of four teachers, which will of necessity be maintained in the future.

The development of this school has been marked by the sending out into the different fields of church work many graduates up to the year 1917, a period of eleven years.

The present school building was erected in 1907, and may be valued at two thousand dollars. The building is located a mile northwest of Fairmount, in a beautiful grove, with plenty of shade and water.

Close by is a large tabernacle, with a seating capacity of two thousand, known as Bethel Tabernacle, where State and National conferences of the church are held from time to time.

The Institute has a library of three hundred and fifty well-selected volumes.

(Editor's Note.—One of the men who in a modest and unostentatious way contributed liberally of his time and means to the building of local churches and other deserving institutions was Ivy Luther. Although not one of the group of pioneers who came to this community in the early day, his steadfast loyalty and never-failing interest in all enterprises to help his adopted Township have left a marked impression upon the people with whom he passed his active life. He was a Southerner by birth, Randolph County, North Carolina, being the place of his nativity. Born on February 22, 1834, of German parentage, he was educated in the common schools of North Carolina. On August

28, 1855, he was married to Miss Sarah Stuart. To this union one son and four daughters were born, namely, Dorothy E.; Narcissa G., wife of Elias Bundy, a prominent attorney of Marion; James A., a stockholder and director of the National Drain Tile Company, of Terre Haute, Indiana; Emma L., wife of Alvin B. Scott, glass manufacturer of Fairmount. One daughter, Julia, died at six years of age in North Carolina. Mr. Luther and family came to Henry County, Indiana, in

ANCIL E. RATLIFF President of the Board of Trustees of Fairmount Academy, was born near Amboy, in Miami County, March 27, 1862. With his parents, Joseph and Mary (Lamb) Ratliff, he came to Fairmount Township in 1870. He worked on his father's farm and attended school in Fairmount. He later entered Amboy Academy, and was a student at Earlham College. Mr. Ratliff has always affiliated with the Republican party, and is a prominent member of the Society of Friends, serving as Clerk of the Yearly Meeting. He has served as County Surveyor and was elected by the people of Grant County to the State Legislature, making an excellent record in the session of 1910-'11. Mr. Ratliff is a progressive farmer, owning 170 acres of fine land in Liberty Township, where he now resides. He has for many years been active and effective in his work for reform legislation, and has done a vast deal of good in helping to develop a community spirit in his neighborhood. This spirit has helped to benefit socially and in material matters where mutual helpfulness counts for everything worth while.

1866, where they remained for several years. On October 21, 1872, the family removed to Grant County and settled in Fairmount Township, where they purchased eighty acres of land located just south of Fairmount corporation. Here they identified themselves with all good movements and have been factors in the upbuilding of the town and surrounding community. Ivy Luther died on April 13, 1914, leaving behind the memory of an upright life and a noble example of rectitude and usefulness.)

CHAPTER XXX.

BUILDING FOWLERTON.

THE SUCCESSFUL development of natural gas in various parts of Grant County stimulated enterprising men in many neighborhoods to make explorations for fuel. Nature had never before provided heat and illumination which were at once so reasonable in price or so convenient for commercial and domestic purposes.

For many years fuel in the gas belt was a matter of nominal expense, while the simple turning of a key designed for the purpose tapped a reservoir of unlimited quantities, day and night.

For illuminating purposes, natural gas was quite an improvement over the coaloil lamp. Great flambeaus were frequently seen along highways and in the streets, lighting up an area equal in extent to a city block.

It was while excitement was running high that towns sprang up much as Western cities would appear in a single night.

In 1896 B. F. Leach built the first house on the present site of Fowlerton.

Previous to this time a postoffice had been established in that neighborhood called Leach, after the well known family of that name, whose members were numerous and influential.

The first industry established in the community was a tile mill, erected in 1895 by Elbert and Jefferson Fowler.

In 1896 John L. Smith started a saw-mill and William J. and Charles E. Leach owned and operated a grain elevator. About the same time B. F. Leach began work on a bottle factory on land donated by William J. Leach.

In 1899 Favre Brothers started the Fowlerton Window Glass Factory.

P. A. Dailey started a saw-mill about 1906. The Royal Window Factory was established soon after, and the Industrial Window Glass Factory came a little later. D. L. Adams bought the Dailey saw-mill about 1909, and after rebuilding and remodeling, converted it into a hoop and saw-mill. This hoop-mill burned in the summer of 1917 and was not rebuilt. These industries were all attracted by the discovery of natural gas in that territory in apparently unlimited quantities.

The Fowlerton Canning Company opened a canning factory about 1904, which was later operated by W. R. Bailey. It has since been made into a modern plant by the Fowlerton Packing Company, J. F. Morris in charge.

The Chicago, Indiana & Eastern Railroad, in 1897, erected a depot on the northwest corner of the Henry Simons farm, now owned by Oliver P. Buller. This building was, in 1900, moved to the present junction of the Big Four and Pennsylvania railroads in Fairmount.

The Cincinnati, Richmond & Muncie Railroad, afterward known as the Chicago, Cincinnati & Louisville, was projected in 1900. This line connected Cincinnati and Chicago and proved to be of immense benefit to Fowlerton as a trading point. During the years 1901 and 1902 Fowlerton was the northern terminal station. The road has since been taken over and operated by the Chesapeake & Ohio and made a part of its system.

John Borrey owned and operated a brick factory in Fowlerton about 1902.

E. D. Fowler, Oliver P. Buller, William A. Miller, Jacob Dame, Allen Virgin, M. F. Partridge, Clyde Partridge and Will C. Smith have served as postmaster, Clyde Partridge having succeeded Smith in 1917.

Among the first merchants who located in Fowlerton were Doc Philpott, John Carter, William Millspaugh, Isaac Key, S. D. Key, J. A. Hardesty & Co., M. F. Partridge & Co., Moses Barnhart, Elias A. Wilhelm and William Dunlap & Son.

J. A. Roberts served as Justice of the Peace, having been appointed in 1892.

Former Township Trustee Joel O. Duling writes from Fowlerton, under date of September 22, 1917:

"These old records need no explanation, as they explain themselves. I give them to you so that you can see when, where, how and by whom the first school house was built in this locality."

As copied from the old records by Mr. Duling, the facts are as here set forth:

"At a school meeting held in District No. 4, in Congressional Township No. 23, Range No. 8 East, at the house of Jonathan F. Reeder, first we took up the subject of whether we should build a District school house or not, and the votes taken, yeas, 12; noes, none; blank. Second, on motion we agree to build on a donation of land made by Abraham Myers, in the center of our District, at the northeast corner of his land. On motion the votes taken, yeas, 12; noes, blank. Third, on motion we unanimously agree to build our school house within ourselves and to make it 18x20 feet, of round logs, the work to be completed against the 30th of November, 1840; yeas, 12, unanimous vote. Fourth, on motion we unanimously agree to support a free school three months in the year. Voters present: George W. Simons, Thomas Reynolds and William Leach, District Trustees; Abraham Myers, Joseph Corn, James Leach, Jonathan F. Reeder, Samuel Myers, Isaac Myers, Jacob Myers, Elijah M. Searl and John Leach. On motion adjourned May the 9th, 1840. George W. Simons, Chairman; Wm. Leach, District Clerk."

Another record, made by the same hand, as Clerk, is shown as follows:

"December 4, 1840. After due notice having been given there was a school meeting held in our school house, in District No. 4, in Congressional Township No. 23, Range 8 East. William Leach took the chair. First, we unanimously agree to commence our school on Monday, the 7th day of December, 1840. Second, on motion we agree to employ John Simons at ten dollars a month and board him. He is to teach seventy-two days for a quarter. Third, on motion Thomas Reynolds and Wm. Leach appoints George W. Simons District Treasurer. Voters present: A. Myers, J. Myers, W. Sade, James Leach and John Leach. Wm. Leach, Clerk. 10 votes."

On July 20, 1898, B. F. Leach and others called a meeting for the purpose of talking over matters in relation to the erection of a new school house at Fowlerton.

A petition was prepared, the necessary signatures procured and presented to Trustee Joseph Ratliff.

Owing to the lateness of the season the petition was not acted upon by the Trustee.

The petitioners appealed to County Superintendent Alex Thompson. The Superintendent agreed with the view the Trustee had taken of the situation, and conceded that while the necessity for the improvement might exist, the season was late and there was not sufficient time in which to erect and equip a suitable building for school purposes before the time fixed for the beginning of the fall term.

In the summer of 1899, however, the first two rooms of the present commodious brick structure were completed. Will W. Ware was selected principal of this school. The first year the building proved to be inadequate to accommodate all patrons. A frame school house was moved from the north to meet the demands.

In the summer of 1907 Trustee Alvin J. Wilson added two more rooms, which have since served the purpose to the satisfaction of patrons and pupils.

Building Fowlerton.

In 1900 so much confusion arose over the difference in the name of the town and the name of the postoffice that steps were taken to adjust the matter in a way that would be satisfactory. Several names were suggested. A letter was addressed to the Postoffice Department by Warren M. Crawford asking that suggestions be made that would aid them in the matter. It was finally agreed that the postoffice be given the name of Fowlerton, a settlement of the question which seemed to be satisfactory to citizens generally. And so the name Leach was dropped, and since 1902 the town and the postoffice have borne the same name—Fowlerton.

Fowlerton was incorporated by authority of the Board of County Commissioners on the first Monday in April, 1903.

Ancil Ratliff made a preliminary survey of forty acres of the original site. George A. Fletcher, surveyor and civil engineer, was employed, in February, 1903, to run the corporation lines and make a map of the territory included in the proposed town.

Elias A. Wilhelm took a census of the inhabitants thirty days previous to this time, the same being certified to by him as correct.

The petition for incorporation was presented to the Board of Commissioners on March 2, 1903. The territory set apart for the purpose embraced land owned partly by Ellis Wright, partly by Frank H. Kirkwood and partly by William J. Leach.

On Tuesday, March 17, 1903, the election was held, the date having been fixed by the Commissioners. Elbert D. Fowler, August Schmidt and Palmer J. Wall were selected to have charge of the election. The result of the voting showed one hundred and twenty-three for incorporation and six against it.

The first election of officers was held between the hours of 6 a. m. and 6 p. m. on May 4, 1903, in Barnhart's block. The election board consisted of Elias A. Wilhelm, inspector ; William Gorton and Matthew Costello, judges ; Allen Virgin, clerk, and S. A. Marriott, sheriff.

The result of the balloting was as follows:
Clerk and Treasurer, James Chapman.
Marshal, Joseph Henisse.
Trustees, First Ward, James P. Brown; Second Ward, William Mitchener; Third Ward, Elbert D. Fowler.

The Methodist Protestant Church was organized in 1900. The members of the denomination who had previous to this time been attending services at Salem transferred their membership and influence to Fowlerton. The result is a strong church organization. Among the first members were John Duling and wife, Joel O. Duling, Solomon Duling and wife and William Duling and wife. Rev. McCaslan was the first pastor. The church was remodeled in 1914, and is now one of the strongest congregations in the Township.

The United Brethren organized a church in 1897. The charter members were R. W. White and wife, Mrs. Lavada Malone, William A. Miller and wife, John G. Corn and wife, Oliver P. Buller and wife, George Fear and wife, Henry Garrison, Mrs. Rebecca J. Corn, Frank Garrison and wife and Lewis Hayden and wife. Rev. John Rector was the first pastor.

The Baptist Church was organized in 1910. The charter members were William J. Leach and wife, Clark Leach and wife, Mrs. Levi Simons, Mrs. Naomi Deeren, Mrs. Margaret Corn, Mrs. Joanna Gregg, Mrs. Martha C. Hancock and John Leach and wife. Noah Ford was the pastor.

The Wesleyan Methodist Church was organized in 1912, with Rev. W. D. Baker, pastor. Charter members were W. L. Dickerson and wife, L. G. Richards and wife, Charles Malone and wife, George Fear and Alva Dickerson and wife.

John A. Hardesty was commissioned a notary public by Governor Marshall in 1909.

The Fowlerton Bank was established in October, 1916, with Maurice Warner as President; John F. P. Thurston, Vice-President; Oscar A. Vinson, Cashier, and Frank M. Hundley, Assistant Cashier.

Fowlerton is the only town in Grant County that has a park.

CHAPTER XXXI.

COMMUNICATIONS AND COMMENT.

PROF. ALVIN SEALE TO DR. A. HENLEY.

Dear Friend Dr. Alpheus Henley:

I see by the interesting letters that you are sending to *The Fairmount News* that yourself and wife and Richard are in Melbourne, Florida. So, for ye sake of auld lang syne, I am going to write you a letter.

Probably you were the first person I saw in this "wourld," as you were our family physician for as long a period as I can remember.

How is the good wife, Louisa? I have a warm spot in my heart for her. I remember she was always thinking of good things for us boys to eat, and when I left Fairmount on my bicycle for the Leland Stanford University, in California, she made for me a most convenient little case with thread, pins, buttons and such handy things in it. That little case has been with me over a large part of the world since then. I have since retired it with a pension for faithful service.

For the past ten years I have been in the Philippine Islands as Chief of all their Fisheries. A very good position and most interesting work. Among the things accomplished in this time I can only state a few.

I found and described more than one hundred new species of fishes. I took the black bass (the one you have in Florida) and stocked the lakes and streams of the Islands with it. They had no good fish in their streams. I started fish ponds and fish cultural work. I introduced from the Hawaiian Islands the "mosquito fish," a little fish that prefers mosquito larvae to any other food. I took over improved nets for the commercial fishermen. I took up the canning industry and got a sardine cannery started. I made a survey of the pearl beds and platted them on the map and got a pearl button factory, employing more than two hundred people, started. I opened up the sponge fisheries; have written forty-two scientific and commercial papers relating to the fisheries. And, just before leaving Manila, I drew the plans and superintended the building of a fine $20,000 aquarium, which is a good success.

So, you see, I have not had much time for anything outside my work, although the work has been good fun and much like play, for it has taken me to all the islands of the Philippines—to Borneo, China, Japan, Australia, and other places.

I even found time to go sea fishing, which is fine sport, and one has excellent success with this kind of fishing in the Philippines. We get Spanish mackerel of sixty pounds, barracuda of one hundred and five pounds, crovilla of eighty pounds, tuna, sea bass and albacore—all fine game fishes.

ALVIN SEALE

Zoologist, was born in Fairmount Township in 1871. He is the son of John and Amy (Davidson) Seale, the father emigrating from England in 1849. Prof. Seale attended the Fairmount public schools, and in 1892 graduated from Fairmount Academy. He received the degree of Bachelor of Arts from Leland Stanford University at a later date, and for ten years served as Chief of the Department of Fisheries for the Philippine Government; Professor in the Museum of Comparative Zoology at Harvard University; co-worker with Dr. Fufitu, of Japan, on the cultivation of pearls, and author of forty-two scientific publications. In politics he affiliates with the Republican party, and is a birthright member of the Friends Church. He is a member of the Far Eastern Medical Association, member of American Association for Advancement of Science, National Geographical Society, Biological Society of Washington, American Society of Ichthyologists, and one of the founders of Stanford Zoological Club. "The more I delve into science," asserts Prof. Seale, "the more reverence I have for the simple teachings of Christ." In speaking of military matters and wars he expresses the sentiments of early Quakers in this very strong language. "I have never been forced by militarism to kill any of my fellowmen, thank God. And I would not trade this record for Grant's or Lee's, or Kaiser William's." Prof. Seale has traveled much in pursuit of scientific knowledge. He served as the zoologist on a scientific expedition to Point Barrow and the Arctic in 1895; was in charge of a scientific expedition to the South Seas and Australia in 1900; curator at the Bishop Museum in Honolulu in 1899; in charge of a scientific expedition to Alaska for the University of California in 1906. He has visited practically all the large Island groups of the Pacific, also New Zealand, Australia, Siberia, China, Japan, Formosa and Borneo, besides every State and large city in the United States. Prof. Seale was married on June 23, 1909, in California, to Miss Ethel Alice Prouty, of Windsor, Vermont. His residence address is Cambridge, Mass., and his business address is San Augustine Ranch, Santa Cruz, California.

About six months ago I received a cable from Harvard University, offering me a good position on their staff to do special scientific research in their Museum of Comparative Zoology. This is a fine place.

The museum was founded by Louis Agassiz and I find lots of specimens here collected by him.

I have been in the tropics for fourteen years, and so find Boston climate rather cold. I shall not care to stay here very long. In fact, I have just received rather a tempting offer from my own alma mater at Palo Alto, California, so I may return there within the next year.

I saved enough money in the Philippines to buy me one of the nicest ranches in California—the San Augustine. It is located just a little way out of the town of Santa Cruz, on Monterey Bay, in California. It has a fine bearing orchard of six hundred trees, a nice bungalow, a trout stream with real trout in it, a mineral spring and sixty of those great California big trees on it. I now have it rented, but that is where I am going to spend most of the remaining portion of my life, and as it is within easy reach of Palo Alto, Stanford University, it makes the offer from that place all the more tempting.

I frequently receive letters from my uncle, William P. Seale. He writes an interesting letter, but he misses my father sadly.

* * * * * *

Do you know probably no one was ever loved more by his children than our dear old father was. And the best of it is my memory of him is never sad, for I always remember some funny story, or incident, he would always tell us. His was truly a successful life. Everyone loved him, and I don't think he ever had an evil thought towards a man in all his life. I treasure his memory.

I would be glad to get a letter from you telling me of your life in Florida. When I was down there you had a place on Indian River, or near that place. I went up it with Ora Bogue one time.

With kindest regards to all, from

ALVIN SEALE.

Harvard University, Cambridge, Massachusetts, January 22, 1917.

(Editor's Note.—The writer is indebted to Dr. A. Henley for permission to print this interesting letter. It is a private communication. Those who are acquainted with Prof. Seale, and are aware of his innate modesty about his professional achievements, will understand from the very nature of the letter that it was not written for publication.)

John Seale, Sr., was born in the village of Stock, near Chelmsford, in the County of Essex, about thirty-five miles northeast of London, England, December 27, 1827, and died at Whittier, California, December 19, 1914, at the age of eighty-six years, eleven months and twenty-two days. His father, Elijah John Seale, was born May 13, 1804, in Beech Street, London, and the mother, Elizabeth (Radley) Seale, was born August 29, 1804, at Purleigh, Essex County, England. At the age of fifteen the subject of this sketch was apprenticed to a farmer named John Jasper Bull. Upon the completion of his apprenticeship he returned to his father's home at Plaistow Lodge, Essex. In 1848 John Jasper and Elizabeth Emson Bull came to America and entered a home-

THE BIG SNOW
(February 22 and 23, 1914)

The above picture shows the big snow drift along the east side of Main Street, between Washington and Adams Streets. For three or four days traffice on the Interurban was almost entirely interrupted. Country roads were impassable, and in many places people were compelled to dig their way out of their homes. There were no schools open in Fairmount or surrounding country for several days. In many places the snow drifts were more than six feet deep.

stead. This homestead adjoins Fairmount corporation on the west, and was for many years the property of Nathan D. Wilson, later passing into the hands of Mr. Seale. In the home of John J. and Elizabeth Bull lived an only daughter, for whom the young apprentice had formed an ardent affection. This attachment was increased by the separation. Upon reaching his majority John Seale left his native land and crossed the Atlantic on a sailing vessel. The voyage in those days required six weeks. Arriving in New York, he journeyed by river, lake and canal to Lagro, Indiana, and from Lagro by wagon to

Jonesboro, walking from there to the double log house located on the knoll at what is now the west end of Second Street, arriving at the home of his sweetheart on May 12, 1849. In 1850 he was wedded to Miss Eliza Bull. After a brief but exceptionally happy married life the young husband was deprived by death of the object of his devotion. In 1859 he was married to Miss Amy Davidson, and to this union eight children were born, namely: Elizabeth Ann, Sarah Alice, Amy Ellen, Herbert E., and William Perry, all deceased; Elijah John, Mary Anna Hancock and Isaac Alvin, the first two residing at Fairmount and the latter at Cambridge, Massachusetts. April 18, 1874, the wife and mother died. September 21, 1875, he was again married, to Asenath, daughter of Joseph and Miriam (Newby) Rich. Three children were born of this marriage, namely: Dr. Joseph Pearle Seale, of Fairmount, and Bertha S. Trueblood and Clista Seale, both residing at Whittier, California.

THE WAYNE TRAIL.

I think Joseph W. Baldwin gave the name Fairmount to your town. Mincher Cox gave it the name of Pucker, but it has long since outgrown that name.

I am sure Greely Bell and Dr. A. Henley have located the Fort Wayne road correctly. It ran through Summitville, and angling through the Kelsay farm, now owned by Mrs. Sluder, and thence northeast past the old Union school house and the farm then owned by Henry Osborn, and kept on the west side of the prairie past the farm of Otho Selby, and near Lake Galatia. I think it crossed the river at Wilson's ford.

I was deeply interested in your Sunday hike, and especially in that part of it relating to Back Creek Cemetery. Sleeping here for more than sixty years lies my grandfather, Jimmy Martin, who was a soldier in the War of 1812, and was present at Hull's disgraceful surrender. Here also sleep my uncle and aunt, who passed to their reward when your Township was in its infancy.

As I read the pathetic story of the young wife and the soldier and his sweetheart who slumber there, I am reminded of Knox's beautiful poem:

> O, why should the spirit of mortal be proud?
> Like a swift-fleeting meteor, a fast-flying cloud;
> A flash of the lightning, a break of the wave,
> Man passes from life to his rest in the grave.

> The maid on whose cheek, on whose brow, in whose eye,
> Shone beauty and pleasure—her triumphs are by;
> And the memory of those who loved her and praised,
> Are alike from the minds of the living erased.

I knew Thomas Wilson and was his schoolmate. He gave his life in defense of his country.

Reflections awakened by memories such as your correspondents describe teaches us the frailty of man's hopes and the uncertainty of his undertakings.   J. M. HUNDLEY.

Summitville, Indiana, February 2, 1917.

FEVER AND AGUE.

During the fifties and part of the sixties everyone, with very few exceptions (I don't remember an exception), had the ague. One would begin about 9 a. m. to chill. I don't think it was possible to apply covering enough to relieve the chill for one hour, more or less. Then a severe headache and high fever for from two to four hours. The same thing over every alternate day until broken with quinine.

Another grade of ague was the third-day chills, which was harder to stop. Ague was in its prime from August to November. I remember my father had the third day kind. Some recommended whiskey with wild cherry and dogwood bark, sarsaparilla root, prickly ash berries (I don't remember what else). So it was decided I should go to Galatia after the whiskey.

They were using our horses tramping out wheat. John Helton said I could go past his house (on the north part of John Heavilin's farm), and his wife, Sarah, would saddle his old mare for me. She buckled a strap through the handle of the jug and around the horn of the saddle. I started southeast across Charles Child's place, N. A. Wilson's, through my own; saw one little field on Thomas D. Duling's farm, struck a trail on the west bank of the prairie, followed it northeast, came through Selby farm, then the Norton farm; all the cleared land was to my left.

There was a saw-mill to my right in the second bottom, as I remember it. One house stood west of the mill, one nearly north. At the last house I asked the way to Galatia. The lady said I was in town then. She told me where the store was. It was four or five rods southeast of Bert Carroll's dwelling. I don't think there was an acre of cleared land in and adjoining town. I got my jug filled and gave the storekeeper a quarter. I don't think I saw over twenty-five acres of cleared land on the trip of over three miles. My memory is blank in regard to benefits received.

THOMAS WINSLOW.

Jonesboro, Indiana, February 12, 1917.

(Editor's Note.—The writer of the above communication is a grandson of Thomas Winslow, who came to Fairmount Township in 1836. Milton Winslow, father of the contributor, was a Friends minister, and wrote a volume of poems which were widely read and appreciated. Reference is made by Hon. Edgar L. Goldthwait to this book of rhymes.

A PIONEER DOCTOR.

Our dear father, John Seale, as you know, was one of those grand old pioneers. He came to Fairmount in May, 1849.

Father once told me a story about old Dr. Horne. It seems Dr. Horne had an excessively long nose, regarding which he was quite sensitive. This, together with a somewhat peppery disposition, made him the subject of frequent pioneer jokes. At that time he lived near Wilson's ford.

One night, very late, some of these early wits were passing his house and they called out:

"Dr. Horne! Oh, Dr. Horne!"

The doctor was awakened and stuck his head out the window only to be told to—

"Please take your nose in so we can get past your house!"

Our father's memory is a most happy one, for even in those rough times he always saw the bright side to everything, and if there was anything funny he remembered it to tell us youngsters.

ALVIN SEALE.

Harvard University, Cambridge, Massachusetts, February 9, 1917.

(Editor's Note.—Prof. Seale is the son of the late John Seale. Prof. Seale has acquired international reputation as a scientist, being at the present time a member of the faculty of Harvard University. With Dr. David Starr Jordan he has collaborated in the production of a number of standard works on natural science which are found in most large scientific libraries throughout the United States and Europe. The late John Seale is all and more than his gifted son has described him to be. An Englishman by birth, he possessed the courtly manners and grace of a polished gentleman. He probably never said a harmful word of any man. He was always cheerful and optimistic, and memories of this grand old man's kindly consideration of others will linger as long as there are people left in this community who knew him and his gentle ways.

BACK CREEK AT FLOOD TIDE
(March 24, 1913)

The high waters covered adjacent lots and near-by streets to a depth in places of several feet. It was the opinion of pioneers then living that within their recollection the overflow had not been equalled in extent of territory covered or destruction of property. A heavy rain for several days brought on the disaster. Several families along the creek were compelled to move their belongings to the second story of their dwellings. The waters raced like a torrent through Mill and Third Streets. A part of the concrete bridge spanning Third Street was washed away. Walnut Street was flooded by the overflow of Puddin' Creek. Basements were flooded and many furnaces put out of commission. Water stood three inches deep in the basement of the Methodist Episcopal Church. Fairmount Public Schools were temporarily closed and only a few students were able to reach the Academy.

WRITES OF DROWNING.

I see that William Baldwin writes of the drowning of Cyrus Puckett and Reuben Bookout at Weesner's ford. It was Calvin Bookout, the father of Reuben Bookout. I will write of it as I remember it.

Puckett rode his horse in the river and when he got in deep water he became frightened and got separated from his horse. It was soon seen that he was drowning. Bookout, without removing his clothing, went to help him. Although a good swimmer, his clothing hindered him, and they both drowned.

Puckett was about seventeen years old, was a son of Greenleaf Puckett, and lived on the farm now owned by Joseph Poole. Bookout was about fifty, and lived on the farm now owned by Otto Wells.

I saw the bodies as they were being taken home through Fairmount.

BERT WIMMER.

Jonesboro, Indiana, February 12, 1917.

(Editor's Note.—Mr. Wimmer here refers to a tragedy which created a good deal of excitement back in the early seventies. It was the first case of a double drowning, perhaps, which had occurred in the Township up to that time. The funerals of the two men were attended by throngs of people. In those days it was the custom for people generally to drop their work and attend funerals, contrary to the habit which now prevails. Mr. Wimmer's father, Isaac Wimmer, was born in Pennsylvania in 1802. From Pennsylvania he moved with his family to Henry County, Indiana, and in 1865 came to Grant County. Peter Wimmer, grandfather of Bert Wimmer, served as a drummer boy with Pennsylvania troops in the War of the Revolution.

LYNX OVER THE DOOR.

I shall never forget the old tanyard, where my father worked for so many years. Many times I have helped him. I used to help pump water in the vats. One time I was jumping, and I think Martha Gossett, Sallie Hollingsworth, now Kelsay, and I jumped in. But the vat was full of hides and I got out as soon as possible.

One time my father and Uncle Billy Brewer went out hunting. Uncle Billy killed a wildcat, or some called it a Canadian lynx. My father had it stuffed and put it over the tanyard door. Everybody who passed that way stopped to see it. It surely was a sight.

MRS. AMANDA SMILEY.

Kiefer, Oklahoma, April 1, 1917.

(Editor's Note.—Mrs. Smiley is a daughter of Nathan and Nancy Little, well remembered and highly respected citizens of Fairmount many years ago. They played well their part in the early development and progress of the Township. Many will recall vividly to mind the lynx which used to hang over the door when Nathan Little owned the tanyard which stood out on East Washington Street.

OLD BRICK CHURCH.

The first ague I ever had Dr. Philip Patterson doctored me. Dr. Philip Patterson was the first doctor I ever saw in Fairmount. He lived

BACK CREEK ON A RAMPAGE
(March 24, 1913)

Looking north from the West Eighth Street bridge. The larger tree in the foreground marks the location of the old swimmin' hole. This favorite retreat for small boys during summer months in the seventies was obscured from public view by a large pile of saw-dust from the saw-mill near by. As a result of high waters Back Creek school was closed for a few days.

where Isaiah Jay's business is now located. Later on, Dr. Patterson and Dr. Pierce doctored together. Later on, Dr. Pierce moved to Jonesboro. He was the father of Jack Pierce and Mrs. Buck Mann.

I helped to make the brick that was used in the old Friends Church that was torn down a few years ago where the new one now stands. After Jonathan Baldwin and Walker Winslow finished making brick they fixed a wagon and Jonathan Baldwin, Walker Winslow, Joe Little and I went to the State Fair. We stayed all night at Jimmy Cammack's, in Hamilton County. We took it by turns, one at a time, to stay with the wagon while in the city.

Dr. White married Solomon Parsons' daughter, I think. My recollection is they didn't stay in Fairmount very long.

The first school I went to in Fairmount was taught by Exum Morris. The school house is the house O. R. Scott and William Lindsey use for their office. The Friends held their meetings there. The next school I went to was taught by Joseph Knight. The next was taught by Jacob Carter. The house stood near George Montgomery's house. That was the first school taught in that house. The next two schools were taught by William Neal.

After that school, Nathan Vinson built the house on East Washington Street. William Hollingsworth moved the old house from North Walnut Street to just east of Flanagan's store, on East Washington Street, just east of where William Lewis's shoe-shop is now located. It was used for furniture and undertaking business.

ALEX LITTLE.

State Soldiers' Home, Indiana, January 26, 1917.

FAIRMOUNT MINING COMPANY.

I give below the names of the charter stockholders of the Fairmount Mining Company.

After canvassing the town three or four times, pleading with business men to put their shoulders (their names to a subscription paper for stock) to the wheel of a local business enterprise the result was as follows:

Dr. Alpheus Henley, Levi Scott, C. R. Small, Thomas J. Nixon, John Flanagan, Dr. W. H. Hubbard, Kimbrough Bros., Jonathan P. Winslow, Moses Mark.

These men were called to meet in the law office of Charles M. Ratliff, in the front room upstairs over the store occupied by A. F. Norton, where Ribble Bros. are now located.

Being much discouraged with so few subscribers for stock in the company, after a spirited discussion it was decided to order an assessment of thirty-five dollars each for expense of completing an organization. This being completed, another assessment, sufficient to put down a gas well, was made, and "Jumbo" was the result.

C. R. SMALL.

Greenville, North Carolina, January 4, 1917.

(Editor's Note.—"Jumbo" created considerable excitement in his palmy days. Excursions were run from different directions to see this wonder of nature, which was brought forth by the intelligent perseverance of forward-looking men who were willing to back their judgment with finances sufficient to carry through the project.)

VOICE FROM IDAHO.

You asked me to write in your album,
I hardly know where to begin,
For there is nothing original in me
Unless it is original sin.

But to say that I am interested in the buiding of a Township would be putting it in mild form. How could I help but be? I am learning about my grandparents. It seems that I am descended from four of the oldest Quaker families in Grant County.

Sister Ruth Carey told of our mother's parents. Our father and William S. Elliott's father were brothers, making William and me first cousins. I tell people that if I am not a full-blooded Quaker I must be fifteen-sixteenths. Well, I am proud of that, all right, but when I stop to think it over, have I held up the standard? I am afraid not.

I can not help but think of the changes since the days of our grandparents. Now, I see that Grandfather Knight was listed in the top ratio when old Back Creek meeting house was built. He would put his family on a horse and walk at their side. I expect if we coud get the records of Mississinewa Friends meeting, Grandfather Elliott's record would be about the same.

I was at preaching two weeks ago at Melba and there were five automobiles and three Fords there. Grandfather walked and let his family ride a horse. I hope we are just as good, but you know we live in faster times.   E. R. ELLIOTT.

Melba, Idaho, April 27, 1917.

THE BIG TREE.

The contributions of my friends, Dr. A. Henley, T. B. McDonald and J. M. Hundley, as well as many others who have written interestingly of the very early days in that section, have really restored, in the mind's eye, the somberness, as well as the glory, of the forest primeval, with which the first settlers had to contend in the struggle to subdue the wilderness. These pen pictures of those early days, handed down in book form, will no doubt find a place and be read in many homes of this and future times. Yet there must have been joy, as well as inspiration, among the hardy pioneers who came with sturdy determination to subdue and to build not only homes for themselves, but a monument to their memory. To them there must have been a joy in conquering nature, which feeling gives a zest to life.

Now a word along another line. The "hikes" taken by yourself and Mrs. Baldwin I have read with much interest. I used to think there were many things along the country ways about Fairmount that were alluring to the lover of nature. There still remained many forests of majestic mien, some yet in a primitive state, and there were beautiful groves, quiet coverts and vistas of field and forest that appealed to me strongly, and I used to keep my bicycle busy whenever occasion permitted. This method was faster than "hiking," but I grant not so satisfactory in some ways. Your method is more deliberate, and consequently more satisfying, and it teaches the valuable lesson of the benefits of walking that is too much of a lost art.

Now, I have an assignment for Mrs. Baldwin. Some years before I bade farewell to the only place that seemed like home to me, and the memory of which I cherish deeply, I published in *The News* a letter written by Rev. Nixon Rush, who was then on a visit to California—I think his first trip to this coast—in which he gave an account of a trip he and Dr. Henley—I think it was the doctor—made when they were boys, through the forest, to what was called in that day "the big tree," an immense tree that was considered a wonder even in that day, and how they came near being attacked by a drove of wild hogs. I think the direction of the tree was northwest, but am not sure.

J. STIVERS.

San Francisco, California, April 22, 1917.

(Editor's Note.—The tree to which Mr. Stivers refers attracted much attention in pioneer days, so large was its trunk and so extensive were its spreading branches. The tree was located several miles northwest of Fairmount, but the exact spot is unknown to the writer. Robert Seeley is authority for the statement that the "big tree" referred to in the communication from J. Stivers stood in the northeast corner of Green Township on land entered by John Pattison and now owned by the Newkirk heirs. The tree—a walnut—was sold by William Pattison to a man by the name of William Kidd. It was sawed into heavy boards at a saw-mill owned by Davis & Burrier. The boards of solid walnut were shipped to New York City to be used as counters for stores. The tree was a beauty and was sound from root to top. At the end of the first twelve-foot log it measured more than nine feet in diameter. The tree, at the time it was visited by Dr. A. Henley and Nixon Rush, stood in the Miami Indian Reservation. The country out there was then an unbroken wilderness. Mr. Seeley formerly lived in the vicinity of the "big tree," which he remembers well. He also remembers the Indians, who kept the "Reserve" as a hunting-ground. They would come there from their village over about Jalapa for the purpose of hunting and for making maple sugar. The men would hunt and the women would make the sugar and syrup. The "bucks" would hire white men to make the wooden troughs into which the sugar-water flowed from the trees. The Indians were fine hunters and could get a deer where no one else could find it.)

THE MAN ON THE RAIL.

At one time in the '70's I helped to carry a man out of Fairmount who was hauling a load of saloon fixtures to the old Methodist Episcopal Church building, which now stands at the southeast corner of Second and Main Streets.

Fred Cartwright and Andy Morris were trying to get a saloon in our little Quaker town. Cartwright went a roundabout way and got in here. He reached Sam Fritch's house, where Sam and Fred were entertaining one another. The man had left his team and fixtures down in the south part of town and walked up the street to see if the coast was clear.

While he was standing on the corner of Washington and Main Streets the word came what his business was. It created quite an excitement, and men, women and children were up in arms.

While they were discussing what to do with the man I came up with the rail and run it between the gentleman's lower limbs. Alex Pickard was then living. He was standing at the right place to catch hold of the other end of the rail. Someone held him on and Pickard and I took him to his wagon, turned his team towards Summitville and started him in the direction from where he came.

Cartwright slipped out of town and went the same way.

W. A. PLANCK.

Fairmount, Indiana, January 15, 1917.

(Editor's Note.—Mr. Planck here relates an incident which at the time caused quite a stir. In those days temperance sentiment was strong. There was a determination on the part of many citizens not to permit a saloon to open its doors in Fairmount. At this particular time Mr. Planck worked on the Big Four section with Henry Barber, who was section foreman. Mr. Planck grew up at Point Isabel. His father and mother moved there fifty-eight years ago, when there was "not a stick amiss." Mr. Planck's father built the first cabin in Point Isabel. The cabin was partitioned off for a postoffice and he was appointed postmaster, retaining the place during thirty-two years of his life. W. A. Planck was his father's assistant for a number of years.)

ISAAC ROBERTS.

The name of Isaac Roberts has been mentioned as one of the early settlers in Fairmount. He conducted the first blacksmith shop that was in the town.

Can anyone except myself show any of his work? I have an old hoe that he made for my father while in that shop. My recollection is that the shop was near where Frank Buller's barn is.

JOHN W. COX.

Fairmount, Indiana, February 1, 1917.

OUR FIRST TAILOR.

In looking over the names of persons in business in the early history of Fairmount, I think my father, John Lillibridge, had the first tailor shop, and the building he occupied stood on East Washington Street, where the back part of the Borrey block now stands.

MAY HENLEY.

Fairmount, Indiana, March 8, 1917.

(Editor's Note.—The writer is sure that so far as his recollection goes John Lillibridge was the first tailor to open a shop in Fairmount. Mrs. Henley was formerly Miss May Lillibridge and a sister to the late Charles A. Lillibridge, former Recorder of Grant County.)

CYRUS PUCKETT, NOT JOHN.

Calvin Bookout and Cy Puckett were drowned at a point southeast of Jonesboro. It was Cy Puckett, and not Jonathan Puckett, and it was on Saturday of June Quarterly Meeting. Cy Puckett's brother married my sister.

I remember the corduroy road just about where the Soldiers' Home is now. I used to go with my father, Robert Trader, to Wabash when he hauled wheat to that point.   HARVEY TRADER.

Fairmount, Indiana, March 10, 1917.

EARLY DAYS.

I remember when all the old Friends around Fairmount came to Back Creek meeting. Joseph Winslow sat head of the meeting and David Stanfield sat next. The gallery was nearly full; in fact, one end of the church was filled. But when the meeting at Fairmount was started it took almost half the members.

I remember well before there was a house in Fairmount. At the cross-roads, a little to the east, a large poplar tree stood in the edge of the road. The first house I remember, Joseph W. Baldwin built. He put a store in the west end of it. It was the Seth Winslow corner. After a few houses were built, before the town was named, I think Jonathan Baldwin was the man that suggested the nickname "Pucker." But the town soon outgrew that.

My father was a strong anti-slavery man in his time. As long as he lived he kept a station on the Underground Railroad. I have seen a great many runaway negroes eating at our house—at one time eight. I have seen a great many slave hunters go through our lane past the house with their bloodhounds, but they never came in. One morning I remember well, after we had breakfast, a slave came and asked mother for something to eat. The slave sat down to the table, and while there a company of men with two dogs rode through the lane going east. The negro looked out of the door and said to mother:

"There goes my old massa!"

Just as they got out of sight the escaped slave went to the north door and took across the meadow toward the church as fast as he could run. We never heard of him being caught.

Father died in the summer of 1849. My mother had her dowry on the old home and lived there until I was grown and married.

I married Malinda Knight, daughter of Benjamin Knight, in the fall of 1864. We moved to Marshall County, Iowa, in the spring. In 1896 we came to Salem, Oregon. CHARLES BALDWIN.

Salem, Oregon, April 18, 1917.

(Editor's Note.—The writer of the above communication is a son of Charles Baldwin, who resided for many years in the Back Creek neighborhood in the early day.)

REFRESHENS MEMORY.

I was noticing in one of the letters to *The News* the statement that the first Friends brick meeting house was built by Samuel Radley (he was my uncle) and Phineas Henley (he was my father-in-law). That was quite correct, but it was a mistake about the brick being hauled from Jonesboro. The brick were made in the field across the road opposite to where Robert Bogue's red barn used to stand. It was in Jonathan Baldwin's field, and the old gate stood a piece north, and the brick kiln was several rods east. The lime was burned at Jonesboro, a little west of the main part of the town, in the creek bottom. It was burned by an Irishman named Crilley, and his assistant was Quincy Collins, a Staffordshire man who used to make boots and shoes when Crilley did not need him in the lime business.

There were fifty thousand brick. I know these to be facts, so have told the straight of it. I gave the hauling as my part of the subscription, free, towards the new meeting house.

WILLIAM P. SEALE.

Whittier, California, March 19, 1917.

BOYHOOD DAYS.

I have just received a copy of *The News,* and after feasting on it for a while have remailed it to my mother at Whittier.

My mind is carried back to boyhood days, to the fishing, skating and swimming at the old creek; to "June Quarterly" at Back Creek, with the busy time at the old toll gate; to the times when we used to gather ferns in the woods and by Lake Galatia for use in making mottoes.

Well do I remember when the old "Jumbo" gas well was ablaze for weeks and could be heard for twenty miles, when one could see to read

a newspaper outdoors any time of the night in Fairmount, and, as *The News* at that time expressed it, "even the chickens, not being able to discern night from day, did not go to roost, but would drop dead from sheer exhaustion."
LEMBERT T. ADELL.

Greenfield, California, April 8, 1917.

(Editor's Note.—Mr. Adell is the son of Jacob and Tacie (Pemberton) Adell, who lived for many years on North Main Street. Bert and his mother went West many years ago, after the death of his father. He is now a prosperous dairyman near Greenfield, California. Jacob Adell, in his time, was an expert penman and made mottoes. Many of these mottoes may still be found in the homes of Fairmount people. He did a great deal of scroll work and many marriage certificates, artistically designed, were executed with his pen.)

THE PLANK ROAD.

The plank road was between Deer Creek Hill and the Marion Cemetery, if I remember, as we hauled our wheat to Lagro in those days. In after years we changed our wheat market to Wabash, where we sold it to Whiteside. We also hauled our peaches and apples to Wabash. I have gone with my brother, Thomas, to Wabash at different times.

As Mr. Hundley says, we generally went with three or more teams at a time, as there generally was someone who had a balky horse and had to have help on the hill, which has been spoken of so often. We would drive a few feet on the hill, and the driver generally walked at the side of the wagon while going up the hill so as to be ready to chock the wagon when we stopped to let the horses get wind, and then make another pull. In this way we would get up the hill. If we went to Lagro we would camp out in the wagon over night, and I would watch the canal boats and trains during the night.

If any of your readers can tell who built the Fairmount Woolen Mill and operated it at first I would like to know, as I think George Eckfelt was the first and I do not remember who was the next. William Wilkinson and Reece & Haisley operated it one time and William Wardwell operated it one time, but do not remember the parties in rotation.
JOHN A. WILSON.

Logansport, Indiana, March 3, 1917.

A CHARACTERISTIC LETTER.

My Dear Friend Edgar: Thine of the 1st was received, with enclosures, and I am ashamed to answer at so late a date. But I am not very well; hence my excuse.

Drop in. You know it is very cold, and thee would be very lucky to be set up alongside of a piping-hot bowl of beef soup, made of 28-cent beef, reinforced with 11-cent onions, 10-cent cabbage and potatoes at $2.70 a bushel. Excuse me. Allow me to add another ladle to thy bowl; thee seems hungry. And now is this not a delicious exhibition of the cost of high living?

But when we are through with the high cost of living we will go to the sitting-room, which is all over the house. Thee can enjoy thyself with a chapter on theology from *Barclay's Apology,* or a thrilling religious experience from *Fox's Journal.* They are both convenient—not hard to find.

When thee gets through translating this thee will not want me to contribute to "The Making of a Township."

IREDELL.

Columbia City, Indiana, February 17, 1917.

(Editor's Note.—Iredell B. Rush, author of this characteristically jovial letter, will be remembered by a great many people back at his old home. Mr. Rush, as a young man, entered the banking business at Marion, as an employe of Adam Wolfe, prominent in his day as one of the foremost financiers of this section of Indiana. From Marion, Mr. Rush went to Columbia City, where he has spent the greater part of his active business career as a banker. He is a son of Nixon Rush, Sr., and a grandson of Azel Rush, who came to this country in the early day. Long before the Civil War Azel Rush, who lived at the time in North Carolina, freed thirty slaves as a matter of conscientious duty.)

JOHN J. BULL.

I read with much interest the article written by E. L. Goldthwait and very much appreciated his kind words in regard to the life and character of my uncle, John J. Bull.

Yes, E. L. Goldthwait, my uncle had a large orchard, and there are two pear trees and two or three apple trees still standing. His paralyzed arm gave him a great deal of trouble for many years and finally affected his whole body. Eight and one-half years of entire helplessness were spent at my father's, where he died, in the spring of 1873.

ELIZABETH PEACOCK.

Fairmount, Indiana, February 17, 1917.

(Editor's Note.—Mrs. Peacock is a daughter of Samuel and Mary (Bull) Radley, English Friends who came to Fairmount Township when Mrs. Peacock was a child. Mrs. Peacock is familiar with the development of this Township since the early days when the first pioneers were making the way for others who followed.)

MARY ANN TAYLOR MORROW.

I do not want Mary Ann Taylor's name left out of the list, because she was my first teacher, and although she made me stand on the stove with a girl one time, and another time I had to stand on the floor with a "dunce-cap" on my head, as a punishment for misdemeanors, I remember her with a degree of affection and respect that do not attach to the name of any other of my early teachers.

She "boarded around" a week at a place, and we children all liked her so well that we were all glad when it came her time to "stay at our house," and we were very jealous of each other, for fear she would spend more time at some other home than at ours.

Of course this sounds odd for this day and time, but at that time the public school terms were short, sometimes only three or four months, and the summers were filled in by subscription terms, attended mostly by small boys and girls, as the older ones had to stay at home and work.

This teacher was a young, sixteen-year-old girl, very pretty, as I remember her, and very efficient as a teacher for primary grades.

Mary Ann Taylor married Joseph Morrow, a lawyer, in Marion, and is now living there.

E. J. COX.

Maitland, Florida, February 8, 1917.

BRINGS BACK OLD TIMES.

Allow me to say "The Making of a Township" brings old times back to my mind as new as if it were today. I remember thirty-five years ago, when we lived in the woods and rolled big log-heaps. My grandfather, George Mason, entered land in Fairmount Township. He had a log house hewed out of logs two feet wide.

H. J. DICKERSON.

Litchville, North Dakota, March 29, 1917.

BACK IN THE FIFTIES.

In looking over an expense account kept by my father (Jesse E. Wilson) from 1856 to 1864, I find the following names of persons doing business in or near Fairmount in 1856—Joshua Mercer, Henry Mercer and Samuel Heavenridge.

In 1857—Micajah Frances, Josiah Bradway, James Johnson, Jesse Reece, Daniel Hollingsworth, Ira Kendall, Levi Pierce, James Quinn, Dr. Philip Patterson, Seaberry Lines, Austin Williams, Elijah Herrold, Jack Reel, Hopkins Richardson, Joseph Bennett and Alfred Waldron.

In 1858—Solomon Parsons, James Turner, Henry Harvey, John Crowell, George Doyle, John Scarry, Hugh Findley, William Wright, Robert Hannah and Frances Lytle.

In 1859—Dr. White, Caleb Neal, Mincher Cox, Alexander Jordan, John Mathers and Ward McNeir. In this same year Micajah Wilson went into business in partnership with Henry Harvey and were still in business in 1864.

The name of Jonathan P. Winslow was mentioned for the first time in 1860. Other names of persons who lived in or near Fairmount from 1860 to 1864 are: Henry Long, Enoch Thomas, George Eckfelt, Dr. David S. Elliott, Joseph Brandon, Dr. John T. Horne, Harmon Pemberton, Thomas Moon, Joseph Rush, Joseph Hollingsworth, Skid Horne and Joseph Milliner.

I think my grandfather, John Wilson, died some time in the early sixties in a house located on the northwest corner of the lot now owned by Dr. D. A. Holliday. About all I remember about my grandfather was the red flannel back to the vest he wore.

Another name not before mentioned is "Toddy" (Solomon) Thomas, the first toll gate keeper I ever saw. He, too, left a lasting impression on my mind by the knit cap he wore and the smooth way he had cutting pennies into half pennies to make change. He lived about where the I. O. O. F. Building now stands. The toll gate was located about where the W. A. Beasely house now stands on South Main Street.

In the expense book before mentioned my father refers to a house and lot as "my house in the log yard," or "my house south of the gristmill." Among the names of tenants who occupied the house from 1859 to 1864 are Joseph Brandon, William Dove, Ward McNeir, Joseph Milliner, Henley Winslow and William Hollingsworth, as a cabinet shop.

Some of the persons whose names I mention were in business for a number of years. I remember my father speaking of almost every man.

This record was discontinued in 1864, but as I "settled" there myself October 5, 1858, the record was taken up again.

C. M. WILSON.

Alexandria, Indiana, February 25, 1917.

FIRST COPY OF THE NEWS.

I have a copy of the first graduating exercises of the Fairmount schools, given in the spring of 1884. If you cannot find it in your files I will copy it and send to you later in the game. I also have the original petition filed with the School Board asking for a Thanksgiving vacation so that the boys might go "rabbit hunting," about 1880.

It is with much pride that I look back to the time when Joel Reece pulled the first copy of *The News* off the old Washington hand press, and know that I was present at its birth.

N. D. ELLIOTT.

Salem, Oregon, February 8, 1917.

DID THEIR PART.

In the account book referred to in my previous letter I find the date of death of two hundred and ninety-two persons who had lived in or near Fairmount and had done well their part in "The Making of a Township."

After looking over the list of names I find to my surprise I knew the most of them, and many whom I had a long time ago forgotten.

This record began with the name of Daniel Hollingsworth, who died on the lot adjoining the Traction Station on the north, in Fairmount, June 8, 1866. This record ended with the name of Margaret Pucket, who died March 24, 1883, and the mother of Cyrus Puckett, who was drowned with Calvin Bookout in June, 1873.

I knew both Bookout and Puckett, and I attended the funeral of Puckett, which was held on Sunday.

Among the long list of names referred to are three or four others whose lives had a tragic ending.

C. M. WILSON.

Alexandria, Indiana, March 7, 1917.

RE-ROOFING OF BACK CREEK MEETING HOUSE.

In order that the list of teachers who have taught school in Fairmount Township may be as complete as possible I will send in the names of a few who taught at old Back Creek from 1854 to 1864. They are Asa T. Baldwin, Quincy Baldwin, Melissa Pierce, Miriam Henley, Sarah Hockett, Levi Coppock, Joel Davis, Mary Ann Coppock, Daniel Lawrence, Jane Pruitt and George Winslow.

In the year of 1859 or 1860 the old Back Creek church needed a new roof on it, and Jack Winslow took the contract to re-roof it for $40, and he bought a large ash tree of my father, Henry Winslow, and my twin brother and I sawed the blocks. We were so small that we had to have blocks to stand on so we could reach the top of the log. He hired a colored man by the name of Pleas Weaver to make the shingles, which, after being riven were dressed with a drawing knife.

Well do I remember when my father kept a slave two weeks who was trying to make escape from his master, and he was so afraid of being re-captured that whenever the door was opened he would hide. He made brooms for my father, and after the war was over he became a citizen of Mill Township and died near Jonesboro.

In those days it was not very satisfactory among the Friends for their children to have fiddles, as they were called then, but my brother Levi had one, and in order that it might not be confiscated by his father he kept it hid in the cheat box of the fanning mill.

Josiah Winslow.

Fairmount, Indiana, February 20, 1917.

(Editor's Note.—Mr. Winslow here refers to the objections of Friends as a denomination to musical instruments either in the home or in connection with church services. Today instruments are found in homes of the modern Quaker who can afford them, as well as being generally used in connection with religious services. Mr. Winslow is a grandson of Joseph Winslow, who settled in 1829 on Back Creek.)

THE OLD SCHOOL HOUSE.

I have not been in Fairmount for many years, but the room in my heart marked "Fairmount" is still as "warm as toast." When I think of the old school house, where the steps went up and down over the fence (where I fell and cracked my arm), I can just see the children come trooping in. To me, they look just as they did then. I am afraid I would not know them now.

Just think, I had an enrollment of ninety-two the first year, ninety-four the second year, and ninety-six the third, and my hair is not very gray, even now. PEARLIE CHAMP MILES.

Dublin, Indiana, February 20, 1917.

ISAAC MEEK.

Do you remember Rev. Isaac Meek, who used to live in the southeast corner of the square opposite Flanagan's store, or one block east and one block south of said store? He was a circuit rider for the Wesleyan Methodist Church. He was an old man there when I knew him, but I don't know if he was among Fairmount's pioneers. He used to preach at Hodson's Chapel and Howell's school house, both places northwest of Fairmount.

H. H. MILLER.

Fargo, North Dakota, February 20, 1917.

(Editor's Note.—The writer recollects Isaac Meek very distinctly. He was a preacher who preached with much fervor. He was regarded as a man of absolute sincerity and was respected by all who knew him. In his day and generation he did a great work for the Wesleyan Methodist Church, and there are many members of this denomination still living who will recall his memory with gratitude and veneration.

INTERESTED IN STORY.

These little histories afford the club women many interesting facts in hunting material for club papers, and stories illustrating the sturdy characters from which we sprung. I am studying the early churches of Indiana, the mission, circuit riders, and your story will be gladly received. ETTA CHARLES.

Alexandria, Indiana, January 13, 1917.

(Editor's Note.—Dr. Charles is a daughter of the late Dr. Henry Charles, who for many years was a successful physician here. He was also a recorded minister in the Society of Friends. Dr. Etta Charles is one of the first woman physicians in this section of the State. She has built up a large and lucrative practice at Alexandria and throughout Madison County. She is much in demand as a speaker by different

County, District and State Medical Societies. The perseverance and determination to succeed in the practice of her profession, which has earned for her both the confidence and respect of a wide circle of acquaintances and friends in central Indiana mark her as a woman of strong character and unsual ability.)

DESERVED TRIBUTE.

As one of the few who now remain that were schoolmates of your grand old man, Dr. Alpheus Henley, I want to congratulate you upon your happy characterization of this good and worthy man.

In every community there is found some one who towers above his fellows and commands the universal love and respect of all who know him. This commanding place in society is sometimes the result of natural endowments which exalt their possessor above less fortunate associates, or it may be due to educational and social advantages not open to others. While these things may and often do give their possessor a place in public esteem which he could never have obtained by his own exertion, it should never be forgotten that a life of unselfish service and devotion to humanity is more to be admired and respected than one, however successful, over which its possessor had only such control as the forces of nature or the power of inherited wealth had given him.

The writer knew your grand old man when he was a country boy in the common schools of your Township and was acquainted with his father, Phineas Henley, who was one of your early Quaker pioneers, and himself a grand old man. I shall not attempt to trace the course of Dr. Henley through his struggle for a professional education, but suffice it to say that his energy and indomitable courage enabled him to overcome obstacles which surrounded him in his pioneer environment and to establish himself in his chosen profession.

He chose as the field of his life work the home of his boyhood and the scenes of his early struggles, in which he, no doubt, received a justly merited material reward for his services. His most lasting and enduring recompense can truly be said to consist of the esteem, love and confidence in which he is held by every man, woman and child who knew him.

No man ever lived in your town who rendered so much faithful and unselfish service to his fellow man as he did, and many times this service was rendered without recompense or hope of reward other than a consciousness of duty well done. I have no powers of description which will enable me to portray the hardship and labor he endured as he rode on horseback or traveled on foot through mud, rain and the intense cold of winter as he ministered to his afflicted and suffering neighbors. No question was ever asked as to the payment of fees and no one was ever refused medical aid because he chanced to be poor.

I venture to say that his gratuitous services rendered the suffering poor of your Township amounted to thousands of dollars. Dr. Henley, as we knew him, had traits of character which endeared him to all who knew him well. He was ever frank and outspoken. There was no guile in his heart. He was honest in his actions. He was pure in his life. He was tender, sympathetic and obliging, slow, perhaps, to make friends, but his unselfishness bound those he made to him with hooks of steel.

President Lincoln once said, "So long as I have been here I have not willingly planted a thorn in any man's bosom." I think it may be truly said that Dr. Henley never carelessly or willingly wounded the feelings of a human being.

I am conscious of the fact that both Dr. Henley and myself are on the western slope, and fast descending toward life's setting sun and, therefore, believing as I do, that life would be much sweeter, I cannot refrain from adding my tribute of love, kind appreciation and respect for your grand old man, Dr. Alpheus Henley.

May the consciousness of a life well spent and the knowledge that there lives and blooms in the hearts of his hosts of friends in your town and Township sincere sentiments of gratitude and appreciation be to him a solace in his declining years, as sweet as the orange blossoms which blow and as beautiful as the roses which bloom in his Southern home is the prayer of his friend, comrade and schoolmate.

J. M. HUNDLEY.

Summitville, Indiana, March 12, 1917.

CHAPTER XXXII.

PERSONAL RECOLLECTIONS.

THE ORIGINAL settlers of that productive spot were different from others—unique, clannish if you please, and set in their ways, and firm in their religious leanings. All were Quakers, opposed to slavery, which made them, naturally, Abolitionists, or Republicans. I never knew a Quaker Democrat—nor a black one.

Under our statute law a license to sell liquor was always turned down by a Quaker County Commissioner, for the simple reason that no applicant was ever considered "fit" to sell booze, and two out of the three on the Board made the county "dry," and it continued so for a generation, distinguishing Grant as about the only dry county in Indiana.

It was only when our party got cold feet on the Prohibition question, as defined by that club-footed Friend, Baxter, from Wayne County, and a Republican Representative in the State Legislature, that a division in the old party became ominous, but we pretended to make light of it. Our program was to ignore the issue. I was editor of the Republican organ here in those days and found the temperance road a hard one to travel, so, like the others, I kept as still as I could, notwithstanding these alleged reformers shot it into me on every occasion.

I remember my neighbor and friend, Dora Wright,[*] a good speaker, went up to Fairmount to open the campaign, about 1884. He had a fine audience that night and a good speech committed to memory, and you may be sure it was orthodox. The audience seemed unduly aroused and every applause came in just at the right time, until Jonathan P. Winslow arose to a point of order.

"Dora!" he exclaimed, raising himself to his full height (six and a half feet), "we've had enough of this bloody-shirt politics! What we want to know," he cried out with vigor, "is thy attitude on the temperance question. Now, will thee tell us?"

Dora wasn't used to hectoring, but in as dignified and parliamentary way as he could command he begged the gentleman's indulgence until he was through with the matter in hand, when he would take up that part of his speech and discuss it fully.

---

[*]Hon. A. T. Wright, better known among his personal and political friends as "Dora," was an excellent orator. In 1880 he was elected to represent Grant County in the State Legislature, being re-elected in 1883. In his second term he was the nominee of the Republicans for Speaker of the House.

But he didn't want to talk about the temperance question, and didn't intend to. He looked benignantly around at the audience and began to drink water, and wandered, and dismissed the audience, finally realizing, he said, that he had kept them up too long.

After that speech Dora's acquaintances down here in Marion would stop him now and then and ask him about his attitude on the temperance question, whereupon Dora would explode and say unkind things of Jonathan.

You knew Mahlon Neal, a very thrifty old Quaker who lived about four miles northwest of Fairmount, on a big farm. Mahlon had much money, and the reputation of having stowed away about the house still more. One night, while Mahlon and his daughter were sitting in front of the open fire, a half-dozen sons of Belial, all masked and holding revolvers in their hands, rushed in on him and demanded his money. It wasn't the old man's nature to be disturbed. He never moved off his chair, but turned his head to the armed robbers and looked them over seriously.

"Won't thee sit down?" he said.

The robbers became disconcerted; the daughter slipped out without being noticed and made a beeline for the dinner-bell hanging from a tall pole, to a rope within her reach, and such a disturbance followed in all the farm houses nearby that every rogue "flew the coop" and the incident ended forever then and there, and no harm done.

EDGAR L. GOLDTHWAIT

Whose kindly criticism and friendly interest in the writer's efforts is largely responsible for this volume, is a member of one of Grant County's oldest families. Mr. Goldthwait was born in Marion, August 7, 1850. At the age of twelve years he began to learn the printer's trade. For forty years he was actively identified with the publishing business and a part of that time engaged in editorial work. For sixteen years he was editor of The Marion Chronicle, which became a power in Indiana Republican politics under Mr. Goldthwait's management.

One of my old friends up there was Milton Winslow,* the poet. I published a volume of his rhymes one time. They were real entertaining. He was strong on temperance and religion and his contribution was a faithful reflection of his opinions.

Do you remember Bishop Milton Wright, of the United Brethren Church? His sons (mere boys) invented one of the marvelous machines of the age—the flying machine—now adopted by every warring nation on earth. Lord Kitchener spoke of it as the greatest addition in warfare known since the invention of gunpowder. These boys deserve a big place in history.

The Quakers are the only American people who ever gave substantial recognition to the colored folk. When they settled here first, sixty-odd years ago, they found homes and protection, and here they thrived, on the whole, better than they have since. The Underground Railroad led through Quakerdom, while nine-tenths of the other counties of Indiana wouldn't allow a black man within their borders. History doesn't take account of this boycott.

I would be somewhat remiss if, on this occasion, I would forget my old friends, Walker Winslow and Henley Winslow, who conducted the Wild West stage between Marion and Anderson in War days. The trip was made daily—thirty miles—and by it we depended wholly for War news, and soldiers came and went to and fro on War errands. Sometimes they were wounded, or ill, or paroled from Southern prisons.

---

*Milton Winslow, farmer and prominent minister of the Society of Friends, was born in Randolph County, North Carolina, May 21, 1821, and died at his home in Fairmount, November 15, 1893. His parents were Thomas and Nancy (Nixon) Winslow, who came to Fairmount Township in 1836, when Milton was fifteen years old. He was educated in the common schools of North Carolina and Indiana. He helped his father during the summer season to clear the farm and take care of the crops. With the exception of three years he lived in Wayne County and two years spent in Michigan, his entire life, after he came with his parents in 1836, was passed in Fairmount Township. He cast his first Presidential vote in 1844 for Henry Clay, the Whig candidate. In 1856 he supported Gen. John C. Fremont, and continued to affiliate with the Republican party until 1884, when he identified himself with the Prohibitionists and remained loyal to this party until his death. He was a birthright member of the Society of Friends. On April 23, 1846, he was married at Dover, in Wayne County, Indiana, to Miss Mary (Johnson) Roberts, daughter of Walter and Hannah (Johnson) Roberts, who had emigrated to Indiana from a Quaker settlement in South Carolina. Mary (Roberts) Winslow was born July 15, 1818, and died July 20, 1906, at her home in Fairmount. On August 2, 1847, Walter and Hannah Roberts deeded to their daughter eighty acres of land in Grant County. Milton Winslow was a man of superior attainments. Not only did he preach the Gospel with power and eloquence, but he possessed literary ability of high order. In 1892 he issued a volume of poems entitled, "Poems for Everybody," which had a large circulation and wide popularity.

The stage was a daily tragedy. Sometimes a dead body was brought home, and almost always the driver of the four horses and the big lumbering stage made his first stop at the postoffice, where Jim Nolan "received" in the midst of an anxious crowd, as many women as men, and it was midnight often before the mail was finally delivered.

Often I met the stage at Deer Creek Hill, where one of the brothers would deliver to me a bundle of *The Indianapolis Daily Journals.* When the news was extra exciting we'd hear the cannon firing at Wabash or Anderson, and the highway on both sides was wildly stirred, and the stage watched for. The papers I'd peddle out at ten cents up, according to the demand, were usually read aloud to the typical audience of those days. God keep their memories green! We haven't seen the like of it in our country for half a century, and no American ever wishes to see it again.

It was worth while to know 'Cajah Wilson, a gardener. He peddled his products about and gave good measure always.

"I have no half-peck measure with me," he once said to a prospective customer, "so I'll pour the 'taters here on the floor and then thee take one and I'll take one, and divide alike," and so they did in the most satisfactory way; and he knew all the news along the route from Fairmount to Marion, and his visits were always welcome. Besides, he was strong on religion and Prohibition, and wouldn't shut up.

Another one was John J. Bull, a large land owner of Fairmount. He must have had bully good orchards scattered around over his farms. His apples looked like they were made ready for the county fair. He would stop in front of a residence and announce his wares.

"Will thee buy some apples today?" Alongside where he sat in the wagon behind his fat team a stick was fastened, on top of which was a sample apple. He didn't need to ring his bell or cry his products; people knew him and his purpose. They were acquainted with that fawn-colored hat, his shad-belly coat and homespun trousers, and even (in my time) his affliction—a paralytic, useless arm. He was, I am told, not a Carolina Quaker, but an English one. He was without guile—Fairmount had no better citizen, and that is saying a great deal.

It didn't take much of a metamorphosis to create young Quakers into dudes when their combs were red. They were our barbers' best customers. Their hair was groomed, mustaches dyed, boots shined, neckties given special attention—verily, I say that Solomon couldn't come it over them. Do you remember Iredell Rush, Steve Baldwin, *et al.*? I never knew the girls in those days. I was too young to know the difference between demureness and indifference. I only know that the plethoric homes up there had not a piano, organ, fiddle or song book.

And now, Ed, haven't I gone far enough into my reminiscences of the past to fill a space in your history of a township?

EDGAR L. GOLDTHWAIT.

Marion, Indiana, February 2, 1917.

(Editor's Note.—Mr. Goldthwait was for many years editor of *The Marion Chronicle*, during a period of its wide popularity and influence. He is now living in well-earned retirement, enjoying the comforts of life, with a competency ample, the result of a successful business career. No one in Grant County possesses a more intimate knowledge of the political issues during the time that he was at the head of the Republican organ of Grant County than he.)

A VARIETY OF THINGS.

Fairmount did not contain more than ten or twelve houses in the year 1853. In fact, as I remember it, there were but seven dwelling houses in the town proper, one of which, located on the present site of the Flanagan store, was occupied by my father.

On the opposite side of the street, on the corner now occupied by a drug store, was the general store of Joseph W. Baldwin. Directly across the street, on the corner now occupied by the Fairmount State Bank, was the store of Isaac Stanfield.

James Cammack was the owner of the saw-mill, one of the up-and-down variety. Cammack lived in a frame building on the mill lot.

James Johnson was the engineer at the saw-mill and lived in a log cabin west of the mill.

William Hundley, father of the writer, was the only blacksmith in town, and his shop stood on the site where a saloon was blown up some years ago.

This shop was built by Isaac Roberts and my father, in the year 1853. Isaac Roberts at that time lived in Fairmount. Andrew Leverton was my uncle and lived with my father until he entered the army, in the year 1861, as a member of Company C, Tenth Indiana Infantry. He was killed at Chickamauga.

John Benbow lived on what I think is now West Washington Street.

William Hall lived somewhere near where the office of Glenn Henley is now located.

David Stanfield lived just south of the Hall home, but he lived on a farm and was not then a citizen of your town.

Jonathan Baldwin lived just north of the town limits, but not included in the town.

Joseph W. Baldwin lived in one end of the building occupied by his store.

Tom Barnhouse came about 1854, and was the first photographer.

Solomon Parsons came into town about 1855 and engaged in shoemaking, and also kept a small hotel on Main Street. His shoeshop was in the same building.

The same year—1854 or 1855—came Seaberry Lines (or Dad Lines as he was known). He had a small grocery and also kept a hotel, and was located about where the Hunt furniture store used to stand.

George Doyle came about this time and located on the corner west of the Montgomery & Buchanan marble shop, with a grocery store and a supply of wet goods, including an abundance of sod-corn whiskey. I think this marks the advent of this disturber of human happiness into your community.

Daniel Ridgeway came about 1855 and located a tanyard in the north part of town.

Nathan Little also had a tanyard, east of town, but not then within the corporation limits.

Albert, Allen, Calvin and William Dillon lived north of town, as did their father, Jesse Dillon. The Dillons were gunsmiths and were, in 1855 and 1856, in the shop owned by my father, just west of where W. F. Buller's bakery stands. This was a new shop and very much larger than the one at first located on Main Street.

In the year 1855 William and Vincent Wright built a store about where A. R. Long's office now stands, and it was this store that Jonathan P. Winslow bought when he came, in the year 1860.

Thomas J. Parker did not come to Fairmount until after the close of the Civil War.

The first physician in town, as I now remember, was Dr. White. I do not recall his given name. Next came Dr. Philip Patterson, about 1854 or 1855. I think Dr. David S. Elliott came about the beginning of the Civil War. I can very distinctly remember that Dr. Horne and Dr. Meek, of Jonesboro, did the medical practice in Fairmount for the first two years after I located there, or from 1853 to 1855.

Alexander Pickard did not come to town until long after I had gone away, in the year 1857.

As a small boy I played around my father's shop, and became quite well acquainted with not only the men of the town, but of the Township as well. I can now recall and locate the following pioneers:

West of town were Nathan D. and Jesse E. Wilson, Daniel Thomas, Nixon Rush, Phineas Henley, Lindsey Buller and John Wilson.

South of town were Carter Hasting, John Smith, Andrew Buller, Calvin Bookout, James and Thomas Lytle, Greenleaf Puckett, John Plasters, Morris Payne, David Smithson, Harvey Davis and Bernard McDonald.

East of town were Nathan Little, Hopkins Richardson, Zimri Richardson, Jonathan Richardson, John Bull, Jesse Winslow, Nixon Winslow, Milton Winslow, William G. Lewis, Henry Osborn, John Buller, Andrew Levell, Jackson Mann, and Simon Kauffman (on the Jack Ink farm).

North of town were Jesse Dillon, Allen Dillon, Thomas Newby, Seth Winslow, Thomas Winslow, Thomas Baldwin, William Pierce and John Phillips.

I am sure that Fairmount did not contain more than ten or twelve houses in the year 1853. I think some confusion may arise from the fact that Fairmount grew very rapidly and was quite a considerable village when the writer removed from there, in 1857. I am not writing this as a contribution to your "Making of a Township," but only as a means of exciting inquiry and criticism in order that the facts, as far as may be possible, may be ascertained. I think it has well been said that man's progress in the past has been made possible by his ability to improve upon the mistakes of his ancestors.

J. M. HUNDLEY.

Summitville, Indiana, January 15, 1917.

JESSE WILSON'S RIFLE.

My friend Hundley takes me to task for leaving the early farmer to the mercy of the winds while cleaning their grain. The method I mentioned was the easier but the method Jim mentioned was used in cases of necessity.

The tread mill consisted of a wheel in the form of a cylinder furnished with some twenty-four steps around its circumference and turned on its axis by the tread of horses or oxen. Two horses were generally used to furnish power sufficient to run a chaff piler. Those tread mills were in common use up to 1870 to saw wood for the railroads that used wood for fuel, and this included all the roads passing through Indiana.

I was pilot of the first coal-burning engine that ever passed over the Pan Handle road from Columbus, Ohio, to Logansport. It was a Rogers engine No. 10. This was in 1869, I think.

Speaking of threshing machines, John Ferree, who lived near Little Ridge, once owned a thresher called the Traveler. Four or six horses were used to propel the machine, which was pulled around the field, the grain being thrown in the cylinders as the machine moved along, the straw being scattered behind the machine. The power was gotten by friction. This machine was not a success.

Brother Hundley must have seen this machine, for if J. M. Hundley or Ceph Bennett failed to see anything when we were boys it was hidden. Just to show how the boys would find melon patches in the early days (I don't mean Hundley or Bennett, of course), they would climb a tree on the edge of a clearing, where they suspected a melon patch might be. In this way they could locate the exact spot where melons could be had, with little risk of being discovered.

There were more shoemakers than any other mechanics in the pioneer days. Some had shops and some went from house to house during the fall and early winter months. Richard Mott (or Daddy Mott, as he was called) was the first one I remember. He made the shoes for father's family for years. James Farrington, Evander Farrington and Berry Farrington were all good shoemakers. Berry Farrington died recently at Ottumwa, Iowa. I have often met him and talked with him of our boyhood days. There are possibly some at Fairmount who will remember him. He was successful in business and lived comfortably for many years. My recollection is that all the shoe lasts were made straight, and neither right nor left. Neither were they made in sections, as now. Both boots and shoes were heavy—no split leather, no shoe polish—only tallow or coon grease. Good wool socks, no overshoes, no damp feet. Thus the pioneers would go the coldest days perfectly comfortable. We do not recall who made shoes in Fairmount in 1854-1858.

Carpenters were plentiful. Jude Smithson, his brother Jake, Nathan Vinson, Alfred Waldron, and, I believe, Alex. Henley and I. B. Rush both worked at the trade when they were young men.

Albert Dillon was a gunsmith.

Nathan Little, Micah Baldwin, J. R. Smith were tanners.

Robert Kelsay was a stone cutter.

William Hollingsworth was a cabinet-maker.

Those mentioned all lived at or near Fairmount prior to 1861. All were good workmen. There were many others whom we have forgotten. No doubt there is evidence of the handiwork of all these men yet to be found in or near Fairmount, with perhaps the exception of the shoemaker or tanner.

The first guns that the Dillons made were flint-locks, as percussion caps were not in general use until 1850. When a boy I owned a gun made by Albert Dillon, and I have an idea that the rifle Jesse Wilson owned when the people of Fairmount thought that the town was going to be raided by the rebels was made by Dillon.

It was told of Jesse that when he was asked to help defend the town he told the ones who went to him:

"I am a man of peace, but if thee needs the gun I will tell thee where thee can find it."

The first blacksmith shop was William Hundley's, and the shop was in Fairmount. At that time charcoal was almost entirely used by the blacksmiths for forge work. They made everything by hand. Horse nails, horseshoes, rivets and all the tools that they used were hand-made—axes, hammers, knives and many other tools.

It was not all smiths that could do every kind of work. Some were more skilled than others. Joe Bennett I recollect best, for the reason that he did my father's work longer than any other smith. Joe was drafted, with many others, to go to the army. I think he was assigned to the Twenty-fourth Battery. I recollect of hearing him preach the Sunday before he left for the army. He told his hearers that he was going to leave his Bible at home and take up the sword. My recollection is that Joe came home and regained his Bible.

It is now fifty-two years since the things occurred that I am trying to write about. My memory, I find, is a little faulty. I have no way of refreshing my memory, and it is five hundred miles to anyone who could assist me.

The first saw-mill at Fairmount was of the sash pattern. It was a lazy man's job to run one of those saws, as they were so very slow and the logs were large. I have seen most of the block where *The News* office now stands covered with immense logs and the old mill going at snail gait sawing them into lumber.

The first circular saw-mill that I remember stood almost west of the Friends Church and on the bank of Back Creek. I think it was in 1864. After the sash saw-mill came one called the Muley, and this was much faster, and soon came into general use. Then came the portable mill with the circular saw of today.

In the early sixties I remember that Jesse E. Wilson had planted peach trees along his fences for some distance on each side of the road near his residence. In the peach season I have seen those trees loaded with the finest fruit imaginable. No one who knew Jesse would take one of those peaches without asking for it, but there were boys not a mile from him that would go miles to take his peaches or pears. The boys spoken of were not bad boys, but were mischievous and loved adventure, and finally grew to manhood to be the best citizens of the community. T. B. McDONALD.

Lovilia, Iowa.

PIONEERS AND EARLY SCHOOL DAYS.

A public speaker once told me that if you want to interest your audience tell them something they already know. This I will, undoubtedly do.

My mother died in the fall of 1856. My brother Winslow and myself went and lived for a time with Uncle Milton Wilson, Nate's father. He had just bought of Tommy Powell the farm now owned by John Kelsay. The house was west of the present residence. Tommy was an Englishman. I think he was a relative of John Bull and Samuel Radley, who were also from England.

Tommy Powell's wife was a Winslow (Aunt Betsey, we called her), a sister of Uncle Jesse Winslow, who lived east of Fairmount. She was afterwards the wife of Samuel Dillon.

My brother and I attended my first school at old Back Creek, north of town, the winter of 1856-1857. Asa T. Baldwin was the teacher. To my surprise he had no "gads" in sight, nor did he use any during the term. Some of the scholars near me were Jesse Dillon, now living in Marion, George Whybrew, David Winslow, Bill Baldwin, Lank Baldwin and many others. We attended Friends services at the old meeting house, then standing, on First day and Fourth day. There was hardly anything said by any one during services for two hours.

The school boys, when playing at recess, would try to see who could crawl through the air holes at the foundation of the old church. Many a boy went through all right, but swelled up until he could not get out, and what a yell they did make under the old church until rescued. The big boys and the teacher would have him come out craw-fish style, and one get hold of each leg and pull him out. The boy was then warned to not try it again, or if he did he would get a licking. But they were trying it again at each play time.

Aunt Rachel Newby lived on the Lewis Fankboner farm. The buildings were north of the present ones. We boys, at her request, would stop and warm by the big fireplace on our way to and from school. This was a small thing, but we never once forgot her for her kindness. It is the little things that people do that count, after all, even down to the present day.

Soon afterwards we went back home to live, south of town, my father having married. Our school days were afterwards spent at Back Creek, southwest of Fairmount. The early teachers were Milton McHatton, George Pierce, Jesse Reece, Keturah Baldwin, Columbus Moore, Foster Davis, Lancaster D. Baldwin, William Baldwin, and some others I may have overlooked. The school houses were log, and very poorly ventilated, but were, for that day, pretty comfortable.

The games played at school in those days were "three-cornered cat," "black man," and "bull pen," but the real game was "town ball." Instead of a baseball bat, a paddle made of oak timber one inch thick and six to ten inches wide, made with a handle, was the bat. There were bases. Two were asked to choose up, or select the players from the crowd. Some one would take a chip of wood and spit on one side and one of the "choosers" would say "wet," the other "dry." They would then toss the chip in the air, and if "wet" was up the one taking that would have first choice of players, and if "dry," the second choice, and so on.

Nathan D. Cox and T. B. McDonald were usually first and second choice, as they were two who could break the paddle or knock the ball over the big white oak tree near by. No one ever caught the ball. Instead of a pitcher he was known as the one "giving balls." If he threw a ball so the batter with his big, wide paddle could not hit it, he was immediately fired and someone else put in to "give balls," so they could hit them. In baseball, which sprang from old "town ball," men are now paid $10,000 to $20,000 annually to pitch a ball they cannot hit, and when he cannot do this he is let out.

We had no umpire in "town ball," and when a player did not like the way the game was going he just got mad and quit and would not play. There were always plenty to take his place. Even to this day there are persons who will not play unless things go to suit them. However, I do not know of any such in Fairmount Township.

The Wesleyans held church in the school house for some time, but finally cleared away about one-half an acre in a very thick woods near by and built the frame church which is now standing to the west on the range line. To clear away the heavy trees for the church was quite a task. However, by the help of Uncle Jonathan Baldwin's pair of big, red oxen, from town, and twenty-five or thirty men who knew what an ax was made for, it was soon done.

The early Wesleyan preachers that I now call to mind who preached at this place were Aaron Worth, now living at Fountain City, Thomas Brelsford, Isaac Meek, Emsley Brookshire, father of Thomas J. Brookshire, William Lacey, and many others I do not now recall. Aaron Worth was then the big preacher of all, and Isaac Meek was very popular and much loved by everybody, especially the young, on account of his Indian, bear and deer stories in conversation. He could talk all kinds of Indian language.

The boys in the neighborhood often had a heated argument as to who was the biggest and best preacher. It was finally decided in favor of a new preacher, whom I do not now recall, for the reason we could hear him nearly a mile away.

There was not very much land cleared in the early settlement of the Township, so the farming was on a very small scale, indeed. On the high places along Back Creek and east of Fairmount along the old prairie was about the only land high enough to farm. The very best black elm land lay idle for years and was rated as worthless, on account of its being covered with water all the year. Today this low, level black land has been drained until it is doubtful if the sun shines on better anywhere.

The farmers raised corn, wheat, flax, buckwheat, sugar cane, but not much stock. The farms averaged one cow, six to ten hogs, two horses and fifteen to twenty head of sheep.

Hogs ran wild and were hunted and killed in the woods when wanted for meat. They were large and thin. There was no danger of getting too much fat in those days. They were what the packers prize so highly today as strictly "bacon hogs."

The farmers had but little to sell in those days. Not many fed over five or ten hogs, and the man who had twenty-five or thirty hogs to market was considered a big stock grower.

Jeans suits made from wool off their own sheep were the clothing. No overcoats, underwear, overshoes or anything in the way of fine dress was in evidence. The women wore calico and flannel and fancy gingham dresses for Sunday.

Neighbors were quite well acquainted and knew one another better than they do today. All would lend any tool or horse. Neighbors visited much more than at present. The whole family would walk a mile and stay and visit a neighbor until bed time, and then return home with a hickory bark torch or a tin lantern punched full of holes and a candle inside for light.

The early merchants in Fairmount bought coon skins, sheep pelts, beeswax, sorghum, flax-seed, feathers, dried peaches and apples, rags, eggs, butter, sheep and beef tallow.

At the tanyard of Micah Baldwin and William Hall they sold oak bark. The farmers of the Township in the early days raised quite an amount of sugar cane, some as much as five or ten acres. Nearly all raised some to make molasses or sorghum. It was an easy crop to grow. After the cane was done growing and the heads ripened and turned black late in the fall, they went through with corn cutters and cut off the heads about one foot from the heads and let them fall on the ground. They next went through with a sharp-edged board and stripped the cane. The cane was then cut close to the ground and hauled to the cane mill, which consisted of two rollers together made of a sugar tree. A lever was fastened at the top of these rollers and a horse hitched, going round and round, and the mill making a noise you could hear a mile or more. You could often hear ten or twelve of these mills in a neighborhood.

The molasses, or sorghum, was easily made, and was usually quite thick and would not run. It was generally put in a large pan, or bowl, in the center of the table, and when any one wanted sorghum, they harpooned it with a knife or fork, and wound out what they desired. And permit me to say that with sausage made from hogs, butter made from cows, and hot biscuits or corn bread it was not very bad.

The people are very much the same wherever you go, from Maine to California. Every place has its good and bad citizens. A very large majority are for the very best interests of all the people everywhere and all the time. However, I am of the opinion that from the day of the entry of the land to the present time, there has lived and are living more of the right kind of people in Fairmount Township and vicinity than any place where the sun shines.

Cyrus W. Neal.

Marion, Indiana, December 26, 1916.

FROM A NOTE BOOK.

I can claim to be a pioneer in one respect, at least, a pioneer in collecting historical facts.

You will receive a small note book filled with facts which I collected in February—just twenty years ago. Most of the facts are about our own family, and will not, therefore, be of general interest. The men whom I interviewed in 1897 were my father, Nixon Rush, Calvin Rush, Sr., James Scott, Elwood Rush, Bernard McDonald and Nathan Little. These were good men and great. Let us ever remember them.

I can give some information which should be of interest to young as well as old. It may not be known to many people that there once lived in Fairmount a man who, I believe, was one of the greatest athletes this country ever produced. If he were a young man now, attending one of our colleges, his picture would be published in all the leading papers of America. This man was James Scott.

When I was in my teens the boy who could beat us all in the running hop, step and jump or the running two hops and a jump, was Wick Winslow. Any of us boys would have traded our homes—families included—for Wick's ability to run and jump.

Among the older boys the great heroes were John and Charles E. White. They could have all the sidewalk any time they wanted it—provided, of course, that there happened to be a sidewalk. Yet none of these heroes—no matter how large the circle of admirers—ever boasted of going more than forty-two feet in a running hop, step and jump, or the more popular two hops and a jump. After several weeks' practice I once made thirty-seven feet myself, but I tore my suspenders in doing it.

My father often told me of the "barn-raisings" when he was a boy. Someone would nearly always start to jump in order to get James Scott and his brother started. As father expressed it, "they jumped as if they had wings." He also told me that on one occasion James Scott jumped against the State champion at Indianapolis and won. And so, in February, just twenty years ago, I went to see James Scott and I wrote in my little red note book his story as he gave it:

"It was the first Monday in August," related James. "Henry Clay was the candidate for President that year. Our wheat was all gathered in the barn and father allowed me to go and see my uncle, who lived at Indianapolis.

"The best jumper in the State was there, and he wanted to bet me ten dollars that he could beat me. I did not want to bet, but the fellow would not jump unless I would bet. So I took his bet. It was on the ground where the Court House now stands. There was a little slope to the land. It was not quite level. We each had three trials. I jumped twice. The first time I jumped sixty feet, and the second time I jumped sixty-two feet. It was the running hop, step and jump. He could not equal my second jump. I jumped fifty-eight feet at Marion when they were laying the foundation for the first Court House. I could jump twenty-five feet at running broad jump on level ground. I could jump from sill to sill when the sills were ten feet apart, and in the haymow I have jumped from one sill to another where the sills were eight feet apart. I could go thirty-three feet on level ground in three jumps standing. I could jump over a pole six inches higher than my head. My brother Stephen could jump thirty-six feet in three jumps, standing."

These were the figures given to me by the quiet old man whose life's journey was nearly run. There was no trace of boastfulness. The exact accuracy of the distances could not, of course, be depended on. They were probably measured by a short ruler, and the measurements were taken from heel to heel, instead of the present method of measurement, and this would reduce each record six or eight inches. Moreover, the ground may not always have been exactly level. But if an untrained farmer lad, wearing heavy shoes which his father probably made, could jump such distances, what records he could have made under one of our great athletic trainers in a college or university.

James Scott also gave me these historical facts about Fairmount:

"Old David Stanfield laid out the first lots of Fairmount and named the place. Stanfield's barn was in the exact location of John Dickey's home. The house was northeast of the barn. It was at the place where Harmon Buller now lives, back of Mattie Wright's home. I was then Justice of the Peace. Stanfield made the plot and sold lots before having the plot recorded, and I came near having trouble. He sold James Cammack a few acres to build a mill where Jap Wheeler's mill now stands. The lots sold for five, ten and fifteen dollars apiece. Joseph W. Baldwin bought a lot from Jonathan Baldwin, just north of Flanagan's store, and built there the first store ever built in Fairmount."

From all of the men interviewed I gained the following information regarding my great grandfather, Azel Rush. Azel was light complexioned, tall, slim, and a little stooped. He had blue eyes, a strong voice and was autocratic. He was an old-fashioned Quaker.

In 1848 he sold the larger part of his North Carolina farm for $3,000, and, after paying his debts, he hid $500 of the money in a barrel and started to Indiana with the barrel. The money was in the form of notes. As he became fearful that it would be stolen he took each note and cut it into two pieces. He then took two envelopes and put a part of each note in each envelope and mailed the money to Indiana, paying the customary postage of ten cents a letter.

Apparently the notes were redeemed all right, for he bought the Henry Doherty farm and paid six dollars an acre for it. He then returned to North Carolina and the next year brought his wife and three youngest sons. The boys drove a big four-horse Carolina wagon, and Azel and his wife rode in a carriage.

Elwood Rush was one of the boys. He told me that they left Carolina on September 15, 1849, and arrived on October 21, and that they crossed but one railroad track in making the trip. Uncle Elwood laughed when he quoted John Plasters as saying that "Azel Rush was smarter than any of his boys."

Bernard McDonald also told me interesting things about Azel. I have this in my note book:

"I remember once he came to me while I was working in a field. It was just before he made his last trip to Carolina. He wanted to borrow twenty dollars. I gave it to him and asked no security. During the course of our conversation he spoke of the fact that William Henry Harrison was for a time a medical student under his cousin, Dr. Benjamin Rush, of Philadelphia. He also spoke of Zachary Taylor, whom I knew well, having boarded with him for two or three years. I knew William Henry Harrison quite well, and I also knew Benjamin Harrison as a slender-legged boy."

It may be of interest to know how the Rushes came to have the Rush Hill farm. This is the way my uncle, Calvin Rush, told it to me twenty years ago:

"When my father, Iredell Rush, came to Indiana, he stopped one year in Henry County, where he made $100, which he saved. He then came to Grant County and paid the $100 for eighty acres, which are now a part of the Frank Presnall farm. One year later he decided to enter the eighty acres just south of his farm, the land on which Rush Hill and the Academy are located, but he had no money. Hearing that a man by the name of Dempsey Bailey was planning also to get the land, Iredell hastened to the home of a friend by the name of Hiatt, who lived, I think, in Henry County. Hiatt took down the family Bible, which was his bank, gave grandfather the money which he needed and told him to hurry. Grandfather rode all night and reached Fort Wayne early in the morning. The land was quickly secured and the money paid, and as he was leaving the court house, Dempsey Bailey walked in. His first log house was sixteen by twenty feet, with a stick and clay chimney. The first year he cleared a few acres, belled the horse and turned him loose and he and Seth Winslow hunted venison, bear and wild honey all winter."

CALVIN C. RUSH.

Philadelphia, Pennsylvania, February 28, 1917.

(Editor's Note.—This article is contributed by Dr. Calvin C. Rush, son of the late Nixon Rush, and grandson of Iredell Rush. Iredell Rush entered land in Fairmount Township March 16, 1831. Dr. Rush is a successful physician, now located at Philadelphia, the home of a distinguished relative, Dr. Benjamin Rush. In this contribution one of Indiana's athletes of pioneer days is introduced. The late James Scott, father of O. R. Scott, was for many years prior to his death a citizen of Fairmount.)

MEMORIES OF THE PAST.

I have been reading "The Making of a Township" and have been quite interested in many of the letters and notes, as they bring to my mind many circumstances which I well remember, and others which I have heard older persons relate.

I remember the house raisings, the log rollings, the quiltings, the wool pickings, when we spun, colored and wove much of the cloth for our clothing, when most of the cooking was done by the fireplace, with which all the houses were provided (many families not owning a cookstove), when we dropped all our corn by hand and covered it with the hoe, when the grain was cut with scythe and cradle and bound by hand, and many other customs of early days.

Many things were not convenient, but in looking back upon those times I always think of them as the good old days when neighbors were much more congenial and helpful to each other than at the present time. One of the undesirable things was the bad roads.

I remember well the corduroy bridges, which consisted of small logs laid across the road as close together as possible in the worst places, sometimes lasting for quite a distance, making very rough traveling, but beat being stuck in the mud.

Another thing was the ague, as I have good reason to remember, being a victim myself, missing the chill only a few weeks in more than a year. Then there were the swarms of mosquitoes that infested this country in those days, when some of the ponds of water never dried up. We had to make smoke at the doors of our homes summer evenings to keep the mosquitoes out of the house, screens being unheard of at that time; but all these, like the log cabins, are things of the past.

Well do I remember the stirring events at the beginning of the Civil War, when many of our bravest and best young men responded to the call of Uncle Sam, going away, many to return no more; of how we anxiously awaited the coming of the old stage coach, bringing the mail in those days, and how later on its coming brought to some of our hearts the greatest sorrow we had ever known.

I knew Rev. Isaac Meek well for years. Have heard him preach many a sermon at Howell's school house and other places. I think he was a pioneer. I have been told that he was a friend of the Indians, hunted with them, could speak their language, and they said he was the only white man they ever knew who always told the truth.

I remember hearing an Indian minister preach at Wesleyan Back Creek, Rev. Meek interpreting the sermon. That has been more than forty years ago. Later Meek moved to Iowa, with his good wife, Ruth, where he passed to the better land several years ago.

CATHARINE BULLER.

Fairmount, Indiana, March 5, 1917.

CHOLERA IN 1849.

Charles Baldwin sat head of Back Creek meeting for a short time about eighty-four years ago. He also taught school at Back Creek in 1833. Grandfather Baldwin moved from New Garden, Wayne County, this State, and settled on the Crabb farm, later known as the John Himelick farm, opposite the McCormick graveyard, where he lived one year.

The McCormick graveyard is where people were buried who died of the cholera in 1849. David Weesner, who was the father of Mrs. Lacy Ann Knight, Mrs. Seth Thomas and Micajah, Elihu and David Weesner, died of this disease. Alex Dolman was another man who died of this disease. Altogether a dozen died of cholera and everybody in the settlement was alarmed and panic-stricken for fear of the spread of the epidemic, which might take everybody before it.

David Weesner ran a tanyard at the time of his death above Jonesboro, on the river, at what was known as Weesner's ford.

WILLIAM BALDWIN.

Marion, Indiana.

DISAPPEARANCE OF TOM WINSLOW.

I now remember that J. P. Winslow had a son, Tom, who went away with me when I went to the army. He was too young to be enlisted, but he went with our company till we reached Murfreesboro, Tennessee, where we were surrounded by Forrest's Cavalry and were under fire for several days. On the first day that firing began, Tom left us and said he was going to make his way back to Nashville. I understand he has never been heard from since. I am sure I have neither seen nor heard from him since, and have often wondered what became of him. J. M. HUNDLEY.

Summitville, Indiana.

THE M'CORMICK PLACE.

With many others, I am interested in the articles you are publishing about Fairmount and Fairmount Township and will add a mite to them.

In the winter of 1855 and 1856, when I was barely in my 'teens, I visited an uncle and family who then lived near New Cumberland. While there I went with a cousin to mill at Jonesboro and passed the Robert McCormick place. I have always remembered it from the fact that across the road from the buildings—north—were traces of fencing for a deer park. As I remember the fencing it was of stakes or light rails standing at an angle of about forty-five degrees. Whether it was built that way or leaned from decay I did not know. I also got the story some way that the east line of the enclosure was a steep creek bank, down which the deer could jump, but could not jump out—making a kind of deer trap.

I also remember seeing a railroad bridge across a creek or ravine south of the road we traveled—I think in the McCormick neighborhood. It was for a proposed road from Cincinnati to Chicago, but never completed. The work on that line was, doubtless, the first railroad work ever done in Fairmount Township. Probably some one can give further facts concerning it.

Years later, while I was a resident of Marion, and Joseph W. Baldwin lived near, I heard him say that he had the honor of giving Fairmount its name. He was then living in the embryo town, and the question of a name came up. He had been reading of the Fairmount Water Works, at Philadelphia, and the word "Fairmount" had struck his fancy and he suggested it as a name, and it was adopted.

Since writing the above paragraph, I thought there might be a mistake in it, and that Fairmount derived its name from the Township. I, therefore, got my Grant County maps and history, published in 1876. I found from them that the original plat of the town was filed on December 28, 1850, and that it was then in Liberty Township; and in the year 1855 the Township was formed by taking from Liberty the territory east of the line between Ranges 7 and 8, and a small Township on the east called Union, and the new Township was named Fairmount, and that the Township name was derived from the name of the town. I also notice that the naming of the town was credited to William Neal. Joseph W. Baldwin was then the only "merchant prince" of the new town, and William Neal doubtless surveyed and made the plat, and doubtless both had a voice in giving the name.

In looking up this matter, I was surprised at the number of changes made in township boundaries of the county before they settled down to present shape. I doubt if many people now living in Grant County know that once there were Townships known as Union, Madison, Grant and Knox. M. F. TINGLEY.

Wabash, Indiana, January 25, 1917.

(Editor's Note.—In September, 1867, Mr. Tingley purchased the only printing office then in Grant County and commenced the publication of *The Marion Chronicle*. He was an active and resolute friend of public improvements. Not only with his pen, but with his means, he assisted in the good work. With but one exception he was an original stockholder in every gravel-road company organized in the county since he became a citizen of it. He was a persistent and indefatigable advocate of the movement to secure the Cincinnati, Wabash & Michigan and the Toledo, St. Louis & Western railroads. Under his editorship *The Chronicle* stood out boldly for honesty and efficiency in municipal and county government, the policy of the paper exerting a marked influence upon the wise and economical expenditure of public funds. Mr. Tingley disposed of his newspaper property in 1884.)

SALOON DID NOT COME.

I remember the hardships of my father and mother in Fairmount Township, when the woods were full of squirrels, deer and wild turkeys. Those dear old pioneers suffered much without a murmur. No sacrifice was too great for those dear old people.

I remember when nobody was rich and nobody was poor—everybody good and nobody bad. I do not now recall a single crime that was ever committed in the old neighborhood.

I remember the first horse thief I ever heard of. He stole Uncle Iredell Rush's horse. But the horse thief did not live in Fairmount Township. The men of the neighborhood got their horses and started on the trail. Some of them got as far as Anderson and others a little farther, then became discouraged and went back. My father, Nixon Rush, Sr., and Micajah Wilson went to Noblesville, I think it was, and found the horse in a feed stable. Father told the sheriff about it and said:

"I will go and call the horse by name, and if he nickers I shall claim the horse."

So father called: "Tobe! Stand around!"

And the horse jumped around and nickered.

The horse knew father's voice.

The sheriff then arrested the thief and they took him to Marion and put him in the lock-up.

Robert and Ruth Brazelton were the first colored people I ever saw. My father had great respect for the colored people. One time we had a colored woman by the name of Celia Brown to work for us, and she would always eat at the table with us. One day we had company. The man was not fond of the negro. When dinner was ready father told all to come to dinner, but Mr. —— did not come. Father asked why. Mr. —— said:

"I will not eat with that negro."

Father said:

"All right. Thee is worse than my hogs, for the white ones will eat with the black ones and will not growl. So thee just wait until we get through."

Father made one of the first coffins, if not the very first one, ever made in Fairmount Township. It seemed to us children that everybody would die at night, for away in the night we would hear someone call:

"Nixon! Nixon! We want thee to make a coffin" for so and so.

They would bring a measuring stick in and set it up in the corner of the room where we children lay in our trundle-beds. Father would get up and go to work. He always prepared his own glue, planed and sandpapered the boards, stained them, and sometimes lined the coffin. (I well remember he lined Uncle Jonathan Jones's coffin.) Then he would take the coffin to the home and stay and help until after the burial, and never charge a cent. Those were days of long, long ago.

The first frame house I ever saw, my father built it—the one at Rush Hill where Walter W. Rush now lives. He built several other frame houses in Fairmount Township.

I was one of the crusaders. Well do I remember when we heard a saloon was to come to Fairmount. So, to give the alarm when the man was seen driving into town, the bells were to ring. The key of the Methodist Church was at my house, across the street from the church, and some one came running up and said:

"The saloon is coming!"

So I took the key, went to the church, and commenced to ring the bell. In a few minutes a dozen or more men and women were there to help me. Martin Crilley, I think, rang the Wesleyan Church bell. All the bells in town were soon ringing. There were only two church bells in town then. Walker Winslow and Jonathan P. Winslow rang their dinner bells. So the saloon did not get very far in town then.

My first school teacher was William Neal. He used the whip most always on the boys. One day Millie Morris and I were getting our "heart lessons," as they were called in those days. We had to say them on Friday afternoons, each week. We were saying ours out too loud, and William threw the ruler at us. He told me to put one end in my mouth and Millie to put the other end in her mouth, and we carried it up to him. He gave us a hit on the hands with it and told us to go sit down and not say our "heart lessons" and get our school lessons.

Margaret E. Raper.

Indianapolis, Indiana, March 31, 1917.

(Editor's Note.—This communication is interesting in that the writer refers to school management in the early days, and also reveals the strong sentiment existing from the very first against the liquor business.)

WANTS HIS PANTS BACK.

I recall incidents from hearing my father relate them. (This is his birthday anniversary. He was born the 30th of March, 1810, in South Carolina.) His father, Charles Baldwin, moved to New Garden, now Fountain City, Wayne County, Indiana, in 1814. My father, when a boy, learned the hatter's trade in Richmond. His father accumulated some cattle and other personal property, and on account of a shortage of feed, in the spring of 1830, he moved, with his large family, consisting of Susannah, who married Jesse Dillon; Thomas, my father;

Mary, who married Lancaster Bell; John; Sarah, who became the wife of Vernon Stanfield; Jane, who married a brother of Vernon Stanfield, I forget his name; Lindsey; Hyra; Abigail, who married Nathan Morris, and Quincy—ten in all. On the 30th day of March, 1830, the day my father was twenty years old, they struck camp on the shores of Lake Galatia to get feed for their cattle, as there was some prairie grass around the edge of the lake.

As soon as he gained his majority father walked through the woods by aid of a compass and the numbers of Townships and Sections blazed on the trees to Ft. Wayne, as that was the location of the United States Land Office, and entered eighty acres of land, now known as the McDonald farm, south of Fairmount. He afterwards entered eighty acres just south of Fairmount, where John Rhoads lives.

I remember when I was a small boy we lived in Jonesboro. I went up to visit my uncles, Henry and Phil Davis. I took my Sunday pants along. I was to start home in time to get there before night. I stopped in Fairmount to play with Micah Baldwin's boys. They were "wild and woolly and full of fleas and hard to curry below the knees" when it came to a rough-and-tumble play. I forgot it was getting late. It was sundown when I left the boys and started down the pike afoot, with my extra pants tied up with a strap swung over my back.

I got along fine until I came to Back Creek graveyard, where now is the resting-place of my father and mother, grandparents on both sides, also of some of my sisters and brother, and many other relatives and friends. I saw the white tombstones loom up in the dark; also a white cow lying down close to the fence. I shied over to the east side of the pike, keeping my eye on the white cow, but did not see a black cow lying on the east side, and ran up against her and fell over her, when she jumped up and bawled. I thought the devil had me sure. I threw away my pants and have not seen them to this day. If you know of anyone finding them please send them to me, as I am in need of a good pair of Sunday breeches.

A. J. BALDWIN.

Salem, Oregon, March 30, 1917.

(Editor's Note.—The writer of this communication is best known to the older residents of Fairmount and Marion as Anan or "Specs." Anan has always been known for his humorous bent of mind, and this letter will be recognized by his friends and relatives as very characteristic.)

LOST IN THE WILDERNESS.

Upon the earnest solicitation of her son, Dr. Calvin C. Rush, Mrs. Louisia (Winslow) Rush, in 1904, wrote for the benefit of her children and grandchildren brief reminiscences of her early life. A few extracts are here given:

"My grandfather, Joseph Winslow, and family of eight children came to Fairmount Township in 1829 direct from Randolph County, North Carolina. They took farms along Back Creek, so named by them after their old stream at home in North Carolina.

"The journey through the timber was very difficult. There were no roads and no bridges.

"Reaching the Mississinewa, near its source, the party made a raft and came down the river as far as where Jonesboro now stands. Traveling south a short distance, they came to a cabin occupied by John Russell. Here they stopped for the night.

"Living in the midst of relatives, and having no reason to rove, I was never outside of Grant County until I was eighteen years old.

"In my earliest recollection there were deer, wolves, bears, coons, wild cats, lynx, panthers, 'possums, groundhogs, squirrels, otters, beavers, muskrats and many other native animals.

"On one occasion my grandmother, Peninah Winslow, was at the home of her daughter, Caroline Newby, to assist her during sickness. They lived only one hundred rods apart. About sundown grandmother started home. She got turned around and was lost. As the timber and underbrush were very thick, she knew that it was useless to go farther until it should get light again, so she climbed some bushes draped in grapevines, and there she lodged for the night.

"No one was uneasy about her, for her folks at home supposed she had remained with her daughter, and her daughter supposed she was at home. So, amidst the biting of mosquitoes and the growling of wolves, she lodged, rather than slept, that night. The next morning the sun and the creek gave her an index to her home, where she arrived a little later.

"Once my mother was riding horseback near the same place. Her horse became a little restless. Looking up, my mother saw a panther in a tree, eyeing her and the horse, just ready to spring. But it didn't attack them.

"One night our young dog treed a panther resting on some low bushes a few rods from our house. As soon as it was light my father took a gun and shot the animal.

"The next morning my father, Daniel Winslow, went to the spring to wash, before breakfast. He had on neither hat nor coat and there was a little snow on the ground. Seeing some wild turkeys in the trees, my father ran to get his gun. When the turkeys flew he chased them, and thus lost his bearings. By this time the snow was melting and he could not retrace his steps. So, in the immense forest, he took notice of the moss on the north side of the trees. Going in a northwest direction about four miles, he came to the stream now known as Deer Creek. Naturally supposing that it would empty into the river, he followed it to its mouth, then went up-stream to where they had left the raft, and from there back to the cabin, reaching his destination at 2 o'clock in the afternoon, quite ready for his breakfast. The folks were just starting out to hunt him.

"The woods furnished gooseberries, plums, wild onions, crabapples, nuts, as well as sassafras, for variety. Had it not been for climatic conditions, which caused ague and fever before the country was cleared and ditched, we would have had many blessings."

ANIMALS AND BIRDS OF THE FOREST.

Before 1841 wolves had been so bad farmers did not venture to keep sheep. Now they began to want them. Father was a lover of sheep and he bought a flock of about thirty. We had to corral them every night. I soon learned my business to go after them and put them in their pen, which was not large, but high, so a wolf could not climb over. One night they strayed out and wolves got among them, playing havoc. Six were killed outright, others crippled. Farmers organized in companies and killed the wolves, and thrilling stories and wonderful adventures would be repeated over and over. About this time an old bear and cubs were discovered a few miles west. A company of men went to the Big Woods, and soon found it was not a joke. The bears had just left their den in search of food. The two cubs were fat, yet outran the men, who shot as they ran, without effect—a flight of that kind for about eight miles, the old mother staying along with her cubs. At last they came to a large oak tree and the bears climbed to the top. About twenty-five men were now on hand, keeping reasonable distance. They began to shoot. Father, with his old flintlock, had a good aim. The cubs fell. The mother, in view of the situation, opened her mouth, gnarling her teeth and drawing herself in a bunch, fell to the ground. Then she sprang to her feet with open mouth, and the men could hear gnashing of teeth and snarly growl as she came swift and fast in leaps. Just at the right time a ball penerated her heart. The forest rang with yells.

One day, when my father was returning from Jonesboro, he spied a large eagle on the old school house chimney. Quickly he got his gun, then as near as possible. I remember, though a very small boy, father's coming home, the great bird in hand. He measured seven feet from tip to tip, with big head and large eyes, his feet and legs full of porcupine quills, showing that some time or other he had tackled a big porcupine.

Hundreds of times have I listened to find a moment's interval that I could not hear a bird sing. In the summer time the woods would chime with melody, not a moment but some little warbler would be happy. I took great comfort in listening. Bluebirds were very numerous, tomtit, pewee, catbird, robin, the jaybird in the top of the tree, a neighbor to the hawks and crow, not far off the owl's "who-who." I did not like the woodpecker family—they were numerous, cruel and destructive, though they coud make a noise in their way. There was a very large kind of woodcock, now almost extinct, nearly as large as a prairie hen, that had a coarse voice. To me, the pheasant made a lonesome noise, sounding like distant thunder. With the cooing of the dove a solemn feeling would pervade my tender heart. I remember I would think of Heaven. Above all, the pigeon took the lead in number. Millions of them would visit our country in the spring and fall. To me it was a halo of joy when the pigeons would come, drove after drove. At times the sun could not shine until they had passed. They would alight on trees, so many as to break off great limbs. We had our different kinds of traps. Great numbers would alight in our fields in search of food, then fly over each other, then alight, looking like a rolling, glistening, high-tide wave. Quail were very numerous. Their "Bob White" was to be heard from morning till night. In cutting grass we one day found sixty eggs, another day ninety-six.

Often a drove of pheasants would fly around and alight on the cherry trees near the house, and in the spring we heard the "gobble-gobble" of wild turkeys in the distance. Squirrels were to be heard almost constantly in the daytime. It was my lot to protect the corn from them and the birds by going around the field before breakfast sounding the alarm, "Hooppee, shoe ye, yo, show show shoe, ye yo!" with the rattletrap in hand. That was made with a big notched wheel fixed in a frame, a board a foot and a half long so placed that as I turned the wheel with a crank it made all the noise to my desire. After all this, the different kinds of birds and squirrels would take every hill, so we would have to replant three and four times to get a stand of corn. Squirrels had homes in large trees in the fields, and there they would carry the corn. Late corn they did not trouble so much, for by that time they would go to the woods and give us a little rest.

To take the place of the first rude camp, my father built a good, strong house. The timber to the south was thick, tall, beautiful. I can remember when almost the entire country was a wilderness of great forest trees. It is like a dream to me when I think of those towering, majestic trees that had stood unmolested for ages, so thick and dense, defying the storms and the Indian's tomahawk. I have never visited a country, never heard of any land with such variety of large trees—towering oak, a few rods away a fine, straight poplar; close by a grand old sugar maple, a rugged elm; a little lower down a few big walnut and sycamore; then again a cluster of oaks, with all kinds mixed in between,—till we had a mass of timber through which the sun's rays could hardly reach the ground to make a shadow.

The undergrowth was ironwood, beech trees, shellbark and hickory, cherry that grew very straight and slender, locust of the thorny kind, but without many thorns, because in the shade the thorns could not grow well, a variety of "saplins" that would run up straight and beautiful. Then, to make it more like a jungle, the spicebrush was very thick—a bush that would sprout up from the roots, six or eight feet high. I have seen the woods so dense a deer could hardly run through. It was interesting to see the large bucks, with great heads of horns, run through the woods with their horns folded over their backs, their noses stuck right straight out, dodging things.

Not all the woods were like this. There were places more open. Later, the big fires, the axe, the cattle browsing, finally thinned out the brush. While cutting his timber my father could kill game without hunting—the deer would come to browse, the turkeys would pass in droves. They had plenty of the very best of food, though at first it was almost impossible to get corn and wheat ground, and at times their bread was hominy. But few people know anything about pioneer life. It is one continual struggle, yet I sometimes think it is the happiest life, if one will only take it just as it comes. I often heard my parents say they were the best days of their lives.

Often there was scarcity of food for stock in winter and we had to resort to cutting down lin (linden) and elm for cattle and horses to browse.

What has become of the millions of pigeons that migrated in the spring and fall is a mystery. They were a slightly larger and longer bird than our tamer pigeon, and darker.

Deer would visit the fields after night. I could hear them in the corn. My father and Uncle Seth Winslow were extra-good marksmen and often helped their neighbors to save crops. Wolves and panthers prowled around, raccoon, opossum, mink and weasel were all cunning and moved about in the dark. In the fall my father hunted bees and gathered much wild honey.

I was about four years old when our big dog got his mouth full of porcupine quills while coon hunting. The dogs had caught a big porcupine before the men could help and had their mouths full of quills. My dog's head was put between the rails of the high fence and men held his feet and head, then my father with the nippers pulled out the big quills one by one, the dog howling at a terrible rate. I thought my good old dog would die.

Occasionally the Indians would come around, and they were great beggars. They made a wild appearance in our cabin, folding their old blankets around their dusky bodies, watching a chance to steal something. Mother was a good hand to satisfy their wants.

In the winter of 1848 James Cammack came to our home from Wayne County to locate a saw-mill in this country. Father went with him to look out a location. They finally settled near Back Creek, where Fairmount now stands. Soon, Joseph W. Baldwin started a very small store. The mill was a success. Logs were brought here from ten miles around to be sawed into planks. I well remember the building of the first house in Fairmount.

My mother was an exhorter in the church, quoting Scripture readily, and dwelling much on the rich things in store for the righteous, she standing upright, very straight in a plain Friends costume of the old fashion, with a white shawl, and always a white cap with a modest plait or fold, which gave her a dignified appearance.

Our good mothers and sisters spun with little wheels, my mother spinning till midnight. When but a little boy I could hear the "buzz" of the wheel all times of the night—it was the way our shirts and little coats were made.

—*From the Journal of Rev. Nixon Rush.*

CHAPTER XXXIII.

FRAGMENTS.

The first death occurring in the Township was that of a child of Charles Baldwin, of scarlet fever.

Caroline, wife of Exum Newby, was the first person buried in old Back Creek Graveyard. Her death occurred on September 24, 1831.

The first saloon I ever saw was in Fairmount, where Ab. Jones' residence now stands. The next saloon in Fairmount was started by Paul Williams in a little shanty which stood where N. A. Wilson's store now is. I remember how they got rid of it. My mother and some other ladies took their knitting and a chair and sat in front by turns and knit him out.

EZRA F. VINSON.

Jonathan P. Winslow, my father, was Trustee when the two-story frame school house was built. Many thought it entirely too big, that there would never be children enough to fill it. But when William Pusey (who can tell who the other two teachers were?) Cal Thornburg and Mary Winslow Bogue started in there wasn't many vacant seats. Jesse E. Wilson and J. P. had quite a time running after Captain Wells to get him headed for Fairmount with the Cincinnati, Wabash & Michigan Railroad. They used to go to Goshen and Elkhart to attend railroad meetings. It took about three days to make the round trip. They would go to Harrisburg (Gas City), take the train for Logansport, and I don't know where from Logansport, but it took about twenty-four hours to get to Goshen or Elkhart from Fairmount. Father spent about $500 attending these meetings.

J. A. WINSLOW.

Ontario, Oregon, March 27, 1917.

"**It will be strange** to the people of today to think that at one time here the squirrels were so bad that the people had to make shooting matches to get them out of the way," writes the late William G. Lewis, in his book of reminiscences. "Two men would choose the gunners and they would choose a driver. The driver was not supposed to carry a gun, but this rule was not always carried out. I chose for my driver old Uncle Lewis Harrison. He was a soldier in the War of 1812, a good shot and used a flint-lock gun. The squirrel was very apt to drop when he shot. Lewis Harrison was the father of Luther Harrison and Mrs. Henry Deshon. The first day we killed eighty-seven squirrels, crows, owls and hawks. A crow would count for five squirrels, an owl and hawk the same. The squirrels would work on the corn in the spring and in the fall. The fields were not large, and woods all around, so they had a good chance. My father was paid fifty cents a day and ammunition found for shooting squirrels around the fields of the Simonses and the Todds. They were all gray squirrels. The fox squirrels came in long afterwards. They were not so plentiful and they were more shy than the gray squirrels. The blackbirds were very numerous and destructive to grain, wheat and oats suffering most. The farmers used to make what they called a horse fiddle. It turned with a crank and made a noise that could be heard quite a distance. The noise did not frighten quite everything to death, but it would scare these pests away. We would take this rattle trap and go around the field several times a day in order to scare the intruders away. Wild turkeys were very plentiful, and bad on corn. The hunter would take his gun and slip around the field and many times get a turkey. And sometimes they would build a pen and dig a trench for them to go in, cover the top over, and when Mr. Turkey would go inside he did not know how to get out. A great many were caught in this way. I heard my father say he caught nine at one time."

WILLIAM G. LEWIS.

Fairmount in 1853.—As I remember it I settled here August 12, 1853 (was a featherweight on that date, weighing only eight and one-half pounds), on the lot where Dale's hardware store now stands. My father, Nathan Vinson, was the first carpenter in Fairmount, and he was building the old barn on the Joseph Ratliff farm. I think Milton Winslow owned it then. The first old settlers I remember were "Dippy" Baldwin, Seaberry Lines, Mincher Cox and Micajah Wilson.

EZRA F. VINSON.

From Iowa in Covered Wagon.—My name is David, or D. L. I am named for my grandfather, David Stanfield, and Lancaster Bell, an uncle. I was born in Linn County, Iowa, in 1854, and came to Marshall County in 1867, where I have resided most of the time since. When I was about five years old our family drove to Indiana in a covered wagon, leaving here in the fall and returning in the spring. The roads were very bad, and it was a long, hard journey. Grandfather was in poor health, which caused us to go. This is the only time I ever saw him or Indiana. He recovered from this sickness and lived a few years after. My father's name was Samuel Vernon Stanfield. My father had a brother, David, who, while in a row boat, went over the dam and was drowned at Union, Iowa, before the Civil War. I never knew very much about my Indiana relatives. My mother was a Baldwin. Both parents died at Clear Lake, Iowa.

D. L. STANFIELD.

Union, Iowa, March 24, 1917.

Jack Brunt was generally on the safe side of the guessing in his hog buying. His death a short time ago, leaving more than $1,000,000, would indicate that his judgment in business affairs had generally redounded to his benefit. He gave $125,000 to the erection of a Young Men's Christian Association building in Anderson. So, if he sometimes got the better of the pioneer in his guessing, he has returned to their posterity many fold blessings in the furthering of a cause which will no doubt bless generations yet unborn. Jack, as he was called, while he was a quaint character and not always understood, wore the rough side out, and his work in buying and driving the hogs of your early pioneers to market was a blessing attended with many hardships on his part, and one which a man of less sturdy character would have hesitated to have undertaken.

J. M. HUNDLEY.

David Smithson, one of the early pioneers, once related in my presence that when he was married his wife's people objected to David taking their daughter for a wife. The young folks were determined to marry. David said that inasmuch as Betsy was willing, there could be no harm in stealing her (eloping, as it is called nowadays). He told that about midnight he rode his horse to the home of Betsy's parents. She came out and got on the horse behind David and rode a number of miles, where they were married. I never knew how David squared himself with the church, as at that time it was against rules to marry outside of meeting. My mother had a birthright in the Friends Church, but was disowned when she married a Catholic. She later joined the Wesleyan Methodists and died in that faith. I am told that father was a member of the Friends Church at the time of his death. I only mention this to show what time has done.

T. B. McDonald.

Road Building.—Prior to 1854 there had been but little, if any, agitation for the improvement of roads. Such highways as had up to that year been opened for travel were built along the ridges, where the land was high and dry. This accounts, to a large extent, for the angling, crooked roads of the early days. It was not until several years after work was started on a more extensive scale that efforts were made to build roads on Range and Township lines, making travel easier and the highways straighter. The Jonesboro and Fairmount turnpike was projected in 1860, being the first gravel road constructed. Jesse E. Wilson and Jonathan P. Winslow were among the promoters and organizers of the company which built this pike. In 1869 the Marion and Liberty gravel-road was constructed to Center school house in Liberty Township. The work progressed rapidly after these pikes were built, and has ever since occupied much of the attention of all classes of citizens. The Liberty and Fairmount pike was promoted in 1869 by William S. Elliott, Jesse E. Wilson and Elwood Arnett. These men sold $4,000 worth of stock, and the work proceeded. William S. Elliott served as Secretary and Treasurer of the Company.

Sarah Baldwin, in 1845, rode horseback from Fairmount to Richmond to attend Indiana Yearly Meeting of Friends. The route was south to Alexandria, then to Middletown and on through New Castle. On this journey she was accompanied by her father, Nathan Morris, and Milton Winslow was along a part of the time. Winslow was on his way to Wayne County to see his best girl, Mary Roberts, who later became his wife and the mother of Thomas Winslow, now living on a farm two miles and a half northeast of Fairmount.

Amaziah Beeson, in 1830, operated a copper distillery two miles east of Fairmount. He also built the first brick house ever erected in Fairmount Township. Daniel Thomas built the second one. This house is now occupied by William A. Beasley and family. Beeson distilled sassafras, horehound, peppermint, golden rod and pennyroyal, the extract being used for medicines. Dennis Montgomery was employed as Beeson's assistant.

Otho Selby built a frame school house about three miles northeast of Fairmount, in 1850, on land now owned by John Selby. This is where Otho Selby first taught school. It was sometimes referred to as the Prairie Seminary.

Jonathan Baldwin, in 1858, built the big two-story frame house on the old Baldwin homestead. The original Baldwin cabin, which stood near the hackberry tree, was torn down and removed to the northeast corner of Second and Main Streets, which was afterwards used as the finishing room of the old tan-yard. In 1883, Robert Bogue bought ten acres of the Baldwin homestead.

The Wide-a-Wakes were active in 1856. Henry Clay made a speech at Marion in this year. Among those who went to hear him were Jonathan Baldwin and family and Mary Hall Hollingsworth. In 1856 William Hall lived on the Henley lot, on South Main Street.

William Hall kept the first toll-gate about the year 1859. The gate was located just south of town, but was afterwards moved across the street, to the east side, where Solomon Thomas collected toll until his death, in 1873.

There was a Methodist Episcopal Church at Bethel, many years ago. In the Bethel graveyard lie the remains of John Suduth, a soldier of the Revolutionary War.

The Big Tree.—The big tree seems to loom up again. I had almost forgotten it until Jack Stivers mentioned the tree in his communication. I am equally at a loss to know what tree Stivers alludes to, as Nixon Rush and I saw three large trees which were very nearly the same diameter. Two were oak and the one Seeley speaks of was black walnut. One of the oak trees stood not a great way from our homestead cabin in Kansas. It was an immense tree, not so tall as the walnut, but had a number of large limbs that came out a pretty regular distance that circled the body of the tree. By the aid of an Indian ladder one could reach the first big limb, then by a spiral climb around the body of the tree from limb to limb one could gradually ascend as high as one cared to. There was a large opening in the body of the tree about forty feet from the ground which we thought would be a good place to find a fat coon, as we were a little short of meat. So we arranged to go up. Mr. Coon was not in at that hour, although the evidence was good that he frequented the retreat. The other oak stood near a mile west of the Wesleyan Campgrounds, on the west end of the south eighty of the land that Iredell B. Rush owned a few years ago west of the Range line. It, too, was a coon den, but too tall to climb or too large to cut down. I think James Nixon managed to burn it down when he owned the place. Nixon Rush and I were often investigating something that was a little out of the ordinary.

A. HENLEY.

Melbourne, Florida, May 29, 1917.

Fairmount Township has furnished several Grant County officials. J. H. Parker served two terms as County Treasurer; Thomas Winslow served as County Assessor; William Hall, Samuel C. Wilson, J. J. McEvoy, M. S. Friend and Oliver P. Buller have each served as Representatives in the State Legislature; Charles C. Lyons was elected for a term of four years in the State Senate and Solomon Thomas, Edmund Duling, Jonathan P. Winslow, John Kelsay and T. J. Lucas have all at different periods represented Fairmount Township and the Third District on the County Board of Commissioners.

Fairmount in May, 1853.—I will just scribble down a few words of things as I remember them and as I saw them when I arrived in Fairmount in May, 1853. David Stanfield lived on his farm, just south of town. The first house north of the Stanfield home, close to what is now Dr. Glenn Henley's place, was occupied by William Hall, and he was then the Postmaster. I remember Mr. and Mrs. Hall distinctly, as I used to have to pay twenty-five cents for every letter I got from home. Then there was a little reddish brown house just across the street. Solomon Parsons was living in it. I think some of Gonner Knight's were staying with him. Anyhow, Knight's folks got me to bring a parcel from Malden, England, and I delivered it to Mr. Parsons. He was mending some shoes when I took the parcel to the house. Joseph W. Baldwin had a little store on the corner of the Seth Winslow lot, and Isaac Stanfield lived across the street where the Robert Bogue store was. The old Friends Meeting House was west and a little north. I settled with my brother, John Seale, on the farm west of Nathan D. Wilson's and lived there seven years. I remember we had quite a time. If we needed a doctor we had to go to Jonesboro to get one. Dr. Horne, Dr. Meek and old Dr. Johnson practiced then. They used to ride horseback all the time. Jonathan Baldwin lived north of town in 1853. Nathan Vinson was the main carpenter and Isaac Roberts used to work with Vinson. Roberts was a blacksmith. I think Daniel Ridgeway started a tanyard in 1854, and James Cammack started a saw-mill. It was an up-and-down sash saw.

WILLIAM P. SEALE.

Whittier, California, January 26, 1917.

Exempt from Execution.—My friend, George Pence, former Auditor of Bartholomew County, was kind enough to draw my attention to the following schedule of property which by law might escape seizure for debt in our great-grandfathers' day. I thought it might be of interest:

An Act to Exempt Certain Property from Execution
(Approved December 24, 1818)

One spinning wheel and reel, one Bible, one bed and the necessary bedding for one bed, six chairs, one dinner pot, one bake oven, one frying pan, one kitchen table with the necessary articles of table and cupboard and furniture to an amount not exceeding ten dollars, one cow and calf, one sow and pigs, six sheep with the wool growing thereon or the yarn and cloth made thereof, any amount of flax (being the growth of half an acre of ground in one year or the cloth and yarn made thereof), and breadstuff, meat and salt sufficient to supply the family three months, also their wearing apparel, one chopping axe, and one weeding hoe, provided the property exempted shall not exceed the value of $100.

THOMAS DEAN BARR.

Indianapolis, Indiana, May 9, 1917.

Jack Brunt bought hogs in the south part of Fairmount Township from 1858 to 1868 and how much longer I do not know. He often received hogs at my father's farm during this time. A few farmers wanted to know how much their hogs weighed. They realized that the buyer was a better judge of the weight and had the advantage in guessing the weight. The means of weighing were very crude at that time. Father purchased a 600 pound beam.. A box was made which would hold two hogs (if they were not too large). The beam was fastened to a pole, which was fastened to a tripod. The leverage was so arranged that one man could easily suspend the box so that the weight could be ascertained. This was slow work but it satisfied the people who desired to know the correct weight. Often it would require two or three days to receive the hogs contracted for. They were driven to Anderson to be shipped. Jack Brunt told the writer that the Irishman and his Quaker neighbors always had good hogs.

T. B. McDonald.

A great many who were not pioneer inhabitants of the Township were directly connected with its interests and made frequent visits to Fairmount, social, religious and for business, my father often for all three—usually accompanied by my mother, who had near relatives in Fairmount, among them Amy Seale, who was a first cousin. My uncle, Joshua Freeman, grandfather of Arthur Brewer, was said by Nixon Rush to have killed the last bear known in that region. Uncle Joshua was a typical pioneer hunter, trapper and fisher, and was with that company away out on the Santa Fe trail along with Nixon Rush, Dr. A. Henley, and others. Uncle Joshua went to the Civil War and came home to die, in 1862. His widow married Lindsey Buller. His old log cabin used to be standing out Little Ridge way when I first came to Fairmount, but is now torn down, I believe. But that is in Liberty, not in Fairmount Township. Last fall a covered one-horse wagon pulled by a gray mare and bearing the sign, "Stove repairs," stopped at our place. Needing some repairs on our kitchen range we gave the man a job and asked him to dinner. In the course of the conversation I remarked that I was from Indiana. He was a talkative man. "I used to live in Indiana," he remarked. I told him I was from Fairmount, near Marion. He said, "Well! I lived near Marion when a boy. I was a desperate young scalawag whom no one thought could be managed, and so I was placed in the home of an old Quaker named Coggeshall. I guess they thought he could reform me. He lived, as near as I can remember now, about six miles in a southerly direction from Marion."

Anna Freeman Garretson.

Friendswood, Texas, April 15, 1917.

It is not material whether young Puckett's name was John, Jonathan or Cyrus. The historical fact of importance to your story is that the drowning took place at some point in the Mississinnewa River, and that Calvin Bookout, a respected pioneer of your Township, gave his life in a heroic effort to save the young man. Had this event occurred in more recent years it would no doubt have been recognized by the Carnegie Hero Commission and Bookout would have been given a place in the records of this laudable undertaking. I am not of the opinion that it is material as to just where the plank road began or where it terminated. The historical fact which we have sought to point out was the short sightedness of the builders of this expensive and short-lived road,

DAVID JONES AND FAMILY

An example of grit and perseverance. In the picture are shown Mr. and Mrs. Jones and their nine sons and daughters, namely: Hon. William M. Jones, of Liberty Township; Dr. Ben Jones, of LaPorte, Indiana; Rev. Thomas Elsa Jones, now a Friends missionary to Japan; Dr. Eli Jones, of Hammond, Indiana; Miss Ora Jones, teacher in High School, Liberty Center, Indiana; Miss Orpha Jones, student at Earlham College; Rene Jones, student at Colorado College, Colorado Springs, Colorado; Frances and Fred, at home. Mr. and Mrs. Jones have retired from the farm and now reside on Henley Avenue, Fairmount.

when there was an abundance of gravel and other road building materials close at hand. This lesson is especially important at this time, when the State and Nation are entering upon road building in a comprehensive and substantial way. I was much interested in Mrs. Buller's communication, and heartily agree with her that there was much more sociability and generosity displayed in these days of long ago than in recent years. Your hardy pioneers lived close to nature and recognized the Fatherhood of God and the brotherhood of man. They were not then absorbed in money-getting, which is the present-day curse of our Nation and will ruin us as it has ruined all the Nations of the past who have forgotten God and worshipped only Mammon. I knew Anna Parsons, and was her schoolmate. Her father, Solomon Parsons, was killed on the railroad within twenty rods of where I now live. I have read with much interest the communications of Dr. A. Henley, and note that he says that those who put their lands into the railroad speculation about which I have before written lost them. I was not sure of this, and am glad that this fact is established. There were four of David Smithson's sons in the Union army, namely, Judiah, Jehu, Isaac and Seth. Jehu belonged to Company B, One Hundred and Thirtieth Indiana Infantry and died at Chattanooga, Tenn., May 18, 1864. Seth belonged to Company E, One Hundred and Fortieth Indiana Infantry, and died at Columbia, Tenn., January 9, 1865. One of the primitive means of making meal was the grater, a contrivance made of a conical piece of tin, perforated with holes, over which the corn in the ear was drawn, the meal falling upon the board to which this was attached, and running thence down this board into the vessel or container designed to hold the meal. I am pleased that some of my writing has provoked criticism, and am sure that it would hardly be expected that some difference of opinion would fail to arise. I once heard an old man say that if everybody was of the same opinion, all would want his wife, Betsy, but if all knew her as he did no one would want her. I am sometimes inclined to the opinion that this may be true of my contributions to "The Making of a Township." I hope that I may be of assistance in resurrecting some of the things of the past which the present generation should know. If we cannot discover all of the truth we will do well to restore some of the things which are destined soon to be lost if not recorded now, as the generation having knowledge of your early settlers is rapidly passing to the Great Beyond.

J. M. HUNDLEY.

The first picture gallery that we can call to mind was operated by L. D. Cossand. It was on wheels and stood south of where Dr. Glenn Henley's office now stands. At that time the photographs of today were not taken, so far as we know. They were called

Daguerreotypes, taken on copper plates. Cossand was an eccentric person and was a bachelor, very reserved, and seldom seen away from his car. The young people loved to tease him, and they played all kinds of tricks on him. It took time to get a dozen pictures, as one had to sit for each picture separately, and the chances were that no two pictures would be exactly alike. In getting a picture you would have to sit perfectly quiet from two to five minutes. Now they get your picture on the run. This is a fair sample of how the times have changed. It has been said that one Thomas Barnhouse was the first person to take pictures in Fairmount. The only thing that we remember about Barnhouse was the house that he built just across the street from the present Interurban station. What made us remember this particular building was the ornamental cornice. It was different from the heavy cornice of that day, being light and of ornamental work. If there is anyone who remembers this house when it was new I wish they would describe it and give date of building.

T. B. McDonald.

Solomon Thomas served as Commissioner from the Third District one term, 1832-1835; Edmund Duling was Commissioner from 1864 to 1866, inclusive; Jonathan P. Winslow served as Commissioner from 1873 to 1877; John Kelsay served from 1903 to 1907; Thomas J. Lucas served from 1907 to 1910, and was re-elected the second time for the term of 1913-1916.

James Montgomery came in 1830 and entered land in 1837. He was a persistent hunter and trapper, and never failed to get his share of the game on his expeditions into the forest. In the winter of 1840, perhaps December of that year, Montgomery tracked a bear in the snow about two miles and a half south of Fairmount. He summoned John Weston, Solomon Thomas and Jacob Davis, and they started in pursuit. The bear, which proved to be one of the biggest yet seen in this settlement, was overtaken and killed. The carcass was brought to James Montgomery's home, skinned and cut up into meat and divided among his neighbors.

Lindsey Buller, Francis Lytle, Henry Harvey, James Lytle, Lewis Jones and Thomas Winslow, while out hunting in 1840, killed a bear west of where the town of Summitville now stands. It was a ferocious female, and put up a terrific encounter. The brute was finally subdued and killed. The carcass was brought late at night to the cabin of Harvey Davis, where the bear was skinned and prepared for food. Mrs. Davis cooked a mess of bear meat for the hungry hunters which was for many years the talk of the entire settlement.

The first marriage license issued in Grant County was granted to John Smith, son of Caleb Smith, and Mary Ann Thomas, daughter of Solomon Thomas. Caleb Smith, father of the groom, who had been elected Associate Judge of the Circuit Court August 8, walked from his home near Jonesboro to the Solomon Thomas cabin, on Lake Galatia farm, to perform the ceremony, which occurred September 8, 1831.

The Union Grave-yard is located on land entered by Solomon Thomas, in 1835, the land now comprising a part of the farm at present owned by David L. Payne, situated three miles southeast of Fairmount. Among the early pioneers buried in this grave-yard are James Montgomery, Martha Creek and Anna Brewer, wife of Aaron Brewer, daughters of Solomon Thomas; Isaiah Edgerton, Thomas Edgerton, William Edgerton, Harmon Lytle and a small son, and Alvah Herrold.

A headstone still stands in Union Grave-yard bearing the inscription which follows: "Alvah, son of Elijah and Rachel Herrold, died May 25, 1844, aged two years, eight months and twenty-five days. This to wait is far from contention, where no soul can dream of dissension." The quotation is from an old hymn book that was in general use in the early day at church services. Solomon Thomas laid out this grave-yard, which comprises about half an acre of land, and donated the ground to Union U. B. Church.

A mistake was made about a part of the grist mill boiler being found in my father's creek bottom; it was my Uncle Nathan's farm, which was between the mill and father's farm. But the weight off the safety valve was in the creek bottom on the south side of the road. I do not know whether the land was Daniel Thomas's or the Stanfield's. I think the miller's name was McNeir, or something like that. My father's first grandson by the name of Wilson is our son, Raymond, of Leadville, Col.

J. A. Wilson.

Logansport, Indiana, February 15, 1917.

I am proud of my heritage, and it is a source of great pride to me to know that my grandparents were identified with and had a part in the building up of Grant County. I believe my mother once told me that at one time her father, Samuel Dillon, was Trustee of Fairmount Township. I remember well many of these grand and venerable folks of whom you write, and the recollection of their cheery and helpful dispositions shall always be a source of inspiration to me.

H. L. CAREY.

Marshalltown, Iowa, April 9, 1917.

Blowing Chaff.—They did not wait for the wind, but two of them held a sheet, or piece of canvas at either end, and kept it moving in such a way as to make a good stiff breeze and a third man poured the wheat and chaff in front of this contrivance in such a way as to have it blow the chaff away and let the wheat fall to the ground, or floor, as the case may be. I wonder if the reader ever saw a chaff piler thresher operating with a tread-mill horse power? That was the first kind of horse power machine I ever saw, and it was a barbarous affair—a regular horse killer. I think I will refer your readers to an encyclopedia for a description of this wonderful machine. Or perhaps some of your school boys who study mechanics can tell you about this contrivance.

J. M. HUNDLEY.

Dentists.—I am interested in getting a complete list of dentists that have practiced in Fairmount. I can remember Drs. Jay, Dale, N. S. Cox, C. M. Wilson, W. N. Ratliff, M. E. Ratliff, O. D. Cartwright, J. A. Pearcy and S. T. Rigsbee. Speaking of Fowlerton, my brother Ancil and I surveyed and platted the first addition to the town. I was also head chain man in the surveying gang that run the prospective line for the C. I. & E. Railroad under the engineer, Sam Houston. One branch we surveyed from Matthews to Red Key, and the other to Muncie from Matthews, or rather the old town of New Cumberland, as it was then. I don't feel old, but when I look back and think of the many changes that have taken place since my boyhood days around Fairmount, I begin to realize that the years are passing away.

M. E. RATLIFF.

Cassopolis, Michigan, March 17, 1917.

I can remember one teacher whose name I have not seen on the list, Elijah Elliott, who taught at Wesleyan Back Creek. I also remember my first and last teachers, who live in Fairmount. They are Angelina (Harvey) Pearson, 1863, and Sallie (Hollingsworth) Kelsay, 1876. I remember Isaac Meek. He used to come to our house and bring an Indian with him, I think it was Me-shin-go-me-sia. He would preach and then Brother Meek would interpret it. He lived in the house that William Dillon built. It stands on the alley east of the N. A. Wilson Block, or, as was known then, the George Eckfelt property. It was Cy Puckett instead of Jonathan Puckett who was drowned in the river south of the tin plate factory at Gas City. There were six persons drowned at the same place. I can not recall but one name of the other four. This name was McKinney, west of town. In 1888 Ed Cassell was drowned in Lake Galatia. Zack Little, Dan McPherson and myself recovered the body.

SYLVESTER SMITHSON.

Fairmount, Indiana, March 17, 1917.

Some Corrections.—Robert Brazelton and family of five children lived on the place now owned by John Flanagan, at the cross roads west of the Wesleyan Campgrounds, as early as 1850, and possibly some earlier. Nelse Brazelton was the eldest son. He went to school where I did, at the first district school house built in the Township. Bob, as we always called him, and his wife, Ruth, were slaves in the South. Ruth was a smart darkey and a favorite with her master, a Mr. Hill, who gave her her freedom. He also aided her in buying Bob, her husband, who was held by a neighboring planter, the price being $200. I think they had no children at the time they left the South or they might not have gotten off so easily. Nelse was a proud, gay, young Negro, liked fine clothes, was a good worker, and I think learned the barber trade. He drifted into Michigan. James Redding, the colored man that Hundley speaks of as having a wagon shop at Jesse Winslow's, was from North Carolina. Redding was a very clean, decent, honest Negro. Every one spoke well of Jim Redding and liked him. Jim knew his place and was not above his color. Jesse Winslow was one of those positive, impartial, unprejudiced characters who had the courage of his convictions. He had but little use for pro-slavery principles. While Redding was living with Jesse there came a young man, a rebel sympathizer, from the South, and wanted work. I think Jesse gave him a contract, and when meal time came round Redding ate his meals with the family. When this fellow saw the colored face would be at the table, he made objections, saying he was not going to eat with a Negro. "Very well," said Jesse, "thee can sit in the parlor, and when Jim has done his meal thee can eat." The fellow took in the situation and sat down with the family. The projected plank road from Jonesboro to Marion, at south end, commenced at the top of Deer Creek Hill, on north side, or near the top, and ran north to some point near the Pan Handle Railroad crossing of the State road, or it might have been the south corporate line of Marion at that date. The enterprise was not a success and was abandoned as a failure. David Stanfield's original farm joined the Nixon Winslow farm on the east until the Cincinnati, Wabash and Michigan Railroad was built, which divided the two farms. David sold twenty acres in the northeast corner to Jonathan P. Winslow. What I have written in this communication, I think, is correct, but if others think different all right.

A. HENLEY.

Melbourne, Florida, March 13, 1917.

Solomon Thomas, who appears to have been a leading figure in the pioneer days of the settlement, owned a half section of land southeast of Fairmount. Thomas planted eleven acres in orchard. About forty acres were dammed for a fish pond. Neighbors persistently protested against this pond, claiming it was insanitary and not good for the health of the locality. In course of time Thomas yielded to the representations and importunities of his neighbors and permitted it to be drained. The Thomas land, of which the farm now owned by David L. Payne forms a part, was entered on November 5, 1835.

Elijah Ward, in 1836, entered the land where the Ward cabin, which he built, now stands.

David Lewis was a relative of Davy Crockett. His wife, Nancy (George) Lewis, was related to Daniel Boone.

Frederick Ice refused to sell corn to people who had the money to pay for it, but held his grain for neighbors less fortunate, who had neither food nor the money with which to buy. This trait of character and consideration for his people shows a custom which prevailed in the pioneer day, but not now so prevalent. Frederick Ice was well-to-do. He owned 1,700 acres of land in the edge of Delaware and Madison counties, just across the Grant County line.

William G. Lewis was a courageous man in his day, and while ruffians might seek trouble with others, they rarely ever purposely provoked him.

David Lewis donated the land on which Sugar Grove Church was located, on the county line road, on the farm now owned by Daniel Johnson.

Union Church was built in 1843 or 1844.

A custom had been handed down to make the teacher treat on Christmas day. We laid our plans in advance. The bigger boys would take the lead, and would be at the school house in good time on Christmas morning, make a fire and wait. Then you could see the teacher come sauntering along, of course expecting trouble. From ten to twenty boys and girls would be inside, a big boy at the door to make the demand, "treat or be ducked," then all the boys and girls would rush out around the teacher, who would sometimes quietly submit and buy candy or a bushel of apples—generally apples if they were very good and scarce. One of our teachers turned around and went home. All hands took after him. He outran, and as he ran dismissed the school, saying: "I will be back tomorrow. I claim pay for my day's work." One teacher refused to treat The boys gathered him up, took him to the creek and cut a hole in the ice, but he begged and exclaimed, "I will treat." On one occasion the master came late with a bushel of apples and threw them on the snow—then the scrambling for apples! We respected the master that would treat. Before we had steel pens we had to write with goose quills. The master had to make our pens. It was his business to know how to make a good pen, and he took pride in it. I remember watching the teacher with a dozen quills and fine pen knife at work. How carefully he would scrape the quill, cut in the right shape, then split as he would place the quill on his thumb nail. When the quill would have to be repaired, get dull or we bore down too hard, then we would go to the master, hand him the quill—he knew just what to do and how to please. It was common for the teacher to carry his rule during school hours. Why he did so I can't tell. One thing children had to do—that was to go to meeting to worship. If we did not like to go, that made no difference. Back Creek Meeting House was our place to go. Father and mother would ride horseback, one would ride behind mother and sometimes two behind father.

Nixon Rush, Jr.

CHAPTER XXXIV.

RAMBLES OVER THE TOWNSHIP.

(By Mrs. Myra Rush Baldwin)

"THERE'S some flour or something on the back of your cap," said the Better Half as we trudged along the tarvia road northward Sunday morning.

"Well, your fuzzy, wuzzy cap is in the same shape," was the answer.

So, we each took off our caps and there, sure enough, was a fluffy white coating sticking to the wool and the fur of our headgear.

It was frost, or frozen moisture, from the fog that seemed to be hovering over the whole world.

In fact, that fog was so heavy that you could taste it and even smell it.

Wonder if a London fog can be tasted and smelled?

It was such a frosty morning, too, and every little twig of tree and blade of grass fairly trembled under loads of dainty, white flakes of rime.

We stopped at old Back Creek graveyard to get some dates from inscriptions on the headstones.

We started in at the very oldest part, away over in the southwest corner. It was here that we found this inscription:

"Caroline, wife of Exum Newby, daughter of Joseph and Penina Winslow, died the twenty-fourth day of the ninth month, 1831, aged twenty-one years, nine months and twenty-nine days."

"But that doesn't tell us anything," you say.

Oh, yes, but it does.

It tells the story of the first tragedy that happened in the little settlement in the wilderness.

Can you not visualize it all—the lonely little mound on the hillside, overlooking the creek, with the unbroken forest all around and the September wind whispering in the tall trees above?

Only one grave, for it was the first in the burying ground, and a young mother slept there alone, with the autumn leaves falling gently all about her.

Through the forest to the north, in a little clearing, on what is now the Ancil Winslow farm, stood the cabin of Caroline's father, Joseph Winslow—the "Uncle Josie" Winslow, who came from

North Carolina in a four-horse wagon, bringing with him $2,600 with which he entered land from the Government at $1.25 an acre for himself and for his seven sons and daughters, away back in 1829.

Aside from Robert McCormick, over on the river, "Uncle Josie" and his family were the very first of the early pioneers to settle in Fairmount Township.

To the south, on what is now the Fankboner farm, stood another cabin, Caroline's own home, on the land given her by her father, the same "Josie" Winslow.

Then, farther to the south, through the big woods, was the home of her brother, Seth Winslow.

Another brother, Matthew Winslow, and two sisters, Mrs. Aaron Hill and Mrs. Solomon Knight, lived farther to the north and east, while still farther down the creek lived Daniel Winslow and at home with "Uncle Josie" was Henry, and these were also brothers.

So, you can see, that for the first interment in old Back Creek graveyard, there were only relatives in the funeral party, with the exception of a very few neighbors, who had arrived in the new settlement in 1830 and 1831, previous to the young wife's death.

The little log church nearby was built that same year of 1831. Soon other graves were made near the lonely one on the bluff and a four-rail fence was built around the little plot. As the numbers increased the rail fence had to be moved over time and time again, until the graveyard attained to its present size.

Ah! Caroline, you were left alone on the hillside that September day, eighty-five years ago, with the birds and the little, wild animals of the forest as your companions. But, today, near you and all about you are the graves of your father and mother, your husband, brothers and sisters, their children and their children's children, many of them, and you are no longer alone.

In the same old part of the burying ground, on the edge of the bluff, we also found the grave of Thomas Wilson, a Quaker boy, son of Jesse and Hannah Wilson. He died of fever contracted while serving with the Northern army in the South during the Civil War. Separated from him by only a grave or two, lies his sweetheart of long ago, who died two years after he passed away—of a broken heart, 'tis said.

Another stone marks the grave of one of the earliest of the pioneers, snatched away in the prime of life, his untimely death being caused by a mistake a clerk made when he filled a prescription with the wrong kind of medicine.

It is not particularly beautiful, this old graveyard of ours, but it is sacred ground to all descendants of the pioneers.

> "For beneath these stones are resting,
> Folded in their last long sleep,
> Men who toiled that we might prosper,
> Men who sowed that we might reap."

It was awfully cold standing out there in the frosty grass, Sunday morning, so the writer ran in to the home of Isaiah Thomas, nearby, to warm her feet by a good gas fire for a minute. It gave her a chance, anyway, to have a nice visit with Aunt Carrie Thomas and Mrs. Hattie Atkinson.

Then we journeyed onward and soon turned east toward the Lin Wilson home.

We were so attracted by the appearance of the handsome bungalow which John Devine has made out of the old house on his farm that we could not resist the temptation to stop and investigate a little. The house is almost completed and it certainly is beautiful and convenient.

We lived a lot in the past last Sunday, but if you could have seen us, along about one o'clock, sitting with the Lin Wilson family, around the dining room table, from which good, country "eats" were fast disappearing, you would have thought rightly that we were existing very much in the present, also.

With "Uncle Sammy" Wilson we could easily live over the years of the early history of Grant County, for, with possibly one exception, Emeline Lewis, Mr. Wilson has resided in Fairmount Township longer than any other person now living. He is in his eighty-third year and his memory is excellent.

After the happy time in the hospitable Wilson home we turned our steps homeward, using the Interurban track for a thoroughfare, as the sun had come out and the roads were muddy.

However, at the next crossing we deviated a little in order to make a visit at the home of Mr. and Mrs. Will Kirkpatrick, which is also the home of Mr. and Mrs. Robert Wilson.

There we found Mrs. Eunice Wilson, once President of the Indiana Woman's Christian Temperance Union, still unable to leave a sick bed which she has occupied for several months. She is cheerful and happy, in spite of it all, with her spirit still undaunted and her intellect still bright and untarnished. "Of such is the kingdom of Heaven."

Another stop was made at the Mrs. Angelina Pearson home where reminiscences were again indulged in and a quiet hour enjoyed.

To round out a happy and never-to-be forgotten day we wended our way, after reaching home, to the Wesleyan Church to hear that "veteran of the Cross," Aaron Worth, preach.

Did you ever see a "splatter-work" motto like Jacob Adell used to make? You can see one hanging over the organ, back of the pulpit, in the new Wesleyan Church.

When we entered the door Rev. Worth was standing in the pulpit, shading his eyes with one hand and looking out over the congregation towards the entrance.

No doubt he was watching the people as they came in, but to the writer, who has a fanciful imagination, it seemed that Mr. Worth was standing near the brink of eternity, looking across into the celestial city "whose builder and maker is God."

M. B.

February 1, 1917.

"Starting out on a hike, are you?" asked George Cleveland Sunday afternoon as we, dressed in our oldest "duds," passed him on our way to Fowlerton.

"Yep," was the answer. "We'd ride in automobiles if they weren't so slow." Mr. Cleveland was just entering his automobile.

Our way led us east on Washington Street. It used to be called Main Cross street or something like that in the old days. Before it was paved East Washington Street was the muddiest street in all the world.

Sometimes, in her dreams, M. B. lives over the old school days and she can just see Walk Winslow's horses and his cab floundering through the mud in front of Ryland Ratliff's house, the horses' sinking in the mire to their knees and the wheels of the cab to the hubs, and often the old plank walk comes back in memory—the rickety plank walk leading to the school house and sometimes overflowing with water from Puddin' Creek. Then the stretches of open country that lay between the main part of town and Jonathan Winslow's home, too, appear in the dreams and we school children are once more afraid of falling off the board walk into the swirling waters of Puddin' Creek.

Sunday we noticed a few changes on the road between Fairmount and Fowlerton. John Fox and family have moved to the N. A. Wilson farm, Mr. and Mrs. Miles Rush having left the place and moved to town. The farm is now gay with the laughter of children, for Mr. and Mrs. Fox have a large family.

Across the road, in the big, new barn belonging to Dr. C. N. Brown and Ed Brown, there were other merry doings, for several other children were playing and romping and having good times as only children in the country can have.

Off to the south we could see the old Monahan home and the residence of James Blair.

A field belonging to Dr. Brown and his brother was alive with young Durocs. You could almost see the pile of dollars the young porkers represented.

We noticed that Joe Holloway has a new cement garage, built where it is the handiest, right near the road.

Coming to East Branch school house we decided to rest a minute. The door was unlocked and we walked in.

We were on historic ground there, for nearby was the old Anthony Wayne trail, so well known in pioneer days.

A cyclone, too, visited the neighborhood once and demolished the McCoy home, the wreck attracting much attention at the time.

Another change noted on the way was the dismantled condition of the old East pumping station. The buildings are in ruins now.

The writer half closed her eyes and tried to imagine that she was passing the ruins of an old German castle, the pools of water all about representing the moat.

It was a fine afternoon for walking. Overhead the deep blue of the sky, the fluffy, feathery, white clouds and the bright sunshine seemed to say, "Summer," but the crisp air, the thin ice on the pools of water, the browns and grays of the landscape and the bare branches of the trees all whispered, "It is winter still."

M. B.

January 8, 1917.

We traveled "The Friendly Road" last Sunday—not "The Friendly Road" of which David Grayson writes in such an entertaining manner, but the dear, old Fairmount-Jonesboro pike.

And such a friendly road it is!

Beside it live many of our friends and relatives and often, from passing automobiles and buggies, there come to us cheery greetings and the sight of waving handkerchiefs as we walk along.

Besides being friendly the road is enchanting—it is not exact and straight with the world, but it curves and angles and meanders at will, following the old trail made through the forest by the early pioneers. To straighten that old road would be nothing short of desecration.

And, then, think of the memories that cluster around this old thoroughfare, built at such cost of labor by our grandfathers and great-grandfathers!

It was along this road that we used to go to June Quarterly meeting. What memories that suggests!

It has always been a favorite driveway for lads and lassies in their courtship days. Buggies were used in the old days, but now it's automobiles.

Some of us have traveled this road to our own weddings or to witness the marriage of our friends. More often have we formed a part of sad processions that wended their way to the two burying grounds that border it on the west.

Ah, yes, it is a friendly road and a sacred one to many of us.

The weather man tried to make the road unfriendly to us last Sunday, but without success, for we enjoyed the walk in spite of the blizzard which raged and roared all about us.

We were dressed for cold weather and as we started early in the morning and boarded an Interurban car near the Lin Wilson home, we escaped the worst of the storm.

There is something exhilarating about facing the elements which never fails to bring a feeling of elation and joy to one's heart.

From the time we left our own door until we arrived at the crossing near the Wilson home we saw only two people, a boy in a lot in the north end of town, where two queer-looking crosses suggested Calvary's hill near Jerusalem.

The other person was Richard Dillon, who was on his way to feed the stock at the old Allen Dillon homestead.

For once The News hikers had the whole road to themselves and seemingly the whole world for a time, for everyone seemed to be shut in their own homes.

Arriving in Marion we found the County seat fairly storm-bound.

One fellow on the street car said "The old ground hog surely saw his shadder this time." "Well, if he didn't he was blind," was the answer made by a dirty-faced Irishman, who was hugging the stove, trying to keep warm.

Another man said, "I'm mighty glad I wore my cap."

"But it isn't doing you any good, for you haven't it down over your ears," said his female companion.

"If I were bare-headed you'd see whether it was doing me any good or not," was the rather illogical answer.

In due course of time we arrived at the home of Mr. and Mrs. William Baldwin, where we spent the day.

Mr. and Mrs. Baldwin live in a brick cottage at the very beginning or else the very ending of Branson Street in South Marion.

The house was built long ago by Jesse Small, father of C. R. Small, and contains much walnut timber and fine old-fashioned presses.

Mr. Baldwin once had a nursery there and all about are several cedar and pine trees, even in the yards of adjoining residence property.

We heard many stories of pioneer times that day, for Mr. Baldwin "grew up with the country."

He can tell about the tragedies and the work and the fun of the early days and of the pranks he and his brother "Lank" used to play.

We were greatly interested in Mr. Baldwin's stories of the "Underground Railway," for his grandfather, Charles Baldwin, and his father, Lindsey Baldwin, were friends of the slaves.

Once upon a time two runaway slaves were hidden in the attic of Lindsey Baldwin's home when three men, disguised as peddlers, arrived from three different directions.

After hanging around awhile and being assured that no slaves were hidden in the house the three men departed.

When the slaves were told of the visit one of them exclaimed, "Yes, sah, one of dem was my massa, too," for he, listening beneath the rafters, had recognized the voice of his master.   M. B.

February 8, 1917.

The new tarvia road stretched before us, white and shining in the moonlight.

And such moonlight!

Even Orion and the Dipper looked dim in the light of the glorious queen of the night.

But Jupiter, floating along by the side of the queen, refused to be outshone. He seemed to be defiantly saying, "You 'dassent' make me look dim and insignificant. I'm Jupiter, I am."

And the wind! It kept up a continual music in our ears as we swung along northward. The wind loves to play on the telephone wires—a singing, musical song, near each pole where wide arms stretch forth seemingly to catch the sounds.

But dearer to the wind even than the telephone wires are the pines and the cedars. How it sings through the waving branches, sometimes mournful and sad and sometimes with a sound like falling water!

On our moonlight walk to Jonesboro, Tuesday evening, the wind in the telephone wires made ringing, singing music for us all the way. At the old homesteads the cedars, grouped on the lawns, sang us songs suggestive of the far distant seashore and of glittering, gleaming waterfalls in far away canyons and glens.

It is impossible for The News hikers to walk along the Fairmount-Jonesboro pike without recalling the past. The road, once only a trail through the mighty forest, connecting the pioneer settlements, has ever been closely identified with the making of Grant County.

Along it, in the early days, the pioneer's horse waded knee-deep in mud as the Southern Grant County resident wended his way to the gristmill at Jonesboro, or journeyed to Marion to pay his taxes.

Then, as times improved, the road was graveled and tollgates were established. Trying to evade a few cents of toll by going the mud roads or by rushing past the tollgates were common occurrences in those days.

It was along this road that the children of the pioneers were taken in big wagons to Harrisburg, now Gas City, to get their first glimpse of a railroad engine and train. How ferocious and fierce the old engine looked as it puffed and screeched its way up to the Pan Handle station! That was long before Fairmount had a railroad.

As we passed the old Joel Wright place, now the LaRue farm, where Ed Stout lives, old Quarterly meeting days came back and the yard seemed full of visiting Friends gathered at the hospitable home for dinner. We could almost see diminutive Aunt Adeline Wright bustling around in the kitchen preparing the feast for the hungry visitors.

Once, when a "general" meeting was held at old Back Creek, the neighboring homes were simply packed with guests. The writer remembers that one night thirty visiting Friends were entertained at "Rush Hill." They naturally overflowed all the beds and many slept on pallets on the floor.

But those days are forever gone and the sturdy pioneers have departed with them.

"We shall never see their like again; those sturdy, honest, economical, God-fearing pioneers are of the past!" said the Better Half as we left old Back Creek graveyard behind, its stones gleaming white in the moonlight.

M. B.

December 7, 1916.

"Are you folks hunting up names of soldiers to enlist?" was asked of us Sunday afternoon as we were snooping around away over on the Muncie pike.

We had to acknowledge our non-belligerent mission. People just cannot understand why any one can enjoy the mere act of walking along the country roads or across fields.

We covered so much territory and had such varied experiences Sunday that it is a difficult matter to know just what to write and what to leave unwritten.

In a little corner of Fairmount Township which juts out toward the river beyond the Muncie pike, a pioneer burying ground lies on the edge of a deep ravine. This is old Bethel graveyard—not more than a mile from the Fankboner burial place—one of the oldest in the Township.

Unlike the latter graveyard it is readily accessible and is easily seen from the road. It is also less neglected, being enclosed with a fence, and interments are still occasionally made there.

The headstones are tall and flat and old-fashioned and sometimes the carving on them is odd and queer.

"Isaac Sudduth, old Revolutioner, died November 27, 1854, aged ninety-nine years," is the inscription we noticed on one headstone.

We had heard, an hour or two previously, from the lips of Mr. Sudduth's great-granddaughter, Mrs. F. M. Haynes, a bit of his life's story and so we know that the words, "Old Revolutioner," meant that he had served in the Revolutionary War.

Mrs. Haynes could, as a little girl, remember her great-grandfather, who lacked only a few months of living to be one hundred years old.

"He would sit by the fire," she said, "and when grandmother would ask him how he felt he would say, 'I'm all right, only I'm just waiting.' One morning he sat down to his breakfast as usual. He had his knife in one hand and his fork in the other. Suddenly the knife and fork dropped to the floor, his head fell forward and the 'Old Revolutioner's' time of waiting was over.

Mr. and Mrs. Haynes told us many things as we sat in their low-ceiled, walnut-finished sitting room while the quiet Sabbath afternoon hours slipped swiftly away.

And Mr. Haynes played some tunes on his fiddle—he doesn't call it a violin. He plays by note and he likes to use an old-time hymn book in which the notes are the old-fashioned kind.

Many people know where the old Daniel Coleman homestead stands, back a short distance from the Muncie pike. This is where Mrs. Haynes was born and, with the exception of about two years, it has always been her home. It is there that she will probably end her days.

Over in Bethel graveyard, which was originally a part of the farm of her father, Daniel Coleman, who deeded the ground to the community for a burial place, lies her great-grandfather, Isaac Sudduth, both her grandfathers, Thomas Coleman and Gabriel Johnson, and many others of her kindred.

In a far corner of the graveyard, where an evergreen tree droops over the headstones and where the weeds are kept cut and every thing is in order, lie many members of one of the oldest of the Township families—the Dulings.

Many other pioneer families are represented, including the Selbys, the Masons and the Weesners.

At the corner, where the little, short road leads off from the Muncie pike toward the old cemetery, C. A. Buffington and his family reside. By-the-way, the farm once belonged to Nathan Beals, a former Fairmount man, and he and his wife lived there for many years.

In a barnlot on the Buffington farm stands just about the most interesting relic in the Township. That is nothing more nor less than a part of the old McCormick tavern, celebrated in local history as the first hostelry in Southern Grant County. There is no doubt about its identity, for a number of the older residents of the Township remember when the building was moved from the McCormick farm, now owned by Eugene Wilson, to its present site. The old logs of which it is constructed certainly show that they have been visited by the storms of many winters, so weather-beaten are they.

Before we reached the Bethel graveyard, we climbed some fences, crossed a stream, clambered up a bluff, skirted a plowed field and finally landed in the old Fankboner burying ground—our second visit to this historic place.

We found that, since our last visit, the urn which adorned the

IN THE QUAKER COSTUMES OF THEIR GRANDMOTHERS
(Olive Rush and Mrs. Myra Baldwin at Rush Hill.)

top of the Robert McCormick monument has been broken off and is now lying on the ground. Otherwise there had been no changes and the place was as quiet as ever, only the singing of the birds and the noise of automobiles, passing on roads beyond the trees, breaking the stillness. Below the bluff the little stream wends its way through the ravine and the wind-flowers nod in the afternoon breeze just as they have done for centuries.

It was a glorious day for a walk and we enjoyed every minute of it, from the time we left the Pennsylvania station at Fowlerton until we reached home long after darkness had fallen.

It was "some" walk, too, as you will realize when we tell you that it included the distance from Fowlerton to the Robert Reeder home, back to Fowlerton again, north to East Bethel church, east to the Lake school house, north to the two old graveyards mentioned above and the Haynes residence, then back home, past East Bethel, then along the angling road that finally merges into the Heavilin highway that extends from Eighth Street eastward.

On the angling road—a new one for us—we passed the Johnnie Flanagan and the Hiram Gardner homes, where the peace of a Sabbath twilight hovered. Mr. Gardner has a new automobile and the family, no doubt, had not returned from a ride, for a dozen calves in the barnyard told us, by their actions, that they thought it was just about supper time for them.

Two or three clean, handsome buggies in front of the Flanagan residence looked as though they might tell a story to us, too, if they only dared. But we didn't ask any questions.

Once, early in the afternoon, we stood on a slightly elevated place where we could see the depressions—the sites of the bogs of the early days.

Half closing our eyes we could almost see the split-board sunbonnets of the pioneer women as they gathered cranberries in the marshes. Over in the vicinity of Lake Galatia we used to gather bushels and bushels of the best hazel nuts, too. Gone are the cranberry marshes and the hazel nut bushes and the bogs, never to return.

Going still farther back in time, as we gazed over the little valley on the old Gift farm, through which Barren Creek flows, we could almost see immense animals—the mammoth, the mastodon and the giant beaver—floundering around in the mud and finally sinking to their death in the mire. Their bones, in some cases, remained throughout the centuries.

Many of these old-time bogs have been recently plowed and so black is the soil, that, at a distance, it has almost a blue tinge.

One of the unusual features of the hike Sunday was the fact that an invitation to join us was actually accepted for once. Mrs. John Delong, whose home we passed on the road north of the Lake school house, joined us in our visit to the old Fankboner graveyard.

By-the-way, a boy over near the school house knew where the "Boner" graveyard was but he couldn't tell the location of the Fankboner burying ground.

Mrs. Delong is a niece of Aunt Gabrilla Havens and she has two aunts buried in the old cemetery whose tragic history she told us.

One named Ursula Clark, aged fifteen, and the other, Polly Clark, aged twenty, came to the new country with their parents, J. H. and S. B. Clark. They took cold on the trip through the forests, hasty consumption set in and one died in June, 1838, and the other in September of the same year.

This is only one short story of the hardships of the early pioneer period.

All along the way, Sunday, whenever we passed a bit of woodland, wild flowers gladdened our eyes and the odor of blossoming orchards clustered about the farm houses, caused us to inhale deeply.

With hands full of red-bud blossoms, bluebells, crow's-foot, lamb's-tongue, wood-anemone, violets and spring-beauties, we thought how glorious it is to be alive in the spring-time!

M. B.

May 17, 1917.

In the course of our journeyings last Sunday—we were in an automobile—we came across the home of a hermit.

It is a tiny house facing a graveyard.

The neighbor women all say that the hermit is a splendid housekeeper and that the washings he puts out are really quite wonderful.

After hearing the story regarding the inmate M. B. looked at the tiny house with almost an overpowering sense of curiosity.

A jaunt across the woods after some glorious branches of redbud in bloom brought us close to the house but we caught no glimpse of its solitary occupant.

A saucy mountain "boomer," perched upon the top rail of a ladder leaning against the rear of the house chattered, daring us to come closer.

Perhaps it was the spirit of the hermit embodied for a time in the squirrel daring us to come closer.

Mischievous boys sometimes, it is said, tease the man, whereupon he rushes out of the tiny house while the boys run for their very lives.

With the headstones of the pioneers of the community guarding his front door and with the trees of the forest primeval shadowing the house in the rear the hermit lives all alone with his thoughts.

Before reaching the tiny house by the graveyard we journeyed over a new road for us—the one that passes Lake Galatia on the east.

We left the car on the roadside and, traversing a ploughed field, we reached the lake—the former "Pool of Siloam," so called by the Spiritualists.

Looking across the lake toward the west the view was rather attractive, with the rays of the afternoon sun glistening on the water.

All about us, though, as we looked at the shore line at our feet, were deep holes in the boggy ground where a false step might prove disastrous. The soil was shaky and we knew that we were standing on a thin covering of decayed vegetation.

Time was when it was really dangerous to fool around in the vicinity of Lake Galatia, so treacherous were the boggy shores. More than one fellow has been pulled out of the muck as he gradually sank to his doom. And there are stories galore of horses and cattle sinking in the boggy ground.

The pioneers really thought that the lake had no bottom.

However, after one or two people had been drowned there and their bodies had been recovered the old superstitious idea that the lake was bottomless was finally dispelled.

Once the lake covered much more ground than it does now and at one time a project for making a summer resort of the place was undertaken by some Marion men.

Like the building of a great Spiritualistic city on its shore, undertaken in the early history of the Township, it, too, fell through with and the hope of future greatness for Lake Galatia vanished.

In spite of the work done by drainage, in spite of the well-developed farms and good homes in the vicinity, a spirit of loneliness broods over Lake Galatia. It is something almost tangible and it grips the visitor with imaginary talons and sometimes makes you want to run from the place. M. B.

May 24, 1917.

We snooped around in the east end of the Township again last Sunday.

We left town by the Eighth Street road and walked to Fowlerton by easy stages, returning in the afternoon by the same road, an unusual thing for us to do. It was a ten-mile walk altogether—a fairly long walk for muscles grown rather soft from lack of systematic hiking these days.

Away over by the Solomon Duling homestead two freckled faced boys were fishing under the bridge which spans the Duling branch just before it empties into Barren Creek. They were catching pretty good sized fish, too.

The young fishermen, the playful lambs, the wild flowers and the birds all said that spring has come, in spite of the fact that farmers are behind with their work and many fields remain unbroken.

We had a nice walk and learned many things.

The most scientific of the modern scientific ways of raising baby chicks was one of the interesting things we learned on the trip.

In Mrs. Lowry Glass' poultry yard we learned that to be absolutely up-to-date in chicken-raising you must feed the little chicks as scientifically and with as much system as a modern mother cares for her baby.

The baby chicks must have certain kinds of food—balanced rations, if you please—administered to them at stated intervals and in stated amounts. Moreover, the temperature of their brooders must be kept just so-so.

Mrs. Glass' father, Thomas Duling, seeing the new-fangled drinking fountain empty, started to fill it from the pump at the splendid drilled well on the place.

He was stopped with a "No, no! the water has to be 'doped' before it is put in the fountain," from his daughter.

And, truly, Mrs. Glass has as fine a lot of baby chicks as any one need care to see—little Plymouth Rocks and Rhode Island Reds—as contented and happy and healthy, the three hundred of them, as though they had a score of scratching, fluffed-up, real, live mothers.

Mr. and Mrs. Glass are raising a lamb by hand and it, too, is fed scientifically, at certain hours of the day.

The hens on the farm are quite orderly, for they lay their eggs in the nests made for them and not all over creation as hens used to do when we had to hunt eggs in the old days.

Mrs. Glass is partial to the incubator way of hatching eggs and the brooder way of raising chickens, for the results are so much more satisfactory, she says.

The newest fad in brooders is a hard coal heater with a drum or reflector, or whatever they call it, which throws the heat to the ground and under which the baby chicks hover.

Sunday we all wondered how Arthur Brewer was getting along with his hundreds of hatching eggs and baby chicks.

We had such a fine time at the Duling home. Mr. and Mrs. Glass and Mr. Duling all have the same home, and a lovely home it is, too, with a wonderful, beautiful, grassy lawn and well kept grounds.

There is one other daughter, Mrs. Milton Rich, in the family, and she and her husband, who live in the neighborhood, were also Sunday afternoon callers.

On the way to Fowlerton, in the morning, we passed the J. O. Duling farm and saw the brick and stone which mark the place where the old Duling home once stood.

When the house burned last winter one of the loveliest old landmarks in the entire Township was destroyed, for the interior finish of the building, woodwork, presses, closets and the fine old stairway were of solid walnut, almost worth its weight in gold these days.

For almost a mile we followed the Chesapeake & Ohio Railroad as it cuts cat-a-cornered across the fields.

Looking at the fine land enclosed in the right-of-way of the railroad we thought of the wastefulness of the American people.

Some day it will be different and the land along the railroads will be cultivated as it is in Germany and other countries in Europe.

Why, there was enough coal—good, big chunks—scattered along that railroad within the space of a few miles to keep a family warm an entire year.

We Americans don't know what it is to economize.

We had dinner Sunday in Fowlerton at the restaurant kept by Mrs. Schmidt, the French woman who has a German name.

On the trip over we stopped for a short time at the Thomas Winslow home and on the return trip we had a little visit with Mr. and Mrs. Wayne Heavilin and the latter's mother, Mrs. Newt Wells, whose girlhood home, the old Flanagan farm, now owned by Charles Child, adjoins the Heavilin place. John Heavilin and his son, Wayne, have leveled and graded the roadside along their farm and have sowed it in clover and grass, making it like a lawn. They will keep it mowed and incidentally get the hay for their pains—a fine plan for others to follow.

Wayne Heavilin has come to it. After holding out for three or four years against an automobile because he likes a driving horse so well he has at last succumbed and a green automobile takes the family for an airing now and then.

"It's a new kind—a metallic Elizabeth," says Mr. Heavilin, "but it gets over the ground all right."

The walk home in the evening was especially enjoyable.

Violets and spring beauties blooming, meadow larks singing and robins trying to sing, a tinge of green appearing on the forest trees, a southwest wind blowing and perfect roads—these and other glorious accessories made the walk a pleasant one.

We faced a sunset sky. Swinging above the purple and rose and pink of the horizon there shone the narrowest, silver crescent you ever saw. It looked like a curved eye-lash.

And the Better Half said, "The moon is hanging on by an eye-lash." M. B.

April 26, 1917.

One ambition of our lives has been realized. We've been entertained in a real-for-sure log-house—not the fancy kind like we've lodged in at the Glacier National Park and the Grand Canyon of the Colorado, but one built more than sixty years ago for a real family home.

It was at Chap Duling's and the visit happened unexpectedly to us last Sunday.

We went to Fowlerton on the 9 o'clock train Sunday morning. A certain old, red sweater—the finest thing to walk in you ever saw—and an old, blue overcoat are surely getting to be quite familiar to the people of Fowlerton by this time.

After a short visit with S. D. Key at his store we wandered into the Methodist Protestant Sunday School and remained for the church service.

There we saw many familiar faces and were greeted by members of such well-known families as the following: Partridge, Nottingham, Duling, Glass, Compton, Simons, Corn, Smith, Scotten, Brown and others. All gave us such a cordial welcome that it was indeed a pleasure to meet with such whole-hearted and wholesome people.

D. C. (Chap) Duling is the efficient superintendent of the Sunday School and Rev. A. E. Scotten is the pastor of the church.

There was an attendance of 134 at the Sunday School and about the same number heard Rev. A. E. Scotten deliver a good sermon at the morning service.

The key-note of the discourse was the thought that "mountain-top experiences" should prepare the Christian for service to mankind in the valley below.

A very good choir furnished the singing with John King at the piano.

We especially liked Mr. King's work as an accompanist. While he works hard during the week on the farm he has time to keep up his music and is always at his place at the piano when the hour comes for Sunday morning service.

We liked the interior of the church, the plain, tinted walls being especially restful.

Preaching services are held every other Sunday morning, alternating with Pleasant Grove Church in the country southwest. However, evening services are conducted every Sunday at Fowlerton, with the pastor in charge.

Having received a cordial dinner invitation from Mr. and Mrs. Chap Duling we departed from our usual custom and accepted. A short walk took us to the home—one of the most interesting we have yet visited. And the dinner—well, the ambrosia and the nectar of the gods could not have been more delicious and, doubtless, were far less satisfying. Real country ham, chicken and everything—but we desist from further description.

Aside from the old house, made of huge logs, the lawn is the most attractive feature of the place, although the grounds all about are well-kept.

Mr. Duling has had an immense pile of old rails and scattered timber sawed for fuel, so that the high price of coal has less terror for him than for many other people. We noticed other large piles of wood at other homes along the way, many of them the result of the big sleet storm of March 13.

From the Chap Duling home we hiked to the William Duling residence, about three-quarters of a mile east on the same road. There we had a good visit with Mr. and Mrs. Duling and their children, Mrs. Charles Hobbs, of Upland; Mrs. Wright, of Washington, D. C., and Mr. and Mrs. Glenn Duling.

William Duling will soon celebrate his eightieth birthday. He owns several hundred acres of fine land and is one of the oldest remaining members of a family, highly esteemed since the early settling of the east end of the Township.

We found that we were not the only hikers out Sunday for Mrs. Hobbs had walked from her residence in Upland in the morning to the home of her parents—a distance of six miles.

After our visit at the Duling home we turned our steps toward the setting sun and hiked into Fairmount.

The Dulings had not seen the last of us, however, for on the way homeward, we stopped at both the Soloman Duling and Thomas Duling residences.

Everybody who is conversant with the neighborhood knows where Solomon Duling lives. It is a lovely place—set quite a distance back from the road, with a beautiful, rolling, grassy meadow in front and a bubbling brook singing at the foot of a wooded hill. The house is finished on the inside with walnut and there are old-fashioned presses and round, home-made rugs to give the proper tone to the interior.

Mr. and Mrs. Duling have had with them, for several weeks, a little victim of the New Castle tornado, the son of an adopted daughter, whose home was partially demolished by the wind.

May 3, 1917. M. B.

Just about the time man decides that he is the supreme lord of creation along comes Nature and the Power back of Nature and they give Mr. Man a slap in the face and tell him to "go 'way back and sit down."

This thought was uppermost in our minds as we walked along the road Sunday evening, our eyes opening wider and wider as fresh evidences of the devastation wrought by the sleet storm of the thirteenth kept presenting themselves.

And the thought of the New Castle and the New Albany tornadoes strengthened our belief in the theory of man's helplessness in the face of the fury of the elements.

Scores of telephone poles lying prostrate on the ground or snapped off by the weight of the sleet, and great trees, broken and maimed by the storm, silently told us of Nature's power when she "gets her back up."

The woods along the way reminded us of pictures we had seen of the famous forests of France after the Germans had raided portions of that country early in the present war.

Indeed, in their helpless, forlorn, mangled condition the trees somewhat resembled the maimed soldiers returning home from the front.

Twilight had come on as we passed between the woods on the old Seth Winslow farm and the woods on the Fankboner place.

We tried our best to find the trail through the trees where a beautiful road used to wind in and out on the Seth Winslow farm, and because all traces seemed to be entirely obliterated our hearts grew heavy.

In the half-darkness under the trees we could almost see a wagon coming behind two fat horses, along that winding road.

In the wagon, on the spring seat, sat a father and mother, while behind, their little legs cramped by sitting on the floor, a group of children peered over the sides, their faces all aglow with wonder at the bigness of the world.

And that's the way we used to go to Back Creek Quarterly meeting.

Another scene visualized itself Sunday evening, and that was a long string of vehicles, many of them big farm wagons, making a procession more than a mile in length.

That was Grandmother Jay's funeral procession on its way to Back Creek.

People do not attend funerals like they used to.

It is change, change, everywhere, and all the time.

The swish of the south wind in the bare branches of the trees, the distant barking of a dog, the croaking of a frog heightened the lonesomeness that crept over us at the thought of change—never-ceasing change.

Then we glanced above where myriads of stars greeted our vision and there gleamed Orion and the Pleiades just like they used to shine in the old days. The stars seem never to change. And there, also, was the bright crescent of the new moon, shining as of yore.

And although we saw her over our left shoulder—an ill omen—she gave us courage, even in a world so full of change.

Preceding our walk we sat for an hour or two on a log in the Rush Hill woods.

Here, in the bright sunshine of a glorious day, with the hope of spring in the south wind's whisper, we held sweet communion with Nature

Incidentally, we acquired a few rheumatic pains because of the dampness emanating from that old, rotten log.

M. B.

March 29, 1917.

We journeyed Sunday afternoon only so far as the John Peacock residence, for the wind blew bitterly cold from the northwest and all the earth was tightly grasped in Father Winter's frosty arms.

John Peacock is a farmer who knows how to farm and his home and all its surroundings tell of comfort and of prosperity.

With two immense up-to-date barns and with a large house, filled with all the modern conveniences, truly here are found "all the comforts of home."

As Mrs Elizabeth Peacock told us of her early life in the wilderness, for she came to Grant County from England when she was a little girl, we could not refrain from contrasting the conditions of those early pioneer days and of her life at the present time.

One phase of pioneer life was significantly brought out in the conversation, Sunday, and that was the homesickness, to say nothing of the loneliness, with which the women of those days had to contend.

Looking out upon a little patch of ground, where the "sticktights" grew waist high, with the forest all around the clearing, Mrs. Samuel Radley, mother of Mrs. Peacock, must have often longed for the well-kept gardens and the green lanes of old England.

When she looked about the little log hut in which she lived, her thoughts must often have wandered to the beautiful, stately brick house near London, which was her home before she came to America.

Mrs. Peacock has a photograph of this lovely old house.

When Mrs. Radley left England she brought with her some pretty white bed spreads to beautify her new home in America.

It was truly discouraging—this trying to beautify a home in the wilderness—for every time it rained the water soaked through the mud daubing between the logs of the cabin and stained the bed spreads.

To add to the homesickness, it took a long time for a letter to come from England, often as long as three months. Moreover, it cost twenty-five cents to buy postage for each letter in those days, and twenty-five cent pieces weren't found growing on bushes then any more than they are now.

This phase of pioneer life was again referred to by Mrs. Jane Hobbs, a little later in the afternoon, when we stopped at her cottage on North Main Street after our pleasant call at the Peacock home.

"I just can't make you understand how it was," said Mrs. Hobbs. "Why, just to think, between here and Carter Hasting's, south of town, except for a very short time in the middle of the summer, the ground was covered with mud and water in which the wagons sank to their hubs."

As the houses were few and far between companionship between neighbors and friends was limited. That is why the pioneers used to hitch the horses to the wagon and "piling the children in," would go to a neighbor's house and stay all day. Hence, also, came the custom of Sunday visiting on a large scale.

When Mrs. Hobbs, as a little girl, moved with her mother from Morgan County, their relatives in that county tried to dissuade them from leaving a civilized county for a place so "backwoodsy" as Grant County.

"Now," Mrs. Hobbs says, "Morgan County is farther behind Grant County in every respect than she was ahead of her in those days."

One of the interesting incidents of the early days was the coming of John Bull to Indiana.

In England, where Mr. Bull resided (from his name you'd naturally guess where he lived), stories of vast wealth to be obtained in the new world were prevalent. Influenced by these Mr. Bull came to Indiana and bought up vast tracts of land, some of it in Grant County.

If he were alive today—we saw his tombstone in the old Back Creek graveyard the other Sunday—he could tell us whether he ever felt disappointed or not.

It is safe to say, however, that if he were alive today and had all that land in his possession his fondest dreams would have come true.

John Bull brought his family with him across the seas. In that family was a young lady, who, when she left England, left a lover behind. The lover followed her to Grant County, and that is why John Seale, Sr., who died a few years ago in Whittier, Cal., ever came to Indiana. M. B.

February 15, 1917.

Forty years ago or a little more, possibly forty-two years ago, a bevy of Southern Grant County girls joined a parade which went to a political rally in Marion. It was a Presidential election and a rally in those days was a wonderful event. Parades were formed of which big floats and gaily decorated wagons were principal features.

At this particular time the girls dressed themselves in the gayest of colors, possibly the colors of the American flag. They crowded into a big float and gaily started off in the parade for the county seat.

All went well until the ravine just on the southern edge of Jonesboro was reached when the horses, becoming frightened, gave a lunge which sent the huge wagon with its load of girls, their laughter turned to cries of fright, down the side of the steep grade to the bottom of the ravine. Many of the girls were injured and some of them never fully recovered from the effects of the accident.

The memory of this incident was renewed in our minds on last Sunday's walk, which was made from Fairmount to Jonesboro late in the afternoon.

The ravine, wooded on one side of the road, with Back Creek at the bottom of the grade, is a beauty spot, but we never pass that way without thinking of the tragedy of those early days.

Most of the girls started on the trip under protest from their mothers and this tragedy was often used as a warning to all of us who were younger not to disobey our parents for fear some dreadful thing would happen to us.

Half the distance last Sunday was made after dark, but this did not lessen the pleasure of the trip. Reflections on the clouds from the lights in Marion and Jonesboro looked like an aurora borealis. The reflections and the snow made a half light out of which trees and buildings emerged almost ghost-like. The lights of a through freight and several Interurban cars, passing on our right, glided past like long, glowing serpents.

As we passed old Back Creek graveyard and looked over toward the headstones the Better Half said: "What would those earliest pioneers think if they could come suddenly to life and see the trains and Interurban cars, the automobiles, electric lights and all the other wonders of modern life?"

When you stop to listen you will notice that night sounds differ from day sounds. From a tree near the Ancil Winslow farm a screech owl answered its mate away over in the Aaron Newby woods. A boy's whistle pierced the air and the through freight almost made the earth tremble with its rumbling noise.

On the south edge of Jonesboro, just after you pass the ravine of tragedy, you come to one of the landmarks on the Fairmount-Jonesboro pike. This is the Joe Hill homestead, set far back in a grove of evergreen trees. East and a little to the south of this fine, old place there was once a cemetery, every vestige of which seems to have disappeared.

As we reached Main Street in Jonesboro church bells were calling people to the evening services. Otherwise a Sabbath quiet brooded over the little town. M. B.

January 7, 1915.

"You go out on this road, but there's no way of getting there except by livery," answered the man at Lafontaine when we stepped off the Interurban car at 7 o'clock Sunday morning and inquired the way to Jalapa.

We did not take the trouble to tell the man that we had in mind a twenty-five mile walk for that day, but moved on in the direction he indicated.

As we proceeded on our way we followed the crooked road, winding in and out, up and down, through the picturesque country. We enjoyed the scenery and the happy warbling of the birds as we journeyed along. The land was carpeted with the green of a luxuriant growth and everywhere there was a promise, this early May morning, of a bountiful harvest for both man and beast.

Here and there, as we trudged along, we caught a glimpse of far-away hills. The distances were blue and dim and misty. The unimproved road which we followed, a part of the way to the Indian burying-ground, was narrow and winding and enchanting, with wild strawberries, wind-flowers, white violets and sweet williams blooming along the fences.

A bright-faced boy of fourteen, riding in a storm buggy, for it had the appearance of rain, stopped long enough on his way to Lafontaine, to give us directions and to put us on the right track.

After leaving Lafontaine we had been traveling south and west, but in order to reach the old Indian burying-ground we turned toward the east. A few minutes' walk brought us to a gently sloping hill at the top of which stands a weather-beaten frame church and in the rear gleam the white monuments and headstones of the wire-fenced graveyard. Nearby is a brick school house.

As we sat resting on the stone steps of the old Indian church we half closed our eyes and imagined we could see the Indians stalking through the ravines and gliding in and out among the trees. How they must have loved this beautiful country with its hills and little valleys and the river flowing gently between the tree-lined bluffs!

And where are they now? A few of the last of the Miamis lie in the burying-ground in the rear of the little church, their souls far away in the "happy hunting-grounds." A cocoon on the twig of a bush, emblematic of a future life and the inscriptions on the tombstones within the rough enclosure, brought to our minds sweet thoughts of immortality.

A tall monolith marks the spot where Meshingomesia, the last chief of the Miamis, lies buried. The inscription on the stone, neatly chiseled in plain letters, reads:

<blockquote>
"Me-shin-go-me-sia
Died December 16, 1879
Aged about ninety-eight years
</blockquote>

He united with the Baptist Church and was baptized the second Sunday in June, 1861, and lived a consistent Christian until he was taken from the church militant to the church triumphant in heaven."

The acorn-like ornament which adorned the top of the monument, as is the case with several others nearby, has fallen to the ground. The vandal fingers of souvenir hunters have also left their depredating marks on the stone which stands at the head of the final resting place of this kindly old man.

By the side of the old chief lies buried his wife, Ta-ke-e-quah, who died September 15, 1879, aged about ninety-four years. Other names noted on the headstones of this quaint spot were C. Peconga, Ka-ge-to-no-quah, Coon Bundy, Chapendoceah, Shapadosia, Shap and Dosia. We wondered if the last two were not contractions of Chapendoceah. Then there were Aw-taw-waw-taw and Ta-wa-ta.

We were told that only two families of Indians now reside in the country which was once their reservation and they are not full-blooded, by any means.

Mrs. James Lugar, a half-breed who married a white man, told us that her own family and a family by the name of Walters are the only representatives of her people in the neighborhood. The Walters family, we were told, were more French than Indian.

Mrs. Lugar has the reputation in her neighborhood of being an extra fine cook. Several little grandchildren in the Lugar family show the Indian strain in their jet-black eyes, straight hair and swarthy complexions.

Not far from the Indian burying-ground is the old Mississinewa batttlefield. A little ravine leads from the field down into the river. We were told by Earl Renbarger, who received the information from his grandfather, that down this ravine the Indians were pursued into the river after the battle, which took place in the winter of 1812.

The battlefield is located on the farm owned by William R. Brock, whose residence stands near the river, in an ideally beautiful spot, across from Conner's mill. A fine grove is situated near the mill on the opposite bank of the river and the grassy slope beneath the trees makes a fine camping place.

Just over the hill lies Jalapa which we reached in time to attend morning services at the Methodist Episcopal Church. We thought that surely for once we would be in a place where no one knew us, but we had scarcely gotten outside the door after services before Frank Ferguson came up and spoke to us. Mr. Ferguson and his family have just returned from a four-years' residence in Dinuba, Cal., glad to be back on Indiana soil once more. They live on a farm near Jalapa.

We visited Bausel Nichols, aged eighty-two, who has lived in Jalapa for more than forty years. He knew Meshingomesia well and spoke highly of the old chief's character. He said that Meshingomesia was a kind old man and that he was heavy-set. The old Indian remembered the Mississinewa battle and told Mr. Nichols that his mother and himself hid under a brush heap during the fighting.

Mr. Nichols was a blacksmith for many years and he used to shoe the ponies of the Indians who lived on the reservation. He said that some of the Indians drank heavily, which made them very mean and hard to get along with.

Mr. Nichols could remember nothing about Joachin Miller, the poet of the Sierras, who once lived in Jalapa.

After the nice little visit with Mr. Nichols we proceeded homeward. "It was a long, long way," and we went southeast, south and then east, then south and east again, making turn after turn on the trip homeward. We ate our noon-time lunch as we walked along the road.

There are many Renbargers in the Jalapa neighborhood, but we saw no familiar faces on the way until we had almost reached Oak Ridge.

We passed "Hardscrabble Ranch" and came within sight of Marion, which lay to the east. As we proceeded, to our right we could see the Studebaker elevator and the church at Roseburg, with the fine old Samuel Burrier homestead nearby. The Sidney Harvey farm is near Roseburg and we passed the beautiful home of their son, Ross Harvey, near the road.

We made a little stop at the home of Henry Shockey. Mr. and Mrs. Shockey were very kind, but they, like many other people, could not see any fun in walking.

Not far from the Shockey home is the O. M. Bish bungalow.

Further back we had passed the Mount Olive Church and school house and, after passing the Roseburg neighborhood, we came to the West Branch Church and school house Number 10. In this neighborhood we saw the beautiful homes of Con Shugart, Nelia Ratliff, Harvey Ratliff, Bert Malott and others.

After we passed the E. Harris farm we turned east again and crossed the Liberty pike and turned south once more, passing the Bethel or District No. 1 school house. To the west we recognized Bethel Church.

Near the bridge which spans Deer Creek on this road stands the ruins of an old-time residence. In the twilight it looked gaunt and gloomy and a fit place for ghosts.

On the way we passed the C. H. Jay, the A. Ferree, the E. Goodykoontz, the F. E. Haisley, the Samuel Hipes, the Louisa Haisley and the Ves Benbow farms and reached Oak Ridge school house just about dark. Samuel Hipes owns the farm which once belonged to the late Elwood Haisley.

We had met Mrs. Mary Gibson, her son and his family in an automobile on the road before we reached Bethel school house. To her question of how far we had walked we answered, "We are almost afraid to tell you for fear you'll not believe us."

Not far from Oak Ridge Glenn Collett passed in a buggy. His kind invitation to ride into town was declined. It must be admitted, however, that the invitation was a great temptation and the declining thereof was the result of a grim determination to make the walk the record-breaking one of the series.

Amusing incidents always occur on a trip like that of Sunday. While we were traversing the road which runs cat-a-cornered from Jalapa to Marion, at one of the Renbarger homes, a woman told us that she thought we'd better hire someone to take us into Fairmount and that we would change our minds about walking the entire distance long before we reached our destination.

Once when we stopped to rest, the Better Half stretched himself on a pile of rails with his feet elevated towards the road. A horse driven by a young lady in a buggy, became so frightened at the sight that it ran away, the incident almost ending in a tragedy.

Just before Oak Ridge was reached we sat down on a bridge to rest. Some young fellow, paraphrasing Longfellow's "The Bridge" yelled out, "We sat on the bridge at midnight." He evidently thought we were a couple of sweethearts, making love in the twilight.

After leaving Oak Ridge the remaining four miles back home were traveled in the darkness. The first glimpse of Fairmount's street lights was a truly welcome sight.   M. B.

May 13, 1915.

P-r-o-s-p-e-r-i-t-y is written all over Fairmount and Liberty Townships. You can see it in the rich soil, in the big gray and white and red barns, in the spacious homes, in the well-improved roads, in the rushing automobiles, in the sleek, fat, blooded stock and in the happy faces of the hospitable people who inhabit this garden-spot of Indiana.

The objective point of the hike on Sunday, March 14, was the country home of B. F. Dickey, five miles west and one mile south of Fairmount, with Little Ridge Church as an interesting and profitable stopping-place on the way.

Leaving *The News* office and going west on Washington Street the first thing to attract our attention was Andy Horine, in a big apron, assisting in the morning housework at his home, for which we gave him due praise.

L. E. Nolder's chickens, alfalfa patch, fat pig and pretty home were next noted and then we glanced northward to the former homes of Jesse and Nathan Wilson. Of the pioneer homes, standing almost in one straight line, north and south, redeemed from the wilderness by Iredell Rush, Jesse Wilson, Nathan Wilson and

Daniel Thomas, only one, Rush Hill, is owned and occupied by descendants of the original owners of the respective farms.

Continuing the journey we passed the E. J. Seale bungalow, off to the north, the Perry Seale home to the west and the Joshua Hollingsworth residence, the latter notable for its fine view of Fairmount.

Near the Perry Seale residence there once stood a little school house in the woods where M. B., her sister, Mary Wilson and Hannah Wilson, learned their first reading lesson under the tutoring of Myra Dillon Charles. The three whose names are mentioned long ago ceased to learn lessons in earthly lore and for them no longer do the leaves rustle nor the birds sing as they did on those spring mornings in the forest where the school house stood.

A little stop was made at the Daniel Thomas farm now owned by W. A. Beasley. Not far from the home once stood one of the school houses of the early pioneer period where our forefathers learned their A, B, C's. About the old brick residence on the farm linger many memories of stories full of the element of human interest.

The sun shone brightly and the robins, song sparrows and meadow larks filled the air with their music as we continued westward past the William G. Moon place, the James Bell, the Milton T. Cox and the John Cox farms. In the grove on the latter farm several buckets were catching the precious sugar water for maple syrup. John, Milton and Vollie Cox, three brothers, live in the same neighborhood in a sort of clan fellowship which we noted several times during the day in other communities among other relationships.

Where the road juts a little to the south there stands a log house and there is also one on the Mort Buller farm, the histories of which we did not learn.

Mort Buller not only has a splendid home on his farm but he has prepared an unusually good cottage and barn for his tenant. Mr. Buller's farm, "Oakwood," formerly owned by "Jozie" Rich, is a good one, and he has added improvement after improvement to the house and barn until there isn't much lacking now.

Turning south after leaving the Buller farm we passed the "Doc" Buller home and the tile mill. The little cluster of houses around the mill reminded us of settlements in the mining districts of Pennsylvania.

At the corner, where we turned to the west, is the Little Ridge school house, with the John Gambriel farm to the south. Before reaching Little Ridge Church we passed the beautiful homes of Joseph Whitely and Ancil E. Ratliff. With all the modern conveniences in the way of heat, light, baths, sleeping porches, telephones and hard wood floors, city residences have little that these homes do not possess.

Little Ridge Church stands in a pretty grove with a little graveyard nearby. As at Deer Creek and Back Creek we found graves of relatives, this time a great-grandfather who was buried in this quiet spot in 1859—a man who braved the hardships of pioneer life in the forests and swamps of Liberty Township. Wright and Harvey are the names most frequently repeated on the stones of this little graveyard and a tangle of myrtle covers the mounds under the old cedar trees.

Mart Trader met the pedestrians near the cemetery gate at the close of Sunday school and his cordial welcome was seconded by a number of others as we entered the door of the church. The Little Ridge people form one big family; they have never had a neighborhood feud and they are thoroughly democratic. These features were all in evidence at the Sunday services when many of the members of the congregation had a voice in the proceedings. No more hospitable a people can be found anywhere and the cheery greetings, urgent dinner invitations and the spirit of friendliness shown us sent a glow to our hearts.

After the services, continuing our course westward, we passed the homes of Clayton Wright, Arthur Brewer and Denny Winslow, while off to the left we saw the farms of Will Harvey, Hiram Harvey and Mrs. Etta Doherty. The latter lives on the farm once owned by her great-grandfather, Azel Rush, through the edge of which ran the eastern boundary line of the old Miami Indian reservation.

Walter Corwin lives on the Gaunt farm. The Gaunt family was once a factor in the neighborhood and, later, in the county, but the members have now all moved away.

The same is true of the Wells family, for whom the Wells school house, situated just south of the Gaunt farm, was named. Only John Caldwell's family represents the Wells' in the community at the present time.

"This is surely where Ben Dickey lives," we said, as we reached a farm where the golden corn was fairly bursting its bins, where the Duroc shoats were so fat and sleek they glistened in the sunshine and where the backs of the high-grade cattle were as straight as boards. And such it proved to be. Set far back from the road, in a beautiful grove, the house has an ideal location. Here we met with a warm welcome. Surrounded by his family, Mr. Dickey was quietly celebrating his seventy-fourth birthday anniversary on the farm which has been his home for forty-four years. Besides the home place he has two or three other farms.

Continuing westward for a quarter of a mile we came to the road leading north toward Hackleman. Off to the south we could see the Chris Behymer home as we made the turn.

We then reached one of the most picturesque homes in Grant county—the John Dickey farm, now the property of Will Lindsey. Set back from the road, in a grove of wonderful trees, adjoining a bit of the forest primeval, the place reminded us of pictures we had seen of old English estates. The large brick house is approached by a graveled driveway, and around the orchard to the south is set a little row of cedar trees, the whole making as beautiful a picture as anyone would care to see.

As we approached Hackleman we could see the modern residences on the Sam Leer and the William Miller farms, the one on the latter occupied by O. E. Curless and family. The store at Hackleman is owned by Ol Banister, a brother of George Banister, of this city.

Alfred Kemmer's new home, built in bungalow style, with everything strictly up-to-date and of the best, is located a short distance east of Hackleman. It was near this point that an automobile passed us and a voice, which we recognized as that of Nick Brookshire, called out, "It's a long, long way from Tipperary." Several kind invitations to ride were extended during the trip but all were declined.

Just before reaching Center school house and church, which are admirably located, we arrived at the comfortable home of J. N. Gibson and family. A half-hour was pleasantly spent here in conversation and in listening to music furnished by Misses Alma and Pauline Gibson.

A stretch of tarvia begins at Center and continues east to the Range Line road. Tarvia roads are fine for automobiles, but when it comes to hiking give us the good, old country roads every time. We passed the homes of George Yale and Ralph Rybolt, the latter having recently moved to the Noble farm. The brick house, which is the home of Robert Moon and family, is nicely located and Jack

McCombs has a fine home a little farther down the road. The homes of Elmer Comer, Charles Collins, who lives on the Seale farm, and the farm of Allie Rich were also passed. George Jones owns a good farm, known to the older residents as the Elwood Arnett place. His mother, Mrs. Mariah Jones, lives on the farm farther to the east which she has owned for many years.

Alva Johnson is the owner of more than two hundred acres of the finest kind of Liberty Township land. The home of Mrs. Susannah Scott is in this neighborhood. We came to a little Whybrew settlement when we passed the Mort Whybrew and the Mrs. Will Whybrew farms.

Where the Hackleman road intersects the Range Line road there once stood a school house. In this school house one of the hikers learned early lessons in his boyhood. The roof of this old building, scarred and crumpled by the passing of the years, is still in existence and is used as a covering for a shed.

By the way, this road which leads past the Academy and on west through Hackleman, follows a direct line into Lafayette.

In this cursory write-up of a day's journey many adjectives are used, but it is almost impossible to describe anything in Fairmount and Liberty Townships without the use of superlatives. M. B.

March 18, 1915.

The country east of Fairmount in the early days was known as "the prairie country east of town." To our childish imagination it was a land of enchantment, for there were cranberry marshes, hazel thickets, the lake and the river, all of them objective points for many merry picnic parties. Barren Creek—"Barn" Creek, we used to say—meandered through the prairie, too. Our last "hike" took us through this enchanted land, but how changed it is from the old days! Never a cranberry is found now, and the marshes where they grew were drained long ago. In the old days a person could stand on the edge of the boggy marsh, jump up and down and shake the ground for yards around.

The tangle of hazel bushes where we once found delicious hazel nuts can be seen no more, and as for the prairie it looks much like the rest of the country now; but in the pioneer days the wonderful big trees did not cover the ground there as they did in west of town and Liberty Township. The lake, too, has been drained and is only about half its original size, and the ground is not so boggy as it once was. Ugh! how we used to shiver with the fear of going down in that mud and never getting out again! Only the river is left as in the old days, and even it is changed—the water is not as clear as in pioneer days. There are too many factories along its course.

The objective point of Sunday's walk was Matthews, with Fowlerton as a good stopping point for church services and for dinner.

Leaving home at 7:20 in the morning we went north on Main street. The first thing that particularly attracted our attention was the new garage Charlie Thomas is building at his home. We turned east on Eighth, going past the pile of melted glass and brick which marks the site of the old Wilson and McCullough glass factory. We saw four or five such heaps at different places during the day—silent reminders of the old boom days.

We passed the Angelina Pearson home, the little thirty-acre patch of ground owned by Charles T. Parker, where Frank Parker lives and the Horace Reeve home. It was early morning and Mr. Reeve was doing his chores about the barn, as was also John Peacock at his farm a little farther east. Mr. Peacock had just hitched his horse to the carriage for Sunday school. The animal had gone through the same performance so many years that she knew every turn to be made, so that driving was unnecessary, only a word now and then being required. Joseph Ratliff raised his family of boys on the next farm, where his step-son, Nathan Thomas, now lives.

John Heavilin lives on the old Daniel Whybrew farm of one hundred acres which he owns. Nearby is the pretty cottage of his son Wayne, who is associated with him. They raise much stock, hogs and cattle especially. The original log cabin of the Whybrew family is back of the barn, being now used as an out-building.

Milt Nicholson lives on the Charles Child place, which is situated at the cross roads. The road here, running north and south, was once the worst old corduroy imaginable.

A little stop was made at the Thomas Winslow home, south of the road. With Mr. Winslow's assistance we were able to locate the beautiful homes of Thomas Duling, J. B. Compton and Henry Morrish on our left. Proceeding eastward we came to a rolling stretch of country and passed the homes of Will Monahan and Burr Leach. Off to the north on a little hill we saw the home of Fred Briggs, the "onion" man. In the bottom land, which once was so swampy that it was considered worthless, Mr. Briggs raises the finest kind of onions for the Snider people. The ground is fine for tomatoes, too, and corn as well.

Crossing Barren Creek and coming to an ideal location for a residence, we recognized the old Edmund Duling place, the present home of Solomon Duling. Stopping for a little chat we were informed by Mr. Duling that he was born sixty-four years ago in a log cabin which stood to the south of the present building. He also told us that the old cranberry marshes used to be north and a little to the east of the Duling farm, on the Major Norton farm and near Lake Galatia.

Mr. Duling lives in a regular Duling settlement, Chap, Virgil, Thomas, William and others living in the neighborhood. Milton Rich has a fine home in this neighborhood, to the north of the road.

Turning south, a walk of a few minutes brought us to Fowlerton. First we went in the Methodist Protestant Church, where a large and interesting Sunday school was in progress. John W. Himelick is superintendent of the school and seems to have affairs well in hand. The church, which has been nicely remodeled, holds a personal interest for the pedestrians, for on a June morning several years ago, a certain fair-haired boy here received his diploma from the township schools.

It was Rev. Heitz's day at Grant and there were no services at the Fowlerton Church, so we wended our way over to the Wesleyan Church, where Mrs. Emma Payne is pastor. Here we found the same situation, as Mrs. Payne was preaching in Summitville that day, so we went to the only other church in town—the United Brethren.

On the way we stopped at the store of Solomon D. Key for a few minutes. Mr. Key has his own religious ideas. While not a Seventh Day Adventist, nor a member of any other church, he believes in observing the seventh day as a day of rest, so he keeps his store closed on Saturdays and open on Sundays. During our half-hour's stay, Mr. Key made several sales, amounting in all to as much as $5 or $6.

Rev. Carter is pastor of the U. B. Church. It was quarterly conference day, however, and the presiding elder of the district was in charge. The church had just experienced a revival and a fervent testimony service formed a part of the morning's worship, with plenty of "Amens" interspersed at intervals.

Following the services we had dinner at a little eating place kept by Mr. and Mrs. Schmidt, natives of France, who came to Grant County in the boom days. Mrs. Schmidt speaks broken English, but her husband understands very little of the language. An interesting hour was spent with them. The reason their name is of German origin lies in the fact that Mr. Schmidt came from Alsace, the much disputed country of northeast France or southwest Germany, as the case may be.

The road from Fowlerton to Matthews lies for the most part through a gently rolling country, which becomes especially picturesque as the river is approached. After leaving Fowlerton we passed the Frank Kirkwood farm, where Walter Kirkwood lives, the Willard Dickerson and the John Dye homes.

Then we saw a large, handsome house, recently improved, with big porches and an out-doors sleeping room and we wondered whose it could be until we discovered the name, Ellis Wright, on the mail box. We passed a pleasant half-hour with Mr. Wright and his family. Talk about your beautiful country homes! Here is one that is not surpassed in miles and miles around. We were especially interested in the beautiful tinted walls, as the interior decorating was done entirely by Miss Myrl Wright, the work equaling that of any professional and the stenciling, the patterns for which she made herself, far excelling most professional work. Each room is different and each has a character all its own.

To the northwest we could see, from the porch of the Wright residence, the house on the Milton Wright farm, which is being prepared for the home of Ovid Reeder and Miss Myrl Wright, who are soon to be married. From the Wright home we could also see the homes on the Wilson Simons and the Levi Simons farms. Harry Winans lives on the next farm east of the Ellis Wright place.

Near where the road makes a little jut is a bit of forest where many of the giant trees lie or lean from their stumps just as they were twisted in a cyclone which struck the neighborhood a few years ago.

A home that attracted our attention, because of its neatness and evidence of prosperity proved to be the home of Adrial Simons and family. Then we soon came to the John Sanders farm, another pretty home. Just before reaching Matthews we passed the farm of one hundred and thirty-five acres owned by T. J. Lucas, of Fairmount.

New Harmony Primitive Baptist Church is beautifully located near Matthews, close to a well kept cemetery overlooking a deep ravine. On the headstones we found the names of many well known families, Richards, Dunn, Couch, Cory, Hayden, Kibbey, Leach and others.

Leaving the cemetery we entered Matthews by a winding road which skirts a ravine and the river. We passed the homes of T. Richards and J. Richards and then came to one of the most picturesque places of all, the residence of John Slater, with its pretty lawn and driveways and its outlook on the river. Mr. Slater's family is especially well known in Fairmount, his children, Mrs. Margaret Newberger, Miss Minda Slater and Joe Slater all having graduated at the Academy.

Matthews has cement walks and brick streets and is a good looking little town.

After we boarded the Pennsylvania evening train for home we passed the site of Palmer Winslow's glass factory, a pile of melted glass and brick showing its former location. We also saw the little brick office which he once used, now fast going to ruin, and the house that was the former home of David A. Baldwin and his family.

We had a little chat with A. E. Wilson, the genial conductor on the train. Mr. Wilson married Miss Mattie Wheeler, a former Fairmount girl. They now live in Converse.

The hike was one long to be remembered. M. B.

March 25, 1915.

"Over the hills to the poor house we wended our weary way" last Sunday. If our readers could have seen us as we climbed the last hill before we reached the main entrance to the grounds where the unfortunates of the county are kept they would wonder why we ever were permitted to leave after we once got inside, for, as warm and dusty as we were we certainly looked like fit subjects for permanent residence.

After finding an attendant we were escorted up the broad steps to the main entrance of the building. On the portico above us, as we mounted the steps, stood a feeble minded man who yelled out, "Oh, you lazy bones!" We are still wondering whether the appellation was meant for us or for the attendant.

Sunday is not visitors' day any more. So many people formed the habit of going on Sunday to visit the institution that the superintendent and his family could get no rest, so an edict was posted that there would be no more Sunday visitors.

However, we met Superintendent Bowles and Dr. Ross, of Gas City, the Infirmary physician. The latter told us that there are always several sick and many infirm people in the institution. We were also told by the superintendent that at least one-third of the inmates are feeble minded and irresponsible.

The farm and the grounds are beautiful. The building is in excellent condition and everything is kept very clean. However, our hearts went out in sympathy for all connected with the place, including those in authority.

As we turned from the gateway, in a backward glance, we saw, in an upper window, the white head of an old, old man buried in his arms as they rested upon the sill. He may have been asleep or he may have been only resting, but so pathetic was the attitude that to us the figure of the man seemed to embody the spirit of the place. Forsaken by relatives and friends he must pass the remaining days of his life as a ward of the county. The picture remained with us all day and will continue to do so for many, many days to come.

Another vivid incident preceded this one only a short time. Near the Infirmary flows Walnut Creek, which is spanned by a pretty bridge. As we sat near the creek resting by the roadside, an automobile filled with men rushed by and came to a sudden halt in the middle of the bridge. Evidently a visit had been made to Gas City, for beer bottles were drawn thick and fast from the bottom of the automobile and, after being drained of their contents, were hurled over the bridge into the creek, striking the water with a great splash.

The men evidently thought we were thirsty, too, for they offered the "better half" a bottle, but did not seem to be offended at the refusal to accept. In commenting upon the incident later in the day, the "better half" said, "Those young fellows are paving the way to the County Infirmary or some such institution unless they mend their ways." Worst of all, they had a child—a little boy—with them.

April 29, 1915.

APPENDIX

How Public Lands Were Surveyed.

(From *Niles' Register,* April 12, 1817.)

Captain Jared Mansfield, U. S. A., succeeded Rufus Putnam, the first Surveyor-General, in 1803. It was necessary for him to survey the Vincennes Indian Grant of 1795, confirmed in 1803. But as the tract was surrounded by Indian lands, cut off from the other surveys and remote from the Ohio river, he was at a loss as to how to proceed. If he tried to survey the tract in conformance with the lines east of the Greenville Treaty line, he felt sure that when the lines were connected after the Indian title to the intervening land was secured there would be great confusion, and if he merely surveyed the tract as a unit he would destroy any uniformity of surveys in the Indiana Territory. He therefore decided to base the surveys upon great lines which could control all future surveys in that region. To this end he ran the Second Principal Meridian through the northeast corner of the cession. For a base line he used a line running from the westernmost corner of Clark's grant on the Ohio—the nearest surveyed land.

This was the beginning of the combination of principal meridians and base lines which have been used in all later surveys. Both had been used before—Mansfield perfected the system and applied his brilliant talents to the astronomical location of the important points from which surrounding surveys could be made. The Second Principal Meridian governed the surveys in Indiana and those in Illinois to the western boundary of the fourteenth range. West from that line to the Mississippi and Illinois rivers the surveys have been based on the Third Principal Meridian, which runs from the mouth of the Ohio river.

The north and south lines are run by the true meridian, and the east and west lines at right angles therefrom, as far as practicable, in closing. But as the east and west lines are made the closing lines of the sections or townships, they frequently vary a little from those points, being run from one section or township corner to another. The lines are well marked by having all those trees which fall in the line notched with two notches on each side where the line cuts, and all or most of the trees on each side of the line and near it blazed on two sides, diagonally or quartering towards the line.

At the section corners there are posts set, having as many notches cut on two sides of them as they are miles distant from the township boundary, where the sectional lines commenced. At the township corners the posts have six notches made on each of the four sides facing the lines. Wherever a tree falls exactly in the corner, it supplies the place of a post, and is marked in the same manner. The places of the posts are perpetuated thus: At each corner the courses are taken to two trees in opposite directions as nearly as may be, and their distance from the post measured. These trees are called "bearing trees" (witness trees) and are blazed on the side next the post, and one notch made with an axe in the blaze. But in prairies, or other places where there are no trees within a convenient distance for bearings, a mound of earth is raised at each corner, not less than two and a half feet high, nor less than that in diameter at the base, in which the moundposts are placed.

At the section corners the numbers of each section, together with the numbers of the township and range, are marked with a marking iron (such as are used in mills and warehouses) on a bearing or other trees standing within the section near to the corner, thus: A blaze large enough for the purpose is made on the tree, and on the blaze the letter R is made, with the number of the range annexed; below this the letter T, with the number of the township; and under that the number of the section, without any letter to denote it. To the number of the township the letter N or S is added, according as the township lies north or south of the baseline; and to the number of the range the letter E or W as the range may be east or west of the principal meridian. By proper attention to these numbers and marks a purchaser is enabled to know the quarter and number of the section he wishes to enter, and the number of the township and range in which it lies. . . .

The quarter-section corners are established in the same manner that the section corners are, but no marks are made for the numbers of the section, township and range; "1-4 S" only is marked on the post.

The deputy surveyors are required to note particularly and to enter in their field books the courses and distances of all lines which they may run; the names and estimated diameters of all corner or bearing trees, and all those trees which fall in the lines, called station or line trees, together with the courses or distances of the bearing trees from their respective corners, with the proper letters and numbers marked on them; all rivers, creeks, springs and smaller streams of water, with their width and the course they run in crossing the line, and whether navigable, rapid, or otherwise; also the face of the country, whether level, hilly or mountainous; the kinds of timber and undergrowth with which the land may be covered, and the quality of the soil; all lakes, ponds, swamps, peat or turf grounds, coal beds, stone quarries; uncommon, natural or artificial productions, such as remains of ancient fortifications, mounds, precipices, caves, etc., all rapids, cascades, or falls of water; minerals, ores, fossils, etc.; the true situation of all mines, salt licks, salt springs, and mill-sites which may come to their knowledge. From the returns of the surveys thus made a complete knowledge of the country may be obtained, and maps thereof drawn with the greatest accuracy. The field notes of the surveyors, together with the plats and descriptions, made out therefrom, are filed in the office of the surveyor-general of the United States, or of the principal surveyors for the territories of Mississippi, Illinois, and Missouri.

Some Old Recipes.

(From *The Medical Investigator,* 1847.)

For Cholera Infantum.

Take a double handful of dewberry roots, a double handful of the root of cranesbill and two gallons of witchhazel leaves, boil these articles separately till the strength is all extracted; then strain, and pour the whole into one vessel, and boil down to a quart; add a pint of the best French brandy, and a pound of loaf sugar. Dose, from a tablespoonful to a wine glassful; repeated according to circumstances, and continued until the action on the bowels is fully checked.

Tincture of Lobelia.

Fill a jar with green herb, well bruised and pressed, and for every quart which the jar will contain add three or four pods of common red pepper, then pour on good whiskey enough to cover the herb, and let it stand for use. The longer it stands the stronger it becomes. This forms an excellent remedy in phthisic, croup, whooping-cough, bad colds, and all catarrhal affections, and is perfectly safe in its effects on all ages and conditions of persons.

For Yellow Jaundice.

Take a double handful of wild cherry tree bark, of the roots; the same quantity of yellow poplar bark, of the roots; of sarsaparilla roots; of the bark of the red sumach roots; half the quantity of bitter root. Boil these ingredients in two gallons of water until it is reduced to half a gallon; pour off and strain the liquid. Then boil or simmer down to one pint; add this to one gallon of hard cider; shake it well; then add two ounces of garden madder, or the madder of the shops. Commence with half a wine glassful three times a day, increasing the dose gradually to half a teacupful or even more in bad cases. When you have drunk half, add another half-gallon of cider.

Opening of the Wabash and Erie Canal.

(From the *Indiana Journal,* July 31, 1835.)

Canal navigation in Indiana has now fairly commenced. Thirty-two miles of the Wabash and Erie canal, extending from the dam across the Little St. Joseph river to Huntington on the Wabash are now completed and boats are regularly running thereon. This interesting event was celebrated in a becoming manner on the 4th inst. On the 2nd three boats left this place for Huntington for the purpose of bringing up such citizens of the lower end of the line as might wish to attend the celebration. The arrival of these boats in Huntington was hailed with the liveliest demonstrations of joy.

The next day the boats returned to Ft. Wayne, and were met and saluted by a detachment of militia, under the command of Capt. Rudisil; the salutes were returned by Capt. Fate's artillery, who came from Huntington with the boats. On the morning of the 4th a procession was formed in front of the Washington Hall and proceeded to the canal, where they embarked on the boats prepared for the occasion, and took a trip to the Feeder dam, seven miles distant. No less than 500 individuals, including a large portion of the fair sex, were present on the occasion. Among the guests were Gen. Tipton, of the U. S. Senate, and Col. Stansberry, of the U. S. Topographical Engineers, who was one of the party who first surveyed the route of the canal. Governor Noble was prevented by ill health from attending. Governor Lucas, of Ohio, was invited, but was prevented by the pressure of official business from being present.

The company landed at the dam, where salutes were fired by the military and some toasts were given. On the health of the canal commissioners being drunk, D. Burr, Esq., returned thanks, and in a short but animated address depicted the difficulties which our infant State had encountered in the commencement of a work of such magnitude as this canal, and the advantages that might reasonably be anticipated from its speedy completion. Gen. Tipton being called upon, delivered a short speech, in wihch he contrasted the present appearance of this section of country—where cultivated farms and cheerful villages meet the eye in every direction—with what it was at the time the canal was first contemplated, when the whole country from Lake Erie to the Wabash was one unbroken wilderness.

The company then returned to Ft. Wayne, where the Declaration of Independence was read by L. B. Wilson, and an oration delivered by Hon. H. McCulloch. A large company afterwards partook of a public dinner prepared for the occasion. The day was uncommonly fine, and nothing happened to disturb the harmony and good feeling which were manifested by all.

The Irish were observed by the citizens to be in the habit of nightly assembling in the secluded places in the woods; and all who could in any way procure arms were providing themselves with them. Three kegs of powder were forcibly taken from a wagon on the highway; the houses of some of the citizens were entered and the owners compelled to give up their guns; and the lives of others were threatened who refused to give up their arms. Several outrages were committed by these deluded ruffians upon each other; and Mr. Brady, a canal contractor, was fired at, but fortunately without effect, by a wretch named Sullivan, who, we are informed, took a prominent part in the disturbances in Maryland last year, and is also deeply implicated in the murders committed at Williamsburgh, Pa., four years ago.

The contest was intended to have taken place on the 12th inst., the anniversary of the battle of the Boyne. On the 10th the "Corkonians" assembled at Lagro, to the number of about three hundred, most of whom were armed; at the same time about two hundred and fifty armed "Fardowns" advanced to Wabash, seven miles from Lagro, on their way to attack their adversaries. D. Burr, Esq., canal commissioner, and some other citizens of the neighborhood, succeeded in inducing the two parties to suspend their intended fight for two days, in order to give them an opportunity of making some amicable arrangement. In the meantime expresses were sent to Fort Wayne and Logansport, requesting assistance to suppress the disturbances and protect the citizens from the dangers to which they would be exposed if the two parties should come in contact.

The express arrived here (Fort Wayne) on Saturday the 11th, and the appeal was promptly responded to by our citizens. The drum beat to arms, and in two hours a company of sixty-three men, well armed and furnished with ammunition and provisions, were on their march for the scene of action. Col. J. Spencer was elected to command the expedition; Adam Hull was elected first lieutenant, Samuel Edsell second lieutenant, and H. Rudisil ensign. The company embarked in a canal boat and arrived at Huntington about midnight; next morning they marched forward on their route, reinforced by a company from Huntington, under the command of Capt. Murray.

On hearing of the arrival of the volunteers, the Irish dispersed into the woods, and the next day most of them returned to their work, fully satisfied that they could not trample on the laws of the State with impunity, and that if they attempted to proceed any further in their mad career they would inevitably meet with the punishment due to such lawless proceedings.

Lincoln in Indiana.

(From the Indianapolis *Daily Journal*, February 12, 1861.)

(Lincoln's Speech at the State Line.)

Gentlemen of Indiana: I am happy to meet you on this occasion, and enter again the State of my early life, and almost my nativity. I am under many obligations to you for your kind reception, and to Indiana for the aid she has rendered the cause which I think eminently a just one.

Gentlemen, I shall address you at greater length at Indianapolis, but not much greater. Again, gentlemen, I thank you for your warm-hearted reception.

Leaving the crowd, amid the firing of cannon, and the waving of flags and handkerchiefs, the train left the State line. It was greeted by similar crowds at Attica, and other points on the road.

(At Lafayette.)

When the train arrived at Lafayette another monster crowd welcomed the incoming president, and while the trains were switching preparatory to transferring passengers and baggage, Mr. Lincoln made a short speech in response to the loud cries of the assembled multitude.

Crowds greeted the train at every station between Lafayette and Indianapolis, and at every place where it stopped Mr. Lincoln showed himself on the platform of the cars and spoke a few words to the people.

(At Indianapolis.)

When the train came in sight of this city its arrival was announced by the roar of artillery. Thirty-four rounds were fired in honor of the thirty-four States of the Union.

At five o'clock the train stopped at the crossing of Washington street, where it was met by members of the legislature, the officers of State, the City Council, the military company of the city, the Fire Department of Indianapolis and thousands of men, women and children on foot, in carriages and on horseback. Every part of the State was represented, and every political party, by hundreds and thousands of persons.

(Reception of the President-Elect.)

When Mr. Lincoln left the cars and made his appearance where he could be seen, deafening cheers arose that sounded above the roar of the cannon and the loudest blasts of the bands playing in the vicinity. The President-elect was welcomed by Governor Morton in the following speech:

(Governor Morton's Speech.)

Sir: On behalf of the people of Indiana I bid you welcome. They avail themselves of this occasion to offer their tribute of high respect to your character as a man, and as a statesman, and in your person to honor the high office to which you have been elected.

In every free government there will be differences of opinion, and these differences result in the formation of parties; but when the voice of the people has been expressed through the forms of the Constitution, all patriots yield to it obedience. Submission to the popular will is the essential principle of Republican government, and so vital is this principle that it admits of but one exception, which is revolution. To weaken it is anarchy; to destroy it is despotism. It recognizes no appeal beyond the ballot-box; and while it is preserved, Liberty may be wounded but never slain.

To this principle the people of Indiana, men of all parties, are loyal, and they here welcome you as the Chief Magistrate-elect of the Republic.

When our fathers framed the Constitution they declared it was to form a more perfect union, establish justice, and to secure the blessings of liberty to themselves and their posterity, and for these considerations we proclaim our purpose to maintain that Constitution inviolate as it came from their hands.

This Union has been the idol of our hopes; the parent of our prosperity; our shield and protection abroad, and our title to the respect and consideration of the world. May it be preserved is the prayer of every patriotic heart in Indiana, and that it shall be, the determination.

(Reply of the President-Elect.)

Governor Morton and Fellow Citizens of the State of Indiana:

Most heartily do I thank you for this magnificent reception, and while I cannot take to myself any share of the compliment thus paid, more than that which pertains to a mere instrument, an accidental instrument, perhaps I should say, of a great cause, I yet must look upon it as a most magnificent reception, and as such most heartily do I thank you for it. You have been pleased to address yourself to me chiefly in behalf of this glorious Union in which we live, in all of which you have my hearty sympathy, and, as far as may be within my power, will have, one and inseparably, my hearty consideration; while I do not expect, upon this occasion, or until I get to Washington, to attempt any lengthy speech, I will only say that to the salvation of this Union there needs but one single thing, the hearts of a people like yours. (Applause.)

The people, when they arise in mass in behalf of the Union, and the liberties of their country, truly it may be said, "The gates of hell can not prevail against them." (Renewed applause.) In all trying positions in which I shall be placed, and doubtless I shall be placed in many such, my reliance will be placed upon you, and the people of the United States—and I wish you to remember, now and forever, that it is your business, and not mine; that if the Union of these States, and the liberties of this people, shall be lost, it is but little to any one man of fifty-two years of age, but a great deal to the thirty millions of people who inhabit these United States, and to their posterity in all coming time. It is your business to rise up and preserve the Union and liberty for yourselves, and not for me.

I desire they should be constitutionally performed. I, as already intimated, am but an accidental instrument, temporary, and to serve but for a limited time, and I appeal to you again to constantly bear in mind that with you, and not with politicians, not with presidents, not with officeseekers, but with you, is the question: Shall the Union and shall the liberties of this country be preserved to the latest generations? (Cheers.)

Indiana.

(From *Indiana's Gift to the Battleship Indiana*; poem by
James Whitcomb Riley, 1896.)

Our Land—our Home!—the common home indeed
  Of soil-born children and adopted ones—
  The stately daughters and the stalwart sons
Of Industry:—All greeting and godspeed!
O home to proudly live for, and, if need
  Be, proudly die for, with the roar of guns
  Blent with our latest prayer.—So died men once. . . . .
Lo, Peace! . . . As we look on the land they freed—
Its harvests all in ocean-overflow
    Poured round autumnal coasts in billowy gold—
    Its corn and wine and balmed fruits and flow'rs,—
We know the exaltation that they know
    Who now, steadfast inheritors, behold
      The Land Elysian, marveling "This is ours!"

NAMES OF COUNTY OFFICERS, FROM THE ORGANIZATION OF GRANT COUNTY, IN 1831, UP TO THE PRESENT TIME (1917)

Date	Circuit Judge	Associate Judge	Associate Judge	Probate Judge	Clerk
1831	Charles H. Test	Samuel McClure	Caleb Smith		Jesse Vermilya
1832	Charles H. Test	Samuel McClure	Caleb Smith		Riley Marshall
1833	Charles H. Test	Samuel McClure	Caleb Smith		Riley Marshall
1834	Charles H. Test	Samuel McClure	Caleb Smith		Riley Marshall
1835	Charles H. Test	Daniel James	Caleb Smith		Riley Marshall
1836	Samuel Bigger	Daniel James	Caleb Smith		Riley Marshall
*1837	Samuel Bigger	William Massey	Caleb Smith	James Trimble	Riley Marshall
1838	Samuel Bigger	William Massey	Caleb Smith	James Trimble	M. Jones (a)
1839	David Kilgore	William Massey	Caleb Smith	B. C. Hogin	J. Trimble
					E. G. Carey
1840	David Kilgore	William Massey	Caleb Smith	B. C. Hogin	E. G. Carey
†1841	David Kilgore	William Massey	Caleb Smith	B. C. Hogin	E. G. Carey
1842	David Kilgore	William Massey	Caleb Smith	B. C. Hogin	E. G. Carey
1843	David Kilgore	William Massey	Caleb Smith	B. C. Hogin	E. G. Carey
1844	David Kilgore	William Massey	Caleb Smith	J. W. Goldthait	E. G. Carey
				George F. Dunn	
1845	David Kilgore	Benj. F. Furnish	Caleb Smith	George F. Dunn	A. Steele (c)
1846	Jeremiah Smith	Benj. F. Furnish	Caleb Smith	George F. Dunn	A. Steele
1847	Jeremiah Smith	Benj. F. Furnish	Caleb Smith	George F. Dunn	A. Steele
1848	Jeremiah Smith	Benj. F. Furnish	Caleb Smith	Frederick P. Lucas	A. Steele
1849	Jeremiah Smith	Benj. F. Furnish	Caleb Smith	Frederick P. Lucas	A. Steele
1850	Jeremiah Smith	Benj. F. Furnish	Caleb Smith	Frederick P. Lucas	J. W. Brown
1851	Jeremiah Smith	Benj. F. Furnish	Henly James	Frederick P. Lucas	J. W. Brown
‡1852	J. Anthony	Benj. F. Furnish	Henly James	Frederick P. Lucas	J. W. Brown
	J. U. Petit				
‖1853	J. U. Petit	Superior Judge		Walter March	J. W. Brown
1854	J. Brownlee			Walter March	J. W. Brown
	J. M. Wallace				
1855	J. M. Wallace			Walter March	J. W. Brown
1856	J. M. Wallace			Henry S. Kelley	R. B. Jones (b)
1857	J. M. Wallace			Henry S. Kelley	R. B. Jones
1858	J. M. Wallace			Henry S. Kelley	R. B. Jones
1859	J. M. Wallace			Henry S. Kelley	R. B. Jones
1860	H. P. Biddle			John Green	R. B. Jones
1861	H. P. Biddle			John Green	R. B. Jones
1862	H. P. Biddle			John Green	Byron H. Jones
1863	H. P. Biddle			John Green	Byron H. Jones
1864	H. P. Biddle			William Garver	Byron H. Jones
1865	H. P. Biddle			William Garver	Byron H. Jones
1866	J. S. Buckles			William Garver	Joseph A. Morrow
1867	J. S. Buckles			William Garver	Joseph A. Morrow
1868	J. S. Buckles			William Garver	Joseph A. Morrow
1869	J. S. Buckles			William Garver	Joseph A. Morrow
1870	Joshua Mellett			William Garver	M. S. Marsh
1871	Joshua Mellett			William Garver	M. S. Marsh
1872	Joshua Mellett			William Garver	M. S. Marsh
§1873	James R. Slack			William Garver	M. S. Marsh
1874	James R. Slack				M. S. Marsh
1875	James R. Slack				M. S. Marsh
1876	James R. Slack				M. S. Marsh

* From 1831 to 1837 the Associate Judges were ex-officio Probate Judges, and transacted Probate business.
† April term (1852) the Associate Judges were discontinued, President Judge thereafter continuing as Circuit Judge.
‡ In 1853 the new constitution changed the office of Probate Judge to Common Pleas Judge.
‖ Up to 1841 one person filled both the offices of Clerk and Auditor. In 1838, for a time, Morton Jones also filled the additional office of Recorder.
§ In 1873 Common Pleas Judge was abolished and business thereof transferred to the Circuit Courts.
(a and b) Deceased in office. (c, d, e and f) Resigned.
(v) David P. Alder was Surveyor from a short time after organization of County until 1846.
(x) Previous to 1857 record of Coroners imperfect and uncertain.

Date	Circuit Judge	Associate Judge	Associate Judge	Probate Judge	Clerk
1877	James R. Slack				M. S. Marsh
1878	James R. Slack				John H. Zahn
1879	James R. Slack				John H. Zahn
1880	James R. Slack				John H. Zahn
1881	Milton Sailor				John H. Zahn
1882	Milton Sailor				John H. Zahn
1883	Milton Sailor				Cyrus W. Neal
1884	Milton Sailor				Cyrus W. Neal
1885	W. H. Carroll				Cyrus W. Neal
1886	W. H. Carroll				Cyrus W. Neal
1887	R. T. St. John				Wm. Feighner
1888	R. T. St. John				Wm. Feighner
1889	R. T. St. John				Wm. Feighner
1890	R. T. St. John				Wm. Feighner
1891	R. T. St. John				Wilson Addington
1892	R. T. St. John				Wilson Addington
1893	Jos. L. Custer				Wilson Addington
1894	Jos. L. Custer				Wilson Addington
1895	Jos. L. Custer				Evan H. Ferree
1896	Jos. L. Custer				Evan H. Ferree
1897	Jos. L. Custer				Evan H. Ferree
1898	H. J. Paulus				Evan H. Ferree
1899	H. J. Paulus	Hiram Brownlee			Will T. Cammack
1900	H. J. Paulus	Hiram Brownlee			Will T. Cammack
1901	H. J. Paulus	Hiram Brownlee			Will T. Cammack
1902	H. J. Paulus	Hiram Brownlee			Will T. Cammack
1903	H. J. Paulus	B. F. Harness			Dr. M. M. Wall
1904	H. J. Paulus	B. F. Harness			Dr. M. M. Wall
1905	H. J. Paulus	B. F. Harness			Dr. M. M. Wall
1906	H. J. Paulus	B. F. Harness			Dr. M. M. Wall
1907	H. J. Paulus	P. H. Elliott			John D. Ferree
1908	H. J. Paulus	P. H. Elliott			John D. Ferree
1909	H. J. Paulus	P. H. Elliott			John D. Ferree
1910	H. J. Paulus	P. H. Elliott			John D. Ferree
1911	H. J. Paulus	Robt. Van Atta			Fred Drake
1912	H. J. Paulus	Robt. Van Atta			Fred Drake
1913	H. J. Paulus	Robt. Van Atta			Fred Drake
1914	H. J. Paulus	Robt. Van Atta			Fred Drake
1915	H. J. Paulus	Robt. Van Atta			Wm. S. Malott
1916	J. Frank Charles	Robt. Van Atta			Wm. S. Malott
1917	J. Frank Charles	Robt. Van Atta			Wm. S. Malott

Date	Auditor	Recorder	Treasurer	Sheriff	Circuit Prosecuting Attorney
1831	Jesse Vermilya	Benjamin Knight	David Branson	Benjamin Berry	
1832	Riley Marshall	Benjamin Knight	David Branson	Benjamin Berry	
1833	Riley Marshall	Benjamin Knight	John Beard	William J. Barnett	H. Gregg
1834	Riley Marshall	Benjamin Knight	Eli Overman	William J. Barnett	William J. Brown
1835	Riley Marshall	Benjamin Knight	Frederick Eltzroth	William J. Barnett	William J. Brown
1836	Riley Marshall	Benjamin Knight	Frederick Eltzroth	William J. Barnett	William J. Brown
1837	Riley Marshall	Benjamin Knight	Frederick Eltzroth	Eb G. Carey	S. W. Parker
1838	Morton Jones	Morton Jones	Isaac Bedsaul	Eb G. Carey	S. W. Parker
1839	E. G. Carey	William C. Jones	Isaac Bedsaul	Henly James	J. T. Elliott
		Thomas J. Neal			
1840	E. G. Carey	Thomas J. Neal	George W. Webster	Henly James	J. T. Elliott
1841	John Gilbert	Thomas J. Neal	Redden Chance	Henly James	Jeremiah Smith
1842	John Gilbert	Thomas J. Neal	Redden Chance	Henly James	John M. Wallace
1843	John Gilbert	Thomas J. Neal	Redden Chance	John Hodge	John M. Wallace
1844	John Gilbert	Thomas J. Neal	B. W. Ruley	John Hodge	John Davis
1845	John Gilbert	Thomas J. Neal	B. W. Ruley	John Hodge	John Davis
1846	James Brownlee	Thomas J. Neal	B. W. Ruley	John Hodge	Joseph S. Buckles
1847	James Brownlee	Thomas J. Neal	B. W. Ruley	Zimri Reynolds	Joseph S. Buckles
1848	James Brownlee	Thomas J. Neal	B. W. Ruley	Zimri Reynolds	Isaiah M. Harlan
1849	James Brownlee	Thomas J. Neal	B. W. Ruley	Zimri Reynolds	Isaiah M. Harlan
1850	James Brownlee	Thomas J. Neal	B. W. Ruley	Zimri Reynolds	Isaiah M. Harlan
1851	James Brownlee	Thomas J. Neal	B. W. Ruley	Alexander Buchanan	David Moss
1852	James Brownlee	Thomas J. Neal	B. W. Ruley	Alexander Buchanan	Silas Colgrove
1853	James Brownlee	Daniel Morris	Jacob Whisler	Alexander Buchanan	J. M. Connell
					I. M. Harlan
1854	James Brownlee	Daniel Morris	Jacob Whisler	Alexander Buchanan	I. M. Harlan
1855	John C. Harlan	Daniel Morris	Ephraim Smith	Alexander Buchanan	Osias Blake
1856	John C. Harlan	Daniel Morris	Ephraim Smith	Alexander Buchanan	Isaiah M. Harlan
1857	John C. Harlan	George Swope	William C. Miles	Calvin B. McRae	Isaiah M. Harlan
1858	John C. Harlan	George Swope	William C. Miles	Calvin B. McRae	R. P. De Hart
1859	Thomas Dean	George Swope	David W. Jones	Calvin B. McRae	R. P. De Hart
1860	Thomas Dean	George Swope	David W. Jones	Calvin B. McRae	M. H. Kidd
1861	Thomas Dean	John H. Zahn	William C. Miles	B. C. Hiatt (b)	M. H. Kidd
1862	Thomas Dean	John H. Zahn	William C. Miles	B. C. Hiatt	T. C. Whiteside
1863	William Neal	John H. Zahn	D. Culbertson	Benj. Crowell	T. C. Whiteside
				L. H. Elliott	
1864	William Neal	John H. Zahn	D. Culbertson	L. H. Elliott	Dudley Chase
1865	William Neal	John H. Zahn	James Brownlee	L. H. Elliott	
1866	William Neal	John H. Zahn	James Brownlee	L. H. Elliott	L. M. Goodwin
1867	William Neal	John H. Zahn	J. C. Nottingham	Alexander Buchanan	L. M. Goodwin
1868	William Neal	John H. Zahn	J. C. Nottingham	Alexander Buchanan	David Chambers
1869	William Neal	Zach. M. Harris	Reuel J. Gauntt	Alexander Buchanan	David Chambers
1870	William Neal	Zach. M. Harris	Reuel J. Gauntt	John F. Jones	David Chambers
1871	John Ratliff	Zach. M. Harris	Reuel J. Gauntt	John F. Jones	David Chambers
1872	John Ratliff	Zach. M. Harris	Reuel J. Gauntt	L. D. Baldwin	David Chambers
1873	John Ratliff	A. M. Baldwin	Jesse H. Nelson	L. D. Baldwin	Alfred Moore
1874	John Ratliff	A. M. Baldwin	Jesse H. Nelson	L. D. Baldwin	Alfred Moore
1875	Joseph W. Stout	A. M. Baldwin	Isaiah M. Cox	L. D. Baldwin	Alfred Moore
1876	Joseph W. Stout	A. M. Baldwin	Isaiah M. Cox	M. Fankboner	Alfred Moore

Date	Auditor	Recorder	Treasurer	Sheriff	Circuit Prosecuting Attorney
1877	Joseph W. Stout	A. M. Baldwin	Isaiah M. Cox	M. Fankboner	Alfred Moore
1878	Joseph W. Stout	A. M. Baldwin	J. P. Campbell	Benj. R. Norman	Chas. Watkins
1879	Joseph W. Stout	A. M. Baldwin	J. P. Campbell	Benj. R. Norma	Chas. Watkins
1880	Joseph W. Stout	A. M. Baldwin	J. P. Campbell	Ashbury E. Eyestone	Chas. Watkins
1881	Joseph W. Stout	A. M. Baldwin	W. I. Milner	Ashbury E. Eyestone	Chas. Watkins
1882	Joseph W. Stout	Benj. Hamaker	W. I. Milner	Ashbury E. Eyestone	A. E. Steele
1883	Joseph W. Stout	Benj. Hamaker	I. M. Cox	Chas. Lenfesty	A. E. Steele
1884	John N. Turner	Benj. Hamaker	I. M. Cox	Chas. Lenfesty	Geo. W. Gibson
1885	John N. Turner	Benj. Hamaker	H. D. Reasoner	Orange R. Holman	Geo. W. Gibson
1886	John N. Turner	Benj. Hamaker	H. D. Reasoner	Orange R. Holman	Sidney W. Cantwe
1887	John N. Turner	Benj. Hamaker	H. D. Reasoner	Wm. G. Wilson	Sidney W. Cantwe
1888	J. W. Miles	Benj. Hamaker	H. D. Reasoner	Wm. G. Wilson	Sidney W. Cantwe
		C. A. Lillibridge			
1889	J. W. Miles	C. A. Lillibridge	J. H. Parker	Robert S. Jones	Sidney W. Cantwe
				Alf McFeeley	
1890	J. W. Miles	Frank Rybolt	J. H. Parker	Alf McFeeley	C. M. Ratliff
1891	J. W. Miles	Frank Rybolt	J. H. Parker	John Sanders	C. M. Ratliff
1892	Geo. A. Osborn	Frank Rybolt	J. H. Parker	John Sanders	C. M. Ratliff
1893	Geo. A. Osborn	Frank Rybolt	W. E. Heal	John T. Williams	O. L. Cline
1894	Geo. A. Osborn	C. A. Lillibridge	W. E. Heal	John T. Williams	O. L. Cline
1895	Geo. A. Osborn	C. A. Lillibridge	W. E. Heal	A. C. Alexander	Elias Bundy
1896	John Wilson	C. A. Lillibridge	H. D. Reasoner	A. C. Alexander	Elias Bundy
1897	John Wilson	C. A. Lillibridge	W. D. Steele	A. C. Alexander	Wm. M. Amsden
1898	John Wilson	J. F. Carmichael	W. D. Steele	A. C. Alexander	Wm. M. Amsden
1899	John Wilson	J. F. Carmichael	W. D. Steele	C. C. Bradford	Wm. M. Amsden
1900	Geo. A. Modlin	J. F. Carmichael	W. D. Steele	C. C. Bradford	Wm. M. Amsden
1901	Geo. A. Modlin	J. F. Carmichael	Ellsworth Harvey	C. C. Bradford	Wm. M. Amsden
1902	Geo. A. Modlin	H. O. P. Cline	Ellsworth Harvey	C. C. Bradford	Grant Dentler
1903	Geo. A. Modlin	H. O. P. Cline	Ellsworth Harvey	Clark Mills	Grant Dentler
1904	Harry Goldthait	H. O. P. Cline	Ellsworth Harvey	Clark Mills	Grant Dentler
1905	Harry Goldthait	H. O. P. Cline	Walter S. Neal	Clark Mills	Grant Dentler
			Walter S. Neal	Clark Mills	E. E. Friedline
1906	Harry Goldthait	Elmer E. Veach			
1907	Harry Goldthait	Elmer E. Veach	Walter S. Neal	J. B. McGuffin	E. E. Friedline
1908	Andrew Y. Stout	Elmer E. Veach	Walter S. Neal	J. B. McGuffin	Wilbur E. Williams
1909	Andrew Y. Stout	Elmer E. Veach	Wm. H. Sanders	Tony George	Wilbur E. Williams
1910	Andrew Y. Stout	Jos. Clouse	Wm. H. Sanders	Tony George	Geo. M. Coon
1911	Andrew Y. Stout	Jos. Clouse	Wm. H. Sanders	Tony George	Geo. M. Coon
1912	Edwin H. Kimball	Jos. Clouse	Wm. H. Sanders	Tony George	Geo. M. Coon
1913	Edwin H. Kimball	Jos. Clouse	Uz McMurtrie	Y. F. White	Geo. M. Coon
1914	Edwin H. Kimball	Chas. E. Davis	Uz McMurtrie	Y. F. White	Wilbur E. Williams
1915	Edwin H. Kimball	Chas. E. Davis	Uz McMurtrie	Oliver P. Wright	Wilbur E. Williams
1916	Mort McRae	Chas. E. Davis	Uz McMurtrie	Oliver P. Wright	Wilbur E. Williams
1917	Mort McRae	Chas. E. Davis	Luther Worl	Oliver P. Wright	Wilbur E. Williams

Date	Surveyor	Coroner	First District Commissioners	Second District Commissioners	Third District Commissioners
1831	(v)	(x)	Jeremiah Sutton	Reason Malott	David Adamson
1832			Jeremiah Sutton	Silas Overman	Solomon Thomas
1833			Charles Hummel	Silas Overman	Solomon Thomas
1834			Charles Hummel	Silas Overman	Solomon Thomas
1835			Charles Hummel	William Roberds	Solomon Thomas
1836			James Barnett	William Roberds	Thomas Kirkwood
1837			James Barnett	John James	Thomas Kirkwood
1838			James Barnett	James Sweetser	John Russell
1839			Wm. E. Hendricks	James Sweetser	Samuel N. Woolman
1840			Wm. E. Hendricks	Benjamin Morgan	Joseph B. Allen
					William H. Smith
1841			Wm. E. Hendricks	Benjamin Morgan	Thomas Dean
1842			Stephen D. Hall	Greenup F. Holman	Thomas Dean
1843			Stephen D. Hall	Greenup F. Holman	Thomas Dean
1844			Stephen D. Hall	Greenup F. Holman	Thomas Coleman
1845			Samuel Doyle	Thomas Wall	Thomas Coleman
1846	Ephraim Smith		Samuel Doyle	Thomas Wall	Thomas Coleman
1847	Ephraim Smith		Samuel Doyle	Robert Griffin	J. L. Dolman
1848	Ephraim Smith		Robert H. Lenfesty	Robert Griffin	J. L. Dolman
1849	John Ratliff		Robert H. Lenfesty	Robert Griffin	Robert Wilson
					Spencer Reeder
1850	John Ratliff		Robert H. Lenfesty	William C. Miles	Spencer Reeder
1851	John Ratliff		Robert H. Lenfesty	William C. Miles	Spencer Reeder
1852	Robert B. Jones		Robert H. Lenfesty	William C. Miles	
					Joshua Canon
1853	Robert B. Jones		Robert H. Lenfesty	Robert Griffin	
					Daniel Coleman
1854	William Neal		Robert H. Lenfesty	Robert Griffin	
					Daniel Coleman
1855	William Neal		Robert H. Lenfesty	Robert Griffin	Hugh Hamilton
1856	William Neal		John Secrist	Robert Beatty	Hugh Hamilton
1857	William Neal	Calvin W. Ward	John Secrist	Robert Beatty	Hugh Hamilton
1858	William Neal	Calvin W. Ward	John Secrist	Robert Beatty	George Cairens
1859	William Neal	Calvin W. Ward	John Secrist	Robert Beatty	George Cairens
1860	William Neal	Calvin W. Ward	Jonathan Seegar	Robert Beatty	George Cairens
1861	William Neal	N. D. Holman	Jonathan Seegar	Robert Beatty	George Cairens
1862	A. C. Overman	N. D. Holman	Jonathan Seegar	Charles S. Tibbits	George Cairens
1863	A. C. Overman	N. D. Holman	John Spears	Charles S. Tibbits	
					George Cairens
1864	A. C. Overman	N. D. Holman	John Spears	Charles S. Tibbits	Edmund Duling
1865	A. C. Overman	Benjamin Crowell	John Spears	John Secrist	Edmund Duling
1866	A. C. Overman	Benjamin Crowell	Jacob Minnick (e)	John Secrist	Edmund Duling
1867	A. C. Overman	Benjamin Crowell	Jacob Minnick	John Secrist	Piner Evans
1868	L. M. Overman	Benjamin Crowell	Jacob Minnick	John Secrist	Piner Evans
1869	L. M. Overman	Benjamin Crowell	Jacob Minnick	John Secrist	Piner Evans
1870	Benajah C. Harris	Benjamin Crowell	Jacob Minnick	John Secris	William Wharton
1871	Benajah C. Harris	Benjamin Crowell	D. F. Wharton (f)	Robert Beatty	William Wharton
1872	David Overman	Daniel Jay	D. F. Wharton	Robert Beatty	William Wharton
1873	David Overman	Daniel Jay	D. F. Wharton	Robert Beatty	J. P. Winslow
1874	William Neal	Benjamin Crowell	Nicholas D. Holman	George White	J. P. Winslow
1875	William Neal	Benjamin Crowell	Nicholas D. Holman	George White	J. P. Winslow
1876	William Neal	Benjamin Crowell	Nicholas D. Holman	George White	J. P. Winslow

Date	Surveyor	Coroner	First District Commissioners	Second District Commissioners	Third District Commissioners
1877	William Neal	Benjamin Crowell	Nicholas D. Holman	George White	J. P. Winslow
1878	Elias C. Murray	A. A. Hamilton	Nicholas D. Holman	George White	J. P. Winslow
1879	Elias C. Murray	A. A. Hamilton	Nicholas D. Holman	George White	J. P. Winslow
1880	Elias C. Murray	A. A. Hamilton	Nicholas D. Holman		B. F. Stevens
1881	Elias C. Murray	A. A. Hamilton	Nicholas D. Holman	Abijah C. Jay	B. F. Stevens
1882	Elias C. Murray	A. A. Hamilton	James F. Charles	Abijah C. Jay	
1883	Elias C. Murray	Daniel Jay	James F. Charles	Abijah C. Jay	Geo. Needler
1884	Elias C. Murray	Daniel Jay	James F. Charles	Geo. B. Sweetser	Geo. Needler
1885	Lindley M. Overman	Isaac Hamilton	James F. Charles	Geo. B. Sweetser	Geo. Needler
1886	Lindley M. Overman	Isaac Hamilton	James F. Charles	Geo. B. Sweetser	Wm. R. Coomier
1887	Lindley M. Overman	Jos. L. Lord	James F. Charles	Benajah Harris	Wm. R. Coomier
1888	Lindley M. Overman	Jos. L. Lord	Eph. Creviston	Benajah Harris	Wm. R. Coomier
1889	John Swisher	Isaac Hamilton	Eph. Creviston	Benajah Harris	James Peele
1890	John Swisher	Isaac Hamilton	Eph. Creviston	Benajah Harris	James Peele
1891	Aneil E. Ratliff	Christopher Porter	Albert W. Stephens	Benajah Harris	James Peele
1892	Aneil E. Ratliff	Christopher Porter	Albert W. Stephens	Benajah Harris	Wm. R. Coomier
1893	Aneil E. Ratliff	James Boyd	Albert W. Stephens	Frank W. Chase	Wm. R. Coomier
1894	Aneil E. Ratliff	James Boyd	Joseph Lugar	Frank W. Chase	Wm. R. Coomier
1895	Wm. S. Freel	H. J. Work	Joseph Lugar	Frank W. Chase	Isaac W. Carter
1896	Wm. S. Freel	H. J. Work	Joseph Lugar	Frank W. Chase	Isaac W. Carter
1897	Aneil R. Smith	C. B. Vigus	Joseph Lugar	Frank W. Chase	Isaac W. Carter
1898	Aneil R. Smith	G. D. Kimball	Joseph Lugar	Frank W. Chase	Isaac W. Carter
1899	Aneil R. Smith	Dr. J. S. Whitson	Joseph Lugar	P. A. Hoover	Isaac W. Carter
1900	Aneil R. Smith	Dr. J. S. Whitson	John T. Williams	P. A. Hoover	Isaac W. Carter
1901	Frank M. Baldwin	Dr. J. S. Whitson	John T. Williams		John Kelsay
1902	Frank M. Baldwin	Dr. J. S. Whitson	John T. Williams	Elihu Pemberton*	John Kelsay
1903	Cortez Knight	Geo. W. Davis	John T. Williams	Elihu Pemberton	John Kelsay
1904	Cortez Knight	Geo. W. Davis	John T. Williams	Elihu Pemberton	John Kelsay
1905	Cortez Knight	Geo. W. Davis	John T. Williams	Elihu Pemberton	John Kelsay
1906	Cortez Knight	Geo. W. Davis	Wm. K. Frazier	John Kiley* John Wilson*	John Kelsay
1907	Fremont Wilson	Geo. R. Daniels	Wm. K. Frazier	John Wilson	Thos. J. Lucas
1908	Fremont Wilson	Geo. R. Daniels	Wm. K. Frazier	John Wilson	Thos. J. Lucas
1909	Fremont Wilson		Wm. K. Frazier	John Wilson	
1910	Fremont Wilson		Wm. K. Frazier	John Wilson* Wm. Baldwin	Thos. J. Lucas Ves Benbow
1911	Fremont Wilson	V. V. Cameron	Wm. K. Frazier	Isaiah Wall	Ves Benbow
1912	Fremont Wilson	V. V. Cameron	O. M. Brumfiel	Isaiah Wall	Ves Benbow
1913	Denver L. Horner	V. V. Cameron	O. M. Brumfiel	Isaiah Wall	Thos. J. Lucas
1914	Denver L. Horner	V. V. Cameron	O. M. Brumfiel	Chas. C. Nelson	Thos. J. Lucas
1915	Clarkson D. Smith	Ernest M. Zimmer	O. M. Brumfiel	Chas. C. Nelson	Thos. J. Lucas
1916	Clarkson D. Smith	Ernest M. Zimmer	O. M. Brumfiel	Chas. C. Nelson	Adam Cline
1917	Phil J. Middleton	Ernest M. Zimmer	O. M. Brumfiel	John A. Frazier	Adam Cline

PASSING OF THE PIONEERS.

They're going fast, those hearts so rare,
Those hearts we love, those lives so fair,
And pure and free from evil deeds,
And from the sins which passion breeds:
They wrought, transformed with tireless hands
A wilderness to fertile lands.
Each leaves to those who bear his name
A legacy of brighter fame
Than could be won in worldly strife—
The memory of an upright life.

MARK BALDWIN.

December, 1908.

CONTENTS

Chapter		Page
I.	BLAZING THE WAY	
	First White Man	17
	The Wayne Trail	19
	Dave Conner	21
	Treaty of Greenville	23
	Death of General Wayne	23
	Death of Little Turtle	23
II.	BATTLE OF THE MISSISSINEWA	
	Bearing upon Early Settlement	24
	War of 1812	24
	Location of Battlefield	24
	Account of the Battle	25
	Importance of the Engagement	26
	Privations of the Soldiers	28
	Attacked by Indians	29
	Gallantry of Captain Trotter	30
	Memorial Asked For	33
III.	ME-SHIN-GO-ME-SIA, CHIEF OF THE MIAMIS	
	Year of His Birth	35
	Date of His Death	35
	Remarks of E. P. McClure	36
	Letter from Maj. George W. Steele	37
	Letter from Dr. T. R. Brady	37
	Letter from Hon. Edgar L. Goldthwait	38
	Opinion of Phineas Henley	38
	Letter from Mrs. Flitcraft	38
	Burial near Jalapa	39
IV.	THE FIRST SETTLERS	
	Making the Best of It	40
	Building the Cabin	42
	Arrival of Robert McCormick	44
	Josiah Dille	45
	James H. Clark Buys Dille Land	45
	Mrs. Gabrille Havens	46
V.	LOCATING ON BACK CREEK	
	Stories Grandfather Tells	47
	Center of Activity Shifts	47
	Causes that Led to Unrest	47

Chapter		Page
	Source of Back Creek	48
	Joseph Winslow Enters Land	48
	Charles Baldwin	50
	Solomon Thomas	50
	Iredell Rush	50
	John Benbow	50
	Nathan Morris	50
	Thomas Morris	50
	Thomas Harvey	50
	Jesse Harvey	50
	Henry Osborn	50
	Thomas Baldwin	50
	Daniel Baldwin	50
	Benjamin Benbow	50
	Father of Twenty-two	50
	Progeny Extinct	51
	Back Creek Meeting-house	51
	Possibilities of Race Suicide	53
	Country Settles Rapidly	53
	Entries from 1835 to 1840	53
	Letter from T. B. McDonald	54
	A Young Quaker Poet	56
	Jack Winslow's Reaper	56
	Back Creek Graveyard	57
VI.	CLOTHING, FOOD AND SHELTER	
	Sowing Flax Seed	58
	John T. Morris	58
	Rotting the Flax	59
	Making Cloth	59
	Wild Game	60
	Forty Miles to Mill	60
	Hog Hunting	61
	Fire Hunting	61
	Log Rollings	62
	Pioneer Games	62
	Building Log Cabins	63
	Cooking Utensils	63
	Asa T. Baldwin	64
	Living in One Room	65
	Dash of Frolic and Romance	65
VII.	DAVID AND NANCY LEWIS	
	Arrival at McCormick's Tavern	66
	From Wilson's Ford to Lafayette	66
	Related to Davy Crockett	67
	William G. Lewis	67
	Mrs. Emeline Lewis	68

Chapter		Page
	Postoffice at AI	68
	Greenberry Postoffice Discontinued	68
	The First Postmaster of Fairmount	69
	Solomon Thomas	69
	First Marriage License	70
	John Smith	70
	Mary Ann Smith	70
	Judge Caleb Smith	70
	First County Commissioner from Third District	71
VIII.	BUILDING ROADS	
	Wabash & Erie Canal	72
	The Plank Road	72
	Gravel Road Projected	72
	Marketing Hogs	72
	Jonesboro & Fairmount Turnpike	73
	Officers of Turnpike Company	73
	Jonathan P. Winslow	75
	Joseph W. Hill	75
	Daniel Winslow	75
	Receipts for Toll	75
	Letter from Dr. A. Henley	76
	William S. Elliott	77
	Draining the Land	77
	John Selby Makes Test	78
	Capt. John F. Jones	80
IX.	GLIMPSES OF PIONEER LIFE	
	Mrs. Lydia Morris Arnold	82
	Pioneer Farmers	82
	Early Storekeepers	83
	First Clock and Cook Stove	83
	William Neal	83
	Studying Out Loud	83
	Games at School	84
	"Prepare for Meeting"	84
	"Meeting Clothes"	85
	Cincinnati a Trading Point	85
	Oxen Used for Logging	86
	Gathering Thorns	86
	Hog Killing Time	87
	Corn Planting	88
	Sugar and Molasses	88
	Raising Broom Corn	89
	Plowing for Wheat	89
	Tin Lanterns	89
	Borrowing Fire	90
	Making Soap	90

Chapter		Page
	To Iowa in a Covered Wagon	91
	"Quite Eccentric"	92
	A Regular Book Worm	93
	Thomas W. Newby	94
	Getting Married	94
	From $100 in 1846 to $130,000 in 1911	95
	Housekeeping Without Cook Stove or Clock	96
	Maj. B. V. Norton	96
	Trading Milk Cow for Clock	97
	Snow on the Cover	97
X.	PERSONAL CHARACTERISTICS OF FIRST SETTLERS	
	John and Mary Wilson	98
	Hanley and Betsy Broyles	99
	Trading in Land	99
	Jonathan Wilcuts	100
	Martin Bates	101
	Bernard McDonald	101
	David and Betsy Smithson	101
	Thomas and Lydia Baldwin	102
	Jesse E. and Nathan D. Wilson	102
	Daniel and Christian Baldwin	102
	Nathan and Miriam Morris	102
	Dugan and Elizabeth Rush	103
	Seth and Mary Winslow	103
	Jacob and Dorinda Hale	104
	Peter and Sarah Rich	104
	Iredell and Elizabeth Rush	104
	William and Keziah Osborn	104
	Thomas Harvey, Sr., and Wife, Anna	105
	Exum Newby	105
	Matthew and Anna Winslow	106
	Charles and Eunice Baldwin	106
	Jesse Morris	107
	Dr. William Lomax	107
	Daniel Frazier	107
	Lewis and Sarah Moorman	108
	Jabez H. Moore	108
	Lancaster and Mary Bell	108
	Jesse and Lydia Harvey	108
	Solomon and Rachel Parsons	108
	Gonner and Elizabeth Knight	109
	John Lee	109
	Amaziah Beeson	109
	Timothy Kelley	109
	Henry and Jesse Winslow	110
	Charles Hinshaw	110
	Hopkins and Elizabeth Richardson	111
	William Winslow	111

Chapter		Page
XI.	HAVING TO DO WITH A WIDE VARIETY OF SUBJECTS	
	First Railroad Project	112
	A Losing Venture	112
	No Use for an Irishman	112
	No Sluggards Here	112
	Manner of Cooking	114
	Spinning the Thread	115
	Tanning Cow Hides	116
	The Itinerant Shoemaker	116
	Muskets Used in War of 1812	116
	Accused of Selling Wet Goods	117
	Making Tallow Candles	118
	Uncle Seth Could Pinch	119
	Milton McHatton	120
	John Rush	120
	William R. Woollen	121
	"A Little English Miss"	122
	"Worst Places Called Corduroy"	123
	Running Past the Tollgate	124
	Fluctuating Value of the Dollar	125
XII.	DAVID STANFIELD AND NAMING OF FAIRMOUNT	
	Diary of David Stanfield	126
	Elizabeth Stanfield	127
	Turned Something Up	128
	A Persistent Bible Student	130
	Naming Fairmount	131
	Lots Platted in 1850	132
	First Home in Corporation	133
XIII.	EIGHTEEN FIFTY-TWO TO EIGHTEEN SIXTY-THREE	
	Letter from Hon. James M. Hundley	134
	Jonathan Baldwin	135
	What Col. Robert G. Ingersoll Said	136
	Dwelling of James Cammack	137
	First Public Improvement	138
	Daniel Ridgeway's Tanyard	139
	Stage Line Established	140
	First Free School in Town	141
	Courts and Jails Unnecessary	142
XIV.	THE UNDERGROUND RAILROAD	
	Slavery in 1620	144
	England Emancipates 800,000	144
	Fugitive Slave Law	145
	Active Agents	145
	Pendleton and Marion Stations	146
	Feeling Against Slavery	146

Chapter		Page
	The Know Nothings	147
	Nelson Brazleton	147
	Letter from Mrs. Angelina Pearson	148
	Runaway Slaves	149
	Station at Charles Baldwin's	149
	Seven Slaves to Bradford's	150
	The Last "Consignment"	151
XV.	THE SPIRITUALISTIC MOVEMENT	
	The Town of Galatia	152
	Otho Selby, Surveyor	152
	The Galatia Messenger	152
	Robert Nose's Story	153
	Pool of Siloam	153
	Morgan O. Lewis	154
	Fine Fishing	154
	Reaches Grant County	155
	Railroad Surveyed	156
	Scrip Issued	157
	Railroad Bubble Bursts	158
XVI.	TEMPERANCE AGITATION	
	First Temperance Meeting	159
	William G. Lewis	159
	Andy Morris Retreats	159
	Dave Capper Defiant	161
	Returns to Harrisburgh	162
	Friends Meeting in 1831	163
	Building Back Creek Meeting-house	163
	"June Quarterly"	163
	Methodist Church Organized	164
	The United Brethren	165
	Wesleyan Methodists	166
	Baptist Church Organized	167
	Fairmount Friends Set Up Meeting	167
	Robert W. Trader	167
	Berean Bible Class	169
	Mrs. Elizabeth Peacock	169
	Isaac Meek	172
	Married in Friends Meeting	172
	Churches in Fairmount	173
XVII.	EARLY SCHOOLS AND SCHOOL TEACHERS	
	School at Back Creek in 1831	176
	Thomas D. Duling, Sr.	176
	Teachers of Pioneer Days	177
	Mary Ann Taylor	178
	John R. Little	180

Chapter		Page
	Roster of Teachers	181
	Robert W. Himelick	183
	Otho Selby, Teacher	185
	Letter from Mrs. Pickard	187
	Letter from Ruth T. Carey	188
	Letter from Myra Baldwin	188
	Letter from D. W. Lawrence	189
	Letter from Solomon Duling	189
	Letter from Harry Suman	190
	Letter from J. H. Baldwin	191
	Letter from Adrial Simons	192
	Letter from Mrs. Mary A. Morrow	194
XVIII.	WILLIAM LEACH AND HIS DESCENDANTS	
	Paper by David G. Lewis	195
	Facts by Claud Leach	196
	Marriage of William Leach	197
	Soldier in War of 1812	197
	Neighbors of William Leach	197
	McCormick Tavern a Landmark	197
	Family of William Leach	198
	An Andrew Jackson Democrat	199
	William J. Leach	200
XIX.	AN INFLUENTIAL PEOPLE	
	Active Promoter of Town	202
	Marriage of Jonathan P. Winslow	203
	Pays Security Debt	204
	Opens Store	204
	Palmer Winslow, Manufacturer	204
	Captain Clark in Revolutionary War	205
	Nixon Winslow, Farmer and Banker	206
XX.	CAPT. DAVID L. PAYNE	
	Son of William and Celia (Lewis) Payne	209
	The Payne Homestead	209
	Wit, Precocity and Initiative	209
	Mrs. George W. Bowers, Early Teacher	210
	Leaves Old Home for Kansas	210
	Enlists in Kansas Cavalry	211
	Joins Gen. George Custer	211
	Elected to Kansas Legislature	211
	Favors the Opening of Oklahoma Territory	211
	Printing Press Seized	212
	Tribute by an Old Friend	213
	Death at Wellington, Kansas	219
XXI.	DULINGS, REEDERS AND SIMONSES	
	Cleared Twelve Acres of Ground for Two-Horse Wagon	220
	No Denomination Barred	221

Chapter		Page
	Finished in Walnut	221
	Paper by Bishop Milton Wright	223
	A Pioneer Peacemaker	227
	Editor *Religious Telescope*	227
	The Wright Brothers	228
	Textbooks Used in Schools	229
	A Roosevelt Family	231
	Paper by John H. Simons	232
	On Foot to Ft. Wayne	232
	"Wolves Howling on the Outside"	233
	Death of Henry Simons	234
	Barren Creek Christian Church	234
XXII.	THE WILSONS	
	Ancestry Traced Nearly Two Hundred Years	235
	Letter from Webster Parry	236
	Came with William Penn	238
	Head of the Society of Friends	238
	Letter from William S. Elliott	238
	Walnut and Poplar for Rails	239
	Hauled Wheat to Wabash	240
	Noisy Visit of Red Skins	242
	Marriage of Lindsey and Jane Wilson	244
	Poor Prospects	246
	President Indiana W. C. T. U.	246
	An Energetic and Painstaking Farmer	248
	Makes Good at Salem	248
	Second and Third Generations	250
XXIII.	FAIRMOUNT TOWNSHIP SOLDIERS	
	War of the Revolution	251
	War of 1812	251
	War with Mexico	251
	Civil War	251
	First to Volunteer	254
	Andrew Rhoads	258
	Letter from T. B. McDonald	260
	Letter from Hon. J. M. Hundley	260
	Additional Names by Jesse Haisley	264
	Letter from Mrs. Lydia Smithson	265
	Letter from Dr. A. Henley	265
	Letter from John L. Rhoads	266
	Fought at Gettysburg	268
	"Over Eighteen"	270
	A Confederate Soldier	271
	War with Spain	271
	War with Germany	272
	Sergeant in the Philippines	273
	Our Lieutenant-Colonel	274

Chapter		Page
XXIV.	FAIRMOUNT TOWNSHIP AND FAIRMOUNT CORPORATION	
	Organization, September, 1851	275
	Territory Set Aside for Purpose	275
	Topography of Township	275
	Descendant of Capt John Smith	276
	Boundary Lines Fixed in 1863	277
	Corduroy Roads Replaced	278
	Road Districts in 1854	278
	Henry Harvey, Township Trustee	279
	Census of 1860	280
	Move for Incorporation	281
	Vote Favorable to Incorporation	281
	Election of Officers	282
	Board of Trustees Meet	282
	By-Laws Adopted	282
	Census of 1870	284
	Wages of Teachers	285
	Corporation Officials from 1871 to 1917	286
	School Trustees	288
	Assessors and Marshals	289
	Health Officers	290
XXV.	THE TANYARD, HOME GUARDS AND QUAKER ARSENAL—CAMMACK'S SAW-MILL—THE EXPLOSION	
	First Tanyard in 1846	291
	Tanning a Cowhide	291
	Headquarters for Abolitionists	292
	The Quaker Arsenal	292
	The Home Guards	293
	Letter from Hon. J. M. Hundley	295
	Cammack's Saw-mill	296
	The Explosion	296
	Letter from M. A. Hiatt	297
XXVI.	TRANSPORTATION PROBLEMS AND PIONEER MERCHANTS	
	Letter from T. B. McDonald	299
	Harness and Wagons Were Home Made	299
	People Went Horseback or on Foot	300
	Letter from Hon. J. M. Hundley	300
	"The Mill Boy of the Slashes"	301
	Freighting from Anderson	302
	Marion and Anderson Stage	302
	The "Artemas Ward" and the "Lincoln"	302
	Walker Winslow Brings News of Lincoln's Death	304
	An Angry Union Soldier	304
	Letter from Mrs. Jennie Jones	305

Chapter		Page
	Projecting the Interurban	305
	Joseph W. Baldwin Opens Store	307
	Early Merchants	307
	Business Directory of 1877	307
	Letter from Dr. A. Henley	308
	John Bull and His Gold	309
	Present Fairmount Business Men	310
	Successful Career of N. W. Edwards	311
XXVII.	FAIRMOUNT PHYSICIANS — FIRST POSTMASTER— NEWSPAPERS — ORGANIZATION OF CORNET BANDS	
	Dr. Alpheus Henley	313
	Practitioners of the Early Day	315
	In Other Fields	316
	Location of First Postoffice	318
	Fairmount's Only Postmistress	319
	An Early Newspaper	319
	The Fairmount News	320
	The Fairmount Times	320
	J. Stivers	320
	The Child's Golden Voice	321
	The Fowlerton Index	321
	Cal Sinninger, Vitriolic	321
	Blanche Hockett Organizes First Cornet Band in 1870	321
	Other Bands	321
	Notable Success in Dentistry	322
XXVIII.	ORGANIZATION OF BANKS—DEVELOPMENT OF NATURAL GAS—BUILDING THE WATER WORKS—LOCATING INDUSTRIES	
	Fairmount Bank Organized	325
	The Fairmount Mining Company	325
	"Penetrated Trenton Rock"	327
	James G. Blaine Sees "Jumbo"	329
	Agitation for Water Works	330
	Building the Cincinnati, Wabash & Michigan Railroad	331
	The Chicago, Indiana & Eastern	332
	Advertising the Town	333
	Locating Snider Preserve Plant	335
	Establishing Bell Bottle Company	337
	The Commercial Club	337
	Organizing Fair Association	337
XXIX.	FAIRMOUNT ACADEMY—HIGH SCHOOL—WESLEYAN THEOLOGICAL SEMINARY	
	Move to Establish Academy	339
	Jesse Hiatt Makes Suggestion	339
	Location Selected	339

Chapter		Page
	Board of Trustees Chosen	339
	Academy Opens	341
	Class of 1888	341
	Academy Basketball Team	345
	High School Receives Commission	345
	High School Basketball Team	346
	First High School Graduates	347
	Origin of Fairmount Bible School	347
	Early Promoters	347
	Small Beginnings	348
	Present School Building	348
	A Modest Benefactor	348
	Reformer and Community Builder	349
XXX.	BUILDING FOWLERTON	
	The First House	350
	Locating Industries	350
	Chicago, Indiana & Eastern	351
	Cincinnati, Richmond & Muncie	351
	Letter from Joel O. Duling	351
	A School Meeting in 1840	352
	Confusion over Name of Town	353
	Fowlerton Incorporated	353
	Election of Officers	353
	Organization of Churches	353
	The Fowlerton Bank Established	354
	Fowlerton Park	354
XXXI.	COMMUNICATIONS AND COMMENT	
	Letter from Alvin Seale to Dr. A. Henley	355
	The Big Snow	358
	The Wayne Trail	359
	Fever and Ague	360
	A Pioneer Doctor	361
	Back Creek at Flood Tide	362
	The Drowning	362
	Lynx Over the Door	363
	Old Brick Church	364
	Fairmount Mining Company	365
	Voice from Idaho	366
	The Big Tree	366
	The Man on the Rail	368
	Isaac Roberts	369
	Our First Tailor	369
	Cyrus Puckett	370
	Early Days	370
	Refreshens Memory	371
	Boyhood Days	371

Chapter		Page
	The Plank Road	372
	A Characteristic Letter	373
	John J. Bull	373
	Mary Ann Taylor Morrow	374
	Brings Back Old Times	374
	Back in the Fifties	375
	First Copy of *The News*	376
	Did Their Part	376
	Re-roofing Back Creek Meeting-house	377
	The Old School House	377
	Isaac Meek	378
	Facts for Club Women	378
	Deserved Tribute	379
XXXII.	PERSONAL RECOLLECTIONS	
	Letter from Hon. Edgar L. Goldthwait	381
	Letter from Hon. James M. Hundley	385
	Jesse Wilson's Rifle	387
	Pioneers and Early School Days	390
	From a Note Book	393
	Memories of the Past	397
	Cholera in 1849	398
	Disappearance of Tom Winslow	399
	The McCormick Place	399
	Saloon Did Not Come	400
	Wants His Pants Back	402
	Lost in the Wilderness	404
	Animals and Birds of the Forest	405
XXXIII.	FRAGMENTS	
	The First Death	409
	Burial of Young Wife	409
	The First Saloon	409
	The Big Frame School House	409
	The Troublesome Squirrel	409
	Fairmount in 1853	410
	From Iowa in Wagon	410
	On Safe Side of the Guessing	411
	David Smithson's Bride	411
	Road Building	412
	To Richmond on Horseback	412
	Beeson's Copper Distillery	412
	The Prairie Seminary	413
	Jonathan Baldwin	413
	The Wide-a-Wakes	413
	The First Tollgate	413
	Remarks About Big Tree	413
	Many County Officials from Fairmount	414
	May, 1853	414

Chapter		Page
	Exempt from Execution	415
	When Jack Brunt Bought Hogs	415
	Many Who Were Not Pioneers	416
	Gave Life for Young Friend	416
	Example of Grit and Perseverance	417
	First Picture Gallery	418
	Solomon Thomas, Commissioner	419
	James Montgomery	419
	Bear Hunting in 1840	419
	Locate Union Graveyard	420
	Blowing Chaff	421
	Some Corrections	422
	Elijah Ward	423
	David Lewis	423
	Frederick Ice	423
	William G. Lewis	424
	Making the Teacher Treat	424
XXXIV.	RAMBLES OVER THE TOWNSHIP	
	At Back Creek Graveyard	425
	The Old Plank Walk	428
	The Friendly Road	429
	Moonlight Walk to Jonesboro	432
	Old Bethel Graveyard	433
	Hiking in an Automobile	437
	Feeding Chicks Scientifically	439
	Dinner in a Real Log House	441
	"Go Way Back and Sit Down"	443
	A Farmer Who Knows How to Farm	445
	Disastrous End of a Frolic	447
	LaFontaine to Fairmount	448
	At the Grave of Me-shin-go-me-sia	449

INDEX

A.

A custom handed down, 424.
Adams, Benny, freighter, 301.
Adamson, Jesse, 60.
A "detector," uses of, 158.
African Methodist Episcopal Church, organized, 175; charter members of, 175.
Ambition realized, 441.
An English Miss, at Wesleyan Back Creek, 122.
"A flash in the pan," 117.
Animals and birds of the forest, 405.
Anthony Wayne trail, 18.
A part of the old McCormick Tavern, 434.
A pioneer doctor, 361.
Apples, source of profit, 112.
A regular book worm, 93.
Army musket, used for hunting, 62.
Arnold, Mrs. Lydia Morris, birth of, 82; letter from, 186.
"As near alike as two peas," 92.
At the Renbarger home, 452.
Audible studying, 120.
Autumn day in 1853, 139.

B.

Back Creek, source of, 48; once called Winslow Creek, 49; impenetrable swamp, 137; at flood tide, 362; on a rampage, 364.
Back Creek Meeting-house, 51; monthly meeting opened, 51; plans for new structure, 51; ratio of apportionment fixed, 51; plans approved, 52; house completed, 52.
Bailey, Dempsey, 99.
Baker, Rev. W. D., 347.
Baldwin, Asa T., native of Township, 63; taught school, 63; death of, 64.
Baldwin, Charles, enters land, 50; election inspector, 69; mentioned, 82, 91; family of, 106; location of land, 106; his two-wheeeld covered gig, 106; slaves in care of, 149; slave owners in close pursuit, 149.
Baldwin, Daniel, enters land, 50; wife and family, 102; land now north half of Fairmount, 102; mentioned, 82, 91, 128, 133.
Baldwin, David, hauling freight from Anderson, 302.
Baldwin, Eunice, mentioned, 85, 91.
Baldwin, J. H., letter from, 191.
Baldwin, Jonathan, hotel, 91; sketch of, 135; extremely hospitable, 135; pillar of Wesleyan Methodist Church, 135; religiously inclined, 135; twice married, 135; death of, 135; superintendent ditching Back Creek, 138; builds home on Main Street, 138; mentioned, 146.
Baldwin, Joseph W., starts store, 83; mentioned, 117, 130; birth of, 308; sold land to John Bull, 309; death of, 310.
Baldwin, Micah, mentioned, 90; buys tanyard, 139.
Baldwin, Lindsey, mentioned, 85.
Baldwin, Mark, mentioned, 47, 56; verse by, 57.
Baldwin, Myra Rush, letter from, 188; rambles over Township, 425.
Baldwin, Quincy, mentioned, 150.
Baldwin, Sarah, mentioned, 412.
Baldwin, Susannah, taught school in 1831; mentioned, 176.
Baldwin, Thomas, enters land, 50; mentioned, 101, 102, 133.
Bankers, not necessary, 142.
Banks, organization of, 325.
Baptist Church of Fairmount, organized, 174; charter members, 174.
Baptist Church, organization of in Township, 167; first members of, 167.
Barr, Daisy, 163.
Barr, T. D., letter from, 415.
Bartholomew, Ephraim, sketch of, 266.
Bates, Martin, 99; buys land, 101; builds frame house, 101; stock in railroad, 101; bubble bursts, 101; moves to Iowa, 101; to Kansas, 101.
Battle of Mississinewa, 24; in Pleasant Township, 24; bearing upon early settlement, 24.
Beck, John, buys land, 109.
Beck Mike, freighter, 301.
Beeson, Amaziah, a chemist, 109; built brick house, 109.
Beeson, Charles, 109.
Bell, Lancaster, mentioned, 108.

494

Index.

Berean Bible Class, 169.
Best and noblest sons give lives, 147.
Big Tree, 366.
Blowing Chaff, 421.
Blaine, James G., visits Fairmount, 328; sees "Jumbo," 329.
Bogue, Mrs. Elizabeth, 138.
Bogue, Jesse, stayed with it, 162.
Bogue, Mary Winslow, 122.
Bogue, Robert, 138.
"Books! books! books!" 83.
Boone, Daniel, cousin to, 66.
"Borrowing fire," 90.
Boyhood days, 371.
Brunt, Jack, mentioned, 411, 415.
Beasley, William A., mentioned, 102.
Bell, Alson M., sketch of, 271.
Belling, horses, cattle and sheep, 119.
Benbow, Benjamin, enters land, 50; mentioned, 101, 102, 176.
Benbow, John, enters land, 50; erects first log house, 128.
Bethel Graveyard, 44.
Black molasses, home-made, 125.
Blacksmiths, early, 141.
Bookout, Calvin, mentioned, 101.
Boots, Martin, mentioned, 60.
Bowers, George, minister, 141; 153; ejects drunken hoodlum, 154; mentioned, 164.
Bradford, Moses, 146; slaves conveyed to, 149.
Brady, Dr. T. R., 26; letter from, 37.
Branson, Thomas, on night expedition, 62.
Brazelton, Nelson, mentioned, 147.
Brazelton, Robert, mentioned, 87.
Bread, substitutes for, 99.
Broyles, Hanley and wife, 99.
Brush drag, devised, 154.
Buchanan, James, mentioned, 146.
Bull, John J., mentioned, 373.
Butler, George W., miller, 137; home of, 137.

C.

Cammack, James, builds saw-mill, 83; mentioned, 291, 296; home of, 137.
Campbell, Lieut.-Col. John B., expedition commanded by, 27; attacked by Indians, 28; expedition successful, 28; his return march, 31; death of, 33.
Candles, making of, 118.
Capper, Dave, defiant, 161; moved out, 162; back to Harrisburg as bells tolled, 162.
Carey, H. L., letter from, 421.
Carey, John, 85.
Carey, Lydia, 85.
Carey, Ruth T., letter from, 188.

Carpenters, early, 141.
Carter, Dr. Thomas J., sketch of, 318.
Cartwright, Fred, 159.
Cattle and sheep markets, 85.
Census of 1860, 280; census of 1870, 284; census of 1875, 284.
Chamness, E. B., teacher, 153; at Alexandria, 154.
Chamness, William, starts town at Lake Galatia, 152; 153; estate of, 221; issues periodical, 319.
Charles, Dr. Etta, sketch of, 316; letter from, 378.
Che-cum-wah, 36.
Chicago, Indiana & Eastern Railroad, built, 332.
Chicken raising, 439.
Cholera in 1849, 398.
Christian Church of Fairmount, organized, 174; first members, 174.
Cincinnati Wabash & Michigan Railroad, came in 1875, 140.
Cincinnati Wabash & Michigan Railroad, constructed, 331.
Citizens Telephone Company, organized, 338.
Clark, James H., buys land, 45.
Clothing, how pioneers provided themselves with, 58; clothing the family, 114.
Coleman, Daniel and Mary, donate land for Bethel Graveyard, 44; Justice of the Peace, 44.
Coleman, Thomas, 44.
Commercial Club, organization of, 337.
Congregational Church of Fairmount, organized, 174; charter members, 174.
Conner, Dave, 21; courage of, 23.
Cooking, manner of, 114.
Cook stove and clock, the first, 83.
Corn planting, 88.
Corrections, some, 422.
Cornwallis, General, surrender of, 17.
Cotton and flannel, 84.
Courts and jails, unnecessary, 142.
Crockett, Davy, cousin to, 67.
Cross, Micajah, erects cabin, 152.
Cox, Garfield, wins honors, 342.
Cox, Eli J., sketch of, 193.

D.

Dailey, Solomon T., mentioned, 73.
Davis, Foster, teacher, 122; never kept a whip, 122.
Davis, Harvey, mentioned, 122; services at home of, 166; school house built on farm of, 166.
Davis, Henry, mentioned, 101.
Dean, Cal, mentioned, 101.
Decorous in meeting, 84.
Dentistry, profession of, 322, 323.

Index. 495

Device to prepare food, 99.
Dicks, Nathan, mentioned, 176, 220.
Did their part, 376.
Dille, Ichabod, mentioned, 45; Justice of the Peace, 69.
Dille, Josiah, mentioned, 45, 47.
Dillon, Allen, mentioned, 91.
Dillon, Jesse, mentioned, 82, 102, 108.
Dillon, Richard, mentioned, 38.
Dillon, Sammy, mentioned, 82, 91.
Directory of 1877, 307.
Disappearance of Tom Winslow, 399.
Diversion for boys, 62.
Dodging the tollgate, 124.
Dolman, Alex, mentioned, 152.
Doyle, George, grocer, 117.
Drainage, perfecting of, 124.
Dred Scott decision, 148.
Drowning, the, 362.
"Dry as the Sahara Desert," 117.
Dulings, Reeders and Simonses, 220.
Duling, Edmund and Eliza, 176; sketch of, 221.
Duling, Solomon, letter from, 189.
Duling, Thomas D., Sr., mentioned, 176; birth of, 220; marriage of, 220; grandfather soldier of Revolutionary War, 220; came to Township, 220; abolitionist, 221; promoter of M. P. Church, 221; teacher, 221; Township Trustee, 221; no denomination barred, 221.
Duling, Thomas D., Jr., sketch of, 223.
Duling, Wm. M., 222; political affiliations, 222; sketch of, 222.

E.

Early days, 370.
East Branch meeting, 173.
East Branch school house, 18.
East end of Township, 438.
Eastern speculators, 109.
Edwards, Nathan W., 173; birth of, 311; education, 312; teacher, 312; locates in Fairmount, 312; marriage of, 312; elected Clerk and Treasurer, 312; member School Board, 312; death of, 311.
Edwards, Xen H., 272; sketch of, 336.
Eighteen fifty-two to eighteen sixty-three, 134.
Election first held, 69; at McCormick Tavern, 69.
Elliott, Dr. David S., sketch of, 316.
Elliott, Nathan D. W., sketch of, 248.
Elliott, William S., pioneer tile manufacturer, 77; overcomes foolish objections, 77; faith fully rewarded, 78; birth of, 79; of Quaker ancestry, 79; becomes a soldier, 79; on important details, 80; mustered out, 80; Trustee White's Institute, 81; article by, 239.
Emancipation of slaves in England, 144.
Exempt from execution, 415.
Explosion, the, 291, 296; scared for once, 297.

F.

Fair Association, organized, 337.
Fairmount business and professional men of 1917, 310.
Fairmount in May, 1853, 414.
Fairmount, naming of, 131; letter concerning it from Mrs. Alvin Wilson, 131; letter from Dr. A. Henley, 131; letter from J. N. Elliott, 132.
Fairmount Academy, move to establish, 339; location reported, 339; Trustees elected, 339; opened for instruction, 341; class of 1888, 341; basketball team, 345.
Fairmount Bible School, origin of, 347; promoters named, 347; small beginning, 348; successful outcome, 348.
Fairmount Cornet Band, first organized, 321; second, 321; third and last, 321.
Fairmount corporation, petition for election, 281; election authorized and incorporation voted for, 281; officers chosen and installed, 282; By-Laws adopted, 282; names of officials, 1871 to 1917, 286; School Trustees, 288; Assessors and Marshals, 289; Health Officers, 290.
Fairmount High School receives commission, 345; R. W. Himelick first Superintendent, 347; basketball team, 346.
Fairmount Mining Company, organization of, 325; contract let for drilling, 327; penetrating Trenton Rock, 327; letter from C. R. Small, 365.
Fairmount Township, how organized, 275; territory set aside for purpose, 275; topography of, 275; re-organization of, 276; boundary lines same as 1863, 277.
Fairmount Township soldiers, 251.
Fairmount Wesleyan Methodist Church, organized, 174.
Fankboner Graveyard, location of, 41.
Farmer who knows how to farm, 445.
Fever and ague, 360.
Fifties, back in the, 375.
Fireplaces, 90.
"First big money," 86.
Flanagan, John, sketch of, 328.
Flanagan, John H., mentioned, 18, 19.
Flax, preparing for the loom, 114.

Flitcraft, Mrs. John, 38.
Fire hunting, 61.
Food, how obtained by pioneers, 60.
Ft. Wayne act establishing land office at, 20.
Fowlerton, building of, 350; first house built, 350; Leach, 350; the tile mill, 350; C. I. & E. and C. R. & M. Railroads, 350; first merchants, 350; school building, 350; confusion over name of town, 351; incorporation and election of officers, 353; churches organized, 353; bank established, 354.
Fragments, 409.
Frazier, Daniel, and family, 107; lost in the forest, 107; found in sycamore log, 108.
Friends meeting for worship, set up, 167; frame church built, 167; where located, 167.
Friends ministers, recorded, 172.
Frolic ends in disaster, 447.
From a note book, 393.
Fugitive Slave Law, 145.
Furnish, Benj. F., Associate Judge, 167.

G.

Games at school, 84.
Garretson, Anna Freeman, letter from, 416.
Gerard fails, 153.
Giant Hackberry, 140.
Glimpses of pioneer life, 82.
Goldthwait, Hon. Edgar L., letter from, 38; sketch of, 382.
Gossett, Z. M., mentioned, 75.
Grant postoffice, established, 69.
Gravel road, first built, 140.
Grave of Me-shin-go-me-sia, 449.
Greenberry Postoffice, 68; discontinuance of, 68; moved to Jonesboro, 69.

H.

Hale, Jacob and Dorinda, and family. 104; remove to Kansas, 104.
Hall, William, first Fairmount postmaster, 69; minister, 141; called to church work, 165; sketch of, 166; in Legislature, 166; Township Treasurer, 278.
Hamtramck, Col. John F., named Ft-Wayne, 23.
"Hardscrabble Ranch," 451.
Harmar, General, victory over, 17.
Harrison, Gen. William Henry, interview with Tecumseh, 24; trouble with Indians, 26; decides on vigorous action, 27.

Harvey, Anna, mentioned, 85.
Harvey, Henry, 92; keeps store, 117; elected Trustee, 279.
Harvey, Jesse, enters land, 50, 85.
Harvey, Jesse, Sr., and Lydia, 108; death of, 108.
Harvey, John S., dangerous mission, 149; successfully performed, 150.
Harvey, Thomas, enters land, 50; mentioned, 85; family of, 105.
Hasting's Carter, reaper at, 56; mentioned, 123.
Hasting, Carter, 165.
Havens, Mrs. Gabrille, 44; parents intimate friends of the McCormicks, 44; accounts for apparent discrepancy in dates, 44.
Havens, Peter, 152.
Haynes, Francis Marion, 44; Civil War veteran, 44; supports dry movement, 44.
Haynes, Mrs. Rachel Coleman, 44.
Headquarters for veterans, 137.
Heavenridge, Samuel, mentioned, 123.
Heavilin, John, postmaster at Greenberry, 69.
Henley, Dr. Alpheus, on mission to Huntington, 20; contribution, 43; assignment of stock to, 75; letter from, 76; mother of, 85; letter from, 98; letter from, 308; last of pioneer physicians, 313; friend of Capt. D. L. Payne, 313; names soldiers, 265.
Henley, Aunt Polly, 85.
Henley, Phineas, mentioned, 38; death of, 103; 170.
Hiatt, M. A., letter from, 297.
Hill, Aaron, mentioned, 82, 150.
Hill, Daniel, 150; seven slaves to Bradford's, 150; heroism personified, 151; the last "consignment," 151.
Hill, Joseph W., mentioned, 74.
Hill, Thomas, mentioned, 107.
Himelick, Robert W., sketch of, 183.
Hinshaw, Charles, buys land, 110; drowning of young man, 110; moved to Kansas, 110.
Hog hunting, 61.
Hog killing time, 87.
Hollingsworth, Eleanor, medium, 152.
Hollingsworth, Enos, mentioned, 152.
Hollingsworth, John B., sketch of, 254.
Hollingsworth, Joseph, mentioned, 152.
Hollingsworth, Moses, builds cabin, 152.
Hollingsworth, William, cabinet maker, 141; made caskets, 141; old church bought, 173.
Home Guards, 291, 292.

Index.   497

Hopkins, General, failure of, 27.
Horse stolen, 401.
House raisings, 62.
Houses few and far between, 446.
Houses first built, 83.
Hundley, James M., letter from, 134; native of Ohio, 134; son of William Hundley, 134; memory first dawns, 134; sketch of, 136; able speaker and writer, 136; in Civil War, 136; letter from, 144, 156; names soldiers; letter from, 295; member of Home Guards, 296; letter from, 300.
Hundley, William, arrival of, 134, 146.
Hunt, Carl D., account of battle prepared by, 25.
Hunter, outfit of, 117.

I.

Ice, Frederick, mentioned, 423.
Inducements to locate factories, 333; 335.
Industries, locating, 331, 332, 333.
In miniature, 143.
Interurban, promoting the, 305; plan organized by Clodfelter, 305; the power house, 306.

J.

Jalapa to Marion, 452.
Joliet, in the region of the Kankakee swamps, 17.
Jonesboro and Fairmount Turnpike Company, building of, 73; first officers of elected, 73; names of shareholders, 73; position of officer not regarded lightly, 74; sold to county, 76; first gravel road built in county, 76.
Jonesboro to Wabash, 72.
Jones, David and family, 417.
Jones, Jane, minister, 82, 134.
Jones, Jennie W., letter from, 305.
Jones, Capt. John F., in Civil War, 79; commands company, 79; interview with Pleasanton, 80; guarding water tank, 80; office of, 137; brave soldier, 137; popular with comrades, 137; obtained pensions for veterans, 137.
Jones, Joseph, postmaster at Greenberry, 69.
Jones, Dr. Robert Benjamin, sketch of, 317.
Jones, Rufus M., 47.
Jones, Samuel, 82; blacksmith, 134.
"June Quarterly," 164.
Jupiter, 431.

K.

Karwin, Billy, mentioned, 21, 141.
Kelley, Timothy, 20, 21; family of, 109; settled near Lake Galatia, 109; cranberry marsh, 109.
Kelsay, John, mentioned, 103.
Kelsay, Robert, mentioned, 142.
Kelsay, Smith, mentioned, 142.
Killed a bear, 419.
Knight, Gonner, an Englishman, 109.
Knight, Dr. John C., mentioned, 109.
Knight, Sallie, mentioned, 85.
Knight, Solomon, mentioned, 82, 84, 85.
Knight, Joseph, mentioned, 93.
Know Nothings, 147; secret meetings of, 147; in Bill Wright's barn, 147.

L.

LaFontaine to Fairmount, 448.
Lake Galatia, 18, 19; fine fishing at, 154.
Lancaster, James, opens store, 152.
Land entries, 1835 to 1840, 53.
Lantern, made of tin, 118.
LaRue, Gilbert, sketch of, 332.
LaSalle, in the region of the Kankakee Swamps, 17.
Latch string out, 64.
Lawrence, D. W., letter from, 189.
Lawyers, none, 142.
Leach, Edmund, mentioned, 176; homestead of, 196.
Leach, Claud, mentioned, 196, 200.
Leach, Esom, mentioned, 112.
Leach, Lewis and Payne boys, 112.
Leach, William, church organized at home of, 167; descendants of, 195; enters land, 195; marriage of, 197; God-fearing man, 199, death of, 200.
Leach, William J., sketch of, 199; mentioned, 200, 201.
Lee, John, mentioned, 21, 92; emigrates to Iowa, 109.
Letter, a characteristic, 373.
Level, Bob, mentioned, 92.
Lewellen, John, Methodist minister, 172.
Lewelling's Mill, 60.
Lewis, David, mentioned, 18, 66; accident to family, 66; moved into Baldwin cabin, 66; to LaFayette for meal, 66; class leader, 67; charter member M. E. Church, 67; ever ready to assist, 68.
Lewis, David G., 195; sketch of, 281.
Lewis, Emeline, mentioned, 68.
Lewis, Morgan O., mentioned, 154.
Lewis, William G., sketch of, 67;

mentioned, 69, 112, 141; first effort of in public, 159; mentioned, 410.
Lewis, William R., mentioned, 69.
Lines, Seaberry, storekeeper, 117; hotel keeper, 142; what he would say, 158.
Little, John R., sketch of, 180.
Little, Nathan, starts tanyard, 139.
Little Turtle, defeats St. Clair, 18; died at Ft. Wayne, 23; sword and medal presented to, 23.
Log Cabins, how built, 63.
Log Rollings, 62, 119.
Lomax, Dr. William, operates without anaesthetics, 107.
Lost in the wilderness, 404.
Lucas, Dr. Carl D., birth of, 322; education, 322; marriage of, 323; notably successful, 322.
Lucas, Elijah, Justice of the Peace, 69.
Lucas, Thomas J., 278.
Luther, Ivy, sketch of, 348.
Lynx over the door, 363.
Lytle, Frank, Jr., emigrates to Iowa, 101.
Lytle, James, settles on Dean place, 101; sold to John Smith, 101; moved to Iowa, 101; death of, 101.

M.

Making coffins, 401.
Making soap, 90.
Man on the rail, 368.
Map of Fairmount Township, 277.
Marketing hogs, 73.
Marquette, James, visits northern Indiana, 17.
Marion & Mississinewa Valley Railroad, 156; evidences on Carroll farm, 156; fac-simile of scrip, 157.
Married in meeting, 172.
Marriage License, the first, 420.
McClure, E. P., 26, 36.
McClure, Robert, clerked for Conner, 23.
McClure, Samuel, mentioned, 36, 146.
McCormick, Robert, arrival of, 44; enters land, 44; mentioned, 47.
McCormick Tavern, frontispiece, 15; original site of, 42; postoffice at, 68.
McCoy, Jacob, mentioned, 19, 21, 176.
McCoy, Willis, mentioned, 18.
McDonald, Bernard, buys Bates land, 101; moved to Grant County, 112;
McDonald, T. B., letter from, 54; letter from, 72; letter from, 112;
sketch of, 113; names of soldiers, 260; letter from, 299.
McHatton, Milt, teacher, 120.
Meek, Isaac, Wesleyan minister, 172; mentioned, 378.
Memories of the past, 397.
Merchants, early Fairmount, 141.
M. E. Church of Fairmount, organized, 173; charter members, 173; frame church built, 173; brick church erected, 173; present structure completed, 173.
Methodist Episcopal Church, charter members of, 164.
Me-shin-go-me-sia, birth of, 35; death of, 35; eldest of ten children, 36; remarkable man, 36; buried near Jalapa, 39.
Me-to-cin-yah, father of Me-shin-go-me-sia, 36.
Modern Fairmount home, 272.
Montgomery, Dennis, mentioned, 159.
Montgomery, James, mentioned, 419.
Moonlight walk to Jonesboro, 432.
Moore, Aquilla, mentioned, 20.
Moore, Georgia, mentioned, 20.
Moore, Jabez H., mentioned, 108; good citizen and community builder, 108.
Moorman, Lewis and Sarah, 108; location of land, 108.
Morris, Aaron, mentioned, 92.
Morris, Andy, tests a matter, 159; accedes to terms, 161; starts south, 161.
Morris, Caleb, mentioned, 92; exhorter, 164.
Morris, Jesse, injury to, 107; foot amputated, 107.
Morris, John T., birth of, 58; came to Grant County, 58; taught school, 58; died, 58; mentioned, 59.
Morris, Luther, opens saloon, 162; building destroyed, 162; remonstrance ends saloon business, 162.
Morris, Miriam, 85; death of, 92.
Morris, Nathan, birth of, 53; moved to Wayne County, Indiana, 53; enters land in Fairmount Township, 50; father of twenty-two children, 50; death of, 53; mentioned, 85; first minister, 163.
Morris, Robert A., sketch of, 329.
Morris, Thomas, enters land, 50; mentioned, 92, 102.
Morrow, Mrs. Mary A., mentioned, 194, 374.
Mott, Granville, mentioned, 142.
Music, Abe, mentioned, 20.

N.

Names of teachers, 181.
Neal, Cyrus W., letter from, 129.
Neal, Eli, mentioned, 122.
Neal, Mahlon, mentioned, 382.
Neal, William, teacher, 83, 141, 179.
Need of stable currency, 158.
Newby, Caroline, death of, 425.
Newby, Exum, enters land, 50; location of land, 105; site donated by, 163.
Newby, Rachel, mentioned, 82, 85.
Newby, Aaron, article by, 94.
Newby, Thomas W., birth of, 94; buys 80 acres, 94; death of, 95.
News, first copy of the, 376.
Nichols, Bausel, mentioned, 450.
Nickerson, Rev. H. S., mentioned, 160.
Nixon, James, mentioned, 123.
Norton, Frank, elected leader, 161; courageous and determined, 161.
Norton, Major B. V., mentioned, 19.
Nose, George, mentioned, 220.
Nose, Robert, relates incident, 153.

O.

"Oh, foolish Galatians," sermon on spiritualism, 153.
Old brick church, 364.
"Old Revolutioner," 433.
Old swimmin' hole, 307.
Old times, brings back, 374.
One of the stopping points, 85.
Only school room, 141.
Organization of churches, 159.
Osborn, Charles, head of meeting, 163.
Osborn, Henry, mentioned, 20; enters land, 50; to LaFayette, 66; services at cabin of, 164.
Osborn, Thomas, mentioned, 66.
Osborn, William and Keziah and family, 104; death of, 104.
Overman, Reuben, on night expedition, 62.
Oxen driven by Indian, 86.

P.

Paper dollar, uncertain value of, 125.
Parker, Allen, sketch of, 274.
Parker, Charles, mentioned, 18; important contribution of, 22.
Parker, Joseph H., mentioned, 18.
Parker, Thomas J., mentioned, 18.
Parry, Webster, letter from, 236.
Parsons, Solomon, Justice of the Peace, 69; buys land, 108; valuable man, 108; hotel keeper, 142.
Patterson, Dr. Joseph W., birth of, 323; ancestry, 323; education, 323; marriage of, 324; second marriage, 324; long period of service for community, 324; death of, 324; advocates water works, 330.
Patterson, Dr. Philip, 146.
Payne, David L., farm of, 68.
Payne, Capt. David L., parentage, 209; birth of, 209; education, 209; picturesque in personal appearance, 209; precocious and witty, 209; Payne homestead, 209; related to Davy Crocket, —; father of strict disciplinarian, 209; his boyhood teachers, 210; goes West, 210; in Border-Ruffian War, 211; in Civil War, 211; joins command of General Custer, 211; elected to Legislature, 211; starts agitation for opening of Oklahoma to settlement, 211; taken to Ft. Smith, 212; seize printing press, 212; tribute by a friend of, 213; death of, 219.
Payne, Henry Elsberry, sketch of, 210.
Peacock, Abigail, mentioned, 92.
Peacock, Elizabeth, paper by, 169; clerk of Fairmount meeting, 171.
Peacock, John, mentioned, 92.
Pearson, Angelina, mentioned, 85; teacher, 122; letter from, 148; sketch of, 148; born in Township, 148; marriage, 148; at Lake Galatia, 155.
Pearson, Herbert, sketch of, 150.
Pens, writing, 120.
Personal characteristics of pioneers, 98.
Phillips, John, loses land, 101.
Physicians, early Fairmount, 141.
Physicians, names of, 315.
Pickard, Alex, 159.
Pickard, Caroline Smith, letter from, 187.
Picture gallery, the first, 418.
Pierce, George, teacher, 122.
Pioneers and early school days, 390.
Planck, W. A., letter from, 150.
Plank road, the, 372.
Pool of Siloam, 152, 153.
Posey, Wade, mentioned, 164.
Postmasters, names of, 318.
Pierce, William R., mentioned, 74, 91.
Plowing for wheat, 89.
Postoffice at AI, opened, 71.
Powell, Thomas, mentioned, 103.
"Prepare for meeting," 84.
Pucket, Cyrus, not John, 370.
Pugsley, Rev. John, mentioned, 165.
Pursued into the river, 450.

Q.

Qualifications of a teacher, 84.
Quaker Arsenal, 291, 292.
Quaker costumes of their grandmothers, 435.

R.

Radley, Samuel, mentioned, 170.
Railroad projected, 112; right-of-way cut out, 112; cross ties and bridge timber hauled, 112; farmers lose their lands, 112.
Raising silk worms, 87.
Rambles over the Township, 425.
Ratliff, Ancil E., sketch of, 349.
Ratliff, Dr. M. E., letter from, 421.
Ratliff, Joseph, sketch of, 280.
Reece, Jesse, minister and superintendent of Sabbath School, 172.
Reece, Joel, founds *The Fairmount News*, 320.
Recollections, personal, 381.
Reeder, George, death of, 224; death of wife, 224; his ancestors, 224.
Reeder, Jonathan Franklin, enters land, 223; marriage of, 222.
Reeder, Robert B., birth of, 231; education, 231; successful farmer, 231; political affiliations, 231; marriage of, 231; family of, 231.
Reeder, Wm. H. H., 177; enters land, 223; abhorrence of wrong, 225; marriage of, 226; family of, 226; homestead, 227; peacemaker, 227; Justice of the Peace, 227; register of school taught, 228; text books used, 229; death of, 231.
Refreshens memory, 371.
Relfe, Joseph Warren, birth of, 276; assessor ten years, 276; political affiliations, 276; Capt. John Smith maternal ancestor, 276.
Re-roofing Back Creek Meetinghouse, 377.
Rhoads, Andrew, sketch of, 258; first Township soldier killed in Civil War, 258; early shoemaker, 266.
Rhoads, John L., letter from, 266.
Ribble, W. Hort, sketch of, 273.
Rich, Peter and Sarah, and family, 104; death of, 104.
Richardson, Hopkins and Elizabeth, and family, 111; deer hunter, 111; horse trader, 111.
Ridgeway, Daniel, locates tanyard, 139; sells out, 139.
Rifle, Jesse Wilson's, 387.
Road building, 72.
Road building, 412.
Road districts, 278.

Roberts, Isaac, blacksmith, 134.
Roberts, Isaac, mentioned, 369.
Rush, Dr. Calvin C., sketch of, 317.
Rush, Charles Everett, librarian, 344.
Rush, Dugan and Elizabeth, 103; moved to Iowa, 103; death of Dugan, 103; family return, 103.
Rush, Elizabeth, 85; married Thomas Jay, 104.
Rush, Iredell, enters land, 50, 82; location of land taken by, 104; death of, 104.
Rush, John, teacher, 120.
Rush, Nixon, Jr., mentioned, 75, 141; among first to respond, 161; in consultation, 162; birth of, 342; marriage of, 342.
Rush, Olive, work of, 343.

S.

Saloon did not come, 400.
Scarry, John, grocer, 117; hotel keeper, 142.
School house, the old, 377.
Schools, subscription, 120.
Scott, Alvin B., manufacturer, 334.
Scott, Levi, sketch of, 326.
Scott, Major-General, with troops, join General Wayne, 18; may have passed through Fairmount Township, 18.
Seale, Alvin, letter of to Dr. A. Henley, 355; sketch of, 355; sea fishing, 356; writes scientific and commercial papers, 355.
Seale, John, Sr., sketch of, 357.
Seale, Wm. P., 415.
Second and third generations, 55.
Seekins, Rev. W. J., mentioned, 348.
Selby, Eli, editor *Galatia Messenger*, 152, 154.
Selby, John, birth of, 327; education of, 327; in Civil War, 327; marriage of, 327; tests the tile, 78; mentioned, 18, 19, 20.
Selby, Otho, 21; land of, 110; an educator, 110; locates streets and blocks, 152, 156; sketch of, 185.
Selby, Victor A., mentioned, 19, 20.
Shoemakers, early, 141.
Shoes, making of, 116.
Simons, Adrial, letter from, 192.
Simons, Bingham, mentioned, 233.
Simons, Henry, birth of, 232; on foot to Grant County, 232; three days to Ft. Wayne, 232; death of, 232; buys land, 233; marriage of, 233; builds cabin, 233; howling wolves, 233; family of, 233; death of wife, 233; second marriage of, 233; death of

wife, 233; ancestor in War of Revolution, 234; Barren Creek Christian Church organized, 234.
Simons, John H., article by, 232; names pioneers, 234.
Slavery shot to death, 147.
Smith, Curtis W., mentioned, 70.
Smith, Ira M., secures license, 162; building destroyed, 162; returns to Marion, 162.
Smith, John, son of Judge Caleb Smith, 70; first marriage license issued to, 70; death of, 70, 101.
Smith, Mary Ann, daughter of Solomon Thomas, 70; death of, 70.
Smithson, David and Betsy, family of, 101, 119; mentioned, 411.
Smithson, Lydia, Mrs., letter from, 265.
Smithson, Sylvester, mentioned, 422.
Smook, Eli, pioneer preacher, good Samaritan, 301.
Snider Preserve plant located, 336.
Snow, the big, 358.
Sorghum, introduction of, 124.
Spiritualist movement, 152; reaches Fairmount Township, 155.
Stage line, established, 140; out of business, 140.
Stanfield, Charles, active at Lake Galatia, 152.
Stanfield, David, 83, 85, 101, 102; birth of, 126; marriage of, 126; children of, 126; plain of dress, 127; recorded minister, 127; purity of character, 128; death of, 129; diary of, 130; at Indiana Yearly meeting, 130; preaches at Cincinnati, 130; bill of expenses, 130; persistent Bible student, 130.
Stanfield, D. L., mentioned, 411.
Stanfield, Elizabeth, birth of, 127; death of, 127.
Stanfield, Isaac, mentioned, 20, 83; builds flouring mill, 138.
Stanfield, Vernon, mentioned, 20.
Stanzas of Gray's Elegy, 142.
State Bank of Indiana, failure of, 158; worthless money, 158.
St. Cecilia's Catholic Church, organized, 174; charter members, 174.
St. Clair, Gen. Arthur, delegate to Continental Congress, 17; first Governor of Northwest Territory, 17; Commander-in-Chief U. S. Army, 18; resigns command, 18; succeeded by General Wayne, 18.
Steele, Major George W., letter from, 37.
Stivers, J., sketch of, 320.
Stone cutters and monument builders, 142.

Store, principal stock in, 117.
Stories Grandfather Tells, 47.
Strange, Hon. John T., introduces bill providing for memorial, 33.
"Studying out loud," 83.
Sudduth, Isaac, soldier in War of Revolution, 44; died at age of 99, 44.
Sugar and molasses, 88.
"Sugaring off," 88.
Suman, Harry, letter from, 190.
Sutton, Jep, Conner's clerk, 23.
Sweetser, James, clerked for Conner, 23.

T.

Taking grist to mill, 88.
Tailor, our first, 369.
Tanning the cowhide, 291.
Tanyards, the, 291; last of the, 294.
Taxable property in 1876, 280.
Taylor, Aaron, Catherine and Martha, mentioned, 165.
Taylor, William, mentioned, 179.
Taylor, Mary Ann, mentioned, 178, 221.
Teachers at Back Creek, 176.
Teachers, pay of, 120.
Tecumseh, interview with Gen. William Henry Harrison, 24; warrior, statesman, orator, 24; pretext of, 24.
Temperance agitation and episodes, 159.
Term of Trustee changed, 279.
Text books of pioneer schools, 84.
Tharp, Rev. Alfred, class organized by 166.
"The big sleet storm," 443.
To Back Creek Quarterly, 444.
The Child's Golden Voice, issued, 321.
The Daily Journal, 321.
The Fairmount News, first issue, 320.
The Fowlerton Index, 321.
The Fowlerton Independent, 321.
The Fowlerton Review, 321.
"The Friendly Road," 429.
The gad, how used, 120.
The Galatia Messenger, 152, 319.
The McCormick place, 399.
"The Mill Boy of the Slashes," 301
Thomas, Daniel, mentioned, 102.
Thomas, Isaiah, mentioned, 150.
Thomas, Solomon, 20; enters land, 50; sells land at Lake Galatia, 68; establishes post office at Al, 68; builds horse mill, 69; year of birth, 69; family of, 69; Commissioner, 71; death of, 71; burial of at Back Creek, 71; moved to Iowa, 92; kept toll gate, 124; horse mill of, 138;

tannery built by, 152; church built on farm of, 165.
Thorn, James C., sketch of, 269.
Thorn, Louisa Payne, mentioned, 152.
Thought the devil had him, 403.
Things, a variety of, 385.
Thread, spinning the, 115.
Threshing, 89.
Tile machine, introduction of, 77.
Timber, disposing of, 118.
"Time is money," 83.
Tin lanterns, 89.
Tollgates, location of, 124.
Town plat, original, 132; additions made, 132, 133.
Township Trustes, names of, 280.
Trader, Robert W., sketch of, 167.
Trading in land, 99.
Transportation, problem of, 299; vehicles scarce, 300.
Treaty of Greenville, 23; present at, 23.
Tribute, deserved, 379.

U.

Underground Railroad, 144, 145; station in Fairmount, 145; stations at Pendleton and Marion, 146.
United Brethren Church, organization of, 165; charter members of, 165.

V.

Vestal, Aaron, sells land, 220.
Vetor, John, mentioned, 251.
Vinson, Ezra F., mentioned, 409, 410.
Vinson, Nathan, hotelkeeper, 142.
Voice from Idaho, 366.

W.

Wabash and Erie Canal, construction of, 72.
Wabash, hauling wheat to, 300.
Wagons, stiff tongued affairs, 85.
Waite, Sullivan T., mentioned, 75.
Wants his pants back, 402.
Ward, Elijah, first class leader at Sugar Grove, 164.
War of 1812. soldiers of, 251.
War with Germany, soldiers of, 272.
War with Mexico, soldiers of, 251.
War of the Rebellion, soldiers of, 251.
War of the Revolution, soldiers of, 251.
War with Spain, soldiers of, 271.
Washington, General George, 23.

Water works, election to decide on, 331.
Wayne, General, supersedes St. Clair, 18; saved Lafayette, 18; cut out road, 19; advance from Ft. Defiance, 23; victory of, 23; died December 14, 1796, 23.
Wayne road, 19, 359.
Weaver, Alpheus, teacher, 93.
Weesner, Micajah, mentioned, 152.
Wellington, William, carpenter and student, 90; at Lake Galatia, 152.
Wesleyan Back Creek, school house, 120.
Wesleyan Methodist Church, organized, 166.
Weston, John, mentioned, 66.
Weston, Joseph, class leader, 164.
Wheeler, Jasper N., miller, 137.
Wilcuts, Jonathan, mentioned, 99, 100, 101.
Wildcat banking, day of, 158.
Williams, Aaron, tanner, 116.
Wilsons, ancestry of, 235; from North Carolina, 236; of Quaker stock, 237; probably with William Penn, 238.
Wilson, Mrs. Eunice, birth of, 246; arrival of parents and family, 245; teaching school, 246; marriage of, 246; chosen President Grant County W. C. T. U., 246; elected President State W. C. T. U., 246; capacity as a leader, 246; good work for humanity, 246.
Wilson's ford, 18, 44.
Wilson, Jesse E., 74, 75, 82, 102; superintendent ditching, 138; birth of, 238; marriage of, 238; head of Society of Friends, 238; active in temperance work, 239; supported public improvements, 239; liberal in helping poor; death of, 239.
Wilson, Jeses Webster, sketch of, 250.
Wilson, John, mentioned, 71; family of, 98; arrival of, 98; energetic and enthusiastic, 98; death of, 99; birth of, 241.
Wilson, J. and M. E., mentioned, 44.
Wilson, John A., letter from, 420.
Wilson, John Harvey, mentioned, 102, 140.
Wilson, Lindsey, 101; birth of, 243; marriage of, 244; in Civil War, 244; family of, 244; death of wife of, 244; death of, 243; good citizen and considerate of the rights of others. 245;
Wilson, Lin, birth of, 247; education, 247; marriage of, 247; up-to-date farmer, 248; worker in many organizations, 248.

Index.

Wilson, Nathan D., 82, 102; clerk of Fairmount meeting, 171; birth of, 239; marriage of, 239; settled many estates, 240; assessed Township, 240; hauled equipment from Cincinnati, 240; family of, 240; wife of, 240; death of, 241.
Wilson, Robert, postmaster at Greenberry, 69.
Wilson, Samuel C., 71; birth of, 241; education of, 242; the clock peddler, 242; noisy Indians, 242; descriptions of fugitive slaves, 242; stuck in the mud, 243; the Cincinnati market, 243; Underground Railroad stations, 243; political affiliations, 243; member Indiana Legislature, 243; marriage of, 243; death of wife, 243.
Winslow, Anna, mentioned, 85.
Winslow, Daniel, mentioned, 74.
Winslow, Joseph A., mentioned, 409
Winslow, Henry, Sr., land of, 110.
Winslow, H. W., buys stage line, 302; the "Artemus Ward," and the "Lincoln," 302; sketch of, 303; important news carried, 303; assassination of Lincoln, 304; an angry soldier, 304; birth of, 303; marriage of, 303; death of, 303, 383.
Winslow, Henry, mentioned, 50; land donated by, 163.
Winslow, Jack, mentioned, 56, 93.
Winslow, Jonathan P., mentioned, 74, 75, 122, 139, 140; vigilant oversight, 161, 162; builds school house, 278; farmer and merchant, 202; birth of, 202; death of, 202; parentage, 202; education of, 202; first visit to Township, 202; political affiliations, 203; start to Fairmount, 204; opens store, 204; home of, 205.
Winslow, Joseph, enters land, 48; founded Friends meeting, 48; liberal supporter of educational movements, 48; death of, 48; mentioned, 82, 84; location of, 105; Friends meeting at cabin of, 163.
Winslow, Levi, birth of, 207; carpenter and builder, 208.
Winslow, Martha, mentioned, 85, 93.
Winslow, Matthew, enters land, 49, 82, 106.
Winslow, Milton, mentioned, 19, 141; first superintendent of Sabbath school, 171; volume of poems, 383; sketch of, 383.
Winslow, Nixon, 101; farmer and banker, 206; community builder, 206; birth of, 206; death of, 206; buys land, 206; President of Citizens Exchange Bank, 206; political affiliations, 206; drafted, 206.
Winslow, Palmer, prosperous manufacturer, 204.
Winslow, Seth, enters land, 50; mentioned, 82; location of. land, 103; builds hewed log house, 119; pinched hard, 119; superintendent ditching, 138.
Winslow, Thomas, mentioned, 18.
Winslow, Thomas, Sr., mentioned, 85, 103; death of, 103.
Winslow, William, location of, 111; moved to Iowa, 111.
Wool picking, 86.
Woolen mill, building of, 139.
Woollen, William R., sketch of, 121; birth of, 121; marriage, 121; second marriage, 122; death of, 121; sterling qualities of, 122.
Wright, Adeline, mentioned, 75.
Wright, Hon. A. T., mentioned, 381.
Wright, Bishop Milton, article by, 223; sketch of, 226; birth of, 226; death of, 226; editor *Religious Telescope*, 227.
Wright, Joel B., sketch of, 344.

www.ingramcontent.com/pod-product-compliance
Lightning Source LLC
Chambersburg PA
CBHW051333230426
43668CB00010B/1251